POCKET GOSPELS
AND ACTS OF
THE APOSTLES

New American Bible

United States
Conference of Catholic Bishops

POCKET GOSPELS
AND ACTS OF
THE APOSTLES

New American Bible

United States
Conference of Catholic Bishops

POCKET GOSPELS
AND ACTS OF THE APOSTLES

New American Bible

United States
Conference of Catholic Bishops

Washington, DC

NEW TESTAMENT

Nihil Obstat:

Stephen J. Hartdegen, OFM, LSS
Censor Deputatus

Imprimatur:

+James A. Hickey, STD, JCD
Archbishop of Washington
August 27, 1986

First printing, May 2014

ISBN 978-1-60137-481-3

TABLE OF
CONTENTS

ABBREVIATIONS

Acts	Acts	1 Kings	1 Kgs
Amos	Am	2 Kings	2 Kgs
Baruch	Bar	Lamentations	Lam
1 Chronicles	1 Chr	Leviticus	Lv
2 Chronicles	2 Chr	Luke	Lk
Colossians	Col	1 Maccabees	1 Mc
1 Corinthians	1 Cor	2 Maccabees	2 Mc
2 Corinthians	2 Cor	Malachi	Mal
Daniel	Dn	Mark	Mk
Deuteronomy	Dt	Matthew	Mt
Ecclesiastes	Eccl	Micah	Mi
Ephesians	Eph	Nahum	Na
Esther	Est	Nehemiah	Neh
Exodus	Ex	Numbers	Nm
Ezekiel	Ez	Obadiah	Ob
Ezra	Ezr	1 Peter	1 Pt
Galatians	Gal	2 Peter	2 Pt
Genesis	Gn	Philemon	Phlm
Habakkuk	Hb	Philippians	Phil
Haggai	Hg	Proverbs	Prv
Hebrews	Heb	Psalms	Ps
Hosea	Hos	Revelation	Rev
Isaiah	Is	Romans	Rom
James	Jas	Ruth	Ru
Jeremiah	Jer	1 Samuel	1 Sm
Job	Jb	2 Samuel	2 Sm
Joel	Jl	Sirach	Sir
1 John	1 Jn	Song of Songs	Sg
2 John	2 Jn	1 Thessalonians	1 Thes
3 John	3 Jn	2 Thessalonians	2 Thes
John	Jn	1 Timothy	1 Tm
Jonah	Jon	2 Timothy	2 Tm
Joshua	Jos	Titus	Ti
Jude	Jude	Tobit	Tb
Judges	Jgs	Wisdom	Wis
Judith	Jdt	Zechariah	Zec
		Zephaniah	Zep

"The joy of the Gospel fills the hearts
and lives of all who encounter Jesus."

—Pope Francis

THE GOSPELS

The collection of writings that constitutes the New Testament begins with four gospels. Next comes the Acts of the Apostles, followed by twenty-one letters that are attributed to Paul, James, Peter, John, and Jude. Finally, at the end of the early church's scriptures stands the Revelation to John. Virtually all Christians agree that these twenty-seven books constitute the "canon," a term that means "rule" and designates the list of writings that are regarded as authoritative for Christian faith and life.

It is the purpose of this introduction to describe those features that are common to the four gospels. A similar treatment of the letters of the New Testament is provided in the two introductions that appear before the Letter to the Romans and before the Letter of James, respectively. The Acts of the Apostles, a work that is both historical and theological, and Revelation, an apocalyptic work, have no counterparts in the New Testament; the special introductions prefixed to these books treat of the literary characteristics proper to each of them.

While the New Testament contains four writings called "gospels," there is in reality only one gospel running through all of the Christian scriptures, the gospel of and about Jesus Christ. Our English word "gospel" translates the Greek term *euangelion*, meaning "good news." This noun was used in the plural by the Greek translators of the Old Testament to render the Hebrew term for "good news" (2 Sm 4:10; possibly also 2 Sm 18:20, 25). But it is the corresponding verb *euangelizomai*, "to proclaim good news," that was especially significant in preparing for the New Testament idea of "gospel," since this term is used by Deutero-Isaiah of announcing the great victory of God that was to establish his universal kingship and inaugurate the new age (Is 40:9; 52:7; 61:1).

Paul used the word *euangelion* to designate the message that he and the other apostles proclaimed, the "gospel of God" (Rom 1:1; 15:16; 2 Cor 11:7; 1 Thes 2:2, 8, 9). He often referred to it simply as "the gospel" (Rom 1:16; 10:16; 11:28; etc) or, because of its content and origin, as "the gospel of Christ" (Rom 15:19; 1 Cor 9:12; 1 Thes 3:2; etc). Because of its personal meaning for him and his own particular manner of telling the story about Jesus Christ and of explaining the significance of his cross and resurrection, Paul also referred to this message as "my gospel" (Rom 2:16; cf. Gal 1:11; 2:2) or "our gospel" (2 Cor 4:3; 1 Thes 1:5; 2 Thes 2:14).

It was Mark, as far as we know, who first applied the term "gospel" to a book telling the story of Jesus; see Mk 1:1 and the note there. This form of presenting Jesus' life, works, teachings, passion, and resurrection was developed further by the other evangelists; see the Introduction to each gospel. The first three of the canonical gospels, Matthew, Mark, and Luke, are so similar at many points when viewed together, particularly when arranged in parallel columns or lines, that they are called "synoptic" gospels, from the Greek word for such a general view. The fourth gospel, John, often differs significantly from the synoptics in outline and approach. This work never uses the word "gospel" or its corresponding verb; nevertheless, its message concerns the same Jesus, and the reader is urged to believe in him as the Messiah, "that through this belief you may have life in his name" (Jn 20:31).

From the second century onward, the practice arose of designating each of these four books as a "gospel," understood as a title, and of adding a phrase with a name that identified the traditional author, e.g., "The Gospel according to Matthew." The arrangement of the canon that was adopted, with the four gospels grouped together at the beginning followed by Acts, provides a massive focus upon Jesus and allows Acts to serve as a framework for the letters of the New Testament. This order, however, conceals the fact that Luke's two volumes, a gospel and Acts, were intended by their author to go together. It further obscures the point that Paul's letters were written before any of our gospels, though the sayings and deeds of Jesus stand behind all the New Testament writings.

THE GOSPEL
ACCORDING
TO MATTHEW

INTRODUCTION

The position of the Gospel according to Matthew as the first of the four gospels in the New Testament reflects both the view that it was the first to be written, a view that goes back to the late second century A.D., and the esteem in which it was held by the church; no other was so frequently quoted in the noncanonical literature of earliest Christianity. Although the majority of scholars now reject the opinion about the time of its composition, the high estimation of this work remains. The reason for that becomes clear upon study of the way in which Matthew presents his story of Jesus, the demands of Christian discipleship, and the breaking-in of the new and final age through the ministry but particularly through the death and resurrection of Jesus.

The gospel begins with a narrative prologue (Mt 1:1–2:23), the first part of which is a genealogy of Jesus starting with Abraham, the father of Israel (Mt 1:1–17). Yet at the beginning of that genealogy Jesus is designated as "the son of David, the son of Abraham" (Mt 1:1). The kingly ancestor who lived about a thousand years after Abraham is named first, for this is the genealogy of Jesus Christ, the Messiah, the royal anointed one (Mt 1:16). In the first of the episodes of the infancy

5

narrative that follow the genealogy, the mystery of Jesus' person is declared. He is conceived of a virgin by the power of the Spirit of God (Mt 1:18–25). The first of the gospel's fulfillment citations, whose purpose it is to show that he was the one to whom the prophecies of Israel were pointing, occurs here (Mt 1:23): he shall be named Emmanuel, for in him God is with us.

The announcement of the birth of this newborn king of the Jews greatly troubles not only King Herod but all Jerusalem (Mt 2:1–3), yet the Gentile magi are overjoyed to find him and offer him their homage and their gifts (Mt 2:10–11). Thus his ultimate rejection by the mass of his own people and his acceptance by the Gentile nations is foreshadowed. He must be taken to Egypt to escape the murderous plan of Herod. By his sojourn there and his subsequent return after the king's death he relives the Exodus experience of Israel. The words of the Lord spoken through the prophet Hosea, "Out of Egypt I called my son," are fulfilled in him (Mt 2:15); if Israel was God's son, Jesus is so in a way far surpassing the dignity of that nation, as his marvelous birth and the unfolding of his story show (see Mt 3:17; 4:1–11; 11:27; 14:33; 16:16; 27:54). Back in the land of Israel, he must be taken to Nazareth in Galilee because of the danger to his life in Judea, where Herod's son Archelaus is now ruling (Mt 2:22–23). The sufferings of Jesus in the infancy narrative anticipate those of his passion, and if his life is spared in spite of the dangers, it is because his destiny is finally to give it on the cross as "a ransom for many" (Mt 20:28). Thus the word of the angel will be fulfilled, ". . . he will save his people from their sins" (Mt 1:21; cf. Mt 26:28).

In Mt 4:12 Matthew begins his account of the ministry of Jesus, introducing it by the preparatory preaching of John the Baptist (Mt 3:1–12), the baptism of Jesus that culminates in

God's proclaiming him his "beloved Son" (Mt 3:13–17), and the temptation in which he proves his true sonship by his victory over the devil's attempt to deflect him from the way of obedience to the Father (Mt 4:1–11). The central message of Jesus' preaching is the coming of the kingdom of heaven and the need for repentance, a complete change of heart and conduct, on the part of those who are to receive this great gift of God (Mt 4:17). Galilee is the setting for most of his ministry; he leaves there for Judea only in Mt 19:1, and his ministry in Jerusalem, the goal of his journey, is limited to a few days (Mt 21:1–25:46).

In this extensive material there are five great discourses of Jesus, each concluding with the formula "When Jesus finished these words" or one closely similar (Mt 7:28; 11:1; 13:53; 19:1; 26:1). These are an important structure of the gospel. In every case the discourse is preceded by a narrative section, each narrative and discourse together constituting a "book" of the gospel. The discourses are, respectively, the "Sermon on the Mount" (Mt 5:3–7:27), the missionary discourse (Mt 10:5–42), the parable discourse (Mt 13:3–52), the "church order" discourse (Mt 18:3–35), and the eschatological discourse (Mt 24:4–25:46). In large measure the material of these discourses came to Matthew from his tradition, but his work in modifying and adding to what he had received is abundantly evident. No other evangelist gives the teaching of Jesus with such elegance and order as he.

In the "Sermon on the Mount" the theme of righteousness is prominent, and even at this early stage of the ministry the note of opposition is struck between Jesus and the Pharisees, who are designated as "the hypocrites" (Mt 6:2, 5, 16). The righteousness of his disciples must surpass that of the scribes and Pharisees; otherwise, in spite of their alleged following of Jesus, they will not enter into the kingdom of heaven (Mt 5:20). Righteousness means doing the will of the heavenly Father (Mt 7:21), and his will is proclaimed in a manner that is startling to all who have identified it with the law of Moses. The antitheses of the Sermon (Mt 5:21–48) both accept (Mt 5:21–30, 43–48) and reject (Mt 5:31–42) elements of that law, and in the former case the understanding of the law's demands is deepened and extended. The antitheses are the best commentary on the meaning of Jesus' claim that he has come not to abolish but to fulfill the law (Mt 5:17). What is meant by fulfillment of the law is not the demand to keep it exactly as it stood before the coming of Jesus, but rather his bringing the law to be a lasting expression of the will of God, and in that fulfillment there is much that will pass away. Should this appear contradictory to his saying that "until heaven and earth pass away" not even the smallest part of the law will pass (Mt 5:18), that time of fulfillment is not the dissolution of the universe but the coming of the new age, which will occur with Jesus' death and resurrection. While righteousness in the new age will continue to mean conduct that is in accordance with the law, it will be conduct in accordance with the law as expounded and interpreted by Jesus (cf. Mt 28:20, ". . . all that I have commanded you").

Though Jesus speaks harshly about the Pharisees in the Sermon, his judgment is not solely a condemnation of them. The Pharisees are portrayed as a negative example for his disciples, and his condemnation of those who claim to belong to him while disobeying his word is no less severe (Mt 7:21–23, 26–27).

In Mt 4:23 a summary statement of Jesus' activity speaks not only of his teaching and proclaiming the gospel but of his "curing every disease and illness among the people"; this is repeated almost verbatim in Mt 9:35. The narrative section that follows the Sermon on the Mount (Mt 8:1–9:38) is composed principally of accounts of those merciful deeds of Jesus, but it is far from being simply a collection of stories about miraculous cures. The nature of the community that Jesus will establish is shown; it will always be under the protection of him whose power can deal with all dangers (Mt 8:23–27), but it is only for those who are prepared to follow him at whatever cost (Mt 8:16–22), not only believing Israelites but Gentiles who have come to faith in him (Mt 8:10–12). The disciples begin to have some insight, however imperfect, into the mystery of Jesus' person. They wonder about him whom "the winds and the sea obey" (Mt 8:27), and they witness his bold declaration of the forgiveness of the paralytic's sins (Mt 9:2). That episode of the narrative moves on two levels. When the crowd sees the cure that testifies to the authority of Jesus, the Son of Man, to forgive sins (Mt 9:6), they glorify God "who had given such authority to human beings" (Mt 9:8). The forgiveness of sins is now not the prerogative of Jesus alone but of "human beings," that is, of the disciples who constitute the community of Jesus, the church. The ecclesial character of this narrative section could hardly be more plainly indicated.

The end of the section prepares for the discourse on the church's mission (Mt 10:5–42). Jesus is moved to pity at the sight of the crowds who are like sheep without a shepherd (Mt 9:36), and he sends out the twelve disciples to make the proclamation with which his own ministry began, "The kingdom of heaven is at hand" (Mt 10:7; cf. Mt 4:17), and to drive out demons and cure the sick as he has done (Mt 10:1). Their mission is limited to Israel (Mt 10:5–6) as Jesus' own was (Mt 15:24), yet in Mt 15:16 that perspective broadens and the discourse begins to speak of the mission that the disciples will have after the resurrection and of the severe persecution that will attend it (Mt 10:18). Again, the discourse moves on two levels: that of the time of Jesus and that of the time of the church.

The narrative section of the third book (Mt 11:2–12:50) deals with the growing opposition to Jesus. Hostility toward him has already been manifested (Mt 8:10; 9:3, 10–13, 34), but here it becomes more intense. The rejection of Jesus comes, as before, from Pharisees, who take "counsel against him to put him to death" (Mt 12:14) and repeat their earlier accusation that he drives out demons because he is in league with demonic power (Mt 12:22–24). But they are not alone in their rejection. Jesus complains of the lack of faith of "this generation" of Israelites (Mt 11:16–19) and reproaches the towns "where most of his mighty deeds had been done" for not heeding his call to repentance (Mt 11:20–24). This dark picture is relieved by Jesus' praise of the Father who has enabled "the childlike" to accept him (Mt 11:25–27), but on the whole the story is one of opposition to his word and blindness to the meaning of his deeds. The whole section ends with his declaring that not even the most intimate blood relationship with him counts for anything; his only true relatives are those who do the will of his heavenly Father (Mt 12:48–50).

The narrative of rejection leads up to the parable discourse (Mt 13:3–52). The reason given for Jesus' speaking to the crowds in parables is that they have hardened themselves against his clear teaching, unlike the disciples to whom knowledge of "the mysteries of the kingdom has been granted" (Mt 13:10–16). In Mt 13:36 he dismisses the crowds and continues the discourse to his disciples alone, who claim, at the end, to have understood all that he has said (Mt 13:51). But, lest the impression be given that the church of Jesus is made up only of true disciples, the explanation of the parable of the weeds among the wheat (Mt 13:37–43), as well as the parable of the net thrown into the sea "which collects fish of every kind" (Mt 13:47–49), shows that it is composed of both the righteous and the wicked, and that separation between the two will be made only at the time of the final judgment.

In the narrative that constitutes the first part of the fourth book of the gospel (Mt 13:54–17:27), Jesus is shown preparing for the establishment of his church with its teaching authority that will supplant the blind guidance of the Pharisees (Mt 15:13–14), whose teaching, curiously said to be that of the Sadducees also, is repudiated by Jesus as the norm for his disciples (Mt 16:6, 11–12). The church of Jesus will be built on Peter (Mt 16:18), who will be given authority to bind and loose on earth, an authority whose exercise will be confirmed in heaven (Mt 16:19). The metaphor of binding and loosing has a variety of meanings, among them that of giving authoritative teaching. This promise is made to Peter directly after he has confessed Jesus to be the Messiah, the Son of the living God (Mt 16:16), a confession that he has made as the result of revelation given to him by the heavenly Father (Mt 16:17); Matthew's ecclesiology is based on his high christology.

Directly after that confession Jesus begins to instruct his disciples about how he must go the way of suffering and death (Mt 16:21). Peter, who has been praised for his confession, protests against this and receives from Jesus the sharpest of rebukes for attempting to deflect Jesus from his God-appointed destiny. The future rock upon whom the church will be built is still a man of "little faith" (see Mt 14:31). Both he and the other disciples must know not only that Jesus will have to suffer and die but that they too will have to follow him on the way of the cross if they are truly to be his disciples (Mt 16:24–25).

The discourse following this narrative (Mt 18:1–35) is often called the "church order" discourse, although that title is perhaps misleading since the emphasis is not on the structure of the church but on the care that the disciples must have for one another in respect to guarding each other's faith in Jesus (Mt 18:6–7), to seeking out those who have wandered from the fold (Mt 18:10–14), and to repeated forgiving of their fellow disciples who have offended them (Mt 18:21–35). But there is also the obligation to correct the sinful fellow Christian and, should one refuse to be corrected, separation from the community is demanded (Mt 18:15–18).

The narrative of the fifth book (Mt 19:1–23:39) begins with the departure of Jesus and his disciples from Galilee for Jerusalem. In the course of their journey Jesus for the third time predicts the passion that awaits him at Jerusalem and also his resurrection (Mt 20:17–19). At his entrance into the city he is hailed as the Son of David by the crowds accompanying him (Mt 21:9). He cleanses the temple (Mt 21:12–17), and in the few days of his Jerusalem ministry he engages in a series of controversies with the Jewish religious leaders (Mt 21:23–27; 22:15–22, 23–33, 34–40, 41–46), meanwhile speaking parables against them (Mt 21:28–32, 33–46), against all those Israelites who have rejected God's invitation to the messianic banquet (Mt 22:1–10), and against all, Jew and Gentile, who have accepted but have shown themselves unworthy of it

(Mt 22:11–14). Once again, the perspective of the evangelist includes not only the time of Jesus' ministry but that of the preaching of the gospel after his resurrection. The narrative culminates in Jesus' denunciation of the scribes and Pharisees, reflecting not only his own opposition to them but that of Matthew's church (Mt 23:1–36), and in Jesus' lament over Jerusalem (Mt 23:37–39).

In the discourse of the fifth book (Mt 24:1–25:46), the last of the great structural discourses of the gospel, Jesus predicts the destruction of the temple and his own final coming. The time of the latter is unknown (Mt 24:36, 44), and the disciples are exhorted in various parables to live in readiness for it, a readiness that entails faithful attention to the duties of the interim period (Mt 24:45–25:30). The coming of Jesus will bring with it the great judgment by which the everlasting destiny of all will be determined (Mt 25:31–46).

The story of Jesus' passion and resurrection (Mt 26:1–28:20), the climax of the gospel, throws light on all that has preceded. In Matthew "righteousness" means both the faithful response to the will of God demanded of all to whom that will is announced and also the saving activity of God for his people (see Mt 3:15; 5:6; 6:33). The passion supremely exemplifies both meanings of that central Matthean word. In Jesus' absolute faithfulness to the Father's will that he drink the cup of suffering (Mt 26:39), the incomparable model for Christian obedience is given; in his death "for the forgiveness of sins" (Mt 26:28), the saving power of God is manifested as never before.

Matthew's portrayal of Jesus in his passion combines both the majestic serenity of the obedient Son who goes his destined way in fulfillment of the scriptures (Mt 26:52–54), confident of his ultimate vindication by God, and the depths of fear and abandonment that he feels in face of death (Mt 26:38–39; 27:46). These two aspects are expressed by an Old Testament theme that occurs often in the narrative, i.e., the portrait of the suffering Righteous One who complains to God in his misery, but is certain of eventual deliverance from his terrible ordeal.

The passion-resurrection of God's Son means nothing less than the turn of the ages, a new stage of history, the coming of the Son of Man in his kingdom (Mt 28:18; cf. Mt 16:28). That is the sense of the apocalyptic signs that accompany Jesus' death (Mt 27:51–53) and resurrection (Mt 28:2). Although the old age continues, as it will until the manifestation of Jesus' triumph at his parousia, the final age has now begun. This is known only to those who have seen the Risen One and to those, both Jews and Gentiles, who have believed in their announcement of Jesus' triumph and have themselves become his disciples (cf. Mt 28:19). To them he is constantly, though invisibly, present (Mt 28:20), verifying the name Emmanuel, "God is with us" (cf. Mt 1:23).

The questions of authorship, sources, and the time of composition of this gospel have received many answers, none of which can claim more a greater or lesser degree of probability. The one now favored by the majority of scholars is the following.

The ancient tradition that the author was the disciple and apostle of Jesus named Matthew (see Mt 10:3) is untenable because the gospel is based, in large part, on the Gospel according to Mark (almost all the verses of that gospel have been utilized in this), and it is hardly likely that a companion of Jesus would have followed so extensively an account that came from one who admittedly never had such an association rather than rely on his own memories. The attribution of the gospel to the disciple Matthew may have been due to his having been responsible for some of the traditions found in it, but that is far from certain.

The unknown author, whom we shall continue to call Matthew for the sake of convenience, drew not only upon the Gospel according to Mark but upon a large body of material (principally, sayings of Jesus) not found in Mark that corresponds, sometimes exactly, to material found also in the Gospel according to Luke. This material, called "Q" (probably from the first letter of the German word Quelle, meaning "source"), represents traditions, written and oral, used by both Matthew and Luke. Mark and Q are sources common to the two other synoptic gospels; hence the name the "Two-Source Theory" given to this explanation of the relation among the synoptics.

In addition to what Matthew drew from Mark and Q, his gospel contains material that is found only there. This is often designated "M," written or oral tradition that was available to the author. Since Mark was written shortly before or shortly after A.D. 70 (see Introduction to Mark), Matthew was composed certainly after that date, which marks the fall of Jerusalem to the Romans at the time of the First Jewish Revolt (A.D. 66–70), and probably at least a decade later since Matthew's use of Mark presupposes a wide diffusion of that gospel. The post-A.D. 70 date is confirmed within the text by Mt 22:7, which refers to the destruction of Jerusalem.

As for the place where the gospel was composed, a plausible suggestion is that it was Antioch, the capital of the Roman province of Syria. That large and important city had a mixed population of Greek-speaking Gentiles and Jews. The tensions between

Jewish and Gentile Christians there in the time of Paul (see Gal 2:1–14) in respect to Christian obligation to observe Mosaic law are partially similar to tensions that can be seen between the two groups in Matthew's gospel. The church of Matthew, originally strongly Jewish Christian, had become one in which Gentile Christians were predominant. His gospel answers the question how obedience to the will of God is to be expressed by those who live after the "turn of the ages," the death and resurrection of Jesus.

The principal divisions of the Gospel according to Matthew are the following:

I.   The Infancy Narrative (1:1–2:23)
II.   The Proclamation of the Kingdom (3:1–7:29)
III. Ministry and Mission in Galilee (8:1–11:1)
IV.   Opposition from Israel (11:2–13:53)
V.   Jesus, the Kingdom, and the Church (13:54–18:35)
VI.   Ministry in Judea and Jerusalem (19:1–25:46)
VII. The Passion and Resurrection (26:1–28:20)

I. THE INFANCY NARRATIVE

CHAPTER 1

The Genealogy of Jesus.[*] [1a]The book of the genealogy of Jesus Christ, the son of David, the son of Abraham.[*]

[2b]Abraham became the father of Isaac, Isaac the father of Jacob, Jacob the father of Judah and his brothers.[c] [3]Judah became the father of Perez and Zerah, whose mother was Tamar.[d] Perez became the father of Hezron, Hezron the father of Ram, [4e]Ram the father of Amminadab. Amminadab became the father of Nahshon, Nahshon the father of Salmon, [5f]Salmon the father of Boaz, whose mother was Rahab. Boaz became the father of Obed, whose mother was Ruth. Obed became the father of Jesse, [6g]Jesse the father of David the king.

David became the father of Solomon, whose mother had been the wife of Uriah.

[7*h]Solomon became the father of Rehoboam, Rehoboam the father of Abijah, Abijah the father of Asaph. [8]Asaph became the father of Jehoshaphat, Jehoshaphat the father of Joram, Joram the father of Uzziah. [9]Uzziah became the father of Jotham, Jotham the father of Ahaz, Ahaz the father of Hezekiah. [10]Hezekiah became the father of Manasseh, Manasseh the father of Amos,[*] Amos the father of Josiah. [11]Josiah became the father of Jechoniah and his brothers at the time of the Babylonian exile.

[12i]After the Babylonian exile, Jechoniah became the father of Shealtiel, Shealtiel the father of Zerubbabel, [13]Zerubbabel the father of Abiud. Abiud became the father of Eliakim, Eliakim the father of Azor, [14]Azor the father of Zadok. Zadok became the father of Achim, Achim the father of Eliud, [15]Eliud the father of Eleazar. Eleazar became the father of

Matthan, Matthan the father of Jacob, [16]Jacob the father of Joseph, the husband of <u>Mary</u>. <u>Of her</u> was born Jesus who is called the Messiah.

[17]Thus the total number of generations from Abraham to David is fourteen generations; from David to the Babylonian exile, fourteen generations; from the Babylonian exile to the Messiah, fourteen generations.*

The Birth of Jesus. [18]Now this is how the birth of Jesus Christ came about. When his mother Mary was betrothed to Joseph,* but before they lived together, she was found with child through the holy Spirit. [19]Joseph her husband, since he was a righteous man,* yet unwilling to expose her to shame, decided to divorce her quietly. [20j]Such was his intention when, behold, the angel of the Lord* appeared to him in a dream and said, "Joseph, son of David, do not be afraid to take Mary your wife into your home. For it is through the holy Spirit that this child has been conceived in her. [21]She will bear a son and you are to name him Jesus,* because he will save his people from their sins." [22]All this took place to fulfill what the Lord had said through the prophet:

[23*k]"Behold, the virgin shall
    be with child and bear
    a son,
and they shall name him
    Emmanuel,"

which means "God is with us." [24]When Joseph awoke, he did as the angel of the Lord had commanded him and took his wife into his home. [25]He had no relations with her until she bore a son,* and he named him Jesus.[l]

---

a.   [1:1] Gn 5:1; 1 Chr 17:11; Gn 22:18.
b.   [1:2–17] Lk 3:23–38.
c.   [1:2] Gn 21:3; 25:26; 29:35; 1 Chr 2:1.
d.   [1:3] Gn 38:29–30; Ru 4:18; 1 Chr 2:4–9.
e.   [1:4] Ru 4:19–20; 1 Chr 2:10–11.
f.   [1:5] Ru 4:21–22; 1 Chr 2:11–12.
g.   [1:6] 2 Sm 12:24; 1 Chr 2:15; 3:5.
h.   [1:7–11] 2 Kgs 25:1–21; 1 Chr 3:10–15.
i.   [1:12–16] 1 Chr 3:16–19.
j.   [1:20] 2:13, 19; Lk 1:35.
k.   [1:23] Is 7:14 LXX.
l.   [1:25] Lk 2:7.

CHAPTER 2

The Visit of the Magi.*

¹When Jesus was born in Bethlehem of Judea, in the days of King Herod,* behold, magi from the east arrived in Jerusalem, ²saying, "Where is the newborn king of the Jews? We saw his star* at its rising and have come to do him homage."ᵃ ³When King Herod heard this, he was greatly troubled, and all Jerusalem with him. ⁴Assembling all the chief priests and the scribes of the people, he inquired of them where the Messiah was to be born.* ⁵ᵇThey said to him, "In Bethlehem of Judea, for thus it has been written through the prophet:

⁶"And you, Bethlehem,
    land of Judah,
  are by no means least
    among the rulers of
    Judah;
since from you shall come
  a ruler,

who is to shepherd my
  people Israel.'"

⁷Then Herod called the magi secretly and ascertained from them the time of the star's appearance. ⁸He sent them to Bethlehem and said, "Go and search diligently for the child. When you have found him, bring me word, that I too may go and do him homage." ⁹After their audience with the king they set out. And behold, the star that they had seen at its rising preceded them, until it came and stopped over the place where the child was. ¹⁰They were overjoyed at seeing the star, ¹¹ᶜand on entering the house they saw the child with Mary his mother. They prostrated themselves and did him homage. Then they opened their treasures and offered him gifts of gold, frankincense, and myrrh. ¹²And having been warned in a dream not to return to

Herod, they departed for their country by another way.

The Flight to Egypt. [13*]When they had departed, behold, the angel of the Lord appeared to Joseph in a dream and said, "Rise, take the child and his mother, flee to Egypt,* and stay there until I tell you. Herod is going to search for the child to destroy him." [14]Joseph rose and took the child and his mother by night and departed for Egypt. [15*]He stayed there until the death of Herod, that what the Lord had said through the prophet[d] might be fulfilled, "Out of Egypt I called my son."

The Massacre of the Infants. [16]When Herod realized that he had been deceived by the magi, he became furious. He ordered the massacre of all the boys in Bethlehem and its vicinity two years old and under, in accordance with the time he had ascertained from the magi. [17]Then was fulfilled what had been said through Jeremiah the prophet:

[18*e]"A voice was heard in
  Ramah,
    sobbing and loud
      lamentation;
Rachel weeping for her
  children,
    and she would not be
      consoled,
    since they were no
      more."

The Return from Egypt. [19]When Herod had died, behold, the angel of the Lord appeared in a dream to Joseph in Egypt [20]and said,[f] "Rise, take the child and his mother and go to the land of Israel, for those who sought the child's life are dead."* [21]He rose, took the child and his mother, and went to the land of Israel. [22]But when he heard that Archelaus was ruling over Judea in place of his father Herod,* he was afraid to go back there. And because he had been warned in a dream, he departed for the region of Galilee. ²³*ᵍHe went and dwelt in a town called Nazareth, so that what had been spoken through the prophets might be fulfilled, "He shall be called a Nazorean."

a. [2:2] Nm 24:17.
b. [2:5–6] Mi 5:1; 2 Sm 5:2.
c. [2:11] Ps 72:10–11, 15; Is 60:6.
d. [2:15] Hos 11:1.
e. [2:18] Jer 31:15.
f. [2:20] Ex 4:19.
g. [2:23] 13:54; Mk 1:9; Lk 2:39; 4:34; Jn 19:19.

II. THE PROCLAMATION OF THE KINGDOM

CHAPTER 3

The Preaching of John the Baptist.*ᵃ ¹In those days John the Baptist appeared, preaching in the desert of Judea* ²[and] saying, "Repent,* for the kingdom of heaven is at hand!"ᵇ ³It was of him that the prophet Isaiahᶜ had spoken when he said:

"A voice of one crying out
    in the desert,
'Prepare the way of the
    Lord,
    make straight his
    paths.'"

⁴*ᵈJohn wore clothing made of camel's hair and had a leather belt around his waist. His food was locusts and wild honey. ⁵At that time Jerusalem, all Judea, and the whole region around the Jordan were going out to him ⁶and were being baptized by him in the Jordan River as they acknowledged their sins.*

⁷When he saw many of the Pharisees and Sadducees* coming to his baptism, he said to them, "You brood of vipers! Who warned you to flee from the coming wrath?ᵉ ⁸Produce good fruit as evidence of your repentance. ⁹And do not presume to say to yourselves, 'We have Abraham as our father.' For I tell you, God can raise up children to Abraham from these stones.ᶠ ¹⁰Even now the ax lies at the root of the trees. Therefore every tree that does not

bear good fruit will be cut down and thrown into the fire. [11g]I am baptizing you with water, for repentance, but the one who is coming after me is mightier than I. I am not worthy to carry his sandals. He will baptize you with the holy Spirit and fire.[*] [12*h]His winnowing fan is in his hand. He will clear his threshing floor and gather his wheat into his barn, but the chaff he will burn with unquenchable fire."

The Baptism of Jesus.[*] [13i]Then Jesus came from Galilee to John at the Jordan to be baptized by him. [14*]John tried to prevent him, saying, "I need to be baptized by you, and yet you are coming to me?" [15]Jesus said to him in reply, "Allow it now, for thus it is fitting for us to fulfill all righteousness." Then he allowed him. [16*j]After Jesus was baptized, he came up from the water and behold, the heavens were opened [for him], and he saw the Spirit of God descending like a dove [and] coming upon him. [17]And a voice came from the heavens, saying, "This is my beloved Son,[*] with whom I am well pleased."[k]

a. [3:1–12] Mk 1:2–8; Lk 3:2–17.
b. [3:2] 4:17; 10:7.
c. [3:3] Is 40:3.
d. [3:4] 11:7–8; 2 Kgs 1:8; Zec 13:4.
e. [3:7] 12:34; 23:33; Is 59:5.
f. [3:9] Jn 8:33, 39; Rom 9:7–8; Gal 4:21–31.
g. [3:11] Jn 1:26–27, 33; Acts 1:5.
h. [3:12] 13:30; Is 41:16; Jer 15:7.
i. [3:13–17] Mk 1:9–11; Lk 3:21–22; Jn 1:31–34.
j. [3:16] Is 42:1.
k. [3:17] 12:18; 17:5; Gn 22:2; Ps 2:7; Is 42:1.

CHAPTER 4

The Temptation of Jesus. [1*a]Then Jesus was led by the Spirit into the desert to be tempted by the devil. [2b]He fasted for forty days and forty nights,[*] and afterwards he was hungry. [3]The tempter approached and said to him, "If you are the Son of God, command that these stones become loaves of bread." [4]He said in reply, "It is written:[c]

'One does not live by
    bread alone,
  but by every word that

comes forth from the mouth of God.'"

5Then the devil took him to the holy city, and made him stand on the parapet of the temple, 6and said to him, "If you are the Son of God, throw yourself down. For it is written:

'He will command his
    angels concerning
    you'
and 'with their hands
    they will support you,
lest you dash your foot
    against a stone.'"d

7Jesus answered him, "Again it is written, 'You shall not put the Lord, your God, to the test.'"e 8Then the devil took him up to a very high mountain, and showed him all the kingdoms of the world in their magnificence, 9and he said to him, "All these I shall give to you, if you will prostrate yourself and worship me.'" 10At this, Jesus said

to him, "Get away, Satan! It is written:

'The Lord, your God, shall
    you worship
    and him alone shall you
    serve.'"f

11Then the devil left him and, behold, angels came and ministered to him.

The Beginning of the Galilean Ministry. 12gWhen he heard that John had been arrested, he withdrew to Galilee. 13He left Nazareth and went to live in Capernaum by the sea, in the region of Zebulun and Naphtali,h 14that what had been said through Isaiah the prophet might be fulfilled:

15"Land of Zebulun and
    land of Naphtali,i
the way to the sea,
    beyond the Jordan,
    Galilee of the Gentiles,
16the people who sit in
    darkness
have seen a great light,
on those dwelling in a

land overshadowed by
death
light has arisen."[j]

[17*]From that time on, Jesus began to preach and say,[k] "Repent, for the kingdom of heaven is at hand."

The Call of the First Disciples.[*] [18l]As he was walking by the Sea of Galilee, he saw two brothers, Simon who is called Peter, and his brother Andrew, casting a net into the sea; they were fishermen. [19]He said to them, "Come after me, and I will make you fishers of men." [20*]At once they left their nets and followed him. [21]He walked along from there and saw two other brothers, James, the son of Zebedee, and his brother John. They were in a boat, with their father Zebedee, mending their nets. He called them, [22]and immediately they left their boat and their father and followed him.

Ministering to a Great Multitude.[*] [23]He went around all of Galilee, teaching in their synagogues,[*] proclaiming the gospel of the kingdom, and curing every disease and illness among the people.[m] [24*]His fame spread to all of Syria, and they brought to him all who were sick with various diseases and racked with pain, those who were possessed, lunatics, and paralytics, and he cured them. [25n]And great crowds from Galilee, the Decapolis,[*] Jerusalem, and Judea, and from beyond the Jordan followed him.

---

a. [4:1–11] Mk 1:12–13; Lk 4:1–13.
b. [4:2] Ex 24:18; Dt 8:2.
c. [4:4] Dt 8:3.
d. [4:6] Ps 91:11–12.
e. [4:7] Dt 6:16.
f. [4:10] 16:23; Dt 6:13.
g. [4:12–13] Mk 1:14–15; Lk 4:14, 31.
h. [4:13] Jn 2:12.
i. [4:15–16] Is 8:23 LXX; 9:1.
j. [4:16] Lk 1:79.
k. [4:17] 3:2.
l. [4:18–22] Mk 1:16–20; Lk 5:1–11.
m. [4:23] 9:35; Mk 1:39; Lk 4:15, 44.
n. [4:25] Mk 3:7–8; Lk 6:17–19.

CHAPTER 5

The Sermon on the Mount.[*] [1*]When he saw the crowds,[*]

he went up the mountain, and after he had sat down, his disciples came to him. ²He began to teach them, saying:

The Beatitudes*

³"Blessed are the poor in
    spirit,*
  for theirs is the kingdom
    of heaven.ᵃ
⁴*Blessed are they who
    mourn,ᵇ
  for they will be
    comforted.
⁵*Blessed are the meek,ᶜ
  for they will inherit the
    land.
⁶Blessed are they who
    hunger and thirst for
    righteousness,*
  for they will be satisfied.
⁷Blessed are the merciful,
  for they will be shown
    mercy.ᵈ
⁸*Blessed are the clean of
    heart,ᵉ
  for they will see God.
⁹Blessed are the
    peacemakers,
  for they will be called
    children of God.

¹⁰Blessed are they who are
    persecuted for the
    sake of righteousness,*
  for theirs is the kingdom
    of heaven.ᶠ

¹¹Blessed are you when they insult you and persecute you and utter every kind of evil against you [falsely] because of me.ᵍ ¹²Rejoice and be glad, for your reward will be great in heaven.ʰ Thus they persecuted the prophets who were before you.

The Similes of Salt and Light.*

¹³ⁱ"You are the salt of the earth. But if salt loses its taste, with what can it be seasoned? It is no longer good for anything but to be thrown out and trampled underfoot.* ¹⁴You are the light of the world. A city set on a mountain cannot be hidden.ʲ ¹⁵Nor do they light a lamp and then put it under a bushel basket; it is set on a lampstand, where it gives light to all in the house.ᵏ ¹⁶Just so, your light must shine before

others, that they may see your good deeds and glorify your heavenly Father.[l]

Teaching About the Law. [17]"Do not think that I have come to abolish the law or the prophets. I have come not to abolish but to fulfill. [18]Amen, I say to you, until heaven and earth pass away, not the smallest letter or the smallest part of a letter will pass from the law, until all things have taken place.[m] [19]Therefore, whoever breaks one of the least of these commandments and teaches others to do so will be called least in the kingdom of heaven. But whoever obeys and teaches these commandments will be called greatest in the kingdom of heaven.[*] [20]I tell you, unless your righteousness surpasses that of the scribes and Pharisees, you will not enter into the kingdom of heaven.

Teaching About Anger.[*] [21]"You have heard that it was said to your ancestors,[n] 'You shall not kill; and whoever kills will be liable to judgment.' [22]But I say to you, whoever is angry[*] with his brother will be liable to judgment,[o] and whoever says to his brother, 'Raqa,' will be answerable to the Sanhedrin, and whoever says, 'You fool,' will be liable to fiery Gehenna. [23]Therefore, if you bring your gift to the altar, and there recall that your brother has anything against you,[p] [24]leave your gift there at the altar, go first and be reconciled with your brother, and then come and offer your gift. [25]Settle with your opponent quickly while on the way to court with him.[q] Otherwise your opponent will hand you over to the judge, and the judge will hand you over to the guard, and you will be thrown into prison. [26]Amen, I say to you, you will not be released until you have paid the last penny.

Teaching About Adultery.
²⁷*"You have heard that it was said,ʳ 'You shall not commit adultery.' ²⁸But I say to you, everyone who looks at a woman with lust has already committed adultery with her in his heart. ²⁹If your right eye causes you to sin, tear it out and throw it away.ˢ It is better for you to lose one of your members than to have your whole body thrown into Gehenna. ³⁰And if your right hand causes you to sin, cut it off and throw it away. It is better for you to lose one of your members than to have your whole body go into Gehenna.

[handwritten: wife]

Teaching About Divorce.
³¹*"It was also said, 'Whoever divorces his wife must give her a bill of divorce.'ᵗ ³²But I say to you, whoever divorces his wife (unless the marriage is unlawful) causes her to commit adultery, and whoever marries a divorced woman commits adultery.ᵘ

Teaching About Oaths.
³³*ᵛ"Again you have heard that it was said to your ancestors, 'Do not take a false oath, but make good to the Lord all that you vow.' ³⁴ʷBut I say to you, do not swear at all;ᵗ not by heaven, for it is God's throne; ³⁵nor by the earth, for it is his footstool; nor by Jerusalem, for it is the city of the great King. ³⁶Do not swear by your head, for you cannot make a single hair white or black. ³⁷Let your 'Yes' mean 'Yes,' and your 'No' mean 'No.' Anything more is from the evil one.

Teaching About Retaliation.
³⁸*"You have heard that it was said,ˣ 'An eye for an eye and a tooth for a tooth.' ³⁹ʸBut I say to you, offer no resistance to one who is evil. When someone strikes you on [your] right cheek, turn the other one to him as well. ⁴⁰If anyone wants to go to law with you over your tunic, hand him your cloak as well. ⁴¹Should

anyone press you into service for one mile,* go with him for two miles.*z* 42Give to the one who asks of you, and do not turn your back on one who wants to borrow.*a*

Love of Enemies.* 43b"You have heard that it was said, 'You shall love your neighbor and hate your enemy.'*c* 44But I say to you, love your enemies, and pray for those who persecute you, 45that you may be children of your heavenly Father, (for he makes his sun rise on the bad and the good, and causes rain to fall on the just and the unjust.) 46For if you love those who love you, what recompense will you have? Do not the tax collectors* do the same? 47And if you greet your brothers only, what is unusual about that? Do not the pagans do the same?* 48So be perfect,* just as your heavenly Father is perfect.*d*

a. [5:3–12] Lk 6:20–23.
b. [5:4] Is 61:2–3; Rev 21:4.
c. [5:5] Gn 13:15; Ps 37:11.
d. [5:7] 18:33; Jas 2:13.
e. [5:8] Ps 24:4–5; 73:1.
f. [5:10] 1 Pt 2:20; 3:14; 4:14.
g. [5:11] 10:22; Acts 5:41.
h. [5:12] 2 Chr 36:16; Heb 11:32–38; Jas 5:10.
i. [5:13] Mk 9:50; Lk 14:34–35.
j. [5:14] Jn 8:12.
k. [5:15] Mk 4:21; Lk 8:16; 11:33.
l. [5:16] Jn 3:21.
m. [5:18] Lk 16:17.
n. [5:21] Ex 20:13; Dt 5:17.
o. [5:22] Jas 1:19–20.
p. [5:23] Mk 11:25.
q. [5:25–26] 18:34–35; Lk 12:58–59.
r. [5:27] Ex 20:14; Dt 5:18.
s. [5:29–30] 18:8–9; Mk 9:43–47.
t. [5:31] 19:3–9; Dt 24:1.
u. [5:32] Lk 16:18; 1 Cor 7:10–11.
v. [5:33] Lv 19:12; Nm 30:3.
w. [5:34–37] Ps 48:3; Sir 23:9; Js 66:1; Jas 5:12.
x. [5:38] Ex 21:24; Lv 24:19–20.
y. [5:39–42] Lk 6:29–30.
z. [5:41] Lam 3:30.
a. [5:42] Dt 15:7–8.
b. [5:43–48] Lk 6:27, 32–36.
c. [5:43] Lv 19:18.
d. [5:48] Lv 11:44; 19:2; Dt 18:13; 1 Pt 1:16; 1 Jn 3:3.

CHAPTER 6

Teaching About Almsgiving.* 1"[But] take care not to perform righteous deeds in order that people may see them;*a* otherwise, you will have no recompense from your heavenly Father. 2When you give alms, do not blow a trumpet before you, as the hypocrites* do in the synagogues and in the streets to win the praise of others. Amen, I say to you, they have received their reward.*b* 3But when you give alms, do not let your left hand know what your right is doing, [4]so that your almsgiving may be secret. And your Father who sees in secret will repay you.

Teaching About Prayer. [5]"When you pray, do not be like the hypocrites, who love to stand and pray in the synagogues and on street corners so that others may see them. Amen, I say to you, they have received their reward. [6]But when you pray, go to your inner room, close the door, and pray to your Father in secret. And your Father who sees in secret will repay you. [7]*In praying, do not babble like the pagans, who think that they will be heard because of their many words.* [8]Do not be like them. Your Father knows what you need before you ask him.

The Lord's Prayer. [9]*"This is how you are to pray:[c]

Our Father in heaven,*
    hallowed be your name,
[10]your kingdom come,*
    your will be done,
        on earth as in
            heaven.[d]
[11]*eGive us today our
    daily bread;
[12]and forgive us our
    debts,*
        as we forgive our
            debtors;[f]
[13]and do not subject us
    to the final test,*
        but deliver us from
            the evil one.[g]

[14]*If you forgive others their transgressions, your heavenly Father will forgive you.[h] [15]But if you do not forgive others, neither will your Father forgive your transgressions.[i]

Teaching About Fasting. [16]"When you fast,* do not look gloomy like the hypocrites. They neglect their appearance, so that they may appear to others to be fasting. Amen, I say to you, they have received their reward. [17]But when you fast, anoint your head and wash your face, [18]so that you may not appear to others to be fasting, except to your Father who is hidden. And your Father who sees what is hidden will repay you.

Treasure in Heaven. [19]"Do not store up for yourselves treasures on earth, where moth and decay destroy, and thieves break in and steal.[j] [20]But store up treasures in heaven, where neither moth nor decay destroys, nor thieves break in and steal. [21]For where your treasure is, there also will your heart be.[k]

The Light of the Body. [22]"The lamp of the body is the eye. If your eye is sound, your whole body will be filled with light; [23]but if your eye is bad, your whole body will be in darkness. And if the light in you is darkness, how great will the darkness be.[l]

God and Money. [24]"No one can serve two masters.[m] He will either hate one and love the other, or be devoted to one and despise the other. You cannot serve God and mammon.

Dependence on God. [25n]"Therefore I tell you, do not worry about your life, what you will eat [or drink], or about your body, what you will wear. Is not life more than food and the body more than clothing? [26]Look at the birds in the sky; they do not sow or reap, they gather nothing into barns, yet your heavenly Father feeds them. Are not you more important than they?[o] [27]Can any of you by worrying add a single moment to your life-span?* [28]Why are you anxious about clothes? Learn from the way the wild flowers grow. They do not work or spin. [29]But I tell you that not even Solomon in all his splendor was clothed like one of them. [30]*If God so clothes the grass of the field, which grows today and is thrown into the oven tomorrow, will he not much more provide for you, O you of little faith? [31]So do not worry and say, 'What are we to eat?' or 'What are we to drink?' or 'What are we to wear?' [32]All these things the pagans seek. Your heavenly Father knows that you need them all. [33]But <u>seek first the kingdom [of God] and his righteousness,</u>* and all these things will be given you besides. ([34]Do not worry about tomorrow; tomorrow will take care of itself. <u>Sufficient for a day is its own evil.</u>)

a. [6:1] 23:5.
b. [6:2] Jn 12:43.
c. [6:9–13] Lk 11:2–4.
d. [6:10] 26:42.
e. [6:11] Prv 30:8–9.
f. [6:12] 18:21–22; Sir 28:2.
g. [6:13] Jn 17:15; 2 Thes 3:3.
h. [6:14] 18:35; Sir 28:1–5; Mk 11:25.
i. [6:15] Jas 2:13.
j. [6:19] Jas 5:2–3.
k. [6:20–21] Lk 12:33–34.
l. [6:22–23] Lk 11:34–36.
m. [6:24] Lk 16:13.
n. [6:25–33] Lk 12:22–31.
o. [6:26] Ps 145:15–16; 147:9.

CHAPTER 7

Judging Others. [1]*a*"<u>Stop judging,</u>* that you may not be judged.*b* [2]For as you judge, so will you be judged, and the measure with which you measure will be measured out to you.*c* [3]Why do you notice the splinter in your brother's eye, but do not perceive the wooden beam in your own eye? [4]How can you say to your brother, 'Let me remove that splinter from your eye,' while the wooden beam is in your eye? [5]You hypocrite,* remove the wooden beam from your eye first; then you will see clearly to remove the splinter from your brother's eye.

Pearls Before Swine. [6]"Do not give what is holy to dogs,* or throw your pearls before swine, lest they trample them underfoot, and turn and tear you to pieces.*d*

The Answer to Prayers. [7]*e*"Ask and it will be given to you; seek and you will find; knock and the door will be opened to you.*f* [8]For everyone who asks, receives; and the one who seeks, finds; and to the one who knocks, the door will be opened.*g* [9]Which one of you would hand his son a stone when he asks for a loaf of bread,* [10]or a snake when he asks for a fish? [11]If you then, who are wicked, know how to give good gifts to your children, how much more will your heavenly Father give good things to those who ask him.[h]

The Golden Rule. [12*]"Do to others whatever you would have them do to you.[i] This is the law and the prophets.

The Narrow Gate. [13*]"Enter through the narrow gate;* for the gate is wide and the road broad that leads to destruction, and those who enter through it are many.[j] [14]How narrow the gate and constricted the road that leads to life. And those who find it are few.

False Prophets.* [15]"Beware of false prophets, who come to you in sheep's clothing, but underneath are ravenous wolves.[k] [16l]By their fruits you will know them. Do people pick grapes from thornbushes, or figs from thistles? [17]Just so, every good tree bears good fruit, and a rotten tree bears bad fruit. [18]A good tree cannot bear bad fruit, nor can a rotten tree bear good fruit. [19]Every tree that does not bear good fruit will be cut down and thrown into the fire. [20]So by their fruits you will know them.[m]

The True Disciple. [21]"Not everyone who says to me, 'Lord, Lord,' will enter the kingdom of heaven,* but only the one who does the will of my Father in heaven.[n] [22]Many will say to me on that day,[o] 'Lord, Lord, did we not prophesy in your name? Did we not drive out demons in your name? Did we not do mighty deeds in your name?'[p] [23]Then I will declare to them solemnly, 'I never knew you.* Depart from me, you evildoers.'[q]

The Two Foundations. [24*]"Everyone who listens to these words of mine and acts on them will be like a wise man who built his house on rock.[r] [25]The rain fell, the floods came, and the winds blew and buffeted the house.[s] But it did not collapse; it had been set solidly on rock. [26]And everyone who listens to these words of mine but does not act on them will be like a fool who built his house on sand. [27]The rain fell, the floods came, and the winds blew and buffeted the house. And it collapsed and was completely ruined."

[28]*When Jesus finished these words, the crowds were astonished at his teaching, [29]*[t]for he taught them as one having authority, and not as their scribes.

a. [7:1–5] Lk 6:37–38, 41–42.
b. [7:1] Rom 2:1–2; 1 Cor 4:5.
c. [7:2] Wis 12:22; Mk 4:24.
d. [7:6] Prv 23:9.
e. [7:7–11] Mk 11:24; Lk 11:9–13.
f. [7:7] 18:19.
g. [7:8] Lk 18:1–8; Jn 14:13.
h. [7:11] 1 Jn 5:14–15.
i. [7:12] Lk 6:31.
j. [7:13] Lk 13:24.
k. [7:15] 2 Pt 2:1.
l. [7:16–17] 12:33; Lk 6:43–44.
m. [7:20] 3:10.
n. [7:21] Is 29:13; Lk 6:46.
o. [7:22–23] Lk 13:26–27.
p. [7:22] 25:11–12.
q. [7:23] Ps 5:5; 6:9.
r. [7:24–27] Lk 6:47–49.
s. [7:25–26] Prv 10:25.
t. [7:29] Mk 1:22; Lk 4:32.

III. MINISTRY AND MISSION IN GALILEE*

CHAPTER 8

The Cleansing of a Leper. [1]*When Jesus came down from the mountain, great crowds followed him. [2]And then a leper* approached, did him homage, and said, "Lord, if you wish, you can make me clean." [3]He stretched out his hand, touched him, and said, "I will do it. Be made clean." His leprosy was cleansed immediately. [4]*Then Jesus said to him, ("See that you tell no one, but go show yourself to the priest, and offer the gift that Moses prescribed;[b] that will be proof for them.")

The Healing of a Centurion's Servant.* [5c]When he entered Capernaum,* a centurion approached him and appealed to him, [6]saying, "Lord, my servant is lying at home paralyzed, suffering dreadfully." [7]He said to him, "I will come and cure him." [8]The centurion said in reply,* "Lord, I am not worthy to have you enter under my roof; only say the word and my servant will be healed. [9]For I too am a person subject to authority, with soldiers subject to me. And I say to one, 'Go,' and he goes; and to another, 'Come here,' and he comes; and to my slave, 'Do this,' and he does it." [10]When Jesus heard this, he was amazed and said to those following him, "Amen, I say to you, in no one in Israel* have I found such faith. [11d]I say to you,* many will come from the east and the west, and will recline with Abraham, Isaac, and Jacob at the banquet in the kingdom of heaven, [12]but the children of the kingdom will be driven out into the outer darkness, where there will be wailing and grinding of teeth." [13]And Jesus said to the centurion, "You may go; as you have believed, let it be done for you." And at that very hour [his] servant was healed.

The Cure of Peter's Mother-in-Law.* [14e]Jesus entered the house of Peter, and saw his mother-in-law lying in bed with a fever. [15]He touched her hand, the fever left her, and she rose and waited on him.[f]

Other Healings. [16]When it was evening, they brought him many who were possessed by demons, and he drove out the spirits by a word* and cured all the sick, [17]to fulfill what had been said by Isaiah the prophet:*[g]

"He took away our infirmities
    and bore our diseases."

The Would-be Followers of Jesus.* [18h]When Jesus saw a crowd around him, he gave orders to cross to the other side.* [19i]A scribe approached and said to him, "Teacher,* I will follow you wherever you go." [20]Jesus answered him, "Foxes have dens and birds of the sky have nests, but the Son of Man* has nowhere to rest his head." [21]Another of [his] disciples said to him, "Lord, let me go first and bury my father." [22]*But Jesus answered him, "Follow me, and let the dead bury their dead."

The Calming of the Storm at Sea. [23]*jHe got into a boat and his disciples followed him. [24]Suddenly a violent storm* came up on the sea, so that the boat was being swamped by waves; but he was asleep. [25]kThey came and woke him, saying, "Lord, save us!* We are perishing!" [26]He said to them, "Why are you terrified, O you of little faith?"* Then he got up, rebuked the winds and the sea, and there was great calm. [27]The men were amazed and said, "What sort of man is this, whom even the winds and the sea obey?"

The Healing of the Gadarene Demoniacs. [28]lWhen he came to the other side, to the territory of the Gadarenes,* two demoniacs who were coming from the tombs met him. They were so savage that no one could travel by that road. [29]They cried out, "What have you to do with us,* Son of God? Have you come here to torment us before the appointed time?" [30]Some distance away a herd of many swine was feeding.* [31]The demons pleaded with him, "If you drive us out, send us into the herd of swine."m [32]And he said to them, "Go then!" They came out and entered the swine, and the whole herd rushed down the steep bank into the sea where they drowned. [33]The swineherds ran away, and when they came to the town they reported everything, including what had happened to the demoniacs. [34]Thereupon the whole town came out to meet Jesus, and when they saw him they begged him to leave their district.

a. [8:1–4] Mk 1:40–44; Lk 5:12–14.
b. [8:4] Lv 14:2–32; Lk 17:14.
c. [8:5–13] Lk 7:1–10; Jn 4:46–53.
d. [8:11–12] 13:42, 50; 22:13; 24:51; 25:30; Lk 13:28–29.
e. [8:14–16] Mk 1:29–34; Lk 4:38–41.
f. [8:15] 9:25.
g. [8:17] Is 53:4.
h. [8:18] Mk 4:35.
i. [8:19–22] Lk 9:57–60.
j. [8:23–27] Mk 4:35–40; Lk 8:22–25.
k. [8:25–26] Ps 107:28–29.
l. [8:28–34] Mk 5:1–17; Lk 8:26–37.
m. [8:31] Lk 4:34, 41.

CHAPTER 9

The Healing of a Paralytic. ¹*ᵃHe entered a boat, made the crossing, and came into his own town. ²And there people brought to him a paralytic lying on a stretcher. When Jesus saw their faith, he said to the paralytic, "Courage, child, your sins are forgiven."ᵇ ³At that, some of the scribes* said to themselves, "This man is blaspheming." ⁴Jesus knew what they were thinking, and said, "Why do you harbor evil thoughts? ⁵Which is easier, to say, 'Your sins are forgiven,' or to say, 'Rise and walk'? ⁶*But that you may know that the Son of Man has authority on earth to forgive sins"—he then said to the paralytic, "Rise, pick up your stretcher, and go home."ᶜ ⁷He rose and went home. ⁸*When the crowds saw this they were struck with awe and glorified God who had given such authority to human beings.

The Call of Matthew.* ⁹As Jesus passed on from there,ᵈ he saw a man named Matthew* sitting at the customs post. He said to him, "Follow me." And he got up and followed him. (¹⁰While he was at table in his house,* many tax collectors and <u>sinners</u> came and sat with Jesus and his disciples.ᵉ) ¹¹The Pharisees saw this and said to his disciples, "Why does your teacher* eat with tax collectors and sinners?" ¹²He heard this and said, "Those who are well do not need a physician, but the sick do.* ¹³<u>Go and learn the meaning of the words,ᶠ 'I desire mercy, not sacrifice.'</u>* <u>I did not come to call the righteous but sinners.</u>"

The Question About Fasting. [14g]Then the disciples of John approached him and said, "Why do we and the Pharisees fast [much], but your disciples do not fast?" [15]Jesus answered them, "Can the wedding guests mourn as long as the bridegroom is with them? The days will come when the bridegroom is taken away from them, and then they will fast.* [16]No one patches an old cloak with a piece of unshrunken cloth,* for its fullness pulls away from the cloak and the tear gets worse. [17]People do not put new wine into old wineskins. Otherwise the skins burst, the wine spills out, and the skins are ruined. Rather, they pour new wine into fresh wineskins, and both are preserved."

The Official's Daughter and the Woman with a Hemorrhage. [18*]While he was saying these things to them,[h] an official* came forward, knelt down before him, and said, "My daughter has just died. But come, lay your hand on her, and she will live." [19]Jesus rose and followed him, and so did his disciples. [20]A woman suffering hemorrhages for twelve years came up behind him and touched the tassel* on his cloak. [21]She said to herself, "If only I can touch his cloak, I shall be cured."[i] [22]Jesus turned around and saw her, and said, "Courage, daughter! Your faith has saved you." And from that hour the woman was cured.

[23]When Jesus arrived at the official's house and saw the flute players and the crowd who were making a commotion, [24]he said, "Go away! The girl is not dead but sleeping."* And they ridiculed him. [25]When the crowd was put out, he came and took her by the hand, and the little girl arose. [26]And news of this spread throughout all that land.

The Healing of Two Blind Men.[*] [27j]And as Jesus passed on from there, two blind men followed [him], crying out, "Son of David,[*] have pity on us!"[k] [28]When he entered the house, the blind men approached him and Jesus said to them, "Do you believe that I can do this?" "Yes, Lord," they said to him. [29]Then he touched their eyes and said, "Let it be done for you according to your faith." [30]And their eyes were opened. Jesus warned them sternly, "See that no one knows about this." [31]But they went out and spread word of him through all that land.

The Healing of a Mute Person. [32l]As they were going out,[*] a demoniac who could not speak was brought to him, [33]and when the demon was driven out the mute person spoke. The crowds were amazed and said, "Nothing like this has ever been seen in Israel."[m] [34*]But the Pharisees said,[n] "He drives out demons by the prince of demons."

The Compassion of Jesus. [35*o]Jesus went around to all the towns and villages, teaching in their synagogues, proclaiming the gospel of the kingdom, and curing every disease and illness. [36p]At the sight of the crowds, his heart was moved with pity for them because they were troubled and abandoned,[*] like sheep without a shepherd. [37*q]Then he said to his disciples, "The harvest is abundant but the laborers are few; [38]so ask the master of the harvest to send out laborers for his harvest."

a. [9:1–8] Mk 2:3–12; Lk 5:18–26.
b. [9:2] Lk 7:48.
c. [9:6] Jn 5:27.
d. [9:9–13] Mk 2:14–17; Lk 5:27–32.
e. [9:10] 11:19; Lk 15:1–2.
f. [9:13] 12:7; Hos 6:6.
g. [9:14–17] Mk 2:18–22; Lk 5:33–39.
h. [9:18–26] Mk 5:22–43; Lk 8:41–56.
i. [9:21] 14:36; Nm 15:37.
j. [9:27–31] 20:29–34.
k. [9:27] 15:22.
l. [9:32–34] 12:22–24; Lk 11:14–15.
m. [9:33] Mk 2:12; 7:37.
n. [9:34] 10:25; Mk 3:22.
o. [9:35] 4:23; Lk 8:1.
p. [9:36] Nm 27:17; 1 Kgs 22:17; Jer 50:6; Ez 34:5; Mk 6:34.
q. [9:37–38] Lk 10:2; Jn 4:35.

CHAPTER 10

The Mission of the Twelve. [1]"Then he summoned his twelve disciples* and gave them authority over unclean spirits to drive them out and to cure every disease and every illness.[a] [2]The names of the twelve apostles* are these: first, Simon called Peter, and his brother Andrew; James, the son of Zebedee, and his brother John; [3]Philip and Bartholomew, Thomas and Matthew the tax collector; James, the son of Alphaeus, and Thaddeus; [4]Simon the Cananean, and Judas Iscariot who betrayed him.

The Commissioning of the Twelve. [5b]Jesus sent out these twelve* after instructing them thus, "Do not go into pagan territory or enter a Samaritan town. [6]Go rather to the lost sheep of the house of Israel. [7]As you go, make this proclamation: 'The kingdom of heaven is at hand.'[d] [8]*Cure the sick, raise the dead, cleanse lepers, drive out demons. Without cost you have received; without cost you are to give.) [9e]Do not take gold or silver or copper for your belts; [10f]no sack for the journey, or a second tunic, or sandals, or walking stick. The laborer deserves his keep. [11g]Whatever town or village you enter, look for a worthy person in it, and stay there until you leave. [12]As you enter a house, wish it peace. [13]If the house is worthy, let your peace come upon it; if not, let your peace return to you.* [14h]Whoever will not receive you or listen to your words— go outside that house or town and shake the dust from your feet. [15]Amen, I say to you, it will be more tolerable for the land of Sodom and Gomorrah on the day of judgment than for that town.[i]

Coming Persecutions. [16j]"Behold, I am sending you like sheep in the midst of wolves; so be shrewd as serpents and simple as doves. [17*]But beware of people,[k] for they will hand you over to courts and scourge you in their synagogues,[l] [18]and you will be led before governors and kings for my sake as a witness before them and the pagans. [19]When they hand you over, do not worry about how you are to speak or what you are to say. You will be given at that moment what you are to say.[m] [20]For it will not be you who speak but the Spirit of your Father speaking through you. [21*n]Brother will hand over brother to death, and the father his child; children will rise up against parents and have them put to death. [22]You will be hated by all because of my name, but whoever endures to the end[*] will be saved. [23]When they persecute you in one town, flee to another. Amen, I say to you, you will not finish the towns of Israel before the Son of Man comes.[*] [24o]No disciple is above his teacher, no slave above his master. [25]It is enough for the disciple that he become like his teacher, for the slave that he become like his master. If they have called the master of the house Beelzebul,[*] how much more those of his household!

Courage Under Persecution. [26p]"Therefore do not be afraid of them. Nothing is concealed that will not be revealed, nor secret that will not be known.[*q] [27]What I say to you in the darkness, speak in the light; what you hear whispered, proclaim on the housetops. [28]And do not be afraid of those who kill the body but cannot kill the soul; rather, be afraid of the one who can destroy both soul and body in Gehenna.[r] [29]Are not two sparrows sold for a small coin? Yet not one of them falls to the ground without your Father's knowledge. [30]Even all the hairs of your head are counted. [31]So do not be afraid; you are worth more than many sparrows. [32]*Everyone who acknowledges me before others I will acknowledge before my heavenly Father. [33]But whoever denies me before others, I will deny before my heavenly Father.[s]

Jesus: A Cause of Division. [34]*"Do not think that I have come to bring peace upon the earth. I have come to bring not peace but the sword. [35]For I have come to set

a man 'against his father,
   a daughter against her
      mother,
and a daughter-in-
      law against her
      mother-in-law;
   [36]and one's enemies
      will be those of his
      household.'

The Conditions of Discipleship. [37u]*"Whoever loves father or mother more than me is not worthy of me, and whoever loves son or

daughter more than me is not worthy of me; [38]and whoever does not <u>take up his cross</u>* <u>and follow after me</u> is not worthy of me. [39]*[v]Whoever finds his life will lose it, and whoever loses his life for my sake will find it.

Rewards. [40]"Whoever receives you receives me,* and whoever receives me receives the one who sent me.[w] [41]*Whoever receives a prophet because he is a prophet will receive a prophet's reward, and whoever receives a righteous man because he is righteous will receive a righteous man's reward. [42]And whoever gives only a cup of cold water to one of these little ones to drink because he is a disciple—amen, I say to you, he will surely not lose his reward."[x]

a. [10:1–4] Mk 3:14–19; Lk 6:13–16; Acts 1:13.
b. [10:5–15] Mk 6:7–13; Lk 9:1–6.
c. [10:6] 15:24.
d. [10:7] 3:2; 4:17.
e. [10:9–10] Mk 6:8–9; Lk 9:3; 10:4.
f. [10:10] Lk 10:7; 1 Cor 9:14; 1 Tm 5:18.
g. [10:11–15] Mk 6:10–11; Lk 9:4–5; 10:5–12.
h. [10:14] Acts 13:51; 18:6.
i. [10:15] 11:24; Gn 19:1–29; Jude 7.

j. [10:16] Lk 10:3.
k. [10:17–22] Mk 13:9–13; Lk 21:12–19.
l. [10:17] Acts 5:40.
m. [10:19] Ex 4:11–12; Jer 1:6–10; Lk 12:11–12.
n. [10:21–22] 24:9, 13.
o. [10:24–25] Lk 6:40; Jn 13:16; 15:20.
p. [10:26–33] Lk 12:2–9.
q. [10:26] Mk 4:22; Lk 8:17; 1 Tm 5:25.
r. [10:28] Jas 4:12.
s. [10:33] Mk 8:38; Lk 9:26; 2 Tm 2:12; Rev 3:5.
t. [10:34–35] Lk 12:51–53.
u. [10:37–39] 16:24–25; Lk 14:26–27.
v. [10:39] Mk 8:35; Lk 9:24; Jn 12:25.
w. [10:40] Lk 10:16; Jn 12:44; 13:20.
x. [10:42] 25:40; Mk 9:41.

CHAPTER 11

¹When Jesus finished giving these commands to his twelve disciples,* he went away from that place to teach and to preach in their towns.

IV. OPPOSITION FROM ISRAEL

The Messengers from John the Baptist. ²*ᵃWhen John heard in prison* of the works of the Messiah, he sent his disciples to him ³*with this question, "Are you the one who is to come, or should we look for another?" ⁴Jesus said to them in reply, "Go and tell John what you hear and see: ⁵*the blind regain their sight, the lame walk, lepers are cleansed, the deaf hear, the dead are raised, and the poor have the good news proclaimed to them.ᵇ ⁶And blessed is the one who takes no offense at me."

Jesus' Testimony to John.* ⁷As they were going off, Jesus began to speak to the crowds about John, "What did you go out to the desert to see? A reed swayed by the wind?ᶜ ⁸Then what did you go out to see? Someone dressed in fine clothing? Those who wear fine clothing are in royal palaces. ⁹Then why did you go out? To see a prophet?* Yes, I tell you, and more than a prophet. ¹⁰This is the one about whom it is written:

'Behold, I am sending my
　　messenger ahead of
　　you;
he will prepare your way
　　before you.'ᵈ

¹¹Amen, I say to you, among those born of women there has been none greater than

John the Baptist; yet the least in the kingdom of heaven is greater than he.* ¹²From the days of John the Baptist until now, the kingdom of heaven suffers violence,* and the violent are taking it by force.ᵉ ¹³All the prophets and the law* prophesied up to the time of John. ¹⁴And if you are willing to accept it, he is Elijah, the one who is to come.ᶠ ¹⁵Whoever has ears ought to hear.

¹⁶ᵍ"To what shall I compare this generation?* It is like children who sit in marketplaces and call to one another, ¹⁷'We played the flute for you, but you did not dance, we sang a dirge but you did not mourn.' ¹⁸For John came neither eating nor drinking, and they said, 'He is possessed by a demon.'ʰ ¹⁹The Son of Man came eating and drinking and they said, 'Look, he is a glutton and a drunkard, a friend of tax collectors and sinners.' But wisdom is vindicated by her works."ⁱ

Reproaches to Unrepentant Towns. ²⁰ʲThen he began to reproach the towns where most of his mighty deeds had been done, since they had not repented. ²¹"Woe to you, Chorazin! Woe to you, Bethsaida! For if the mighty deeds done in your midst had been done in Tyre and Sidon,* they would long ago have repented in sackcloth and ashes.ᵏ ²²But I tell you, it will be more tolerable for Tyre and Sidon on the day of judgment than for you. ²³And as for you, Capernaum:

'Will you be exalted to
    heaven?'ˡ
You will go down to the
    netherworld.'

For if the mighty deeds done in your midst had been done in Sodom, it would have remained until this day. ²⁴But I tell you, it will be more tolerable for the land of Sodom on the day of judgment than for you."ᵐ

The Praise of the Father.
[25]nAt that time Jesus said in reply,* "I give praise to you, Father, Lord of heaven and earth, for although you have hidden these things from the wise and the learned you have revealed them to the childlike. [26]Yes, Father, such has been your gracious will. [27]All things have been handed over to me by my Father. No one knows the Son except the Father, and no one knows the Father except the Son and anyone to whom the Son wishes to reveal him.[o]

The Gentle Mastery of Christ. [28]*"Come to me, all you who labor and are burdened,* and I will give you rest. [29]*pTake my yoke upon you and learn from me, for I am meek and humble of heart; and you will find rest for yourselves. [30]For my yoke is easy, and my burden light."

a. [11:2–11] Lk 7:18–28.
b. [11:5] Is 26:19; 29:18–19; 35:5–6; 61:1.
c. [11:7] 3:3, 5.
d. [11:10] Ex 23:20; Mal 3:1; Mk 1:2; Lk 1:76.
e. [11:12] Lk 16:16.

f. [11:14] 17:10–13; Mal 3:23; Lk 1:17.
g. [11:16–19] Lk 7:31–35.
h. [11:18] Lk 1:15.
i. [11:19] 9:10–11.
j. [11:20–24] Lk 10:12–15.
k. [11:21] Jl 4:4–7.
l. [11:23] Is 14:13–15.
m. [11:24] 10:15.
n. [11:25–27] Lk 10:21–22.
o. [11:27] Jn 3:35; 6:46; 7:28; 10:15.
p. [11:29] Sir 51:26; Jer 6:16.

CHAPTER 12

Picking Grain on the Sabbath. [1]*At that time Jesus was going through a field of grain on the sabbath.[a] His disciples were hungry and began to pick the heads* of grain and eat them.[b] [2]When the Pharisees saw this, they said to him, "See, your disciples are doing what is unlawful to do on the sabbath." [3]He said to them,* "Have you not read what David[c] did when he and his companions were hungry, [4]how he went into the house of God and ate the bread of offering,[d] which neither he nor his companions but only the priests could lawfully eat? [5]*Or have you not read in the law that on the sabbath the priests serving in the temple violate the sabbath and are innocent?*e* 6I say to you, something greater than the temple is here. 7If you knew what this meant, 'I desire mercy, not sacrifice,'f you would not have condemned these innocent men. 8*g*For the Son of Man is Lord of the sabbath."

The Man with a Withered Hand. 9*h*Moving on from there, he went into their synagogue. 10And behold, there was a man there who had a withered hand. They questioned him, "Is it lawful to cure on the sabbath?"* so that they might accuse him. 11He said to them, "Which one of you who has a sheep that falls into a pit on the sabbath will not take hold of it and lift it out? 12How much more valuable a person is than a sheep. So it is lawful to do good on the sabbath." 13Then he said to the man, "Stretch out your hand." He stretched it out, and it was restored as sound as the other. 14But the Pharisees* went out and took counsel against him to put him to death.*i*

The Chosen Servant.* 15When Jesus realized this, he withdrew from that place. Many [people] followed him, and he cured them all,* 16but he warned them not to make him known. 17This was to fulfill what had been spoken through Isaiah the prophet:

18"Behold, my servant
    whom I have chosen,*j*
  my beloved in whom I
    delight;
I shall place my spirit
    upon him,
  and he will proclaim
    justice to the Gentiles.
19He will not contend* or
    cry out,
  nor will anyone hear his
    voice in the streets.
20A bruised reed he will
    not break,
  a smoldering wick he
    will not quench,
until he brings justice to

victory.
²¹And in his name the
Gentiles will hope."*

Jesus and Beelzebul.[*] ^{22k}Then
they brought to him a demo-
niac who was blind and
mute. He cured the mute
person so that he could
speak and see. ^{23*l}All the
crowd was astounded, and
said, "Could this perhaps be
the Son of David?" ^{24*m}But
when the Pharisees heard
this, they said, "This man
drives out demons only by
the power of Beelzebul, the
prince of demons." ²⁵ⁿBut he
knew what they were think-
ing and said to them,[*] "Every
kingdom divided against
itself will be laid waste, and
no town or house divided
against itself will stand. ²⁶And
if Satan drives out Satan, he is
divided against himself; how,
then, will his kingdom stand?
²⁷And if I drive out demons
by Beelzebul, by whom do
your own people[*] drive them
out? Therefore they will be
your judges. ^{28*o}But if it is by
the Spirit of God that I drive
out demons, then the kingdom of God has come upon
you. ^{29*}How can anyone enter
a strong man's house and steal
his property, unless he first
ties up the strong man? Then
he can plunder his house.
^{30*p}Whoever is not with me
is against me, and whoever
does not gather with me scat-
ters. ^{31q}Therefore, I say to you,
every sin and blasphemy will
be forgiven people, but blasphemy against the Spirit[*] will
not be forgiven. ³²And whoever speaks a word against
the Son of Man will be forgiven; but whoever speaks
against the holy Spirit will
not be forgiven, either in this
age or in the age to come.

A Tree and Its Fruits.
^{33r}"Either declare[*] the tree
good and its fruit is good, or
declare the tree rotten and
its fruit is rotten, for a tree
is known by its fruit. ^{34*s}You
brood of vipers, how can you

say good things when you are evil? For from the fullness of the heart the mouth speaks. ³⁵A good person brings forth good out of a store of goodness, but an evil person brings forth evil out of a store of evil. ^{36*}I tell you, on the day of judgment people will render an account for every careless word they speak. ³⁷By your words you will be acquitted, and by your words you will be condemned."

The Demand for a Sign.[*] ³⁸Then some of the scribes and Pharisees said to him, "Teacher,[*] we wish to see a sign from you."^u ³⁹He said to them in reply, "An evil and unfaithful[*] generation seeks a sign, but no sign will be given it except the sign of Jonah the prophet. ⁴⁰Just as Jonah was in the belly of the whale three days and three nights,[*] so will the Son of Man be in the heart of the earth three days and three nights. ^{41*}At the judgment, the men of Nineveh will arise with this generation and condemn it, because they repented at the preaching of Jonah; and there is something greater than Jonah here. ⁴²At the judgment the queen of the south will arise with this generation and condemn it, because she came from the ends of the earth to hear the wisdom of Solomon; and there is something greater than Solomon here.^v

The Return of the Unclean Spirit.[*] ^{43w}"When an unclean spirit goes out of a person it roams through arid regions searching for rest but finds none. ⁴⁴Then it says, 'I will return to my home from which I came.' But upon returning, it finds it empty, swept clean, and put in order. ⁴⁵Then it goes and brings back with itself seven other spirits more evil than itself, and they move in and dwell there; and the last condition of that person is worse than the first. Thus it will be with this evil generation."

The True Family of Jesus.*

⁴⁶ˣWhile he was still speaking to the crowds, his mother and his brothers appeared outside, wishing to speak with him. ⁴⁷[Someone told him, "Your mother and your brothers are standing outside, asking to speak with you."]* ⁴⁸But he said in reply to the one who told him, "Who is my mother? Who are my brothers?" ⁴⁹And stretching out his hand toward his disciples, he said, "Here are my mother and my brothers. ⁵⁰For whoever does the will of my heavenly Father is my brother, and sister, and mother."

a. [12:1–8] Mk 2:23–28; Lk 6:1–5.
b. [12:1] Dt 23:26.
c. [12:3–4] 1 Sm 21:2–7.
d. [12:4] Lv 24:5–9.
e. [12:5] Lv 24:8; Nm 28:9–10.
f. [12:7] Hos 6:6.
g. [12:8] Jn 5:16–17.
h. [12:9–13] Mk 3:1–6; Lk 6:6–11.
i. [12:14] Jn 5:18.
j. [12:18–21] Is 42:1–4.
k. [12:22–24] 9:32–34; Lk 11:14–15.
l. [12:23] 9:27.
m. [12:24] 10:25; Mk 3:22.
n. [12:25–29] Mk 3:23–27; Lk 11:17–22.
o. [12:28] Lk 11:20.
p. [12:30] Lk 11:23.
q. [12:31–32] Mk 3:28–30; Lk 12:10.
r. [12:33–35] Lk 6:43–45.
s. [12:34] 3:7; 23:33; 15:11–12; Lk 3:7.
t. [12:36–37] Jas 3:1–2.
u. [12:38–42] 16:1–4; Jon 2:1; 3:1–10; Mk 8:11–12; Lk 11:29–32.
v. [12:42] 1 Kgs 10:1–10.
w. [12:43–45] Lk 11:24–26.
x. [12:46–50] Mk 3:31–35; Lk 8:19–21.

CHAPTER 13

The Parable of the Sower.

¹*On that day, Jesus went out of the house and sat down by the sea.ᵃ ²Such large crowds gathered around him that he got into a boat and sat down, and the whole crowd stood along the shore. ³*And he spoke to them at length in parables,* saying: "A sower went out to sow. ⁴And as he sowed, some seed fell on the path, and birds came and ate it up. ⁵Some fell on rocky ground, where it had little soil. It sprang up at once because the soil was not deep, ⁶and when the sun rose it was scorched, and it withered for lack of roots. ⁷Some seed fell among thorns, and the thorns grew up and choked it. ⁸But some seed fell on

rich soil, and produced fruit, a hundred or sixty or thirtyfold. [9]Whoever has ears ought to hear."

The Purpose of Parables.

[10]The disciples approached him and said, "Why do you speak to them in parables?" [11]He said to them in reply, "Because knowledge of the mysteries of the kingdom of heaven has been granted to you, but to them it has not been granted. [12b]To anyone who has, more will be given* and he will grow rich; from anyone who has not, even what he has will be taken away. [13*c]This is why I speak to them in parables, because 'they look but do not see and hear but do not listen or understand.' [14d]Isaiah's prophecy is fulfilled in them, which says:

'You shall indeed hear but
    not understand,
  you shall indeed look
    but never see.
[15]Gross is the heart of this

people,
  they will hardly hear
    with their ears,
  they have closed their
    eyes,
  lest they see with
    their eyes
  and hear with their ears
 and understand with
    their heart and be
    converted,
  and I heal them.'

The Privilege of Discipleship.* [16e]"But blessed are your eyes, because they see, and your ears, because they hear. [17]Amen, I say to you, many prophets and righteous people longed to see what you see but did not see it, and to hear what you hear but did not hear it.

The Explanation of the Parable of the Sower.* [18f]"Hear then the parable of the sower. [19]The seed sown on the path is the one who hears the word of the kingdom without understanding it, and the evil

one comes and steals away what was sown in his heart. ²⁰The seed sown on rocky ground is the one who hears the word and receives it at once with joy. ²¹But he has no root and lasts only for a time. When some tribulation or persecution comes because of the word, he immediately falls away. ²²The seed sown among thorns is the one who hears the word, but then (worldly anxiety and the lure of riches choke the word and it bears no fruit.) ²³But the seed sown on rich soil is the one who hears the word and understands it, who indeed bears fruit and yields a hundred or sixty or thirtyfold."

The Parable of the Weeds Among the Wheat. ²⁴He proposed another parable to them.* "The kingdom of heaven may be likened to a man who sowed good seed in his field. ²⁵While everyone was asleep his enemy came and sowed weeds* all through the wheat, and then went off. ²⁶When the crop grew and bore fruit, the weeds appeared as well. ²⁷The slaves of the householder came to him and said, 'Master, did you not sow good seed in your field? Where have the weeds come from?' ²⁸He answered, 'An enemy has done this.' His slaves said to him, 'Do you want us to go and pull them up?' ²⁹He replied, 'No, if you pull up the weeds you might uproot the wheat along with them. ³⁰Let them grow together until harvest;' then at harvest time I will say to the harvesters, "First collect the weeds and tie them in bundles for burning; but gather the wheat into my barn."'"ᵍ

The Parable of the Mustard Seed.* ³¹ʰHe proposed another parable to them. "The kingdom of heaven is like a mustard seed that a person took and sowed in a field. ³²ⁱIt is the smallest of all the seeds, yet when full-grown it is the largest of plants. It becomes a large bush, and the 'birds of the sky come and dwell in its branches.'"

The Parable of the Yeast. [33]He spoke to them another parable. "The kingdom of heaven is like yeast* that a woman took and mixed with three measures of wheat flour until the whole batch was leavened."[j]

The Use of Parables. [34*k]All these things Jesus spoke to the crowds in parables. He spoke to them only in parables, [35]to fulfill what had been said through the prophet:*

"I will open my mouth in parables,
I will announce what has lain hidden from the foundation [of the world]."[l]

The Explanation of the Parable of the Weeds. [36]Then, dismissing the crowds,* he went into the house. His disciples approached him and said, "Explain to us the parable of the weeds in the field." [37*]He said in reply, "He who sows good seed is the Son of Man, [38]the field is the world,* the good seed the children of the kingdom. The weeds are the children of the evil one, [39]and the enemy who sows them is the devil. The harvest is the end of the age,* and the harvesters are angels. [40]Just as weeds are collected and burned [up] with fire, so will it be at the end of the age. [41]The Son of Man will send his angels, and they will collect out of his kingdom* (all who cause others to sin and all evildoers.) [42m]They will throw them into the fiery furnace, where there will be wailing and grinding of teeth. [43*n]Then the righteous will shine like the sun in the kingdom of their Father. Whoever has ears ought to hear.

More Parables.[*] 440"The kingdom of heaven is like a treasure buried in a field,[*] which a person finds and hides again, and out of joy goes and sells all that he has and buys that field. 45Again, the kingdom of heaven is like a merchant searching for fine pearls. 46When he finds a pearl of great price, he goes and sells all that he has and buys it. 47Again, the kingdom of heaven is like a net thrown into the sea, which collects fish of every kind. 48When it is full they haul it ashore and sit down to put what is good into buckets. What is bad they throw away. 49Thus it will be at the end of the age. The angels will go out and separate the wicked from the righteous 50and throw them into the fiery furnace, where there will be wailing and grinding of teeth.

Treasures New and Old. 51"Do you understand[*] all these things?" They answered,

"Yes." 52[*]And he replied, "Then every scribe who has been instructed in the kingdom of heaven is like the head of a household who brings from his storeroom both the new and the old." 53When Jesus finished these parables, he went away from there.

V. JESUS, THE KINGDOM, AND THE CHURCH

The Rejection at Nazareth. 54[*]He came to his native place and taught the people in their synagogue.[p] They were astonished[*] and said, "Where did this man get such wisdom and mighty deeds?[q] 55Is he not the carpenter's son? Is not his mother named Mary and his brothers James, Joseph, Simon, and Judas?[r] 56Are not his sisters all with us? Where did this man get all this?" 57And they took offense at him. But Jesus said to them, "A prophet is not without honor except in his native place and in his own house."[s] [58]And he did not work many mighty deeds there because of their lack of faith.

a. [13:1–15] Mk 4:1–12; Lk 8:4–10.
b. [13;12] 25:29; Mk 4:25; Lk 8:18; 19:26.
c. [13:13] Jn 9:39.
d. [13:14–15] Is 6:9–10; Jn 12:40; Acts 28:26–27; Rom 11:8.
e. [13:16–17] Lk 10:23–24; 1 Pt 1:10–12.
f. [13:18–23] Mk 4:13–20; Lk 8:11–15.
g. [13:30] 3:12.
h. [13:31–32] Mk 4:30–32; Lk 13:18–19.
i. [13:32] Ez 17:23; 31:6; Dn 4:7–9, 17–19.
j. [13:33] Lk 13:20–21.
k. [13:34–35] Mk 4:33–34.
l. [13:35] Ps 78:2.
m. [13:42] 8:12; Rev 21:8.
n. [13:43] Dn 12:3.
o. [13:44–45] Prv 2:4; 4:7.
p. [13:54–58] Mk 6:1–6; Lk 4:16–30.
q. [13:54] 2:23; Jn 1:46; 7:15.
r. [13:55] 12:46; 27:56; Jn 6:42.
s. [13:57] Jn 4:44.

CHAPTER 14

Herod's Opinion of Jesus. [1][*a]At that time Herod the tetrarch[*b] heard of the reputation of Jesus[c] [2]and said to his servants, "This man is John the Baptist. He has been raised from the dead; that is why mighty powers are at work in him."

The Death of John the Baptist. [3][d]Now Herod had arrested John, bound [him], and put him in prison on account of Herodias,[*] the wife of his brother Philip, [4][e]for John had said to him, "It is not lawful for you to have her." [5][f]Although he wanted to kill him, he feared the people, for they regarded him as a prophet. [6]But at a birthday celebration for Herod, the daughter of Herodias performed a dance before the guests and delighted Herod [7]so much that he swore to give her whatever she might ask for. [8]Prompted by her mother, she said, "Give me here on a platter the head of John the Baptist." [9]The king was distressed, but because of his oaths and the guests who were present, he ordered that it be given, [10]and he had John beheaded in the prison. [11]His head was brought in on a platter and given to the girl, who took it to her mother. [12]His disciples came and took away the corpse and buried him; and they went and told Jesus.

The Return of the Twelve and the Feeding of the Five Thousand. [13g]When Jesus heard of it, he <u>withdrew</u> in a boat <u>to a deserted place by himself</u>. The crowds heard of this and followed him on foot from their towns. [14]When he disembarked and saw the vast crowd, ⟨his heart was moved with pity for them, and he cured their sick.⟩ [15]When it was evening, the disciples approached him and said, "This is a deserted place and it is already late; dismiss the crowds so that they can go to the villages and buy food for themselves." [16][Jesus] said to them, "There is no need for them to go away; give them some food yourselves." [17]But they said to him, "Five loaves and two fish are all we have here." [18]Then he said, "Bring them here to me," [19]and he ordered the crowds to sit down on the grass. Taking[*] the five loaves and the two fish, and looking up to heaven, he said the blessing, broke the loaves, and gave them to the disciples, who in turn gave them to the crowds. [20]They all ate and were satisfied, and they picked up the fragments left over[*]—twelve wicker baskets full. [21]Those who ate were about five thousand men, not counting women and children.

The Walking on the Water. [*] [22h]Then he made the disciples get into the boat and precede him to the other side, while he dismissed the crowds. [23i]After doing so, <u>he went up on the mountain by himself to pray</u>. When it was evening he was there alone. [24]Meanwhile the boat, already a few miles offshore, was being tossed about by the waves, for the wind was against it. [25]During the fourth watch of the night,[*] he came toward them, walking on the sea. [26]When the disciples saw him walking on the sea they were terrified. "It is a ghost," they said, and they cried out in fear. [27]At once [Jesus] spoke to them, "Take courage, it is I;* do not be afraid." ²⁸Peter said to him in reply, "Lord, if it is you, command me to come to you on the water." ²⁹He said, "Come." Peter got out of the boat and began to walk on the water toward Jesus. ³⁰ʲBut when he saw how [strong] the wind was he became frightened; and, beginning to sink, he cried out, "Lord, save me!" ³¹Immediately Jesus stretched out his hand and caught him, and said to him, "O you of little faith,* why did you doubt?" ³²After they got into the boat, the wind died down. ³³*ᵏThose who were in the boat did him homage, saying, "Truly, you are the Son of God."

The Healings at Gennesaret. ³⁴ˡAfter making the crossing, they came to land at Gennesaret. ³⁵When the men of that place recognized him, they sent word to all the surrounding country. People brought to him all those who were sick ³⁶ᵐand begged him that they might touch only the tassel on his cloak, and as many as touched it were healed.

---

a. [14:1–12] Mk 6:14–29.
b. [14:1–2] Lk 9:7–9.
c. [14:1] Lk 3:1.
d. [14:3–4] Lk 3:19–20.
e. [14:4] Lv 18:16; 20:21.
f. [14:5] 21:26.
g. [14:13–21] 15:32–38; Mk 6:32–44; Lk 9:10–17; Jn 6:1–13.
h. [14:22–33] Mk 6:45–52; Jn 6:16–21.
i. [14:23] Mk 1:35; Lk 5:16; 6:12.
j. [14:30–31] 8:25–26.
k. [14:33] 16:16.
l. [14:34–36] Mk 6:53–56.
m. [14:36] 9:20–22.

CHAPTER 15

The Tradition of the Elders.* ¹ᵃThen Pharisees and scribes came to Jesus from Jerusalem and said, ²ᵇ"Why do your disciples break the tradition of the elders?* They do not wash [their] hands when they eat a meal." ³He said to them in reply, "And why do you break the commandment of God* for the sake of your tradition? ⁴ᶜFor God said, 'Honor your father and your mother,' and 'Whoever curses father or mother shall die.' ⁵*But you say, 'Whoever says to father or mother, "Any support you might have had from me is dedicated to God," [6]need not honor his father.' You have nullified the word of God for the sake of your tradition. [7]Hypocrites, well did Isaiah prophesy about you when he said:

[8d]"This people honors me
    with their lips,*
 but their hearts are far
    from me;
[9e]in vain do they worship
    me,
 teaching as doctrines
    human precepts.'"

[10f]He summoned the crowd and said to them, "Hear and understand. [11]It is not what enters one's mouth that defiles that person; but what comes out of the mouth is what defiles one." [12]Then his disciples approached and said to him, "Do you know that the Pharisees took offense when they heard what you said?" [13]He said in reply,* "Every plant that my heavenly Father has not planted will be uprooted. [14g]Let them alone; they are blind guides [of the blind]. If a blind person leads a blind person, both will fall into a pit." [15]Then Peter* said to him in reply, "Explain [this] parable to us." [16]He said to them, "Are even you still without understanding? [17]Do you not realize that everything that enters the mouth passes into the stomach and is expelled into the latrine? [18h]But the things that come out of the mouth come from the heart, and they defile. [19]*For from the heart come evil thoughts, murder, adultery, unchastity, theft, false witness, blasphemy. [20]These are what defile a person, but to eat with unwashed hands does not defile."

The Canaanite Woman's Faith.* [21i]Then Jesus went from that place and withdrew to the region of Tyre and Sidon. [22]And behold, a Canaanite woman of that district came and called out, "Have pity on me, Lord, Son of David! My daughter is tormented by a demon." [23]But he did not say a word in answer to her. His disciples came and asked him, "Send her away, for she keeps calling out after us." [24]*He said in reply, "I was sent only to the lost sheep of the house of Israel." [25]*But the woman came and did him homage, saying, "Lord, help me." [26]He said in reply, "It is not right to take the food of the children* and throw it to the dogs." [27]She said, "Please, Lord, for even the dogs eat the scraps that fall from the table of their masters." [28]*Then Jesus said to her in reply, "O woman, great is your faith!* Let it be done for you as you wish." And her daughter was healed from that hour.

The Healing of Many People. [29]Moving on from there Jesus walked by the Sea of Galilee, went up on the mountain, and sat down there. [30]*Great crowds came to him, having with them the lame, the blind, the deformed, the mute, and many others. They placed them at his feet, and he cured them. [31]The crowds were amazed when they saw the mute speaking, the deformed made whole, the lame walking, and the blind able to see, and they glorified the God of Israel.

The Feeding of the Four Thousand.* [32]*Jesus summoned his disciples and said, "My heart is moved with pity for the crowd, for they have been with me now for three days and have nothing to eat. I do not want to send them away hungry, for fear they may collapse on the way." [33]The disciples said to him, "Where could we ever get enough bread in this deserted place to satisfy such a crowd?" [34]Jesus said to them, "How many loaves do you have?"

"Seven," they replied, "and a few fish." ³⁵He ordered the crowd to sit down on the ground. ³⁶Then he took the seven loaves and the fish, gave thanks,* broke the loaves, and gave them to the disciples, who in turn gave them to the crowds. ³⁷ⁿThey all ate and were satisfied. They picked up the fragments left over— seven baskets full. ³⁸Those who ate were four thousand men, not counting women and children. ³⁹And when he had dismissed the crowds, he got into the boat and came to the district of Magadan.

a. [15:1–20] Mk 7:1–23.
b. [15:2] Lk 11:38.
c. [15:4] Ex 20:12; 21:17; Lv 20:9; Dt 5:16; Prv 20:20.
d. [15:8] Is 29:13 LXX.
e. [15:9] Col 2:23.
f. [15:10] Mk 7:14.
g. [15:14] 23:16, 19, 24; Lk 6:39; Jn 9:40.
h. [15:18] 12:34.
i. [15:21–28] Mk 7:24–30.
j. [15:25] 10:6.
k. [15:28] 8:10.
l. [15:30] Is 35:5–6.
m. [15:32–39] Mk 8:1–10.
n. [15:37] 16:10.

CHAPTER 16

The Demand for a Sign. ¹*ᵃThe Pharisees and Sadducees came and, to test him, asked him to show them a sign from heaven. ²ᵇHe said to them in reply, "[In the evening you say, 'Tomorrow will be fair, for the sky is red'; ³ᵇand, in the morning, 'Today will be stormy, for the sky is red and threatening.' You know how to judge the appearance of the sky, but you cannot judge the signs of the times.] ⁴ᶜAn evil and unfaithful generation seeks a sign, but no sign will be given it except the sign of Jonah.'" Then he left them and went away.

The Leaven of the Pharisees and Sadducees. ⁵ᵈIn coming to the other side of the sea,* the disciples had forgotten to bring bread. ⁶ᵉJesus said to them, "Look out, and beware of the leaven* of the Pharisees and Sadducees." ⁷"They concluded among themselves, saying, "It is because we have brought no bread." ⁸When Jesus became aware of this he said, "You of little faith, why do you conclude among yourselves that it is because you have no bread? [9f]Do you not yet <u>understand</u>, and do you not <u>remember</u> the five loaves for the five thousand, and how many wicker baskets you took up? [10g]Or the seven loaves for the four thousand, and how many baskets you took up? [11]How do you not comprehend that I was not speaking to you about bread? Beware of the leaven of the Pharisees and Sadducees." [12]Then they understood[*] that he was not telling them to beware of the leaven of bread, but of the teaching of the Pharisees and Sadducees.

Peter's Confession About Jesus.[*] [13h]When Jesus went into the region of Caesarea Philippi[*] he asked his disciples, "Who do people say that the Son of Man is?" [14i]They replied, "Some say John the Baptist,[*] others Elijah, still others Jeremiah or one of the prophets." [15]He said to them,

"But who do you say that I am?" [16*j]Simon Peter said in reply, "You are the Messiah, the Son of the living God." [17]Jesus said to him in reply, "Blessed are you, Simon son of Jonah. For flesh and blood[*] has not revealed this to you, but my heavenly Father. [18k]And so I say to you, you are Peter, and upon this rock I will build my church,[*] and the gates of the netherworld shall not prevail against it. [19l]I will give you the keys to the kingdom of heaven.[*] Whatever you bind on earth shall be bound in heaven; and whatever you loose on earth shall be loosed in heaven." [20*m]Then he strictly ordered his disciples to tell no one that he was the Messiah.

The First Prediction of the Passion.[*] [21n]From that time on, Jesus began to show his disciples that he[*] must go to Jerusalem and <u>suffer greatly</u> from the elders, the chief priests, and the scribes, and be killed and on the third day be raised.[o] 22*Then Peter took him aside and began to rebuke him, "God forbid, Lord! No such thing shall ever happen to you." 23pHe turned and said to Peter, "Get behind me, Satan! You are an obstacle to me. You are thinking not as God does, but as human beings do."

The Conditions of Discipleship.* 24qThen Jesus said to his disciples, "Whoever wishes to come after me must deny himself,* take up his cross, and follow me. 25rFor whoever wishes to save his life will lose it, but whoever loses his life for my sake will find it.* 26What profit would there be for one to gain the whole world and forfeit his life? Or what can one give in exchange for his life? 27*sFor the Son of Man will come with his angels in his Father's glory, and then he will repay everyone according to his conduct. 28*Amen, I say to

you, there are some standing here who will not taste death until they see the Son of Man coming in his kingdom."

a. [16:1–10] Mk 8:11–21.
b. [16:3] Lk 12:54–56.
c. [16:4] 12:39; Jon 2:1.
d. [16:5–12] Mk 8:14–21.
e. [16:6] Lk 12:1.
f. [16:9] 14:17–21; Jn 6:9.
g. [16:10] 15:34–38.
h. [16:13–16] Mk 8:27–29; Lk 9:18–20.
i. [16:14] 14:2.
j. [16:16] Jn 6:69.
k. [16:18] Jn 1:42.
l. [16:19] Is 22:22; Rev 3:7.
m. [16:20] Mk 8:30; Lk 9:21.
n. [16:21–28] Mk 8:31–9:1; Lk 9:22–27.
o. [16:21] 17:22–23; 20:17–19.
p. [16:23] 4:10.
q. [16:24] Lk 14:27.
r. [16:25] Lk 17:33; Jn 12:25.
s. [16:27] 25:31–33; Jb 34:11; Ps 62:13; Jer 17:10; 2 Thes 1:7–8.

CHAPTER 17

The Transfiguration of Jesus.* 1aAfter six days Jesus took Peter, James, and John his brother, and led them up a high mountain by themselves.* 2*bAnd he was transfigured before them; his face shone like the sun and his clothes became white as light. 3*And behold, Moses and Elijah appeared to them, conversing with him. 4Then Peter said to Jesus in reply,

"Lord, it is good that we are here. If you wish, I will make three tents* here, one for you, one for Moses, and one for Elijah." 5c*While he was still speaking, behold, a bright cloud cast a shadow over them,* then from the cloud came a voice that said, "This is my beloved Son, with whom I am well pleased; listen to him."* 6*When the disciples heard this, they fell prostrate and were very much afraid. 7But Jesus came and touched them, saying, "Rise, and do not be afraid." 8And when the disciples raised their eyes, they saw no one else but Jesus alone.

The Coming of Elijah.* 9d*As they were coming down from the mountain, Jesus charged them, "Do not tell the vision* to anyone until the Son of Man has been raised from the dead." 10*eThen the disciples asked him, "Why do the scribes say that Elijah must come first?" 11fHe said

in reply,* "Elijah will indeed come and restore all things; 12gbut I tell you that Elijah has already come, and they did not recognize him but did to him whatever they pleased. So also will the Son of Man suffer at their hands." 13*Then the disciples understood that he was speaking to them of John the Baptist.

The Healing of a Boy with a Demon.* 14hWhen they came to the crowd a man approached, knelt down before him, 15and said, "Lord, have pity on my son, for he is a lunatic* and suffers severely; often he falls into fire, and often into water. 16I brought him to your disciples, but they could not cure him." 17iJesus said in reply, "O faithless and perverse* generation, how long will I be with you? How long will I endure you? Bring him here to me." 18Jesus rebuked him and the demon came out of him,* and from that hour the boy was cured. ¹⁹Then the disciples approached Jesus in private and said, "Why could we not drive it out?" ²⁰*ʲHe said to them, "Because of your little faith. Amen, I say to you, if you have faith the size of a mustard seed, you will say to this mountain, 'Move from here to there,' and it will move. Nothing will be impossible for you." [²¹]*

The Second Prediction of the Passion.* ²²ᵏAs they were gathering in Galilee, Jesus said to them, "The Son of Man is to be handed over to men, ²³and they will kill him, and he will be raised on the third day." And they were overwhelmed with grief.

Payment of the Temple Tax.* ²⁴ˡWhen they came to Capernaum, the collectors of the temple tax* approached Peter and said, "Doesn't your teacher pay the temple tax?" ²⁵"Yes," he said.* When he came into the house, before he had time to speak, Jesus asked him, "What is your opinion, Simon? From whom do the kings of the earth take tolls or census tax? From their subjects or from foreigners?" ²⁶*When he said, "From foreigners," Jesus said to him, "Then the subjects are exempt. ²⁷But that we may not offend them,* go to the sea, drop in a hook, and take the first fish that comes up. Open its mouth and you will find a coin worth twice the temple tax. Give that to them for me and for you."

a. [17:1–8] Mk 9:2–8; Lk 9:28–36.
b. [17:2] 28:3; Dn 7:9; 10:6; Rev 4:4; 7:9; 19:14.
c. [17:5] 3:17; Dt 18:15; 2 Pt 1:17.
d. [17:9–13] Mk 9:9–13.
e. [17:10] Mal 3:23–24.
f. [17:11] Lk 1:17.
g. [17:12–13] 11:14.
h. [17:14–21] Mk 9:14–29; Lk 9:37–43.
i. [17:17] Dt 32:5 LXX.
j. [17:20] 21:21; Lk 17:6; 1 Cor 13:2.
k. [17:22–23] 16:21; 20:18–19.
l. [17:24] Ex 30:11–16; Neh 10:33.

CHAPTER 18*

The Greatest in the Kingdom. ¹ᵃAt that time the disciples* approached Jesus and said, "Who is the greatest in the kingdom of heaven?" ²He called a child over, placed it in their midst, 36band said, "Amen, I say to you, unless you turn and become like children,* you will not enter the kingdom of heaven. 4cWhoever humbles himself like this child is the greatest in the kingdom of heaven. 5*And whoever receives one child such as this in my name receives me.)

Temptations to Sin. 6d"Whoever causes one of these little ones* who believe in me to sin, it would be better for him to have a great millstone hung around his neck and to be drowned in the depths of the sea. 7*Woe to the world because of things that cause sin! Such things must come, but woe to the one through whom they come! 8eIf your hand or foot causes you to sin,* cut it off and throw it away. It is better for you to enter into life maimed or crippled than with two hands or two feet to be thrown into eternal fire. 9And if your eye causes you to sin, tear it out and throw it away. It is better for you to enter into life with one eye than with two eyes to be thrown into fiery Gehenna.

The Parable of the Lost Sheep. 10f"See that you do not despise one of these little ones,* for I say to you that their angels in heaven always look upon the face of my heavenly Father. [11]g* 12What is your opinion? If a man has a hundred sheep and one of them goes astray, will he not leave the ninety-nine in the hills and go in search of the stray? 13And if he finds it, amen, I say to you, he rejoices more over it than over the ninety-nine that did not stray. 14In just the same way, it is not the will of your heavenly Father that one of these little ones be lost.

A Brother Who Sins. 15h"If your brother* sins [against you], go and tell him his fault between you and him alone. If he listens to you, you have won over your brother. [16]*'If he does not listen, take one or two others along with you, so that 'every fact may be established on the testimony of two or three witnesses.' [17]'If he refuses to listen to them, tell the church.* If he refuses to listen even to the church, then treat him as you would a Gentile or a tax collector. [18]*kAmen, I say to you, whatever you bind on earth shall be bound in heaven, and whatever you loose on earth shall be loosed in heaven. [19]*lAgain, [amen,] I say to you, if two of you agree on earth about anything for which they are to pray, it shall be granted to them by my heavenly Father. [20]*mFor where two or three are gathered together in my name, there am I in the midst of them."

The Parable of the Unforgiving Servant.* [21]nThen Peter approaching asked him, "Lord, if my brother sins against me, how often must I forgive him? As many as seven times?" [22]*Jesus answered, "I say to you, not seven times but seventy-seven times. [23]oThat is why the kingdom of heaven may be likened to a king who decided to settle accounts with his servants. [24]*When he began the accounting, a debtor was brought before him who owed him a huge amount. [25]Since he had no way of paying it back, his master ordered him to be sold, along with his wife, his children, and all his property, in payment of the debt. [26]*At that, the servant fell down, did him homage, and said, 'Be patient with me, and I will pay you back in full.' [27]Moved with compassion the master of that servant let him go and forgave him the loan. [28]When that servant had left, he found one of his fellow servants who owed

him a much smaller amount.*
He seized him and started
to choke him, demanding,
'Pay back what you owe.'
[29]Falling to his knees, his
fellow servant begged him,
'Be patient with me, and I
will pay you back.' [30]But he
refused. Instead, he had him
put in prison until he paid
back the debt. [31]Now when
his fellow servants saw what
had happened, they were
deeply disturbed, and went
to their master and reported
the whole affair. [32]His master
summoned him and said to
him, 'You wicked servant! I
forgave you your entire debt
because you begged me to.
[33p]Should you not have had
pity on your fellow servant, as
I had pity on you?' [34]Then in
anger his master handed him
over to the torturers until he
should pay back the whole
debt.* [35*q]So will my heavenly
Father do to you, unless each
of you forgives his brother
from his heart."

a. [18:1–5] Mk 9:36–37; Lk 9:46–48.
b. [18:3] 19:14; Mk 10:15; Lk 18:17.
c. [18:4] 23:12.
d. [18:6–7] Mk 9:42; Lk 17:1–2.
e. [18:8–9] 5:29–30; Mk 9:43–47.
f. [18:10–14] Ez 34:1–3, 16; Lk 15:3–7.
g. [18:11] Lk 19:10.
h. [18:15] Lv 19:17; Sir 19:13; Gal 6:1.
i. [18:16] Dt 19:15; Jn 8:17; 1 Tm 5:19.
j. [18:17] 1 Cor 5:1–13.
k. [18:18] 16:19; Jn 20:23.
l. [18:19] 7:7–8; Jn 15:7.
m. [18:20] 1 Cor 5:4.
n. [18:21–22] 6:12; Lk 17:4.
o. [18:23] 25:19.
p. [18:33] Sir 28:4.
q. [18:35] 6:15; Jas 2:13.

VI. MINISTRY IN JUDEA AND JERUSALEM

CHAPTER 19

Marriage and Divorce.
[1*]When Jesus* finished these
words,* he left Galilee and
went to the district of Judea
across the Jordan. [2]Great
crowds followed him, and
he cured them there. [3a]Some
Pharisees approached him,
and tested him,* saying, "Is
it lawful for a man to divorce
his wife for any cause whatever?" [4*b]He said in reply,
"Have you not read that
from the beginning the Creator 'made them male and

female' [5c]and said, 'For this reason a man shall leave his father and mother and be joined to his wife, and the two shall become one flesh'? [6]So they are no longer two, but one flesh. Therefore, what God has joined together, no human being must separate." [7*d]They said to him, "Then why did Moses command that the man give the woman a bill of divorce and dismiss [her]?" [8]He said to them, "Because of the hardness of your hearts Moses allowed you to divorce your wives, but from the beginning it was not so. [9e]I say to you,* whoever divorces his wife (unless the marriage is unlawful) and marries another commits adultery." [10][His] disciples said to him, "If that is the case of a man with his wife, it is better not to marry." [11]He answered, "Not all can accept [this] word,* but only those to whom that is granted. [12]Some are incapable of marriage because they were born so; some, because they were made so by others; some, because they have renounced marriage* for the sake of the kingdom of heaven. Whoever can accept this ought to accept it."

Blessing of the Children.* [13f]Then children were brought to him that he might lay his hands on them and pray. The disciples rebuked them, [14g]but Jesus said, "Let the children come to me, and do not prevent them; for the kingdom of heaven belongs to such as these." [15]After he placed his hands on them, he went away.

The Rich Young Man.* [16h]Now someone approached him and said, "Teacher, what good must I do to gain eternal life?" [17]He answered him, "Why do you ask me about the good? There is only One who is good.* If you wish to enter into life, keep the commandments." [18*i]He asked him, "Which ones?" And

5 of 10 Commandments
+ Love neighbor

Jesus replied, (" 'You shall not kill; you shall not commit adultery; you shall not steal; you shall not bear false witness; ¹⁹honor your father and your mother'; and 'you shall love your neighbor as yourself.")²⁰*The young man said to him, "All of these I have observed. What do I still lack?" ²¹ʲJesus said to him, "If you wish to be perfect, go, sell what you have and give to [the] poor, and you will have treasure in heaven. Then come, follow me." ²²When the young man heard this statement, he went away sad, for he had many possessions. ²³*Then Jesus said to his disciples, "Amen, I say to you, it will be hard for one who is rich to enter the kingdom of heaven. ²⁴ᵏAgain I say to you, it is easier for a camel to pass through the eye of a needle than for one who is rich to enter the kingdom of God." ²⁵*When the disciples heard this, they were greatly astonished and said, "Who then can be saved?" ²⁶ˡJesus looked at them and said, "For human beings this is impossible, but for God all things are possible." ²⁷ᵐThen Peter said to him in reply, "We have given up everything and followed you. What will there be for us?" ²⁸ⁿJesus said to them, "Amen, I say to you that you who have followed me, in the new age, when the Son of Man is seated on his throne of glory, will yourselves sit on twelve thrones, judging the twelve tribes of Israel. ²⁹And everyone who has given up houses or brothers or sisters or father or mother or children or lands for the sake of my name will receive a hundred times more, and will inherit eternal life. (³⁰*ºBut many who are first will be last, and the last will be first.)

20:16

a. [19:3–9] Mk 10:2–12.
b. [19:4] Gn 1:27.
c. [19:5] Gn 2:24; 1 Cor 6:16; Eph 5:31.
d. [19:7] Dt 24:1–4.
e. [19:9] 5:32; Lk 16:18; 1 Cor 7:10–11.
f. [19:13–15] Mk 10:13–16; Lk 18:15–17.
g. [19:14] 18:3; Acts 8:36.
h. [19:16–30] Mk 10:17–31; Lk 18:18–30.
i. [19:18–19] Ex 20:12–16; Dt 5:16–20 / Lv 19:18; Rom 13:9.

j. [19:21] 5:48; 6:20.
k. [19:24] 7:14.
l. [19:26] Gn 18:14; Jb 42:2; Lk 1:37.
m. [19:27] 4:20, 22.
n. [19:28] 25:31; Dn 7:9, 22; Lk 22:30; Rev 3:21; 20:4.
o. [19:30] 20:16.

CHAPTER 20

The Workers in the Vineyard.[*] ¹"The kingdom of heaven is like a landowner who went out at dawn to hire laborers for his vineyard. ²After agreeing with them for the usual daily wage, he sent them into his vineyard. ³Going out about nine o'clock, he saw others standing idle in the marketplace, ⁴and he said to them, 'You too go into my vineyard, and I will give you what is just.' ⁵So they went off. [And] he went out again around noon, and around three o'clock, and did likewise. ⁶Going out about five o'clock, he found others standing around, and said to them, 'Why do you stand here idle all day?' ⁷They answered, 'Because no one has hired us.' He said to them,

'You too go into my vineyard.' ⁸*ᵃWhen it was evening the owner of the vineyard said to his foreman, 'Summon the laborers and give them their pay, beginning with the last and ending with the first.' ⁹When those who had started about five o'clock came, each received the usual daily wage. ¹⁰So when the first came, they thought that they would receive more, but each of them also got the usual wage. ¹¹And on receiving it they grumbled against the landowner, ¹²saying, 'These last ones worked only one hour, and you have made them equal to us, who bore the day's burden and the heat.' ¹³He said to one of them in reply, 'My friend, I am not cheating you.' Did you not agree with me for the usual daily wage? ¹⁴Take what is yours and go. What if I wish to give this last one the same as you? ¹⁵[Or] am I not free to do as I wish with my own money? Are you envious because I am gener-ous?' [16]"Thus, the last will be first, and the first will be last."

The Third Prediction of the Passion.* [17b]As Jesus was going up to Jerusalem, he took the twelve [disciples] aside by themselves, and said to them on the way, [18]"Behold, we are going up to Jerusalem, and the Son of Man will be handed over to the chief priests and the scribes, and they will condemn him to death, [19]and hand him over to the Gentiles to be mocked and scourged and crucified, and he will be raised on the third day."

The Request of James and John.* [20c]Then the mother* of the sons of Zebedee app-roached him with her sons and did him homage, wish-ing to ask him for something. [21]He said to her, "What do you wish?" She answered him, "Command that these two sons of mine sit, one at your right and the other at your left,

in your kingdom." [22]Jesus said in reply, "You do not know what you are asking.* Can you drink the cup that I am going to drink?" They said to him, "We can." [23]He replied, "My cup you will indeed drink, but to sit at my right and at my left [, this] is not mine to give but is for those for whom it has been prepared by my Father." [24d]When the ten heard this, they became indignant at the two brothers. [25]But Jesus summoned them and said, "You know that the rulers of the Gentiles lord it over them, and the great ones make their authority over them felt. [26]But it shall not be so among you. Rather, whoever wishes to be great among you shall be your servant; [27e]whoever wishes to be first among you shall be your slave. [28f]Just so, the Son of Man did not come to be served but to serve and to give his life as a ransom* for many."

The Healing of Two Blind Men.* [29g]As they left Jericho, a great crowd followed him. [30h]Two blind men were sitting by the roadside, and when they heard that Jesus was passing by, they cried out, "[Lord,][*] Son of David, have pity on us!" [31]The crowd warned them to be silent, but they called out all the more, "Lord, Son of David, have pity on us!" [32]Jesus stopped and called them and said, "What do you want me to do for you?" [33]They answered him, "Lord, let our eyes be opened." [34]Moved with pity, Jesus touched their eyes. Immediately they received their sight, and followed him.

a. [20:8] Lv 19:13; Dt 24:15.
b. [20:17–19] 16:21; 17:22–23; Mk 10:32–34; Lk 18:31–33.
c. [20:20–28] Mk 10:35–45.
d. [20:24–27] Lk 22:25–27.
e. [20:27] Mk 9:35.
f. [20:28] 26:28; Is 53:12; Rom 5:6; 1 Tm 2:6.
g. [20:29–34] Mk 10:46–52; Lk 18:35–43.
h. [20:30] 9:27.

CHAPTER 21

The Entry into Jerusalem.[*] [1a]When they drew near Jerusalem and came to Bethphage[*] on the Mount of Olives, Jesus sent two disciples, [2]saying to them, "Go into the village opposite you, and immediately you will find an ass tethered, and a colt with her.[*] Untie them and bring them here to me. [3]And if anyone should say anything to you, reply, 'The master has need of them.' Then he will send them at once." [4]This happened so that what had been spoken through the prophet might be fulfilled:

[5b]"Say to daughter Zion,
'Behold, your king comes
    to you,
  meek and riding on an
    ass,
    and on a colt, the
    foal of a beast of
    burden.'"

[6]The disciples went and did as Jesus had ordered them. [7]They brought the ass and the colt and laid their cloaks over them, and he sat upon them. [8c]The very large crowd spread

their cloaks on the road, while others cut branches from the trees and strewed them on the road. ⁹ᵈThe crowds preceding him and those following kept crying out and saying:

"Hosanna* to the Son of
  David;
    blessed is he who comes
    in the name of the
    Lord;
hosanna in the highest."

¹⁰And when he entered Jerusalem the whole city was shaken* and asked, "Who is this?" ¹¹And the crowds replied, "This is Jesus the prophet,* from Nazareth in Galilee."

The Cleansing of the Temple.* ¹²ᵉJesus entered the temple area and drove out all those engaged in selling and buying there. He overturned the tables of the money changers and the seats of those who were selling doves.*
¹³ᵍAnd he said to them, "It is written:

'My house shall be a house
  of prayer,'*
    but you are making it a
    den of thieves.'"

¹⁴ʰThe blind and the lame* approached him in the temple area, and he cured them. ¹⁵When the chief priests and the scribes saw the wondrous things* he was doing, and the children crying out in the temple area, "Hosanna to the Son of David," they were indignant ¹⁶ⁱand said to him, "Do you hear what they are saying?" Jesus said to them, "Yes; and have you never read the text, 'Out of the mouths of infants and nurslings you have brought forth praise'?" ¹⁷And leaving them, he went out of the city to Bethany, and there he spent the night.

The Cursing of the Fig Tree.*
¹⁸ʲWhen he was going back to the city in the morning, he was hungry. ¹⁹ᵏSeeing a fig tree by the road, he went over to it, but found nothing on it except leaves. And he said to

it, "May no fruit ever come from you again." And immediately the fig tree withered. [20]When the disciples saw this, they were amazed and said, "How was it that the fig tree withered immediately?" [21][*l]Jesus said to them in reply, "Amen, I say to you, if you have faith and do not waver, not only will you do what has been done to the fig tree, but even if you say to this mountain, 'Be lifted up and thrown into the sea,' it will be done. [22][m]Whatever you ask for in prayer with faith, you will receive."

The Authority of Jesus Questioned.[*] [23][n]When he had come into the temple area, the chief priests and the elders of the people approached him as he was teaching and said, "By what authority are you doing these things?[*] And who gave you this authority?"[o] [24]Jesus said to them in reply, "I shall ask you one question,[*] and if you answer it for me, then I

shall tell you by what authority I do these things. [25]Where was John's baptism from? Was it of heavenly or of human origin?" They discussed this among themselves and said, "If we say 'Of heavenly origin,' he will say to us, 'Then why did you not believe him?' [26][*p]But if we say, 'Of human origin,' we fear the crowd, for they all regard John as a prophet." [27]So they said to Jesus in reply, "We do not know." He himself said to them, "Neither shall I tell you by what authority I do these things.[*]

The Parable of the Two Sons.[*] [28]"What is your opinion? A man had two sons. He came to the first and said, 'Son, go out and work in the vineyard today.' [29]He said in reply, 'I will not,' but afterwards he changed his mind and went. [30]The man came to the other son and gave the same order. He said in reply, 'Yes, sir,' but did not go. [31]Which of the two did his father's will?"

They answered, "The first." Jesus said to them, "Amen, I say to you, tax collectors and prostitutes are entering the kingdom of God before you. ³²*ᑫWhen John came to you in the way of righteousness, you did not believe him; but tax collectors and prostitutes did. Yet even when you saw that, you did not later change your minds and believe him.

The Parable of the Tenants.ˣ ³³ʳ"Hear another parable. There was a landowner who planted a vineyard,ˣ put a hedge around it, dug a wine press in it, and built a tower. Then he leased it to tenants and went on a journey.ˢ ³⁴When vintage time drew near, he sent his servantsˣ to the tenants to obtain his produce. ³⁵But the tenants seized the servants and one they beat, another they killed, and a third they stoned. ³⁶Again he sent other servants, more numerous than the first ones, but they treated them in the same way. ³⁷Finally, he sent his son to them, thinking, 'They will respect my son.' ³⁸*But when the tenants saw the son, they said to one another, 'This is the heir. Come, let us kill him and acquire his inheritance.' ³⁹*ᵗThey seized him, threw him out of the vineyard, and killed him. ⁴⁰What will the owner of the vineyard do to those tenants when he comes?" ⁴¹They answeredˣ him, "He will put those wretched men to a wretched death and lease his vineyard to other tenants who will give him the produce at the proper times." ⁴²*ᵘJesus said to them, "Did you never read in the scriptures:

'The stone that the build-
    ers rejected
  has become the
    cornerstone;
by the Lord has this been
    done,
  and it is wonderful in
    our eyes'?

⁴³"Therefore, I say to you, the kingdom of God will be taken away from you and given to a people that will produce its fruit. ⁴⁴['The one who falls on this stone will be dashed to pieces; and it will crush anyone on whom it falls.]"
⁴⁵When the chief priests and the Pharisees* heard his parables, they knew that he was speaking about them. ⁴⁶And although they were attempting to arrest him, they feared the crowds, for they regarded him as a prophet.

a. [21:1–11] Mk 11:1–11; Lk 19:28–38; Jn 12:12–15.
b. [21:5] Is 62:11; Zec 9:9.
c. [21:8] 2 Kgs 9:13.
d. [21:9] Ps 118:25–26.
e. [21:12–17] Mk 11:15–19; Lk 19:45–48; Jn 2:14–22.
f. [21:13] Lv 5:7.
g. [21:13] Is 56:7; Jer 7:11.
h. [21:14] 2 Sm 5:8 LXX.
i. [21:16] Ps 8:2 LXX; Wis 10:21.
j. [21:18–22] Mk 11:12–14, 20–24.
k. [21:19] Jer 8:13; Lk 13:6–9.
l. [21:21] 17:20; Lk 17:6.
m. [21:22] 7:7; 1 Jn 3:22.
n. [21:23–27] Mk 11:27–33; Lk 20:1–8.
o. [21:23] Jn 2:18.
p. [21:26] 14:5.
q. [21:32] Lk 7:29–30.
r. [21:33–46] Mk 12:1–12; Lk 20:9–19.
s. [21:33] Is 5:1–2, 7.
t. [21:39] Heb 13:12.
u. [21:42] Ps 118:22–23; Is 28:16; Acts 4:11; 1 Pt 2:7.

CHAPTER 22

The Parable of the Wedding Feast. * ¹ᵃJesus again in reply spoke to them in parables, saying, ²"The kingdom of heaven may be likened to a king who gave a wedding feast* for his son. ³*He dispatched his servants to summon the invited guests to the feast, but they refused to come. ⁴A second time he sent other servants, saying, 'Tell those invited: "Behold, I have prepared my banquet, my calves and fattened cattle are killed, and everything is ready; come to the feast."' ⁵Some ignored the invitation and went away, one to his farm, another to his business. ⁶ᵇThe rest laid hold of his servants, mistreated them, and killed them. ⁷*The king was enraged and sent his troops, destroyed those murderers, and burned their city. ⁸Then he said to his servants, 'The feast is ready, but those who were invited were not worthy to come. ⁹Go out, therefore, into the main roads and invite to the feast whomever you find.' ¹⁰The servants went out into the streets and gathered all they found, (bad and good alike,) and the hall was filled with guests. ¹¹*But when the king came in to meet the guests he saw a man there not dressed in a wedding garment. ¹²He said to him, 'My friend, how is it that you came in here without a wedding garment?' But he was reduced to silence. ¹³*ᶜThen the king said to his attendants, 'Bind his hands and feet, and cast him into the darkness outside, where there will be wailing and grinding of teeth.' ¹⁴Many are invited, but few are chosen."

Paying Taxes to the Emperor.* ¹⁵ᵈThen the Pharisees* went off and plotted how they might entrap him in speech. ¹⁶They sent their disciples to him, with the Herodians,* saying, "Teacher, we know that you are a truthful man and that you teach the way of God in accordance with the truth. And you are not concerned with anyone's opinion, for you do not regard a person's status. ¹⁷*Tell us, then, what is your opinion: Is it lawful to pay the census tax to Caesar or not?" ¹⁸Knowing their malice, Jesus said, "Why are you testing me, you hypocrites? ¹⁹*Show me the coin that pays the census tax." Then they handed him the Roman coin. ²⁰He said to them, "Whose image is this and whose inscription?" ²¹ᵉThey replied, "Caesar's." At that he said to them, "Then repay to Caesar what belongs to Caesar and to God what belongs to God." ²²When they heard this they were amazed, and leaving him they went away.

The Question About the Resurrection.* ²³*On that day Sadducees approached him, saying that there is no resurrection.* They put this question to him, 24g saying, "Teacher, Moses said, 'If a man dies* without children, his brother shall marry his wife and raise up descendants for his brother.' 25Now there were seven brothers among us. The first married and died and, having no descendants, left his wife to his brother. 26The same happened with the second and the third, through all seven. 27Finally the woman died. 28Now at the resurrection, of the seven, whose wife will she be? For they all had been married to her." 29*Jesus said to them in reply, "You are misled because you do not know the scriptures or the power of God. 30At the resurrection they neither marry nor are given in marriage but are like the angels in heaven. 31And concerning the resurrection of the dead, have you not read what was said to you* by God, 32h'I am the God of Abraham, the God of Isaac, and the God of Jacob'? He is not the God of the dead but of the living." 33When the crowds heard this, they were astonished at his teaching.

The Greatest Commandment.* 34i When the Pharisees heard that he had silenced the Sadducees, they gathered together, 35and one of them [a scholar of the law]* tested him by asking, 36"Teacher,* which commandment in the law is the greatest?" 37jHe said to him,* "You shall love the Lord, your God, with all your heart, with all your soul, and with all your mind. 38This is the greatest and the first commandment. 39kThe second is like it:* You shall love your neighbor as yourself. 40*lThe whole law and the prophets depend on these two commandments."

The Question About David's Son.* 41mWhile the Pharisees were gathered together, Jesus questioned them,* 42*saying, "What is your opinion about the Messiah? Whose son is he?" They replied, "David's." 43He said to them, "How, then, does David, inspired by the Spirit, call him 'lord,' saying:

44n"The Lord said to my lord,

"Sit at my right hand until I place your enemies under your feet'"?

45*If David calls him 'lord,' how can he be his son?" 46oNo one was able to answer him a word, nor from that day on did anyone dare to ask him any more questions.

a. [22:1–14] Lk 14:15–24.
b. [22:6] 21:35.
c. [22:13] 8:12; 25:30.
d. [22:15–22] Mk 12:13–17; Lk 20:20–26.
e. [22:21] Rom 13:7.
f. [22:23–33] Mk 12:18–27; Lk 20:27–40.
g. [22:24] Gn 38:8; Dt 25:5–6.
h. [22:32] Ex 3:6.
i. [22:34–40] Mk 12:28–34; Lk 10:25–28.
j. [22:37] Dt 6:5.
k. [22:39] Lv 19:18; Jas 2:8.
l. [22:40] Rom 13:8–10; Gal 5:14.
m. [22:41–46] Mk 12:35–37; Lk 20:41–44.
n. [22:44] Ps 110:1; Acts 2:35; Heb 1:13.
o. [22:46] Lk 20:40.

CHAPTER 23*

Denunciation of the Scribes and Pharisees. 1aThen Jesus spoke to the crowds and to his disciples, 2*saying, "The scribes and the Pharisees have taken their seat on the chair of Moses. 3Therefore, do and observe all things whatsoever they tell you, but do not follow their example. For they preach but they do not practice. 4bThey tie up heavy burdens* [hard to carry] and lay them on people's shoulders, but they will not lift a finger to move them. 5*cAll their works are performed to be seen. They widen their phylacteries and lengthen their tassels. 6*dThey love places of honor at banquets, seats of honor in synagogues, 7greetings in marketplaces, and the salutation 'Rabbi.' 8*As for you, do not be called 'Rabbi.' You have but one teacher, and you are all brothers. 9Call no one on earth your father; you have but one Father in heaven. 10Do not be called 'Master'; you have but one master, the Messiah. 11eThe greatest among you must be your servant. 12fWhoever exalts himself will be humbled; but whoever humbles himself will be exalted.

[13]*g*"Woe to you, scribes and Pharisees, you hypocrites. You lock the kingdom of heaven* before human beings. You do not enter yourselves, nor do you allow entrance to those trying to enter.)[14]*

[15]*"Woe to you, scribes and Pharisees, you hypocrites. You traverse sea and land to make one convert, and when that happens you make him a child of Gehenna twice as much as yourselves.

[16]*h*"Woe to you, blind guides, who say, 'If one swears by the temple, it means nothing, but if one swears by the gold of the temple, one is obligated.' [17]Blind fools, which is greater, the gold, or the temple that made the gold sacred? [18]And you say, 'If one swears by the altar, it means nothing, but if one swears by the gift on the altar, one is obligated.' [19]You blind ones, which is greater, the gift, or the altar

that makes the gift sacred? [20]*i*One who swears by the altar swears by it and all that is upon it; [21]one who swears by the temple swears by it and by him who dwells in it; [22]one who swears by heaven swears by the throne of God and by him who is seated on it.

[23]*j*"Woe to you, scribes and Pharisees, you hypocrites. You pay tithes* of mint and dill and cummin, and have neglected the weightier things of the law: judgment and mercy and fidelity.)[But] these you should have done, without neglecting the others. [24]*k*Blind guides, who strain out the gnat and swallow the camel!

[25]*l*"Woe to you, scribes and Pharisees, you hypocrites. You cleanse the outside of cup and dish, but inside they are full of plunder and self-indulgence. [26]Blind Pharisee, cleanse first the inside of the cup, so that the outside also may be clean.

[27]*"Woe to you, scribes and Pharisees, you hypocrites. You are like whitewashed tombs, which appear beautiful on the outside, but inside are full of dead men's bones and every kind of filth. [28m]Even so, on the outside you appear righteous, but inside you are filled with hypocrisy and evildoing.

[29]*"Woe to you, scribes and Pharisees, you hypocrites. You build the tombs of the prophets and adorn the memorials of the righteous, [30n]and you say, 'If we had lived in the days of our ancestors, we would not have joined them in shedding the prophets' blood.' [31o]Thus you bear witness against yourselves that you are the children of those who murdered the prophets; [32]now fill up what your ancestors measured out! [33p]You serpents, you brood of vipers, how can you flee from the judgment of Gehenna? [34]*[q]Therefore, behold, I send to you prophets and wise men and scribes; some of them you will kill and crucify, some of them you will scourge in your synagogues and pursue from town to town, [35]so that there may come upon you all the righteous blood shed upon earth, from the righteous blood of Abel to the blood of Zechariah, the son of Barachiah, whom you murdered between the sanctuary and the altar. [36]Amen, I say to you, all these things will come upon this generation.

The Lament over Jerusalem.*
[37]*"Jerusalem, Jerusalem, you who kill the prophets and stone those sent to you, how many times I yearned to gather your children together, as a hen gathers her young under her wings, but you were unwilling! [38t]Behold, your house will be abandoned, desolate. [39u]I tell you, you will not see me again until you say, 'Blessed is

he who comes in the name of the Lord.'"

a. [23:1–39] Mk 12:38–39; Lk 11:37–52; 13:34–35.
b. [23:4] Lk 11:46.
c. [23:5] 6:1–6; Ex 13:9, 16; Nm 15:38–39; Dt 6:8; 11:18.
d. [23:6–7] Mk 12:38–39; Lk 11:43; 20:46.
e. [23:11] 20:26.
f. [23:12] Lk 14:11; 18:14.
g. [23:13] Lk 11:52.
h. [23:16] 15:14.
i. [23:20–22] 5:34–35.
j. [23:23] Lv 27:30; Dt 14:22; Lk 11:42.
k. [23:24] Lv 11:41–45.
l. [23:25–26] Mk 7:4; Lk 11:39.
m. [23:28] Lk 16:15; 18:9.
n. [23:30] Lk 11:47.
o. [23:31] Acts 7:52.
p. [23:33] 3:7; 12:34.
q. [23:34–36] 5:12; Gn 4:8; 2 Chr 24:20–22; Zec 1:1; Lk 11:49–51; Rev 18:24.
r. [23:37–39] Lk 13:34–35; 19:41–44.
s. [23:37] 21:35.
t. [23:38] Jer 12:7.
u. [23:39] Ps 118:26.

CHAPTER 24

The Destruction of the Temple Foretold. [1]*[a]Jesus left the temple area and was going away, when his disciples approached him to point out the temple buildings. [2]*He said to them in reply, "You see all these things, do you not? Amen, I say to you, there will not be left here a stone upon another stone that will not be thrown down."

The Beginning of Calamities. [3]As he was sitting on the Mount of Olives,* the disciples approached him privately and said, "Tell us, when will this happen, and what sign will there be of your coming, and of the end of the age?" [4]*Jesus said to them in reply, "See that no one deceives you. [5]For many will come in my name, saying, 'I am the Messiah,' and they will deceive many. [6b]You will hear of wars* and reports of wars; see that you are not alarmed, for these things must happen, but it will not yet be the end. [7c]Nation will rise against nation, and kingdom against kingdom; there will be famines and earthquakes from place to place. [8]*All these are the beginning of the labor_pains. [9]*[d]Then they will hand you over to persecution, and they will kill you. You will be hated by all nations because of my name. [10]And then many will be led into sin; they will betray and hate one another. [11]Many false prophets will arise and deceive many; [12]and because of the increase of evildoing, the love of many will grow cold. [13e]But the one who perseveres to the end will be saved. [14f]And this gospel of the kingdom will be preached throughout the world as a witness to all nations,[*] and then the end will come.

The Great Tribulation.[*] [15g]"When you see the desolating abomination[*] spoken of through Daniel the prophet standing in the holy place (let the reader understand), [16]then those in Judea must flee[*] to the mountains, [17*h]a person on the housetop must not go down to get things out of his house, [18]a person in the field must not return to get his cloak. [19]Woe to pregnant women and nursing mothers in those days. [20*]Pray that your flight not be in winter or on the sabbath, [21*i]for at that time there will be great tribulation, such as has not been since the beginning of the world until now, nor ever will be. [22]And if those days had not been shortened, no one would be saved; but for the sake of the elect they will be shortened. [23j]If anyone says to you then, 'Look, here is the Messiah!' or, 'There he is!' do not believe it. [24]False messiahs and false prophets will arise, and they will perform signs and wonders so great as to deceive, if that were possible, even the elect. [25]Behold, I have told it to you beforehand. [26]So if they say to you, 'He is in the desert,' do not go out there; if they say, 'He is in the inner rooms,' do not believe it.[*] [27k]For just as lightning comes from the east and is seen as far as the west, so will the coming of the Son of Man be. [28]Wherever the corpse is, there the vultures will gather.

The Coming of the Son of Man. [29][i]"Immediately after the tribulation of those days,

the sun will be darkened,
   and the moon will not
      give its light,
and the stars will fall from
   the sky,
   and the powers of
      the heavens will be
      shaken.

[30][m]And then the sign of the Son of Man[*] will appear in heaven, and all the tribes of the earth will mourn, and they will see the Son of Man coming upon the clouds of heaven with power and great glory. [31][n]And he will send out his angels[*] with a trumpet blast, and they will gather his elect from the four winds, from one end of the heavens to the other.

The Lesson of the Fig Tree.[*] [32]"Learn a lesson from the fig tree. When its branch becomes tender and sprouts leaves, you know that summer is near. [33]In the same way, when you see all these things, know that he is near, at the gates. [34]Amen, I say to you, this generation[*] will not pass away until all these things have taken place. [35][o]Heaven and earth will pass away, but my words will not pass away.

The Unknown Day and Hour.[*] [36][p]"But of that day and hour no one knows, neither the angels of heaven, nor the Son,[*] but the Father alone. [37][q]For as it was in the days of Noah, so it will be at the coming of the Son of Man. [38]In [those] days before the flood, they were eating and drinking, marrying and giving in marriage, up to the day that Noah entered the ark. [39]They did not know until the flood came and carried them all away. So will it be [also] at the coming of the Son of Man. [40][r]Two men will be out in the field; one will be taken, and one will be left. [41]Two women will be grinding at the mill; one will be taken, and one will be left. ⁴²*^sTherefore, stay awake! For you do not know on which day your Lord will come. ⁴³*Be sure of this: if the master of the house had known the hour of night when the thief was coming, he would have stayed awake and not let his house be broken into. ⁴⁴So too, you also must be prepared, for at an hour you do not expect, the Son of Man will come.

The Faithful or the Unfaithful Servant.[*] ⁴⁵^u"Who, then, is the faithful and prudent servant, whom the master has put in charge of his household to distribute to them their food at the proper time?[*] ⁴⁶Blessed is that servant whom his master on his arrival finds doing so. ⁴⁷Amen, I say to you, he will put him in charge of all his property. ⁴⁸*But if that wicked servant says to himself, 'My master is long delayed,'

⁴⁹and begins to beat his fellow servants, and eat and drink with drunkards, ⁵⁰the servant's master will come on an unexpected day and at an unknown hour ⁵¹^vand will punish him severely[*] and assign him a place with the hypocrites, where there will be wailing and grinding of teeth.

---

a. [24:1–44] Mk 13:1–37; Lk 21:5–36.
b. [24:6] Dn 2:28 LXX.
c. [24:7] Is 19:2.
d. [24:9] 10:17.
e. [24:13] 10:22.
f. [24:14] 28:19; Rom 10:18.
g. [24:15] Dn 9:27; 11:31; 12:11; Mk 13:14.
h. [24:17] Lk 17:31.
i. [24:21] Dn 12:1.
j. [24:23] Lk 17:23.
k. [24:27–28] Lk 17:24, 37.
l. [24:29] Is 13:10, 13; Ez 32:7; Am 8:9.
m. [24:30] Dn 7:13; Zec 12:12–14; Rev 1:7.
n. [24:31] Is 27:13; 1 Cor 15:52; 1 Thes 4:16.
o. [24:35] Is 40:8.
p. [24:36] Acts 1:7.
q. [24:37–39] Gn 6:5–7:23; Lk 17:26–27; 2 Pt 3:6.
r. [24:40–41] Lk 17:34–35.
s. [24:42–44] 25:13; Lk 12:39–40.
t. [24:43] 1 Thes 5:2.
u. [24:45–51] Lk 12:41–46.
v. [24:51] 13:42; 25:30.

CHAPTER 25

The Parable of the Ten Virgins.[*] ¹"Then[*] the kingdom of heaven will be like ten virgins who took their lamps and went out to meet the bridegroom. [2*]Five of them were foolish and five were wise. [3]The foolish ones, when taking their lamps, brought no oil with them, [4]but the wise brought flasks of oil with their lamps. [5]Since the bridegroom was long delayed, they all became drowsy and fell asleep. [6]At midnight, there was a cry, 'Behold, the bridegroom! Come out to meet him!' [7]Then all those virgins got up and trimmed their lamps. [8]The foolish ones said to the wise, 'Give us some of your oil, for our lamps are going out.' [9]But the wise ones replied, 'No, for there may not be enough for us and you. Go instead to the merchants and buy some for yourselves.' [10]While they went off to buy it, the bridegroom came and those who were ready went into the wedding feast with him. Then the door was locked. [11*a]Afterwards the other virgins came and said, 'Lord, Lord, open the door for us!' [12]But he said in reply,

'Amen, I say to you, I do not know you.' [13b]Therefore, stay awake,* for you know neither the day nor the hour.

The Parable of the Talents.[*]
[14c]"It will be as when a man who was going on a journey* called in his servants and entrusted his possessions to them. [15]To one he gave five talents;* to another, two; to a third, one—to each according to his ability. Then he went away. Immediately [16]the one who received five talents went and traded with them, and made another five. [17]Likewise, the one who received two made another two. [18*]But the man who received one went off and dug a hole in the ground and buried his master's money. [19]After a long time the master of those servants came back and settled accounts with them. [20]The one who had received five talents came forward bringing the additional five.* He said, 'Master,

you gave me five talents. See, I have made five more.' [21d]His master said to him, 'Well done, my good and faithful servant. Since you were faithful in small matters, I will give you great responsibilities. Come, share your master's joy.' [22][Then] the one who had received two talents also came forward and said, 'Master, you gave me two talents. See, I have made two more.' [23]His master said to him, 'Well done, my good and faithful servant. Since you were faithful in small matters, I will give you great responsibilities. Come, share your master's joy.' [24]Then the one who had received the one talent came forward and said, 'Master, I knew you were a demanding person, harvesting where you did not plant and gathering where you did not scatter; [25]so out of fear I went off and buried your talent in the ground. Here it is back.' [26]His master said to him in reply, 'You wicked, lazy servant!* So you knew that I harvest where I did not plant and gather where I did not scatter? [27]Should you not then have put my money in the bank so that I could have got it back with interest on my return? [28]Now then! Take the talent from him and give it to the one with ten. [29*e]For to everyone who has, more will be given and he will grow rich; but from the one who has not, even what he has will be taken away. [30*]And throw this useless servant into the darkness outside, where there will be wailing and grinding of teeth.'

The Judgment of the Nations.[*] [31f]"When the Son of Man comes in his glory, and all the angels with him, he will sit upon his glorious throne, [32g]and all the nations* will be assembled before him. And he will separate them one from another, as a shepherd separates the sheep from the goats. [33]He will place the sheep on his right and the goats on his left. ³⁴Then the king will say to those on his right, 'Come, you who are blessed by my Father. Inherit the kingdom prepared for you from the foundation of the world. ^{35h}For I was hungry and you gave me food, I was thirsty and you gave me drink, a stranger and you welcomed me, ³⁶naked and you clothed me, ill and you cared for me, in prison and you visited me.' ³⁷Then the righteous* will answer him and say, 'Lord, when did we see you hungry and feed you, or thirsty and give you drink? ³⁸When did we see you a stranger and welcome you, or naked and clothe you? ³⁹When did we see you ill or in prison, and visit you?' ⁴⁰ⁱAnd the king will say to them in reply, 'Amen, I say to you, whatever you did for one of these least brothers of mine, you did for me.' ^{41*j}Then he will say to those on his left, 'Depart from me, you accursed, into the eternal fire prepared for the devil and his angels. ^{42k}For I was hungry and you gave me no food, I was thirsty and you gave me no drink, ⁴³a stranger and you gave me no welcome, naked and you gave me no clothing, ill and in prison, and you did not care for me.' ⁴⁴Then they will answer and say, 'Lord, when did we see you hungry or thirsty or a stranger or naked or ill or in prison, and not minister to your needs?' ⁴⁵He will answer them, 'Amen, I say to you, what you did not do for one of these least ones, you did not do for me.' ^{46l}And these will go off to eternal punishment, but the righteous to eternal life."

---

a. [25:11–12] 7:21, 23; Lk 13:25–27.
b. [25:13] 24:42; Mk 13:33.
c. [25:14–30] Lk 19:12–27.
d. [25:21] Lk 16:10.
e. [25:29] 13:12; Mk 4:25; Lk 8:18; 19:26.
f. [25:31] 16:27; Dt 33:2 LXX.
g. [25:32] Ez 34:17.
h. [25:35–36] Is 58:7; Ez 18:7.
i. [25:40] 10:40, 42.
j. [25:41] 7:23; Lk 13:27.
k. [25:42–43] Jb 22:7; Jas 2:15–16.
l. [25:46] Dn 12:2.

VII. THE PASSION AND RESURRECTION

CHAPTER 26

The Conspiracy Against Jesus. [1*]When Jesus finished all these words,* he said to his disciples, [2a]"You know that in two days' time it will be Passover, and the Son of Man will be handed over to be crucified." [3*]Then the chief priests and the elders of the people assembled in the palace of the high priest, who was called Caiaphas, [4b]and they consulted together to arrest Jesus by treachery and put him to death. [5]But they said, "Not during the festival,* that there may not be a riot among the people."

The Anointing at Bethany.* [6c]Now when Jesus was in Bethany in the house of Simon the leper, [7a]a woman came up to him with an alabaster jar of costly perfumed oil, and poured it on his head while he was reclining at table. [8]When the disciples saw this, they were indignant and said, "Why this waste? [9]It could have been sold for much, and the money given to the poor." [10]Since Jesus knew this, he said to them, "Why do you make trouble for the woman? She has done a good thing for me. [11d]The poor you will always have with you; but you will not always have me. [12]In pouring this perfumed oil upon my body, she did it to prepare me for burial. [13]Amen, I say to you, wherever this gospel is proclaimed in the whole world, what she has done will be spoken of, in memory of her."

The Betrayal by Judas. [14e]Then one of the Twelve, who was called Judas Iscariot,* went to the chief priests [15*f]and said, "What are you willing to give me if I hand him over to you?" They paid him thirty pieces of silver, [16]and from that time on he looked for an opportunity to hand him over.

Preparations for the Passover. [17g]On the first day of the Feast of Unleavened Bread,* the disciples approached Jesus and said, "Where do you want us to prepare for you to eat the Passover?"[h] [18]He said, "Go into the city to a certain man and tell him, 'The teacher says, "My appointed time draws near; in your house I shall celebrate the Passover with my disciples."'" [19]The disciples then did as Jesus had ordered, and prepared the Passover.

The Betrayer. [20]When it was evening, he reclined at table with the Twelve. [21]And while they were eating, he said, "Amen, I say to you, one of you will betray me."* [22]Deeply distressed at this, they began to say to him one after another, "Surely it is not I, Lord?" [23]He said in reply, "He

who has dipped his hand into the dish with me is the one who will betray me. [24*i]The Son of Man indeed goes, as it is written of him, but woe to that man by whom the Son of Man is betrayed. It would be better for that man if he had never been born." [25*]Then Judas, his betrayer, said in reply, "Surely it is not I, Rabbi?" He answered, "You have said so."

The Lord's Supper. [26*j]While they were eating, Jesus took bread, said the blessing, broke it, and giving it to his disciples said, "Take and eat; this is my body."[*k] [27]Then he took a cup, gave thanks,* and gave it to them, saying, "Drink from it, all of you, [28l]for this is my blood of the covenant, which will be shed on behalf of many for the forgiveness of sins. [29*]I tell you, from now on I shall not drink this fruit of the vine until the day when I drink it with you new in the kingdom of my

Father." [30*]Then, after singing a hymn, they went out to the Mount of Olives.

Peter's Denial Foretold. [31m]Then Jesus said to them, "This night all of you will have your faith in me shaken,[*] for it is written:[n]

'I will strike the shepherd,
    and the sheep of
        the flock will be
            dispersed';

[32]but after I have been raised up, I shall go before you to Galilee." [33]Peter said to him in reply, "Though all may have their faith in you shaken, mine will never be." [34*o]Jesus said to him, "Amen, I say to you, this very night before the cock crows, you will deny me three times."[p] [35]Peter said to him, "Even though I should have to die with you, I will not deny you." And all the disciples spoke likewise.

The Agony in the Garden. [36*q]Then Jesus came with them to a place called Gethsemane,[*] and he said to his disciples, "Sit here while I go over there and pray."[r] [37s]He took along Peter and the two sons of Zebedee,[*] and began to feel sorrow and distress. [38t]Then he said to them, "My soul is sorrowful even to death.[*] Remain here and keep watch with me." [39u]He advanced a little and fell prostrate in prayer, saying, "My Father,[*] if it is possible, let this cup pass from me; yet, not as I will, but as you will." [40]When he returned to his disciples he found them asleep. He said to Peter, "So you could not keep watch with me for one hour? [41]Watch and pray that you may not undergo the test.[*] The spirit is willing, but the flesh is weak." [42*v]Withdrawing a second time, he prayed again, "My Father, if it is not possible that this cup pass without my drinking it, your will be done!" [43]Then he returned once more and found them asleep, for they could not keep their eyes open. [44]He left them and withdrew again and prayed a third time, saying the same thing again. [45w]Then he returned to his disciples and said to them, "Are you still sleeping and taking your rest? Behold, the hour is at hand when the Son of Man is to be handed over to sinners. [46]Get up, let us go. Look, my betrayer is at hand."

The Betrayal and Arrest of Jesus. [47x]While he was still speaking, Judas, one of the Twelve, arrived, accompanied by a large crowd, with swords and clubs, who had come from the chief priests and the elders of the people. [48]His betrayer had arranged a sign with them, saying, "The man I shall kiss is the one; arrest him." [49]Immediately he went over to Jesus and said, "Hail, Rabbi!" and he kissed him. [50]Jesus answered him, "Friend, do what you have come

for." Then stepping forward they laid hands on Jesus and arrested him. [51]And behold, one of those who accompanied Jesus put his hand to his sword, drew it, and struck the high priest's servant, cutting off his ear. [52]Then Jesus said to him, "Put your sword back into its sheath, for all who take the sword will perish by the sword. [53]Do you think that I cannot call upon my Father and he will not provide me at this moment with more than twelve legions of angels? [54]But then how would the scriptures be fulfilled which say that it must come to pass in this way?" [55*]At that hour Jesus said to the crowds, "Have you come out as against a robber, with swords and clubs to seize me? Day after day I sat teaching in the temple area, yet you did not arrest me. [56y]But all this has come to pass that the writings of the prophets may be fulfilled." Then all the disciples left him and fled.

Jesus Before the Sanhedrin.[*]
[57z]Those who had arrested Jesus led him away to Caiaphas[*] the high priest, where the scribes and the elders were assembled. [58]Peter was following him at a distance as far as the high priest's courtyard, and going inside he sat down with the servants to see the outcome. [59]The chief priests and the entire Sanhedrin[*] kept trying to obtain false testimony against Jesus in order to put him to death, [60a]but they found none, though many false witnesses came forward. Finally two[*] came forward [61]who stated, "This man said, 'I can destroy the temple of God and within three days rebuild it.'" [62]The high priest rose and addressed him, "Have you no answer? What are these men testifying against you?" [63b]But Jesus was silent.[*] Then the high priest said to him, "I order you to tell us under oath before the living God whether you are the Messiah, the Son of God." [64c]Jesus said to him in reply, "You have said so.[*] But I tell you:

From now on you will see
'the Son of Man
    seated at the right hand
        of the Power'
and 'coming on the
    clouds of heaven.'"

[65]Then the high priest tore his robes and said, "He has blasphemed![*] What further need have we of witnesses? You have now heard the blasphemy; [66]what is your opinion?" They said in reply, "He deserves to die!" [67*d]Then they spat in his face and struck him, while some slapped him, [68]saying, "Prophesy for us, Messiah: who is it that struck you?"

Peter's Denial of Jesus.
[69e]Now Peter was sitting outside in the courtyard. One of the maids came over to him and said, "You too were with Jesus the Galilean." [70*]But he denied it in front of everyone,

saying, "I do not know what you are talking about!" 71As he went out to the gate, another girl saw him and said to those who were there, "This man was with Jesus the Nazorean." 72Again he denied it with an oath, "I do not know the man!" 73*A little later the bystanders came over and said to Peter, "Surely you too are one of them; even your speech gives you away." 74At that he began to curse and to swear, "I do not know the man." And immediately a cock crowed. 75fThen Peter remembered the word that Jesus had spoken: "Before the cock crows you will deny me three times." He went out and began to weep bitterly.

a. [26:2–5] Mk 14:1–2; Lk 22:1–2.
b. [26:4] Jn 11:47–53.
c. [26:6–13] Mk 14:3–9; Jn 12:1–8.
d. [26:11] Dt 15:11.
e. [26:14–16] Mk 14:10–11; Lk 22:3–6.
f. [26:15] Zec 11:12.
g. [26:17–25] Mk 14:12–21; Lk 22:7–23.
h. [26:17] Ex 12:14–20.
i. [26:24] Is 53:8–10.
j. [26:26–30] Mk 14:22–26; Lk 22:14–23; 1 Cor 11:23–25.
k. [26:26–27] 1 Cor 10:16.
l. [26:28] Ex 24:8; Is 53:12.
m. [26:31–35] Mk 14:7–31.
n. [26:31] Zec 13:7; Jn 16:32.
o. [26:34–35] Lk 22:33–34; Jn 13:37–38.
p. [26:34] 26:69–75.
q. [26:36–46] Mk 14:32–42; Lk 22:39–46.
r. [26:36] Jn 18:1.
s. [26:37–39] Heb 5:7.
t. [26:38] Ps 42:6, 12; Jon 4:9.
u. [26:39] Jn 4:34; 6:38; Phil 2:8.
v. [26:42] 6:10; Heb 10:9.
w. [26:45] Jn 12:23; 13:1; 17:1.
x. [26:47–56] Mk 14:43–50; Lk 22:47–53; Jn 18:3–11.
y. [26:56] 26:31.
z. [26:57–68] Mk 14:53–65; Lk 22:54–55, 63–71; Jn 18:12–14, 19–24.
a. [26:60–61] Dt 19:15; Jn 2:19; Acts 6:14.
b. [26:63] Is 53:7.
c. [26:64] Ps 110:1; Dn 7:13.
d. [26:67] Wis 2:19; Is 50:6.
e. [26:69–75] Mk 14:66–72; Lk 22:56–62; Jn 18:17–18, 25–27.
f. [26:75] 26:34.

CHAPTER 27

Jesus Before Pilate. 1*When it was morning,a all the chief priests and the elders of the people took counsel* against Jesus to put him to death. 2They bound him, led him away, and handed him over to Pilate, the governor.

The Death of Judas. 3bThen Judas, his betrayer, seeing that Jesus had been condemned, deeply regretted what he had done. He returned the thirty pieces of silver* to the chief priests and elders,c 4saying, "I have sinned in betraying innocent blood." They said,

"What is that to us? Look to it yourself." ⁵*Flinging the money into the temple, he departed and went off and hanged himself. ⁶The chief priests gathered up the money, but said, "It is not lawful to deposit this in the temple treasury, for it is the price of blood." ⁷After consultation, they used it to buy the potter's field as a burial place for foreigners. ⁸That is why that field even today is called the Field of Blood. ⁹Then was fulfilled what had been said through Jeremiah the prophet,* "And they took the thirty pieces of silver, the value of a man with a price on his head, a price set by some of the Israelites, ¹⁰ᵈand they paid it out for the potter's field just as the Lord had commanded me."

Jesus Questioned by Pilate.
¹¹ᵉNow Jesus stood before the governor, and he questioned him, *"Are you the king of the Jews?"* Jesus said, "You say so." ¹²ᶠAnd when he was accused by the chief priests and elders,* he made no answer. ¹³Then Pilate said to him, "Do you not hear how many things they are testifying against you?" ¹⁴But he did not answer him one word, so that the governor was greatly amazed.

The Sentence of Death.
¹⁵*ᵍNow on the occasion of the feast the governor was accustomed to release to the crowd one prisoner whom they wished. ¹⁶*And at that time they had a notorious prisoner called [Jesus] Barabbas. ¹⁷So when they had assembled, Pilate said to them, "Which one do you want me to release to you, [Jesus] Barabbas, or Jesus called Messiah?" ¹⁸*For he knew that it was out of envy that they had handed him over. ¹⁹*While he was still seated on the bench, his wife sent him a message, "Have nothing to do with that righteous man. I suffered much

in a dream today because of him." [20h]The chief priests and the elders persuaded the crowds to ask for Barabbas but to destroy Jesus. [21]The governor said to them in reply, "Which of the two do you want me to release to you?" They answered, "Barabbas!" [22*]Pilate said to them, "Then what shall I do with Jesus called Messiah?" They all said, "Let him be crucified!" [23]But he said, "Why? What evil has he done?" They only shouted the louder, "Let him be crucified!" [24*i]When Pilate saw that he was not succeeding at all, but that a riot was breaking out instead, he took water and washed his hands in the sight of the crowd, saying, "I am innocent of this man's blood. Look to it yourselves." [25]And the whole people said in reply, "His blood be upon us and upon our children." [26]Then he released Barabbas to them, but after he had Jesus scourged,* he handed him over to be crucified.

Mockery by the Soldiers. [27j]Then the soldiers of the governor took Jesus inside the praetorium* and gathered the whole cohort around him. [28]They stripped off his clothes and threw a scarlet military cloak* about him. [29k]Weaving a crown out of thorns,* they placed it on his head, and a reed in his right hand. And kneeling before him, they mocked him, saying, "Hail, King of the Jews!" [30l]They spat upon him* and took the reed and kept striking him on the head. [31]And when they had mocked him, they stripped him of the cloak, dressed him in his own clothes, and led him off to crucify him.

The Way of the Cross.* [32m]As they were going out, they met a Cyrenian named Simon; this man they pressed into service to carry his cross.

The Crucifixion. [33n]And when they came to a place called Golgotha (which means Place of the Skull), [34o]they gave Jesus wine to drink mixed with gall.* But when he had tasted it, he refused to drink. [35p]After they had crucified him, they divided his garments* by casting lots; [36]then they sat down and kept watch over him there. [37]And they placed over his head the written charge* against him: This is Jesus, the King of the Jews. [38]Two revolutionaries* were crucified with him, one on his right and the other on his left. [39*q]Those passing by reviled him, shaking their heads [40r]and saying, "You who would destroy the temple and rebuild it in three days, save yourself, if you are the Son of God, [and] come down from the cross!" [41]Likewise the chief priests with the scribes and elders mocked him and said, [42]"He saved others; he cannot save himself. So he is the king of Israel!* Let him come down from the cross now, and we will believe in him. [43*s]He trusted in God; let him deliver him now if he wants him. For he said, 'I am the Son of God.'" [44]The revolutionaries who were crucified with him also kept abusing him in the same way.

The Death of Jesus. [45*t]From noon onward,[u] darkness came over the whole land until three in the afternoon. [46v]And about three o'clock Jesus cried out in a loud voice, "*Eli, Eli, lema sabachthani?*"* which means, "My God, my God, why have you forsaken me?" [47*]Some of the bystanders who heard it said, "This one is calling for Elijah." [48w]Immediately one of them ran to get a sponge; he soaked it in wine, and putting it on a reed, gave it to him to drink. [49]But the rest said, "Wait, let us see if Elijah comes to save him." [50*]But Jesus cried out again in a loud voice, and gave up his spirit. [51x]And behold, the veil of the sanctuary was torn in two from top to bottom.* The earth quaked, rocks were split, [52y]tombs were opened, and the bodies of many saints who had fallen asleep were raised. [53]And coming forth from their tombs after his resurrection, they entered the holy city and appeared to many. [54*]The centurion and the men with him who were keeping watch over Jesus feared greatly when they saw the earthquake and all that was happening, and they said, "Truly, this was the Son of God!" [55]There were many women there, looking on from a distance,* who had followed Jesus from Galilee, ministering to him. [56z]Among them were Mary Magdalene and Mary the mother of James and Joseph, and the mother of the sons of Zebedee.

The Burial of Jesus.* [57a]When it was evening, there came a rich man from Arimathea named Joseph, who was himself a disciple of Jesus.[b] [58]He went to Pilate and asked for the body of Jesus; then Pilate ordered it to be handed over. [59]Taking the body, Joseph wrapped it [in] clean linen [60]and laid it in his new tomb that he had hewn in the rock. Then he rolled a huge stone across the entrance to the tomb and departed. [61]But Mary Magdalene and the other Mary remained sitting there, facing the tomb.

The Guard at the Tomb.* [62]The next day, the one following the day of preparation,* the chief priests and the Pharisees gathered before Pilate [63c]and said, "Sir, we remember that this impostor while still alive said, 'After three days I will be raised up.' [64]Give orders, then, that the grave be secured until the third day, lest his disciples come and steal him and say to the people, 'He has been raised from the dead.' This last imposture would be worse than the first.'" [65]Pilate said to them, "The guard is yours;* go secure it as best you can." [66]So they went and secured the tomb by fixing a seal to the stone and setting the guard.

a. [27:1–2] Mk 15:1; Lk 23:1; Jn 18:28.
b. [27:3–10] Acts 1:18–19.
c. [27:3] 26:15.
d. [27:10] Zec 11:12–13.
e. [27:11–14] Mk 15:2–5; Lk 23:2–3; Jn 18:29–38.
f. [27:12] Is 53:7.
g. [27:15–26] Mk 15:6–15; Lk 23:17–25; Jn 18:39–19:16.
h. [27:20] Acts 3:14.
i. [27:24] Dt 21:1–8.
j. [27:27–31] Mk 15:16–20; Jn 19:2–3.
k. [27:29] 27:11.
l. [27:30] Is 50:6.
m. [27:32] Mk 15:21; Lk 23:26.
n. [27:33–44] Mk 15:22–32; Lk 23:32–38; Jn 19:17–19, 23–24.
o. [27:34] Ps 69:21.
p. [27:35] Ps 22:19.
q. [27:39] Ps 22:8.
r. [27:40] 4:3, 6; 26:61.
s. [27:43] Ps 22:9; Wis 2:12–20.
t. [27:45–46] Mk 15:33–41; Lk 23:44–49; Jn 19:28–30.
u. [27:45] Am 8:9.
v. [27:46] Ps 22:2.
w. [27:48] Ps 69:21.
x. [27:51] Ex 26:31–36; Ps 68:9; 77:19.
y. [27:52] Dn 12:1–3.
z. [27:56] 13:55.
a. [27:57–61] Mk 15:42–47; Lk 23:50–56; Jn 19:38–42.
b. [27:57] Is 53:9.
c. [27:63] 12:40; 16:21; 17:23; 20:19.

CHAPTER 28*

The Resurrection of Jesus. [1a]After the sabbath, as the first day of the week was dawning,* Mary Magdalene and the other Mary came to see the tomb. [2*b]And behold, there was a great earthquake; for an angel of the Lord descended from heaven, approached, rolled back the stone, and sat upon it. [3c]His appearance was like lightning and his clothing was white as snow. [4]The guards were shaken with fear of him and became like dead men. [5]Then the angel said to the women in reply, "Do not be afraid! I know that you are seeking Jesus the crucified. [6*]He is not here, for he has been raised just as he said. Come and see the place where he lay. [7d]Then go quickly and tell his disciples, 'He has been raised from the dead, and he is going before you to Galilee; there you will see him.' Behold, I have told you." [8]Then they went away quickly from the tomb, fearful yet overjoyed, and ran to announce* this to his disciples. [9*e]And behold, Jesus met them on their way and greeted them.

They approached, embraced his feet, and did him homage. [10]Then Jesus said to them, "Do not be afraid. Go tell my brothers to go to Galilee, and there they will see me."

The Report of the Guard.[*] [11]While they were going, some of the guard went into the city and told the chief priests all that had happened. [12]They assembled with the elders and took counsel; then they gave a large sum of money to the soldiers, [13]telling them, "You are to say, 'His disciples came by night and stole him while we were asleep.' [14]And if this gets to the ears of the governor, we will satisfy [him] and keep you out of trouble." [15]The soldiers took the money and did as they were instructed. And this story has circulated among the Jews to the present [day].

The Commissioning of the Disciples.[*] [16f]The eleven[*] disciples went to Galilee, to the mountain to which Jesus had ordered them. [17*]When they saw him, they worshiped, but they doubted. [18g]Then Jesus approached and said to them, "All power in heaven and on earth has been given to me. [19h]Go, therefore,[*] and make disciples of all nations, baptizing them in the name of the Father, and of the Son, and of the holy Spirit, [20i]teaching them to observe all that I have commanded you.[*] And behold, I am with you always, until the end of the age."

a. [28:1–10] Mk 16:1–8; Lk 24:1–12; Jn 20:1–10.
b. [28:2] 25:51.
c. [28:3] 17:2.
d. [28:7] 26:32.
e. [28:9–10] Jn 20:17.
f. [28:16–20] Mk 16:14–16; Lk 24:36–49; Jn 20:19–23.
g. [28:18] Dn 7:14 LXX.
h. [28:19] Acts 1:8.
i. [28:20] 1:23; 13:39; 24:3.

Notes

* [1:1–2:23] The infancy narrative forms the prologue of the gospel. Consisting of a genealogy and five stories, it presents the coming of Jesus as the climax of Israel's history, and the events of his conception, birth, and early childhood as the fulfillment of Old Testament prophecy. The genealogy is probably traditional material that Matthew edited. In its first two sections (Mt 1:2–11) it was drawn from Ru 4:18–22; 1 Chr 1–3. Except for Jechoniah, Shealtiel, and Zerubbabel, none of the names in the third section (Mt 1:12–16) is found

in any Old Testament genealogy. While the gene-alogy shows the continuity of God's providential plan from Abraham on, discontinuity is also present. The women Tamar (Mt 1:3), Rahab and Ruth (Mt 1:5), and the wife of Uriah, Bathsheba (Mt 1:6), bore their sons through unions that were in varying degrees strange and unexpected. These "irregularities" culminate in the supreme "irregu-larity" of the Messiah's birth of a virgin mother; the age of fulfillment is inaugurated by a creative act of God.

Drawing upon both biblical tradition and Jew-ish stories, Matthew portrays Jesus as reliving the Exodus experience of Israel and the persecutions of Moses. His rejection by his own people and his passion are foreshadowed by the troubled reaction of "all Jerusalem" to the question of the magi who are seeking the "newborn king of the Jews" (Mt 2:2–3), and by Herod's attempt to have him killed. The magi who do him homage prefigure the Gen-tiles who will accept the preaching of the gospel. The infancy narrative proclaims who Jesus is, the savior of his people from their sins (Mt 1:21), Emmanuel in whom "God is with us" (Mt 1:23), and the Son of God (Mt 2:15).

* [1:1] **The Son of David, the son of Abraham:** two links of the genealogical chain are singled out. Although the later, David is placed first in order to emphasize that Jesus is the royal Messiah. The mention of Abraham may be due not only to his being the father of the nation Israel but to Mat-thew's interest in the universal scope of Jesus' mis-sion; cf. Gn 22:18 ". . . in your descendants all the nations of the earth shall find blessing."

* [1:7] The successor of Abijah was not Asaph but Asa (see 1 Chr 3:10). Some textual witnesses read the latter name; however, **Asaph** is better attested. Matthew may have deliberately intro-duced the psalmist Asaph into the genealogy (and in Mt 1:10 the prophet Amos) in order to show that Jesus is the fulfillment not only of the promises made to David (see 2 Sm 7) but of all the Old Testament.

* [1:10] **Amos:** some textual witnesses read **Amon,** who was the actual successor of Manasseh (see 1 Chr 3:14).

* [1:17] Matthew is concerned with fourteen generations, probably because fourteen is the numerical value of the Hebrew letters forming the name of David. In the second section of the genealogy (Mt 1:6b–11), three kings of Judah, Ahaziah, Joash, and Amaziah, have been omit-ted (see 1 Chr 3:11–12), so that there are four-teen generations in that section. Yet the third (Mt 1:12-16) apparently has only thirteen. Since Matthew here emphasizes that each section has fourteen, it is unlikely that the thirteen of the last was due to his oversight. Some scholars suggest that **Jesus who is called the Messiah** (Mt 1:16b) doubles the final member of the chain: **Jesus,** born within the

family of David, opens up the new age as **Messiah,** so that in fact there are fourteen generations in the third section. This is perhaps too subtle, and the hypothesis of a slip not on the part of Matthew but of a later scribe seems likely. On **Messiah,** see note on Lk 2:11.

* [1:18–25] This first story of the infancy narra-tive spells out what is summarily indicated in Mt 1:16. The virginal conception of Jesus is the work of the Spirit of God. Joseph's decision to divorce Mary is overcome by the heavenly command that he take her into his home and accept the child as his own. The natural genealogical line is broken but the promises to David are fulfilled; through Joseph's adoption the child belongs to the family of David. Matthew sees the virginal conception as the fulfillment of Is 7:14.

* [1:18] **Betrothed to Joseph:** betrothal was the first part of the marriage, constituting a man and woman as husband and wife. Subsequent infidel-ity was considered adultery. The betrothal was followed some months later by the husband's tak-ing his wife into his home, at which time normal married life began.

* [1:19] **A righteous man:** as a devout observer of the Mosaic law, Joseph wished to break his union with someone whom he suspected of gross violation of the law. It is commonly said that the law required him to do so, but the texts usually given in support of that view, e.g., Dt 22:20–21 do not clearly pertain to Joseph's situation. **Unwilling to expose her to shame:** the penalty for proved adultery was death by stoning; cf. Dt 22:21–23.

* [1:20] **The angel of the Lord:** in the Old Testa-ment a common designation of God's communi-cation with a human being. **In a dream:** see Mt 2:13, 19, 22. These dreams may be meant to recall the dreams of Joseph, son of Jacob the patriarch (Gn 37:5–11, 19). A closer parallel is the dream of Amram, father of Moses, related by Josephus (*Antiquities* 2:212, 215–16).

* [1:21] **Jesus:** in first-century Judaism the Hebrew name Joshua (Greek *Iēsous*) meaning "Yahweh helps" was interpreted as "Yahweh saves."

* [1:23] **God is with us:** God's promise of deliv-erance to Judah in Isaiah's time is seen by Matthew as fulfilled in the birth of Jesus, in whom God is with his people. The name Emmanuel is alluded to at the end of the gospel where the risen Jesus assures his disciples of his continued presence, ". . . I am with you always, until the end of the age" (Mt 28:20).

* [1:25] **Until she bore a son:** the evangelist is concerned to emphasize that Joseph was not responsible for the conception of Jesus. The Greek word translated "until" does not imply normal marital conduct after Jesus' birth, nor does it exclude it.

* [2:1–12] The future rejection of Jesus by Israel and his acceptance by the Gentiles are retrojected into this scene of the narrative.

* [2:1] **In the days of King Herod**: Herod reigned from 37 to 4 B.C. **Magi**: originally a designation of the Persian priestly caste, the word became used of those who were regarded as having more than human knowledge. Matthew's magi are astrologers.

* [2:2] **We saw his star**: it was a common ancient belief that a new star appeared at the time of a ruler's birth. Matthew also draws upon the Old Testament story of Balaam, who had prophesied that "A star shall advance from Jacob" (Nm 24:17), though there the star means not an astral phenomenon but the king himself.

* [2:4] Herod's consultation with the chief priests and scribes has some similarity to a Jewish legend about the child Moses in which the "sacred scribes" warn Pharaoh about the imminent birth of one who will deliver Israel from Egypt and the king makes plans to destroy them.

* [2:11] Cf. Ps 72:10, 15; Is 60:6. These Old Testament texts led to the interpretation of the magi as kings.

* [2:13–23] Biblical and nonbiblical traditions about Moses are here applied to the child Jesus, though the dominant Old Testament type is not Moses but Israel (Mt 2:15).

* [2:13] **Flee to Egypt**: Egypt was a traditional place of refuge for those fleeing from danger in Palestine (see 1 Kgs 11:40; Jer 26:21), but the main reason why the child is to be taken to Egypt is that he may relive the Exodus experience of Israel.

* [2:15] The fulfillment citation is taken from Hos 11:1. Israel, God's son, was called out of Egypt at the time of the Exodus; Jesus, the Son of God, will similarly be called out of that land in a new exodus. The father-son relationship between God and the nation is set in a higher key. Here the son is not a group adopted as "son of God," but the child who, as conceived by the holy Spirit, stands in unique relation to God. He is son of David and of Abraham, of Mary and of Joseph, but, above all, of God.

* [2:18] Jer 31:15 portrays Rachel, wife of the patriarch Jacob, weeping for her children taken into exile at the time of the Assyrian invasion of the northern kingdom (722–21 B.C.). Bethlehem was traditionally identified with Ephrath, the place near which Rachel was buried (see Gn 35:19; 48:7), and the mourning of Rachel is here applied to her lost children of a later age. **Ramah**: about six miles north of Jerusalem. The lamentation of Rachel is so great as to be heard at a far distance.

* [2:20] **For those who sought the child's life are dead**: Moses, who had fled from Egypt because the Pharaoh sought to kill him (see Ex 2:15), was told to return there, "for all the men who sought your life are dead" (Ex 4:19).

* [2:22] With the agreement of the emperor Augustus, Archelaus received half of his father's kingdom, including Judea, after Herod's death. He had the title "ethnarch" (i.e., "ruler of a nation") and reigned from 4 B.C. to A.D. 6.

* [2:23] **Nazareth . . . he shall be called a Nazorean**: the tradition of Jesus' residence in Nazareth was firmly established, and Matthew sees it as being in accordance with the foreannounced plan of God. The town of Nazareth is not mentioned in the Old Testament, and no such prophecy can be found there. The vague expression "through the prophets" may be due to Matthew's seeing a connection between Nazareth and certain texts in which there are words with a remote similarity to the name of that town. Some such Old Testament texts are Is 11:1 where the Davidic king of the future is called "a bud" (*nēṣer*) that shall blossom from the roots of Jesse, and Jgs 13:5, 7 where Samson, the future deliverer of Israel from the Philistines, is called one who shall be consecrated (a *nāzîr*) to God.

* [3:1–12] Here Matthew takes up the order of Jesus' ministry found in the gospel of Mark, beginning with the preparatory preaching of John the Baptist.

* [3:1] Unlike Luke, Matthew says nothing of the Baptist's origins and does not make him a relative of Jesus. **The desert of Judea**: the barren region west of the Dead Sea extending up the Jordan valley.

* [3:2] **Repent**: the Baptist calls for a change of heart and conduct, a turning of one's life from rebellion to obedience towards God. **The kingdom of heaven is at hand**: "heaven" (lit., "the heavens") is a substitute for the name "God" that was avoided by devout Jews of the time out of reverence. The expression "the kingdom of heaven" occurs only in the gospel of Matthew. It means the effective rule of God over his people. In its fullness it includes not only human obedience to God's word, but the triumph of God over physical evils, supremely over death. In the expectation found in Jewish apocalyptic, the kingdom was to be ushered in by a judgment in which sinners would be condemned and perish, an expectation shared by the Baptist. This was modified in Christian understanding where the kingdom was seen as being established in stages, culminating with the parousia of Jesus.

* [3:3] See note on Jn 1:23.

* [3:4] The clothing of John recalls the austere dress of the prophet Elijah (2 Kgs 1:8). The expectation of the return of Elijah from heaven to prepare Israel for the final manifestation of God's kingdom was widespread, and according to Matthew this expectation was fulfilled in the Baptist's ministry (Mt 11:14; 17:11–13).

* [3:6] Ritual washing was practiced by various groups in Palestine between 150 B.C. and A.D. 250. John's baptism may have been related to the purificatory washings of the Essenes at Qumran.

* [3:7] **Pharisees and Sadducees**: the former were marked by devotion to the law, written and oral, and the scribes, experts in the law, belonged predominantly to this group. The Sadducees were the priestly aristocratic party, centered in Jerusalem. They accepted as scripture only the first five books of the Old Testament, followed only the letter of the law, rejected the oral legal traditions, and were opposed to teachings not found in the Pentateuch, such as the resurrection of the dead. Matthew links both of these groups together as enemies of Jesus (Mt 16:1, 6, 11, 12; cf. Mk 8:11–13, 15). The threatening words that follow are addressed to them rather than to "the crowds" as in Lk 3:7. **The coming wrath**: the judgment that will bring about the destruction of unrepentant sinners.

* [3:11] **Baptize you with the holy Spirit and fire**: the water baptism of John will be followed by an "immersion" of the repentant in the cleansing power of the Spirit of God, and of the unrepentant in the destroying power of God's judgment. However, some see **the holy Spirit** and **fire** as synonymous, and the effect of this "baptism" as either purification or destruction. See note on Lk 3:16.

* [3:12] The discrimination between the good and the bad is compared to the procedure by which a farmer separates wheat and chaff. The **winnowing fan** was a forklike shovel with which the threshed wheat was thrown into the air. The kernels fell to the ground; the light chaff, blown off by the wind, was gathered and burned up.

* [3:13–17] The baptism of Jesus is the occasion on which he is equipped for his ministry by the holy Spirit and proclaimed to be the Son of God.

* [3:14–15] This dialogue, peculiar to Matthew, reveals John's awareness of Jesus' superiority to him as the mightier one who is coming and who will baptize with the holy Spirit (Mt 3:11). His reluctance to admit Jesus among the sinners whom he is baptizing with water is overcome by Jesus' response. **To fulfill all righteousness**: in this gospel to **fulfill** usually refers to fulfillment of prophecy, and **righteousness** to moral conduct in conformity with God's will. Here, however, as in Mt 5:6; 6:33, **righteousness** seems to mean the saving activity of God. **To fulfill all righteousness** is to submit to the plan of God for the salvation of the human race. This involves Jesus' identification with sinners; hence the propriety of his accepting John's baptism.

* [3:16] **The Spirit . . . coming upon him**: cf. Is 42:1.

* [3:17] **This is my beloved Son**: the Marcan address to Jesus (Mk 1:11) is changed into a proclamation. The Father's voice speaks in terms that reflect Is 42:1; Ps 2:7; Gn 22:2.

* [4:1–11] Jesus, proclaimed Son of God at his baptism, is subjected to a triple temptation. Obedience to the Father is a characteristic of true sonship, and Jesus is tempted by the devil to rebel against God, overtly in the third case, more subtly in the first two. Each refusal of Jesus is expressed in language taken from the Book of Deuteronomy (Dt 8:3; 6:13, 16). The testings of Jesus resemble those of Israel during the wandering in the desert and later in Canaan, and the victory of Jesus, the true Israel and the true Son, contrasts with the failure of the ancient and disobedient "son," the old Israel. In the temptation account Matthew is almost identical with Luke; both seem to have drawn upon the same source.

* [4:2] **Forty days and forty nights**: the same time as that during which Moses remained on Sinai (Ex 24:18). The time reference, however, seems primarily intended to recall the forty years during which Israel was tempted in the desert (Dt 8:2).

* [4:4] Cf. Dt 8:3. Jesus refuses to use his power for his own benefit and accepts whatever God wills.

* [4:5–7] The devil supports his proposal by an appeal to the scriptures, Ps 91:11a, 12. Unlike Israel (Dt 6:16), Jesus refuses to "test" God by demanding from him an extraordinary show of power.

* [4:9] The worship of Satan to which Jesus is tempted is probably intended to recall Israel's worship of false gods. His refusal is expressed in the words of Dt 6:13.

* [4:12–17] Isaiah's prophecy of the light rising upon Zebulun and Naphtali (Is 8:22–9:1) is fulfilled in Jesus' residence at Capernaum. The territory of these two tribes was the first to be devastated (733–32 B.C.) at the time of the Assyrian invasion. In order to accommodate Jesus' move to Capernaum to the prophecy, Matthew speaks of that town as being "in the region of Zebulun and Naphtali" (Mt 4:13), whereas it was only in the territory of the latter, and he understands the sea of the prophecy, the Mediterranean, as the sea of Galilee.

* [4:17] At the beginning of his preaching Jesus takes up the words of John the Baptist (Mt 3:2) although with a different meaning; in his ministry the kingdom of heaven has already begun to be present (Mt 12:28).

* [4:18–22] The call of the first disciples promises them a share in Jesus' work and entails abandonment of family and former way of life. Three of the four, Simon, James, and John, are distinguished among the disciples by a closer relation with Jesus (Mt 17:1; 26:37).

* [4:20] Here and in Mt 4:22, as in Mark (Mk 1:16–20) and unlike the Lucan account (Lk 5:1–11), the disciples' response is motivated only by Jesus' invitation, an element that emphasizes his mysterious power.

* [4:23–25] This summary of Jesus' ministry concludes the narrative part of the first book of Matthew's gospel (Mt 3–4). The activities of his ministry are teaching, proclaiming the gospel, and healing; cf. Mt 9:35.

* [4:23] **Their synagogues**: Matthew usually designates the Jewish synagogues as **their synagogue(s)** (Mt 9:35; 10:17; 12:9; 13:54) or, in address to Jews, **your synagogues** (Mt 23:34), an indication that he wrote after the break between church and synagogue.

* [4:24] **Syria**: the Roman province to which Palestine belonged.

* [4:25] **The Decapolis**: a federation of Greek cities in Palestine, originally ten in number, all but one east of the Jordan.

---

* [5:1–7:29] The first of the five discourses that are a central part of the structure of this gospel. It is the discourse section of the first book and contains sayings of Jesus derived from Q and from M. The Lucan parallel is in that called "Sermon on the Plain" (Lk 6:20–49), although some of the sayings in Matthew's "Sermon on the Mount" have their parallels in other parts of Luke. The careful topical arrangement of the sermon is probably not due only to Matthew's editing; he seems to have had a structured discourse of Jesus as one of his sources. The form of that source may have been as follows: four beatitudes (Mt 5:3–4, 6, 11–12), a section on the new righteousness with illustrations (Mt 5:17, 20–24, 27–28, 33–48), a section on good works (Mt 6:1–6, 16–18), and three warnings (Mt 7:1–2, 15–21, 24–27).

* [5:1–2] Unlike Luke's sermon, this is addressed not only to the disciples but to the crowds (see Mt 7:28).

* [5:3–12] The form **Blessed are (is)** occurs frequently in the Old Testament in the Wisdom literature and in the psalms. Although modified by Matthew, the first, second, fourth, and ninth beatitudes have Lucan parallels (Mt 5:3 // Lk 6:20; Mt 5:4 // Lk 6:21b; Mt 5:6 // Lk 6:21a; Mt 5:11–12 // Lk 5:22–23). The others were added by the evangelist and are probably his own composition. A few manuscripts, Western and Alexandrian, and many versions and patristic quotations give the second and third beatitudes in inverted order.

* [5:3] **The poor in spirit**: in the Old Testament, the poor ('*anāwîm*) are those who are without material possessions and whose confidence is in God (see Is 61:1; Zep 2:3; in the NAB the word is translated **lowly** and **humble**, respectively, in those texts). Matthew added **in spirit** in order either to indicate that only the devout poor

were meant or to extend the beatitude to all, of whatever social rank, who recognized their complete dependence on God. The same phrase **poor in spirit** is found in the Qumran literature (1QM 14:7).

* [5:4] Cf. Is 61:2, "(The Lord has sent me) . . . to comfort all who mourn." **They will be comforted**: here the passive is a "theological passive" equivalent to the active "God will comfort them"; so also in Mt 5:6, 7.

* [5:5] Cf. Ps 37:11, ". . . the meek shall possess the land." In the psalm "the land" means the land of Palestine; here it means the kingdom.

* [5:6] **For righteousness**: a Matthean addition. For the meaning of **righteousness**, see note on Mt 3:14–15.

* [5:8] Cf. Ps 24:4. Only one "whose heart is clean" can take part in the temple worship. To be with God in the temple is described in Ps 42:3 as "beholding his face," but here the promise to the **clean of heart** is that they will **see God** not in the temple but in the coming kingdom.

* [5:10] **Righteousness** here, as usually in Matthew, means conduct in conformity with God's will.

* [5:12] **The prophets who were before you**: the disciples of Jesus stand in the line of the persecuted prophets of Israel. Some would see the expression as indicating also that Matthew considered all Christian disciples as prophets.

* [5:13–16] By their deeds the disciples are to influence the world for good. They can no more escape notice than **a city set on a mountain**. If they fail in good works, they are as useless as flavorless salt or as a lamp whose light is concealed.

* [5:13] The unusual supposition of salt losing its flavor has led some to suppose that the saying refers to the salt of the Dead Sea that, because chemically impure, could lose its taste.

* [5:17–20] This statement of Jesus' position concerning the Mosaic law is composed of traditional material from Matthew's sermon documentation (see note on Mt 5:1–7:29), other Q material (cf. Mt 18; Lk 16:17), and the evangelist's own editorial touches. **To fulfill** the law appears at first to mean a literal enforcement of the law in the least detail: **until heaven and earth pass away** nothing of the law **will pass** (Mt 5:18). Yet the "passing away" of heaven and earth is not necessarily the end of the world understood, as in much apocalyptic literature, as the dissolution of the existing universe. The "turning of the ages" comes with the apocalyptic event of Jesus' death and resurrection, and those to whom this gospel is addressed are living in the new and final age, prophesied by Isaiah as the time of "new heavens and a new earth" (Is 65:17; 66:22). Meanwhile, during Jesus' ministry when the kingdom is already breaking in, his mission remains within the framework of the law, though with significant anticipation of

the age to come, as the following antitheses (Mt 5:21–48) show.

* [5:19] Probably **these commandments** means those of the Mosaic law. But this is an interim ethic "until heaven and earth pass away."

* [5:21–48] Six examples of the conduct demanded of the Christian disciple. Each deals with a commandment of the law, introduced by **You have heard that it was said to your ancestors** or an equivalent formula, followed by Jesus' teaching in respect to that commandment, **But I say to you;** thus their designation as "antitheses." Three of them accept the Mosaic law but extend or deepen it (Mt 5:21–22; 27–28; 43–44); three reject it as a standard of conduct for the disciples (Mt 5:31–32; 33–37; 38–39).

* [5:21] Cf. Ex 20:13; Dt 5:17. The second part of the verse is not an exact quotation from the Old Testament, but cf. Ex 21:12.

* [5:22–26] Reconciliation with an offended brother is urged in the admonition of Mt 5:23–24 and the parable of Mt 5:25–26 (// Lk 12:58–59). The severity of the judge in the parable is a warning of the fate of unrepentant sinners in the coming judgment by God.

* [5:22] Anger is the motive behind murder, as the insulting epithets are steps that may lead to it. They, as well as the deed, are all forbidden. **Raqa**: an Aramaic word *rêqā'* or *rêqâ* probably meaning "imbecile," "blockhead," a term of abuse. The ascending order of punishment, **judgment** (by a local council?), trial before **the Sanhedrin**, condemnation to **Gehenna**, points to a higher degree of seriousness in each of the offenses. **Sanhedrin**: the highest judicial body of Judaism. **Gehenna**: in Hebrew *gê-hinnōm*, "Valley of Hinnom," or *gê ben-hinnōm*, "Valley of the son of Hinnom," southwest of Jerusalem, the center of an idolatrous cult during the monarchy in which children were offered in sacrifice (see 2 Kgs 23:10; Jer 7:31). In Jos 18:16 (Septuagint, Codex Vaticanus) the Hebrew is transliterated into Greek as *gaienna*, which appears in the New Testament as *geenna*. The concept of punishment of sinners by fire either after death or after the final judgment is found in Jewish apocalyptic literature (e.g., Enoch 90:26) but the name *geenna* is first given to the place of punishment in the New Testament.

* [5:27] See Ex 20:14; Dt 5:18.

* [5:29–30] No sacrifice is too great to avoid total destruction in **Gehenna**.

* [5:31–32] See Dt 24:1–5. The Old Testament commandment that a bill of divorce be given to the woman assumes the legitimacy of divorce itself. It is this that Jesus denies. (**Unless the marriage is unlawful**): this "exceptive clause," as it is often called, occurs also in Mt 19:9, where the Greek is slightly different. There are other sayings of Jesus about divorce that prohibit it absolutely (see Mk 10:11–12; Lk 16:18; cf. 1 Cor 7:10, 11b),

and most scholars agree that they represent the stand of Jesus. Matthew's "exceptive clauses" are understood by some as a modification of the absolute prohibition. It seems, however, that the unlawfulness that Matthew gives as a reason why a marriage must be broken refers to a situation peculiar to his community: the violation of Mosaic law forbidding marriage between persons of certain blood and/or legal relationship (Lv 18:6–18). Marriages of that sort were regarded as incest (*porneia*), but some rabbis allowed Gentile converts to Judaism who had contracted such marriages to remain in them. Matthew's "exceptive clause" is against such permissiveness for Gentile converts to Christianity; cf. the similar prohibition of *porneia* in Acts 15:20, 29. In this interpretation, the clause constitutes no exception to the absolute prohibition of divorce when the marriage is lawful.

* [5:33] This is not an exact quotation of any Old Testament text, but see Ex 20:7; Dt 5:11; Lv 19:12. The purpose of an oath was to guarantee truthfulness by one's calling on God as witness.

* [5:34–36] The use of these oath formularies that avoid the divine name is in fact equivalent to swearing by it, for all the things sworn by are related to God.

* [5:37] **Let your 'Yes' mean 'Yes,' and your 'No' mean 'No'**: literally, "let your speech be 'Yes, yes,' 'No, no.'" Some have understood this as a milder form of oath, permitted by Jesus. In view of Mt 5:34, "Do not swear at all," that is unlikely. **From the evil one**: i.e., from the devil. Oath-taking presupposes a sinful weakness of the human race, namely, the tendency to lie. Jesus demands of his disciples a truthfulness that makes oaths unnecessary.

* [5:38–42] See Lv 24:20. The Old Testament commandment was meant to moderate vengeance; the punishment should not exceed the injury done. Jesus forbids even this proportionate retaliation. Of the five examples that follow, only the first deals directly with retaliation for evil; the others speak of liberality.

* [5:41] Roman garrisons in Palestine had the right to requisition the property and services of the native population.

* [5:43–48] See Lv 19:18. There is no Old Testament commandment demanding hatred of one's enemy, but the "neighbor" of the love commandment was understood as one's fellow countryman. Both in the Old Testament (Ps 139:19–22) and at Qumran (1QS 9:21) hatred of evil persons is assumed to be right. Jesus extends the love commandment to the enemy and the persecutor. His disciples, as children of God, must imitate the example of their Father, who grants his gifts of sun and rain to both the good and the bad.

* [5:46] **Tax collectors**: Jews who were engaged in the collection of indirect taxes such as tolls and customs. See note on Mk 2:14.

* [5:47] Jesus' disciples must not be content with merely usual standards of conduct; see Mt 5:20 where the verb "surpass" (Greek *perisseuō*) is cognate with the **unusual** (*perisson*) of this verse.

* [5:48] **Perfect**: in the gospels this word occurs only in Matthew, here and in Mt 19:21. The Lucan parallel (Lk 6:36) demands that the disciples be **merciful**.

* [6:1–18] The sermon continues with a warning against doing good in order to be seen and gives three examples, almsgiving (Mt 6:2–4), prayer (Mt 6:5–15), and fasting (Mt 6:16–18). In each, the conduct of the hypocrites (Mt 6:2) is contrasted with that demanded of the disciples. The sayings about reward found here and elsewhere (Mt 5:12, 46; 10:41–42) show that this is a genuine element of Christian moral exhortation. Possibly to underline the difference between the Christian idea of reward and that of the hypocrites, the evangelist uses two different Greek verbs to express the rewarding of the disciples and that of the hypocrites; in the latter case it is the verb *apechō*, a commercial term for giving a receipt for what has been paid in full (Mt 6:2, 5, 16).

* [6:2] **The hypocrites**: the scribes and Pharisees, see Mt 23:13, 15, 23, 25, 27, 29. The designation reflects an attitude resulting not only from the controversies at the time of Jesus' ministry but from the opposition between Pharisaic Judaism and the church of Matthew. **They have received their reward**: they desire praise and have received what they were looking for.

* [6:7–15] Matthew inserts into his basic traditional material an expansion of the material on prayer that includes the model prayer, the "Our Father." That prayer is found in Lk 11:2–4 in a different context and in a different form.

* [6:7] The example of what Christian prayer should be like contrasts it now not with the prayer of the hypocrites but with that of **the pagans**. Their babbling probably means their reciting a long list of divine names, hoping that one of them will force a response from the deity.

* [6:9–13] Matthew's form of the "Our Father" follows the liturgical tradition of his church. Luke's less developed form also represents the liturgical tradition known to him, but it is probably closer than Matthew's to the original words of Jesus.

* [6:9] **Our Father in heaven**: this invocation is found in many rabbinic prayers of the post-New Testament period. **Hallowed be your name**: though the "hallowing" of the divine name could be understood as reverence done to God by human praise and by obedience to his will, this is more probably a petition that God hallow his own

name, i.e., that he manifest his glory by an act of power (cf. Ez 36:23), in this case, by the establishment of his kingdom in its fullness.

* [6:10] **Your kingdom come**: this petition sets the tone of the prayer, inclines the balance toward divine rather than human action in the petitions that immediately precede and follow it. **Your will be done, on earth as in heaven**: a petition that the divine purpose to establish the kingdom, a purpose present now **in heaven**, be executed **on earth**.

* [6:11] **Give us today our daily bread**: the rare Greek word *epiousios*, here **daily**, occurs in the New Testament only here and in Lk 11:3. A single occurrence of the word outside of these texts and of literature dependent on them has been claimed, but the claim is highly doubtful. The word may mean **daily** or "future" (other meanings have also been proposed). The latter would conform better to the eschatological tone of the whole prayer. So understood, the petition would be for a speedy coming of the kingdom (**today**), which is often portrayed in both the Old Testament and the New under the image of a feast (Is 25:6; Mt 8:11; 22:1–10; Lk 13:29; 14:15–24).

* [6:12] **Forgive us our debts**: the word **debts** is used metaphorically of sins, "debts" owed to God (see Lk 11:4). The request is probably for forgiveness at the final judgment.

* [6:13] Jewish apocalyptic writings speak of a period of severe trial before the end of the age, sometimes called the "messianic woes." This petition asks that the disciples be spared that **final test**.

* [6:14–15] These verses reflect a set pattern called "Principles of Holy Law." Human action now will be met by a corresponding action of God at the final judgment.

* [6:16] The only fast prescribed in the Mosaic law was that of the Day of Atonement (Lv 16:31), but the practice of regular fasting was common in later Judaism; cf. *Didache* 9:1.

* [6:19–34] The remaining material of this chapter is taken almost entirely from Q. It deals principally with worldly possessions, and the controlling thought is summed up in Mt 6:24: the disciple can serve only one master and must choose between God and wealth (**mammon**). See further the note on Lk 16:9.

* [6:22–23] In this context the parable probably points to the need for the disciple to be enlightened by Jesus' teaching on the transitory nature of earthly riches.

* [6:24] **Mammon**: an Aramaic word meaning wealth or property.

* [6:25–34] Jesus does not deny the reality of human needs (Mt 6:32), but forbids making them the object of anxious care and, in effect, becoming their slave.

* [6:27] **Life-span**: the Greek word can also mean "stature." If it is taken in that sense, the word here translated **moment** (literally, "cubit") must be translated literally as a unit not of time but of spatial measure. The cubit is about eighteen inches.

* [6:30] **Of little faith**: except for the parallel in Lk 12:28, the word translated **of little faith** is found in the New Testament only in Matthew. It is used by him of those who are disciples of Jesus but whose faith in him is not as deep as it should be (see Mt 8:26; 14:31; 16:8 and the cognate noun in Mt 17:20).

* [6:33] **Righteousness**: see note on Mt 3:14–15.

* [7:1–12] In Mt 7:1 Matthew returns to the basic traditional material of the sermon (Lk 6:37–38, 41–42). The governing thought is the correspondence between conduct toward one's fellows and God's conduct toward the one so acting.

* [7:1] This is not a prohibition against recognizing the faults of others, which would be hardly compatible with Mt 7:5, 6 but against passing judgment in a spirit of arrogance, forgetful of one's own faults.

* [7:5] **Hypocrite**: the designation previously given to the scribes and Pharisees is here given to the Christian disciple who is concerned with the faults of another and ignores his own more serious offenses.

* [7:6] **Dogs** and **swine** were Jewish terms of contempt for Gentiles. This saying may originally have derived from a Jewish Christian community opposed to preaching the gospel (**what is holy, pearls**) to Gentiles. In the light of Mt 28:19 that can hardly be Matthew's meaning. He may have taken the saying as applying to a Christian dealing with an obstinately impenitent fellow Christian (Mt 18:17).

* [7:9–10] There is a resemblance between a stone and a round loaf of bread and between a serpent and the scaleless fish called *barbut*.

* [7:12] See Lk 6:31. This saying, known since the eighteenth century as the "Golden Rule," is found in both positive and negative form in pagan and Jewish sources, both earlier and later than the gospel. **This is the law and the prophets** is an addition probably due to the evangelist.

* [7:13–28] The final section of the discourse is composed of a series of antitheses, contrasting two kinds of life within the Christian community, that of those who obey the words of Jesus and that of those who do not. Most of the sayings are from Q and are found also in Luke.

* [7:13–14] The metaphor of the "two ways" was common in pagan philosophy and in the Old Testament. In Christian literature it is found also in the *Didache* (1–6) and the *Epistle of Barnabas* (18–20).

* [7:15–20] Christian disciples who claimed to speak in the name of God are called **prophets** (Mt 7:15) in Mt 10:41; Mt 23:34. They were presumably an important group within the church of Matthew. As in the case of the Old Testament prophets, there were both true and false ones, and for Matthew the difference could be recognized by the quality of their deeds, the **fruits** (Mt 7:16). The mention of **fruits** leads to the comparison with trees, some producing good fruit, others bad.

* [7:21–23] The attack on the false prophets is continued, but is broadened to include those disciples who perform works of healing and exorcism in the name of Jesus (**Lord**) but live evil lives. Entrance into the kingdom is only for those who do the will of the Father. On the day of judgment (**on that day**) the morally corrupt prophets and miracle workers will be rejected by Jesus.

* [7:23] **I never knew you**: cf. Mt 10:33. **Depart from me, you evildoers**: cf. Ps 6:9.

* [7:24–27] The conclusion of the discourse (cf. Lk 6:47–49). Here the relation is not between saying and doing as in Mt 7:15–23 but between hearing and doing, and the words of Jesus are applied to every Christian (**everyone who listens**).

* [7:28–29] **When Jesus finished these words**: this or a similar formula is used by Matthew to conclude each of the five great discourses of Jesus (cf. Mt 11:1; 13:53; 19:1; 26:1).

* [7:29] **Not as their scribes**: scribal instruction was a faithful handing down of the traditions of earlier teachers; Jesus' teaching is based on his own authority. **Their scribes**: for the implications of **their**, see note on Mt 4:23.

* [8:1–9:38] This narrative section of the second book of the gospel is composed of nine miracle stories, most of which are found in Mark, although Matthew does not follow the Marcan order and abbreviates the stories radically. The stories are arranged in three groups of three, each group followed by a section composed principally of sayings of Jesus about discipleship. Mt 9:35 is an almost verbatim repetition of Mt 4:23. Each speaks of Jesus' teaching, preaching, and healing. The teaching and preaching form the content of Mt 5–7; the healing, that of Mt 8–9. Some scholars speak of a portrayal of Jesus as "Messiah of the Word" in Mt 5–7 and "Messiah of the Deed" in Mt 8–9. That is accurate so far as it goes, but there is also a strong emphasis on discipleship in Mt 8–9; these chapters have not only christological but ecclesiological import.

* [8:2] **A leper**: see note on Mk 1:40.

* [8:4] Cf. Lv 14:2–9. **That will be proof for them**: the Greek can also mean "that will be proof against them." It is not clear whether **them** refers to the priests or the people.

* [8:5–13] This story comes from Q (see Lk 7:1–10) and is also reflected in Jn 4:46–54. The similarity between the Q story and the Johannine is due to a common oral tradition, not to a common

literary source. As in the later story of the daughter of the Canaanite woman (Mt 15:21–28) Jesus here breaks with his usual procedure of ministering only to Israelites and anticipates the mission to the Gentiles.

* [8:5] **A centurion**: a military officer commanding a hundred men. He was probably in the service of Herod Antipas, tetrarch of Galilee; see note on Mt 14:1.

* [8:8–9] Acquainted by his position with the force of a command, the centurion expresses faith in the power of Jesus' mere word.

* [8:10] **In no one in Israel**: there is good textual attestation (e.g., Codex Sinaiticus) for a reading identical with that of Lk 7:9, "not even in Israel." But that seems to be due to a harmonization of Matthew with Luke.

* [8:11–12] Matthew inserts into the story a Q saying (see Lk 13:28–29) about the entrance of Gentiles into the kingdom and the exclusion of those Israelites who, though descended from the patriarchs and members of the chosen nation (**the children of the kingdom**), refused to believe in Jesus. **There will be wailing and grinding of teeth**: the first occurrence of a phrase used frequently in this gospel to describe final condemnation (Mt 13:42, 50; 22:13; 24:51; 25:30). It is found elsewhere in the New Testament only in Lk 13:28.

* [8:14–15] Cf. Mk 1:29–31. Unlike Mark, Matthew has no implied request by others for the woman's cure. Jesus acts on his own initiative, and the cured woman rises and waits not on "them" (Mk 1:31) but on **him**.

* [8:16] **By a word**: a Matthean addition to Mk 1:34; cf. 8:8.

* [8:17] This fulfillment citation from Is 53:4 follows the MT, not the LXX. The prophet speaks of the Servant of the Lord who suffers vicariously for the sins ("infirmities") of others; Matthew takes the **infirmities** as physical afflictions.

* [8:18–22] This passage between the first and second series of miracles and following Jesus is taken from Q (see Lk 9:57–62). The third of the three sayings found in the source is absent from Matthew.

* [8:18] **The other side**: i.e., of the Sea of Galilee.

* [8:19] **Teacher**: for Matthew, this designation of Jesus is true, for he has Jesus using it of himself (Mt 10:24, 25; 23:8; 26:18), yet when it is used of him by others they are either his opponents (Mt 9:11; 12:38; 17:24; 22:16, 24, 36) or, as here and in Mt 19:16, well-disposed persons who cannot see more deeply. Thus it reveals an inadequate recognition of who Jesus is.

* [8:20] **Son of Man**: see note on Mk 8:31. This is the first occurrence in Matthew of a term that appears in the New Testament only in sayings of Jesus, except for Acts 7:56 and possibly Mt 9:6 (// Mk 2:10; Lk 5:24). In Matthew it refers to Jesus in his ministry (seven times, as here), in

his passion and resurrection (nine times, e.g., Mt 17:22), and in his glorious coming at the end of the age (thirteen times, e.g., Mt 24:30).

* [8:22] **Let the dead bury their dead**: the demand of Jesus overrides what both the Jewish and the Hellenistic world regarded as a filial obligation of the highest importance. See note on Lk 9:60.

* [8:23] **His disciples followed him**: the first miracle in the second group (Mt 8:23–9:8) is introduced by a verse that links it with the preceding sayings by the catchword "follow." In Mark the initiative in entering the boat is taken by the disciples (Mk 4:35–41); here, Jesus enters first and the disciples follow.

* [8:24] **Storm**: literally, "earthquake," a word commonly used in apocalyptic literature for the shaking of the old world when God brings in his kingdom. All the synoptics use it in depicting the events preceding the parousia of the Son of Man (Mt 24:7; Mk 13:8; Lk 21:11). Matthew has introduced it here and in his account of the death and resurrection of Jesus (Mt 27:51–54; 28:2).

* [8:25] The reverent plea of the disciples contrasts sharply with their reproach of Jesus in Mk 4:38.

* [8:26] **You of little faith**: see note on Mt 6:30. **Great calm**: Jesus' calming the sea may be meant to recall the Old Testament theme of God's control over the chaotic waters (Ps 65:8; 89:10; 93:3–4; 107:29).

* [8:28] **Gadarenes**: this is the reading of Codex Vaticanus, supported by other important textual witnesses. The original reading of Codex Sinaiticus was Gazarenes, later changed to Gergesenes, and a few versions have Gerasenes. Each of these readings points to a different territory connected, respectively, with the cities Gadara, Gergesa, and Gerasa (modern Jerash). There is the same confusion of readings in the parallel texts, Mk 5:1 and Lk 8:26; there the best reading seems to be "Gerasenes," whereas "Gadarenes" is probably the original reading in Matthew. The town of Gadara was about five miles southeast of the Sea of Galilee, and Josephus (*Life* 9:42) refers to it as possessing territory that lay on that sea. **Two demoniacs**: Mark (5:1–20) has one.

* [8:29] **What have you to do with us?**: see note on Jn 2:4. **Before the appointed time**: the notion that evil spirits were allowed by God to afflict human beings until the time of the final judgment is found in Enoch 16:1 and Jubilees 10:7–10.

* [8:30] The tending of pigs, animals considered unclean by Mosaic law (Lv 11:6–7), indicates that the population was Gentile.

---

* [9:1] **His own town**: Capernaum; see Mt 4:13.
* [9:3] **Scribes**: see note on Mk 2:6. Matthew omits the reason given in the Marcan story for the

charge of blasphemy: "Who but God alone can forgive sins?" (Mk 2:7).

* [9:6] It is not clear whether **But that you may know . . . to forgive sins** is intended to be a continuation of the words of Jesus or a parenthetical comment of the evangelist to those who would hear or read this gospel. In any case, Matthew here follows the Marcan text.

* [9:8] **Who had given such authority to human beings**: a significant difference from Mk 2:12 ("They . . . glorified God, saying, 'We have never seen anything like this'"). Matthew's extension to **human beings** of the authority to forgive sins points to the belief that such authority was being claimed by Matthew's church.

* [9:9–17] In this section the order is the same as that of Mk 2:13–22.

* [9:9] **A man named Matthew**: Mark names this tax collector Levi (Mk 2:14). No such name appears in the four lists of the twelve who were the closest companions of Jesus (Mt 10:2–4; Mk 3:16–19; Lk 6:14–16; Acts 1:13 [eleven, because of the defection of Judas Iscariot]), whereas all four list a Matthew, designated in Mt 10:3 as "the tax collector." The evangelist may have changed the "Levi" of his source to **Matthew** so that this man, whose call is given special notice, like that of the first four disciples (Mt 4:18–22), might be included among the twelve. Another reason for the change may be that the disciple Matthew was the source of traditions peculiar to the church for which the evangelist was writing.

* [9:10] **His house**: it is not clear whether **his** refers to Jesus or Matthew. **Tax collectors**: see note on Mt 5:46. Table association with such persons would cause ritual impurity.

* [9:11] **Teacher**: see note on Mt 8:19.

* [9:12] See note on Mk 2:17.

* [9:13] **Go and learn . . . not sacrifice**: Matthew adds the prophetic statement of Hos 6:6 to the Marcan account (see also Mt 12:7). If mercy is superior to the temple sacrifices, how much more to the laws of ritual impurity.

* [9:15] Fasting is a sign of mourning and would be as inappropriate at this time of joy, when Jesus is proclaiming the kingdom, as it would be at a marriage feast. Yet the saying looks forward to the time when Jesus will no longer be with the disciples visibly, the time of Matthew's church. **Then they will fast**: see *Didache* 8:1.

* [9:16–17] Each of these parables speaks of the unsuitability of attempting to combine the old and the new. Jesus' teaching is not a patching up of Judaism, nor can the gospel be contained within the limits of Mosaic law.

* [9:18–34] In this third group of miracles, the first (Mt 9:18–26) is clearly dependent on Mark (Mk 5:21–43). Though it tells of two miracles, the cure of the woman had already been included within the story of the raising of the official's daughter, so that the two were probably regarded as a single unit. The other miracles seem to have been derived from Mark and Q, respectively, though there Matthew's own editing is much more evident.

* [9:18] **Official**: literally, "ruler." Mark calls him "one of the synagogue officials" (Mk 5:22). **My daughter has just died**: Matthew heightens the Marcan "my daughter is at the point of death" (Mk 5:23).

* [9:20] **Tassel**: possibly "fringe." The Mosaic law prescribed that tassels be worn on the corners of one's garment as a reminder to keep the commandments (see Nm 15:37–39; Dt 22:12).

* [9:24] **Sleeping**: sleep is a biblical metaphor for death (see Ps 87:6 LXX; Dn 12:2; 1 Thes 5:10). Jesus' statement is not a denial of the child's real death, but an assurance that she will be roused from her sleep of death.

* [9:27–31] This story was probably composed by Matthew out of Mark's story of the healing of a blind man named Bartimaeus (Mk 10:46–52). Mark places the event late in Jesus' ministry, just before his entrance into Jerusalem, and Matthew has followed his Marcan source at that point in his gospel also (see Mt 20:29–34). In each of the Matthean stories the single blind man of Mark becomes two. The reason why Matthew would have given a double version of the Marcan story and placed the earlier one here may be that he wished to add a story of Jesus' curing the blind at this point in order to prepare for Jesus' answer to the emissaries of the Baptist (Mt 11:4–6) in which Jesus, recounting his works, begins with his giving sight to the blind.

* [9:27] **Son of David**: this messianic title is connected once with the healing power of Jesus in Mark (Mk 10:47–48) and Luke (Lk 18:38–39) but more frequently in Matthew (see also Mt 12:23; 15:22; 20:30–31).

* [9:32–34] The source of this story seems to be Q (see Lk 11:14–15). As in the preceding healing of the blind, Matthew has two versions of this healing, the later in Mt 12:22–24 and the earlier here.

* [9:34] This spiteful accusation foreshadows the growing opposition to Jesus in Mt 11 and 12.

* [9:35] See notes on Mt 4:23–25; Mt 8:1–9:38.

* [9:36] See Mk 6:34; Nm 27:17; 1 Kgs 22:17.

* [9:37–38] This Q saying (see Lk 10:2) is only imperfectly related to this context. It presupposes that only God (**the master of the harvest**) can take the initiative in sending out preachers of the gospel, whereas in Matthew's setting it leads into Mt 10 where Jesus does so.

---

* [10:1–11:1] After an introductory narrative (Mt 10:1–4), the second of the discourses of the gospel. It deals with the mission now to be undertaken by the disciples (Mt 10:5–15), but the

perspective broadens and includes the missionary activity of the church between the time of the resurrection and the parousia.

* [10:1] **His twelve disciples**: although, unlike Mark (Mk 3:13–14) and Luke (Lk 6:12–16), Matthew has no story of Jesus' choosing the Twelve, he assumes that the group is known to the reader. The earliest New Testament text to speak of it is 1 Cor 15:5. The number probably is meant to recall the twelve tribes of Israel and implies Jesus' authority to call all Israel into the kingdom. While Luke (Lk 6:13) and probably Mark (Mk 4:10, 34) distinguish between the Twelve and a larger group also termed disciples, Matthew tends to identify the disciples and the Twelve. **Authority . . . every illness**: activities the same as those of Jesus; see Mt 4:23; Mt 9:35; 10:8. The Twelve also share in his proclamation of the kingdom (Mt 10:7). But although he teaches (Mt 4:23; 7:28; 9:35), they do not. Their commission to teach comes only after Jesus' resurrection, after they have been fully instructed by him (Mt 28:20).

* [10:2–4] Here, for the only time in Matthew, the Twelve are designated **apostles**. The word "apostle" means "one who is sent," and therefore fits the situation here described. In the Pauline letters, the place where the term occurs most frequently in the New Testament, it means primarily one who has seen the risen Lord and has been commissioned to proclaim the resurrection. With slight variants in Luke and Acts, the names of those who belong to this group are the same in the four lists given in the New Testament (see note on Mt 9:9). **Cananean**: this represents an Aramaic word meaning "zealot." The meaning of that designation is unclear (see note on Lk 6:15).

* [10:5–6] Like Jesus (Mt 15:24), the Twelve are sent only to Israel. This saying may reflect an original Jewish Christian refusal of the mission to the Gentiles, but for Matthew it expresses rather the limitation that Jesus himself observed during his ministry.

* [10:8–11] The Twelve have received their own call and mission through God's gift, and the benefits they confer are likewise to be given freely. They are not to take with them money, provisions, or unnecessary clothing; their lodging and food will be provided by those who receive them.

* [10:13] The greeting of peace is conceived of not merely as a salutation but as an effective word. If it finds no worthy recipient, it will return to the speaker.

* [10:14] **Shake the dust from your feet**: this gesture indicates a complete disassociation from such unbelievers.

* [10:17] The persecutions attendant upon the post-resurrection mission now begin to be spoken of. Here Matthew brings into the discourse sayings found in Mk 13 which deals with events preceding the parousia.

* [10:21] See Mi 7:6 which is cited in Mt 10:35, 36.

* [10:22] **To the end**: the original meaning was probably "until the parousia." But it is not likely that Matthew expected no missionary disciples to suffer death before then, since he envisages the martyrdom of other Christians (Mt 10:21). For him, **the end** is probably that of the individual's life (see Mt 10:28).

* [10:23] **Before the Son of Man comes**: since the coming of the Son of Man at the end of the age had not taken place when this gospel was written, much less during the mission of the Twelve during Jesus' ministry, Matthew cannot have meant the coming to refer to the parousia. It is difficult to know what he understood it to be: perhaps the "proleptic parousia" of Mt 28:16–20, or the destruction of the temple in A.D. 70, viewed as a coming of Jesus in judgment on unbelieving Israel.

* [10:25] **Beelzebul**: see Mt 9:34 for the charge linking Jesus with "the prince of demons," who is named **Beelzebul** in Mt 12:24. The meaning of the name is uncertain; possibly, "lord of the house."

* [10:26] The **concealed** and **secret** coming of the kingdom is to be proclaimed by them, and no fear must be allowed to deter them from that proclamation.

* [10:32–33] In the Q parallel (Lk 12:8–9), the Son of Man will acknowledge those who have acknowledged Jesus, and those who deny him will be denied (by the Son of Man) before the angels of God at the judgment. Here Jesus and the Son of Man are identified, and the acknowledgment or denial will be before his heavenly Father.

* [10:38] The first mention of the cross in Matthew, explicitly that of the disciple, but implicitly that of Jesus (**and follow after me**). Crucifixion was a form of capital punishment used by the Romans for offenders who were not Roman citizens.

* [10:39] One who denies Jesus in order to save one's earthly life will be condemned to everlasting destruction; loss of earthly life for Jesus' sake will be rewarded by everlasting life in the kingdom.

* [10:40–42] All who receive the disciples of Jesus receive him, and God who sent him, and will be rewarded accordingly.

* [10:41] **A prophet**: one who speaks in the name of God; here, the Christian prophets who proclaim the gospel. **Righteous man**: since righteousness is demanded of all the disciples, it is difficult to take the **righteous man** of this verse and **one of these little ones** (Mt 10:42) as indicating different groups within the followers of Jesus. Probably all three designations are used here of Christian missionaries as such.

---

* [11:1] The closing formula of the discourse refers back to the original addressees, the Twelve.

* [11:2–12:50] The narrative section of the third book deals with the growing opposition to Jesus. It is largely devoted to disputes and attacks relating to faith and discipleship and thus contains much sayings-material, drawn in large part from Q.

* [11:2] **In prison**: see Mt 4:12; 14:1–12. **The works of the Messiah**: the deeds of Mt 8–9.

* [11:3] The question probably expresses a doubt of the Baptist that Jesus is **the one who is to come** (cf. Mal 3:1) because his mission has not been one of fiery judgment as John had expected (Mt 3:2).

* [11:5–6] Jesus' response is taken from passages of Isaiah (Is 26:19; 29:18–19; 35:5–6; 61:1) that picture the time of salvation as marked by deeds such as those that Jesus is doing. The beatitude is a warning to the Baptist not to disbelieve because his expectations have not been met.

* [11:7–19] Jesus' rebuke of John is counterbalanced by a reminder of the greatness of the Baptist's function (Mt 11:7–15) that is followed by a complaint about those who have heeded neither John nor Jesus (Mt 11:16–19).

* [11:9–10] In common Jewish belief there had been no prophecy in Israel since the last of the Old Testament prophets, Malachi. The coming of a new prophet was eagerly awaited, and Jesus agrees that John was such. Yet he was **more than a prophet**, for he was the precursor of the one who would bring in the new and final age. The Old Testament quotation is a combination of Mal 3:1; Ex 23:20 with the significant change that the **before me** of Malachi becomes **before you**. The messenger now precedes not God, as in the original, but Jesus.

* [11:11] John's preeminent greatness lies in his function of announcing the imminence of the kingdom (Mt 3:1). But to be in the kingdom is so great a privilege that the least who has it is greater than the Baptist.

* [11:12] The meaning of this difficult saying is probably that the opponents of Jesus are trying to prevent people from accepting the kingdom and to snatch it away from those who have received it.

* [11:13] **All the prophets and the law**: Matthew inverts the usual order, "law and prophets," and says that both have **prophesied**. This emphasis on the prophetic character of the law points to its fulfillment in the teaching of Jesus and the transitory nature of some of its commandments (see note on Mt 5:17–20).

* [11:16–19] See Lk 7:31–35. The meaning of the parable (Mt 11:16–17) and its explanation (Mt 11:18–19b) is much disputed. A plausible view is that the **children** of the parable are two groups, one of which proposes different entertainments to the other that will not agree with either proposal. The first represents John, Jesus, and their disciples; the second those who reject John for his asceticism and Jesus for his table association with those despised by the religiously observant.

Mt 11:19c (**her works**) forms an inclusion with Mt 11:2 ("the works of the Messiah"). The original form of the saying is better preserved in Lk 7:35 ". . . wisdom is vindicated by all her children." There John and Jesus are the children of Wisdom; here the works of Jesus the Messiah are those of divine Wisdom, of which he is the embodiment. Some important textual witnesses, however, have essentially the same reading as in Luke.

* [11:21] Tyre and Sidon were pagan cities denounced for their wickedness in the Old Testament; cf. Jl 4:4–7.

* [11:23] Capernaum's pride and punishment are described in language taken from the taunt song against the king of Babylon (Is 14:13–15).

* [11:25–27] This Q saying, identical with Lk 10:21–22 except for minor variations, introduces a joyous note into this section, so dominated by the theme of unbelief. **While the wise and the learned**, the scribes and Pharisees, have rejected Jesus' preaching and the significance of his mighty deeds, **the childlike** have accepted them. Acceptance depends upon the Father's revelation, but this is granted to those who are open to receive it and refused to the arrogant. Jesus can speak of all mysteries because he is **the Son** and there is perfect reciprocity of knowledge between him and the Father; what has been **handed over** to him is revealed only to those whom he wishes.

* [11:28–29] These verses are peculiar to Matthew and are similar to Ben Sirach's invitation to learn wisdom and submit to her yoke (Sir 51:23, 26).

* [11:28] **Who labor and are burdened**: burdened by the law as expounded by the scribes and Pharisees (Mt 23:4).

* [11:29] In place of the yoke of the law, complicated by scribal interpretation, Jesus invites the burdened to take the yoke of obedience to his word, under which they **will find rest**; cf. Jer 6:16.

---

* [12:1–14] Matthew here returns to the Marcan order that he left in Mt 9:18. The two stories depend on Mk 2:23–28; 3:1–6, respectively, and are the only places in either gospel that deal explicitly with Jesus' attitude toward sabbath observance.

* [12:1–2] The picking of the heads of grain is here equated with reaping, which was forbidden on the sabbath (Ex 34:21).

* [12:3–4] See 1 Sm 21:2–7. In the Marcan parallel (Mk 2:25–26) the high priest is called Abiathar, although in 1 Samuel this action is attributed to Ahimelech. The Old Testament story is not about a violation of the sabbath rest; its pertinence to this dispute is that a violation of the law was permissible because of David's men being without food.

* [12:5–6] This and the following argument (Mt 12:7) are peculiar to Matthew. The temple service

seems to be the changing of the showbread on the sabbath (Lv 24:8) and the doubling on the sabbath of the usual daily holocausts (Nm 28:9–10). The argument is that the law itself requires work that breaks the sabbath rest, because of the higher duty of temple service. If temple duties outweigh the sabbath law, how much more does the presence of Jesus, with his proclamation of the kingdom (**something greater than the temple**), justify the conduct of his disciples.

* [12:7] See note on Mt 9:13.

* [12:8] The ultimate justification for the disciples' violation of the sabbath rest is that Jesus, the Son of Man, has supreme authority over the law.

* [12:10] Rabbinic tradition later than the gospels allowed relief to be given to a sufferer on the sabbath if life was in danger. This may also have been the view of Jesus' Pharisaic contemporaries. But the case here is not about one in danger of death.

* [12:11] Matthew omits the question posed by Jesus in Mk 3:4 and substitutes one about rescuing a sheep on the sabbath, similar to that in Lk 14:5.

* [12:14] See Mk 3:6. Here the plan to bring about Jesus' death is attributed to the Pharisees only. This is probably due to the situation of Matthew's church, when the sole opponents were the Pharisees.

* [12:15–21] Matthew follows Mk 3:7–12 but summarizes his source in two verses (Mt 12:15, 16) that pick up the withdrawal, the healings, and the command for silence. To this he adds a fulfillment citation from the first Servant Song (Is 42:1–4) that does not correspond exactly to either the Hebrew or the LXX of that passage. It is the longest Old Testament citation in this gospel, emphasizing the meekness of Jesus, the Servant of the Lord, and foretelling the extension of his mission to the Gentiles.

* [12:15] Jesus' knowledge of the Pharisees' plot and his healing all are peculiar to Matthew.

* [12:19] The servant's not contending is seen as fulfilled in Jesus' withdrawal from the disputes narrated in Mt 12:1–14.

* [12:21] Except for a minor detail, Matthew here follows the LXX, although the meaning of the Hebrew ("the coastlands will wait for his teaching") is similar.

* [12:22–32] For the exorcism, see note on Mt 9:32–34. The long discussion combines Marcan and Q material (Mk 3:22–30; Lk 11:19–20, 23; 12:10). Mk 3:20–21 is omitted, with a consequent lessening of the sharpness of Mt 12:48.

* [12:23] See note on Mt 9:27.

* [12:24] See note on Mt 10:25.

* [12:25–26] Jesus' first response to the Pharisees' charge is that if it were true, Satan would be destroying his own kingdom.

* [12:27] Besides pointing out the absurdity of the charge, Jesus asks how the work of Jewish

exorcists (**your own people**) is to be interpreted. Are they, too, to be charged with collusion with Beelzebul? For an example of Jewish exorcism see Josephus, *Antiquities* 8:42–49.

* [12:28] The Q parallel (Lk 11:20) speaks of the "finger" rather than of the "spirit" of God. While the difference is probably due to Matthew's editing, he retains **the kingdom of God** rather than changing it to his usual "kingdom of heaven." **Has come upon you**: see Mt 4:17.

* [12:29] A short parable illustrates what Jesus is doing. The **strong man** is Satan, whom Jesus has tied up and whose **house** he is plundering. Jewish expectation was that Satan would be chained up in the last days (Rev 20:2); Jesus' exorcisms indicate that those days have begun.

* [12:30] This saying, already attached to the preceding verses in Q (see Lk 11:23), warns that there can be no neutrality where Jesus is concerned. Its pertinence in a context where Jesus is addressing not the neutral but the bitterly opposed is not clear. The accusation of scattering, however, does fit the situation. Jesus is the shepherd of God's people (Mt 2:6), his mission is to the lost sheep of Israel (Mt 15:24); the Pharisees, who oppose him, are guilty of scattering the sheep.

* [12:31] **Blasphemy against the Spirit**: the sin of attributing to Satan (Mt 12:24) what is the work of the Spirit of God (Mt 12:28).

* [12:33] **Declare**: literally, "make." The meaning of this verse is obscure. Possibly it is a challenge to the Pharisees either to declare Jesus and his exorcisms good or both of them bad. A tree is known by its fruit; if the fruit is good, so must the tree be, If the driving out of demons is good, so must its source be.

* [12:34] The admission of Jesus' goodness cannot be made by the Pharisees, for they are evil, and the words that proceed from their evil hearts cannot be good.

* [12:36–37] If on the day of judgment people will be held accountable for even their **careless** words, the vicious accusations of the Pharisees will surely lead to their condemnation.

* [12:38–42] This section is mainly from Q (see Lk 11:29–32). Mk 8:11–12, which Matthew has followed in Mt 16:1–4, has a similar demand for a sign. The scribes and Pharisees refuse to accept the exorcisms of Jesus as authentication of his claims and demand a sign that will end all possibility of doubt. Jesus' response is that no such sign will be given. Because his opponents are evil and see him as an agent of Satan, nothing will convince them.

* [12:38] **Teacher**: see note on Mt 8:19. In Mt 16:1 the request is for a sign "from heaven" (Mk 8:11).

* [12:39] **Unfaithful**: literally, "adulterous." The covenant between God and Israel was portrayed

as a marriage bond, and unfaithfulness to the covenant as adultery; cf. Hos 2:4–14; Jer 3:6–10.

* [12:40] See Jon 2:1. While in Q the sign was simply Jonah's preaching to the Ninevites (Lk 11:30, 32), Matthew here adds Jonah's sojourn **in the belly of the whale** for **three days and three nights**, a prefigurement of Jesus' sojourn in the abode of the dead and, implicitly, of his resurrection.

* [12:41–42] The Ninevites who **repented** (see Jon 3:1–10) and **the queen of the south** (i.e., of Sheba; see 1 Kgs 10:1–13) were pagans who responded to lesser opportunities than have been offered to Israel in the ministry of Jesus, **something greater than Jonah** or **Solomon**. At the final judgment they will condemn the faithless **generation** that has rejected him.

* [12:43–45] Another Q passage; cf. Mt 11:24–26. Jesus' ministry has broken Satan's hold over Israel, but the refusal of **this evil generation** to accept him will lead to a worse situation than what preceded his coming.

* [12:46–50] See Mk 3:31–35. Matthew has omitted Mk 3:20–21 which is taken up in Mk 3:31 (see note on Mt 12:22–32), yet the point of the story is the same in both gospels: natural kinship with Jesus counts for nothing; only one who **does the will** of his **heavenly Father** belongs to his true family.

* [12:47] This verse is omitted in some important textual witnesses, including Codex Sinaiticus (original reading) and Codex Vaticanus.

---

* [13:1–53] The discourse in parables is the third great discourse of Jesus in Matthew and constitutes the second part of the third book of the gospel. Matthew follows the Marcan outline (Mk 4:1–35) but has only two of Mark's parables, the five others being from Q and M. In addition to the seven parables, the discourse gives the reason why Jesus uses this type of speech (Mt 13:10–15), declares the blessedness of those who understand his teaching (Mt 13:16–17), explains the parable of the sower (Mt 13:18–23) and of the weeds (Mt 13:36–43), and ends with a concluding statement to the disciples (Mt 13:51–52).

* [13:3–8] Since in Palestine sowing often preceded plowing, much of the seed is scattered on ground that is unsuitable. Yet while much is wasted, the seed that falls on good ground bears fruit in extraordinarily large measure. The point of the parable is that, in spite of some failure because of opposition and indifference, the message of Jesus about the coming of the kingdom will have enormous success.

* [13:3] **In parables**: the word "parable" (Greek *parabolē*) is used in the LXX to translate the Hebrew *māshāl*, a designation covering a wide variety of literary forms such as axioms, proverbs, similitudes, and allegories. In the New Testament

the same breadth of meaning of the word is found, but there it primarily designates stories that are illustrative comparisons between Christian truths and events of everyday life. Sometimes the event has a strange element that is quite different from usual experience (e.g., in Mt 13:33 the enormous amount of dough in the parable of the yeast); this is meant to sharpen the curiosity of the hearer. If each detail of such a story is given a figurative meaning, the story is an allegory. Those who maintain a sharp distinction between parable and allegory insist that a parable has only one point of comparison, and that while parables were characteristic of Jesus' teaching, to see allegorical details in them is to introduce meanings that go beyond their original intention and even falsify it. However, to exclude any allegorical elements from a parable is an excessively rigid mode of interpretation, now abandoned by many scholars.

* [13:11] Since a parable is figurative speech that demands reflection for understanding, only those who are prepared to explore its meaning can come to know it. To understand is a gift of God, granted to the disciples but not to the crowds. In Semitic fashion, both the disciples' understanding and the crowd's obtuseness are attributed to God. The question of human responsibility for the obtuseness is not dealt with, although it is asserted in Mt 13:13. **The mysteries**: as in Lk 8:10; Mk 4:11 has "the mystery." The word is used in Dn 2:18, 19, 27 and in the Qumran literature (1Qp Hab 7:8; 1QS 3:23; 1QM 3:9) to designate a divine plan or decree affecting the course of history that can be known only when revealed. **Knowledge of the mysteries of the kingdom of heaven** means recognition that the kingdom has become present in the ministry of Jesus.

* [13:12] In the New Testament use of this axiom of practical "wisdom" (see Mt 25:29; Mk 4:25; Lk 8:18; 19:26), the reference transcends the original level. God gives further understanding to one who accepts the revealed mystery; from the one who does not, he will take it away (note the "theological passive," **more will be given, what he has will be taken away**).

* [13:13] **Because 'they look . . . or understand'**: Matthew softens his Marcan source, which states that Jesus speaks in parables so that the crowds may not understand (Mk 4:12), and makes such speaking a punishment given **because** they have not accepted his previous clear teaching. However, his citation of Is 6:9–10 in Mt 13:14 supports the harsher Marcan view.

* [13:16–17] Unlike the unbelieving crowds, the disciples have seen that which the **prophets** and the **righteous** of the Old Testament **longed to see** without having their longing fulfilled.

* [13:18–23] See Mk 4:14–20; Lk 8:11–15. In this explanation of the parable the emphasis is on the various types of soil on which the seed falls,

i.e., on the dispositions with which the preaching of Jesus is received. The second and third types particularly are explained in such a way as to support the view held by many scholars that the explanation derives not from Jesus but from early Christian reflection upon apostasy from the faith that was the consequence of persecution and worldliness, respectively. Others, however, hold that the explanation may come basically from Jesus even though it was developed in the light of later Christian experience. The four types of persons envisaged are (1) those who never accept the word of the kingdom (Mt 13:19); (2) those who believe for a while but fall away because of persecution (Mt 13:20–21); (3) those who believe, but in whom the word is choked by worldly anxiety and the seduction of riches (Mt 13:22); (4) those who respond to the word and produce fruit abundantly (Mt 13:23).

* [13:24–30] This parable is peculiar to Matthew. The comparison in Mt 13:24 does not mean that the kingdom of heaven may be likened simply to the person in question but to the situation narrated in the whole story. The refusal of the householder to allow his slaves to separate the wheat from the weeds while they are still growing is a warning to the disciples not to attempt to anticipate the final judgment of God by a definitive exclusion of sinners from the kingdom. In its present stage it is composed of the good and the bad. The judgment of God alone will eliminate the sinful. Until then there must be patience and the preaching of repentance.

* [13:25] Weeds: darnel, a poisonous weed that in its first stage of growth resembles wheat.

* [13:30] Harvest: a common biblical metaphor for the time of God's judgment; cf. Jer 51:33; Jl 4:13; Hos 6:11.

* [13:31–33] See Mk 4:30–32; Lk 13:18–21. The parables of the mustard seed and the yeast illustrate the same point: the amazing contrast between the small beginnings of the kingdom and its marvelous expansion.

* [13:32] See Dn 4:7–9, 17–19 where the birds nesting in the tree represent the people of Nebuchadnezzar's kingdom. See also Ez 17:23; 31:6.

* [13:33] Except in this Q parable and in Mt 16:12, yeast (or "leaven") is, in New Testament usage, a symbol of corruption (see Mt 16:6, 11–12; Mk 8:15; Lk 12:1; 1 Cor 5:6–8; Gal 5:9). Three measures: an enormous amount, enough to feed a hundred people. The exaggeration of this element of the parable points to the greatness of the kingdom's effect.

* [13:34] Only in parables: see Mt 13:10–15.

* [13:35] The prophet: some textual witnesses read "Isaiah the prophet." The quotation is actually from Ps 78:2; the first line corresponds to the LXX text of the psalm. The psalm's title ascribes it to Asaph, the founder of one of the guilds of temple musicians. He is called "the prophet" (NAB "the seer") in 2 Chr 29:30, but it is doubtful that Matthew averted to that; for him, any Old Testament text that could be seen as fulfilled in Jesus was prophetic.

* [13:36] Dismissing the crowds: the return of Jesus to the house marks a break with the crowds, who represent unbelieving Israel. From now on his attention is directed more and more to his disciples and to their instruction. The rest of the discourse is addressed to them alone.

* [13:37–43] In the explanation of the parable of the weeds emphasis lies on the eschatological end of the wicked, whereas the parable itself concentrates on patience with them until judgment time.

* [13:38] The field is the world: this presupposes the resurrection of Jesus and the granting to him of "all power in heaven and on earth" (Mt 28:18).

* [13:39] The end of the age: this phrase is found only in Matthew (13:40, 49; 24:3; 28:20).

* [13:41] His kingdom: the kingdom of the Son of Man is distinguished from that of the Father (Mt 13:43); see 1 Cor 15:24–25. The church is the place where Jesus' kingdom is manifested, but his royal authority embraces the entire world; see note on Mt 13:38.

* [13:43] See Dn 12:3.

* [13:44–50] The first two of the last three parables of the discourse have the same point. The person who finds a buried treasure and the merchant who finds a pearl of great price sell all that they have to acquire these finds; similarly, the one who understands the supreme value of the kingdom gives up whatever he must to obtain it. The joy with which this is done is made explicit in the first parable, but it may be presumed in the second also. The concluding parable of the fishnet resembles the explanation of the parable of the weeds with its stress upon the final exclusion of evil persons from the kingdom.

* [13:44] In the unsettled conditions of Palestine in Jesus' time, it was not unusual to guard valuables by burying them in the ground.

* [13:51] Matthew typically speaks of the understanding of the disciples.

* [13:52] Since Matthew tends to identify the disciples and the Twelve (see note on Mt 10:1), this saying about the Christian scribe cannot be taken as applicable to all who accept the message of Jesus. While the Twelve are in many ways representative of all who believe in him, they are also distinguished from them in certain respects. The church of Matthew has leaders among whom are a group designated as "scribes" (Mt 23:34). Like the scribes of Israel, these are teachers. It is the Twelve and these their later counterparts to whom this verse applies. The scribe . . . instructed in the kingdom of heaven knows both the teaching of Jesus (the new) and the law and prophets (the

old) and provides in his own teaching **both the new and the old** as interpreted and fulfilled by **the new**. On the translation **head of a household** (for the same Greek word translated **householder** in Mt 13:27), see note on Mt 24:45–51.

* [13:54–17:27] This section is the narrative part of the fourth book of the gospel.

* [13:54–58] After the Sermon on the Mount the crowds are in admiring astonishment at Jesus' teaching (Mt 7:28); here the astonishment is of those who take **offense at him**. Familiarity with his background and family leads them to regard him as pretentious. Matthew modifies his Marcan source (Mt 6:1–6). Jesus is not the carpenter but **the carpenter's son** (Mt 13:55), "and among his own kin" is omitted (Mt 13:57), **he did not work many mighty deeds** in face of such unbelief (Mt 13:58) rather than the Marcan ". . . he was not able to perform any mighty deed there" (Mt 6:5), and there is no mention of his amazement at his townspeople's lack of faith.

* [14:1–12] The murder of the Baptist by Herod Antipas prefigures the death of Jesus (see Mt 17:12). The Marcan source (Mk 6:14–29) is much reduced and in some points changed. In Mark Herod reveres John as a holy man and the desire to kill him is attributed to Herodias (Mk 6:19, 20), whereas here that desire is Herod's from the beginning (Mt 14:5).

* [14:1] **Herod the tetrarch**: Herod Antipas, son of Herod the Great. When the latter died, his territory was divided among three of his surviving sons, Archelaus who received half of it (Mt 2:23), Herod Antipas who became ruler of Galilee and Perea, and Philip who became ruler of northern Transjordan. Since he received a quarter of his father's domain, Antipas is accurately designated **tetrarch** ("ruler of a fourth [part]"), although in Mt 14:9 Matthew repeats the "king" of his Marcan source (Mk 6:26).

* [14:3] Herodias was not the wife of Herod's half-brother Philip but of another half-brother, Herod Boethus. The union was prohibited by Lv 18:16; 20:21. According to Josephus (*Antiquities* 18:116–19), Herod imprisoned and then executed John because he feared that the Baptist's influence over the people might enable him to lead a rebellion.

* [14:13–21] The feeding of the five thousand is the only miracle of Jesus that is recounted in all four gospels. The principal reason for that may be that it was seen as anticipating the Eucharist and the final banquet in the kingdom (Mt 8:11; 26:29), but it looks not only forward but backward, to the feeding of Israel with manna in the desert at the time of the Exodus (Ex 16), a miracle that in some contemporary Jewish expectation would be repeated in the messianic age (2 Bar 29:8). It may

also be meant to recall Elisha's feeding a hundred men with small provisions (2 Kgs 4:42–44).

* [14:19] The **taking**, saying the blessing, breaking, and giving to the disciples correspond to the actions of Jesus over the bread at the Last Supper (Mt 26:26). Since they were usual at any Jewish meal, that correspondence does not necessarily indicate a eucharistic reference here. Matthew's silence about Jesus' dividing the fish among the people (Mk 6:41) is perhaps more significant in that regard.

* [14:20] **The fragments left over**: as in Elisha's miracle, food was **left over** after all had been fed. The word **fragments** (Greek *klasmata*) is used, in the singular, of the broken bread of the Eucharist in *Didache* 9:3–4.

* [14:22–33] The disciples, laboring against the turbulent sea, are saved by Jesus. For his power over the waters, see note on Mt 8:26. Here that power is expressed also by his **walking on the sea** (Mt 14:25; cf. Ps 77:20; Jb 9:8). Matthew has inserted into the Marcan story (Mk 6:45–52) material that belongs to his special traditions on Peter (Mt 14:28–31).

* [14:25] **The fourth watch of the night**: between 3 a.m. and 6 a.m. The Romans divided the twelve hours between 6 p.m. and 6 a.m. into four equal parts called "watches."

* [14:27] **It is I**: see note on Mk 6:50.

* [14:31] **You of little faith**: see note on Mt 6:30. **Why did you doubt?**: the verb is peculiar to Matthew and occurs elsewhere only in Mt 28:17.

* [14:33] This confession is in striking contrast to the Marcan parallel (Mk 6:51) where the disciples are "completely astounded."

* [15:1–20] This dispute begins with the question of the Pharisees and scribes why Jesus' disciples are breaking **the tradition of the elders** about washing one's hands before eating (Mt 15:2). Jesus' counteraccusation accuses his opponents of breaking **the commandment of God for the sake of** their **tradition** (Mt 15:3) and illustrates this by their interpretation of the commandment of the Decalogue concerning parents (Mt 15:4–6). Denouncing them as hypocrites, he applies to them a derogatory prophecy of Isaiah (Mt 15:7–8). Then with a wider audience (**the crowd**, Mt 15:10) he goes beyond the violation of tradition with which the dispute has started. The parable (Mt 15:11) is an attack on the Mosaic law concerning clean and unclean foods, similar to those antitheses that abrogate the law (Mt 5:31–32, 33–34, 38–39). After a warning to his disciples not to follow the moral guidance of the Pharisees (Mt 15:13–14), he explains the **parable** (Mt 15:15) to them, saying that defilement comes not from what **enters the mouth** (Mt 15:17) but from the evil thoughts and deeds that rise from within, **from the heart** (Mt 15:18–20). The last

verse returns to the starting point of the dispute (eating **with unwashed hands**). Because of Matthew's omission of Mk 7:19b, some scholars think that Matthew has weakened the Marcan repudiation of the Mosaic food laws. But that half verse is ambiguous in the Greek, which may be the reason for its omission here.

* [15:2] **The tradition of the elders**: see note on Mk 7:5. The purpose of the handwashing was to remove defilement caused by contact with what was ritually unclean.

* [15:3–4] For the commandment see Ex 20:12 (// Dt 5:16); 21:17. The honoring of one's parents had to do with supporting them in their needs.

* [15:5] See note on Mk 7:11.

* [15:8] The text of Is 29:13 is quoted approximately according to the Septuagint.

* [15:13–14] Jesus leads his disciples away from the teaching authority of the Pharisees.

* [15:15] Matthew specifies **Peter** as the questioner, unlike Mk 7:17. Given his tendency to present the disciples as more understanding than in his Marcan source, it is noteworthy that here he retains the Marcan rebuke, although in a slightly milder form. This may be due to his wish to correct the Jewish Christians within his church who still held to the food laws and thus separated themselves from Gentile Christians who did not observe them.

* [15:19] The Marcan list of thirteen things that defile (Mk 7:21–22) is here reduced to seven that partially cover the content of the Decalogue.

* [15:21–28] See note on Mt 8:5–13.

* [15:24] See note on Mt 10:5–6.

* [15:26] **The children**: the people of Israel. **Dogs**: see note on Mt 7:6.

* [15:28] As in the case of the cure of the centurion's servant (Mt 8:10), Matthew ascribes Jesus' granting the request to the woman's **great faith**, a point not made equally explicit in the Marcan parallel (Mk 7:24–30).

* [15:32–39] Most probably this story is a doublet of that of the feeding of the five thousand (Mt 14:13–21). It differs from it notably only in that Jesus takes the initiative, not the disciples (Mt 15:32), and in the numbers: the crowd has been with Jesus **three days** (Mt 15:32), **seven loaves** are multiplied (Mt 15:36), **seven baskets of fragments** remain after the feeding (Mt 15:37), and **four thousand** men are fed (Mt 15:38).

* [15:36] **Gave thanks**: see Mt 14:19, "said the blessing." There is no difference in meaning. The thanksgiving was a blessing of God for his benefits.

* [16:1] **A sign from heaven**: see note on Mt 12:38–42.

* [16:2–3] The answer of Jesus in these verses is omitted in many important textual witnesses, and it is very uncertain that it is an original part of this gospel. It resembles Lk 12:54–56 and may have been inserted from there. It rebukes the Pharisees and Sadducees who are able to read indications of coming weather but not the indications of the coming kingdom in the signs that Jesus does offer, his mighty deeds and teaching.

* [16:4] See notes on Mt 12:39, 40.

* [16:5–12] Jesus' warning his disciples against **the teaching of the Pharisees and Sadducees** comes immediately before his promise to confer on Peter the authority to bind and to loose on earth (Mt 16:19), an authority that will be confirmed in heaven. Such authority most probably has to do, at least in part, with teaching. The rejection of the teaching authority of the Pharisees (see also Mt 12:12–14) prepares for a new one derived from Jesus.

* [16:6] **Leaven**: see note on Mt 13:33. **Sadducees**: Matthew's Marcan source speaks rather of "the leaven of Herod" (Mk 8:15).

* [16:7–11] The disciples, men **of little faith**, misunderstand Jesus' metaphorical use of **leaven**, forgetting that, as the feeding of the crowds shows, he is not at a loss to provide them with bread.

* [16:12] After his rebuke, the disciples understand that by **leaven** he meant the corrupting influence of the **teaching of the Pharisees and Sadducees**. The evangelist probably understands this **teaching** as common to both groups. Since at the time of Jesus' ministry the two differed widely on points of teaching, e.g., the resurrection of the dead, and at the time of the evangelist the Sadducee party was no longer a force in Judaism, the supposed common teaching fits neither period. The disciples' eventual understanding of Jesus' warning contrasts with their continuing obtuseness in the Marcan parallel (Mk 8:14–21).

* [16:13–20] The Marcan confession of Jesus as Messiah, made by Peter as spokesman for the other disciples (Mk 8:27–29; cf. also Lk 9:18–20), is modified significantly here. The confession is of Jesus both as **Messiah** and as **Son of the living God** (Mt 16:16). Jesus' response, drawn principally from material peculiar to Matthew, attributes the confession to a divine revelation granted to Peter alone (Mt 16:17) and makes him the **rock** on which Jesus **will build** his **church** (Mt 16:18) and the disciple whose authority in the church **on earth** will be confirmed in **heaven**, i.e., by God (Mt 16:19).

* [16:13] **Caesarea Philippi**: situated about twenty miles north of the Sea of Galilee in the territory ruled by Philip, a son of Herod the Great, tetrarch from 4 B.C. until his death in A.D. 34 (see note on Mt 14:1). He rebuilt the town of Paneas, naming it **Caesarea** in honor of the emperor, and **Philippi** ("of Philip") to distinguish it from the seaport in Samaria that was also called Caesarea. **Who do people say that the Son of Man is?**: although the question differs from the Marcan

parallel (Mk 8:27: "Who . . . that I am?"), the meaning is the same, for Jesus here refers to himself as the Son of Man (cf. Mt 16:15).

* [16:14] **John the Baptist**: see Mt 14:2. **Elijah**: cf. Mal 3:23–24; Sir 48:10; and see note on Mt 3:4. **Jeremiah**: an addition of Matthew to the Marcan source.

* [16:16] **The Son of the living God**: see Mt 2:15; 3:17. The addition of this exalted title to the Marcan confession eliminates whatever ambiguity was attached to the title Messiah. This, among other things, supports the view proposed by many scholars that Matthew has here combined his source's confession with a post-resurrectional confession of faith in Jesus as **Son of the living God** that belonged to the appearance of the risen Jesus to Peter; cf. 1 Cor 15:5; Lk 24:34.

* [16:17] **Flesh and blood**: a Semitic expression for human beings, especially in their weakness. **Has not revealed this . . . but my heavenly Father**: that Peter's faith is spoken of as coming not through human means but through a revelation from God is similar to Paul's description of his recognition of who Jesus was; see Gal 1:15–16, ". . . when he [God] . . . was pleased to reveal his Son to me. . . ."

* [16:18] **You are Peter, and upon this rock I will build my church**: the Aramaic word *kēpaʾ* meaning **rock** and transliterated into Greek as *Kēphas* is the name by which Peter is called in the Pauline letters (1 Cor 1:12; 3:22; 9:5; 15:4; Gal 1:18; 2:9, 11, 14) except in Gal 2:7–8 ("Peter"). It is translated as *Petros* ("Peter") in Jn 1:42. The presumed original Aramaic of Jesus' statement would have been, in English, "You are the Rock (*Kēpaʾ*) and upon this rock (*kēpaʾ*) I will build my church." The Greek text probably means the same, for the difference in gender between the masculine noun *petros*, the disciple's new name, and the feminine noun *petra* (rock) may be due simply to the unsuitability of using a feminine noun as the proper name of a male. Although the two words were generally used with slightly different nuances, they were also used interchangeably with the same meaning, "rock." **Church**: this word (Greek *ekklēsia*) occurs in the gospels only here and in Mt 18:17 (twice). There are several possibilities for an Aramaic original. Jesus' **church** means the community that he **will** gather and that, like a building, will have Peter as its solid foundation. That function of Peter consists in his being witness to Jesus as **the Messiah, the Son of the living God. The gates of the netherworld shall not prevail against it**: the netherworld (Greek *Hadēs*, the abode of the dead) is conceived of as a walled city whose **gates** will not close in upon the church of Jesus, i.e., it will not be overcome by the power of death.

* [16:19] **The keys to the kingdom of heaven**: the image of the keys is probably drawn from Is

22:15–25 where Eliakim, who succeeds Shebna as master of the palace, is given "the key of the House of David," which he authoritatively "opens" and "shuts" (Is 22:22). **Whatever you bind . . . loosed in heaven**: there are many instances in rabbinic literature of the binding-loosing imagery. Of the several meanings given there to the metaphor, two are of special importance here: the giving of authoritative teaching, and the lifting or imposing of the ban of excommunication. It is disputed whether the image of **the keys** and that of binding and loosing are different metaphors meaning the same thing. In any case, the promise of the keys is given to Peter alone. In Mt 18:18 all the disciples are given the power of binding and loosing, but the context of that verse suggests that there the power of excommunication alone is intended. That **the keys** are those to the **kingdom of heaven** and that Peter's exercise of authority in the church **on earth** will be confirmed **in heaven** show an intimate connection between, but not an identification of, the church and the **kingdom of heaven**.

* [16:20] Cf. Mk 8:30. Matthew makes explicit that the prohibition has to do with speaking of Jesus as **the Messiah**; see note on Mk 8:27–30.

* [16:21–23] This first prediction of the passion follows Mk 8:31–33 in the main and serves as a corrective to an understanding of Jesus' messiahship as solely one of glory and triumph. By his addition of **from that time on** (Mt 16:21) Matthew has emphasized that Jesus' revelation of his coming suffering and death marks a new phase of the gospel. Neither this nor the two later passion predictions (Mt 17:22–23; 20:17–19) can be taken as sayings that, as they stand, go back to Jesus himself. However, it is probable that he foresaw that his mission would entail suffering and perhaps death, but was confident that he would ultimately be vindicated by God (see Mt 26:29).

* [16:21] **He**: the Marcan parallel (Mk 8:31) has "the Son of Man." Since Matthew has already designated Jesus by that title (Mt 15:13), its omission here is not significant. The Matthean prediction is equally about the sufferings of the Son of Man. **Must**: this necessity is part of the tradition of all the synoptics; cf. Mk 8:31; Lk 9:21. **The elders, the chief priests, and the scribes**: see note on Mk 8:31. **On the third day**: so also Lk 9:22, against the Marcan "after three days" (Mk 8:31). Matthew's formulation is, in the Greek, almost identical with the pre-Pauline fragment of the kerygma in 1 Cor 15:4 and also with Hos 6:2, which many take to be the Old Testament background to the confession that Jesus was raised on **the third day**. Josephus uses "after three days" and "on the third day" interchangeably (*Antiquities* 7:280–81; 8, 3:214, 218) and there is probably no difference in meaning between the two phrases.

* [16:22–23] Peter's refusal to accept Jesus' predicted suffering and death is seen as a satanic

attempt to deflect Jesus from his God-appointed course, and the disciple is addressed in terms that recall Jesus' dismissal of the devil in the temptation account (Mt 4:10: "Get away, Satan!"). Peter's satanic purpose is emphasized by Matthew's addition to the Marcan source of the words **You are an obstacle to me**.

* [16:24–28] A readiness to follow Jesus even to giving up one's life for him is the condition for true discipleship; this will be repaid by him at the final judgment.

* [16:24] **Deny himself**: to deny someone is to disown him (see Mt 10:33; 26:34–35) and to deny oneself is to disown oneself as the center of one's existence.

* [16:25] See notes on Mt 10:38, 39.

* [16:27] The parousia and final judgment are described in Mt 25:31 in terms almost identical with these.

* [16:28] **Coming in his kingdom**: since the **kingdom of the Son of Man** has been described as "the world" and Jesus' sovereignty precedes his final coming in glory (Mt 13:38, 41), the coming in this verse is not the parousia as in the preceding but the manifestation of Jesus' rule after his resurrection; see notes on Mt 13:38, 41.

---

* [17:1–8] The account of the transfiguration confirms that Jesus is the **Son of God** (Mt 17:5) and points to fulfillment of the prediction that he will come **in his Father's glory** at the end of the age (Mt 16:27). It has been explained by some as a resurrection appearance retrojected into the time of Jesus' ministry, but that is not probable since the account lacks many of the usual elements of the resurrection-appearance narratives. It draws upon motifs from the Old Testament and noncanonical Jewish apocalyptic literature that express the presence of the heavenly and the divine, e.g., brilliant light, white garments, and the overshadowing cloud.

* [17:1] These three disciples are also taken apart from the others by Jesus in Gethsemane (Mt 26:37). **A high mountain**: this has been identified with Tabor or Hermon, but probably no specific mountain was intended by the evangelist or by his Marcan source (Mk 9:2). Its meaning is theological rather than geographical, possibly recalling the revelation to Moses on Mount Sinai (Ex 24:12–18) and to Elijah at the same place (1 Kgs 19:8–18; Horeb = Sinai).

* [17:2] **His face shone like the sun**: this is a Matthean addition; cf. Dn 10:6. **His clothes became white as light**: cf. Dn 7:9, where the clothing of God appears "snow bright." For the white garments of other heavenly beings, see Rev 4:4; 7:9; 19:14.

* [17:3] See note on Mk 9:5.

* [17:4] **Three tents**: the booths in which the Israelites lived during the feast of Tabernacles (cf.

Jn 7:2) were meant to recall their ancestors' dwelling in booths during the journey from Egypt to the promised land (Lv 23:39–42). The same Greek word, *skēnē*, here translated **tents**, is used in the LXX for the booths of that feast, and some scholars have suggested that there is an allusion here to that liturgical custom.

* [17:5] **Cloud cast a shadow over them**: see note on Mk 9:7. **This is my beloved Son . . . listen to him**: cf. Mt 3:17. The voice repeats the baptismal proclamation about Jesus, with the addition of the command **listen to him**. The latter is a reference to Dt 18:15 in which the Israelites are commanded to **listen to** the prophet like Moses whom God will raise up for them. The command to listen to Jesus is general, but in this context it probably applies particularly to the preceding predictions of his passion and resurrection (Mt 16:21) and of his coming (Mt 16:27, 28).

* [17:6–7] A Matthean addition; cf. Dn 10:9–10, 18–19.

* [17:9–13] In response to the disciples' question about the expected return of Elijah, Jesus interprets the mission of the Baptist as the fulfillment of that expectation. But that was not suspected by those who opposed and finally killed him, and Jesus predicts a similar fate for himself.

* [17:9] **The vision**: Matthew alone uses this word to describe the transfiguration. **Until the Son of Man has been raised from the dead**: only in the light of Jesus' resurrection can the meaning of his life and mission be truly understood; until then no testimony to **the vision** will lead people to faith.

* [17:10] See notes on Mt 3:4; 16:14.

* [17:11–12] The preceding question and this answer may reflect later controversy with Jews who objected to the Christian claims for Jesus that Elijah had not yet come.

* [17:13] See Mt 11:14.

* [17:14–20] Matthew has greatly shortened the Marcan story (Mk 9:14–29). Leaving aside several details of the boy's illness, he concentrates on the need for faith, not so much on the part of the boy's father (as does Mark, for Matthew omits Mk 9:22b–24) but on that of his own disciples whose inability to drive out the demon is ascribed to their **little faith** (Mt 17:20).

* [17:15] **A lunatic**: this description of the boy is peculiar to Matthew. The word occurs in the New Testament only here and in Mt 4:24 and means one affected or struck by the moon. The symptoms of the boy's illness point to epilepsy, and attacks of this were thought to be caused by phases of the moon.

* [17:17] **Faithless and perverse**: so Matthew and Luke (Lk 9:41) against Mark's **faithless** (Mk 9:19). The Greek word here translated **perverse** is the same as that in Dt 32:5 LXX, where Moses speaks to his people. There is a problem

in knowing to whom the reproach is addressed. Since the Matthean Jesus normally chides his disciples for their **little faith** (as in Mt 17:20), it would appear that the charge of lack of faith could not be made against them and that the reproach is addressed to unbelievers among the Jews. However in Mt 17:20b (**if you have faith the size of a mustard seed**), which is certainly addressed to the disciples, they appear to have not even the smallest faith; if they had, they would have been able to cure the boy. In the light of Mt 17:20b the reproach of Mt 17:17 could have applied to the disciples. There seems to be an inconsistency between the charge of **little faith** in Mt 17:20a and that of not even a little in Mt 17:20b.

* [17:18] **The demon came out of him**: not until this verse does Matthew indicate that the boy's illness is a case of demoniacal possession.

* [17:20] The entire verse is an addition of Matthew who (according to the better attested text) omits the reason given for the disciples' inability in Mk 9:29. **Little faith**: see note on Mt 6:30. **Faith the size of a mustard seed . . . and it will move**: a combination of a Q saying (cf. Lk 17:6) with a Marcan saying (cf. Mk 11:23).

* [17:21] Some manuscripts add, "But this kind does not come out except by prayer and fasting"; this is a variant of the better reading of Mk 9:29.

* [17:22–23] The second passion prediction (cf. Mt 16:21–23) is the least detailed of the three and may be the earliest. In the Marcan parallel the disciples do not understand (Mk 9:32); here they understand and are **overwhelmed with grief** at the prospect of Jesus' death (Mt 17:23).

* [17:24–27] Like Mt 14:28–31 and Mt 16:16b–19, this episode comes from Matthew's special material on Peter. Although the question of **the collectors** concerns Jesus' payment of the **temple tax**, it is put to Peter. It is he who receives instruction from Jesus about freedom from the obligation of payment and yet why it should be made. The means of doing so is provided miraculously. The pericope deals with a problem of Matthew's church, whether its members should pay the temple tax, and the answer is given through a word of Jesus conveyed to Peter. Some scholars see here an example of the teaching authority of Peter exercised in the name of Jesus (see Mt 16:19). The specific problem was a Jewish Christian one and may have arisen when the Matthean church was composed largely of that group.

* [17:24] **The temple tax**: before the destruction of the Jerusalem temple in A.D. 70 every male Jew above nineteen years of age was obliged to make an annual contribution to its upkeep (cf. Ex 30:11–16; Neh 10:33). After the destruction the Romans imposed upon Jews the obligation of paying that tax for the temple of Jupiter Capitolinus. There is disagreement about which period the story deals with.

* [17:25] **From their subjects or from foreigners?**: the Greek word here translated **subjects** literally means "sons."

* [17:26] **Then the subjects are exempt**: just as **subjects** are not bound by laws applying to **foreigners**, neither are Jesus and his disciples, who belong to the kingdom of heaven, bound by the duty of paying the temple tax imposed on those who are not of the kingdom. If the Greek is translated "sons," the freedom of Jesus, the Son of God, and of his disciples, children ("sons") of the kingdom (cf. Mt 13:38), is even more clear.

* [17:27] **That we may not offend them**: though they are exempt (Mt 17:26), Jesus and his disciples are to avoid giving offense; therefore the tax is to be paid. **A coin worth twice the temple tax**: literally, "a stater," a Greek coin worth two double drachmas. Two double drachmas were equal to the Jewish shekel and the tax was a half-shekel. **For me and for you**: not only Jesus but Peter pays the tax, and this example serves as a standard for the conduct of all the disciples.

---

* [18:1–35] This discourse of the fourth book of the gospel is often called the "church order" discourse, but it lacks most of the considerations usually connected with church order, such as various offices in the church and the duties of each, and deals principally with the relations that must obtain among the members of the church. Beginning with the warning that greatness in the **kingdom of heaven** is measured not by rank or power but by childlikeness (Mt 18:1–5), it deals with the care that the disciples must take not to cause the **little ones to sin** or to neglect them if they stray from the community (Mt 18:6–14), the correction of members who sin (Mt 18:15–18), the efficacy of the prayer of the disciples because of the presence of Jesus (Mt 18:19–20), and the forgiveness that must be repeatedly extended to sinful members who repent (Mt 18:21–35).

* [18:1] The initiative is taken not by Jesus as in the Marcan parallel (Mk 9:33–34) but by the disciples. **Kingdom of heaven**: this may mean **the kingdom** in its fullness, i.e., after the parousia and the final judgment. But what follows about causes of sin, church discipline, and forgiveness, all dealing with the present age, suggests that the question has to do with rank also in the church, where the kingdom is manifested here and now, although only partially and by anticipation; see notes on Mt 3:2; 4:17.

* [18:3] **Become like children**: the child is held up as a model for the disciples not because of any supposed innocence of children but because of their complete dependence on, and trust in, their parents. So must the disciples be, in respect to God.

* [18:5] Cf. Mt 10:40.

* [18:6] **One of these little ones**: the thought passes from the child of Mt 18:2–4 to the disciples, **little ones** because of their becoming **like children**. It is difficult to know whether this is a designation of all who are disciples or of those who are insignificant in contrast to others, e.g., the leaders of the community. Since apart from this chapter the designation **little ones** occurs in Matthew only in Mt 10:42 where it means disciples as such, that is its more likely meaning here. **Who believe in me**: since discipleship is impossible without at least some degree of faith, this further specification seems superfluous. However, it serves to indicate that the warning against causing a **little one** to sin is principally directed against whatever would lead such a one to a weakening or loss of faith. The Greek verb *skandalizein*, here translated **causes . . . to sin**, means literally "causes to stumble"; what the stumbling is depends on the context. It is used of falling away from faith in Mt 13:21. According to the better reading of Mk 9:42, **in me** is a Matthean addition to the Marcan source. **It would be better . . . depths of the sea**: cf. Mk 9:42.

* [18:7] This is a Q saying; cf. Lk 17:1. The inevitability of **things that cause sin** (literally, "scandals") does not take away the responsibility for **the one through whom they come**.

* [18:8–9] These verses are a doublet of Mt 5:29–30. In that context they have to do with causes of sexual sin. As in the Marcan source from which they have been drawn (Mk 9:42–48), they differ from the first warning about scandal, which deals with causing another person to sin, for they concern what **causes** oneself **to sin** and they do not seem to be related to another's loss of faith, as the first warning is. It is difficult to know how Matthew understood the logical connection between these verses and Mt 18:6–7.

* [18:10–14] The first and last verses are peculiar to Matthew. The parable itself comes from Q; see Lk 15:3–7. In Luke it serves as justification for Jesus' table-companionship with sinners; here, it is an exhortation for the disciples to seek out fellow disciples who have gone astray. Not only must no one cause a fellow disciple to sin, but those who have strayed must be sought out and, if possible, brought back to the community. The joy of the shepherd on finding the sheep, though not absent in Mt 18:13 is more emphasized in Luke. By his addition of Mt 18:10, 14 Matthew has drawn out explicitly the application of the parable to the care of the **little ones**.

* [18:10] **Their angels in heaven . . . my heavenly Father**: for the Jewish belief in angels as guardians of nations and individuals, see Dn 10:13, 20–21; Tb 5:4–7; 1QH 5:20–22; as intercessors who present the prayers of human beings to God, see Tb 13:12, 15. The high worth of the little ones is indicated by their being represented before God by these heavenly beings.

* [18:11] Some manuscripts add, "For the Son of Man has come to save what was lost"; cf. Mt 9:13. This is practically identical with Lk 19:10 and is probably a copyist's addition from that source.

* [18:15–20] Passing from the duty of Christian disciples toward those who have strayed from their number, the discourse now turns to how they are to deal with one who sins and yet remains within the community. First there is to be private correction (Mt 18:15); if this is unsuccessful, further correction before **two or three witnesses** (Mt 18:16); if this fails, the matter is to be brought before the assembled community (the church), and if the sinner refuses to attend to the correction of **the church**, he is to be expelled (Mt 18:17). The church's judgment will be ratified **in heaven**, i.e., by God (Mt 18:18). This three-step process of correction corresponds, though not exactly, to the procedure of the Qumran community; see 1QS 5:25–6:1; 6:24–7:25; CD 9:2–8. The section ends with a saying about the favorable response of God to prayer, even to that of a very small number, for Jesus is in the midst of any gathering of his disciples, however small (Mt 18:19–20). Whether this prayer has anything to do with the preceding judgment is uncertain.

* [18:15] **Your brother**: a fellow disciple; see Mt 23:8. The bracketed words, **against you**, are widely attested but are not in the important codices Sinaiticus and Vaticanus or in some other textual witnesses. Their omission broadens the type of sin in question. **Won over**: literally, "gained."

* [18:16] Cf. Dt 19:15.

* [18:17] **The church**: the second of the only two instances of this word in the gospels; see note on Mt 16:18. Here it refers not to the entire **church** of Jesus, as in Mt 16:18, but to the local congregation. **Treat him . . . a Gentile or a tax collector**: just as the observant Jew avoided the company of Gentiles and tax collectors, so must the congregation of Christian disciples separate itself from the arrogantly sinful member who refuses to repent even when convicted of his sin by the whole **church**. Such a one is to be set outside the fellowship of the community. The harsh language about **Gentile** and **tax collector** probably reflects a stage of the Matthean **church** when it was principally composed of Jewish Christians. That time had long since passed, but the principle of exclusion for such a sinner remained. Paul makes a similar demand for excommunication in 1 Cor 5:1–13.

* [18:18] Except for the plural of the verbs **bind** and **loose**, this verse is practically identical with Mt 16:19b and many scholars understand it as granting to all the disciples what was previously given to Peter alone. For a different view, based on the different contexts of the two verses, see note on Mt 16:19.

* [18:19–20] Some take these verses as applying to prayer on the occasion of the church's gathering to deal with the sinner of Mt 18:17. Unless an *a fortiori* argument is supposed, this seems unlikely. God's answer to the prayer of **two or three** envisages a different situation from one that involves the entire congregation. In addition, the object of this prayer is expressed in most general terms as **anything for which they are to pray**.

* [18:20] **For where two or three . . . midst of them**: the presence of Jesus guarantees the efficacy of the prayer. This saying is similar to one attributed to a rabbi executed in A.D. 135 at the time of the second Jewish revolt: ". . . When two sit and there are between them the words of the Torah, the divine presence (*Shekinah*) rests upon them" (*Pirqê 'Abôt* 3, 3).

* [18:21–35] The final section of the discourse deals with the forgiveness that the disciples are to give to their fellow disciples who sin against them. To the question of Peter how often forgiveness is to be granted (Mt 18:21), Jesus answers that it is to be given without limit (Mt 18:22) and illustrates this with the parable of the unmerciful servant (Mt 18:23–34), warning that his **heavenly Father** will give those who do not forgive the same treatment as that given to the unmerciful servant (Mt 18:35). Mt 18:21–22 correspond to Lk 17:4; the parable and the final warning are peculiar to Matthew. That the parable did not originally belong to this context is suggested by the fact that it really does not deal with repeated forgiveness, which is the point of Peter's question and Jesus' reply.

* [18:22] **Seventy-seven times**: the Greek corresponds exactly to the LXX of Gn 4:24. There is probably an allusion, by contrast, to the limitless vengeance of Lamech in the Genesis text. In any case, what is demanded of the disciples is limitless forgiveness.

* [18:24] **A huge amount**: literally, "ten thousand talents." The talent was a unit of coinage of high but varying value depending on its metal (gold, silver, copper) and its place of origin. It is mentioned in the New Testament only here and in Mt 25:14–30.

* [18:26] **Pay you back in full**: an empty promise, given the size of the debt.

* [18:28] **A much smaller amount**: literally, "a hundred denarii." A denarius was the normal daily wage of a laborer. The difference between the two debts is enormous and brings out the absurdity of the conduct of the Christian who has received the great forgiveness of God and yet refuses to forgive the relatively minor offenses done to him.

* [18:34] Since the debt is so great as to be unpayable, the punishment will be endless.

* [18:35] The Father's forgiveness, already given, will be withdrawn at the final judgment for those who have not imitated his forgiveness by their own.

* [19:1–23:39] The narrative section of the fifth book of the gospel. The first part (Mt 19:1–20:34) has for its setting the journey of Jesus from Galilee to Jerusalem; the second (Mt 21:1–23:39) deals with Jesus' ministry in Jerusalem up to the final great discourse of the gospel (Mt 24–25). Matthew follows the Marcan sequence of events, though adding material both special to this gospel and drawn from Q. The second part ends with the denunciation of the scribes and Pharisees (Mt 23:1–36) followed by Jesus' lament over Jerusalem (Mt 23:37–39). This long and important speech raises a problem for the view that Matthew is structured around five other discourses of Jesus (see Introduction) and that this one has no such function in the gospel. However, it is to be noted that this speech lacks the customary concluding formula that follows the five discourses (see note on Mt 7:28), and that those discourses are all addressed either exclusively (Mt 10; 18; 24; 25) or primarily (Mt 5–7; 13) to the disciples, whereas this is addressed primarily to the scribes and Pharisees (Mt 23:1–36). Consequently, it seems plausible to maintain that the evangelist did not intend to give it the structural importance of the five other discourses, and that, in spite of its being composed of sayings-material, it belongs to the narrative section of this book. In that regard, it is similar to the sayings-material of Mt 11:7–30. Some have proposed that Matthew wished to regard it as part of the final discourse of Mt 24–25, but the intervening material (Mt 24:1–4) and the change in matter and style of those chapters do not support that view.

* [19:1] In giving Jesus' teaching on divorce (Mt 19:3–9), Matthew here follows his Marcan source (Mk 10:2–12) as he does Q in Mt 5:31–32 (cf. Lk 16:18). Mt 19:10–12 are peculiar to Matthew.

* [19:1] **When Jesus finished these words**: see note on Mt 7:28–29. **The district of Judea across the Jordan**: an inexact designation of the territory. Judea did not extend **across the Jordan**; the territory east of the river was Perea. The route to Jerusalem by way of Perea avoided passage through Samaria.

* [19:3] **Tested him**: the verb is used of attempts of Jesus' opponents to embarrass him by challenging him to do something they think impossible (Mt 16:1; Mk 8:11; Lk 11:16) or by having him say something that they can use against him (Mt 22:18, 35; Mk 10:2; 12:15). **For any cause whatever**: this is peculiar to Matthew and has been interpreted by some as meaning that Jesus was being asked to take sides in the dispute between the schools of Hillel and Shammai on the reasons for divorce, the latter holding a stricter position than the former. It is unlikely, however, that to ask Jesus' opinion about the differing views of two Jewish schools, both highly respected, could

be described as "testing" him, for the reason indicated above.

* [19:4–6] Matthew recasts his Marcan source, omitting Jesus' question about Moses' command (Mk 10:3) and having him recall at once two Genesis texts that show the will and purpose of **the Creator** in making human beings **male and female** (Gn 1:27), namely, that a **man** may be **joined to his wife** in marriage in the intimacy of **one flesh** (Gn 2:24). **What God has** thus **joined** must not be separated by any human being. (The NAB translation of the Hebrew *bāśār* of Gn 2:24 as "body" rather than "flesh" obscures the reference of Matthew to that text.)

* [19:7] See Dt 24:1–4.

* [19:9] Moses' concession to human sinfulness (**the hardness of your hearts,** Mt 19:8) is repudiated by Jesus, and the original will of the Creator is reaffirmed against that concession. (**Unless the marriage is unlawful**): see note on Mt 5:31–32. There is some evidence suggesting that Jesus' absolute prohibition of divorce was paralleled in the Qumran community (see 11QTemple 57:17–19; CD 4:12b–5:14). Matthew removes Mark's setting of this verse as spoken to the disciples alone "in the house" (Mk 10:10) and also his extension of the divorce prohibition to the case of a woman's divorcing her husband (Mk 10:12), probably because in Palestine, unlike the places where Roman and Greek law prevailed, the woman was not allowed to initiate the divorce.

* [19:11] [**This**] **word:** probably the disciples' "**it is better not to marry**" (Mt 19:10). Jesus agrees but says that celibacy is not for all but only for those **to whom that is granted** by God.

* [19:12] **Incapable of marriage:** literally, "eunuchs." Three classes are mentioned, eunuchs from birth, eunuchs by castration, and those who have voluntarily **renounced marriage** (literally, "have made themselves eunuchs") **for the sake of the kingdom,** i.e., to devote themselves entirely to its service. Some scholars take the last class to be those who have been divorced by their spouses and have refused to enter another marriage. But it is more likely that it is rather those who have chosen never to marry, since that suits better the optional nature of the decision: **whoever can . . . ought to accept it.**

* [19:13–15] This account is understood by some as intended to justify the practice of infant baptism. That interpretation is based principally on the command not to **prevent** the children from coming, since that word sometimes has a baptismal connotation in the New Testament; see Acts 8:36.

* [19:16–30] Cf. Mk 10:17–31. This story does not set up a "two-tier" morality, that of those who seek (only) **eternal life** (Mt 19:16) and that of those who **wish to be perfect** (Mt 19:21). It speaks rather of the obstacle that riches constitute

for the following of Jesus and of the impossibility, humanly speaking, for one who has **many possessions** (Mt 19:22) **to enter the kingdom** (Mt 19:24). Actual renunciation of riches is not demanded of all; Matthew counts the rich Joseph of Arimathea as a disciple of Jesus (Mt 27:57). But only the poor in spirit (Mt 5:3) can **enter the kingdom** and, as here, such poverty may entail the sacrifice of one's **possessions.** The Twelve, who **have given up everything** (Mt 19:27) to follow Jesus, will have as their reward a share in Jesus' (the Son of Man's) **judging the twelve tribes of Israel** (Mt 19:28), and all who have similarly sacrificed family or property for his sake **will inherit eternal life** (Mt 19:29).

* [19:16] **Gain eternal life:** this is equivalent to "entering into life" (Mt 19:17) and "being saved" (Mt 19:25); the **life** is that of the new age after the final judgment (see Mt 25:46). It probably is also equivalent here to "entering the kingdom of heaven" (Mt 19:23) or "the kingdom of God" (Mt 19:24), but see notes on Mt 3:2; 4:17; 18:1 for the wider reference of **the kingdom** in Matthew.

* [19:17] By Matthew's reformulation of the Marcan question and reply (Mk 10:17–18) Jesus' repudiation of the term "good" for himself has been softened. Yet the Marcan assertion that "no one is good but God alone" stands, with only unimportant verbal modification.

* [19:18–19] The first five commandments cited are from the Decalogue (see Ex 20:12–16; Dt 5:16–20). Matthew omits Mark's "you shall not defraud" (Mk 10:19; see Dt 24:14) and adds Lv 19:18. This combination of commandments of the Decalogue with Lv 19:18 is partially the same as Paul's enumeration of the demands of Christian morality in Rom 13:9.

* [19:20] **Young man:** in Matthew alone of the synoptics the questioner is said to be a **young man;** thus the Marcan "from my youth" (Mk 10:20) is omitted.

* [19:21] **If you wish to be perfect:** to be perfect is demanded of all Christians; see Mt 5:48. In the case of this man, it involves selling his possessions and giving to the poor; only so can he **follow** Jesus.

* [19:23–24] Riches are an obstacle to entering **the kingdom** that cannot be overcome by human power. The comparison with the impossibility of a camel's passing **through the eye of a needle** should not be mitigated by such suppositions as that **the eye of a needle** means a low or narrow gate. **The kingdom of God:** as in Mt 12:28; 21:31, 43 instead of Matthew's usual **kingdom of heaven.**

* [19:25–26] See note on Mk 10:23–27.

* [19:28] This saying, directed to the Twelve, is from Q; see Lk 22:29–30. **The new age:** the Greek word here translated "new age" occurs in the New Testament only here and in Ti 3:5. Literally, it

means "rebirth" or "regeneration," and is used in Titus of spiritual rebirth through baptism. Here it means the "rebirth" effected by the coming of the kingdom. Since that coming has various stages (see notes on Mt 3:2; 4:17), the **new age** could be taken as referring to the time after the resurrection when the Twelve will govern the true Israel, i.e., the church of Jesus. (For "judge" in the sense of "govern," cf. Jgs 12:8, 9, 11; 15:20; 16:31; Ps 2:10). But since it is connected here with the time when the **Son of Man** will be **seated on his throne of glory**, language that Matthew uses in Mt 25:31 for the time of final judgment, it is more likely that what the Twelve are promised is that they will be joined with Jesus then in judging the people of Israel.

* [19:30] Different interpretations have been given to this saying, which comes from Mk 10:31. In view of Matthew's associating it with the following parable (Mt 20:1–15) and substantially repeating it (in reverse order) at the end of that parable (Mt 20:16), it may be that his meaning is that all who respond to the call of Jesus, at whatever time (**first** or **last**), will be the same in respect to inheriting the benefits of the kingdom, which is the gift of God.

* [20:1–16] This parable is peculiar to Matthew. It is difficult to know whether the evangelist composed it or received it as part of his traditional material and, if the latter is the case, what its original reference was. In its present context its close association with Mt 19:30 suggests that its teaching is the equality of all the disciples in the reward of inheriting eternal life.

* [20:4] **What is just**: although the wage is not stipulated as in the case of those first hired, it will be fair.

* [20:8] **Beginning with the last . . . the first**: this element of the parable has no other purpose than to show how the **first** knew what the **last** were given (Mt 20:12).

* [20:13] **I am not cheating you**: literally, "I am not treating you unjustly."

* [20:14–15] The owner's conduct involves no violation of justice (Mt 20:4, 13), and that all the workers receive the same wage is due only to his generosity to the latest arrivals; the resentment of the first comes from envy.

* [20:16] See note on Mt 19:30.

* [20:17–19] Cf. Mk 10:32–34. This is the third and the most detailed of the passion predictions (Mt 16:21–23; 17:22–23). It speaks of Jesus' being **handed over to the Gentiles** (Mt 27:2), his being **mocked** (Mt 27:27–30), **scourged** (Mt 27:26), and **crucified** (Mt 27:31, 35). In all but the last of these points Matthew agrees with his Marcan source, but whereas Mark speaks of Jesus' being killed (Mk 10:34), Matthew has the specific **to be . . . crucified.**

* [20:20–28] Cf. Mk 10:35–45. The request of the sons of Zebedee, made through their mother, for the highest places of honor in the **kingdom**, and the indignation of **the** other **ten** disciples at this request, show that neither **the two brothers** nor the others have understood that what makes for greatness in the kingdom is not lordly power but humble service. Jesus gives the example, and his ministry of service will reach its highest point when he gives his life for the deliverance of the human race from sin.

* [20:20–21] The reason for Matthew's making **the mother** the petitioner (cf. Mk 10:35) is not clear. Possibly he intends an allusion to Bathsheba's seeking the kingdom for Solomon; see 1 Kgs 1:11–21. **Your kingdom**: see note on Mt 16:28.

* [20:22] **You do not know what you are asking**: the Greek verbs are plural and, with the rest of the verse, indicate that the answer is addressed not to the woman but to her sons. **Drink the cup**: see note on Mk 10:38–40. Matthew omits the Marcan "or be baptized with the baptism with which I am baptized" (Mk 10:38).

* [20:28] **Ransom**: this noun, which occurs in the New Testament only here and in the Marcan parallel (Mk 10:45), does not necessarily express the idea of liberation by payment of some price. The cognate verb is used frequently in the LXX of God's liberating Israel from Egypt or from Babylonia after the Exile; see Ex 6:6; 15:13; Ps 77:16 (76 LXX); Is 43:1; 44:22. The liberation brought by Jesus' death will be **for many**; cf. Is 53:12. **Many** does not mean that some are excluded, but is a Semitism designating the collectivity who benefit from the service of the one, and is equivalent to "all." While there are few verbal contacts between this saying and the fourth Servant Song (Is 52:13–53:12), the ideas of that passage are reflected here.

* [20:29–34] The cure of the blind men is probably symbolic of what will happen to the disciples, now blind to the meaning of Jesus' passion and to the necessity of their sharing his suffering. As the men are given sight, so, after the resurrection, will the disciples come to see that to which they are now blind. Matthew has abbreviated his Marcan source (Mk 10:46–52) and has made Mark's one man two. Such doubling is characteristic of this gospel; see Mt 8:28–34 (// Mk 5:1–20) and the note on Mt 9:27–31.

* [20:30] **[Lord,]**: some important textual witnesses omit this, but that may be because copyists assimilated this verse to Mt 9:27. **Son of David**: see note on Mt 9:27.

* [21:1–11] Jesus' coming to Jerusalem is in accordance with the divine will that he must go there (cf. Mt 16:21) to suffer, die, and be raised. He prepares for his entry into the city in such a way as to make it a fulfillment of the prophecy of Zec 9:9 (Mt 21:2) that emphasizes the humility of the

king who **comes** (Mt 21:5). That prophecy, absent from the Marcan parallel account (Mk 11:1–11) although found also in the Johannine account of the entry (Jn 12:15), is the center of the Matthean story. During the procession from Bethphage to Jerusalem, Jesus is acclaimed as the Davidic messianic king by the crowds who accompany him (Mt 21:9). On his arrival the **whole city was shaken**, and to the inquiry of the amazed populace about Jesus' identity the crowds with him reply that he is **the prophet, from Nazareth in Galilee** (Mt 21:10, 11).

* [21:1] **Bethphage**: a village that can no longer be certainly identified. Mark mentions it before Bethany (Mk 11:1), which suggests that it lay to the east of the latter. **The Mount of Olives**: the hill east of Jerusalem that is spoken of in Zec 14:4 as the place where the Lord will come to rescue Jerusalem from the enemy nations.

* [21:2] **An ass tethered, and a colt with her**: instead of the one animal of Mk 11:2, Matthew has two, as demanded by his understanding of Zec 9:9.

* [21:4–5] **The prophet**: this fulfillment citation is actually composed of two distinct Old Testament texts, Is 62:11 (**Say to daughter Zion**) and Zec 9:9. The **ass** and the **colt** are the same animal in the prophecy, mentioned twice in different ways, the common Hebrew literary device of poetic parallelism. That Matthew takes them as two is one of the reasons why some scholars think that he was a Gentile rather than a Jewish Christian who would presumably not make that mistake (see Introduction).

* [21:7] **Upon them**: upon the two animals; an awkward picture resulting from Matthew's misunderstanding of the prophecy.

* [21:8] **Spread . . . on the road**: cf. 2 Kgs 9:13. There is a similarity between the cutting and strewing of the branches and the festivities of Tabernacles (Lv 23:39–40); see also 2 Mc 10:5–8 where the celebration of the rededication of the temple is compared to that of Tabernacles.

* [21:9] **Hosanna**: the Hebrew means "(O LORD) grant salvation"; see Ps 118:25, but that invocation had become an acclamation of jubilation and welcome. **Blessed is he . . . in the name of the Lord**: see Ps 118:26 and the note on Jn 12:13. **In the highest**: probably only an intensification of the acclamation, although **Hosanna in the highest** could be taken as a prayer, "May God save (him)."

* [21:10] **Was shaken**: in the gospels this verb is peculiar to Matthew where it is used also of the earthquake at the time of the crucifixion (Mt 27:51) and of the terror of the guards of Jesus' tomb at the appearance of the angel (Mt 28:4). For Matthew's use of the cognate noun, see note on Mt 8:24.

* [21:11] **The prophet**: see Mt 16:14 ("one of the prophets") and 21:46.

* [21:12–17] Matthew changes the order of (Mk 11:11, 12, 15) and places the cleansing of the temple on the same day as the entry into Jerusalem, immediately after it. The activities going on in **the temple area** were not secular but connected with the temple worship. Thus Jesus' attack on those so engaged and his charge that they were **making** God's **house of prayer a den of thieves** (Mt 21:12–13) constituted a claim to authority over the religious practices of Israel and were a challenge to the priestly authorities. Mt 21:14–17 are peculiar to Matthew. Jesus' healings and his countenancing the children's cries of praise rouse the indignation of **the chief priests and the scribes** (Mt 21:15). These two groups appear in the infancy narrative (Mt 2:4) and have been mentioned in the first and third passion predictions (Mt 16:21; 20:18). Now, as the passion approaches, they come on the scene again, exhibiting their hostility to Jesus.

* [21:12] These activities were carried on in the court of the Gentiles, the outermost court of **the temple area**. Animals for sacrifice were sold; the **doves** were for those who could not afford a more expensive offering; see Lv 5:7. **Tables of the money changers**: only the coinage of Tyre could be used for the purchases; other money had to be exchanged for that.

* [21:13] '**My house . . . prayer**': cf. Is 56:7. Matthew omits the final words of the quotation, "for all peoples" ("all nations"), possibly because for him the worship of the God of Israel by all nations belongs to the time after the resurrection; see Mt 28:19. **A den of thieves**: the phrase is taken from Jer 7:11.

* [21:14] **The blind and the lame**: according to 2 Sm 5:8 LXX **the blind and the lame** were forbidden to enter "the house of the Lord," the temple. These are the last of Jesus' healings in Matthew.

* [21:15] **The wondrous things**: the healings.

* [21:16] '**Out of the mouths . . . praise**': cf. Ps 8:3 LXX.

* [21:18–22] In Mark the effect of Jesus' cursing the fig tree is not immediate; see Mk 11:14, 20. By making it so, Matthew has heightened the miracle. Jesus' act seems arbitrary and ill-tempered, but it is a prophetic action similar to those of Old Testament prophets that vividly symbolize some part of their preaching; see, e.g., Ez 12:1–20. It is a sign of the judgment that is to come upon the Israel that with all its apparent piety lacks the fruit of good deeds (Mt 3:10) and will soon bear the punishment of its fruitlessness (Mt 21:43). Some scholars propose that this story is the development in tradition of a parable of Jesus about the destiny of a fruitless tree, such as Lk 13:6–9. Jesus' answer to the question of the amazed disciples (Mt 21:20) makes the miracle an example of the

power of prayer made with unwavering **faith** (Mt 21:21–22).

* [21:21] See Mt 17:20.

* [21:23–27] Cf. Mk 11:27–33. This is the first of five controversies between Jesus and the religious authorities of Judaism in Mt 21:23–22:46, presented in the form of questions and answers.

* [21:23] **These things**: probably his entry into the city, his cleansing of the temple, and his healings there.

* [21:24] To reply by counterquestion was common in rabbinical debate.

* [21:26] **We fear . . . as a prophet**: cf. Mt 14:5.

* [21:27] Since through embarrassment on the one hand and fear on the other the religious authorities claim ignorance of the origin of John's baptism, they show themselves incapable of speaking with authority; hence Jesus refuses to discuss with them the grounds of his authority.

* [21:28–32] The series of controversies is interrupted by three parables on the judgment of Israel (Mt 21:28–22:14) of which this, peculiar to Matthew, is the first. The second (Mt 21:33–46) comes from Mark (12:1–12), and the third (Mt 22:1–14) from Q; see Lk 14:15–24. This interruption of the controversies is similar to that in Mark, although Mark has only one parable between the first and second controversy. As regards Matthew's first parable, Mt 21:28–30 if taken by themselves could point simply to the difference between saying and doing, a theme of much importance in this gospel (cf. Mt 7:21; 12:50); that may have been the parable's original reference. However, it is given a more specific application by the addition of Mt 21:31–32. The two sons represent, respectively, the religious leaders and the religious outcasts who followed John's call to repentance. By the answer they give to Jesus' question (Mt 21:31) the leaders condemn themselves. There is much confusion in the textual tradition of the parable. Of the three different forms of the text given by important textual witnesses, one has the leaders answer that the son who agreed to go but did not was the one who did the father's will. Although some scholars accept that as the original reading, their arguments in favor of it seem unconvincing. The choice probably lies only between a reading that puts the son who agrees and then disobeys before the son who at first refuses and then obeys, and the reading followed in the present translation. The witnesses to the latter reading are slightly better than those that support the other.

* [21:31] **Entering . . . before you**: this probably means "they enter; you do not."

* [21:32] Cf. Lk 7:29–30. Although the thought is similar to that of the Lucan text, the formulation is so different that it is improbable that the saying comes from Q. **Came to you . . . way of righteousness**: several meanings are possible: that John himself was righteous, that he taught

righteousness to others, or that he had an important place in God's plan of salvation. For the last, see note on Mt 3:14–15.

* [21:33–46] Cf. Mk 12:1–12. In this parable there is a close correspondence between most of the details of the story and the situation that it illustrates, the dealings of God with his people. Because of that heavy allegorizing, some scholars think that it does not in any way go back to Jesus, but represents the theology of the later church. That judgment applies to the Marcan parallel as well, although the allegorizing has gone farther in Matthew. There are others who believe that while many of the allegorical elements are due to church sources, they have been added to a basic parable spoken by Jesus. This view is now supported by the Gospel of Thomas 65, where a less allegorized and probably more primitive form of the parable is found.

* [21:33] **Planted a vineyard . . . a tower**: cf. Is 5:1–2. The **vineyard** is defined in Is 5:7 as "the house of Israel."

* [21:34–35] **His servants**: Matthew has two sendings of **servants** as against Mark's three sendings of a single servant (Mk 12:2–5a) followed by a statement about the sending of "many others" (Mk 12:2, 5b). That these servants stand for the prophets sent by God to Israel is clearly implied but not made explicit here, but see Mt 23:37. **His produce**: cf. Mk 12:2 "some of the produce." The **produce** is the good works demanded by God, and his claim to them is total.

* [21:38] **Acquire his inheritance**: if a Jewish proselyte died without heir, the tenants of his land would have final claim on it.

* [21:39] **Threw him out . . . and killed him**: the change in the Marcan order where the son is killed and his corpse then thrown out (Mk 12:8) was probably made because of the tradition that Jesus died outside the city of Jerusalem; see Jn 19:17; Heb 13:12.

* [21:41] **They answered**: in Mk 12:9 the question is answered by Jesus himself; here the leaders answer and so condemn themselves; cf. Mt 21:31. Matthew adds that the new **tenants** to whom the vineyard will be transferred **will give** the owner **the produce at the proper times**.

* [21:42] Cf. Ps 118:22–23. The psalm was used in the early church as a prophecy of Jesus' resurrection; see Acts 4:11; 1 Pt 2:7. If, as some think, the original parable ended at Mt 21:39 it was thought necessary to complete it by a reference to Jesus' vindication by God.

* [21:43] Peculiar to Matthew. **Kingdom of God**: see note on Mt 19:23–24. Its presence here instead of Matthew's usual "kingdom of heaven" may indicate that the saying came from Matthew's own traditional material. **A people that will produce its fruit**: believing Israelites and Gentiles, the church of Jesus.

* [21:44] The majority of textual witnesses omit this verse. It is probably an early addition to Matthew from Lk 20:18 with which it is practically identical.

* [21:45] **The Pharisees**: Matthew inserts into the group of Jewish leaders (Mt 21:23) those who represented the Judaism of his own time.

* [22:1–14] This parable is from Q; see Lk 14:15–24. It has been given many allegorical traits by Matthew, e.g., the burning of the **city** of the guests who refused the invitation (Mt 22:7), which corresponds to the destruction of Jerusalem by the Romans in A.D. 70. It has similarities with the preceding parable of the tenants: the sending of two groups of **servants** (Mt 22:3, 4), the murder of the **servants** (Mt 22:6), the punishment of the **murderers** (Mt 22:7), and the entrance of a new group into a privileged situation of which the others had proved themselves unworthy (Mt 22:8–10). The parable ends with a section that is peculiar to Matthew (Mt 22.11–14), which some take as a distinct parable. Matthew presents the **kingdom** in its double aspect, already present and something that can be entered here and now (Mt 22:1–10), and something that will be possessed only by those present members who can stand the scrutiny of the final judgment (Mt 22:11–14). The parable is not only a statement of God's judgment on Israel but a warning to Matthew's church.

* [22:2] **Wedding feast**: the Old Testament's portrayal of final salvation under the image of a banquet (Is 25:6) is taken up also in Mt 8:11; cf. Lk 13:15.

* [22:3–4] **Servants . . . other servants**: probably Christian missionaries in both instances; cf. Mt 23:34.

* [22:7] See note on Mt 22:1–14.

* [22:10] **Bad and good alike**: cf. Mt 13:47.

* [22:11] **A wedding garment**: the repentance, change of heart and mind, that is the condition for entrance into the kingdom (Mt 3:2; 4:17) must be continued in a life of good deeds (Mt 7:21–23).

* [22:13] **Wailing and grinding of teeth**: the Christian who lacks the wedding garment of good deeds will suffer the same fate as those Jews who have rejected Jesus; see note on Mt 8:11–12.

* [22:15–22] The series of controversies between Jesus and the representatives of Judaism (see note on Mt 21:23–27) is resumed. As in the first (Mt 21:23–27), here and in the following disputes Matthew follows his Marcan source with few modifications.

* [22:15] **The Pharisees**: while Matthew retains the Marcan union of Pharisees and Herodians in this account, he clearly emphasizes the Pharisees' part. They alone are mentioned here, and the Herodians are joined with them only in a prepositional phrase of Mt 22:16. **Entrap him in speech**: the question that they will pose is intended to force Jesus to take either a position contrary to that held by the majority of the people or one that will bring him into conflict with the Roman authorities.

* [22:16] **Herodians**: see note on Mk 3:6. They would favor payment of the tax; the Pharisees did not.

* [22:17] **Is it lawful**: the law to which they refer is the law of God.

* [22:19] **They handed him the Roman coin**: their readiness in producing the money implies their use of it and their acceptance of the financial advantages of the Roman administration in Palestine.

* [22:21] **Caesar's**: the emperor Tiberius (A.D. 14–37). **Repay to Caesar what belongs to Caesar**: those who willingly use the coin that is Caesar's should **repay** him in kind. The answer avoids taking sides in the question of the lawfulness of the tax. **To God what belongs to God**: Jesus raises the debate to a new level. Those who have hypocritically asked about tax in respect to its relation to the law of **God** should be concerned rather with repaying God with the good deeds that are his due; cf. Mt 21:41, 43.

* [22:23–33] Here Jesus' opponents are the **Sadducees**, members of the powerful priestly party of his time; see note on Mt 3:7. Denying the resurrection of the dead, a teaching of relatively late origin in Judaism (cf. Dn 12:2), they appeal to a law of the Pentateuch (Dt 25:5–10) and present a case based on it that would make resurrection from the dead ridiculous (Mt 22:24–28). Jesus chides them for knowing neither **the scriptures** nor **the power of God** (Mt 22:29). His argument in respect to God's power contradicts the notion, held even by many proponents as well as by opponents of the teaching, that the life of those raised from the dead would be essentially a continuation of the type of life they had had before death (Mt 22:30). His argument based on the scriptures (Mt 22:31–32) is of a sort that was accepted as valid among Jews of the time.

* [22:23] **Saying that there is no resurrection**: in the Marcan parallel (Mk 22:12, 18) the Sadducees are correctly defined as those "who say there is no resurrection"; see also Lk 20:27. Matthew's rewording of Mark can mean that these particular Sadducees deny the resurrection, which would imply that he was not aware that the denial was characteristic of the party. For some scholars this is an indication of his being a Gentile Christian; see note on Mt 21:4–5.

* [22:24] **'If a man dies . . . his brother'**: this is known as the "law of the levirate," from the Latin *levir*, "brother-in-law." Its purpose was to continue the family line of the deceased brother (Dt 25:6).

* [22:29] The sexual relationships of this world will be transcended; the risen body will be the work of the creative **power of God**.

* [22:31–32] Cf. Ex 3:6. In the Pentateuch, which the Sadducees accepted as normative for Jewish belief and practice, God speaks even now (**to you**) of himself as the God of the patriarchs who died centuries ago. He identifies himself in relation to them, and because of their relation to him, the living God, they too are alive. This might appear no argument for the resurrection, but simply for life after death as conceived in Wis 3:1–3. But the general thought of early first-century Judaism was not influenced by that conception; for it human immortality was connected with the existence of the body.

* [22:34–40] The Marcan parallel (Mk 12:28–34) is an exchange between Jesus and a scribe who is impressed by the way in which Jesus has conducted himself in the previous controversy (Mk 12:28), who compliments him for the answer he gives him (Mk 12:32), and who is said by Jesus to be "not far from the kingdom of God" (Mk 12:34). Matthew has sharpened that scene. The questioner, as the representative of other Pharisees, tests Jesus by his question (Mt 22:34–35), and both his reaction to Jesus' reply and Jesus' commendation of him are lacking.

* [22:35] [**A scholar of the law**]: meaning "scribe." Although this reading is supported by the vast majority of textual witnesses, it is the only time that the Greek word so translated occurs in Matthew. It is relatively frequent in Luke, and there is reason to think that it may have been added here by a copyist since it occurs in the Lucan parallel (Lk 10:25–28). **Tested**: see note on Mt 19:3.

* [22:36] For the devout Jew all the commandments were to be kept with equal care, but there is evidence of preoccupation in Jewish sources with the question put to Jesus.

* [22:37–38] Cf. Dt 6:5. Matthew omits the first part of Mark's fuller quotation (Mk 12:29; Dt 6:4–5), probably because he considered its monotheistic emphasis needless for his church. The love of God must engage the total person (**heart, soul, mind**).

* [22:39] Jesus goes beyond the extent of the question put to him and joins **to the greatest and the first commandment** a second, that of **love** of **neighbor**, Lv 19:18; see note on Mt 19:18–19. This combination of the two commandments may already have been present in Judaism.

* [22:40] The double commandment is the source from which **the whole law and the prophets** are derived.

* [22:41–46] Having answered the questions of his opponents in the preceding three controversies, Jesus now puts a question to them about the sonship of the Messiah. Their easy response (Mt 22:43a) is countered by his quoting a verse of Ps 110 that raises a problem for their response (43b–45). They are unable to solve it and **from that day on** their questioning of him is ended.

* [22:41] **The Pharisees . . . questioned them**: Mark is not specific about who are questioned (Mk 12:35).

* [22:42–44] **David's**: this view of the Pharisees was based on such Old Testament texts as Is 11:1–9; Jer 23:5; and Ez 34:23; see also the extrabiblical Psalms of Solomon 17:21. **How, then . . . saying**: Jesus cites Ps 110:1 accepting the Davidic authorship of the psalm, a common view of his time. The psalm was probably composed for the enthronement of a Davidic king of Judah. Matthew assumes that the Pharisees interpret it as referring to the Messiah, although there is no clear evidence that it was so interpreted in the Judaism of Jesus' time. It was widely used in the early church as referring to the exaltation of the risen Jesus. **My lord**: understood as the Messiah.

* [22:45] Since Matthew presents Jesus both as Messiah (Mt 16:16) and as Son of David (Mt 1:1; see also note on Mt 9:27), the question is not meant to imply Jesus' denial of Davidic sonship. It probably means that although he is the Son of David, he is someone greater, Son of Man and Son of God, and recognized as greater by David who calls him my '**lord**.'

---

* [23:1–39] The final section of the narrative part of the fifth book of the gospel is a denunciation by Jesus of the scribes and the Pharisees (see note on Mt 3:7). It depends in part on Mark and Q (cf. Mk 12:38–39; Lk 11:37–52; 13:34–35), but in the main it is peculiar to Matthew. (For the reasons against considering this extensive body of sayings-material either as one of the structural discourses of this gospel or as part of the one that follows in Mt 24–25, see note on Mt 19:1–23:39.) While the tradition of a deep opposition between Jesus and the Pharisees is well founded, this speech reflects an opposition that goes beyond that of Jesus' ministry and must be seen as expressing the bitter conflict between Pharisaic Judaism and the church of Matthew at the time when the gospel was composed. The complaint often made that the speech ignores the positive qualities of Pharisaism and its better representatives is true, but the complaint overlooks the circumstances that gave rise to the invective. Nor is the speech purely anti-Pharisaic. The evangelist discerns in his church many of the same faults that he finds in its opponents and warns his fellow Christians to look to their own conduct and attitudes.

* [23:2–3] **I have taken their seat . . . Moses**: it is uncertain whether this is simply a metaphor for Mosaic teaching authority or refers to an actual **chair** on which the teacher sat. It has been proved that there was a seat so designated in synagogues of a later period than that of this gospel. **Do and observe . . . they tell you**: since the Matthean

Jesus abrogates Mosaic law (Mt 5:31–42), warns his disciples against the teaching of the Pharisees (Mt 14:1–12), and, in this speech, denounces the Pharisees as blind guides in respect to their teaching on oaths (Mt 23:16–22), this commandment **to observe all things whatsoever they** (the scribes and Pharisees) **tell you** cannot be taken as the evangelist's understanding of the proper standard of conduct for his church. The saying may reflect a period when the Matthean community was largely Jewish Christian and was still seeking to avoid a complete break with the synagogue. Matthew has incorporated this traditional material into the speech in accordance with his view of the course of salvation history, in which he portrays the time of Jesus' ministry as marked by the fidelity to the law, although with significant pointers to the new situation that would exist after his death and resurrection (see note on Mt 5:17–20). The crowds and the disciples (Mt 23:1) are exhorted not to **follow** the **example** of the Jewish leaders, whose deeds do not conform to their teaching (Mt 23:3).

* [23:4] **Tie up heavy burdens**: see note on Mt 11:28.

* [23:5] To the charge of preaching but not practicing (Mt 23:3), Jesus adds that of acting in order to earn praise. The disciples have already been warned against this same fault (see note on Mt 6:1–18). **Phylacteries**: the Mosaic law required that during prayer small boxes containing parchments on which verses of scripture were written be worn on the left forearm and the forehead (see Ex 13:9, 16; Dt 6:8; 11:18). **Tassels**: see note on Mt 9:20. The widening of **phylacteries** and the lengthening of **tassels** were for the purpose of making these evidences of piety more noticeable.

* [23:6–7] Cf. Mk 12:38–39. '**Rabbi**': literally, "my great one," a title of respect for teachers and leaders.

* [23:8–12] These verses, warning against the use of various titles, are addressed to the disciples alone. While only the title '**Rabbi**' has been said to be used in addressing the scribes and Pharisees (Mt 23:7), the implication is that **Father** and '**Master**' also were. The prohibition of these titles to the disciples suggests that their use was present in Matthew's church. The Matthean Jesus forbids not only the titles but the spirit of superiority and pride that is shown by their acceptance. **Whoever exalts . . . will be exalted**: cf. Lk 14:11.

* [23:13–36] This series of seven "woes," directed against the **scribes and Pharisees** and addressed to them, is the heart of the speech. The phrase **woe to** occurs often in the prophetic and apocalyptic literature, expressing horror of a sin and punishment for those who commit it. **Hypocrites**: see note on Mt 6:2. The hypocrisy of the **scribes and Pharisees** consists in the difference between their speech and action (Mt 23:3) and in

demonstrations of piety that have no other purpose than to enhance their reputation as religious persons (Mt 23:5).

* [23:13] **You lock the kingdom of heaven**: cf. Mt 16:19 where Jesus tells Peter that he will give him the keys to the **kingdom of heaven**. The purpose of the authority expressed by that metaphor is to give entrance into the kingdom (the kingdom is closed only to those who reject the authority); here the charge is made that the authority of the **scribes and Pharisees** is exercised in such a way as to be an obstacle to entrance. Cf. Lk 11:52 where the accusation against the "scholars of the law" (Matthew's **scribes**) is that they "have taken away the key of knowledge."

* [23:14] Some manuscripts add a verse here or after Mt 23:12, "Woe to you, scribes and Pharisees, you hypocrites. You devour the houses of widows and, as a pretext, recite lengthy prayers. Because of this, you will receive a very severe condemnation." Cf. Mk 12:40; Lk 20:47. This "woe" is almost identical with Mk 12:40 and seems to be an interpolation derived from that text.

* [23:15] In the first century A.D. until the First Jewish Revolt against Rome (A.D. 66–70), many Pharisees conducted a vigorous missionary campaign among Gentiles. **Convert**: literally, "proselyte," a Gentile who accepted Judaism fully by submitting to circumcision and all other requirements of Mosaic law. **Child of Gehenna**: worthy of everlasting punishment; for **Gehenna**, see note on Mt 5:22. **Twice as much as yourselves**: possibly this refers simply to the zeal of the **convert**, surpassing that of the one who converted him.

* [23:16–22] An attack on that casuistry that declared some oaths binding (**one is obligated**) and others not (**it means nothing**) and held the binding oath to be the one made by something of lesser value (**the gold; the gift on the altar**). Such teaching, which inverts the order of values, reveals the teachers to be **blind guides**; cf. Mt 15:14. Since the Matthean Jesus forbids all oaths to his disciples (Mt 5:33–37), this woe does not set up a standard for Christian moral conduct, but ridicules the Pharisees on their own terms.

* [23:23] The Mosaic law ordered tithing of the produce of the land (Lv 27:30; Dt 14:22–23), and the scribal tradition is said here to have extended this law to even the smallest herbs. The practice is criticized not in itself but because it shows the Pharisees' preoccupation with matters of less importance while they neglect **the weightier things of the law**.

* [23:24] Cf. Lv 11:41–45 that forbids the eating of any "swarming creature." The Pharisees' scrupulosity about minor matters and neglect of greater ones (Mt 23:23) is further brought out by this contrast between straining liquids that might contain a tiny "swarming creature" and yet swallowing **the camel**. The latter was one of the

unclean animals forbidden by the law (Lv 11:4), but it is hardly possible that the scribes and Pharisees are being denounced as guilty of so gross a violation of the food laws. To **swallow the camel** is only a hyperbolic way of speaking of their neglect of what is important.

* [23:25–26] The ritual washing of utensils for dining (cf. Mk 7:4) is turned into a metaphor illustrating a concern for appearances while inner purity is ignored. The **scribes and Pharisees** are compared to cups carefully washed on the outside but filthy within. **Self-indulgence:** the Greek word here translated means lack of self-control, whether in drinking or in sexual conduct.

* [23:27–28] The sixth **woe**, like the preceding one, deals with concern for externals and neglect of what is **inside**. Since contact with dead bodies, even when one was unaware of it, caused ritual impurity (Nm 19:11–22), tombs were whitewashed so that no one would contract such impurity inadvertently.

* [23:29–36] The final **woe** is the most serious indictment of all. It portrays the **scribes and Pharisees** as standing in the same line as their **ancestors** who murdered **the prophets and the righteous.**

* [23:29–32] In spite of honoring the slain dead by building their **tombs** and adorning their **memorials**, and claiming that they would not have joined in their ancestors' crimes if they **had lived in their days**, the scribes and Pharisees are true children of their ancestors and are defiantly ordered by Jesus to **fill up** what those **ancestors measured out**. This order reflects the Jewish notion that there was an allotted measure of suffering that had to be completed before God's final judgment would take place.

* [23:34–36] There are important differences between the Matthean and the Lucan form of this Q material; cf. Lk 11:49–51. In Luke the one who sends the emissaries is the "wisdom of God." If, as many scholars think, that is the original wording of Q, Matthew, by making Jesus the sender, has presented him as the personified divine wisdom. In Luke, wisdom's emissaries are the Old Testament "prophets" and the Christian "apostles." Matthew's **prophets and wise men and scribes** are probably Christian disciples alone; cf. Mt 10:41 and see note on Mt 13:52. **You will kill:** see Mt 24:9. **Scourge in your synagogues . . . town to town:** see Mt 10:17, 23 and the note on Mt 10:17. **All the righteous blood shed upon the earth:** the slaying of the disciples is in continuity with all the shedding of **righteous blood** beginning with that of Abel. The persecution of Jesus' disciples by **this generation** involves the persecutors in the guilt of their murderous ancestors. **The blood of Zechariah:** see note on Lk 11:51. By identifying him as **the son of Barachiah** Matthew understands

him to be Zechariah the Old Testament minor prophet; see Zec 1:1.

* [23:37–39] Cf. Lk 13:34–35. The denunciation of Pharisaic Judaism ends with this lament over **Jerusalem**, which has repeatedly rejected and murdered those whom God has **sent** to her. **How many times:** this may refer to various visits of Jesus to the city, an aspect of his ministry found in John but otherwise not in the synoptics. **As a hen . . . under her wings:** for imagery similar to this, see Ps 17:8; 91:4. **Your house . . . desolate:** probably an allusion to the destruction of the temple in A.D. 70. **You will not see me . . . in the name of the Lord:** Israel will not see Jesus again until he comes in glory for the final judgment. The acclamation has been interpreted in contrasting ways, as an indication that Israel will at last accept Jesus at that time, and as its troubled recognition of him as its dreaded judge who will pronounce its condemnation; in support of the latter view see Mt 24:30.

---

* [24:1–25:46] The discourse of the fifth book, the last of the five around which the gospel is structured. It is called the "eschatological" discourse since it deals with the coming of the new age (the *eschaton*) in its fullness, with events that will precede it, and with how the disciples are to conduct themselves while awaiting an event that is as certain as its exact time is unknown to all but the Father (Mt 24:36). The discourse may be divided into two parts, Mt 24:1–44 and Mt 24:45–25:46. In the first, Matthew follows his Marcan source (Mk 13:1–37) closely. The second is drawn from Q and from the evangelist's own traditional material. Both parts show Matthew's editing of his sources by deletions, additions, and modifications. The vigilant waiting that is emphasized in the second part does not mean a cessation of ordinary activity and concentration only on what is to come, but a faithful accomplishment of duties at hand, with awareness that the end, for which the disciples must always be ready, will entail the great judgment by which the everlasting destiny of all will be determined.

* [24:2] As in Mark, Jesus predicts the destruction of the temple. By omitting the Marcan story of the widow's contribution (Mk 12:41–44) that immediately precedes the prediction in that gospel, Matthew has established a close connection between it and Mt 23:38, ". . . your house will be abandoned desolate."

* [24:3] **The Mount of Olives:** see note on Mt 21:1. **The disciples:** cf. Mk 13:3–4 where only Peter, James, John, and Andrew put the question that is answered by the discourse. In both gospels, however, the question is put **privately:** the ensuing discourse is only for those who are **disciples** of Jesus. **When will this happen . . . end of the age?:** Matthew distinguishes carefully between the destruction of the temple (**this**) and the **coming** of Jesus that will bring **the end of the age**. In Mark the two events are more closely connected, a fact that may be explained by Mark's believing that the one would immediately succeed the other. **Coming**: this translates the Greek word *parousia*, which is used in the gospels only here and in Mt 24:27, 37, 39. It designated the official visit of a ruler to a city or the manifestation of a saving deity, and it was used by Christians to refer to the final coming of Jesus in glory, a term first found in the New Testament with that meaning in 1 Thes 2:19. **The end of the age**: see note on Mt 13:39.

* [24:4–14] This section of the discourse deals with calamities in the world (Mt 24:6–7) and in the church (Mt 24:9–12). The former **must happen** before **the end** comes (Mt 24:6), but they are only the **beginning of the labor pains** (Mt 24:8). (It may be noted that the Greek word translated **the end** in Mt 24:6 and in Mt 24:13–14 is not the same as the phrase "the end of the age" in Mt 24:3, although the meaning is the same.) The latter are sufferings of the church, both from within and without, that will last until **the gospel is preached . . . to all nations**. **Then the end will come** and those who have endured the sufferings with fidelity **will be saved** (Mt 24:13–14).

* [24:6–7] The disturbances mentioned here are a commonplace of apocalyptic language, as is the assurance that they **must happen** (see Dn 2:28 LXX), for that is the plan of God. **Kingdom against kingdom**: see Is 19:2.

* [24:8] **The labor pains**: the tribulations leading up to the end of the age are compared to the pains of a woman about to give birth. There is much attestation for rabbinic use of the phrase "the woes (or birth pains) of the Messiah" after the New Testament period, but in at least one instance it is attributed to a rabbi who lived in the late first century A.D. In this Jewish usage it meant the distress of the time preceding the coming of the Messiah; here, the **labor pains** precede the coming of the Son of Man in glory.

* [24:9–12] Matthew has used Mk 13:9–12 in his missionary discourse (Mt 10:17–21) and omits it here. Besides the sufferings, including death, and the hatred of **all nations** that the disciples will have to endure, there will be worse affliction within the church itself. This is described in Mt 24:10–12, which are peculiar to Matthew. **Will be led into sin**: literally, "will be scandalized," probably meaning that they will become apostates; see Mt 13:21 where "fall away" translates the same Greek word as here. **Betray**: in the Greek this is the same word as the **hand over** of Mt 24:9. The handing over to persecution and hatred from outside will have their counterpart within the church. **False prophets**: these are Christians; see note on Mt 7:15–20. **Evildoing**: see Mt 7:23. Because of the apocalyptic nature of much of this discourse,

the literal meaning of this description of the church should not be pressed too hard. However, there is reason to think that Matthew's addition of these verses reflects in some measure the condition of his community.

* [24:14] Except for the last part (**and then the end will come**), this verse substantially repeats Mk 13:10. The Matthean addition raises a problem since what follows in Mt 24:15–23 refers to the horrors of the First Jewish Revolt including the destruction of the temple, and Matthew, writing after that time, knew that the parousia of Jesus was still in the future. A solution may be that the evangelist saw the events of those verses as foreshadowing the cosmic disturbances that he associates with the parousia (Mt 24:29) so that the period in which the former took place could be understood as belonging to the **end**.

* [24:15–28] Cf. Mk 13:14–23; Lk 17:23–24, 37. A further stage in the tribulations that will precede the coming of the Son of Man, and an answer to the question of Mt 24:3a, "when will this (the destruction of the temple) happen?"

* [24:15] **The desolating abomination**: in 167 B.C. the Syrian king Antiochus IV Epiphanes desecrated the temple by setting up in it a statue of Zeus Olympios (see 1 Mc 1:54). That event is referred to in Dn 12:11 LXX as the "desolating abomination" (NAB "horrible abomination") and the same Greek term is used here; cf. also Dn 9:27; 11:31. Although the desecration had taken place before Daniel was written, it is presented there as a future event, and Matthew sees that "prophecy" fulfilled in the desecration of the temple by the Romans. **In the holy place**: the temple; more precise than Mark's **where he should not** (Mk 13:14). **Let the reader understand**: this parenthetical remark, taken from Mk 13:14 invites the reader to realize the meaning of Daniel's "prophecy."

* [24:16] The tradition that the Christians of Jerusalem fled from that city to Pella, a city of Transjordan, at the time of the First Jewish Revolt is found in Eusebius (*Ecclesiastical History* 3.5.3), who attributes the flight to "a certain oracle given by revelation before the war." The tradition is not improbable but the Matthean command, derived from its Marcan source, is vague in respect to the place of flight (**to the mountains**), although some scholars see it as applicable to the flight to Pella.

* [24:17–19] Haste is essential, and the journey will be particularly difficult for women who are burdened with unborn or infant children.

* [24:20] **On the sabbath**: this addition to **in winter** (cf. Mk 13:18) has been understood as an indication that Matthew was addressed to a church still observing the Mosaic law of sabbath rest and the scribal limitations upon the length of journeys that might lawfully be made on that day. That interpretation conflicts with Matthew's view on sabbath observance (cf. Mt 12:1–14).

The meaning of the addition may be that those undertaking on the sabbath a journey such as the one here ordered would be offending the sensibilities of law-observant Jews and would incur their hostility.

* [24:21] For the unparalleled distress of that time, see Dn 12:1.

* [24:26–28] Claims that the Messiah is to be found in some distant or secret place must be ignored. **The coming of the Son of Man** will be as clear as **lightning** is to all and as **the corpse** of an animal is to **vultures**; cf. Lk 17:24, 37. Here there is clear identification of the **Son of Man** and the Messiah; cf. Mt 24:23.

* [24:29] The answer to the question of Mt 24:3b, "What sign will there be of your coming?" **Immediately after . . . those days**: the shortening of time between the preceding **tribulation** and the parousia has been explained as Matthew's use of a supposed device of Old Testament prophecy whereby certainty that a predicted event will occur is expressed by depicting it as imminent. While it is questionable that that is an acceptable understanding of the Old Testament predictions, it may be applicable here, for Matthew knew that the parousia had not come **immediately after** the fall of Jerusalem, and it is unlikely that he is attributing a mistaken calculation of time to Jesus. **The sun . . . be shaken**: cf. Is 13:10, 13.

* [24:30] **The sign of the Son of Man**: perhaps this means **the sign** that is the glorious appearance **of the Son of Man**; cf. Mt 12:39–40 where "the sign of Jonah" is Jonah's being in the "belly of the whale." **Tribes of the earth will mourn**: peculiar to Matthew; cf. Zec 12:12–14. **Coming upon the clouds . . . glory**: cf. Dn 7:13, although there the "one like a son of man" comes to God to receive kingship; here the **Son of Man** comes from heaven for judgment.

* [24:31] **Send out his angels**: cf. Mt 13:41 where they are sent out to collect the wicked for punishment. **Trumpet blast**: cf. Is 27:13; 1 Thes 4:16.

* [24:32–35] Cf. Mk 13:28–31.

* [24:34] The difficulty raised by this verse cannot be satisfactorily removed by the supposition that **this generation** means the Jewish people throughout the course of their history, much less the entire human race. Perhaps for Matthew it means the **generation** to which he and his community belonged.

* [24:36–44] The statement of Mt 24:34 is now counterbalanced by one that declares that the exact time of the parousia is known only to **the Father** (Mt 24:36), and the disciples are warned to be always ready for it. This section is drawn from Mark and Q (cf. Lk 17:26–27, 34–35; 12:39–40).

* [24:36] Many textual witnesses omit **nor the Son**, which follows Mk 13:32. Since its omission can be explained by reluctance to attribute this ignorance to **the Son**, the reading that includes it is probably original.

* [24:37–39] Cf. Lk 17:26–27. **In the days of Noah**: the Old Testament account of the flood lays no emphasis upon what is central for Matthew, i.e., the unexpected coming of the flood upon those who were unprepared for it.

* [24:40–41] Cf. Lk 17:34–35. **Taken . . . left**: the former probably means **taken** into the kingdom; the latter, **left** for destruction. People in the same situation will be dealt with in opposite ways. In this context, the discrimination between them will be based on their readiness for the coming of the Son of Man.

* [24:42–44] Cf. Lk 12:39–40. The theme of vigilance and readiness is continued with the bold comparison of the Son of Man to a thief who comes to break into a house.

* [24:45–51] The second part of the discourse (see note on Mt 24:1–25:46) begins with this parable of **the faithful** or unfaithful **servant**; cf. Lk 12:41–46. It is addressed to the leaders of Matthew's church; **the servant has** been **put in charge** of his master's **household** (Mt 24:45) even though that household is composed of those who are his **fellow servants** (Mt 24:49).

* [24:45] **To distribute . . . proper time**: readiness for the master's return means a vigilance that is accompanied by faithful performance of the duty assigned.

* [24:48] **My master . . . delayed**: the note of delay is found also in the other parables of this section; cf. Mt 25:5, 19.

* [24:51] **Punish him severely**: the Greek verb, found in the New Testament only here and in the Lucan parallel (Lk 12:46), means, literally, "cut in two." **With the hypocrites**: see note on Mt 6:2. Matthew classes the unfaithful Christian leader with the unbelieving leaders of Judaism. **Wailing and grinding of teeth**: see note on Mt 8:11–12.

---

* [25:1–13] Peculiar to Matthew.

* [25:1] **Then**: at the time of the parousia. **Kingdom . . . will be like**: see note on Mt 13:24–30.

* [25:2–4] **Foolish . . . wise**: cf. the contrasted "wise man" and "fool" of Mt 7:24, 26 where the two are distinguished by good deeds and lack of them, and such deeds may be signified by the **oil** of this parable.

* [25:11–12] **Lord, Lord**: cf. Mt 7:21. **I do not know you**: cf. Mt 7:23 where the Greek verb is different but synonymous.

* [25:13] **Stay awake**: some scholars see this command as an addition to the original parable of Matthew's traditional material, since in Mt 25:5 all the virgins, wise and foolish, fall asleep. But the wise virgins are adequately equipped for their task, and stay awake may mean no more than to be prepared; cf. Mt 24:42, 44.

* [25:14–30] Cf. Lk 19:12–27.

* [25:14] **It will be as when . . . journey**: literally, "For just as a man who was going on a journey". Although the comparison is not completed, the sense is clear; kingdom of heaven is like the situation here described. Faithful use of one's gifts will lead to participation in the fullness of the kingdom, lazy inactivity to exclusion from it.

* [25:15] **Talents**: see note on Mt 18:24.

* [25:18] **Buried his master's money**: see note on Mt 13:44.

* [25:20–23] Although the first two servants have received and doubled large sums, their faithful trading is regarded by the master as fidelity **in small matters** only, compared with **the great responsibilities** now to be given to them. The latter are unspecified. **Share your master's joy**: probably the joy of the banquet of the kingdom; cf. Mt 8:11.

* [25:26–28] **Wicked, lazy servant**: this man's inactivity is not negligible but seriously culpable. As punishment, he loses the gift he had received, that is now given to the first servant, whose possessions are already great.

* [25:29] See note on Mt 13:12 where there is a similar application of this maxim.

* [25:30] See note on Mt 8:11–12.

* [25:31–46] The conclusion of the discourse, which is peculiar to Matthew, portrays the final judgment that will accompany the parousia. Although often called a "parable," it is not really such, for the only parabolic elements are the depiction of **the Son of Man** as a **shepherd** and of **the righteous** and the **wicked** as **sheep** and **goats**, respectively (Mt 25:32–33). The criterion of judgment will be the deeds of mercy that have been done for the **least** of Jesus' **brothers** (Mt 25:40). A difficult and important question is the identification of these **least brothers**. Are they all people who have suffered hunger, thirst, etc. (Mt 25:35, 36) or a particular group of such sufferers? Scholars are divided in their response and arguments can be made for either side. But leaving aside the problem of what the traditional material that Matthew edited may have meant, it seems that a stronger case can be made for the view that in the evangelist's sense the sufferers are Christians, probably Christian missionaries whose sufferings were brought upon them by their preaching of the gospel. The criterion of judgment for **all the nations** is their treatment of those who have borne to the world the message of Jesus, and this means ultimately their acceptance or rejection of Jesus himself; cf. Mt 10:40, "Whoever receives you, receives me." See note on Mt 16:27.

* [25:32] **All the nations**: before the end the gospel will have been preached throughout the world (Mt 24:14); thus the Gentiles will be judged on their response to it. But the phrase **all the nations** includes the Jews also, for at the judgment "the Son of Man . . . will repay everyone according to his conduct" (Mt 16:27).

* [25:37–40] **The righteous** will be astonished that in caring for the needs of the sufferers they were ministering to the **Lord** himself. **One of these least brothers of mine**: cf. Mt 10:42.

* [25:41] **Fire prepared . . . his angels**: cf. 1 Enoch 10:13 where it is said of the evil angels and Semyaza, their leader, "In those days they will lead them into the bottom of the fire—and in torment—in the prison (where) they will be locked up forever."

* [25:44–45] The **accursed** (Mt 25:41) will be likewise astonished that their neglect of the sufferers was neglect of the **Lord** and will receive from him a similar answer.

---

* [26:1–28:20] The five books with alternating narrative and discourse (Mt 3:1–25:46) that give this gospel its distinctive structure lead up to the climactic events that are the center of Christian belief and the origin of the Christian church, the passion and resurrection of Jesus. In his passion narrative (Mt 26 and 27) Matthew follows his Marcan source closely but with omissions (e.g., Mk 14:51–52) and additions (e.g., Mt 27:3–10, 19). Some of the additions indicate that he utilized traditions that he had received from elsewhere; others are due to his own theological insight (e.g., Mt 26:28 ". . . for the forgiveness of sins"; Mt 27:52). In his editing Matthew also altered Mark in some minor details. But there is no need to suppose that he knew any passion narrative other than Mark's.

* [26:1–2] **When Jesus finished all these words**: see note on Mt 7:28–29. **"You know . . . crucified"**: Matthew turns Mark's statement of the time (Mk 14:1) into Jesus' final prediction of his passion. **Passover**: see note on Mk 14:1.

* [26:3] **Caiaphas** was high priest from A.D. 18 to 36.

* [26:5] **Not during the festival**: the plan to delay Jesus' arrest and execution until after **the festival** was not carried out, for according to the synoptics he was arrested on the night of Nisan 14 and put to death the following day. No reason is given why the plan was changed.

* [26:6–13] See notes on Mk 14:3–9 and Jn 12:1–8.

* [26:12] **To prepare me for burial**: cf. Mk 14:8. In accordance with the interpretation of this act as Jesus' **burial** anointing, Matthew, more consistent than Mark, changes the purpose of the visit of the women to Jesus' tomb; they do not go to anoint him (Mk 16:1) but "to see the tomb" (Mt 28:1).

* [26:14] **Iscariot**: see note on Lk 6:16.

* [26:15] The motive of avarice is introduced by Judas' question about the price for betrayal, which is absent in the Marcan source (Mk 14:10–11). **Hand him over**: the same Greek verb is used

to express the saving purpose of God by which Jesus is handed over to death (cf. Mt 17:22; 20:18; 26:2) and the human malice that hands him over. **Thirty pieces of silver**: the price of the betrayal is found only in Matthew. It is derived from Zec 11:12 where it is the wages paid to the rejected shepherd, a cheap price (Zec 11:13). That amount is also the compensation paid to one whose slave has been gored by an ox (Ex 21:32).

* [26:17] **The first day of the Feast of Unleavened Bread**: see note on Mk 14:1. Matthew omits Mark's "when they sacrificed the Passover lamb."

* [26:18] By omitting much of Mk 14:13–15, adding **My appointed time draws near**, and turning the question into a statement, **in your house I shall celebrate the Passover**, Matthew has given this passage a solemnity and majesty greater than that of his source.

* [26:21] Given Matthew's interest in the fulfillment of the Old Testament, it is curious that he omits the Marcan designation of Jesus' betrayer as "one who is eating with me" (Mk 14:18), since that is probably an allusion to Ps 41:10. However, the shocking fact that the betrayer is one who shares table fellowship with Jesus is emphasized in Mt 26:23.

* [26:24] **It would be better . . . born**: the enormity of the deed is such that it would be better not to exist than to do it.

* [26:25] Peculiar to Matthew. **You have said so**: cf. Mt 26:64; 27:11. This is a half-affirmative. Emphasis is laid on the pronoun and the answer implies that the statement would not have been made if the question had not been asked.

* [26:26–29] See note on Mk 14:22–24. The Marcan-Matthean is one of the two major New Testament traditions of the words of Jesus when instituting the Eucharist. The other (and earlier) is the Pauline-Lucan (1 Cor 11:23–25; Lk 22:19–20). Each shows the influence of Christian liturgical usage, but the Marcan-Matthean is more developed in that regard than the Pauline-Lucan. The words over the bread and cup succeed each other without the intervening meal mentioned in 1 Cor 11:25; Lk 22:20; and there is parallelism between the consecratory words (**this is my body . . . this is my blood**). Matthew follows Mark closely but with some changes.

* [26:26] See note on Mt 14:19. **Said the blessing**: a prayer blessing God. **Take and eat**: literally, **Take, eat**. **Eat** is an addition to Mark's "take it" (literally, "take"; Mk 14:22). **This is my body**: the bread is identified with Jesus himself.

* [26:27–28] **Gave thanks**: see note on Mt 15:36. **Gave it to them . . . all of you**: cf. Mk 14:23–24. In the Marcan sequence the disciples drink and then Jesus says the interpretative words. Matthew has changed this into a command to **drink** followed by those words. **My blood**: see Lv 17:11 for the concept that the **blood** is "the seat of life" and that

when placed on the altar it "makes atonement." **Which will be shed**: the present participle, "being shed" or "going to be shed," is future in relation to the Last Supper. **On behalf of**: Greek *peri*; see note on Mk 14:24. **Many**: see note on Mt 20:28. **For the forgiveness of sins**: a Matthean addition. The same phrase occurs in Mk 1:4 in connection with John's baptism but Matthew avoids it there (Mt 3:11). He places it here probably because he wishes to emphasize that it is the sacrificial death of Jesus that brings **forgiveness of sins**.

* [26:29] Although his death will interrupt the table fellowship he has had with the disciples, Jesus confidently predicts his vindication by God and a new table fellowship with them at the banquet of the kingdom.

* [26:30] See note on Mk 14:26.

* [26:31] **Will have . . . shaken**: literally, "will be scandalized in me"; see note on Mt 24:9–12. **I will strike . . . dispersed**: cf. Zec 13:7.

* [26:34] **Before the cock crows**: see note on Mt 14:25. The third watch of the night was called "cockcrow." **Deny me**: see note on Mt 16:24.

* [26:36–56] Cf. Mk 14:32–52. The account of Jesus in Gethsemane is divided between that of his agony (Mt 26:36–46) and that of his betrayal and arrest (Mt 26:47–56). Jesus' **sorrow and distress** (Mt 26:37) in face of death is unrelieved by the presence of his three disciples who, though urged to **watch with** him (Mt 26:38, 41), fall asleep (Mt 26:40, 43). He prays that **if . . . possible** his death may be avoided (Mt 26:39) but that his Father's will be done (Mt 26:39, 42, 44). Knowing then that his death must take place, he announces to his companions that **the hour** for his being **handed over** has come (Mt 26:45). Judas arrives with an armed band provided by the Sanhedrin and greets Jesus with a kiss, the prearranged sign for his identification (Mt 26:47–49). After his arrest, he rebukes a disciple who has attacked the **high priest's servant** with a **sword** (Mt 26:51–54), and chides those who have come out to seize him with **swords and clubs** as if he were a **robber** (Mt 26:55–56). In both rebukes Jesus declares that the treatment he is now receiving is the fulfillment of the scriptures (Mt 26:55, 56). The subsequent flight of **all the disciples** is itself the fulfillment of his own prediction (cf. 31). In this episode, Matthew follows Mark with a few alterations.

* [26:36] **Gethsemane**: the Hebrew name means "oil press" and designates an olive orchard on the western slope of the Mount of Olives; see note on Mt 21:1. The name appears only in Matthew and Mark. The place is called a "garden" in Jn 18:1.

* [26:37] **Peter and the two sons of Zebedee**: cf. Mt 17:1.

* [26:38] Cf. Ps 42:6, 12. In the Septuagint (Ps 41:5, 12) the same Greek word for **sorrowful** is used as here. **To death**: i.e., "enough to die"; cf. Jon 4:9.

* [26:39] **My Father**: see note on Mk 14:36. Matthew omits the Aramaic *'abbā'* and adds the qualifier **my. This cup**: see note on Mk 10:38–40.

* [26:41] **Undergo the test**: see note on Mt 6:13. In that verse "the final test" translates the same Greek word as is here translated **the test**, and these are the only instances of the use of that word in Matthew. It is possible that the passion of Jesus is seen here as an anticipation of the great tribulation that will precede the parousia (see notes on Mt 24:8; 24:21) to which Mt 6:13 refers, and that just as Jesus prays to be delivered from death (Mt 26:39), so he exhorts the disciples to pray that they will not have to **undergo the** great **test** that his passion would be for them. Some scholars, however, understand **not undergo** (literally, "not enter") **the test** as meaning not that the disciples may be spared **the test** but that they may not yield to the temptation of falling away from Jesus because of his passion even though they will have to endure it.

* [26:42] **Your will be done**: cf. Mt 6:10.

* [26:49] **Rabbi**: see note on Mt 23:6–7. Jesus is so addressed twice in Matthew (Mt 26:25), both times by Judas. For the significance of the closely related address "teacher" in Matthew, see note on Mt 8:19.

* [26:55] **Day after day . . . arrest me**: cf. Mk 14:49. This suggests that Jesus had taught for a relatively long period in Jerusalem, whereas Mt 21:1–11 puts his coming to the city for the first time only a few days before.

* [26:57–68] Following Mk 14:53–65 Matthew presents the nighttime appearance of Jesus before the **Sanhedrin** as a real trial. After **many false witnesses** bring charges against him that do not suffice for the death sentence (Mt 26:60), **two came forward** who charge him with claiming to be able to **destroy the temple . . . and within three days** to **rebuild it** (Mt 26:60–61). Jesus makes no answer even when challenged to do so by **the high priest**, who then orders him to declare **under oath . . . whether** he is the **Messiah, the Son of God** (Mt 26:62–63). Matthew changes Mark's clear affirmative response (Mk 14:62) to the same one as that given to Judas (Mt 26:25), but follows Mark almost verbatim in Jesus' predicting that his judges will see him (**the Son of Man**) **seated at the right hand of God and coming on the clouds of heaven** (Mt 26:64). **The high priest** then charges him with blasphemy (Mt 26:65), a charge with which the other members of **the Sanhedrin** agree by declaring that **he deserves to die** (Mt 26:66). They then attack him (Mt 26:67) and mockingly demand that he **prophesy** (Mt 26:68). This account contains elements that are contrary to the judicial procedures prescribed in the Mishnah, the Jewish code of law that dates in written form from ca. A.D. 200, e.g., trial on a feast day, a night session of the court, pronouncement of

a verdict of condemnation at the same session at which testimony was received. Consequently, some scholars regard the account entirely as a creation of the early Christians without historical value. However, it is disputable whether the norms found in the Mishnah were in force at the time of Jesus. More to the point is the question whether the Matthean-Marcan night trial derives from a combination of two separate incidents, a nighttime preliminary investigation (cf. Jn 18:13, 19–24) and a formal trial on the following morning (cf. Lk 22:66–71).

* [26:57] **Caiaphas**: see note on Mt 26:3.

* [26:59] **Sanhedrin**: see note on Lk 22:66.

* [26:60–61] **Two**: cf. Dt 19:15. **I can destroy . . . rebuild it**: there are significant differences from the Marcan parallel (Mk 14:58). Matthew omits "made with hands" and "not made with hands" and changes Mark's "will destroy" and "will build another" to **can destroy** and (can) **rebuild**. The charge is probably based on Jesus' prediction of the temple's destruction; see notes on Mt 23:37–39; 24:2; and Jn 2:19. A similar prediction by Jeremiah was considered as deserving death; cf. Jer 7:1–15; 26:1–8.

* [26:63] **Silent**: possibly an allusion to Is 53:7. **I order you . . . living God**: peculiar to Matthew; cf. Mk 14:61.

* [26:64] **You have said so**: see note on Mt 26:25. **From now on . . . heaven**: the Son of Man who is to be crucified (cf. Mt 20:19) will be seen in glorious majesty (cf. Ps 110:1) and **coming on the clouds of heaven** (cf. Dn 7:13). **The Power**: see note on Mk 14:61–62.

* [26:65] **Blasphemed**: the punishment for **blasphemy** was death by stoning (see Lv 24:10–16). According to the Mishnah, to be guilty of blasphemy one had to pronounce "the Name itself," i.e., Yahweh; cf. *Sanhedrin* 7:4, 5. Those who judge the gospel accounts of Jesus' trial by the later Mishnah standards point out that Jesus uses the surrogate "the Power," and hence no Jewish court would have regarded him as guilty of blasphemy; others hold that the Mishnah's narrow understanding of blasphemy was a later development.

* [26:67–68] The physical abuse, apparently done to Jesus by the members of the Sanhedrin themselves, recalls the sufferings of the Isaian Servant of the Lord; cf. Is 50:6. The mocking challenge to **prophesy** is probably motivated by Jesus' prediction of his future glory (Mt 26:64).

* [26:70] **Denied it in front of everyone**: see Mt 10:33. Peter's repentance (Mt 26:75) saves him from the fearful destiny of which Jesus speaks there.

* [26:73] **Your speech . . . away**: Matthew explicates Mark's "you too are a Galilean" (Mk 14:70).

---

* [27:1–31] Cf. Mk 15:1–20. Matthew's account of the Roman trial before **Pilate** is introduced

by a consultation of the Sanhedrin after which Jesus is **handed over to . . . the governor** (Mt 27:1–2). Matthew follows his Marcan source closely but adds some material that is peculiar to him, the death of **Judas** (Mt 27:3–10), possibly the name **Jesus** as the name of **Barabbas** also (Mt 27:16–17), the intervention of Pilate's **wife** (Mt 27:19), Pilate's washing **his hands** in token of his disclaiming responsibility for Jesus' death (Mt 27:24), and the assuming of that responsibility by **the whole people** (Mt 27:25).

* [27:1] There is scholarly disagreement about the meaning of the Sanhedrin's taking **counsel** (*symboulion elabon*; cf. Mt 12:14; 22:15; 27:7; 28:12); see note on Mk 15:1. Some understand it as a discussion about the strategy for putting their death sentence against Jesus into effect since they lacked the right to do so themselves. Others see it as the occasion for their passing that sentence, holding that Matthew, unlike Mark (Mk 14:64), does not consider that it had been passed in the night session (Mt 26:66). Even in the latter interpretation, their handing **him over to Pilate** is best explained on the hypothesis that they did not have competence to put their sentence into effect, as is stated in Jn 18:31.

* [27:3] **The thirty pieces of silver**: see Mt 26:15.

* [27:5–8] For another tradition about the death of Judas, cf. Acts 1:18–19. The two traditions agree only in the purchase of a field with **the money** paid to Judas for his betrayal of Jesus and the name given to the field, **the Field of Blood**. In Acts Judas himself buys the field and its name comes from his own blood shed in his fatal accident on it. **The potter's field**: this designation of the field is based on the fulfillment citation in Mt 27:10.

* [27:9–10] Cf. Mt 26:15. Matthew's attributing this text to Jeremiah is puzzling, for there is no such text in that book, and **the thirty pieces of silver** thrown by Judas "into the temple" (Mt 27:5) recall rather Zec 11:12–13. It is usually said that the attribution of the text to Jeremiah is due to Matthew's combining the Zechariah text with texts from Jeremiah that speak of a **potter** (Jer 18:2–3), the buying of a **field** (Jer 32:6–9), or the breaking of a potter's flask at Topheth in the valley of Ben-Hinnom with the prediction that it will become a burial place (Jer 19:1–13).

* [27:11] **King of the Jews**: this title is used of Jesus only by pagans. The Matthean instances are, besides this one, Mt 2:2; 27:29, 37. Matthew equates it with "Messiah"; cf. Mt 2:2, 4 and Mt 27:17, 22 where he has changed "the king of the Jews" of his Marcan source (Mk 15:9, 12) to "(Jesus) called Messiah." The normal political connotation of both titles would be of concern to the Roman **governor**. **You say so**: see note on Mt 26:25. An unqualified affirmative response is not

made because Jesus' kingship is not what Pilate would understand it to be.

* [27:12–14] Cf. Mt 26:62–63. As in the trial before the Sanhedrin, Jesus' silence may be meant to recall Is 53:7. **Greatly amazed**: possibly an allusion to Is 52:14–15.

* [27:15–26] The choice that Pilate offers **the crowd** between **Barabbas** and **Jesus** is said to be in accordance with a custom of releasing at the Passover feast **one prisoner** chosen by **the crowd** (Mt 27:15). This custom is mentioned also in Mk 15:6 and Jn 18:39 but not in Luke; see note on Lk 23:17. Outside of the gospels there is no direct attestation of it, and scholars are divided in their judgment of the historical reliability of the claim that there was such a practice.

* [27:16–17] **[Jesus] Barabbas**: it is possible that the double name is the original reading; **Jesus** was a common Jewish name; see note on Mt 1:21. This reading is found in only a few textual witnesses, although its absence in the majority can be explained as an omission of **Jesus** made for reverential reasons. That name is bracketed because of its uncertain textual attestation. The Aramaic name **Barabbas** means "son of the father"; the irony of the choice offered between him and Jesus, the true son of the Father, would be evident to those addressees of Matthew who knew that.

* [27:18] Cf. Mk 14:10. This is an example of the tendency, found in varying degree in all the gospels, to present Pilate in a relatively favorable light and emphasize the hostility of the Jewish authorities and eventually of the people.

* [27:19] Jesus' innocence is declared by a Gentile woman. **In a dream**: in Matthew's infancy narrative, dreams are the means of divine communication; cf. Mt 1:20; 2:12, 13, 19, 22.

* [27:22] **Let him be crucified**: incited by the chief priests and elders (Mt 27:20), the crowds demand that Jesus be executed by crucifixion, a peculiarly horrible form of Roman capital punishment. The Marcan parallel, "Crucify him" (Mk 15:3), addressed to Pilate, is changed by Matthew to the passive, probably to emphasize the responsibility of the crowds.

* [27:24–25] Peculiar to Matthew. **Took water . . . blood**: cf. Dt 21:1–8, the handwashing prescribed in the case of a murder when the killer is unknown. The elders of the city nearest to where the corpse is found must wash their hands, declaring, "Our hands did not shed this blood." **Look to it yourselves**: cf. Mt 27:4. **The whole people**: Matthew sees in those who speak these words the entire people (Greek *laos*) of Israel. **His blood . . . and upon our children**: cf. Jer 26:15. The responsibility for Jesus' death is accepted by the nation that was God's special possession (Ex 19:5), his own **people** (Hos 2:25), and they thereby lose that high privilege; see Mt 21:43 and the note on that verse. The controversy between Matthew's church

and Pharisaic Judaism about which was the true people of God is reflected here. As the Second Vatican Council has pointed out, guilt for Jesus' death is not attributable to all the Jews of his time or to any Jews of later times.

* [27:26] **He had Jesus scourged**: the usual preliminary to crucifixion.

* [27:27] **The praetorium**: the residence of the Roman governor. His usual place of residence was at Caesarea Maritima on the Mediterranean coast, but he went to Jerusalem during the great feasts, when the influx of pilgrims posed the danger of a nationalistic riot. It is disputed whether the **praetorium** in Jerusalem was the old palace of Herod in the west of the city or the fortress of Antonia northwest of the temple area. **The whole cohort**: normally six hundred soldiers.

* [27:28] **Scarlet military cloak**: so Matthew as against the royal purple of Mk 15:17 and Jn 19:2.

* [27:29] **Crown out of thorns**: probably of long **thorns** that stood upright so that it resembled the "radiant" **crown**, a diadem with spikes worn by Hellenistic kings. The soldiers' purpose was mockery, not torture. **A reed**: peculiar to Matthew; a mock scepter.

* [27:30] **Spat upon him**: cf. Mt 26:67 where there also is a possible allusion to Is 50:6.

* [27:32] See note on Mk 15:21. **Cyrenian named Simon**: Cyrenaica was a Roman province on the north coast of Africa and Cyrene was its capital city. The city had a large population of Greek-speaking Jews. **Simon** may have been living in Palestine or have come there for the Passover as a pilgrim. **Pressed into service**: see note on Mt 5:41.

* [27:34] **Wine . . . mixed with gall**: cf. Mk 15:23 where the drink is "wine drugged with myrrh," a narcotic. Matthew's text is probably an inexact allusion to Ps 69:22. That psalm belongs to the class called the individual lament, in which a persecuted just man prays for deliverance in the midst of great suffering and also expresses confidence that his prayer will be heard. That theme of the suffering Just One is frequently applied to the sufferings of Jesus in the passion narratives.

* [27:35] The clothing of an executed criminal went to his executioner(s), but the description of that procedure in the case of Jesus, found in all the gospels, is plainly inspired by Ps 22:19. However, that psalm verse is quoted only in Jn 19:24.

* [27:37] The offense of a person condemned to death by crucifixion was written on a tablet that was displayed on his cross. The **charge** against **Jesus** was that he had claimed to be the **King of the Jews** (cf. Mt 27:11), i.e., the Messiah (cf. Mt 27:17, 22).

* [27:38] **Revolutionaries**: see note on Jn 18:40 where the same Greek word as that found here is used for Barabbas.

* [27:39–40] **Reviled him . . . heads**: cf. Ps 22:8. **You who would destroy . . . three days**; cf. Mt 26:61. **If you are the Son of God**: the same words as those of the devil in the temptation of Jesus; cf. Mt 4:3, 6.

* [27:42] **King of Israel**: in their mocking of Jesus the members of the Sanhedrin call themselves and their people not "the Jews" but **Israel**.

* [27:43] Peculiar to Matthew. **He trusted in God . . . wants him**: cf. Ps 22:9. **He said . . . of God**: probably an allusion to Wis 2:12–20 where the theme of the suffering Just One appears.

* [27:45] Cf. Am 8:9 where on the day of the Lord "the sun will set at midday."

* [27:46] *Eli, Eli, lema sabachthani?*: Jesus cries out in the words of Ps 22:2a, a psalm of lament that is the Old Testament passage most frequently drawn upon in this narrative. In Mark the verse is cited entirely in Aramaic, which Matthew partially retains but changes the invocation of God to the Hebrew *Eli*, possibly because that is more easily related to the statement of the following verse about Jesus' calling for Elijah.

* [27:47] **Elijah**: see note on Mt 3:4. This prophet, taken up into heaven (2 Kgs 2:11), was believed to come to the help of those in distress, but the evidences of that belief are all later than the gospels.

* [27:50] **Gave up his spirit**: cf. the Marcan parallel (Mk 15:37), "breathed his last." Matthew's alteration expresses both Jesus' control over his destiny and his obedient giving up of his life to God.

* [27:51–53] **Veil of the sanctuary . . . bottom**: cf. Mk 15:38; Lk 23:45. Luke puts this event immediately before the death of Jesus. There were two veils in the Mosaic tabernacle on the model of which the temple was constructed, the outer one before the entrance of the Holy Place and the inner one before the Holy of Holies (see Ex 26:31–36). Only the high priest could pass through the latter and that only on the Day of Atonement (see Lv 16:1–18). Probably the torn veil of the gospels is the inner one. The meaning of the scene may be that now, because of Jesus' death, all people have access to the presence of God, or that the temple, its holiest part standing exposed, is now profaned and will soon be destroyed. **The earth quaked . . . appeared to many**: peculiar to Matthew. The earthquake, the splitting of the **rocks**, and especially the resurrection of the dead **saints** indicate the coming of the final age. In the Old Testament the coming of God is frequently portrayed with the imagery of an earthquake (see Ps 68:9; 77:19), and Jesus speaks of the earthquakes that will accompany the "labor pains" that signify the beginning of the dissolution of the old world (Mt 24:7–8). For the expectation of the resurrection of the dead at the coming of the new and final age, see Dn 12:1–3. Matthew knows that the end

of the old age has not yet come (Mt 28:20), but the new age has broken in with the death (and resurrection; cf. the earthquake in Mt 28:2) of Jesus; see note on Mt 16:28. **After his resurrection**: this qualification seems to be due to Matthew's wish to assert the primacy of Jesus' **resurrection** even though he has placed the resurrection of the dead **saints** immediately after Jesus' death.

* [27:54] Cf. Mk 15:39. The Christian confession of faith is made by Gentiles, not only the **centurion**, as in Mark, but the other soldiers **who were keeping watch over Jesus** (cf. Mt 27:36).

* [27:55–56] **Looking on from a distance**: cf. Ps 38:12. **Mary Magdalene . . . Joseph**: these two women are mentioned again in Mt 27:61 and Mt 28:1 and are important as witnesses of the reality of the empty tomb. A **James and Joseph** are referred to in Mt 13:55 as brothers of Jesus.

* [27:57–61] Cf. Mk 15:42–47. Matthew drops Mark's designation of **Joseph** of **Arimathea** as "a distinguished member of the council" (the Sanhedrin), and makes him **a rich man** and **a disciple of Jesus**. The former may be an allusion to Is 53:9 (the Hebrew reading of that text is disputed and the one followed in the NAB OT has nothing about the rich, but they are mentioned in the LXX version). That the tomb was the **new tomb** of **a rich man** and that it was seen by the women are indications of an apologetic intent of Matthew; there could be no question about the identity of Jesus' burial place. **The other Mary**: the mother of James and Joseph (Mt 27:56).

* [27:62–66] Peculiar to Matthew. The story prepares for Mt 28:11–15 and the Jewish charge that the tomb was empty because the disciples had stolen the body (see Mt 28:13, 15).

* [27:62] **The next day . . . preparation**: the sabbath. According to the synoptic chronology, in that year **the day of preparation** (for the sabbath) was the Passover; cf. Mk 15:42. **The Pharisees**: the principal opponents of Jesus during his ministry and, in Matthew's time, of the Christian church, join with **the chief priests** to guarantee against a possible attempt of Jesus' **disciples** to steal his body.

* [27:64] **This last imposture . . . the first**: the claim that Jesus **has been raised from the dead** is clearly the **last imposture; the first** may be either his claim that he would **be raised up** (Mt 27:63) or his claim that he was the one with whose ministry the kingdom of God had come (see Mt 12:28).

* [27:65] **The guard is yours**: literally, "have a guard" or "you have a guard." Either the imperative or the indicative could mean that Pilate granted the petitioners some Roman soldiers as guards, which is the sense of the present translation. However, if the verb is taken as an indicative it could also mean that Pilate told them to use their own Jewish guards.

* [28:1–20] Except for Mt 28:1–8 based on Mk 16:1–8, the material of this final chapter is peculiar to Matthew. Even where he follows Mark, Matthew has altered his source so greatly that a very different impression is given from that of the Marcan account. The two points that are common to the resurrection testimony of all the gospels are that the tomb of Jesus had been found empty and that the risen Jesus had appeared to certain persons, or, in the original form of Mark, that such an appearance was promised as soon to take place (see Mk 16:7). On this central and all-important basis, Matthew has constructed an account that interprets the resurrection as the turning of the ages (Mt 28:2–4), shows the Jewish opposition to Jesus as continuing **to the present** in the claim that the resurrection is a deception perpetrated by the **disciples** who stole his body from the tomb (Mt 28:11–15), and marks a new stage in the mission of **the disciples** once limited to Israel (Mt 10:5–6); now they are to **make disciples of all nations**. In this work they will be strengthened by the presence of the exalted Son of Man, who will be with them **until** the kingdom comes in fullness at **the end of the age** (Mt 28:16–20).

* [28:1] **After the sabbath . . . dawning**: since the sabbath ended at sunset, this could mean in the early evening, for **dawning** can refer to the appearance of the evening star; cf. Lk 23:54. However, it is probable that Matthew means the morning dawn of the day after the sabbath, as in the similar though slightly different text of Mark, "when the sun had risen" (Mk 16:2). **Mary Magdalene and the other Mary**: see notes on Mt 27:55–56; 57–61. **To see the tomb**: cf. Mk 16:1–2 where the purpose of the women's visit is to anoint Jesus' body.

* [28:2–4] Peculiar to Matthew. **A great earthquake**: see note on Mt 27:51–53. **Descended from heaven**: this trait is peculiar to Matthew, although his interpretation of the "young man" of his Marcan source (Mk 16:5) as an **angel** is probably true to Mark's intention; cf. Lk 24:23 where the "two men" of Mt 24:4 are said to be "angels." **Rolled back the stone . . . upon it**: not to allow the risen Jesus to leave the tomb but to make evident that the tomb is empty (see Mt 24:6). Unlike the apocryphal Gospel of Peter (9:35—11:44), the New Testament does not describe the resurrection of Jesus, nor is there anyone who sees it. **His appearance was like lightning . . . snow**: see note on Mt 17:2.

* [28:6–7] Cf. Mk 16:6–7. **Just as he said**: a Matthean addition referring to Jesus' predictions of his resurrection, e.g., Mt 16:21; 17:23; 20:19. **Tell his disciples**: like the angel of the Lord of the infancy narrative, the angel interprets a fact and gives a commandment about what is to be done; cf. Mt 1:20–21. Matthew omits Mark's "and Peter" (Mk 16:7); considering his interest in Peter, this

omission is curious. Perhaps the reason is that the Marcan text may allude to a first appearance of Jesus to Peter alone (cf. 1 Cor 15:5; Lk 24:34) which Matthew has already incorporated into his account of Peter's confession at Caesarea Philippi; see note on Mt 16:16. **He is going . . . Galilee:** like Mk 16:7, a reference to Jesus' prediction at the Last Supper (Mt 26:32; Mk 14:28). Matthew changes Mark's "as he told you" to a declaration of the angel.

* [28:8] Contrast Mk 16:8 where the women in their fear "said nothing to anyone."

* [28:9–10] Although these verses are peculiar to Matthew, there are similarities between them and John's account of the appearance of Jesus to Mary Magdalene (Jn 20:17). In both there is a touching of Jesus' body, and a command of Jesus to bear a message to his disciples, designated as his **brothers.** Matthew may have drawn upon a tradition that appears in a different form in John. Jesus' words to the women are mainly a repetition of those of the angel (Mt 28:5a, 7b).

* [28:11–15] This account indicates that the dispute between Christians and Jews about the empty tomb was not whether the tomb was empty but why.

* [28:16–20] This climactic scene has been called a "proleptic parousia," for it gives a foretaste of the final glorious coming of the Son of Man (Mt 26:64). Then his triumph will be manifest to all; now it is revealed only to **the disciples,** who are commissioned to announce it to **all nations** and bring them to belief in Jesus and obedience to his commandments.

* [28:16] **The eleven:** the number recalls the tragic defection of Judas Iscariot. **To the mountain . . . ordered them:** since the message to the disciples was simply that they were to go to Galilee (Mt 28:10), some think that **the mountain** comes from a tradition of the message known to Matthew and alluded to here. For the significance of **the mountain,** see note on Mt 17:1.

* [28:17] **But they doubted:** the Greek can also be translated, "but some doubted." The verb occurs elsewhere in the New Testament only in Mt 14:31 where it is associated with Peter's being of "little faith." For the meaning of that designation, see note on Mt 6:30.

* [28:18] **All power . . . me:** the Greek word here translated **power** is the same as that found in the LXX translation of Dn 7:13–14 where one "like a son of man" is given **power** and an everlasting kingdom by God. The risen Jesus here claims universal power, i.e., **in heaven and on earth.**

* [28:19] **Therefore:** since universal power belongs to the risen Jesus (Mt 28:18), he gives the eleven a mission that is universal. They are to **make disciples of all nations.** While **all nations** is understood by some scholars as referring only to all Gentiles, it is probable that it included the Jews

as well. **Baptizing them:** baptism is the means of entrance into the community of the risen one, the Church. **In the name of the Father . . . holy Spirit:** this is perhaps the clearest expression in the New Testament of trinitarian belief. It may have been the baptismal formula of Matthew's church, but primarily it designates the effect of baptism, the union of the one baptized with the Father, Son, and holy Spirit.

* [28:20] **All that I have commanded you:** the moral teaching found in this gospel, preeminently that of the Sermon on the Mount (Mt 5–7). The commandments of Jesus are the standard of Christian conduct, not the Mosaic law as such, even though some of the Mosaic commandments have now been invested with the authority of Jesus. **Behold, I am with you always:** the promise of Jesus' real though invisible presence echoes the name Emmanuel given to him in the infancy narrative; see note on Mt 1:23. **End of the age:** see notes on Mt 13:39 and Mt 24:3.

THE GOSPEL ACCORDING TO MARK

INTRODUCTION

This shortest of all New Testament gospels is likely the first to have been written, yet it often tells of Jesus' ministry in more detail than either Matthew or Luke (for example, the miracle stories at Mk 5:1–20 or Mk 9:14–29). It recounts what Jesus did in a vivid style, where one incident follows directly upon another. In this almost breathless narrative, Mark stresses Jesus' message about the kingdom of God now breaking into human life as good news (Mk 1:14–15) and Jesus himself as the gospel of God (Mk 1:1; 8:35; 10:29). Jesus is the Son whom God has sent to rescue humanity by serving and by sacrificing his life (Mk 10:45).

The opening verse about good news in Mark (Mk 1:1) serves as a title for the entire book. The action begins with the appearance of John the Baptist, a messenger of God attested by scripture. But John points to a mightier one, Jesus, at whose baptism God speaks from heaven, declaring Jesus his Son. The Spirit descends upon Jesus, who eventually, it is promised, will baptize "with the holy Spirit." This presentation of who Jesus really is (Mk 1:1–13) is rounded out with a brief reference to the temptation of Jesus and how Satan's attack fails. Jesus as Son of God will be victorious, a point to be remembered as one reads of Jesus' death and the enigmatic ending to Mark's Gospel.

The key verses at Mk 1:14–15, which are programmatic, summarize what Jesus proclaims as gospel: fulfillment, the nearness of the kingdom, and therefore the need for repentance and for faith. After the call of the first four disciples, all fishermen (Mk 1:16–20), we see Jesus engaged in teaching (Mk 1:21, 22, 27), preaching (Mk 1:38, 39), and healing (Mk 1:29–31, 34, 40–45), and exorcising demons (Mk 1:22–27, 34–39). The content of Jesus' teaching is only rarely stated, and then chiefly in parables (Mk 4) about the kingdom. His cures, especially on the sabbath (Mk 3:1–5); his claim, like God, to forgive sins (Mk 2:3–12); his table fellowship with tax collectors and sinners (Mk 2:14–17); and the statement that his followers need not now fast but should rejoice while Jesus is present (Mk 2:18–22), all stir up opposition that will lead to Jesus' death (Mk 3:6).

In Mark, Jesus is portrayed as immensely popular with the people in Galilee during his ministry (Mk 2:2; 3:7; 4:1). He appoints twelve disciples to help preach and drive out demons, just as he does (Mk 3:13–19). He continues to work many miracles; the blocks Mk 4:35–6:44 and Mk 6:45–7:10 are cycles of stories about healings, miracles at the Sea of Galilee, and marvelous feedings of the crowds. Jesus' teaching in Mk 7 exalts the word of God over "the tradition of the elders" and sees defilement as a matter of the heart, not of unclean foods. Yet opposition mounts. Scribes charge that Jesus is possessed by Beelzebul (Mk 3:22). His relatives think him "out of his mind" (Mk 3:21). Jesus' kinship is with those who do the will of God, in a new eschatological family, not even with mother, brothers, or sisters by blood ties (Mk 3:31–35; cf. Mk 6:1–6). But all too often his own disciples do not understand Jesus (Mk 4:13, 40; 6:52; 8:17–21). The fate of John the Baptist (Mk 6:17–29) hints ominously at Jesus' own passion (Mk 9:13; cf. Mk 8:31).

A breakthrough seemingly comes with Peter's confession that Jesus is the Christ (Messiah; Mk 8:27–30). But Jesus himself emphasizes his passion (Mk 8:31; 9:31; 10:33–34), not glory in the kingdom (Mk 10:35–45). Momentarily he is glimpsed in his true identity when he is transfigured before three of the disciples (Mk 9:2–8), but by and large Jesus is depicted in Mark as moving obediently along the way to his cross in Jerusalem. Occasionally there are miracles (Mk 9:17–27; 10:46–52; 11:12–14, 20–21, the only such account in Jerusalem), sometimes teachings (Mk 10:2–11, 23–31), but the greatest concern is with discipleship (Mk 8:34–9:1; 9:33–50). For the disciples do not grasp the mystery being revealed (Mk 9:32; 10:32, 38). One of them will betray him, Judas (Mk 14:10–11, 43–45); one will deny him, Peter (Mk 14:27, 31, 54, 66–72); all eleven men will desert Jesus (Mk 14:27, 50).

The passion account, with its condemnation of Jesus by the Sanhedrin (Mk 14:53, 55–65; 15:1a) and sentencing by Pilate (Mk 15:1b–15), is prefaced with the entry into Jerusalem (Mk 11:1–11), ministry and controversies there (Mk 11:15–12:44), Jesus' Last Supper with the disciples (Mk 14:1–26), and his arrest at Gethsemane (Mk 14:32–52). A chapter of apocalyptic tone about the destruction of the temple (Mk 13:1–2, 14–23) and the coming of the Son of Man (Mk 13:24–27), a discourse filled with promises (Mk 13:11, 31) and admonitions to be watchful (Mk 13:2, 23, 37), is significant for Mark's Gospel, for it helps one see that God, in Jesus, will be victorious after the cross and at the end of history.

The Gospel of Mark ends in the most ancient manuscripts with an abrupt scene at Jesus' tomb, which the women find empty (Mk 16:1–8). His own prophecy of Mk 14:28 is reiterated, that Jesus goes before the disciples into Galilee; "there you will see him." These words may imply resurrection appearances there, or Jesus' parousia there, or the start of Christian mission, or a return to the roots depicted in Mk 1:9, 14–15 in Galilee. Other hands have attached additional endings after Mk 16:8; see note on Mk 16:9–20.

The framework of Mark's Gospel is partly geographical: Galilee (Mk 1:14–9:49), through the area "across the Jordan" (Mk 10:1) and through Jericho (Mk 10:46–52), to Jerusalem (Mk 11:1–16:8). Only rarely does Jesus go into Gentile territory (Mk 5:1–20; 7:24–37), but those who acknowledge him there and the centurion who confesses Jesus at the cross (Mk 15:39) presage the gospel's expansion into the world beyond Palestine.

Mark's Gospel is even more oriented to christology. Jesus is the Son of God (Mk 1:11; 9:7; 15:39; cf. Mk 1:1; 14:61). He is the Messiah, the anointed king of Davidic descent (Mk 12:35; 15:32), the Greek for which, *Christos*, has, by the time Mark wrote, become in effect a proper name (Mk 1:1; 9:41). Jesus is also seen as Son of Man, a term used in Mark not simply as a substitute for "I" or for humanity in general (cf. Mk 2:10, 27–28; 14:21) or with reference to a mighty figure who is to come (Mk 13:26; 14:62), but also in connection with Jesus' predestined, necessary path of suffering and vindication (Mk 8:31; 10:45).

The unfolding of Mark's story about Jesus is sometimes viewed by interpreters as centered around the term "mystery." The word is employed just once, at Mk 4:11, in the singular, and its content there is the kingdom, the open secret that God's reign is now breaking into human life with its reversal of human values. There is a related sense in which Jesus' real identity remained a secret during his lifetime, according to Mark, although demons and demoniacs knew it (Mk 1:24; 3:11; 5:7); Jesus warned against telling of his mighty deeds and revealing his identity (Mk 1:44; 3:12; 5:43; 7:36; 8:26, 30), an injunction sometimes broken (Mk 1:45; cf. Mk 5:19–20). Further, Jesus teaches by parables, according to Mark, in such a way that those "outside" the kingdom do not understand, but only those to whom the mystery has been granted by God.

Mark thus shares with Paul, as well as with other parts of the New Testament, an emphasis on election (Mk 13:20, 22) and upon the gospel as Christ and his cross (cf. 1 Cor 1:23). Yet in Mark the person of Jesus is also depicted with an unaffected naturalness. He reacts to events with authentic human emotion: pity (Mk 1:44), anger (Mk 3:5), triumph (Mk 4:40), sympathy (Mk 5:36; 6:34), surprise (Mk 6:9), admiration (Mk 7:29; 10:21), sadness (Mk 14:33–34), and indignation (Mk 14:48–49).

Although the book is anonymous, apart from the ancient heading "According to Mark" in manuscripts, it has traditionally been assigned to John Mark, in whose mother's house (at Jerusalem) Christians assembled (Acts 12:12). This Mark was a cousin of Barnabas (Col 4:10) and accompanied Barnabas and Paul on a missionary journey (Acts 12:25; 13:3; 15:36–39). He appears in Pauline letters (2 Tm 4:11; Phlm 24) and with Peter (1 Pt 5:13). Papias (ca. A.D. 135) described Mark as Peter's "interpreter," a view found in other patristic writers. Petrine influence should not, however, be exaggerated. The evangelist has put together various oral and possibly written sources— miracle stories, parables, sayings, stories of controversies, and the passion—so as to speak of the crucified Messiah for Mark's own day.

Traditionally, the gospel is said to have been written shortly before A.D. 70 in Rome, at a time of impending persecution and when destruction loomed over Jerusalem. Its audience seems to have been Gentile, unfamiliar with Jewish customs (hence Mk 7:3–4, 11). The book aimed to equip such Christians to stand faithful in the face of persecution (Mk 13:9–13), while going on with the proclamation of the gospel begun in Galilee (Mk 13:10; 14:9). Modern research often proposes as the author an unknown Hellenistic Jewish Christian, possibly in Syria, and perhaps shortly after the year 70.

The principal divisions of the Gospel according to Mark are the following:

I.   The Preparation for the Public Ministry of Jesus
      (1:1–13)
II.   The Mystery of Jesus (1:14–8:26)
III. The Mystery Begins to Be Revealed (8:27–9:32)
IV.   The Full Revelation of the Mystery (9:33–16:8)

      The Longer Ending (16:9–20)
      The Shorter Ending
      The Freer Logion (in the note on 16:9–20)

I. THE PREPARATION FOR THE PUBLIC MINISTRY OF JESUS[*]

CHAPTER 1

[1]The beginning of the gospel of Jesus Christ [the Son of God].[*]

The Preaching of John the Baptist. [2a]As it is written in Isaiah the prophet:[*b]

"Behold, I am sending my
    messenger ahead of
    you;
 he will prepare your
    way.
[3c]A voice of one crying out
    in the desert:
 'Prepare the way of the
    Lord,
 make straight his
    paths.'"

[4]John [the] Baptist appeared in the desert proclaiming a baptism of repentance for the forgiveness of sins. [5]People of the whole Judean countryside and all the inhabitants of Jerusalem were going out to him and were being baptized by him in the Jordan River as they acknowledged their sins. [6]John was clothed in camel's hair, with a leather belt around his waist.[*] He fed on locusts and wild honey. [7]And this is what he proclaimed: "One mightier than I is coming after me. I am not worthy to stoop and loosen the thongs of his sandals. [8*d]I have baptized you with water; he will baptize you with the holy Spirit."

The Baptism of Jesus. [9e]It happened in those days that Jesus came from Nazareth of Galilee and was baptized in the Jordan by John. [10]On coming up out of the water he saw the heavens being torn open and the Spirit, like a dove, descending upon him.[*] [11f]And a voice came from the heavens, "You are my beloved Son; with you I am well pleased."

The Temptation of Jesus.*

¹²At once the Spirit drove him out into the desert,^g ¹³and he remained in the desert for forty days, tempted by Satan. He was among wild beasts, and the angels ministered to him.

II. THE MYSTERY OF JESUS

The Beginning of the Galilean Ministry. ^{14h}After John had been arrested,* Jesus came to Galilee proclaiming the gospel of God: ¹⁵ⁱ"This is the time of fulfillment. The kingdom of God is at hand. Repent, and believe in the gospel."

The Call of the First Disciples.* ^{16j}As he passed by the Sea of Galilee, he saw Simon and his brother Andrew casting their nets into the sea; they were fishermen. ¹⁷Jesus said to them, "Come after me,

and I will make you fishers of men." ¹⁸Then they abandoned their nets and followed him. ¹⁹He walked along a little farther and saw James, the son of Zebedee, and his brother John. They too were in a boat mending their nets. ²⁰Then he called them. So they left their father Zebedee in the boat along with the hired men and followed him.

The Cure of a Demoniac.

^{21*k}Then they came to Capernaum, and on the sabbath he entered the synagogue and taught. ^{22l}The people were astonished at his teaching, for he taught them as one having authority and not as the scribes. ^{23*}In their synagogue was a man with an unclean spirit; ^{24*}he cried out, "What have you to do with us,* Jesus of Nazareth? Have you come to destroy us? I know who you are—the Holy One of God!" ²⁵Jesus rebuked him and said, "Quiet! Come out of him!" ²⁶The unclean spirit

convulsed him and with a loud cry came out of him. ²⁷All were amazed and asked one another, "What is this? A new teaching with authority. He commands even the unclean spirits and they obey him." ²⁸His fame spread everywhere throughout the whole region of Galilee.

The Cure of Simon's Mother-in-Law. ²⁹ᵐOn leaving the synagogue he entered the house of Simon and Andrew with James and John. ³⁰Simon's mother-in-law lay sick with a fever. They immediately told him about her. ³¹He approached, grasped her hand, and helped her up. Then the fever left her and she waited on them.

Other Healings. ³²When it was evening, after sunset, they brought to him all who were ill or possessed by demons. ³³The whole town was gathered at the door. ³⁴He cured many who were sick with various diseases, and he drove out many demons, not permitting them to speak because they knew him.

Jesus Leaves Capernaum. ³⁵ⁿRising very early before dawn, he left and went off to a deserted place, where he prayed. ³⁶Simon and those who were with him pursued him ³⁷and on finding him said, "Everyone is looking for you." ³⁸He told them, "Let us go on to the nearby villages that I may preach there also. For this purpose have I come." ³⁹So he went into their synagogues, preaching and driving out demons throughout the whole of Galilee.

The Cleansing of a Leper. ⁴⁰ᵒA leper* came to him [and kneeling down] begged him and said, "If you wish, you can make me clean." ⁴¹Moved with pity, he stretched out his hand, touched him, and said to him, "I do will it. Be made clean."ᵖ ⁴²The leprosy left him immediately, and he was made clean.�q ⁴³Then, warning him sternly, he dismissed him at once. ⁴⁴Then he said to him, "See that you tell no one anything, but go, show yourself to the priest and offer for your cleansing what Moses prescribed; that will be proof for them."ʳ ⁴⁵The man went away and began to publicize the whole matter. He spread the report abroad so that it was impossible for Jesus to enter a town openly. He remained outside in deserted places, and people kept coming to him from everywhere.

a. [1:2–8] Mt 3:1–11; Lk 3:2–16.
b. [1:2] Mal 3:1.
c. [1:3] Is 40:3; Jn 1:23.
d. [1:8] Jn 1:27; Acts 1:5; 11:16.
e. [1:9–11] Mt 3:13–17; Lk 3:21–23; Jn 1:32–33.
f. [1:11] Ps 2:7.
g. [1:12–13] Mt 4:1–11; Lk 4:1–13.
h. [1:14–15] Mt 4:12–17; Lk 4:14–15.
i. [1:15] Mt 3:2.
j. [1:16–20] Mt 4:18–22; Lk 5:2–11.
k. [1:21–28] Lk 4:31–37.
l. [1:22] Mt 7:28–29.
m. [1:29–34] Mt 8:14–16; Lk 4:38–41.
n. [1:35–39] Lk 4:42–44.
o. [1:40–44] Mt 8:2–4; Lk 5:12–14.
p. [1:41] 5:30.
q. [1:42] Lk 17:14.
r. [1:44] Lv 14:2–32.

CHAPTER 2

The Healing of a Paralytic.
¹*When Jesus returned to Capernaumᵃ after some days, it became known that he was at home.* ²Many gathered together so that there was no longer room for them, not even around the door, and he preached the word to them. ³They came bringing to him a paralytic carried by four men. ⁴Unable to get near Jesus because of the crowd, they opened up the roof above him. After they had broken through, they let down the mat on which the paralytic was lying. ⁵*When Jesus saw their faith, he said to the paralytic, "Child, your sins are forgiven." ⁶*Now some of the scribes were sitting there asking themselves, ⁷"Why does this man speak that way?* He is blaspheming. Who but God alone can forgive sins?"ᵇ ⁸Jesus immediately knew in his mind what they were thinking to themselves, so he said, "Why are you thinking such things in your hearts? ⁹Which is easier, to say to the paralytic, 'Your

sins are forgiven,' or to say, 'Rise, pick up your mat and walk'? [10*]But that you may know that the Son of Man has authority to forgive sins on earth"— [11]he said to the paralytic, "I say to you, rise, pick up your mat, and go home." [12]He rose, picked up his mat at once, and went away in the sight of everyone. They were all astounded and glorified God, saying, "We have never seen anything like this."

The Call of Levi. [13*]"Once again he went out along the sea. All the crowd came to him and he taught them. [14d]As he passed by,* he saw Levi, son of Alphaeus, sitting at the customs post. He said to him, "Follow me." And he got up and followed him. [15]While he was at table in his house,* many tax collectors and sinners sat with Jesus and his disciples; for there were many who followed him. [16*]Some scribes who were Pharisees saw that he was eating with sinners and tax collectors and said to his disciples, "Why does he eat with tax collectors and sinners?" [17]Jesus heard this and said to them [that], "Those who are well do not need a physician,* but the sick do. I did not come to call the righteous but sinners."

The Question About Fasting.[*] [18]The disciples of John and of the Pharisees were accustomed to fast.[e] People came to him and objected, "Why do the disciples of John and the disciples of the Pharisees fast, but your disciples do not fast?" [19]Jesus answered them, "Can the wedding guests fast* while the bridegroom is with them? As long as they have the bridegroom with them they cannot fast. [20]But the days will come when the bridegroom is taken away from them, and then they will fast on that day. [21]No one sews a piece of unshrunken cloth on an old cloak. If he does, its fullness pulls away, the new from the old, and the tear gets worse. ²²Likewise, no one pours new wine into old wineskins. Otherwise, the wine will burst the skins, and both the wine and the skins are ruined. Rather, new wine is poured into fresh wineskins."

The Disciples and the Sabbath. ²³As he was passing through a field of grain on the sabbath, his disciples began to make a path while picking the heads of grain.ᶠ ²⁴At this the Pharisees said to him, "Look, why are they doing what is unlawful on the sabbath?"ᵍ ²⁵He said to them, "Have you never read what David did* when he was in need and he and his companions were hungry? ²⁶How he went into the house of God when Abiathar was high priest and ate the bread of offering that only the priests could lawfully eat, and shared it with his companions?"ʰ ²⁷Then he said to them, "The

sabbath was made for man,* not man for the sabbath.ⁱ ²⁸That is why the Son of Man is lord even of the sabbath."

---

a. [2:1–12] Mt 9:2–8; Lk 5:18–26.
b. [2:7] Is 43:25.
c. [2:13] 4:1.
d. [2:14–17] Mt 9:9–13; Lk 5:27–32.
e. [2:18–22] Mt 9:14–17; Lk 5:33–39.
f. [2:23–28] Mt 12:1–8; Lk 6:1–5.
g. [2:24] Dt 23:25.
h. [2:26] 1 Sm 21:2–7; Lv 24:5–9.
i. [2:27] 2 Mc 5:19.

CHAPTER 3

A Man with a Withered Hand. ¹*Again he entered the synagogue.ᵃ There was a man there who had a withered hand. ²They watched him closely to see if he would cure him on the sabbath so that they might accuse him. ³He said to the man with the withered hand, "Come up here before us." ⁴Then he said to them, "Is it lawful to do good on the sabbath rather than to do evil, to save life rather than to destroy it?" But they remained silent. ⁵Looking around at them with anger and grieved at their hardness of heart, he said to the man,

"Stretch out your hand." He stretched it out and his hand was restored.[b] [6*]The Pharisees went out and immediately took counsel with the Herodians against him to put him to death.

The Mercy of Jesus. [7*]Jesus withdrew toward the sea with his disciples.[c] A large number of people [followed] from Galilee and from Judea. [8]Hearing what he was doing, a large number of people came to him also from Jerusalem, from Idumea, from beyond the Jordan, and from the neighborhood of Tyre and Sidon. [9]He told his disciples to have a boat ready for him because of the crowd, so that they would not crush him. [10]He had cured many and, as a result, those who had diseases were pressing upon him to touch him.[d] [11*]And whenever unclean spirits saw him they would fall down before him and shout, "You are the Son of God."[e] [12]He warned them sternly not to make him known.

The Mission of the Twelve. [13f]He went up the mountain[*] and summoned those whom he wanted and they came to him. [14g]He appointed twelve [whom he also named apostles] that they might be with him[*] and he might send them forth to preach [15]and to have authority to drive out demons: [16*][he appointed the twelve:] Simon, whom he named Peter; [17]James, son of Zebedee, and John the brother of James, whom he named Boanerges, that is, sons of thunder;[h] [18]Andrew, Philip, Bartholomew, Matthew, Thomas, James the son of Alphaeus; Thaddeus, Simon the Cananean, [19]and Judas Iscariot who betrayed him.

Blasphemy of the Scribes. [20*]He came home.[*] Again [the] crowd gathered, making it impossible for them even to eat.[i] [21]When his relatives heard of this they set out to seize him, for they said, "He is out of his mind."[j] [22]The scribes who had come from Jerusalem said, "He is possessed by Beelzebul,"[*] and "By the prince of demons he drives out demons."[k]

Jesus and Beelzebul. [23]Summoning them, he began to speak to them in parables, "How can Satan drive out Satan? [24]If a kingdom is divided against itself, that kingdom cannot stand. [25]And if a house is divided against itself, that house will not be able to stand. [26]And if Satan has risen up against himself and is divided, he cannot stand; that is the end of him. [27]But no one can enter a strong man's house to plunder his property unless he first ties up the strong man. Then he can plunder his house. [28]Amen, I say to you, all sins and all blasphemies that people utter will be forgiven them.[l] [29]But

whoever blasphemes against the holy Spirit[*] will never have forgiveness, but is guilty of an everlasting sin." [30]For they had said, "He has an unclean spirit."

Jesus and His Family. [31][m]His mother and his brothers arrived. Standing outside they sent word to him and called him. [32]A crowd seated around him told him, "Your mother and your brothers[*] [and your sisters] are outside asking for you." [33]But he said to them in reply, "Who are my mother and [my] brothers?" [34]And looking around at those seated in the circle he said, "Here are my mother and my brothers. [35][For] whoever does the will of God is my brother and sister and mother."

---

a.　[3:1–6] Mt 12:9–14; Lk 6:6–11.
b.　[3:5] Lk 14:4.
c.　[3:7–12] Mt 4:23–25; 12:15; Lk 6:17–19.
d.　[3:10] 5:30.
e.　[3:11] 1:34; Lk 4:41.
f.　[3:13–19] Mt 10:1–4; Lk 6:12–16.
g.　[3:14] 6:7.
h.　[3:17] Mt 16:18; Jn 1:42.
i.　[3:20] 2:2.
j.　[3:21] Jn 10:20.
k.　[3:22–30] Mt 12:24–32; Lk 11:15–22; 12:10.
l.　[3:28] Lk 12:10.
m.　[3:31–35] Mt 12:46–50; Lk 8:19–21.

CHAPTER 4

The Parable of the Sower.
[1]*On another occasion[a] he began to teach by the sea.* A very large crowd gathered around him so that he got into a boat on the sea and sat down. And the whole crowd was beside the sea on land.[b] [2]And he taught them at length in parables, and in the course of his instruction he said to them, [3]*"Hear this! A sower went out to sow. [4]And as he sowed, some seed fell on the path, and the birds came and ate it up. [5]Other seed fell on rocky ground where it had little soil. It sprang up at once because the soil was not deep. [6]And when the sun rose, it was scorched and it withered for lack of roots. [7]Some seed fell among thorns, and the thorns grew up and choked it and it produced no grain. [8]And some seed fell on rich soil and produced fruit. It came up and grew and yielded thirty,

sixty, and a hundredfold." [9]He added, "Whoever has ears to hear ought to hear."

The Purpose of the Parables.
[10]And when he was alone, those present along with the Twelve questioned him about the parables. [11]*He answered them, "The mystery of the kingdom of God has been granted to you. But to those outside everything comes in parables, [12]so that

'they may look and see but
    not perceive,
  and hear and listen but
    not understand,
in order that they may not
    be converted and be
    forgiven.'"[c]

[13]*Jesus said to them, "Do you not understand this parable?[d] Then how will you understand any of the parables? [14]The sower sows the word. [15]These are the ones on the path where the word is sown. As soon as they hear, Satan comes at once and

takes away the word sown in them. [16]And these are the ones sown on rocky ground who, when they hear the word, receive it at once with joy. [17]But they have no root; they last only for a time. Then when tribulation or persecution comes because of the word, they quickly fall away. [18]Those sown among thorns are another sort. They are the people who hear the word, [19]but worldly anxiety, the lure of riches, and the craving for other things intrude and choke the word, and it bears no fruit. [20]But those sown on rich soil are the ones who hear the word and accept it and bear fruit thirty and sixty and a hundredfold."

Parable of the Lamp. [21e]He said to them, "Is a lamp brought in to be placed under a bushel basket or under a bed, and not to be placed on a lampstand?[f] [22]For there is nothing hidden except to be made visible; nothing is secret except to come to light.[g] [23]Anyone who has ears to hear ought to hear." [24]He also told them, "Take care what you hear. The measure with which you measure will be measured out to you, and still more will be given to you.[h] [25]To the one who has, more will be given; from the one who has not, even what he has will be taken away."[i]

Seed Grows of Itself. [26]He said, "This is how it is with the kingdom of God; it is as if a man were to scatter seed[j] on the land [27]and would sleep and rise night and day and the seed would sprout and grow, he knows not how. [28]Of its own accord the land yields fruit, first the blade, then the ear, then the full grain in the ear. [29]And when the grain is ripe, he wields the sickle at once, for the harvest has come."

The Mustard Seed. [30k]He said, "To what shall we compare the kingdom of God, or what parable can we use for it? [31]It is like a mustard seed that, when it is sown in the ground, is the smallest of all the seeds on the earth. [32]*But once it is sown, it springs up and becomes the largest of plants and puts forth large branches, so that the birds of the sky can dwell in its shade." [33]With many such parables[i] he spoke the word to them as they were able to understand it. [34]Without parables he did not speak to them, but to his own disciples he explained everything in private.

The Calming of a Storm at Sea. [35]*On that day, as evening drew on, he said to them, "Let us cross to the other side."[m] [36]Leaving the crowd, they took him with them in the boat just as he was. And other boats were with him. [37]A violent squall came up and waves were breaking over the boat, so that it was already filling up. [38]Jesus was in the stern, asleep on a cushion. They woke him and said to him, "Teacher, do you not care that we are perishing?" [39]He woke up, rebuked the wind, and said to the sea, "Quiet! Be still!"* The wind ceased and there was great calm. [40]Then he asked them, "Why are you terrified? Do you not yet have faith?" [41]*[n]They were filled with great awe and said to one another, "Who then is this whom even wind and sea obey?" *God*

a. [4:1–12] Mt 13:1–13; Lk 8:4–10.
b. [4:1] 2:13; Lk 5:1.
c. [4:12] Is 6:9; Jn 12:40; Acts 28:26; Rom 11:8.
d. [4:13–20] Mt 13:18–23; Lk 8:11–15.
e. [4:21–25] Lk 8:16–18.
f. [4:21] Mt 5:15; Lk 11:33.
g. [4:22] Mt 10:26; Lk 12:2.
h. [4:24] Mt 7:2; Lk 6:38.
i. [4:25] Mt 13:12; Lk 19:26.
j. [4:26–29] Jas 5:7.
k. [4:30–32] Mt 13:31–32; Lk 13:18–19.
l. [4:33–34] Mt 13:34.
m. [4:35–40] Mt 8:18, 23–37; Lk 8:22–25.
n. [4:41] 1:27.

CHAPTER 5

The Healing of the Gerasene Demoniac. [1]*[a]They came to the other side of the sea, to the territory of the Gerasenes. [2]When he got out of the boat, at once a man* from the tombs who had an unclean spirit met him. ³The man had been dwelling among the tombs, and no one could restrain him any longer, even with a chain. ⁴In fact, he had frequently been bound with shackles and chains, but the chains had been pulled apart by him and the shackles smashed, and no one was strong enough to subdue him. ⁵Night and day among the tombs and on the hillsides he was always crying out and bruising himself with stones. ⁶Catching sight of Jesus from a distance, he ran up and prostrated himself before him, ⁷crying out in a loud voice, "What have you to do with me,ˣ Jesus, Son of the Most High God? I adjure you by God, do not torment me!" ⁸(He had been saying to him, "Unclean spirit, come out of the man!") ⁹ˣHe asked him, "What is your name?" He replied, "Legion is my name. There are many of us."ᵇ ¹⁰And he pleaded earnestly

with him not to drive them away from that territory.

¹¹Now a large herd of swineˣ was feeding there on the hillside. ¹²And they pleaded with him, "Send us into the swine. Let us enter them." ¹³And he let them, and the unclean spirits came out and entered the swine. The herd of about two thousand rushed down a steep bank into the sea, where they were drowned. ¹⁴The swineherds ran away and reported the incident in the town and throughout the countryside. And people came out to see what had happened. ¹⁵As they approached Jesus, they caught sight of the man who had been possessed by Legion, sitting there clothed and in his right mind. And they were seized with fear. ¹⁶Those who witnessed the incident explained to them what had happened to the possessed man and to the swine. ¹⁷Then they began to beg him to leave their district. ¹⁸As he was getting into the

boat, the man who had been possessed pleaded to remain with him. ¹⁹But he would not permit him but told him instead, "Go home* to your family and announce to them all that the Lord in his pity has done for you." ²⁰Then the man went off and began to proclaim in the Decapolis what Jesus had done for him; and all were amazed.

Jairus's Daughter and the Woman with a Hemorrhage.* ²¹When Jesus had crossed again [in the boat] to the other side, a large crowd gathered around him, and he stayed close to the sea.ᶜ ²²One of the synagogue officials, named Jairus, came forward.ᵈ Seeing him he fell at his feet ²³and pleaded earnestly with him, saying, "My daughter is at the point of death. Please, come lay your hands on her* that she may get well and live." ²⁴He went off with him, and a large crowd followed him and pressed upon him.

²⁵There was a woman afflicted with hemorrhages for twelve years. ²⁶She had suffered greatly at the hands of many doctors and had spent all that she had. Yet she was not helped but only grew worse. ²⁷She had heard about Jesus and came up behind him in the crowd and touched his cloak. ²⁸*She said, "If I but touch his clothes, I shall be cured." ²⁹Immediately her flow of blood dried up. She felt in her body that she was healed of her affliction. ³⁰Jesus, aware at once that power had gone out from him, turned around in the crowd and asked, "Who has touched my clothes?" ³¹But his disciples said to him, "You see how the crowd is pressing upon you, and yet you ask, 'Who touched me?'" ³²And he looked around to see who had done it. ³³The woman, realizing what had happened to her, approached in fear and trembling. She fell down before Jesus and told him the

whole truth. [34]He said to her, "Daughter, your faith has saved you. Go in peace and be cured of your affliction."[e]

[35*]While he was still speaking, people from the synagogue official's house arrived and said, "Your daughter has died; why trouble the teacher any longer?" [36]Disregarding the message that was reported, Jesus said to the synagogue official, "Do not be afraid; just have faith." [37]He did not allow anyone to accompany him inside except Peter, James, and John, the brother of James. [38]When they arrived at the house of the synagogue official, he caught sight of a commotion, people weeping and wailing loudly. [39*f]So he went in and said to them, "Why this commotion and weeping? The child is not dead but asleep." [40]And they ridiculed him. Then he put them all out. He took along the child's father and mother and those who were with him and entered the room where the child was. [41*]He took the child by the hand and said to her, "Talitha koum," which means, "Little girl, I say to you, arise!" [42]The girl, a child of twelve, arose immediately and walked around. [At that] they were utterly astounded. [43]He gave strict orders that no one should know this and said that she should be given something to eat.

---

a. [5:1–20] Mt 8:28–34; Lk 8:26–39.
b. [5:9] Mt 12:45; Lk 8:2; 11:26.
c. [5:21] 2:13.
d. [5:22–43] Mt 9:18–26; Lk 8:41–56.
e. [5:34] Lk 7:30.
f. [5:39–40] Acts 9:40.

CHAPTER 6

The Rejection at Nazareth. [1a]He departed from there and came to his native place,[*] accompanied by his disciples. [2*]When the sabbath came he began to teach in the synagogue, and many who heard him were astonished. They said, "Where did this man get all this? What kind of wisdom has been given him? What mighty deeds are wrought by his hands! ³ᵇIs he not the carpenter,* the son of Mary, and the brother of James and Joses and Judas and Simon? And are not his sisters here with us?" And they took offense at him. ⁴*ᶜJesus said to them, "A prophet is not without honor except in his native place and among his own kin and in his own house." ⁵So he was not able to perform any mighty deed there,* apart from curing a few sick people by laying his hands on them. ⁶He was amazed at their lack of faith.

The Mission of the Twelve. He went around to the villages in the vicinity teaching. ⁷ᵈHe summoned the Twelve* and began to send them out two by two and gave them authority over unclean spirits. ⁸He instructed them to take nothing for the journey but a walking stick—no food, no sack, no money in their belts. ⁹They were, however,

to wear sandals but not a second tunic. ¹⁰He said to them, "Wherever you enter a house, stay there until you leave from there. ¹¹Whatever place does not welcome you or listen to you, leave there and shake the dust off your feet in testimony against them." ¹²So they went off and preached repentance. ¹³They drove out many demons, and they anointed with oil many who were sick*ᵉ and cured them.

Herod's Opinion of Jesus. * ¹⁴King Herod* heard about it, for his fame had become widespread, and people were saying,ᶠ "John the Baptist has been raised from the dead; that is why mighty powers are at work in him."ᵍ ¹⁵Others were saying, "He is Elijah"; still others, "He is a prophet like any of the prophets."ʰ ¹⁶But when Herod learned of it, he said, "It is John whom I beheaded. He has been raised up."

The Death of John the Baptist. [*] [17]Herod was the one who had John arrested and bound in prison on account of Herodias, the wife of his brother Philip, whom he had married.[i] [18]John had said to Herod, "It is not lawful for you to have your brother's wife."[j] [19]Herodias[*] harbored a grudge against him and wanted to kill him but was unable to do so. [20]Herod feared John, knowing him to be a righteous and holy man, and kept him in custody. When he heard him speak he was very much perplexed, yet he liked to listen to him. [21]She had an opportunity one day when Herod, on his birthday, gave a banquet for his courtiers, his military officers, and the leading men of Galilee. [22]Herodias's own daughter came in and performed a dance that delighted Herod and his guests. The king said to the girl, "Ask of me whatever you wish and I will grant it to you." [23]He even swore [many things] to her, "I will grant you whatever you ask of me, even to half of my kingdom."[k] [24]She went out and said to her mother, "What shall I ask for?" She replied, "The head of John the Baptist." [25]The girl hurried back to the king's presence and made her request, "I want you to give me at once on a platter the head of John the Baptist." [26]The king was deeply distressed, but because of his oaths and the guests he did not wish to break his word to her. [27]So he promptly dispatched an executioner with orders to bring back his head. He went off and beheaded him in the prison. [28]He brought in the head on a platter and gave it to the girl. The girl in turn gave it to her mother. [29]When his disciples heard about it, they came and took his body and laid it in a tomb.

The Return of the Twelve. [30]The apostles[*] gathered

together with Jesus and reported all they had done and taught.*[m]* [31]*He said to them, "Come away by yourselves to a deserted place and rest a while." People were coming and going in great numbers, and they had no opportunity even to eat.*[n]* [32]So they went off in the boat by themselves to a deserted place.*[o]* [33]People saw them leaving and many came to know about it. They hastened there on foot from all the towns and arrived at the place before them.

The Feeding of the Five Thousand. [34]When he disembarked and saw the vast crowd, his heart was moved with pity for them, for they were like sheep without a shepherd; and he began to teach them many things. [35]*By now it was already late and his disciples approached him and said, "This is a deserted place and it is already very late. [36]Dismiss them so that

they can go to the surrounding farms and villages and buy themselves something to eat." [37]He said to them in reply, "Give them some food yourselves." But they said to him, "Are we to buy two hundred days' wages worth of food and give it to them to eat?" [38]He asked them, "How many loaves do you have? Go and see." And when they had found out they said, "Five loaves and two fish." [39]So he gave orders to have them sit down in groups on the green grass. [40]*The people took their places in rows by hundreds and by fifties. [41]Then, taking the five loaves and the two fish and looking up to heaven, he said the blessing, broke the loaves, and gave them to [his] disciples to set before the people; he also divided the two fish among them all.* [42]They all ate and were satisfied. [43]And they picked up twelve wicker baskets full of fragments and what was left of the fish. [44]Those who ate [of the loaves] were five thousand men.

The Walking on the Water.[*]
[45]Then he made his disciples get into the boat[p] and precede him to the other side toward Bethsaida,[*] while he dismissed the crowd. [46]*And when he had taken leave of them, he went off to the mountain to pray. [47]When it was evening, the boat was far out on the sea and he was alone on shore. [48]Then he saw that they were tossed about while rowing, for the wind was against them. About the fourth watch of the night, he came toward them walking on the sea.[*] He meant to pass by them. [49]But when they saw him walking on the sea, they thought it was a ghost and cried out. [50]*They had all seen him and were terrified. But at once he spoke with them, "Take courage, it is I, do not be afraid!" [51]He got into the boat with them and the wind died down. They were [completely] astounded.

[52]They had not understood the incident of the loaves.[*] On the contrary, their hearts were hardened.[q]

The Healings at Gennesaret.
[53r]After making the crossing, they came to land at Gennesaret and tied up there. [54]As they were leaving the boat, people immediately recognized him. [55]They scurried about the surrounding country and began to bring in the sick on mats to wherever they heard he was. [56]Whatever villages or towns or countryside he entered, they laid the sick in the marketplaces and begged him that they might touch only the tassel on his cloak; and as many as touched it were healed.[s]

a. [6:1–6] Mt 13:54–58; Lk 4:16–30.
b. [6:3] 15:40; Mt 12:46; Jn 6:42.
c. [6:4] Jn 4:44.
d. [6:7–11] Mt 10:1, 9–14; Lk 9:15; 10:4–11.
e. [6:13] Jas 5:14.
f. [6:14–29] Mt 14:1–12.
g. [6:14–16] Lk 9:7–8.
h. [6:15] Mt 16:14.
i. [6:17] Lk 3:19–20.
j. [6:18] Lv 18:16.
k. [6:23] Est 5:3.
l. [6:27–28] Lk 9:9.
m. [6:30] Lk 9:10.
n. [6:31] 3:20; Mt 14:13; Lk 9:10.
o. [6:32–44] Mt 14:13–21; Lk 9:10–17; Jn 6:1–13.

CHAPTER 7

The Tradition of the Elders.[*] [1]Now when the Pharisees with some scribes who had come from Jerusalem gathered around him,[a] [2]they observed that some of his disciples ate their meals with unclean, that is, unwashed, hands. [3](For the Pharisees and, in fact, all Jews, do not eat without carefully washing their hands,[*] keeping the tradition of the elders. [4]And on coming from the marketplace they do not eat without purifying themselves. And there are many other things that they have traditionally observed, the purification of cups and jugs and kettles [and beds].) [5]So the Pharisees and scribes questioned him, "Why do your disciples not follow the tradition of the elders[*] but instead eat a meal with unclean hands?" [6]He responded, "Well did Isaiah prophesy about you hypocrites, as it is written:[b]

'This people honors me
with their lips,
but their <u>hearts</u> are far
from me;
[7]In vain do they worship
me,
teaching as doctrines
human precepts.'

[8]You disregard God's commandment but cling to human tradition." [9]He went on to say, "How well you have set aside the commandment of God in order to uphold your tradition! [10]For Moses said, 'Honor your father and your mother,' and 'Whoever curses father or mother shall die.'[c] [11]Yet you say, 'If a person says to father or mother, "Any support you might have had from me is *qorban*"'" (meaning, dedicated to God), [12]you allow him to do nothing more for his father or mother. [13]You nullify the word of God in favor of your tradition that

you have handed on. And you do many such things." ¹⁴ᵈHe summoned the crowd again and said to them, "Hear me, all of you, and understand. ¹⁵Nothing that enters one from outside can defile that person; but the things that come out from within are what defile." [¹⁶]*

¹⁷*ᵉWhen he got home away from the crowd his disciples questioned him about the parable. ¹⁸He said to them, "Are even you likewise without understanding? Do you not realize that everything that goes into a person from outside cannot defile, ¹⁹*ᶠsince it enters not the heart but the stomach and passes out into the latrine?" (Thus he declared all foods clean.) ²⁰"But what comes out of a person, that is what defiles. ²¹ᵍFrom within people, from their hearts, come evil thoughts, unchastity, theft, murder, ²²adultery, greed, malice, deceit, licentiousness, envy, blasphemy, arrogance, folly. ²³All these evils come from within and they defile."

The Syrophoenician Woman's Faith. ²⁴ʰFrom that place he went off to the district of Tyre.* He entered a house and wanted no one to know about it, but he could not escape notice. ²⁵Soon a woman whose daughter had an unclean spirit heard about him. She came and fell at his feet. ²⁶The woman was a Greek, a Syrophoenician by birth, and she begged him to drive the demon out of her daughter.ⁱ ²⁷He said to her, "Let the children be fed first.* For it is not right to take the food of the children and throw it to the dogs." ²⁸She replied and said to him, "Lord, even the dogs under the table eat the children's scraps." ²⁹Then he said to her, "For saying this, you may go. The demon has gone out of your daughter." ³⁰When the woman went home, she found the child lying in bed and the demon gone.

The Healing of a Deaf Man.

³¹ʲAgain he left the district of Tyre and went by way of Sidon to the Sea of Galilee, into the district of the Decapolis. ³²And people brought to him a deaf man who had a speech impediment and begged him to lay his hand on him. ³³He took him off by himself away from the crowd. He put his finger into the man's ears and, spitting, touched his tongue; ³⁴then he looked up to heaven and groaned, and said to him, "*Ephphatha*!" (that is, "Be opened!") ³⁵And [immediately] the man's ears were opened, his speech impediment was removed, and he spoke plainly. ³⁶*He ordered them not to tell anyone. But the more he ordered them not to, the more they proclaimed it. ³⁷They were exceedingly astonished and they said, "He has done all things well. He makes the deaf hear and [the] mute speak."ᵏ

c.   [7:10] Ex 21:17; Lv 20:9; Dt 5:16; Eph 6:2.
d.   [7:14–23] Mt 15:10–20.
e.   [7:17] 4:10, 13.
f.   [7:19] Acts 10:15.
g.   [7:21] Jer 17:9.
h.   [7:24–30] Mt 15:21–28.
i.   [7:26] Mt 8:29.
j.   [7:31–37] Mt 15:29–31.
k.   [7:37] Mt 15:31.

CHAPTER 8

The Feeding of the Four Thousand.*

¹In those days when there again was a great crowd without anything to eat,ᵃ he summoned the disciples and said, ²"My heart is moved with pity for the crowd, because they have been with me now for three days and have nothing to eat. ³If I send them away hungry to their homes, they will collapse on the way, and some of them have come a great distance." ⁴His disciples answered him, "Where can anyone get enough bread to satisfy them here in this deserted place?" ⁵Still he asked them, "How many loaves do you have?" "Seven," they replied. ⁶*He ordered the crowd to sit down on

a.   [7:1–23] Mt 15:1–20.
b.   [7:6] Is 29:13.

Disciples didn't learn

the ground. Then, taking the seven loaves he gave thanks, broke them, and gave them to his disciples to distribute, and they distributed them to the crowd. [7]They also had a few fish. He said the blessing over them and ordered them distributed also. [8]They ate and were satisfied. They picked up the fragments left over— seven baskets. [9]There were about four thousand people.

He dismissed them [10]and got into the boat with his disciples and came to the region of Dalmanutha.

The Demand for a Sign. [11]The Pharisees came forward and began to argue with him,[b] seeking from him a sign from heaven to test him.[c] [12]He sighed from the depth of his spirit and said, "Why does this generation seek a sign? Amen, I say to you, no sign will be given to this generation." [13]Then he left them, got into the boat again, and went off to the other shore.

The Leaven of the Pharisees. [14d]They had forgotten to bring bread, and they had only one loaf with them in the boat. [15]He enjoined them, "Watch out, guard against the leaven of the Pharisees and the leaven of Herod." [16]They concluded among themselves that it was because they had no bread. [17]When he became aware of this he said to them, "Why do you conclude that it is because you have no bread? Do you not yet understand or comprehend? Are your hearts hardened?[e] [18]Do you have eyes and not see, ears and not hear? And do you not remember,[f] [19]when I broke the five loaves for the five thousand, how many wicker baskets full of fragments you picked up?" They answered him, "Twelve." [20]"When I broke the seven loaves for the four thousand, how many full baskets of fragments did you pick up?" They answered [him], "Seven." [21]He said to them, "Do you still not understand?"

The Blind Man of Bethsaida.[*] [22]When they arrived at Bethsaida, they brought to him a blind man and begged him to touch him. [23]He took the blind man by the hand and led him outside the village. Putting spittle on his eyes he laid his hands on him and asked, "Do you see anything?"[g] [24]Looking up he replied, "I see people looking like trees and walking." [25]Then he laid hands on his eyes a second time and he saw clearly; his sight was restored and he could see everything distinctly. [26]Then he sent him home and said, "Do not even go into the village."

III. THE MYSTERY BEGINS TO BE REVEALED

Peter's Confession About Jesus.[*] [27]Now Jesus and his disciples set out for the villages of Caesarea Philippi.[h] Along the way he asked his disciples, "Who do people say that I am?" [28]They said in reply, "John the Baptist, others Elijah, still others one of the prophets." [29]And he asked them, "But who do you say that I am?" Peter said to him in reply, "You are the Messiah." [30]Then he warned them not to tell anyone about him.

The First Prediction of the Passion. [31][i]He began to teach them that the Son of Man[*] must suffer greatly and be rejected by the elders, the chief priests, and the scribes, and be killed, and rise after three days. [32]He spoke this openly. Then Peter took him aside and began to rebuke him. [33]At this he turned around and, looking at his disciples, rebuked Peter and said, "Get behind me, Satan. You are thinking not as God does, but as human beings do."

The Conditions of Discipleship. [34]He summoned the crowd with his disciples and said[*] to them, "Whoever wishes to come after me must deny himself, take up his cross, and follow me.[j] [35]For whoever wishes to save his life will lose it, but whoever loses his life for my sake and that of the gospel[*] will save it.[k] [36]What profit is there for one to gain the whole world and forfeit his life? [37]What could one give in exchange for his life? [38]Whoever is ashamed of me and of my words in this faithless and sinful generation, the Son of Man will be ashamed of when he comes in his Father's glory with the holy angels."[l]

a.   [8:1–10] 6:34–44; Mt 15:32–39.
b.   [8:11–13] Mt 12:38–39; 16:1–4.
c.   [8:11] Lk 11:16.
d.   [8:14–21] Mt 16:5–12; Lk 12:1.
e.   [8:17] 4:13.
f.   [8:18] Jer 5:21; Ez 12:2.
g.   [8:23] 7:33; Jn 9:6.
h.   [8:27–30] Mt 16:13–20; Lk 9:18–21.
i.   [8:31–38] Mt 16:21–27; Lk 9:22–26.
j.   [8:34] Mt 10:38–39; 16:24–27; Lk 14:26–27.
k.   [8:35] Jn 12:25.
l.   [8:38] Mt 10:33; Lk 12:8.

CHAPTER 9

[1][*][a]He also said to them, "Amen, I say to you, there are some standing here who will not taste death until they see that the kingdom of God has come in power."

The Transfiguration of Jesus.

[2]After six days Jesus took Peter, James, and John and led them up a high mountain apart by themselves.[b] And he was transfigured before them, [3]and his clothes became dazzling white, such as no fuller on earth could bleach them. [4]Then Elijah appeared to them along with Moses, and they were conversing with Jesus. [5]Then Peter said to Jesus in reply, "Rabbi, it is good that we are here! Let us make three tents: one for you, one for Moses, and one for Elijah." [6]He hardly knew what to say, they were so terrified. [7]Then a cloud came, casting a shadow over them;[*] then from the cloud came a voice, "This is my beloved Son. Listen to him." [8]Suddenly, looking around, they no longer saw anyone but Jesus alone with them.

The Coming of Elijah. [*] ⁹As they were coming down from the mountain, he charged them not to relate what they had seen to anyone, except when the Son of Man had risen from the dead.[c] ¹⁰So they kept the matter to themselves, questioning what rising from the dead meant. ¹¹[d]Then they asked him, "Why do the scribes say that Elijah must come first?" ¹²He told them, "Elijah will indeed come first and <u>restore all</u> things, yet how is it written regarding the Son of Man that he must suffer greatly and be treated with contempt? ¹³But I tell you that Elijah has come and they did to him whatever they pleased, as it is written of him."[e]

The Healing of a Boy with a Demon. [*] ¹⁴When they came to the disciples,[f] they saw a large crowd around them and scribes arguing with them. ¹⁵Immediately on seeing him, the whole crowd was utterly amazed. They ran up to him and greeted him. ¹⁶He asked them, "What are you arguing about with them?" ¹⁷Someone from the crowd answered him, "Teacher, I have brought to you my son possessed by a mute spirit. ¹⁸Wherever it seizes him, it throws him down; he foams at the mouth, grinds his teeth, and becomes rigid. I asked your disciples to drive it out, but they were unable to do so." ¹⁹He said to them in reply, "O faithless generation, how long will I be with you? How long will I endure you? Bring him to me." ²⁰They brought the boy to him. And when he saw him, the spirit immediately threw the boy into convulsions. As he fell to the ground, he began to roll around and foam at the mouth. ²¹Then he questioned his father, "How long has this been happening to him?" He replied, "Since childhood. ²²It has often thrown him into fire and into water to kill him. But if you can do anything, have compassion on us and help us." [23]Jesus said to him, "'If you can!' Everything is possible to one who has faith." [24]Then the boy's father cried out, "I do believe, help my unbelief!" [25]Jesus, on seeing a crowd rapidly gathering, rebuked the unclean spirit and said to it, "Mute and deaf spirit, I command you: come out of him and never enter him again!" [26]Shouting and throwing the boy into convulsions, it came out. He became like a corpse, which caused many to say, "He is dead!" [27]But Jesus took him by the hand, raised him, and he stood up. [28]When he entered the house, his disciples asked him in private, "Why could we not drive it out?" [29]*He said to them, "This kind can only come out through prayer."

The Second Prediction of the Passion. [30]gThey left from there and began a journey through Galilee, but he did not wish anyone to know about it.[h] [31]He was teaching his disciples and telling them, "The Son of Man is to be handed over to men and they will kill him, and three days after his death he will rise." [32]But they did not understand the saying, and they were afraid to question him.

IV. THE FULL REVELATION OF THE MYSTERY

The Greatest in the Kingdom.[*] [33]They came to Capernaum and, once inside the house, he began to ask them, "What were you arguing about on the way?"[i] [34]But they remained silent. They had been discussing among themselves on the way who was the greatest. [35]Then he sat down, called the Twelve, and said to them, "If anyone wishes to be first, he shall be the last of all and the servant of all."[j] [36]Taking a child he placed it in their midst, and putting his arms around it he said to them, 37“Whoever receives one child such as this in my name, receives me; and whoever receives me, receives not me but the One who sent me.”[k]

Another Exorcist.* 38John said to him,[l] “Teacher, we saw someone driving out demons in your name, and we tried to prevent him because he does not follow us.” 39Jesus replied, “Do not prevent him. There is no one who performs a mighty deed in my name who can at the same time speak ill of me. 40For whoever is not against us is for us.[m] 41Anyone who gives you a cup of water to drink because you belong to Christ, amen, I say to you, will surely not lose his reward.[n]

Temptations to Sin. 42[o]“Whoever causes one of these little ones who believe [in me] to sin, it would be better for him if a great millstone were put around his neck and he were thrown into the sea. 43If your hand causes you to sin, cut it off. It is better for you to enter into life maimed than with two hands to go into Gehenna,* into the unquenchable fire. [44]* 45And if your foot causes you to sin, cut it off. It is better for you to enter into life crippled than with two feet to be thrown into Gehenna. [46] 47And if your eye causes you to sin, pluck it out. Better for you to enter into the kingdom of God with one eye than with two eyes to be thrown into Gehenna, 48where ‘their worm does not die, and the fire is not quenched.’[p]

The Simile of Salt. 49*“Everyone will be salted with fire. 50Salt is good, but if salt becomes insipid, with what will you restore its flavor? Keep salt in yourselves and you will have peace with one another.”[q]

---

a. [9:1] Mt 16:28; Lk 9:27.
b. [9:2–13] Mt 17:1–13; Lk 9:28–36.

c. [9:9] 8:31.
d. [9:11–12] Is 53:3; Mal 3:23.
e. [9:13] 1 Kgs 19:2–10.
f. [9:14–29] Mt 17:14–21; Lk 9:37–43.
g. [9:30–32] 8:31; Mt 17:22–23; Lk 9:43–45.
h. [9:30] Jn 7:1.
i. [9:33–37] Mt 18:1–5; Lk 9:46–48.
j. [9:35] Mt 20:27.
k. [9:37] Mt 10:40; 18:5; Jn 13:20.
l. [9:38–41] Nm 11:28; Lk 9:49–50; 1 Cor 12:3.
m. [9:40] Mt 12:30.
n. [9:41] Mt 10:42; 1 Cor 3:23.
o. [9:42–47] Mt 5:29–30; 18:6–9; Lk 17:1–2.
p. [9:48] Is 66:24.
q. [9:50] Lv 2:13; Mt 5:13; Lk 14:34–35; Col 4:6.

CHAPTER 10

Marriage and Divorce. ¹He set out from there and went into the district of Judea [and] across the Jordan. Again crowds gathered around him and, as was his custom, he again taught them. ²The Pharisees approached and asked, "Is it lawful for a husband to divorce his wife?" They were testing him.ᵃ ³He said to them in reply, "What did Moses command you?" ⁴They replied, "Moses permitted him to write a bill of divorce and dismiss her."ᵇ ⁵But Jesus told them, "Because of the hardness of your hearts he wrote you this commandment. ⁶But from the beginning of creation, 'God made them male and female.ᶜ ⁷For this reason a man shall leave his father and mother [and be joined to his wife],ᵈ ⁸and the two shall become one flesh.' So they are no longer two but one flesh. ⁹Therefore what God has joined together, no human being must separate." ¹⁰In the house the disciples again questioned him about this. ¹¹ᵉHe said to them, "Whoever divorces his wife and marries another commits adultery against her; ¹²and if she divorces her husband and marries another, she commits adultery."

Blessing of the Children. ¹³ᶠAnd people were bringing children to him that he might touch them, but the disciples rebuked them.ᵍ ¹⁴When Jesus saw this he became indignant and said to them, "Let the children come to me; do not prevent them, for the kingdom of God belongs to such as these. [15]Amen, I say to you, whoever does not accept the kingdom of God like a child[*] will not enter it."[h] [16]Then he embraced them and blessed them, placing his hands on them.

The Rich Man. [17i]As he was setting out on a journey, a man ran up, knelt down before him, and asked him, "Good teacher, what must I do to inherit eternal life?" [18]Jesus answered him, "Why do you call me good?[*] No one is good but God alone. [19]You know the commandments: 'You shall not kill; you shall not commit adultery; you shall not steal; you shall not bear false witness; you shall not defraud; honor your father and your mother.'"[j] [20]He replied and said to him, "Teacher, all of these I have observed from my youth." [21]Jesus, looking at him, loved him and said to him, "You are lacking in one thing. Go, sell what you have, and give to [the] poor and you will have treasure in heaven; then come, follow me." [22]At that statement his face fell, and he went away sad, for he had many possessions.

[23]Jesus looked around and said to his disciples, "How hard it is for those who have wealth to enter the kingdom of God!"[k] [24]The disciples were amazed at his words. So Jesus again said to them in reply, "Children, how hard it is to enter the kingdom of God! [25]It is easier for a camel to pass through [the] eye of [a] needle than for one who is rich to enter the kingdom of God." [26]They were exceedingly astonished and said among themselves, "Then who can be saved?" [27]Jesus looked at them and said, "For human beings it is impossible, but not for God. All things are possible for God." [28]Peter began to say to him, "We have given up everything and followed you." [29]Jesus said, "Amen, I say to

you, there is no one who has given up house or brothers or sisters or mother or father or children or lands for my sake and for the sake of the gospel [30]who will not receive a hundred times more now in this present age: houses and brothers and sisters and mothers and children and lands, with persecutions, and eternal life in the age to come. [31]But many that are first will be last, and [the] last will be first."[l]

The Third Prediction of the Passion. [32m]They were on the way, going up to Jerusalem, and Jesus went ahead of them. They were amazed, and those who followed were afraid. Taking the Twelve aside again, he began to tell them what was going to happen to him. [33]"Behold, we are going up to Jerusalem, and the Son of Man will be handed over to the chief priests and the scribes, and they will condemn him to death and hand him over to the Gentiles [34]who will mock him, spit upon him, scourge him, and put him to death, but after three days he will rise."

Ambition of James and John. [35n]Then James and John, the sons of Zebedee, came to him and said to him, "Teacher, we want you to do for us whatever we ask of you." [36]He replied, "What do you wish [me] to do for you?" [37]They answered him, "Grant that in your glory we may sit one at your right and the other at your left." [38*o]Jesus said to them, "You do not know what you are asking. Can you drink the cup that I drink or be baptized with the baptism with which I am baptized?" [39]They said to him, "We can." Jesus said to them, "The cup that I drink, you will drink, and with the baptism with which I am baptized, you will be baptized; [40]but to sit at my right or at my left is not

Jesus' humility

mine to give but is for those for whom it has been prepared." ⁴¹When the ten heard this, they became indignant at James and John. ^{42*}Jesus summoned them and said to them,^p "You know that those who are recognized as rulers over the Gentiles lord it over them, and their great ones make their authority over them felt. ⁴³But it shall not be so among you. Rather, whoever wishes to be great among you will be your servant; ⁴⁴whoever wishes to be first among you will be the slave of all. ⁴⁵For the Son of Man did not come to be served but to serve and to give his life as a ransom for many."

The Blind Bartimaeus.*

⁴⁶They came to Jericho.^q And as he was leaving Jericho with his disciples and a sizable crowd, Bartimaeus, a blind man, the son of Timaeus, sat by the roadside begging. ⁴⁷On hearing that it was Jesus of Nazareth, he began to cry out and say, "Jesus, son of David, have pity on me." ⁴⁸And many rebuked him, telling him to be silent. But he kept calling out all the more, "Son of David, have pity on me." ⁴⁹Jesus stopped and said, "Call him." So they called the blind man, saying to him, "Take courage; get up, he is calling you." ⁵⁰He threw aside his cloak, sprang up, and came to Jesus. ⁵¹Jesus said to him in reply, "What do you want me to do for you?" The blind man replied to him, "Master, I want to see." ⁵²Jesus told him, "Go your way; your faith has saved you." Immediately he received his sight and followed him on the way.

a. [10:2–12] Mt 19:3–9.
b. [10:4] Dt 24:1–4.
c. [10:6] Gn 1:27.
d. [10:7–8] Gn 2:24; 1 Cor 6:16; Eph 5:31.
e. [10:11–12] Mt 5:32; Lk 16:18; 1 Cor 7:10–11.
f. [10:13–16] Mt 19:13–15; Lk 18:15–17.
g. [10:13] Lk 9:47.
h. [10:15] Mt 18:3.
i. [10:17–31] Mt 19:16–30; Lk 18:18–30.
j. [10:19] Ex 20:12–16; Dt 5:16–21.
k. [10:23] Prv 11:28.
l. [10:31] Mt 19:30; Lk 13:30.
m. [10:32–34] 8:31; Mt 20:17–19; Lk 18:31–33.
n. [10:35–45] Mt 20:20–28.
o. [10:38] Lk 12:50.
p. [10:42–45] Lk 22:25–27.
q. [10:46–52] Mt 20:29–34; Lk 18:35–43.

CHAPTER 11

The Entry into Jerusalem.[*]
[1]When they drew near to Jerusalem,[a] to Bethphage and Bethany at the Mount of Olives, he sent two of his disciples [2]and said to them, "Go into the village opposite you, and immediately on entering it, you will find a colt tethered on which no one has ever sat. Untie it and bring it here. [3]If anyone should say to you, 'Why are you doing this?' reply, 'The Master has need of it and will send it back here at once.'" [4]So they went off and found a colt tethered at a gate outside on the street, and they untied it. [5]Some of the bystanders said to them, "What are you doing, untying the colt?" [6]They answered them just as Jesus had told them to, and they permitted them to do it. [7]So they brought the colt to Jesus and put their cloaks over it. And he sat on it. [8]Many people spread their cloaks on the road, and others spread leafy branches that they had cut from the fields. [9]Those preceding him as well as those following kept crying out:[b]

"Hosanna!
    Blessed is he who comes
        in the name of the
        Lord!
    [10]Blessed is the kingdom
        of our father David
        that is to come!
Hosanna in the highest!"

[11]He entered Jerusalem and went into the temple area. He looked around at everything and, since it was already late, went out to Bethany with the Twelve.[c]

Jesus Curses a Fig Tree.[*]
[12]The next day as they were leaving Bethany he was hungry.[d] [13]Seeing from a distance a fig tree in leaf, he went over to see if he could find anything on it. When he reached it he found nothing but leaves; it was not the time for figs. [14]And he said to it in

? reply, "May no one ever eat of your fruit again!" And his disciples heard it.

Cleansing of the Temple.[*] ¹⁵They came to Jerusalem,[e] and on entering the temple area he began to drive out those selling and buying there. He overturned the tables of the money changers and the seats of those who were selling doves. ¹⁶He did not permit anyone to carry anything through the temple area. ¹⁷Then he taught them saying, "Is it not written:

'My house shall be called a
     house of prayer for all
     peoples'?
But you have made it a
     den of thieves."[f]

¹⁸The chief priests and the scribes came to hear of it and were seeking a way to put him to death, yet they feared him because the whole crowd was astonished at his teaching. ¹⁹When evening came, they went out of the city.[g]

The Withered Fig Tree. ²⁰[h]Early in the morning, as they were walking along, they saw the fig tree withered to its roots. ²¹Peter remembered and said to him, "Rabbi, look! The fig tree that you cursed has withered." ²²Jesus said to them in reply, "Have faith in God. ²³Amen, I say to you, whoever says to this mountain, 'Be lifted up and thrown into the sea,' and does not doubt in his heart but believes that what he says will happen, it shall be done for him.[i] ²⁴Therefore I tell you, all that you ask for in prayer, believe that you will receive it and it shall be yours.[j] ²⁵When you stand to pray, forgive anyone against whom you have a grievance, so that your heavenly Father may in turn forgive you your transgressions."[k] [26][*]

The Authority of Jesus Questioned.[*] ²⁷They returned once more to Jerusalem.[l] As he was walking in the temple area, the chief priests, the scribes, and the elders approached him ²⁸and said to him, "By what authority are you doing these things? Or who gave you this authority to do them?" ²⁹Jesus said to them, "I shall ask you one question. Answer me, and I will tell you by what authority I do these things. ³⁰Was John's baptism of heavenly or of human origin? Answer me." ³¹They discussed this among themselves and said, "If we say, 'Of heavenly origin,' he will say, '[Then] why did you not believe him?' ³²But shall we say, 'Of human origin'?"—they feared the crowd, for they all thought John really was a prophet. ³³So they said to Jesus in reply, "We do not know." Then Jesus said to them, "Neither shall I tell you by what authority I do these things."

---

a. [11:1–10] Mt 21:1–9; Lk 19:29–38; Jn 12:12–15.
b. [11:9–10] 2 Sm 7:16; Ps 118:26.
c. [11:11] Mt 21:10, 17.
d. [11:12–14] Mt 21:18–20; Lk 13:6–9.
e. [11:15–18] Mt 21:12–13; Lk 19:45–46; Jn 2:14–16.
f. [11:17] Is 56:7; Jer 7:11.
g. [11:19] Lk 21:37.

h. [11:20–24] Mt 21:20–22.
i. [11:23] Mt 17:20–21; Lk 17:6.
j. [11:24] Mt 7:7; Jn 11:22; 14:13.
k. [11:25] Mt 6:14; 18:35.
l. [11:27–33] Mt 21:23–27; Lk 20:1–8.

CHAPTER 12

Parable of the Tenants.[*] ¹He began to speak to them in parables.[a] "A man planted a vineyard, put a hedge around it, dug a wine press, and built a tower. Then he leased it to tenant farmers and left on a journey.[b] ²At the proper time he sent a servant to the tenants to obtain from them some of the produce of the vineyard. ³But they seized him, beat him, and sent him away empty-handed. ⁴Again he sent them another servant. And that one they beat over the head and treated shamefully. ⁵He sent yet another whom they killed. So, too, many others; some they beat, others they killed. ⁶He had one other to send, a beloved son. He sent him to them last of all, thinking, 'They will respect my son.' ⁷But those tenants said to one another, 'This is the heir. Come, let us kill him, and the inheritance will be ours.' [8] So they seized him and killed him, and threw him out of the vineyard. [9] What [then] will the owner of the vineyard do? He will come, put the tenants to death, and give the vineyard to others. [10] Have you not read this scripture passage:[c]

'The stone that the builders rejected
has become the cornerstone;
[11] by the Lord has this been done,
and it is wonderful in our eyes'?"

[12] They were seeking to arrest him, but they feared the crowd, for they realized that he had addressed the parable to them. So they left him and went away.

Paying Taxes to the Emperor.
[13] They sent some Pharisees[d] and Herodians to him to ensnare him[e] in his speech.[*] [14] They came and said to him, "Teacher, we know that you are a truthful man and that you are not concerned with anyone's opinion. You do not regard a person's status but teach the way of God in accordance with the truth. Is it lawful to pay the census tax to Caesar or not? Should we pay or should we not pay?" [15] Knowing their hypocrisy he said to them, "Why are you testing me? Bring me a denarius to look at." [16] They brought one to him and he said to them, "Whose image and inscription is this?" They replied to him, "Caesar's." [17] So Jesus said to them, "Repay to Caesar what belongs to Caesar and to God what belongs to God." They were utterly amazed at him.[f]

The Question About the Resurrection.[*] [18] Some Sadducees, who say there is no resurrection, came to him and put this question to him,

faith & money & Power   heaven & earth

¹⁹saying, "Teacher, Moses wrote for us, 'If someone's brother dies, leaving a wife but no child, his brother must take the wife and raise up descendants for his brother.'ᵍ ²⁰Now there were seven brothers. The first married a woman and died, leaving no descendants. ²¹So the second married her and died, leaving no descendants, and the third likewise. ²²And the seven left no descendants. Last of all the woman also died. ²³At the resurrection [when they arise] whose wife will she be? For all seven had been married to her." ²⁴Jesus said to them, "Are you not misled because you do not know the scriptures or the power of God? ²⁵When they rise from the dead, they neither marry nor are given in marriage, but they are like the angels in heaven. ²⁶As for the dead being raised, have you not read in the Book of Moses, in the passage about the bush, how God told him, 'I am the God of Abraham, [the] God of Isaac, and [the] God of Jacob'?ʰ ²⁷He is not God of the dead but of the living. You are greatly misled."

The Greatest Commandment. ²⁸One of the scribes,ⁱ when he came forward and heard them disputing and saw how well he had answered them, asked him, "Which is the first of all the commandments?" ²⁹Jesus replied, "The first is this: 'Hear, O Israel! The Lord our God is Lord alone! ³⁰You shall love the Lord your God with all your heart, with all your soul, with all your mind, and with all your strength.'ʲ ³¹The second is this: 'You shall love your neighbor as yourself.' There is no other commandment greater than these."ᵏ ³²The scribe said to him, "Well said, teacher. You are right in saying, 'He is One and there is no other than he.' ³³And 'to love him with all your heart, with all your understanding, with all your strength, and to love your neighbor as yourself' is worth more than all burnt offerings and sacrifices."[l] [34]And when Jesus saw that [he] answered with understanding, he said to him, "You are not far from the kingdom of God." And no one dared to ask him any more questions.[m]

The Question About David's Son. [35]As Jesus was teaching in the temple area he said,[n] "How do the scribes claim that the Messiah is the son of David? [36]David himself, inspired by the holy Spirit, said:

'The Lord said to my lord,
  "Sit at my right hand
    until I place your
      enemies under your
        feet."'[o]

[37]David himself calls him 'lord'; so how is he his son?" [The] great crowd heard this with delight.

Denunciation of the Scribes. [38]In the course of his teaching he said,[p] "Beware of the scribes, who like to go around in long robes and accept greetings in the marketplaces, [39]seats of honor in synagogues, and places of honor at banquets. [40]They devour the houses of widows and, as a pretext, recite lengthy prayers. They will receive a very severe condemnation."

The Poor Widow's Contribution. [41]He sat down opposite the treasury and observed how the crowd put money into the treasury.[q] Many rich people put in large sums. [42]A poor widow also came and put in two small coins worth a few cents. [43]Calling his disciples to himself, he said to them, "Amen, I say to you, this poor widow put in more than all the other contributors to the treasury. [44]For they have all contributed from their surplus wealth, but she, from her poverty, has contributed all she had, her whole livelihood."

a. [12:1–12] Mt 21:33–46; Lk 20:9–19.
b. [12:1] Is 5:1–7; Jer 2:21.
c. [12:10–11] Ps 118:22–23; Is 28:16.
d. [12:13–27] Mt 22:15–33; Lk 20:20–39.
e. [12:13] 3:6.
f. [12:17] Rom 13:7.
g. [12:19] Dt 25:5.
h. [12:26] Ex 3:6.
i. [12:28–34] Mt 22:34–40; Lk 10:25–28.
j. [12:30] Dt 6:4–5.
k. [12:31] Lv 19:18; Rom 13:9; Gal 5:14; Jas 2:8.
l. [12:33] Dt 6:4; Ps 40:7–9.
m. [12:34] Mt 22:46; Lk 20:40.
n. [12:35–37] Mt 22:41–45; Lk 20:41–44.
o. [12:36] Ps 110:1.
p. [12:38–40] Mt 23:1–7; Lk 11:43; 20:45–47.
q. [12:41–44] Lk 21:1–4.

CHAPTER 13

The Destruction of the Temple Foretold. [1]As he was making his way out of the temple area one of his disciples said to him, "Look, teacher, what stones and what buildings!"[a] [2]Jesus said to him, "Do you see these great buildings? There will not be one stone left upon another that will not be thrown down."

The Signs of the End. [3]As he was sitting on the Mount of Olives opposite the temple area, Peter, James, John, and Andrew asked him privately,[b] [4]"Tell us, when will this happen, and what sign will there be when all these things are about to come to an end?" [5]Jesus began to say to them, "See that no one deceives you.[c] [6]Many will come in my name saying, 'I am he,' and they will deceive many. [7]When you hear of wars and reports of wars do not be alarmed; such things must happen, but it will not yet be the end. [8]Nation will rise against nation and kingdom against kingdom. There will be earthquakes from place to place and there will be famines. These are the beginnings of the labor pains.

The Coming Persecution. [9]"Watch out for yourselves.[d] They will hand you over to the courts. You will be beaten in synagogues. You will be arraigned before governors and kings because of me, as a witness before them. [10]But the gospel must first be preached to all nations.* [11]When they lead you away and hand you over, do not worry beforehand about what you are to say.[e] But say whatever will be given to you at that hour. For it will not be you who are speaking but the holy Spirit. [12]Brother will hand over brother to death, and the father his child; children will rise up against parents and have them put to death. [13]You will be hated by all because of my name. But the one who perseveres to the end will be saved.

The Great Tribulation. [14f]"When you see the desolating abomination standing* where he should not (let the reader understand), then those in Judea must flee to the mountains,[g] [15][and] a person on a housetop must not go down or enter to get anything out of his house,[h] [16]and a person in a field must not return to get his cloak. [17]Woe to pregnant women and nursing mothers in those days. [18]Pray that this does not happen in winter. [19]For those times will have tribulation such as has not been since the beginning of God's creation until now, nor ever will be.[i] [20]If the Lord had not shortened those days, no one would be saved; but for the sake of the elect whom he chose, he did shorten the days. [21]If anyone says to you then, 'Look, here is the Messiah! Look, there he is!' do not believe it. [22]False messiahs and false prophets will arise and will perform signs and wonders in order to mislead, if that were possible, the elect. [23]Be watchful! I have told it all to you beforehand.

The Coming of the Son of Man. [24j]"But in those days after that tribulation

the sun will be darkened,
  and the moon will not
    give its light,[k]
[25]and the stars will be falling from the sky,

and the powers in
the heavens will be
shaken.

²⁶*ˡAnd then they will see 'the Son of Man coming in the clouds' with great power and glory, ²⁷and then he will send out the angels and gather [his] elect from the four winds, from the end of the earth to the end of the sky.

The Lesson of the Fig Tree.
²⁸ᵐ"Learn a lesson from the fig tree. When its branch becomes tender and sprouts leaves, you know that summer is near. ²⁹In the same way, when you see these things happening, know that he is near, at the gates. ³⁰Amen, I say to you, this generation will not pass away until all these things have taken place. ³¹Heaven and earth will pass away, but my words will not pass away.

Need for Watchfulness. ³²"But of that day or hour, no one knows, neither the angels in heaven, nor the Son, but only the Father. ³³ⁿBe watchful! Be alert! You do not know when the time will come. ³⁴It is like a man traveling abroad. He leaves home and places his servants in charge, each with his work, and orders the gatekeeper to be on the watch.ᵒ ³⁵Watch, therefore; you do not know when the lord of the house is coming, whether in the evening, or at midnight, or at cockcrow, or in the morning. ³⁶May he not come suddenly and find you sleeping. ³⁷What I say to you, I say to all: 'Watch!'"

a. [13:1–2] Mt 24:1–2; Lk 21:5–6.
b. [13:3–8] Mt 24:3–8; Lk 21:7–11.
c. [13:5] Eph 5:6; 2 Thes 2:3.
d. [13:9–13] Mt 24:9–14; Lk 21:12–19.
e. [13:11–12] Mt 10:19–22; Lk 12:11–12.
f. [13:14–23] Mt 24:15–22; Lk 21:20–24.
g. [13:14] Dn 9:27; Mt 24:15.
h. [13:15] Lk 17:31.
i. [13:19] Dn 12:1.
j. [13:24–27] Mt 24:29–31; Lk 21:25–27.
k. [13:24] Is 13:10; Ez 32:7; Jl 2:10.
l. [13:26] 14:62; Dn 7:13–14.
m. [13:28–32] Mt 24:32–36; Lk 21:29–33.
n. [13:33–37] Mt 24:42; 25:13–15.
o. [13:34] Mt 25:14–30; Lk 19:12–27.

CHAPTER 14

The Conspiracy Against Jesus. ¹"The Passover and the

Feast of Unleavened Bread* were to take place in two days' time.*ᵃ So the chief priests and the scribes were seeking a way to arrest him by treachery and put him to death. ²They said, "Not during the festival, for fear that there may be a riot among the people."

The Anointing at Bethany.*
³When he was in Bethany reclining at table in the house of Simon the leper,*ᵇ a woman came with an alabaster jar of perfumed oil, costly genuine spikenard. She broke the alabaster jar and poured it on his head. ⁴There were some who were indignant. "Why has there been this waste of perfumed oil? ⁵It could have been sold for more than three hundred days' wages and the money given to the poor." They were infuriated with her. ⁶Jesus said, "Let her alone. Why do you make trouble for her? She has done a good thing for me. ⁷The poor you will always have with you,

and whenever you wish you can do good to them, but you will not always have me. ⁸She has done what she could. She has anticipated anointing my body for burial. ⁹Amen, I say to you, wherever the gospel is proclaimed to the whole world, what she has done will be told in memory of her."

The Betrayal by Judas.
¹⁰ᶜThen Judas Iscariot, one of the Twelve, went off to the chief priests to hand him over to them. ¹¹When they heard him they were pleased and promised to pay him money. Then he looked for an opportunity to hand him over.

Preparations for the Passover. ¹²ᵈOn the first day of the Feast of Unleavened Bread, when they sacrificed the Passover lamb,* his disciples said to him, "Where do you want us to go and prepare for you to eat the Passover?" ¹³He sent two of his disciples and said to them, "Go into the city and a man will meet you, carrying a jar of water.* Follow him. [14]Wherever he enters, say to the master of the house, 'The Teacher says, "Where is my guest room where I may eat the Passover with my disciples?"' [15]Then he will show you a large upper room furnished and ready. Make the preparations for us there." [16]The disciples then went off, entered the city, and found it just as he had told them; and they prepared the Passover.

The Betrayer. [17e]When it was evening, he came with the Twelve. [18*]And as they reclined at table and were eating, Jesus said, "Amen, I say to you, one of you will betray me, one who is eating with me." [19]They began to be distressed and to say to him, one by one, "Surely it is not I?" [20]He said to them, "One of the Twelve, the one who dips with me into the dish. [21]For the Son of Man indeed goes, as it is written of him,* but

woe to that man by whom the Son of Man is betrayed. It would be better for that man if he had never been born."

The Lord's Supper. [22*]While they were eating,[f] he took bread, said the blessing, broke it, and gave it to them, and said, "Take it; this is my body." [23]Then he took a cup, gave thanks, and gave it to them, and they all drank from it. [24]He said to them, "This is my blood of the covenant, which will be shed* for many. [25]Amen, I say to you, I shall not drink again the fruit of the vine until the day when I drink it new in the kingdom of God." [26]Then, after singing a hymn,* they went out to the Mount of Olives.[g]

Peter's Denial Foretold.* [27]Then Jesus said to them, "All of you will have your faith shaken, for it is written:

'I will strike the shepherd,
    and the sheep will be
        dispersed.'[h]

²⁸But after I have been raised up, I shall go before you to Galilee." ²⁹Peter said to him, "Even though all should have their faith shaken, mine will not be." ³⁰Then Jesus said to him, "Amen, I say to you, this very night before the cock crows twice you will deny me three times." ³¹But he vehemently replied, "Even though I should have to die with you, I will not deny you." And they all spoke similarly.

The Agony in the Garden. ³²*Then they came to a place named Gethsemane,ⁱ and he said to his disciples, "Sit here while I pray."ʲ ³³He took with him Peter, James, and John, and began to be troubled and distressed. ³⁴Then he said to them, "My soul is sorrowful even to death. Remain here and keep watch." ³⁵He advanced a little and fell to the ground and prayed that if it were possible the hour might pass by him; ³⁶he said, "Abba, Father,* all things are possible to you. Take this cup away from me, but not what I will but what you will." ³⁷When he returned he found them asleep. He said to Peter, "Simon, are you asleep? Could you not keep watch for one hour? ³⁸Watch and pray that you may not undergo the test.ᵏ The spirit is willing but the flesh is weak." ³⁹Withdrawing again, he prayed, saying the same thing. ⁴⁰Then he returned once more and found them asleep, for they could not keep their eyes open and did not know what to answer him. ⁴¹He returned a third time and said to them, "Are you still sleeping and taking your rest? It is enough. The hour has come. Behold, the Son of Man is to be handed over to sinners. ⁴²Get up, let us go. See, my betrayer is at hand."

• **The Betrayal and Arrest of Jesus.** ⁴³ˡThen, while he was still speaking, Judas, one of the Twelve, arrived, accompanied by a crowd with swords and clubs who had come from the chief priests, the scribes, and the elders. ⁴⁴His betrayer had arranged a signal with them, saying, "The man I shall kiss is the one; arrest him and lead him away securely." ⁴⁵He came and immediately went over to him and said, "Rabbi." And he kissed him. ⁴⁶At this they laid hands on him and arrested him. ⁴⁷One of the bystanders drew his sword, struck the high priest's servant, and cut off his ear. ⁴⁸Jesus said to them in reply, "Have you come out as against a robber, with swords and clubs, to seize me? ⁴⁹Day after day I was with you teaching in the temple area, yet you did not arrest me; but that the scriptures may be fulfilled." ⁵⁰And they all left him and fled. ⁵¹Now a young man followed him wearing nothing but a linen cloth about his body. They seized him, ⁵²but he left the cloth behind and ran off naked.

Jesus Before the Sanhedrin. ⁵³*ᵐ*They led Jesus away to the high priest, and all the chief priests and the elders and the scribes came together. ⁵⁴Peter followed him at a distance into the high priest's courtyard and was seated with the guards, warming himself at the fire. ⁵⁵The chief priests and the entire Sanhedrin kept trying to obtain testimony against Jesus in order to put him to death, but they found none. ⁵⁶Many gave false witness against him, but their testimony did not agree. ⁵⁷*Some took the stand and testified falsely against him, alleging, ⁵⁸"We heard him say, 'I will destroy this temple made with hands and within three days I will build another not made with hands.'"ⁿ ⁵⁹Even so their testimony did not agree. ⁶⁰The high priest rose before the assembly and questioned

Jesus, saying, "Have you no answer? What are these men testifying against you?" [61*]But he was <u>silent</u> and answered nothing. Again the high priest asked him and said to him, "Are you the Messiah, the son of the Blessed One?" [62]Then Jesus answered, "I am;

⌜and 'you will see the Son of Man
seated at the right hand of the Power
and coming with the clouds of heaven.'"[o]⌟

[63]At that the high priest tore his garments and said, "What further need have we of witnesses? [64]You have heard the <u>blasphemy</u>. What do you think?" They all condemned him as deserving to die. [65]Some began to spit on him. They blindfolded him and struck him and said to him, "Prophesy!" And the guards greeted him with blows.[p]

Peter's Denial of Jesus. [66q]While Peter was below in the courtyard, one of the high priest's maids came along. [67]Seeing Peter warming himself, she looked intently at him and said, "You too were with the Nazarene, Jesus." [68*]But he denied it saying, "I neither know nor understand what you are talking about." So he went out into the outer court. [Then the cock crowed.] [69]The maid saw him and began again to say to the bystanders, "This man is one of them." [70]Once again he denied it. A little later the bystanders said to Peter once more, "Surely you are one of them; for you too are a Galilean." [71]He began to curse and to swear, "I do not know this man about whom you are talking." [72]And immediately a cock crowed a second time. Then Peter remembered the word that Jesus had said to him, "Before the cock crows twice you will deny me three times." He broke down and wept.[r]

a. [14:1–2] Mt 26:2–5; Lk 22:1–2; Jn 11:45–53.
b. [14:3–9] Mt 26:6–13; Jn 12:1–8.
c. [14:10–11] Mt 26:14–16; Lk 22:3–6.
d. [14:12–16] Mt 26:17–19; Lk 22:7–13.
e. [14:17–21] Mt 26:20–24; Lk 22:21–23; Jn
     13:21–26.
f. [14:22–25] Mt 26:26–30; Lk 22:19–20; 1 Cor
     11:23–25.
g. [14:26–31] Mt 26:30–35; Lk 22:34, 39; Jn
     13:36–38.
h. [14:27] Zec 13:7; Jn 16:32.
i. [14:32–42] Mt 26:36–46; Lk 22:40–46.
j. [14:32] Jn 18:1.
k. [14:38] Rom 7:5.
l. [14:43–50] Mt 26:47–56; Lk 22:47–53; Jn
     18:3–11.
m. [14:53–65] Mt 26:57–68; Lk 22:54–55, 63–65,
     67–71; Jn 18:12–13.
n. [14:58] 15:29; 2 Cor 5:1.
o. [14:62] 13:26; Ps 110:1; Dn 7:13; Mt 24:30.
p. [14:65] Lk 22:63–65.
q. [14:66–72] Mt 26:69–75; Lk 22:56–62; Jn 18:16–
     18, 25–27.
r. [14:72] Jn 13:38.

CHAPTER 15

Jesus Before Pilate. [1a]As soon as morning came,[b] the chief priests with the elders and the scribes, that is, the whole Sanhedrin, held a council.[*] They bound Jesus, led him away, and handed him over to Pilate. [2]Pilate questioned him, "Are you the king of the Jews?"[*] He said to him in reply, "You say so." [3]The chief priests accused him of many things. [4]Again Pilate questioned him, "Have you no answer? See how many things they accuse you of." [5]Jesus gave him no further answer, so that Pilate was amazed.

The Sentence of Death.[*] [6]Now on the occasion of the feast he used to release to them one prisoner whom they requested.[c] [7]A man called Barabbas[*] was then in prison along with the rebels who had committed murder in a rebellion. [8]The crowd came forward and began to ask him to do for them as he was accustomed. [9]Pilate answered, "Do you want me to release to you the king of the Jews?" [10]For he knew that it was out of envy that the chief priests had handed him over. [11]But the chief priests stirred up the crowd to have him release Barabbas for them instead. [12]Pilate again said to them in reply, "Then what [do you want] me to do with [the man you call] the king of the Jews?" [13*]They shouted again, "Crucify him." [14]Pilate said to them, "Why? What evil has he done?" They only shouted the louder, "Crucify him." ^{15*}So Pilate, <u>wishing to satisfy the crowd</u>, released Barabbas to them and, after he had Jesus scourged, handed him over to be crucified.

Mockery by the Soldiers. ^{16*d}The soldiers led him away inside the palace, that is, the praetorium, and assembled the whole cohort. ¹⁷They clothed him in purple and, weaving a crown of thorns, placed it on him. ¹⁸They began to salute him with, "Hail, King of the Jews!" ¹⁹and kept striking his head with a reed and spitting upon him. They knelt before him in homage. ²⁰And when they had mocked him, they stripped him of the purple cloak, dressed him in his own clothes, and led him out to crucify him.

The Way of the Cross. ²¹They pressed into service a passerby, Simon, a Cyrenian,* who was coming in from the country, the father of Alexander and Rufus, to carry his cross.^e

The Crucifixion. ^{22f}They brought him to the place of Golgotha (which is translated Place of the Skull). ²³They gave him wine drugged with myrrh, but he did not take it. ^{24*g}Then they crucified him and divided his garments by casting lots for them to see what each should take. ²⁵It was <u>nine o'clock in the morning</u>* when they crucified him. ^{26*}The inscription of the charge against him read, "The King of the Jews." ²⁷With him they crucified two revolutionaries, one on his right and one on his left.^h [²⁸]* ^{29*}Those passing by reviled him, shaking their heads and saying,ⁱ "Aha! You who would destroy the temple and rebuild it in three days, ³⁰save yourself by coming down from the cross." ³¹Likewise the chief priests, with the scribes, mocked him among themselves and said, "He saved others; he cannot save himself. ³²Let the Messiah, the King of Israel, come down now from the cross that we may see and believe." Those who were crucified with him also kept abusing him.[j]

The Death of Jesus. [33]At noon darkness came over the whole land until three in the afternoon. [34]And at three o'clock Jesus cried out in a loud voice, "*Eloi, Eloi, lema sabachthani?*" which is translated, "My God, my God, why have you forsaken me?"[k] [35]Some of the bystanders who heard it said, "Look, he is calling Elijah." [36]One of them ran, soaked a sponge with wine, put it on a reed, and gave it to him to drink, saying, "Wait, let us see if Elijah comes to take him down." [37]Jesus gave a loud cry and breathed his last. [38]The veil of the sanctuary was torn in two from top to bottom. [39]When the centurion who stood facing him saw how he breathed his last he said, "Truly this man was the Son of God!" [40]There were also women looking on from a distance.[m] Among them were Mary Magdalene, Mary the mother of the younger James and of Joses, and Salome. [41]These women had followed him when he was in Galilee and ministered to him. There were also many other women who had come up with him to Jerusalem.

The Burial of Jesus. [42n]When it was already evening, since it was the day of preparation, the day before the sabbath, [43]Joseph of Arimathea, a distinguished member of the council, who was himself awaiting the kingdom of God, came and courageously went to Pilate and asked for the body of Jesus. [44]Pilate was amazed that he was already dead. He summoned the centurion and asked him if Jesus had already died. [45]And when he learned of it from the centurion, he gave the body to Joseph. [46]Having bought a linen cloth, he took him down, wrapped him in the linen cloth and laid him in a tomb that had been hewn out of the rock. Then he rolled a stone against the entrance to the tomb. ⁴⁷Mary Magdalene and Mary the mother of Joses watched where he was laid.

---

a.   [15:1–5] Mt 27:1–2, 11–14; Lk 23:1–3.
b.   [15:1] Jn 18:28.
c.   [15:6–15] Mt 27:15–26; Lk 23:17–25; Jn 18:39–40.
d.   [15:16–20] Mt 27:27–31; Jn 19:2–3.
e.   [15:21] Mt 27:32; Lk 23:26.
f.   [15:22–38] Mt 27:33–51; Lk 23:32–46; Jn 19:17–30.
g.   [15:24] Ps 22:18.
h.   [15:27] Lk 23:33.
i.   [15:29] Jn 2:19.
j.   [15:32] Lk 23:39.
k.   [15:34] Ps 22:2.
l.   [15:39–41] Mt 27:54–56; Lk 23:47–49.
m. [15:40] 6:3; Lk 8:2–3.
n.   [15:42–47] Mt 27:57–61; Lk 23:50–56; Jn 19:38–42.

CHAPTER 16

The Resurrection of Jesus.[*]
¹When the sabbath was over,[a] Mary Magdalene, Mary, the mother of James, and Salome bought spices so that they might go and anoint him.[b] ²Very early when the sun had risen, on the first day of the week, they came to the tomb. ³They were saying to one another, "Who will roll back the stone for us from the entrance to the tomb?" ⁴When they looked up, they saw that the stone had been rolled back; it was very large. ⁵On entering the tomb they saw a young man sitting on the right side, clothed in a white robe, and they were utterly amazed.[c] ⁶He said to them, "Do not be amazed! You seek Jesus of Nazareth, the crucified. He has been raised; he is not here. Behold, the place where they laid him. ⁷But go and tell his disciples and Peter, 'He is going before you to Galilee; there you will see him, as he told you.'"[d] ⁸Then they went out and fled from the tomb, seized with trembling and bewilderment. They said nothing to anyone, for they were afraid.

THE LONGER ENDING[*]

The Appearance to Mary Magdalene. [⁹eWhen he had risen, early on the first day of the week, he appeared first to Mary Magdalene, out of whom he had driven seven demons. [10f]She went and told his companions who were mourning and weeping. [11]When they heard that he was alive and had been seen by her, they did not believe.

The Appearance to Two Disciples. [12g]After this he appeared in another form to two of them walking along on their way to the country. [13]They returned and told the others; but they did not believe them either.

The Commissioning of the Eleven. [14h][But] later, as the eleven were at table, he appeared to them and rebuked them for their unbelief and hardness of heart because they had not believed those who saw him after he had been raised. [15i]He said to them, "Go into the whole world and proclaim the gospel to every creature. [16]Whoever believes and is baptized will be saved; whoever does not believe will be condemned.

[17]These signs will accompany those who believe: in my name they will drive out demons, they will speak new languages. [18]They will pick up serpents [with their hands], and if they drink any deadly thing, it will not harm them. They will lay hands on the sick, and they will recover."[j]

The Ascension of Jesus. [19]So then the Lord Jesus, after he spoke to them, was taken up into heaven and took his seat at the right hand of God.[k] [20]But they went forth and preached everywhere, while the Lord worked with them and confirmed the word through accompanying signs.][l]

THE SHORTER ENDING

[And they reported all the instructions briefly to Peter's companions. Afterwards Jesus himself, through them, sent forth from east to west the sacred and imperishable proclamation of eternal salvation. Amen.]

a. [16:1–8] Mt 28:1–8; Lk 24:1–10; Jn 20:1–10.
b. [16:1–2] Mt 28:1; Lk 23:56.
c. [16:5] Jn 20:12.
d. [16:7] 14:28.
e. [16:9–20] Mt 28:1–10; Jn 20:11–18.
f. [16:10–11] Lk 24:10–11; Jn 20:18.
g. [16:12–14] Lk 24:13–35.
h. [16:14] Lk 24:36–49; Lk Cor 15:5.
i. [16:15–16] 13:10; Mt 28:18–20; Lk 24:47; Jn 20:21.
j. [16:18] Mt 10:1; Lk 10:19; Acts 28:3–6.
k. [16:19] Lk 24:50–53.
l. [16:20] 1 Tm 3:16.

Notes

* [1:1–13] The prologue of the Gospel according to Mark begins with the title (Mk 1:1) followed by three events preparatory to Jesus' preaching: (1) the appearance in the Judean wilderness of John, baptizer, preacher of repentance, and precursor of Jesus (Mk 1:2–8); (2) the baptism of Jesus, at which a voice from heaven acknowledges Jesus to be God's Son, and the holy Spirit descends on him (Mk 1:9–11); (3) the temptation of Jesus by Satan (Mk 1:12–13).

* [1:1] **The gospel of Jesus Christ [the Son of God]**: the "good news" of salvation in and through Jesus, crucified and risen, acknowledged by the Christian community as Messiah (Mk 8:29; 14:61–62) and the Son of God (Mk 1:11; 9:7; 15:39), although some important manuscripts here omit **the Son of God**.

* [1:2–3] Although Mark attributes the prophecy to Isaiah, the text is a combination of Mal 3:1; Is 40:3; Ex 23:20; cf. Mt 11:10; Lk 7:27. John's ministry is seen as God's prelude to the saving mission of his Son. **The way of the Lord**: this prophecy of Deutero-Isaiah concerning the end of the Babylonian exile is here applied to the coming of Jesus; John the Baptist is to prepare the way for him.

* [1:6] **Clothed in camel's hair . . . waist**: the Baptist's garb recalls that of Elijah in 2 Kgs 1:8. Jesus speaks of the Baptist as Elijah who has already come (Mk 9:11–13; Mt 17:10–12; cf. Mal 3:23–24; Lk 1:17).

* [1:8–9] Through the life-giving baptism with the holy Spirit (Mk 1:8), Jesus will create a new people of God. But first he identifies himself with the people of Israel in submitting to John's baptism of repentance and in bearing on their behalf the burden of God's decisive judgment (Mk 1:9;

cf. Mk 1:4). As in the desert of Sinai, so here in the wilderness of Judea, Israel's sonship with God is to be renewed.

* [1:10–11] **He saw the heavens . . . and the Spirit . . . upon him**: indicating divine intervention in fulfillment of promise. Here the descent of the Spirit on Jesus is meant, anointing him for his ministry; cf. Is 11:2; 42:1; 61:1; 63:9. **A voice . . . with you I am well pleased**: God's acknowledgment of Jesus as his unique Son, the object of his love. His approval of Jesus is the assurance that Jesus will fulfill his messianic mission of salvation.

* [1:12–13] The same Spirit who descended on Jesus in his baptism now drives him into the desert for forty days. The result is radical confrontation and temptation by Satan who attempts to frustrate the work of God. The presence of wild beasts may indicate the horror and danger of the desert regarded as the abode of demons or may reflect the paradise motif of harmony among all creatures; cf. Is 11:6–9. The presence of ministering angels to sustain Jesus recalls the angel who guided the Israelites in the desert in the first Exodus (Ex 14:19; 23:20) and the angel who supplied nourishment to Elijah in the wilderness (1 Kgs 19:5–7). The combined forces of good and evil were present to Jesus in the desert. His sustained obedience brings forth the new Israel of God there where Israel's rebellion had brought death and alienation.

* [1:14–15] **After John had been arrested**: in the plan of God, Jesus was not to proclaim the good news of salvation prior to the termination of the Baptist's active mission. **Galilee**: in the Marcan account, scene of the major part of Jesus' public ministry before his arrest and condemnation. **The gospel of God**: not only the good news from God but about God at work in Jesus Christ. **This is the time of fulfillment**: i.e., of God's promises. **The kingdom of God . . . Repent**: see note on Mt 3:2.

* [1:16–20] These verses narrate the call of the first Disciples. See notes on Mt 4:18–22 and Mt 4:20.

* [1:21–45] The account of a single day's ministry of Jesus on a sabbath in and outside the synagogue of Capernaum (Mk 1:21–31) combines teaching and miracles of exorcism and healing. Mention is not made of the content of the teaching but of the effect of astonishment and alarm on the people. Jesus' teaching with authority, making an absolute claim on the hearer, was in the best tradition of the ancient prophets, not of the scribes. The narrative continues with events that evening (Mk 1:32–34; see notes on Mt 8:14–17) and the next day (Mk 1:35–39). The cleansing in Mk 1:40–45 stands as an isolated story.

* [1:23] **An unclean spirit**: so called because of the spirit's resistance to the holiness of God. The spirit knows and fears the power of Jesus to destroy his influence; cf. Mk 1:32, 34; 3:11; 6:13.

* [1:24–25] **The Holy One of God**: not a confession but an attempt to ward off Jesus' power, reflecting the notion that use of the precise name of an opposing spirit would guarantee mastery over him. Jesus silenced the cry of the unclean spirit and drove him out of the man.

* [1:24] **What have you to do with us?**: see note on Jn 2:4.

* [1:40] **A leper**: for the various forms of skin disease, see Lv 13:1–50 and the note on Lv 13:2–4. There are only two instances in the Old Testament in which God is shown to have cured a leper (Nm 12:10–15; 2 Kgs 5:1–14). The law of Moses provided for the ritual purification of a leper. In curing the leper, Jesus assumes that the priests will reinstate the cured man into the religious community. See also note on Lk 5:14.

* [2:1–3:6] This section relates a series of conflicts between Jesus and the scribes and Pharisees in which the growing opposition of the latter leads to their plot to put Jesus to death (Mk 3:6).

* [2:1–2] **He was at home**: to the crowds that gathered in and outside the house Jesus **preached the word**, i.e., the gospel concerning the nearness of the kingdom and the necessity of repentance and faith (Mk 1:14).

* [2:5] It was the faith of the paralytic and those who carried him that moved Jesus to heal the sick man. Accounts of other miracles of Jesus reveal more and more his emphasis on faith as the requisite for exercising his healing powers (Mk 5:34; 9:23–24; 10:52).

* [2:6] **Scribes**: trained in oral interpretation of the written law; in Mark's gospel, adversaries of Jesus, with one exception (Mk 12:28, 34).

* [2:7] **He is blaspheming**: an accusation made here and repeated during the trial of Jesus (Mk 14:60–64).

* [2:10] **But that you may know that the Son of Man . . . on earth**: although Mk 2:8–9 are addressed to the scribes, the sudden interruption of thought and structure in Mk 2:10 seems not addressed to them nor to the paralytic. Moreover, the early public use of the designation "Son of Man" to unbelieving scribes is most unlikely. The most probable explanation is that Mark's insertion of Mk 2:10 is a commentary addressed to Christians for whom the miracle and who already accept in faith that Jesus is Messiah and Son of God.

* [2:13] **He taught them**: see note on Mk 1:21–45.

* [2:14] **As he passed by**: see note on Mk 1:16–20. **Levi, son of Alphaeus**: see note on Mt 9:9. **Customs post**: such tax collectors paid a fixed sum for the right to collect customs duties within their districts. Since whatever they could collect above this amount constituted their profit, the abuse of extortion was widespread among them.

Hence, Jewish customs officials were regarded as sinners (Mk 2:16), outcasts of society, and disgraced along with their families. **He got up and followed him**: i.e., became a disciple of Jesus.

* [2:15] **In his house**: cf. Mk 2:1; Mt 9:10. Lk 5:29 clearly calls it Levi's house.

* [2:16–17] This and the following conflict stories reflect a similar pattern: a statement of fact, a question of protest, and a reply by Jesus.

* [2:17] **Do not need a physician**: this maxim of Jesus with its implied irony was uttered to silence his adversaries who objected that he ate with **tax collectors and sinners** (Mk 2:16). Because the scribes and Pharisees were self-righteous, they were not capable of responding to Jesus' call to repentance and faith in the gospel.

* [2:18–22] This conflict over the question of fasting has the same pattern as Mk 2:16–17; see notes on Mt 9:15; 9:16–17.

* [2:19] **Can the wedding guests fast?**: the bridal metaphor expresses a new relationship of love between God and his people in the person and mission of Jesus to his disciples. It is the inauguration of the new and joyful messianic time of fulfillment and the passing of the old. Any attempt at assimilating the Pharisaic practice of fasting, or of extending the preparatory discipline of John's disciples beyond the arrival of the bridegroom, would be as futile as sewing **a piece of unshrunken cloth on an old cloak** or pouring **new wine into old wineskins** with the resulting destruction of both cloth and wine (Mk 2:21–22). Fasting is rendered superfluous during the earthly ministry of Jesus; cf. Mk 2:20.

* [2:23–28] This conflict regarding the sabbath follows the same pattern as Mk 2:18–22.

* [2:25–26] **Have you never read what David did?**: Jesus defends the action of his disciples on the basis of 1 Sm 21:2–7 in which an exception is made to the regulation of Lv 24:9 because of the extreme hunger of David and his men. According to 1 Samuel, the priest who gave the bread to David was Ahimelech, father of Abiathar.

* [2:27] **The sabbath was made for man**: a reaffirmation of the divine intent of the sabbath to benefit Israel as contrasted with the restrictive Pharisaic tradition added to the law.

* [2:28] **The Son of Man is lord even of the sabbath**: Mark's comment on the theological meaning of the incident is to benefit his Christian readers; see note on Mk 2:10.

* [3:1–5] Here Jesus is again depicted in conflict with his adversaries over the question of sabbath-day observance. His opponents were already ill disposed toward him because they regarded Jesus as a violator of the sabbath. Jesus' question **Is it lawful to do good on the sabbath rather than to do evil?** places the matter in the broader theological context outside the casuistry of the scribes.

The answer is obvious. Jesus heals the man with the withered hand in the sight of all and reduces his opponents to silence; cf. Jn 5:17–18.

* [3:6] In reporting the plot of the Pharisees and Herodians to put Jesus to death after this series of conflicts in Galilee, Mark uses a pattern that recurs in his account of later controversies in Jerusalem (Mk 11:17–18; 12:13–17). The help of the Herodians, supporters of Herod Antipas, tetrarch of Galilee and Perea, is needed to take action against Jesus. Both series of conflicts point to their gravity and to the impending passion of Jesus.

* [3:7–19] This overview of the Galilean ministry manifests the power of Jesus to draw people to himself through his teaching and deeds of power. The crowds of Jews from many regions surround Jesus (Mk 3:7–12). This phenomenon prepares the way for creating a new people of Israel. The choice and mission of the Twelve is the prelude (Mk 3:13–19).

* [3:11–12] See note on Mk 1:24–25.

* [3:13] **He went up the mountain**: here and elsewhere the mountain is associated with solemn moments and acts in the mission and self-revelation of Jesus (Mk 6:46; 9:2–8; 13:3). Jesus acts with authority as he **summoned those whom he wanted and they came to him**.

* [3:14–15] **He appointed twelve [whom he also named apostles] that they might be with him**: literally "he made," i.e., instituted them as apostles to extend his messianic mission through them (Mk 6:7–13). See notes on Mt 10:1 and 10:2–4.

* [3:16] **Simon, whom he named Peter**: Mark indicates that Simon's name was changed on this occasion. Peter is first in all lists of the apostles (Mt 10:2; Lk 6:14; Acts 1:13; cf. 1 Cor 15:5–8).

* [3:20–35] Within the narrative of the coming of Jesus' relatives (Mk 3:20–21) is inserted the account of the unbelieving scribes from Jerusalem who attributed Jesus' power over demons to Beelzebul (Mk 3:22–30); see note on Mk 5:21–43. There were those even among the relatives of Jesus who disbelieved and regarded Jesus as **out of his mind** (Mk 3:21). Against this background, Jesus is informed of the arrival of his mother and brothers [and sisters] (Mk 3:32). He responds by showing that not family ties but doing God's will (Mk 3:35) is decisive in the kingdom; cf. note on Mt 12:46–50.

* [3:20] **He came home**: cf. Mk 2:1–2 and see note on Mk 2:15.

* [3:22] **By Beelzebul**: see note on Mt 10:25. Two accusations are leveled against Jesus: (1) that **he is possessed** by an unclean spirit and (2) **by the prince of demons he drives out demons**. Jesus answers the second charge by a parable (Mk 3:24–27) and responds to the first charge in Mk 3:28–29.

* [3:29] **Whoever blasphemes against the holy Spirit**: this sin is called **an everlasting sin** because it attributes to Satan, who is the power of evil, what is actually the work of the holy Spirit, namely, victory over the demons.

* [3:32] **Your brothers**: see note on Mk 6:3.

* [4:1–34] **In parables** (Mk 4:2): see note on Mt 13:3. The use of parables is typical of Jesus' enigmatic method of teaching the crowds (Mk 4:2–9, 12) as compared with the interpretation of the parables he gives to his disciples (Mk 4:10–25, 33–34) to each group according to its capacity to understand (Mk 4:9–11). The key feature of the parable at hand is the sowing of the seed (Mk 4:3), representing the breakthrough of the kingdom of God into the world. The various types of soil refer to the diversity of response accorded the word of God (Mk 4:4–7). The climax of the parable is the harvest of thirty, sixty, and a hundredfold, indicating the consummation of the kingdom (Mk 4:8). Thus both the present and the future action of God, from the initiation to the fulfillment of the kingdom, is presented through this and other parables (Mk 4:26–29, 30–32).

* [4:1] **By the sea**: the shore of the Sea of Galilee or a boat near the shore (Mk 2:13; 3:7–8) is the place where Mark depicts Jesus teaching the crowds. By contrast the mountain is the scene of Jesus at prayer (Mk 6:46) or in the process of forming his disciples (Mk 3:13; 9:2).

* [4:3–8] See note on Mt 13:3–8.

* [4:11–12] These verses are to be viewed against their background in Mk 3:6, 22 concerning the unbelief and opposition Jesus encountered in his ministry. It is against this background that the distinction in Jesus' method becomes clear of presenting the kingdom to the disbelieving crowd in one manner and to the disciples in another. To the former it is presented in parables and the truth remains hidden; for the latter the parable is interpreted and the mystery is partially revealed because of their faith; see notes on Mt 13:11 and Mt 13:13.

* [4:13–20] See note on Mt 13:18–23.

* [4:26–29] Only Mark records the parable of the seed's growth. Sower and harvester are the same. The emphasis is on the power of the seed to grow of itself without human intervention (Mk 4:27). Mysteriously it produces **blade** and **ear** and **full grain** (Mk 4:28). Thus the kingdom of God initiated by Jesus in proclaiming the word develops quietly yet powerfully until it is fully established by him at the final judgment (Mk 4:29); cf. Rev 14:15.

* [4:32] The universality of the kingdom of God is indicated here; cf. Ez 17:23; 31:6; Dn 4:17–19.

* [4:35–5:43] After the chapter on parables, Mark narrates four miracle stories: Mk 4:35–41;

5:1–20; and two joined together in Mk 5:21–43. See also notes on Mt 8:23–34 and 9:8–26.

* [4:39] **Quiet! Be still!**: as in the case of silencing a demon (Mk 1:25), Jesus rebukes the wind and subdues the turbulence of the sea by a mere word; see note on Mt 8:26.

* [4:41] Jesus is here depicted as exercising power over wind and sea. In the Christian community this event was seen as a sign of Jesus' saving presence amid persecutions that threatened its existence.

* [5:1] **The territory of the Gerasenes**: the reference is to pagan territory; cf. Is 65:1. Another reading is "Gadarenes"; see note on Mt 8:28.

* [5:2–6] The man was an outcast from society, dominated by unclean spirits (Mk 5:8, 13), living among the tombs. The prostration before Jesus (Mk 5:6) indicates Jesus' power over evil spirits.

* [5:7] **What have you to do with me?**: cf. Mk 1:24 and see note on Jn 2:4.

* [5:9] **Legion is my name**: the demons were numerous and the condition of the possessed man was extremely serious; cf. Mt 12:45.

* [5:11] **Herd of swine**: see note on Mt 8:30.

* [5:19] **Go home**: Jesus did not accept the man's request **to remain with him** as a disciple (Mk 5:18), yet invited him to announce to his own people what the Lord had done for him, i.e., proclaim the gospel message to his pagan family; cf. Mk 1:14, 39; 3:14; 13:10.

* [5:21–43] The story of the raising to life of Jairus's daughter is divided into two parts: Mk 5:21–24; 5:35–43. Between these two separated parts the account of the cure of the hemorrhage victim (Mk 5:25–34) is interposed. This technique of intercalating or sandwiching one story within another occurs several times in Mk 3:19b–21; 3:22–30; 3:31–35; 6:6b–13; 6:14–29; 6:30; 11:12–14; 11:15–19; 11:20–25; 14:53; 14:54; 14:55–65; 14:66–73.

* [5:23] **Lay your hands on her**: this act for the purpose of healing is frequent in Mk 6:5; 7:32–35; 8:23–25; 16:18 and is also found in Mt 9:18; Lk 4:40; 13:13; Acts 9:17; 28:8.

* [5:28] Both in the case of Jairus and his daughter (Mk 5:23) and in the case of the hemorrhage victim, the inner conviction that physical contact (Mk 5:30) accompanied by faith in Jesus' saving power could effect a cure was rewarded.

* [5:35] The faith of Jairus was put to a twofold test: (1) that his daughter might be cured and now that she had died, (2) that she might be restored to life. His faith contrasts with the lack of faith of the crowd.

* [5:39] **Not dead but asleep**: the New Testament often refers to death as sleep (Mt 27:52; Jn 11:11; 1 Cor 15:6; 1 Thes 4:13–15); see note on Mt 9:24.

* [5:41] **Arise**: the Greek verb *egeirein* is the verb generally used to express resurrection from death (Mk 6:14, 16; Mt 11:5; Lk 7:14) and Jesus' own resurrection (Mk 16:6; Mt 28:6; Lk 24:6).

* [6:1] **His native place**: the Greek word *patris* here refers to Nazareth (cf. Mk 1:9; Lk 4:16, 23–24) though it can also mean native land.

* [6:2–6] See note on Jn 4:44.

* [6:3] **Is he not the carpenter?**: no other gospel calls Jesus a carpenter. Some witnesses have "the carpenter's son," as in Mt 13:55. **Son of Mary**: contrary to Jewish custom, which calls a man the son of his father, this expression may reflect Mark's own faith that God is the Father of Jesus (Mk 1:1, 11; 8:38; 13:32; 14:36). **The brother of James . . . Simon**: in Semitic usage, the terms "brother," "sister" are applied not only to children of the same parents, but to nephews, nieces, cousins, half-brothers, and half-sisters; cf. Gn 14:16; 29:15; Lv 10:4. While one cannot suppose that the meaning of a Greek word should be sought in the first place from Semitic usage, the Septuagint often translates the Hebrew *'ah* by the Greek word *adelphos*, "brother," as in the cited passages, a fact that may argue for a similar breadth of meaning in some New Testament passages. For instance, there is no doubt that in v 17, "brother" is used of Philip, who was actually the half-brother of Herod Antipas. On the other hand, Mark may have understood the terms literally; see also 3:31–32; Mt 12:46; 13:55–56; Lk 8:19; Jn 7:3, 5. The question of meaning here would not have arisen but for the faith of the church for Mary's perpetual virginity.

* [6:4] **A prophet is not without honor except . . . in his own house**: a saying that finds parallels in other literatures, especially Jewish and Greek, but without reference to a prophet. Comparing himself to previous Hebrew prophets whom the people rejected, Jesus intimates his own eventual rejection by the nation especially in view of the dishonor his own relatives had shown him (Mk 3:21) and now his townspeople as well.

* [6:5] **He was not able to perform any mighty deed there**: according to Mark, Jesus' power could not take effect because of a person's lack of faith.

* [6:7–13] The preparation for the mission of the Twelve is seen in the call (1) of the first disciples to be fishers of men (Mk 1:16–20), (2) then of the Twelve set apart to be with Jesus and to receive authority to preach and expel demons (Mk 3:13–19). Now they are given the specific mission to exercise that authority in word and power as representatives of Jesus during the time of their formation.

* [6:8–9] In Mark the use of a **walking stick** (Mk 6:8) and **sandals** (Mk 6:9) is permitted, but not in Mt 10:10 nor in Lk 10:4. Mark does not mention any prohibition to visit pagan territory and to enter Samaritan towns. These differences indicate

a certain adaptation to conditions in and outside of Palestine and suggest in Mark's account a later activity in the church. For the rest, Jesus required of his apostles a total dependence on God for food and shelter; cf. Mk 6:35–44; 8:1–9.

* [6:10–11] Remaining in the same house as a guest (Mk 6:10) rather than moving to another offering greater comfort avoided any impression of seeking advantage for oneself and prevented dishonor to one's host. Shaking the dust off one's feet served as testimony against those who rejected the call to repentance.

* [6:13] **Anointed with oil . . . cured them**: a common medicinal remedy, but seen here as a vehicle of divine power for healing.

* [6:14–16] The various opinions about Jesus anticipate the theme of his identity that reaches its climax in Mk 8:27–30.

* [6:14] **King Herod**: see note on Mt 14:1.

* [6:17–29] Similarities are to be noted between Mark's account of the imprisonment and death of John the Baptist in this pericope, and that of the passion of Jesus (Mk 15:1–47). Herod and Pilate, each in turn, acknowledges the holiness of life of one over whom he unjustly exercises the power of condemnation and death (Mk 6:26–27; 15:9–10, 14–15). The hatred of Herodias toward John parallels that of the Jewish leaders toward Jesus. After the deaths of John and of Jesus, well-disposed persons request the bodies of the victims of Herod and of Pilate in turn to give them respectful burial (Mk 6:29; 15:45–46).

* [6:19] **Herodias**: see note on Mt 14:3.

* [6:30] **Apostles**: here, and in some manuscripts at Mk 3:14, Mark calls apostles (i.e., those sent forth) the Twelve whom Jesus sends as his emissaries, empowering them to preach, to expel demons, and to cure the sick (Mk 6:13). Only after Pentecost is the title used in the technical sense.

* [6:31–34] The withdrawal of Jesus with his disciples to a desert place to rest attracts a great number of people to follow them. Toward this people of the new exodus Jesus is moved with pity; he satisfies their spiritual hunger by teaching them many things, thus gradually showing himself the faithful shepherd of a new Israel; cf. Nm 27:17; Ez 34:15.

* [6:35–44] See note on Mt 14:13–21. Compare this section with Mk 8:1–9. The various accounts of the multiplication of loaves and fishes, two each in Mark and in Matthew and one each in Luke and in John, indicate the wide interest of the early church in their eucharistic gatherings; see, e.g., Mk 6:41; 8:6; 14:22; and recall also the sign of bread in Ex 16; Dt 8:3–16; Ps 78:24–25; 105:40; Wis 16:20–21.

* [6:40] **The people . . . in rows by hundreds and by fifties**: reminiscent of the groupings of Israelites encamped in the desert (Ex 18:21–25) and of the wilderness tradition of the prophets

depicting the transformation of the wasteland into pastures where the true shepherd feeds his flock (Ez 34:25–26) and makes his people beneficiaries of messianic grace.

* [6:41] On the language of this verse as eucharistic (cf. Mk 14:22), see notes on Mt 14:19, 20. Jesus observed the Jewish table ritual of blessing God before partaking of food.

* [6:45–52] See note on Mt 14:22–33.

* [6:45] **To the other side toward Bethsaida**: a village at the northeastern shore of the Sea of Galilee.

* [6:46] **He went off to the mountain to pray**: see Mk 1:35–38. In Jn 6:15 Jesus withdrew to evade any involvement in the false messianic hopes of the multitude.

* [6:48] **Walking on the sea**: see notes on Mt 14:22–33 and on Jn 6:19.

* [6:50] **It is I, do not be afraid!**: literally, "I am." This may reflect the divine revelatory formula of Ex 3:14; Is 41:4, 10, 14; 43:1–3, 10, 13. Mark implies the hidden identity of Jesus as Son of God.

* [6:52] **They had not understood . . . the loaves**: the revelatory character of this sign and that of the walking on the sea completely escaped the disciples. **Their hearts were hardened**: in Mk 3:5–6 hardness of heart was attributed to those who did not accept Jesus and plotted his death. Here the same disposition prevents the disciples from comprehending Jesus' self-revelation through signs; cf. Mk 8:17.

---

* [7:1–23] See note on Mt 15:1–20. Against the Pharisees' narrow, legalistic, and external practices of piety in matters of purification (Mk 7:2–5), external worship (Mk 7:6–7), and observance of commandments, Jesus sets in opposition the true moral intent of the divine law (Mk 7:8–13). But he goes beyond contrasting the law and Pharisaic interpretation of it. The parable of Mk 7:14–15 in effect sets aside the law itself in respect to clean and unclean food. He thereby opens the way for unity between Jew and Gentile in the kingdom of God, intimated by Jesus' departure for pagan territory beyond Galilee. For similar contrast see Mk 2:1–3:6; 3:20–35; 6:1–6.

* [7:3] **Carefully washing their hands**: refers to ritual purification.

* [7:5] **Tradition of the elders**: the body of detailed, unwritten, human laws regarded by the scribes and Pharisees to have the same binding force as that of the Mosaic law; cf. Gal 1:14.

* [7:11] **Qorban**: a formula for a gift to God, dedicating the offering to the temple, so that the giver might continue to use it for himself but not give it to others, even needy parents.

* [7:16] Mk 7:16, "Anyone who has ears to hear ought to hear," is omitted because it is lacking in some of the best Greek manuscripts and was probably transferred here by scribes from Mk 4:9, 23.

* [7:17] **Away from the crowd . . . the parable**: in this context of privacy the term *parable* refers to something hidden, about to be revealed to the disciples; cf. Mk 4:10–11, 34. Jesus sets the Mosaic food laws in the context of the kingdom of God where they are abrogated, and he declares moral defilement the only cause of uncleanness.

* [7:19] **(Thus he declared all foods clean)**: if this bold declaration goes back to Jesus, its force was not realized among Jewish Christians in the early church; cf. Acts 10:1–11:18.

* [7:24–37] The withdrawal of Jesus to the district of Tyre may have been for a respite (Mk 7:24), but he soon moved onward to Sidon and, by way of the Sea of Galilee, to the Decapolis. These districts provided a Gentile setting for the extension of his ministry of healing because the people there acknowledged his power (Mk 7:29, 37). The actions attributed to Jesus (Mk 7:33–35) were also used by healers of the time.

* [7:27–28] The figure of a household in which children at table are fed first and then their left-over food is given to the dogs under the table is used effectively to acknowledge the prior claim of the Jews to the ministry of Jesus; however, Jesus accedes to the Gentile woman's plea for the cure of her afflicted daughter because of her faith.

* [7:36] **The more they proclaimed it**: the same verb *proclaim* attributed here to the crowd in relation to the miracles of Jesus is elsewhere used in Mark for the preaching of the gospel on the part of Jesus, of his disciples, and of the Christian community (Mk 1:14; 13:10; 14:9). Implied in the action of the crowd is a recognition of the salvific mission of Jesus; see note on Mt 11:5–6.

---

* [8:1–10] The two accounts of the multiplication of loaves and fishes (Mk 8:1–10; 6:31–44) have eucharistic significance. Their similarity of structure and themes but dissimilarity of detail are considered by many to refer to a single event that, however, developed in two distinct traditions, one Jewish Christian and the other Gentile Christian, since Jesus in Mark's presentation (Mk 7:24–37) has extended his saving mission to the Gentiles.

* [8:6] See note on Mk 6:41.

* [8:11–12] The objection of the Pharisees that Jesus' miracles are unsatisfactory for proving the arrival of God's kingdom is comparable to the request of the crowd for a sign in Jn 6:30–31. Jesus' response shows that a sign originating in human demand will not be provided; cf. Nm 14:11, 22.

* [8:15] **The leaven of the Pharisees . . . of Herod**: the corruptive action of leaven (1 Cor 5:6–8; Gal 5:9) was an apt symbol of the evil dispositions both of the Pharisees (Mk 8:11–13; 7:5–13) and of Herod (Mk 6:14–29) toward Jesus. The disciples of Jesus are warned against sharing such rebellious attitudes toward Jesus; cf. Mk 8:17, 21.

* [8:22–26] Jesus' actions and the gradual cure of the blind man probably have the same purpose as in the case of the deaf man (Mk 7:31–37). Some commentators regard the cure as an intended symbol of the gradual enlightenment of the disciples concerning Jesus' messiahship.

* [8:27–30] This episode is the turning point in Mark's account of Jesus in his public ministry. Popular opinions concur in regarding him as a prophet. The disciples by contrast believe him to be the Messiah. Jesus acknowledges this identification but prohibits them from making his messianic office known to avoid confusing it with ambiguous contemporary ideas on the nature of that office. See further the notes on Mt 16:13–20.

* [8:31] **Son of Man**: an enigmatic title. It is used in Dn 7:13–14 as a symbol of "the saints of the Most High," the faithful Israelites who receive the everlasting kingdom from the Ancient One (God). They are represented by a human figure that contrasts with the various beasts who represent the previous kingdoms of the earth. In the Jewish apocryphal books of 1 Enoch and 4 Ezra the "Son of Man" is not, as in Daniel, a group, but a unique figure of extraordinary spiritual endowments, who will be revealed as the one through whom the everlasting kingdom decreed by God will be established. It is possible though doubtful that this individualization of the Son of Man figure had been made in Jesus' time, and therefore his use of the title in that sense is questionable. Of itself, this expression means simply a human being, or, indefinitely, someone, and there are evidences of this use in pre-Christian times. Its use in the New Testament is probably due to Jesus' speaking of himself in that way, "a human being," and the later church's taking this in the sense of the Jewish apocrypha and applying it to him with that meaning. **Rejected by the elders, the chief priests, and the scribes**: the supreme council called the Sanhedrin was made up of seventy-one members of these three groups and presided over by the high priest. It exercised authority over the Jews in religious matters. See note on Mt 8:20.

* [8:34–35] This utterance of Jesus challenges all believers to authentic discipleship and total commitment to himself through self-renunciation and acceptance of the cross of suffering, even to the sacrifice of life itself. **Whoever wishes to save his life will lose it . . . will save it**: an expression of the ambivalence of life and its contrasting destiny. Life seen as mere self-centered earthly existence and lived in denial of Christ ends in destruction, but when lived in loyalty to Christ, despite earthly death, it arrives at fullness of life.

* [8:35] **For my sake and that of the gospel**: Mark here, as at Mk 10:29 equates Jesus with the gospel.

* [9:1] **There are some standing . . . come in power**: understood by some to refer to the establishment by God's power of his kingdom on earth in and through the church; more likely, as understood by others, a reference to the imminent parousia.

* [9:2–8] Mark and Mt 17:1 place the transfiguration of Jesus six days after the first prediction of his passion and death and his instruction to the disciples on the doctrine of the cross; Lk 9:28 has "about eight days." Thus the transfiguration counterbalances the prediction of the passion by affording certain of the disciples insight into the divine glory that Jesus possessed. His glory will overcome his death and that of his disciples; cf. 2 Cor 3:18; 2 Pt 1:16–19. The heavenly voice (Mk 9:7) prepares the disciples to understand that in the divine plan Jesus must die ignominiously before his messianic glory is made manifest; cf. Lk 24:25–27. See further the note on Mt 17:1–8.

* [9:5] Moses and Elijah represent, respectively, law and prophecy in the Old Testament and are linked to Mount Sinai; cf. Ex 19:16–20:17; 1 Kgs 19:2, 8–14. They now appear with Jesus as witnesses to the fulfillment of the law and the prophets taking place in the person of Jesus as he appears in glory.

* [9:7] **A cloud came, casting a shadow over them**: even the disciples enter into the mystery of his glorification. In the Old Testament the cloud covered the meeting tent, indicating the Lord's presence in the midst of his people (Ex 40:34–35) and came to rest upon the temple in Jerusalem at the time of its dedication (1 Kgs 8:10).

* [9:9–13] At the transfiguration of Jesus his disciples had seen Elijah. They were perplexed because, according to the rabbinical interpretation of Mal 3:23–24, Elijah was to come first. Jesus' response shows that Elijah has come, in the person of John the Baptist, to prepare for the day of the Lord. Jesus **must suffer greatly and be treated with contempt** (Mk 9:12) like the Baptist (Mk 9:13); cf. Mk 6:17–29.

* [9:14–29] The disciples' failure to effect a cure seems to reflect unfavorably on Jesus (Mk 9:14–18, 22). In response Jesus exposes their lack of trust in God (Mk 9:19) and scores their lack of prayer (Mk 9:29), i.e., of conscious reliance on God's power when acting in Jesus' name. For Matthew, see note on Mt 17:14–20. Lk 9:37–43 centers attention on Jesus' sovereign power.

* [9:29] **This kind can only come out through prayer**: a variant reading adds "and through fasting."

* [9:33–37] Mark probably intends this incident and the sayings that follow as commentary on the disciples' lack of understanding (Mk 9:32). Their role in Jesus' work is one of service, especially to the poor and lowly. Children were the symbol

Jesus used for the *anawim*, the poor in spirit, the lowly in the Christian community.

* [9:38–41] Jesus warns against jealousy and intolerance toward others, such as exorcists who do **not follow us**. The saying in Mk 9:40 is a broad principle of the divine tolerance. Even the smallest courtesies shown to those who teach in Jesus' name do not go unrewarded.

* [9:43, 45, 47] **Gehenna**: see note on Mt 5:22.

* [9:44, 46] These verses, lacking in some important early manuscripts, are here omitted as scribal additions. They simply repeat Mk 9:48 itself a modified citation of Is 66:24.

* [9:49] **Everyone will be salted with fire**: so the better manuscripts. Some add "every sacrifice will be salted with salt." The purifying and preservative use of salt in food (Lv 2:13) and the refinement effected through fire refer here to comparable effects in the spiritual life of the disciples of Jesus.

* [10:2–9] In the dialogue between Jesus and the Pharisees on the subject of divorce, Jesus declares that the law of Moses permitted divorce (Dt 24:1) only **because of the hardness of your hearts** (Mk 10:4–5). In citing Gn 1:27 and 2:24 Jesus proclaims permanence to be the divine intent from the beginning concerning human marriage (Mk 10:6–8). He reaffirms this with the declaration that **what God has joined together, no human being must separate** (Mk 10:9). See further the notes on Mt 5:31–32; 19:3–9.

* [10:15] **Whoever does not accept the kingdom of God like a child**: i.e., in total dependence upon and obedience to the gospel; cf. Mt 18:3–4.

* [10:18] **Why do you call me good?**: Jesus repudiates the term "good" for himself and directs it to God, the source of all goodness who alone can grant the gift of eternal life; cf. Mt 19:16–17.

* [10:23–27] In the Old Testament wealth and material goods are considered a sign of God's favor (Jb 1:10; Ps 128:1–2; Is 3:10). The words of Jesus in Mk 10:23–25 provoke astonishment among the disciples because of their apparent contradiction of the Old Testament concept (Mk 10:24, 26). Since wealth, power, and merit generate false security, Jesus rejects them utterly as a claim to enter the kingdom. Achievement of salvation is beyond human capability and depends solely on the goodness of God who offers it as a gift (Mk 10:27).

* [10:38–40] **Can you drink the cup . . . I am baptized?**: the metaphor of drinking the cup is used in the Old Testament to refer to acceptance of the destiny assigned by God; see note on Psalm 11:6. In Jesus' case, this involves divine judgment on sin that Jesus the innocent one is to expiate on behalf of the guilty (Mk 14:24; Is 53:5). His baptism is to be his crucifixion and death for the salvation of the human race; cf. Lk 12:50. The request of James and John for a share in the glory

(Mk 10:35–37) must of necessity involve a share in Jesus' sufferings, the endurance of tribulation and suffering for the gospel (Mk 10:39). The authority of assigning places of honor in the kingdom is reserved to God (Mk 10:40).

* [10:42–45] Whatever authority is to be exercised by the disciples must, like that of Jesus, be rendered as service to others (Mk 10:45) rather than for personal aggrandizement (Mk 10:42–44). The service of Jesus is his passion and death for the sins of the human race (Mk 10:45); cf. Mk 14:24; Is 53:11–12; Mt 26:28; Lk 22:19–20.

* [10:46–52] See notes on Mt 9:27–31 and 20:29–34.

* [11:1–11] In Mark's account Jesus takes the initiative in ordering the preparation for his entry into Jerusalem (Mk 11:1–6) even as he later orders the preparation of his last Passover supper (Mk 14:12–16). In Mk 10:9–10 the greeting Jesus receives stops short of proclaiming him Messiah. He is greeted rather as the prophet of the coming messianic kingdom. Contrast Mt 21:9.

* [11:12–14] Jesus' search for fruit on the fig tree recalls the prophets' earlier use of this image to designate Israel; cf. Jer 8:13; 29:17; Jl 1:7; Hos 9:10, 16. Cursing the fig tree is a parable in action representing Jesus' judgment (Mk 11:20) on barren Israel and the fate of Jerusalem for failing to receive his teaching; cf. Is 34:4; Hos 2:14; Lk 13:6–9.

* [11:15–19] See note on Mt 21:12–17.

* [11:26] This verse, which reads, "But if you do not forgive, neither will your heavenly Father forgive your transgressions," is omitted in the best manuscripts. It was probably added by copyists under the influence of Mt 6:15.

* [11:27–33] The mounting hostility toward Jesus came from the chief priests, the scribes, and the elders (Mk 11:27); the Herodians and the Pharisees (Mk 12:13); and the Sadducees (Mk 12:18). By their rejection of God's messengers, John the Baptist and Jesus, they incurred the divine judgment implied in Mk 11:27–33 and confirmed in the parable of the vineyard tenants (Mk 12:1–12).

* [12:1–12] The vineyard denotes Israel (Is 5:1–7). The tenant farmers are the religious leaders of Israel. God is the owner of the vineyard. His servants are his messengers, the prophets. The beloved son is Jesus (Mk 1:11; 9:7; Mt 3:17; 17:5; Lk 3:22; 9:35). The punishment of the tenants refers to the religious leaders, and the transfer of the vineyard to others refers to the people of the new Israel.

* [12:13–34] In the ensuing conflicts (cf. also Mk 2:1–3:6) Jesus vanquishes his adversaries by his responses to their questions and reduces them to silence (Mk 12:34).

* [12:13–17] See note on Mt 22:15–22.
* [12:18–27] See note on Mt 22:23–33.
* [12:28–34] See note on Mt 22:34–40.
* [12:35–37] Jesus questions the claim of the scribes about the Davidic descent of the Messiah, not to deny it (Mt 1:1; Acts 2:20, 34; Rom 1:3; 2 Tm 2:8) but to imply that he is more than this. His superiority derives from his transcendent origin, to which David himself attested when he spoke of the Messiah with the name "Lord" (Ps 110:1). See also note on Mt 22:41–46.

* [12:38–40] See notes on Mk 7:1–23 and Mt 23:1–39.

* [12:41–44] See note on Lk 21:1–4.

* [13:1–2] The reconstructed temple with its precincts, begun under Herod the Great ca. 20 B.C., was completed only some seven years before it was destroyed by fire in A.D. 70 at the hands of the Romans; cf. Jer 26:18; Mt 24:1–2. For the dating of the reconstruction of the temple, see further the note on Jn 2:20.

* [13:3–37] Jesus' prediction of the destruction of the temple (Mk 13:2) provoked questions that the four named disciples put to him in private regarding the time and the sign when all these things are about to come to an end (Mk 13:3–4). The response to their questions was Jesus' eschatological discourse prior to his imminent death. It contained instruction and consolation exhorting the disciples and the church to faith and obedience through the trials that would confront them (Mk 13:5–13). The sign is the presence of the desolating abomination (Mk 13:14; Dn 9:27), i.e., of the Roman power profaning the temple. Flight from Jerusalem is urged rather than defense of the city through misguided messianic hope (Mk 13:14–23). Intervention will occur only after destruction (Mk 13:24–27), which will happen before the end of the first Christian generation (Mk 13:28–31). No one but the Father knows the precise time, or that of the parousia (Mk 13:32); hence the necessity of constant vigilance (Mk 13:33–37). Luke sets the parousia at a later date, after "the time of the Gentiles" (Lk 21:24). See also notes on Mt 24:1–25:46.

* [13:10] The gospel . . . to all nations: the period of the Christian mission.

* [13:14] The participle standing is masculine, in contrast to the neuter at Mt 24:15.

* [13:26] Son of Man . . . with great power and glory: Jesus cites this text from Dn 7:13 in his response to the high priest, Are you the Messiah? (Mk 14:61). In Ex 34:5; Lv 16:2; and Nm 11:25 the clouds indicate the presence of the divinity. Thus in his role of Son of Man, Jesus is a heavenly being who will come in power and glory.

* [14:1–16:8] In the movement of Mark's gospel the cross is depicted as Jesus' way to glory in accordance with the divine will. Thus the passion narrative is seen as the climax of Jesus' ministry.

* [14:1] **The Passover and the Feast of Unleavened Bread**: the connection between the two festivals is reflected in Ex 12:3–20; 34:18; Lv 23:4–8; Nm 9:2–14; 28:16–17; Dt 16:1–8. The Passover commemorated the redemption from slavery and the departure of the Israelites from Egypt by night. It began at sundown after the Passover lamb was sacrificed in the temple in the afternoon of the fourteenth day of the month of Nisan. With the Passover supper on the same evening was associated the eating of unleavened bread. The latter was continued through Nisan 21, a reminder of the affliction of the Israelites and of the haste surrounding their departure. Praise and thanks to God for his goodness in the past were combined at this dual festival with the hope of future salvation. **The chief priests . . . to death**: the intent to put Jesus to death was plotted for a long time but delayed for fear of the crowd (Mk 3:6; 11:18; 12:12).

* [14:3] At Bethany on the Mount of Olives, a few miles from Jerusalem, **in the house of Simon the leper**, Jesus defends a woman's loving action of anointing his head with perfumed oil in view of his impending death and burial as a criminal, in which case his body would not be anointed. See further the note on Jn 12:7. He assures the woman of the remembrance of her deed in the worldwide preaching of the good news.

* [14:12] **The first day of the Feast of Unleavened Bread . . . the Passover lamb**: a less precise designation of the day for sacrificing the Passover lamb as evidenced by some rabbinical literature. For a more exact designation, see note on Mk 14:1. It was actually Nisan 14.

* [14:13] **A man . . . carrying a jar of water**: perhaps a prearranged signal, for only women ordinarily carried water in jars. The Greek word used here, however, implies simply a person and not necessarily a male.

* [14:18] **One of you will betray me, one who is eating with me**: contrasts the intimacy of table fellowship at the Passover meal with the treachery of the traitor; cf. Ps 41:10.

* [14:21] **The Son of Man indeed goes, as it is written of him**: a reference to Ps 41:10 cited by Jesus concerning Judas at the Last Supper; cf. Jn 13:18–19.

* [14:22–24] The actions and words of Jesus express within the framework of the Passover meal and the transition to a new covenant the sacrifice of himself through the offering of his body and blood in anticipation of his passion and death. His **blood of the covenant** both alludes to the ancient rite of Ex 24:4–8 and indicates the new community that the sacrifice of Jesus will bring into being (Mt 26:26–28; Lk 22:19–20; 1 Cor 11:23–25).

* [14:24] **Which will be shed**: see note on Mt 26:27–28. **For many**: the Greek preposition *hyper* is a different one from that at Mt 26:28 but the same as that found at Lk 22:19, 20 and 1 Cor 11:24. The sense of both words is vicarious, and it is difficult in Hellenistic Greek to distinguish between them. For many in the sense of "all," see note on Mt 20:28.

* [14:26] **After singing a hymn**: Ps 114–118, thanksgiving songs concluding the Passover meal.

* [14:27–31] Jesus predicted that the Twelve would waver in their faith, even abandon him, despite their protestations to the contrary. Yet he reassured them that after his resurrection he would regather them in Galilee (Mk 16:7; cf. Mt 26:32; 28:7, 10, 16; Jn 21), where he first summoned them to be his followers as he began to preach the good news (Mk 1:14–20).

* [14:32–34] The disciples who had witnessed the raising to life of the daughter of Jairus (Mk 5:37) and the transfiguration of their Master (Mk 9:2) were now invited to witness his degradation and agony and to watch and pray with him.

* [14:36] **Abba, Father**: an Aramaic term, here also translated by Mark, Jesus' special way of addressing God with filial intimacy. The word *'abba'* seems not to have been used in earlier or contemporaneous Jewish sources to address God without some qualifier. Cf. Rom 8:15; Gal 4:6 for other occurrences of the Aramaic word in the Greek New Testament. **Not what I will but what you will**: note the complete obedient surrender of the human will of Jesus to the divine will of the Father; cf. Jn 4:34; 8:29; Rom 5:19; Phil 2:8; Heb 5:8.

* [14:38] **The spirit is willing but the flesh is weak**: the spirit is drawn to what is good yet found in conflict with the flesh, inclined to sin; cf. Ps 51:7, 12. Everyone is faced with this struggle, the full force of which Jesus accepted on our behalf and, through his bitter passion and death, achieved the victory.

* [14:53] **They led Jesus away . . . came together**: Mark presents a formal assembly of the whole Sanhedrin (chief priests, elders, and scribes) at night, leading to the condemnation of Jesus (Mk 14:64), in contrast to Lk 22:66, 71 where Jesus is condemned in a daytime meeting of the council; see also Jn 18:13, 19–24.

* [14:57–58] See notes on Mt 26:60–61 and Jn 2:19.

* [14:61–62] **The Blessed One**: a surrogate for the divine name, which Jews did not pronounce. **I am**: indicates Jesus' acknowledgment that he is the Messiah and Son of God; cf. Mk 1:1. Contrast Mt 26:64 and Lk 22:67–70, in which Jesus leaves his interrogators to answer their own question. **You will see the Son of Man . . . with the clouds**

of heaven: an allusion to Dn 7:13 and Ps 110:1 portending the enthronement of Jesus as judge in the transcendent glory of God's kingdom. **The Power**: another surrogate for the name of God.

* [14:68] **[Then the cock crowed]**: found in most manuscripts, perhaps in view of Mk 14:30, 72 but omitted in others.

---

* [15:1] **Held a council**: the verb here, *poieō*, can mean either "convene a council" or "take counsel." This reading is preferred to a variant "reached a decision" (cf. Mk 3:6), which Mk 14:64 describes as having happened at the night trial; see note on Mt 27:1–2. **Handed him over to Pilate**: lacking authority to execute their sentence of condemnation (Mk 14:64), the Sanhedrin had recourse to Pilate to have Jesus tried and put to death (Mk 15:15); cf. Jn 18:31.

* [15:2] **The king of the Jews**: in the accounts of the evangelists a certain irony surrounds the use of this title as an accusation against Jesus (see note on Mk 15:26). While Pilate uses this term (Mk 15:2, 9, 12), he is aware of the evil motivation of the chief priests who handed Jesus over for trial and condemnation (Mk 15:10; Lk 23:14–16, 20; Mt 27:18, 24; Jn 18:38; 19:4, 6, 12).

* [15:6–15] See note on Mt 27:15–26.

* [15:7] **Barabbas**: see note on Mt 27:16–17.

* [15:13] **Crucify him**: see note on Mt 27:22.

* [15:15] See note on Mt 27:26.

* [15:16] **Praetorium**: see note on Mt 27:27.

* [15:21] **They pressed into service . . . Simon, a Cyrenian**: a condemned person was constrained to bear his own instrument of torture, at least the crossbeam. The precise naming of Simon and his sons is probably due to their being known among early Christian believers to whom Mark addressed his gospel. See also notes on Mt 27:32; Lk 23:26–32.

* [15:24] See notes on Mt 27:35 and Jn 19:23–25a.

* [15:25] **It was nine o'clock in the morning**: literally, "the third hour," thus between 9 a.m. and 12 noon. Cf. Mk 15:33, 34, 42 for Mark's chronological sequence, which may reflect liturgical or catechetical considerations rather than the precise historical sequence of events; contrast the different chronologies in the other gospels, especially Jn 19:14.

* [15:26] **The inscription . . . the King of the Jews**: the political reason for the death penalty falsely charged by the enemies of Jesus. See further the notes on Mt 27:37 and Jn 19:19.

* [15:28] This verse, "And the scripture was fulfilled that says, 'And he was counted among the wicked,'" is omitted in the earliest and best manuscripts. It contains a citation from Is 53:12 and was probably introduced from Lk 22:37.

* [15:29] See note on Mt 27:39–40.

* [15:34] An Aramaic rendering of Ps 22:2. See also note on Mt 27:46.

* [15:35] **Elijah**: a verbal link with Eloi (Mk 15:34). See note on Mk 9:9–13; cf. Mal 3:23–24. See also note on Mt 27:47.

* [15:38] See note on Mt 27:51–53.

* [15:39] The closing portion of Mark's gospel returns to the theme of its beginning in the Gentile centurion's climactic declaration of belief that Jesus **was the Son of God**. It indicates the fulfillment of the good news announced in the prologue (Mk 1:1) and may be regarded as the firstfruit of the passion and death of Jesus.

* [15:40–41] See note on Mt 27:55–56.

* [15:43] **Joseph of Arimathea**: see note on Mt 27:57–61.

---

* [16:1–8] The purpose of this narrative is to show that the tomb is empty and that Jesus **has been raised** (Mk 16:6) and is **going before you to Galilee** (Mk 16:7) in fulfillment of Mk 14:28. The women find the tomb empty, and an angel stationed there announces to them what has happened. They are told to proclaim the news to Peter and the disciples in order to prepare them for a reunion with him. Mark's composition of the gospel ends at Mk 16:8 with the women telling no one, because they were afraid. This abrupt termination causes some to believe that the original ending of this gospel may have been lost. See the following note.

* [16:9–20] This passage, termed the Longer Ending to the Marcan gospel by comparison with a much briefer conclusion found in some less important manuscripts, has traditionally been accepted as a canonical part of the gospel and was defined as such by the Council of Trent. Early citations of it by the Fathers indicate that it was composed by the second century, although vocabulary and style indicate that it was written by someone other than Mark. It is a general resume of the material concerning the appearances of the risen Jesus, reflecting, in particular, traditions found in Lk 24 and Jn 20.

The Shorter Ending: Found after Mk 16:8 before the Longer Ending in four seventh-to-ninth-century Greek manuscripts as well as in one Old Latin version, where it appears alone without the Longer Ending.

The Freer Logion: Found after Mk 16:14 in a fourth-fifth century manuscript preserved in the Freer Gallery of Art, Washington, DC, this ending was known to Jerome in the fourth century. It reads: "And they excused themselves, saying, 'This age of lawlessness and unbelief is under Satan, who does not allow the truth and power of God to prevail over the unclean things dominated by the spirits [or, does not allow the unclean things to grasp the truth and power of God]. Therefore reveal your righteousness now.'

They spoke to Christ. And Christ responded to them, 'The limit of the years of Satan's power is completed, but other terrible things draw near. And for those who sinned I was handed over to death, that they might return to the truth and no longer sin, in order that they might inherit the spiritual and incorruptible heavenly glory of righteousness. But . . . .'"

THE GOSPEL ACCORDING TO LUKE

INTRODUCTION

The Gospel according to Luke is the first part of a two-volume work that continues the biblical history of God's dealings with humanity found in the Old Testament, showing how God's promises to Israel have been fulfilled in Jesus and how the salvation promised to Israel and accomplished by Jesus has been extended to the Gentiles. The stated purpose of the two volumes is to provide Theophilus and others like him with certainty—assurance—about earlier instruction they have received (Lk 1:4). To accomplish his purpose, Luke shows that the preaching and teaching of the representatives of the early church are grounded in the preaching and teaching of Jesus, who during his historical ministry (Acts 1:21–22) prepared his specially chosen followers and commissioned them to be witnesses to his resurrection and to all else that he did (Acts 10:37–42). This continuity between the historical ministry of Jesus and the ministry of the apostles is Luke's way of guaranteeing the fidelity of the Church's teaching to the teaching of Jesus.

Luke's story of Jesus and the church is dominated by a historical perspective. This history is first of all salvation history. God's divine plan for human salvation was accomplished during the period of Jesus, who through the events of his life (Lk

22:22) fulfilled the Old Testament prophecies (Lk 4:21; 18:31; 22:37; 24:26–27, 44), and this salvation is now extended to all humanity in the period of the church (Acts 4:12). This salvation history, moreover, is a part of human history. Luke relates the story of Jesus and the church to events in contemporary Palestinian (Lk 1:5; 3:1–2; Acts 4:6) and Roman (Lk 2:1–2; 3:1; Acts 11:28; 18:2, 12) history for, as Paul says in Acts 26:26, "this was not done in a corner." Finally, Luke relates the story of Jesus and the church to contemporaneous church history. Luke is concerned with presenting Christianity as a legitimate form of worship in the Roman world, a religion that is capable of meeting the spiritual needs of a world empire like that of Rome. To this end, Luke depicts the Roman governor Pilate declaring Jesus innocent of any wrongdoing three times (Lk 23:4, 14, 22). At the same time Luke argues in Acts that Christianity is the logical development and proper fulfillment of Judaism and is therefore deserving of the same toleration and freedom traditionally accorded Judaism by Rome (Acts 13:16–41; 23:6–9; 24:10–21; 26:2–23).

The prominence given to the period of the church in the story has important consequences for Luke's interpretation of the teachings of Jesus. By presenting the time of the church as a distinct phase of salvation history, Luke accordingly shifts the early Christian emphasis away from the expectation of an imminent parousia to the day-to-day concerns of the Christian community in the world. He does this in the gospel by regularly emphasizing the words "each day" (Lk 9:23; cf. Mk 8:34; Lk 11:3; 16:19; 19:47) in the sayings of Jesus. Although Luke still believes the parousia to be a reality that will come unexpectedly (Lk 12:38, 45–46), he is more concerned with presenting the words and deeds of Jesus as guides for the conduct of Christian disciples in the interim period between the ascension and the parousia and with presenting Jesus himself as the model of Christian life and piety.

Throughout the gospel, Luke calls upon the Christian disciple to identify with the master Jesus, who is caring and tender toward the poor and lowly, the outcast, the sinner, and the afflicted, toward all those who recognize their dependence on God (Lk 4:18; 6:20–23; 7:36–50; 14:12–14; 15:1–32; 16:19–31; 18:9–14; 19:1–10; 21:1–4), but who is severe toward the proud and self-righteous, and particularly toward those who place their material wealth before the service of God and his people (Lk 6:24–26; 12:13–21; 16:13–15, 19–31; 18:9–14, 15–25; cf. Lk 1:50–53). No gospel writer is more concerned than Luke with the mercy and compassion of Jesus (Lk 7:41–43; 10:29–37; 13:6–9; 15:11–32). No gospel writer is more concerned with the role of the Spirit in the life of Jesus and the Christian disciple (Lk 1:35, 41; 2:25–27; 4:1, 14, 18; 10:21; 11:13; 24:49), with the importance of prayer (Lk 3:21; 5:16; 6:12; 9:28; 11:1–13; 18:1–8), or with Jesus' concern for women (Lk 7:11–17, 36–50; 8:2–3; 10:38–42). While Jesus calls all humanity to repent (Lk 5:32; 10:13; 11:32; 13:1–5; 15:7–10; 16:30; 17:3–4; 24:47), he is particularly demanding of those who would be his disciples. Of them he demands absolute and total detachment from family and material possessions (Lk 9:57–62; 12:32–34; 14:25–35). To all who respond in faith and repentance to the word Jesus preaches, he brings salvation (Lk 2:30–32; 3:6; 7:50; 8:48, 50; 17:19; 19:9) and peace (Lk 2:14; 7:50; 8:48; 19:38, 42) and life (Lk 10:25–28; 18:26–30).

Early Christian tradition, from the late second century on, identifies the author of this gospel and of the Acts of the Apostles as Luke, a Syrian from Antioch, who is mentioned in the New Testament in Col 4:14, Phlm 24 and 2 Tm 4:11. The prologue of the gospel makes it clear that Luke is not part of the first generation of Christian disciples but is himself dependent upon the traditions he received from those who were eyewitnesses and ministers of the word (Lk 1:2). His two-volume work marks him as someone who was highly literate both in the Old Testament traditions according to the Greek versions and in Hellenistic Greek writings.

Among the likely sources for the composition of this gospel (Lk 1:3) were the Gospel of Mark, a written collection of sayings of Jesus known also to the author of the Gospel of Matthew (Q; see Introduction to Matthew), and other special traditions that were used by Luke alone among the gospel writers. Some hold that Luke used Mark only as a complementary source for rounding out the material he took from other traditions. Because of its dependence on the Gospel of Mark and because details in Luke's Gospel (Lk 13:35a; 19:43–44; 21:20; 23:28–31) imply that the author was acquainted with the destruction of the city of Jerusalem by the Romans in A.D. 70, the Gospel of Luke is dated by most scholars after that date; many propose A.D. 80–90 as the time of composition.

Luke's consistent substitution of Greek names for the Aramaic or Hebrew names occurring in his sources (e.g., Lk 23:33; Mk 15:22; Lk 18:41; Mk 10:51), his omission from the gospel of specifically Jewish Christian concerns found in his sources (e.g., Mk 7:1–23), his interest in Gentile Christians (Lk 2:30–32; 3:6, 38; 4:16–30; 13:28–30; 14:15–24; 17:11–19; 24:47–48), and his incomplete knowledge of Palestinian geography, customs, and practices are among the characteristics of this gospel that suggest that Luke was a non-Palestinian writing to a non-Palestinian audience that was largely made up of Gentile Christians.

The principal divisions of the Gospel according to Luke are the following:

I. THE PROLOGUE*

CHAPTER 1

¹Since many have undertaken to compile a narrative of the events that have been fulfilled among us,ᵃ ²just as those who were eyewitnesses from the beginning and ministers of the word have handed them down to us,ᵇ)³I too have decided, after investigating everything accurately anew, to write it down in an orderly sequence for you, most excellent Theophilus, ⁴so that you may realize the certainty of the teachings you have received.

II. THE INFANCY NARRATIVE*

Announcement of the Birth of John. ⁵In the days of Herod, King of Judea,* there was a priest named Zechariah of the priestly division of Abijah; his wife was from the daughters of Aaron, and her name was Elizabeth.ᶜ (⁶Both were righteous in the eyes of God, observing all the commandments and ordinances of the Lord blamelessly.)⁷But they had no child,* because Elizabeth was barren and both were advanced in years.ᵈ ⁸Once when he was serving as priest in his division's turn before God, ⁹according to the practice of the priestly service, he was chosen by lot to enter the sanctuary of the Lord to burn incense.ᵉ ¹⁰Then, when the whole assembly of the people was praying outside at the hour of the incense offering, ¹¹the angel of the Lord appeared to him, standing at the right of the altar of incense. ¹²Zechariah was troubled by what he saw, and fear came upon him. ¹³But the angel said to him, "Do not be afraid,* Zechariah, because your prayer has been heard. Your wife Elizabeth will bear you a son, and you shall name him John.ᶠ ¹⁴And you will have joy and gladness, and many will rejoice at his birth, [15]for he will be great in the sight of [the] Lord. He will drink neither wine nor strong drink.* He will be filled with the holy Spirit even from his mother's womb,[g] [16]and he will turn many of the children of Israel to the Lord their God. [17]He will go before him in the spirit and power of Elijah* to turn the hearts of fathers toward children and the disobedient to the understanding of the righteous, to prepare a people fit for the Lord."[h] [18]Then Zechariah said to the angel, "How shall I know this? For I am an old man, and my wife is advanced in years." [19]And the angel said to him in reply, "I am Gabriel,* who stand before God. I was sent to speak to you and to announce to you this good news.[i] [20]But now you will be speechless and unable to talk* until the day these things take place, because you did not believe my words, which will be fulfilled at their proper time."[j]

[21]Meanwhile the people were waiting for Zechariah and were amazed that he stayed so long in the sanctuary. [22]But when he came out, he was unable to speak to them, and they realized that he had seen a vision in the sanctuary. He was gesturing to them but remained mute. [23]Then, when his days of ministry were completed, he went home. [24]After this time his wife Elizabeth conceived, and she went into seclusion for five months, saying, [25]"So has the Lord done for me at a time when he has seen fit to take away my disgrace before others."[k]

Announcement of the Birth of Jesus. * [26]In the sixth month, the angel Gabriel was sent from God to a town of Galilee called Nazareth, [27]to a virgin betrothed to a man named Joseph, of the house of David, and the virgin's name was Mary.*l* ²⁸And coming to her, he said, "Hail, favored one! The Lord is with you."*m* ²⁹But she was greatly troubled at what was said and pondered what sort of greeting this might be. ³⁰Then the angel said to her, "Do not be afraid, Mary, for you have found favor with God. ³¹*n*Behold, you will conceive in your womb and bear a son, and you shall name him Jesus. ³²*o*He will be great and will be called Son of the Most High,* and the Lord God will give him the throne of David his father, ³³and he will rule over the house of Jacob forever, and of his kingdom there will be no end."*p* ³⁴But Mary said to the angel, "How can this be, since I have no relations with a man?"* ³⁵And the angel said to her in reply, "The holy Spirit will come upon you, and the power of the Most High will overshadow you. Therefore the child to be born will be called holy, the Son of God.*q* ³⁶And behold, Elizabeth, your relative, has also conceived* a son in her old age, and this is the sixth month for her who was called barren; ³⁷for nothing will be impossible for God."*r* ³⁸Mary said, "Behold, I am the handmaid of the Lord. May it be done to me according to your word." Then the angel departed from her.

Mary Visits Elizabeth. ³⁹During those days Mary set out and traveled to the hill country in haste to a town of Judah, ⁴⁰where she entered the house of Zechariah and greeted Elizabeth. ⁴¹When Elizabeth heard Mary's greeting, the infant leaped in her womb, and Elizabeth, filled with the holy Spirit,*s* ⁴²cried out in a loud voice and said, "Most blessed are you among women, and blessed is the fruit of your womb.*t* ⁴³And how does this happen to me, that the mother of my Lord* should come to me? ⁴⁴For at the moment the sound of your greeting reached my ears, the infant in my womb leaped for joy. ⁴⁵Blessed are you who believed[*] that what was spoken to you by the Lord would be fulfilled."[u]

The Canticle of Mary. ⁴⁶[v]And Mary said:[*]

["My soul proclaims the greatness of the Lord;[w]
⁴⁷my spirit rejoices in God my savior.[x]
⁴⁸For he has looked upon his handmaid's lowliness;
behold, from now on will all ages call me blessed.[y]
⁴⁹The Mighty One has done great things for me,
and holy is his name.[z]
⁵⁰His mercy is from age to age
to those who fear him.[a]
⁵¹He has shown might with his arm,
dispersed the arrogant of mind and heart.[b]
⁵²He has thrown down the rulers from their thrones
but lifted up the lowly.[c]
⁵³The hungry he has filled with good things;
the rich he has sent away empty.[d]
⁵⁴He has helped Israel his servant,
remembering his mercy,[e]
⁵⁵according to his promise to our fathers,
to Abraham and to his descendants forever."[f]]

⁵⁶Mary remained with her about three months and then returned to her home.

The Birth of John.[*] ⁵⁷When the time arrived for Elizabeth to have her child she gave birth to a son. ⁵⁸Her neighbors and relatives heard that the Lord had shown his great mercy toward her, and they rejoiced with her.[g] ⁵⁹[*]When they came on the eighth day to circumcise[h] the child, they were going to call him

Zechariah after his father, [60]but his mother said in reply, "No. He will be called John."[i] [61]But they answered her, "There is no one among your relatives who has this name." [62]So they made signs, asking his father what he wished him to be called. [63]He asked for a tablet and wrote, "John is his name," and all were amazed. [64]Immediately his mouth was opened, his tongue freed, and he spoke blessing God.[j] [65]Then fear came upon all their neighbors, and all these matters were discussed throughout the hill country of Judea. [66]All who heard these things took them to heart, saying, "What, then, will this child be?" For surely the hand of the Lord was with him.

The Canticle of Zechariah. [67]Then Zechariah his father, filled with the holy Spirit, prophesied, saying:

[68]"Blessed be the Lord, the God of Israel,

for he has visited and
    brought redemption
    to his people.[k]
[69]He has raised up a horn
    for our salvation
within the house of
    David his servant,[l]
[70]even as he promised
    through the mouth
    of his holy prophets
    from of old:
[71]salvation from our
    enemies and from the
    hand of all who hate
    us,[m]
[72]to show mercy to our
    fathers[n]
and to be mindful of his
    holy covenant[o]
[73]and of the oath he swore
    to Abraham our
    father,[p]
and to grant us that,
    [74]rescued from the
    hand of enemies,
without fear we might
    worship him
    [75]in holiness and
    righteousness
before him all our days.[q]
[76]And you, child, will be

called prophet of the
Most High,
for you will go before
the Lord* to prepare
his ways,ʳ
⁷⁷to give his people knowledge of salvation
through the forgiveness
of their sins,
⁷⁸because of the tender
mercy of our Godˢ
by which the daybreak
from on high* will
visit usᵗ
⁷⁹to shine on those who
sit in darkness and
death's shadow,
to guide our feet into
the path of peace."

⁸⁰The child grew and became
strong in spirit, and he was in
the desert until the day of his
manifestation to Israel.ᵘ

a. [1:1–4] Acts 1:1; 1 Cor 15:3.
b. [1:2] 24:48; Jn 15:27; Acts 1:21–22.
c. [1:5] 1 Chr 24:10.
d. [1:7] Gn 18:11; Jgs 13:2–5; 1 Sm 1:5–6.
f. [1:9] Ex 30:7.
f. [1:13] 1:57, 60, 63; Mt 1:20–21.
g. [1:15] 7:33; Nm 6:1–21; Jgs 13:4; 1 Sm 1:11 LXX.
h. [1:17] Sir 48:10; Mal 3:1; 3:23–24; Mt 11:14;
17:11–13.
i. [1:19] Dn 8:16; 9:21.
j. [1:20] 1:45.
k. [1:25] Gn 30:23.
l. [1:27] 2:5; Mt 1:16, 18.

m. [1:28] Jgs 6:12; Ru 2:4; Jdt 13:18.
n. [1:31] Gn 16:11; Jgs 13:3; Is 7:14; Mt 1:21–23.
o. [1:32–33] 2 Sm 7:12, 13, 16; Is 9:7.
p. [1:33] Dn 2:44; 7:14; Mi 4:7; Mt 28:18.
q. [1:35] Mt 1:20.
r. [1:37] Gn 18:14; Jer 32:27; Mt 19:26.
s. [1:41] 1:15; Gn 25:22 LXX.
t. [1:42] 11:27–28; Jgs 5:24; Jdt 13:18; Dt 28:4.
u. [1:45] 1:20.
v. [1:46–55] 1 Sm 2:1–10.
w. [1:46] Ps 35:9; Is 61:10; Heb 3:18.
x. [1:47] Ti 3:4; Jude 25.
y. [1:48] 11:27; 1 Sm 1:11; 2 Sm 16:12; 2 Kgs 14:26;
Ps 113:7.
z. [1:49] Dt 10:21; Ps 71:19; 111:9; 126:2–3.
a. [1:50] Ps 89:2; 103:13, 17.
b. [1:51] Ps 89:10; 118:15; Jer 32:17 (39:17 LXX).
c. [1:52] 1 Sm 2:7; 2 Sm 22:28; Jb 5:11; 12:19; Ps
147:6; Sir 10:14; Jas 4:6; 1 Pt 5:5.
d. [1:53] 1 Sm 2:5; Ps 107:9.
e. [1:54] Ps 98:3; Is 41:8–9.
f. [1:55] Gn 13:15; 17:7; 18:18; 22:17–18; Mi 7:20.
g. [1:58] 1:14.
h. [1:59] 2:21; Gn 17:10, 12; Lv 12:3.
i. [1:60] 1:13.
j. [1:64] 1:20.
k. [1:68] 7:16; Ps 41:13; 72:18; 106:48; 111:9.
l. [1:69] Ps 18:3.
m. [1:71] Ps 106:10.
n. [1:72–73] Gn 17:7; Lv 26:42; Ps 105:8–9; Mi 7:20.
o. [1:72] Ps 106:45–46.
p. [1:73–74] Gn 22:16–17.
q. [1:75] Ti 2:12.
r. [1:76] Is 40:3; Mal 3:1; Mt 3:3; 11:10.
s. [1:78–79] Is 60:1–2.
t. [1:78] Mal 3:20.
u. [1:80] 2:40; Mt 3:1.

CHAPTER 2

The Birth of Jesus. ¹*In
those days a decree went out
from Caesar Augustus* that
the whole world should be
enrolled. ²This was the first
enrollment, when Quirin-
ius was governor of Syria.
³So all went to be enrolled,
each to his own town. ⁴And

Joseph too went up from Galilee from the town of Nazareth to Judea, to the city of David that is called Bethlehem, because he was of the house and family of David,*a* 5to be enrolled with Mary, his betrothed, who was with child.*b* 6While they were there, the time came for her to have her child, 7and she gave birth to her firstborn son.* She wrapped him in swaddling clothes and laid him in a manger, because there was no room for them in the inn.*c*

8*Now there were shepherds in that region living in the fields and keeping the night watch over their flock. 9The angel of the Lord appeared to them and the glory of the Lord shone around them, and they were struck with great fear.*d* 10The angel said to them, "Do not be afraid; for behold, I proclaim to you good news of great joy that will be for all the people. 11*e*For today in the city of David a savior has been born for you who is Messiah and Lord. 12And this will be a sign for you: you will find an infant wrapped in swaddling clothes and lying in a manger." 13And suddenly there was a multitude of the heavenly host with the angel, praising God and saying:

14*"Glory to God in the highest*f*
and on earth peace to those on whom his favor rests."

The Visit of the Shepherds.
15When the angels went away from them to heaven, the shepherds said to one another, "Let us go, then, to Bethlehem to see this thing that has taken place, which the Lord has made known to us." 16So they went in haste and found Mary and Joseph, and the infant lying in the manger. 17When they saw this, they made known the message that had been told

them about this child. [18]All who heard it were amazed by what had been told them by the shepherds. [19]And Mary kept all these things, reflecting on them in her heart. [20]Then the shepherds returned, glorifying and praising God for all they had heard and seen, just as it had been told to them.

The Circumcision and Naming of Jesus. [21]When eight days were completed for his circumcision,* he was named Jesus, the name given him by the angel before he was conceived in the womb.[g]

The Presentation in the Temple. [22]*When the days were completed for their purification* according to the law of Moses, they took him up to Jerusalem to present him to the Lord,[h] [23]just as it is written in the law of the Lord, "Every male that opens the womb shall be consecrated to the Lord,"[i] [24]and to offer the sacrifice of "a pair of turtledoves or two young pigeons," in accordance with the dictate in the law of the Lord.

[25]Now there was a man in Jerusalem whose name was Simeon. This man was righteous and devout, awaiting the consolation of Israel,* and the holy Spirit was upon him. [26]It had been revealed to him by the holy Spirit that he should not see death before he had seen the Messiah of the Lord. [27]He came in the Spirit into the temple; and when the parents brought in the child Jesus to perform the custom of the law in regard to him, [28]he took him into his arms and blessed God, saying:

[29]"Now, Master, you may
    let your servant go
    in peace, according to
    your word,
[30]for my eyes have seen
    your salvation,[j]
[31]which you prepared
    in sight of all the

Nunc Dimitis

peoples,
³²a light for revelation to
    the Gentiles,
and glory for your
    people Israel."ᵏ

³³The child's father and mother were amazed at what was said about him; ³⁴and Simeon blessed them and said to Mary his mother, "Behold, this child is destined for the fall and rise of many in Israel, and to be a sign that will be contradictedˡ ³⁵(and you yourself a sword will pierce)⁎ so that the thoughts of many hearts may be revealed." ³⁶There was also a prophetess, Anna, the daughter of Phanuel, of the tribe of Asher. She was advanced in years, having lived seven years with her husband after her marriage, ³⁷and then as a widow until she was eighty-four. She never left the temple, but worshiped night and day with fasting and prayer. ³⁸And coming forward at that very time, she gave thanks to God and spoke about the child to all who were awaiting the redemption of Jerusalem.ᵐ

The Return to Nazareth. ³⁹When they had fulfilled all the prescriptions of the law of the Lord, they returned to Galilee, to their own town of Nazareth.ⁿ ⁴⁰The child grew and became strong, filled with wisdom; and the favor of God was upon him.ᵒ

The Boy Jesus in the Temple.⁎ ⁴¹Each year his parents went to Jerusalem for the feast of Passover,ᵖ ⁴²and when he was twelve years old, they went up according to festival custom. ⁴³After they had completed its days, as they were returning, the boy Jesus remained behind in Jerusalem, but his parents did not know it. ⁴⁴Thinking that he was in the caravan, they journeyed for a day and looked for him among their relatives and acquaintances, ⁴⁵but not finding him, they returned to Jerusalem to look for him.

⁴⁶After three days they found him in the temple, sitting in the midst of the teachers, listening to them and asking them questions, ⁴⁷and all who heard him were astounded at his understanding and his answers. ⁴⁸When his parents saw him, they were astonished, and his mother said to him, "Son, why have you done this to us? Your father and I have been looking for you with great anxiety." ⁴⁹And he said to them, "Why were you looking for me? Did you not know that I must be in my Father's house?"* ⁵⁰But they did not understand what he said to them. ⁵¹He went down with them and came to Nazareth, and was obedient to them; and his mother kept all these things in her heart.*) (⁵²And Jesus advanced [in] wisdom and age and favor before God and man.*)

a.   [2:4] Mi 5:2; Mt 2:6.
b.   [2:5] 1:27; Mt 1:18.
c.   [2:7] Mt 1:25.
d.   [2:9] 1:11, 26.
e.   [2:11] Mt 1:21; 16:16; Jn 4:42; Acts 2:36; 5:31; Phil 2:11.
f.   [2:14] 19:38.
g.   [2:21] 1:31; Gn 17:12; Mt 1:21.
h.   [2:22–24] Lv 12:2–8.
i.   [2:23] Ex 13:2, 12.
j.   [2:30–31] 3:6; Is 40:5 LXX; 52:10.
k.   [2:32] Is 42:6; 46:13; 49:6; Acts 13:47; 26:23.
l.   [2:34] 12:51; Is 8:14; Jn 9:39; Rom 9:33; 1 Cor 1:23; 1 Pt 2:7–8.
m.   [2:38] Is 52:9.
n.   [2:39] Mt 2:23.
o.   [2:40] 1:80; 2:52.
p.   [2:41] Ex 12:24–27; 23:15; Dt 16:1–8.
q.   [2:51] 2:19.
r.   [2:52] 1:80; 2:40; 1 Sm 2:26.

III. THE PREPARATION FOR THE PUBLIC MINISTRY

CHAPTER 3

The Preaching of John the Baptist. ¹In the fifteenth year of the reign of Tiberius Caesar,* when Pontius Pilate was governor of Judea,ᵃ and Herod was tetrarch of Galilee, and his brother Philip tetrarch of the region of Ituraea and Trachonitis, and Lysanias was tetrarch of Abilene, ²during the high priesthood of Annas and Caiaphas,* the word of God came to Johnᵇ the son of Zechariah in the desert. ³*He went throughout

[the] whole region of the Jordan, (proclaiming a baptism of repentance for the forgiveness of sins,*c*)*4* as it is written in the book of the words of the prophet Isaiah:*d*

"A voice of one crying out
    in the desert:
'Prepare the way of the
    Lord,*e*
make straight his paths.
*5*Every valley shall be filled
    and every mountain and
        hill shall be made low.
The winding roads shall be
    made straight,
    and the rough ways
        made smooth,
*6*and all flesh shall see the
    salvation of God.'"*f*

*7*He said to the crowds who came out to be baptized by him, "You brood of vipers! Who warned you to flee from the coming wrath?*g* *8*Produce good fruits as evidence of your repentance; and do not begin to say to yourselves, 'We have Abraham as our father,' for I tell you, God can raise up children to Abraham from these stones.*h* *9*Even now the ax lies at the root of the trees. Therefore every tree that does not produce good fruit will be cut down and thrown into the fire."*i*

*10*And the crowds asked him, "What then should we do?" *11*He said to them in reply, "Whoever has two tunics should share with the person who has none. And whoever has food should do likewise." *12*Even tax collectors came to be baptized and they said to him, "Teacher, what should we do?"*j* *13*He answered them, "Stop collecting more than what is prescribed." *14*Soldiers also asked him, "And what is it that we should do?" He told them, "Do not practice extortion, do not falsely accuse anyone, and be satisfied with your wages."

*15k*Now the people were filled with expectation, and all were asking in their hearts whether John might be the Messiah. [16*]John answered them all, saying,[l] "I am baptizing you with water, but one mightier than I is coming. I am not worthy to loosen the thongs of his sandals. He will baptize you with the holy Spirit and fire. [17]His winnowing fan[*] is in his hand to clear his threshing floor and to gather the wheat into his barn, but the chaff he will burn with unquenchable fire."[m] [18]Exhorting them in many other ways, he preached good news to the people. [19*]Now Herod the tetrarch,[n] who had been censured by him because of Herodias, his brother's wife, and because of all the evil deeds Herod had committed, [20]added still another to these by [also] putting John in prison.

The Baptism of Jesus.[*] [21o]After all the people had been baptized and Jesus also had been baptized and was praying,[*] heaven was opened [22*p]and the holy Spirit descended upon him in bodily form like a dove. And a voice came from heaven, "You are my beloved Son; with you I am well pleased."

The Genealogy of Jesus.[*] [23q]When Jesus began his ministry he was about thirty years of age. He was the son, as was thought, of Joseph, the son of Heli,[r] [24]the son of Matthat, the son of Levi, the son of Melchi, the son of Jannai, the son of Joseph, [25]the son of Mattathias, the son of Amos, the son of Nahum, the son of Esli, the son of Naggai, [26]the son of Maath, the son of Mattathias, the son of Semein, the son of Josech, the son of Joda, [27]the son of Joanan, the son of Rhesa, the son of Zerubbabel, the son of Shealtiel, the son of Neri,[s] [28]the son of Melchi, the son of Addi, the son of Cosam, the son of Elmadam, the son of Er, [29]the son of Joshua, the son of Eliezer, the son of Jorim, the son of Matthat, the son of Levi, ³⁰the son of Simeon, the son of Judah, the son of Joseph, the son of Jonam, the son of Eliakim, ³¹ᵗthe son of Melea, the son of Menna, the son of Mattatha, the son of Nathan, the son of David,* ³²the son of Jesse,ᵘ the son of Obed, the son of Boaz, the son of Sala, the son of Nahshon, ³³the son of Amminadab, the son of Admin, the son of Arni, the son of Hezron, the son of Perez,ᵛ the son of Judah,ʷ ³⁴the son of Jacob, the son of Isaac, the son of Abraham,ˣ the son of Terah, the son of Nahor, ³⁵the son of Serug, the son of Reu, the son of Peleg, the son of Eber, the son of Shelah, ³⁶the son of Cainan, the son of Arphaxad, the son of Shem,ʸ the son of Noah, the son of Lamech, ³⁷the son of Methuselah, the son of Enoch, the son of Jared, the son of Mahalaleel, the son of Cainan, ³⁸the son of Enos, the son of Seth, the son of Adam,ᶻ the son of God.

a. [3:1–20] Mt 3:1–12; Mk 1:1–8; Jn 1:19–28.
b. [3:2] 1:80.
c. [3:3] Acts 13:24; 19:4.
d. [3:4–6] Is 40:3–5.
e. [3:4] Jn 1:23.
f. [3:6] 2:30–31.
g. [3:7] Mt 12:34.
h. [3:8] Jn 8:39.
i. [3:9] Mt 7:19; Jn 15:6.
j. [3:12] 7:29.
k. [3:15–16] Acts 13:25.
l. [3:16] 7:19–20; Jn 1:27; Acts 1:5; 11:16.
m. [3:17] Mt 3:12.
n. [3:19–20] Mt 14:3–4; Mk 6:17–18.
o. [3:21–22] Mt 3:13–17; Mk 1:9–11.
p. [3:22] 9:35; Ps 2:7; Is 42:1; Mt 12:18; 17:5; Mk 9:7; Jn 1:32; 2 Pt 1:17.
q. [3:23–38] Mt 1:1–17.
r. [3:23] 4:22; Jn 6:42.
s. [3:27] 1 Chr 3:17; Ez 3:2.
t. [3:31] 2 Sm 5:14.
u. [3:31–32] 1 Sm 16:1, 18.
v. [3:31–33] Ru 4:17–22; 1 Chr 2:1–15.
w. [3:33] Gn 29:35; 38:29.
x. [3:34] Gn 21:3; 25:26; 1 Chr 1:34; 28:34.
y. [3:34–36] Gn 11:10–26; 1 Chr 1:24–27.
z. [3:36–38] Gn 4:25–5:32; 1 Chr 1:1–4.

CHAPTER 4

The Temptation of Jesus.* ¹ᵃFilled with the holy Spirit,* Jesus returned from the Jordan and was led by the Spirit into the desert ²for forty days,* to be tempted by the devil. He ate nothing during those days, and when they were over he was hungry.ᵇ ³The devil said to him, "If you are the Son of God, command this stone to become bread." ⁴Jesus answered him, "It is written, 'One does not live by bread alone.'"*c* *5*Then he took him up and showed him all the kingdoms of the world in a single instant. *6*The devil said to him, "I shall give to you all this power and their glory; for it has been handed over to me, and I may give it to whomever I wish.*d* *7*All this will be yours, if you worship me." *8*Jesus said to him in reply, "It is written:

'You shall worship the
     Lord, your God,
   and him alone shall you
     serve.'"*e*

*9*Then he led him to Jerusalem, made him stand on the parapet of the temple, and said to him, "If you are the Son of God, throw yourself down from here, *10*for it is written:

'He will command his
     angels concerning
     you,
   to guard you,'*f*

*11*and:

'With their hands they will
     support you,
   lest you dash your foot
     against a stone.'"*g*

*12*Jesus said to him in reply, "It also says, 'You shall not put the Lord, your God, to the test.'"*h* *13*When the devil had finished every temptation,*i* he departed from him for a time.

IV. THE MINISTRY IN GALILEE

The Beginning of the Galilean Ministry. *14j*Jesus returned to Galilee in the power of the Spirit, and news of him spread throughout the whole region.*k* *15*He taught in their synagogues and was praised by all.

The Rejection at Nazareth.*l* *16*He came to Nazareth, where he had grown up, and went according to his custom* into the synagogue on the sabbath day. He stood up to read *17*and was handed a scroll of the prophet Isaiah. He unrolled the scroll and found the passage where it was written:

[18"The Spirit of the Lord is
    upon me,*
  because he has anointed
      me
    to bring glad tidings
        to the poor.*m*
  He has sent me to proclaim liberty to
      captives
    and recovery of sight to
        the blind,
      to let the oppressed
          go free,
19and to proclaim a year
    acceptable to the
        Lord."   *Jubilee*

20Rolling up the scroll, he handed it back to the attendant and sat down, and the eyes of all in the synagogue looked intently at him. 21He said to them, "Today this scripture passage is fulfilled in your hearing."* 22And all spoke highly of him and were amazed at the gracious words that came from his mouth.

They also asked, "Isn't this the son of Joseph?"*n* 23He said to them, "Surely you will quote me this proverb, 'Physician, cure yourself,' and say, 'Do here in your native place the things that we heard were done in Capernaum.'"* 24And he said, "Amen, I say to you, no prophet is accepted in his own native place. 25*Indeed, I tell you, there were many widows in Israel in the days of Elijah when the sky was closed for three and a half years and a severe famine spread over the entire land.*o* 26It was to none of these that Elijah was sent, but only to a widow in Zarephath*p* in the land of Sidon. 27Again, there were many lepers in Israel during the time of Elisha the prophet; yet not one of them was cleansed, but only Naaman the Syrian."*q* 28When the people in the synagogue heard this, they were all filled with fury. 29They rose up, drove him out of the town, and led him to the brow of the hill on which their town had been built, to hurl him down headlong. ³⁰But he passed through the midst of them and went away.

The Cure of a Demoniac. ³¹*Jesus then went down to Capernaum,ʳ a town of Galilee.ˢ He taught them on the sabbath, ³²and they were astonished at his teaching because he spoke with authority.ᵗ ³³In the synagogue there was a man with the spirit of an unclean demon,ᵘ and he cried out in a loud voice, ³⁴"Ha! What have you to do with us, Jesus of Nazareth? Have you come to destroy us?* I know who you are—the Holy One of God!"ᵛ ³⁵Jesus rebuked him and said, "Be quiet! Come out of him!" Then the demon threw the man down in front of them and came out of him without doing him any harm. ³⁶They were all amazed and said to one another, "What is there about his word? For with

authority and power he commands the unclean spirits, and they come out." ³⁷And news of him spread everywhere in the surrounding region.

The Cure of Simon's Mother-in-Law. ³⁸*After he left the synagogue, he entered the house of Simon.* Simon's mother-in-law was afflicted with a severe fever, and they interceded with him about her. ³⁹He stood over her, rebuked the fever, and it left her. She got up immediately and waited on them.

after Sabbath

Other Healings.ˣ ⁴⁰At sunset, all who had people sick with various diseases brought them to him. He laid his hands on each of them and cured them. ⁴¹*And demons also came out from many, shouting, "You are the Son of God."ʸ But he rebuked them and did not allow them to speak because they knew that he was the Messiah.

Jesus Leaves Capernaum.ᶻ ⁴²*At daybreak, Jesus left and

went to a deserted place. The crowds went looking for him, and when they came to him, they tried to prevent him from leaving them. [43]But he said to them, "To the other towns also I must proclaim the good news of the kingdom of God, because for this purpose I have been sent."[a] [44]And he was preaching in the synagogues of Judea.[*]

a. [4:1–13] Mt 4:1–11; Mk 1:12–13.
b. [4:2] Heb 4:15.
c. [4:4] Dt 8:3.
d. [4:6] Jer 27:5; Mt 28:18.
e. [4:8] Dt 6:13.
f. [4:10] Ps 91:11.
g. [4:11] Ps 91:12.
h. [4:12] Dt 6:16; 1 Cor 10:9.
i. [4:13] 22:3; Jn 13:2, 27; Heb 4:15.
j. [4:14–15] Mt 4:12–17; Mk 1:14–15.
k. [4:14] 5:15; Mt 3:16.
l. [4:16–30] Mt 13:53–58; Mk 6:1–6.
m. [4:18–19] Is 61:1–2; 58:6.
n. [4:22] 3:23; Jn 6:42.
o. [4:25] 1 Kgs 17:1–7; 18:1; Jas 5:17.
p. [4:26] 1 Kgs 17:9.
q. [4:27] 2 Kgs 5:1–14.
r. [4:31–37] Mk 1:21–28.
s. [4:31] Mt 4:13; Jn 2:12.
t. [4:32] Mt 7:28–29.
u. [4:33–34] 8:28; Mt 8:29; Mk 1:23–24; 5:7.
v. [4:34] 4:41; Jn 6:69.
w. [4:38–39] Mt 8:14–15; Mk 1:29–31.
x. [4:40–41] Mt 8:16; Mk 1:32–34.
y. [4:41] 4:34; Mt 8:29; Mk 3:11–12.
z. [4:42–44] Mk 1:35–39.
a. [4:43] 8:1; Mk 1:14–15.

CHAPTER 5

The Call of Simon the Fisherman.[*a] [1b]While the crowd was pressing in on Jesus and listening to the word of God, he was standing by the Lake of Gennesaret. [2]He saw two boats there alongside the lake; the fishermen had disembarked and were washing their nets. [3]Getting into one of the boats, the one belonging to Simon, he asked him to put out a short distance from the shore. Then he sat down and taught the crowds from the boat. [4c]After he had finished speaking, he said to Simon, "Put out into deep water and lower your nets for a catch." [5]Simon said in reply, "Master, we have worked hard all night and have caught nothing, but at your command I will lower the nets." [6]When they had done this, they caught a great number of fish and their nets were tearing. [7]They signaled to their partners in the other boat to come to help them. They came and filled both boats so that they were in danger of sinking. [8]When

Simon Peter saw this, he fell at the knees of Jesus and said, "Depart from me, Lord, for I am a sinful man." ⁹For astonishment at the catch of fish they had made seized him and all those with him, ¹⁰and likewise James and John, the sons of Zebedee, who were partners of Simon. Jesus said to Simon, "Do not be afraid; from now on you will be catching men."ᵈ ¹¹When they brought their boats to the shore, they left everything* and followed him.ᵉ

The Cleansing of a Leper.ᶠ

¹²Now there was a man full of leprosy* in one of the towns where he was; and when he saw Jesus, he fell prostrate, pleaded with him, and said, "Lord, if you wish, you can make me clean." ¹³Jesus stretched out his hand, touched him, and said, "I do will it. Be made clean." And the leprosy left him immediately. ¹⁴Then he ordered him not to tell anyone, but "Go, show yourself to the priest and offer for your cleansing what Moses prescribed;* that will be proof for them."ᵍ ¹⁵The report about him spread all the more, and great crowds assembled to listen to him and to be cured of their ailments, ¹⁶but he would withdraw to deserted places to pray.ʰ

The Healing of a Paralytic.ⁱ

¹⁷*One day as Jesus was teaching, Pharisees* and teachers of the law were sitting there who had come from every village of Galilee and Judea and Jerusalem, and the power of the Lord was with him for healing. ¹⁸And some men brought on a stretcher a man who was paralyzed; they were trying to bring him in and set [him] in his presence. ¹⁹But not finding a way to bring him in because of the crowd, they went up on the roof and lowered him on the stretcher through the tiles* into the middle in front of Jesus. ²⁰When he saw their faith, he

said, "As for you, your sins are forgiven."* ²¹Then the scribes* and Pharisees began to ask themselves, "Who is this who speaks blasphemies? Who but God alone can forgive sins?"ʲ ²²Jesus knew their thoughts and said to them in reply, "What are you thinking in your hearts?ᵏ ²³Which is easier, to say, 'Your sins are forgiven,' or to say, 'Rise and walk'? ²⁴ˡBut that you may know that the Son of Man has authority on earth to forgive sins"—he said to the man who was paralyzed, "I say to you, rise, pick up your stretcher, and go home." ²⁵He stood up immediately before them, picked up what he had been lying on, and went home, glorifying God. ²⁶Then astonishment seized them all and they glorified God, and, struck with awe, they said, "We have seen incredible things today."

The Call of Levi. ᵐ ²⁷After this he went out and saw a tax collector named Levi sitting at the customs post. He said to him, "Follow me." ²⁸And leaving everything behind, he got up and followed him. ²⁹ⁿThen Levi gave a great banquet for him in his house, and a large crowd of tax collectors and others were at table with them. ³⁰The Pharisees and their scribes complained to his disciples, saying, "Why do you eat and drink with tax collectors and sinners?" ³¹Jesus said to them in reply, "Those who are healthy do not need a physician, but the sick do. ³²I have not come to call the righteous to repentance but sinners."

The Question About Fasting. ᵒ ³³And they said to him, "The disciples of John fast often and offer prayers, and the disciples of the Pharisees do the same; but yours eat and drink." ³⁴*Jesus answered them, "Can you make the wedding guests* fast while the bridegroom is with them?

³⁵But the days will come, and when the bridegroom is taken away from them, then they will fast in those days." ^{36*}And he also told them a parable. "No one tears a piece from a new cloak to patch an old one. Otherwise, he will tear the new and the piece from it will not match the old cloak. ³⁷Likewise, no one pours new wine into old wineskins. Otherwise, the new wine will burst the skins, and it will be spilled, and the skins will be ruined. ³⁸Rather, new wine must be poured into fresh wineskins. ³⁹[And] no one who has been drinking old wine desires new, for he says, 'The old is good.'"*

---

a.   [5:1–11] Mt 4:18–22; Mk 1:16–20.
b.   [5:1–3] Mt 13:1–2; Mk 2:13; 3:9–10; 4:1–2.
c.   [5:4–9] Jn 21:1–11.
d.   [5:10] Jer 16:16.
e.   [5:11] Mt 19:27.
f.   [5:12–16] Mt 8:2–4; Mk 1:40–45.
g.   [5:14] 8:56; Lv 14:2–32; Mk 7:36.
h.   [5:16] Mk 1:35.
i.   [5:17–26] Mt 9:1–8; Mk 2:1–12.
j.   [5:21] 7:49; Is 43:25.
k.   [5:22] 6:8; 9:47.
l.   [5:24–25] Jn 5:8–9, 27.
m.   [5:27–32] Mt 9:9–13; Mk 2:13–17.
n.   [5:29–30] 15:1–2.
o.   [5:33–39] Mt 9:14–17; Mk 2:18–22.

CHAPTER 6

Debates About the Sabbath.[*] ^{1a}While he was going through a field of grain on a sabbath, his disciples were picking the heads of grain, rubbing them in their hands, and eating them.^b ²Some Pharisees said, "Why are you doing what is unlawful on the sabbath?" ^{3c}Jesus said to them in reply, "Have you not read what David did when he and those [who were] with him were hungry? ⁴[How] he went into the house of God, took the bread of offering,[*] which only the priests could lawfully eat, ate of it, and shared it with his companions."^d ⁵Then he said to them, ("The Son of Man is lord of the sabbath.")

^{6e}On another sabbath he went into the synagogue and taught, and there was a man there whose right hand was withered. ⁷The scribes and the Pharisees watched him closely to see if he would cure on the sabbath so that they

might discover a reason to accuse him.*^f ⁸But he realized their intentions and said to the man with the withered hand, "Come up and stand before us." And he rose and stood there.^g ⁹Then Jesus said to them, "I ask you, is it <u>lawful to do good</u> on the sabbath rather than to do evil, to save life rather than to destroy it?" ¹⁰Looking around at them all, he then said to him, "Stretch out your hand." He did so and his hand was <u>restored</u>. ¹¹But they became <u>enraged</u> and discussed together what they might do to Jesus.

The Mission of the Twelve.[*] ^{12h}In those days he departed to the <u>mountain to pray</u>, and he spent the night in prayer[*] to God. ¹³When day came, he called his disciples to himself, and from them he chose Twelve,[*] whom he also named apostles: ¹⁴ⁱSimon, whom he named Peter,[*] and his brother Andrew, James, John, Philip, Bartholomew,

¹⁵Matthew, Thomas, James the son of Alphaeus, Simon who was called a Zealot,[*] ¹⁶and Judas the son of James, and Judas Iscariot,[*] who became a traitor.

Ministering to a Great Multitude.^j ^{17*}And he came down with them and stood on a stretch of level ground. A great crowd of his disciples and a large number of the people from all Judea and Jerusalem and the coastal region of Tyre and Sidon ¹⁸came to <u>hear</u> him and to <u>be healed</u> of their diseases; and even those who were tormented by unclean spirits were cured. ¹⁹Everyone in the crowd sought to touch him because <u>power</u> came forth from him and healed them all.

Sermon on the Plain.^k ^{20*}And raising his eyes toward his disciples he said:

"Blessed are you who are <u>poor</u>,[*]

for the <u>kingdom</u> of God
is yours.

²¹Blessed are you who are
now hungry,

for you will be satisfied.
Blessed are you who are
now weeping,

for you will laugh.[l]

²²Blessed are you when
people hate you,
and when they exclude
and insult you,
and denounce your
name as evil
on account of the Son of
Man.[m]

²³Rejoice and leap for joy on
that day! Behold, your reward
will be great in heaven. For
their ancestors treated the
<u>prophets</u> in the same way.[n]

²⁴But woe to you who are
<u>rich</u>,

for you have received
your consolation.[o]

²⁵But woe to you who are
filled now,

for you will be hungry.
Woe to you who laugh

now,

for you will grieve and
weep.[p]

²⁶Woe to you when all
<u>speak well</u> of you,
for their ancestors
treated the <u>false</u>
<u>prophets</u> in this way.[q]

Love of Enemies.[*] ²⁷[r]"But
to you who hear I say, (love
your enemies, do good to
those who hate you,[s] ²⁸bless
those who curse you, pray
for those who mistreat you.[t])
²⁹To the person who strikes
you on one cheek, offer the
other one as well, and from
the person who takes your
cloak, do not withhold even
your tunic. ³⁰Give to everyone who asks of you, and
from the one who takes what
is yours do not demand it
back. ³¹<u>Do to others as you
would have them do to you.</u>[u]
³²For if you love those who
love you, what credit is that
to you? Even sinners love
those who love them. ³³And
if you do good to those who

do good to you, what credit is that to you? Even sinners do the same. ³⁴If you lend money to those from whom you expect repayment, what credit [is] that to you? Even sinners lend to sinners, and get back the same amount.ᵛ ³⁵But rather, love your enemies and do good to them, and lend expecting nothing back; then your reward will be great and you will be children of the Most High, for he himself is kind to the ungrateful and the wicked.ʷ ³⁶Be merciful, just as [also] your Father is merciful.

Judging Others.⁎ ³⁷ˣ"Stop judging and you will not be judged. Stop condemning and you will not be condemned. Forgive and you will be forgiven.ʸ ³⁸Give and gifts will be given to you; a good measure, packed together, shaken down, and overflowing, will be poured into your lap. For the measure with which you measure will in return be measured out to you."ᶻ ³⁹And he told them a parable, "Can a blind person guide a blind person? Will not both fall into a pit?ᵃ ⁴⁰No disciple is superior to the teacher; but when fully trained, every disciple will be like his teacher.ᵇ ⁴¹Why do you notice the splinter in your brother's eye, but do not perceive the wooden beam in your own? ⁴²How can you say to your brother, 'Brother, let me remove that splinter in your eye,' when you do not even notice the wooden beam in your own eye? You hypocrite! Remove the wooden beam from your eye first; then you will see clearly to remove the splinter in your brother's eye.

A Tree Known by Its Fruit.ᶜ ⁴³⁎"A good tree does not bear rotten fruit, nor does a rotten tree bear good fruit. ⁴⁴For every tree is known by its own fruit. For people do not pick figs from thornbushes, nor do they gather grapes from brambles. ⁴⁵A good person out of the store of goodness in his heart produces good, but an evil person out of a store of evil produces evil; for <u>from the fullness of the heart the mouth speaks</u>.

The Two Foundations. ^{46d}"Why do you call me, 'Lord, Lord,' but not <u>do</u> what I command? ^{47*}I will show you what someone is like who comes to me, <u>listens to my words, and acts</u> on them.^e ⁴⁸That one is like a person building a house, who dug deeply and laid the foundation on rock; when the flood came, the river burst against that house but could not shake it because it had been well built. ⁴⁹But the one who listens and does not act is like a person who built a house on the ground without a foundation. When the river burst against it, it

collapsed at once and was completely destroyed."

a. [6:1–5] Mt 12:1–8; Mk 2:23–28.
b. [6:1] Dt 23:26.
c. [6:3–4] 1 Sm 21:1–6.
d. [6:4] Lv 24:5–9.
e. [6:6–11] Mt 12:9–14; Mk 3:1–6.
f. [6:7] 14:1.
g. [6:8] 5:22; 9:47.
h. [6:12–16] Mt 10:1–4; Mk 3:13–19.
i. [6:14–16] Acts 1:13.
j. [6:17–19] Mt 4:23–25; Mk 3:7–10.
k. [6:20–26] Mt 5:1–12.
l. [6:21] Ps 126:5–6; Is 61:3; Jer 31:25; Rev 7:16–17.
m. [6:22] Jn 15:19; 16:2; 1 Pt 4:14.
n. [6:23] 11:47–48; 2 Chr 36:16; Mt 23:30–31.
o. [6:24] Jas 5:1.
p. [6:25] Is 65:13–14.
q. [6:26] Jas 4:4.
r. [6:27–36] Mt 5:38–48.
s. [6:27] Prv 25:21; Rom 12:20–21.
t. [6:28] Rom 12:14; 1 Pt 3:9.
u. [6:31] Mt 7:12.
v. [6:34] Dt 15:7–8.
w. [6:35] Lv 25:35–36.
x. [6:37–42] Mt 7:1–5.
y. [6:37] Mt 6:14; Jas 2:13.
z. [6:38] Mk 4:24.
a. [6:39] Mt 15:14; 23:16–17, 24.
b. [6:40] Mt 10:24–25; Jn 13:16; 15:20.
c. [6:43–45] Mt 7:16–20; 12:33, 35.
d. [6:46] Mt 7:21; Rom 2:13; Jas 1:22.
e. [6:47–49] Mt 7:24–27.

CHAPTER 7

The Healing of a Centurion's Slave.^a ^{1*}When he had finished all his words to the people, he entered Capernaum.[*] ²A <u>centurion</u>[*] there had a slave who was ill and about to die, and he was valuable to him. ³When he heard about Jesus, (he <u>sent elders</u> of the Jews to him,) asking him to come and save the life of his slave. [4]They approached Jesus and strongly urged him to come, saying, "He deserves to have you do this for him, [5]for he loves our nation and he built the synagogue for us." [6]And Jesus went with them, but when he was only a short distance from the house, (the centurion sent friends to tell him,) "Lord, do not trouble yourself, for I am not worthy to have you enter under my roof. [7]Therefore, I did not consider myself worthy to come to you; but say the word and let my servant be healed. [8]For I too am a person subject to authority, with soldiers subject to me. (And I say to one, 'Go,' and he goes; and to another, 'Come here,' and he comes; and to my slave, 'Do this,' and he does it." [9]When Jesus heard this he was amazed at him and, turning, said to the crowd following him, "I tell you, not even in Israel have I found such faith." [10]When the messengers returned to the house, they found the slave in good health.

Raising of the Widow's Son. [11b]Soon afterward he journeyed to a city called Nain, and his disciples and a large crowd accompanied him. [12]As he drew near to the gate of the city, a man who had died was being carried out, the only son of his mother, and she was a widow. A large crowd from the city was with her.[c] [13]When the Lord saw her, he was moved with pity for her and said to her, "Do not weep." [14]He stepped forward and touched the coffin; at this the bearers halted, and he said, "Young man, I tell you, arise!" [15]The dead man sat up and began to speak, and Jesus gave him to his mother.[d] [16]Fear seized them all, and they glorified God, exclaiming, "A great prophet has arisen in our midst," and "God has visited his people."[e] [17]This report about him spread through the whole of Judea and in all the surrounding region.

The Messengers from John the Baptist.[*] 18[f]The disciples of John told him about all these things. John summoned two of his disciples 19and sent them to the Lord to ask, "Are you the one who is to come, or should we look for another?"[g] 20When the men came to him, they said, "John the Baptist has sent us to you to ask, 'Are you the one who is to come, or should we look for another?'" 21At that time he cured many of their diseases, sufferings, and evil spirits; he also granted sight to many who were blind. 22And he said to them in reply, "Go and tell John what you have seen and heard: the blind regain their sight, the lame walk, lepers are cleansed, the deaf hear, the dead are raised, the poor have the good news proclaimed to them.[h] 23And

blessed is the one who takes no offense at me.'"

Jesus' Testimony to John. 24*When the messengers of John had left, Jesus began to speak to the crowds about John.[i] "What did you go out to the desert to see—a reed swayed by the wind? 25Then what did you go out to see? Someone dressed in fine garments? Those who dress luxuriously and live sumptuously are found in royal palaces. 26Then what did you go out to see? A prophet? Yes, I tell you, and more than a prophet.[j] 27This is the one about whom scripture says:

'Behold, I am sending my
    messenger ahead of
    you,
he will prepare your way
    before you.'[k]

28I tell you, among those born of women, no one is greater than John; yet the least in the kingdom of God is greater than he." 29[l](All the people

not one way

who listened, including the tax collectors, and who were baptized with the baptism of John,(acknowledged the righteousness of God;) [30]but the Pharisees and scholars of the law, who were not baptized by him, rejected the plan of God for themselves.)

[31]"Then to what shall I compare the people of this generation? What are they like?[m] [32]They are like children who sit in the marketplace and call to one another,

'We played the flute for you, but you did not dance.
We sang a dirge, but you did not weep.'

[33]For John the Baptist came neither eating food nor drinking wine, and you said, 'He is possessed by a demon.' [34]The Son of Man came eating and drinking and you said, 'Look, he is a glutton and a drunkard, a friend of tax collectors and sinners.'[n] [35]But wisdom is vindicated by all her children."

The Pardon of the Sinful Woman.[*] [36o]A Pharisee invited him to dine with him, and he entered the Pharisee's house and reclined at table.[*] [37]Now there was a sinful woman in the city who learned that he was at table in the house of the Pharisee.[p] Bringing an alabaster flask of ointment,[q] [38]she stood behind him at his feet weeping and began to bathe his feet with her tears. Then she wiped them with her hair, kissed them, and anointed them with the ointment. [39]When the Pharisee who had invited him saw this he said to himself, "If this man were a prophet, he would know who and what sort of woman this is who is touching him, that she is a sinner." [40]Jesus said to him in reply, "Simon, I have something to say to you." "Tell me, teacher," he said. [41]"Two people were in debt to a certain creditor; one owed five hundred days' wages* and the other owed fifty. 42Since they were unable to repay the debt, he forgave it for both. Which of them will love him more?" 43Simon said in reply, "The one, I suppose, whose larger debt was forgiven." He said to him, "You have judged rightly." 44Then he turned to the woman and said to Simon, "Do you see this woman? When I entered your house, you did not give me water for my feet, but she has bathed them with her tears and wiped them with her hair. 45You did not give me a kiss, but she has not ceased kissing my feet since the time I entered. 46You did not anoint my head with oil, but she anointed my feet with ointment. 47So I tell you, her many sins have been forgiven; hence, she has shown great love.* But the one to whom little is forgiven, loves little." 48He said to her, "Your sins are forgiven."r 49The others at table said to themselves, "Who is this who even forgives sins?"s 50But he said to the woman, "Your faith has saved you; go in peace."

a. [7:1–10] Mt 8:5–13; Jn 4:43–54.
b. [7:11–17] 4:25–26; 1 Kgs 17:8–24.
c. [7:12] 8:42; 1 Kgs 17:17.
d. [7:15] 1 Kgs 17:23; 2 Kgs 4:36.
e. [7:16] 1:68; 19:44.
f. [7:18–23] Mt 11:2–6.
g. [7:19] Mal 3:1; Rev 1:4, 8; 4:8.
h. [7:22] 4:18; Is 35:5–6; 61:1.
i. [7:24–30] Mt 11:7–15.
j. [7:26] 1:76.
k. [7:27] Mal 3:1 / Is 40:3.
l. [7:29–30] 3:7, 12; Mt 21:32.
m. [7:31–35] Mt 11:16–19.
n. [7:34] 15:2.
o. [7:36] 11:37; 14:1.
p. [7:37] Mt 26:7; Mk 14:3.
q. [7:37–38] Jn 12:3.
r. [7:48] 5:20; Mt 9:20; Mk 2:5.
s. [7:49] 5:21.

CHAPTER 8

Galilean Women Follow Jesus. * 1Afterward he journeyed from one town and village to another, preaching and proclaiming the good news of the kingdom of God.a Accompanying him were the Twelve 2band some women who had been cured of evil spirits and infirmities, Mary, called Magdalene, from whom seven demons had gone out, 3Joanna, the wife of Herod's steward Chuza, Susanna, and many others who provided for them out of their resources.

The Parable of the Sower.[c] [4]*When a large crowd gathered, with people from one town after another journeying to him, he spoke in a parable.[*] [5]"A sower went out to sow his seed. And as he sowed, some seed fell on the path and was trampled, and the birds of the sky ate it up. [6]Some seed fell on rocky ground, and when it grew, it withered for lack of moisture. [7]Some seed fell among thorns, and the thorns grew with it and choked it. [8]And some seed fell on good soil, and when it grew, it produced fruit a hundredfold." After saying this, he called out, "Whoever has ears to hear ought to hear."[d]

The Purpose of the Parables.[e] [9]Then his disciples asked him what the meaning of this parable might be. [10]He answered, "Knowledge of the mysteries of the kingdom of God has been granted to you; but to the rest, they are made known through parables so that 'they may look but not see, and hear but not understand.'[f]

The Parable of the Sower Explained.[*] [11g]"This is the meaning of the parable. The seed is the word of God.[h] [12]Those on the path are the ones who have heard, but the devil comes and takes away the word from their hearts that they may not believe and be saved. [13]Those on rocky ground are the ones who, when they hear, receive the word with joy, but they have no root; they believe only for a time and fall away in time of trial. [14]As for the seed that fell among thorns, they are the ones who have heard, but as they go along, they are choked by the anxieties and riches and pleasures of life, and they fail to produce mature fruit. [15]But as for the seed that fell on rich soil, they are the ones who, when they have heard the word, embrace it with a generous and good heart, and bear fruit through perseverance.

The Parable of the Lamp.[*] [16]"No one who lights a lamp conceals it with a vessel or sets it under a bed; rather, he places it on a lampstand so that those who enter may see the light.[j] [17]For there is nothing hidden that will not become visible, and nothing secret that will not be known and come to light.[k] [18]Take care, then, how you hear. To anyone who has, more will be given, and from the one who has not, even what he seems to have will be taken away."[l]

Jesus and His Family.[m] [19]Then his mother and his brothers[*] came to him but were unable to join him because of the crowd. [20n]He was told, "Your mother and your brothers are standing outside and they wish to see you." [21]He said to them in reply, "My mother

and my brothers are those who hear the word of God and act on it."[*]

The Calming of a Storm at Sea.[o] [22]One day he got into a boat with his disciples and said to them, "Let us cross to the other side of the lake." So they set sail, [23]and while they were sailing he fell asleep. A squall blew over the lake, and they were taking in water and were in danger. [24]They came and woke him saying, "Master, master, we are perishing!" He awakened, rebuked the wind and the waves, and they subsided and there was a calm. [25]Then he asked them, "Where is your faith?" But they were filled with awe and amazed and said to one another, "Who then is this, who commands even the winds and the sea, and they obey him?"

The Healing of the Gerasene Demoniac.[p] [26]Then they sailed to the territory of the Gerasenes,[*] which is opposite Galilee. ²⁷When he came ashore a man from the town who was possessed by demons met him. For a long time he had not worn clothes; he did not live in a house, but lived among the tombs. ²⁸ᵠWhen he saw Jesus, he cried out and fell down before him; in a loud voice he shouted, "What have you to do with me, Jesus, son of the Most High God? I beg you, do not torment me!" ²⁹For he had ordered the unclean spirit to come out of the man. (It had taken hold of him many times, and he used to be bound with chains and shackles as a restraint, but he would break his bonds and be driven by the demon into deserted places.) ³⁰Then Jesus asked him, "What is your name?"˙ He replied, "Legion," because many demons had entered him. ³¹And they pleaded with him not to order them to depart to the abyss.˙

³²A herd of many swine was feeding there on the hillside, and they pleaded with him to allow them to enter those swine; and he let them. ³³The demons came out of the man and entered the swine, and the herd rushed down the steep bank into the lake and was drowned. ³⁴When the swineherds saw what had happened, they ran away and reported the incident in the town and throughout the countryside. ³⁵People came out to see what had happened and, when they approached Jesus, they discovered the man from whom the demons had come out sitting at his feet.˙ He was clothed and in his right mind, and they were seized with fear. ³⁶Those who witnessed it told them how the possessed man had been saved. ³⁷The entire population of the region of the Gerasenes asked Jesus to leave them because they were seized with great fear. So he got into a boat and returned. ³⁸The man from whom the demons had come

out begged to remain with him, but he sent him away, saying, [39]"Return home and recount what God has done for you." The man went off and proclaimed throughout the whole town what Jesus had done for him.)

Jairus's Daughter and the Woman with a Hemorrhage.[*] [40]When Jesus returned, the crowd welcomed him, for they were all waiting for him. [41]And a man named Jairus, an official of the synagogue, came forward. He fell at the feet of Jesus and begged him to come to his house, [42]because he had an only daughter,[*] about twelve years old, and she was dying. As he went, the crowds almost crushed him. [43]And a woman afflicted with hemorrhages for twelve years,[*] who [had spent her whole livelihood on doctors and] was unable to be cured by anyone, [44]came up behind him and touched the tassel on his cloak.

Immediately her bleeding stopped. [45]Jesus then asked, "Who touched me?" While all were denying it, Peter said, "Master, the crowds are pushing and pressing in upon you." [46]But Jesus said, "Someone has touched me; for I know that power has gone out from me."[s] [47]When the woman realized that she had not escaped notice, she came forward trembling. Falling down before him, she explained in the presence of all the people why she had touched him and how she had been healed immediately. [48]He said to her, "Daughter, your faith has saved you; go in peace."[t]

[49]While he was still speaking, someone from the synagogue official's house arrived and said, "Your daughter is dead; do not trouble the teacher any longer." [50]On hearing this, Jesus answered him, "Do not be afraid; just have faith and she will be saved." [51]When he arrived at the house he allowed no

one to enter with him except Peter and John and James, and the child's father and mother. [52]*uAll were weeping and mourning for her, when he said, "Do not weep any longer, for she is not dead, but sleeping." [53]And they ridiculed him, because they knew that she was dead. [54]But he took her by the hand and called to her, "Child, arise!" [55]Her breath returned and she immediately arose. He then directed that she should be given something to eat. [56]Her parents were astounded, and he instructed them to tell no one what had happened.

a. [8:1] 4:43.
b. [8:2–3] 23:49; 24:10; Mt 27:55–56; Mk 15:40–41; Jn 19:5.
c. [8:4–8] Mt 13:1–9; Mk 4:1–9.
d. [8:8] 14:35; Mt 11:15; 13:43; Mk 4:23.
e. [8:9–10] Mt 13:10–13; Mk 4:10–12.
f. [8:10] Is 6:9.
g. [8:11–15] Mt 13:18–23; Mk 4:13–20.
h. [8:11] 1 Pt 1:23.
i. [8:16–18] Mk 4:21–25.
j. [8:16] 11:33; Mt 5:15.
k. [8:17] 12:2; Mt 10:26.
l. [8:18] 19:26; Mt 13:12; 25:29.
m. [8:19–21] Mt 12:46–50; Mk 3:31–35.
n. [8:20–21] 11:27–28.
o. [8:22–25] Mt 8:18, 23–27; Mk 4:35–41.
p. [8:26–39] Mt 8:28–34; Mk 5:1–20.
q. [8:28–29] 4:33–35; Mt 8:29; Mk 1:23–24.
r. [8:40–56] Mt 9:18–26; Mk 5:21–43.
s. [8:46] 6:19.
t. [8:48] 7:50; 17:19; 18:42.
u. [8:52] 7:13.

CHAPTER 9

The Mission of the Twelve.[*] [1a]He summoned the Twelve and gave them power and authority over all demons and to cure diseases, [2]and he sent them to proclaim the kingdom of God and to heal [the sick]. [3]He said to them, "Take nothing for the journey,[*] neither walking stick, nor sack, nor food, nor money, and let no one take a second tunic. [4]Whatever house you enter, stay there and leave from there.[b] [5]And as for those who do not welcome you, when you leave that town, shake the dust from your feet[*] in testimony against them."[c] [6]Then they set out and went from village to village proclaiming the good news and curing diseases everywhere.

Herod's Opinion of Jesus.[d] [7]*Herod the tetrarch[*] heard about all that was happening, and he was greatly perplexed because some were saying, "John has been raised from

Baptist; others, Elijah; still others, 'One of the ancient prophets has arisen.'[k] [20]Then he said to them, "But who do you say that I am?" Peter said in reply, "The Messiah of God."[ ] [21]He rebuked them and directed them not to tell this to anyone.

The First Prediction of the Passion. [22]He said, "The Son of Man must suffer greatly and be rejected by the elders, the chief priests, and the scribes, and be killed and on the third day be raised."[l]

The Conditions of Discipleship.[m] [23]Then he said to all, "If anyone wishes to come after me, he must deny himself and take up his cross daily[ ] and follow me.[n] [24]For whoever wishes to save his life will lose it, but whoever loses his life for my sake will save it.[o] [25]What profit is there for one to gain the whole world yet lose or forfeit himself? [26]Whoever is ashamed of me and of my words, the

Son of Man will be ashamed of when he comes in his glory and in the glory of the Father and of the holy angels.[p] [27]Truly I say to you, there are some standing here who will not taste death until they see the kingdom of God."

The Transfiguration of Jesus.[ ] [28q]About eight days after he said this, he took Peter, John, and James and went up the mountain to pray.[ ] [29]While he was praying his face changed in appearance and his clothing became dazzling white. [30]And behold, two men were conversing with him, Moses and Elijah,[ ] [31r]who appeared in glory and spoke of his exodus that he was going to accomplish in Jerusalem. [32]Peter and his companions had been overcome by sleep, but becoming fully awake, they saw his glory[ ] and the two men standing with him.[s] [33]As they were about to part from him, Peter said to Jesus, "Master, it is good that we are here; let us the dead";*e* ⁸others were saying, "Elijah has appeared"; still others, "One of the ancient prophets has arisen." ⁹*f*But Herod said, "John I beheaded. Who then is this about whom I hear such things?" And he kept trying to see him.

The Return of the Twelve and the Feeding of the Five Thousand.*g* ¹⁰When the apostles returned, they explained to him what they had done. He took them and withdrew in private to a town called Bethsaida. ¹¹The crowds, meanwhile, learned of this and followed him. He received them and spoke to them about the kingdom of God, and he healed those who needed to be cured.) ¹²As the day was drawing to a close, the Twelve approached him and said, "Dismiss the crowd so that they can go to the surrounding villages and farms and find lodging and provisions; for we are in a deserted place here." [ ] said to them, "Give [ ] some food yourselves." [ ] replied, "Five loaves and [ ] fish are all we have, unle[ss] ourselves go and buy foo[d for] all these people." ¹⁴No[w the] men there numbered [ ] five thousand. Then h[e said] to his disciples, "Have [them] sit down in groups of [ ] fifty." ¹⁵They did so and [ ] them all sit down. ¹⁶Th[en tak]ing* the five loaves a[nd the] two fish, and looking [up to] heaven, he said the b[lessing] over them, broke the[m and] gave them to the disc[iples to] set before the crowd. [They] all ate and were satisf[ied and] when the leftover fra[gments] were picked up, the[y filled] twelve wicker basket[s].

Peter's Confession [About] Jesus. ¹⁸*j*Once wh[en Jesus] was praying in solit[ude and] the disciples were w[ith him,] he asked them, "[Who do] the crowds say tha[t I am?"] ¹⁹They said in reply, [ ] make three tents,* one for you, one for Moses, and one for Elijah." But he did not know what he was saying. ³⁴*While he was still speaking, a cloud came and cast a shadow over them, and they became frightened when they entered the cloud. ³⁵*ᵗThen from the cloud came a voice that said, "This is my chosen Son; listen to him." ³⁶After the voice had spoken, Jesus was found alone. They fell silent and did not at that time* tell anyone what they had seen.

The Healing of a Boy with a Demon.* ³⁷ᵘOn the next day, when they came down from the mountain, a large crowd met him. ³⁸There was a man in the crowd who cried out, "Teacher, I beg you, look at my son; he is my only child. ³⁹For a spirit seizes him and he suddenly screams and it convulses him until he foams at the mouth; it releases him only with difficulty, wearing him out. ⁴⁰I begged your disciples to cast it out but they could not." ⁴¹Jesus said in reply, "O faithless and perverse generation, how long will I be with you and endure you? Bring your son here." ⁴²As he was coming forward, the demon threw him to the ground in a convulsion; but Jesus rebuked the unclean spirit, healed the boy, and returned him to his father. ⁴³And all were astonished by the majesty of God.

The Second Prediction of the Passion.ᵛ While they were all amazed at his every deed, he said to his disciples, ⁴⁴"Pay attention to what I am telling you. The Son of Man is to be handed over to men." ⁴⁵But they did not understand this saying; its meaning was hidden from them so that they should not understand it, and they were afraid to ask him about this saying.

The Greatest in the Kingdom.ʷ ⁴⁶*An argument arose among the disciples about which of them was the greatest.[x] [47]Jesus realized the intention of their hearts and took a child and placed it by his side [48]and said to them, "Whoever receives this child in my name receives me, and whoever receives me receives the one who sent me. For the one who is least among all of you is the one who is the greatest."[y]

Another Exorcist.[z] [49]Then John said in reply, "Master, we saw someone casting out demons in your name and we tried to prevent him because he does not follow in our company." [50]Jesus said to him, "Do not prevent him, for whoever is not against you is for you."

V. THE JOURNEY TO JERUSALEM: LUKE'S TRAVEL NARRATIVE[*]

Departure for Jerusalem; Samaritan Inhospitality. [51]When the days for his being taken up[*] were fulfilled, he resolutely determined to journey to Jerusalem,[a] [52]and he sent messengers ahead of him.[b] On the way they entered a Samaritan village to prepare for his reception there, [53]but they would not welcome him because the destination of his journey was Jerusalem. [54]When the disciples James and John saw this they asked, "Lord, do you want us to call down fire from heaven to consume them?"[c] [55]Jesus turned and rebuked them, [56]and they journeyed to another village.)

The Would-be Followers of Jesus.[*] [57]As they were proceeding on their journey someone said to him, "I will follow you wherever you go." [58]Jesus answered him, "Foxes have dens and birds of the sky have nests, but the Son of Man has nowhere to rest his head." [59]And to another he said, "Follow me." But he replied, "[Lord,] let me go first and bury my father." ⁶⁰But he answered him, "Let the dead bury their dead. But you, go and proclaim the kingdom of God." ⁶¹ᵉAnd another said, "I will follow you, Lord, but first let me say farewell to my family at home." ⁶²[To him] Jesus said, "No one who sets a hand to the plow and looks to what was left behind is fit for the kingdom of God."

a. [9:1–6] Mt 10:1, 5–15; Mk 6:7–13.
b. [9:4] 10:5–7.
c. [9:5] 10:10–11; Acts 13:51.
d. [9:7–9] Mt 14:1–12; Mk 6:14–29.
e. [9:7–8] 9:19; Mt 16:14; Mk 8:28.
f. [9:9] 23:8.
g. [9:10–17] Mt 14:13–21; Mk 6:30–44; Jn 6:1–14.
h. [9:13–17] 2 Kgs 4:42–44.
i. [9:16] 22:19; 24:30–31; Acts 2:42; 20:11; 27:35.
j. [9:18–21] Mt 16:13–20; Mk 8:27–30.
k. [9:19] 9:7–8.
l. [9:22] 24:7, 26; Mt 16:21; 20:18–19; Mk 8:31; 10:33–34.
m. [9:23–27] Mt 16:24–28; Mk 8:34–9:1.
n. [9:23] 14:27; Mt 10:38.
o. [9:24] 17:33; Mt 10:39; Jn 12:25.
p. [9:26] 12:9; Mt 10:33; 2 Tm 2:12.
q. [9:28–36] Mt 17:1–8; Mk 9:2–8.
r. [9:31] 9:22; 13:33.
s. [9:32] Jn 1:14; 2 Pt 1:16.
t. [9:35] 3:22; Dt 18:15; Ps 2:7; Is 42:1; Mt 3:17; 12:18; Mk 1:11; 2 Pt 1:17–18.
u. [9:37–43] Mt 17:14–18; Mk 9:14–27.
v. [9:43–45] 18:32–34; Mt 17:22–23; Mk 9:30–32.
w. [9:46–48] Mt 18:1–5; Mk 9:33–37.
x. [9:46] 22:24.
y. [9:48] 10:16; Mt 10:40; Jn 13:20.
z. [9:49–50] Mk 9:38–40.
a. [9:51] 9:53; 13:22, 33; 17:11; 18:31; 19:28; 24:51; Acts 1:2, 9–11, 22.
b. [9:52] Mal 3:1.
c. [9:57] 2 Kgs 1:10, 12.
d. [9:57–60] Mt 8:19–22.
e. [9:61–62] 1 Kgs 19:20.

CHAPTER 10

The Mission of the Seventy-two. ¹After this the Lord appointed seventy[-two] others whom he sent ahead of him in pairs to every town and place he intended to visit.ᵃ ²He said to them, "The harvest is abundant but the laborers are few; so ask the master of the harvest to send out laborers for his harvest.ᵇ ³Go on your way; behold, I am sending you like lambs among wolves.ᶜ ⁴Carry no money bag,ᵈ no sack, no sandals;ᵉ and greet no one along the way. ⁵Into whatever house you enter, first say, 'Peace to this household.' ⁶If a peaceful person lives there, your peace will rest on him; but if not, it will return to you. ⁷Stay in the same house and eat and drink what is offered to you, for the laborer deserves his payment. Do not move about from one house to another.ᶠ ⁸Whatever town you enter and they welcome you, <u>eat</u> what is set before you,[g] [9]<u>cure</u> the sick in it and say to them, 'The kingdom of God is <u>at hand</u> for you.'[h] [10]Whatever town you enter and they do not receive you, go out into the streets and say,[i] [11]'The dust of your town that clings to our feet, even that we shake off against you.' Yet know this: the kingdom of God is at hand.[j] [12]I tell you, it will be more tolerable for Sodom on that day than for that town.[k]

Reproaches to Unrepentant Towns.[*] [13][l]"Woe to you, Chorazin! Woe to you, Bethsaida![m] For if the mighty deeds done in your midst had been done in Tyre and Sidon, they would long ago have repented, sitting in sackcloth and ashes. [14]But it will be more tolerable for Tyre and Sidon at the judgment than for you. [15][*n]And as for you, Capernaum, 'Will you be exalted to heaven? You will go down to the netherworld.' [16]Whoever

listens to you listens to me. Whoever rejects you rejects me. And whoever rejects me rejects the one who sent me."[o]

Return of the Seventy-two. [17]The seventy[-two] returned rejoicing, and said, "Lord, even the demons are subject to us because of your name." [18]Jesus said, "I have observed Satan fall like lightning[*] from the sky.[p] [19]Behold, I have given you the power 'to tread upon serpents' and scorpions and upon the full force of the enemy and nothing will harm you.[q] [20]Nevertheless, do not rejoice because the spirits are subject to you, but rejoice because your names are written in heaven."[r]

Praise of the Father.[s] [21]At that very moment <u>he rejoiced</u> [in] <u>the holy Spirit</u> and said, "I give you praise, Father, Lord of heaven and earth, for although you have hidden these things from the wise and the learned you have revealed them to the

childlike.* Yes, Father, such has been your gracious will.[t] [22]All things have been handed over to me by my Father. No one knows who the Son is except the Father, and who the Father is except the Son and anyone to whom the Son wishes to reveal him."[u]

The Privileges of Discipleship.[v] [23]Turning to the disciples in private he said, "Blessed are the eyes that see what you see. [24]For I say to you, many prophets and kings desired to see what you see, but did not see it, and to hear what you hear, but did not hear it."

The Greatest Commandment.[w] [25]*There was a scholar of the law* who stood up to test him and said, "Teacher, what must I do to inherit eternal life?"[x] [26]Jesus said to him, "What is written in the law? How do you read it?" [27]He said in reply, "You shall love the Lord, your God, with all your heart, with all your

being, with all your strength, and with all your mind, and your neighbor as yourself."[y] [28]He replied to him, "You have answered correctly; do this and you will live."[z]

The Parable of the Good Samaritan. [29]But because he wished to justify himself, he said to Jesus, "And who is my neighbor?" [30]Jesus replied, "A man fell victim to robbers as he went down from Jerusalem to Jericho. They stripped and beat him and went off leaving him half-dead. [31]*A priest happened to be going down that road, but when he saw him, he passed by on the opposite side. [32]Likewise a Levite came to the place, and when he saw him, he passed by on the opposite side. [33]But a Samaritan traveler who came upon him was moved with compassion at the sight. [34]He approached the victim, poured oil and wine over his wounds and bandaged them. Then he lifted him up on his own animal, took him to an inn and cared for him. ³⁵The next day he took out two silver coins and gave them to the innkeeper with the instruction, 'Take care of him. If you spend more than what I have given you, I shall repay you on my way back.' ³⁶Which of these three, in your opinion, was neighbor to the robbers' victim?" ³⁷He answered, "The one who treated him with mercy." Jesus said to him, "Go and do likewise."

Martha and Mary.[*] ³⁸ᵃAs they continued their journey he entered a village where a woman whose name was Martha welcomed him. ³⁹*She had a sister named Mary [who] sat beside the Lord at his feet listening to him speak. ⁴⁰Martha, burdened with much serving, came to him and said, "Lord, do you not care that my sister has left me by myself to do the serving? Tell her to help

me." ⁴¹The Lord said to her in reply, "Martha, Martha, you are anxious and worried about many things. ⁴²*There is need of only one thing. Mary has chosen the better part and it will not be taken from her."

a. [10:1] Mk 6:7.
b. [10:2] Mt 9:37–38; Jn 4:35.
c. [10:3] Mt 10:16.
d. [10:4–11] Mt 10:7–14.
e. [10:4] 9:3; 2 Kgs 4:29.
f. [10:7] 9:4; Mt 10:10; 1 Cor 9:6–14; 1 Tm 5:18.
g. [10:8] 1 Cor 10:27.
h. [10:9] Mt 3:2; 4:17; Mk 1:15.
i. [10:10–11] 9:5.
j. [10:11] Acts 13:51; 18:6.
k. [10:12] Mt 10:15; 11:24.
l. [10:13–15] Mt 11:20–24.
m. [10:13–14] Is 23; Ez 26–28; Jl 3:4–8; Am 1:1–10; Zec 9:2–4.
n. [10:15] Is 14:13–15.
o. [10:16] Mt 10:40; Jn 5:23; 13:20; 15:23.
p. [10:18] Is 14:12; Jn 12:31; Rev 12:7–12.
q. [10:19] Ps 91:13; Mk 16:18.
r. [10:20] Ex 32:32; Dn 12:1; Mt 7:22; Phil 4:3; Heb 12:23; Rev 3:5; 21:27.
s. [10:21–22] Mt 11:25–27.
t. [10:21] 1 Cor 1:26–28.
u. [10:22] Jn 3:35; 10:15.
v. [10:23–24] Mt 13:16–17.
w. [10:25–28] Mt 22:34–40; Mk 12:28–34.
x. [10:25] 18:18; Mt 19:16; Mk 10:17.
y. [10:27] Lv 19:18; Dt 6:5; 10:12; Jos 22:5; Mt 19:19; 22:37–39; Rom 13:9; Gal 5:14; Jas 2:8.
z. [10:28] Lv 18:5; Prv 19:16; Rom 10:5; Gal 3:12.
a. [10:38–39] Jn 11:1; 12:2–3.

CHAPTER 11

The Lord's Prayer.[a] ¹He was praying in a certain place, and when he had finished, one of his disciples said to him, "Lord, teach us to pray just as John taught his disciples."* ²*He said to them, "When you pray, say:

Father, hallowed be your
    name, (Spirit)
your kingdom come.
³Give us each day our
    daily bread*
⁴and forgive us our sins
    for we ourselves forgive
    everyone in debt to
    us,
    and do not subject us to
    the final test."

Further Teachings on Prayer.ᵇ
⁵And he said to them, "Suppose one of you has a friend to whom he goes at midnight and says, 'Friend, lend me three loaves of bread, ⁶for a friend of mine has arrived at my house from a journey and I have nothing to offer him,' ⁷and he says in reply from within, 'Do not bother me; the door has already been locked and my children and I are already in bed. I cannot get up to give you anything.' ⁸I tell you, if he does not get up to give him the loaves because of their friendship, he will get up to give him whatever he needs because of his persistence.

The Answer to Prayer.ᶜ ⁹"And I tell you, ask and you will receive; seek and you will find; knock and the door will be opened to you.ᵈ ¹⁰For everyone who asks, receives; and the one who seeks, finds; and to the one who knocks, the door will be opened. ¹¹What father among you would hand his son a snake when he asks for a fish? ¹²Or hand him a scorpion when he asks for an egg? ¹³If you then, who are wicked, know how to give good gifts to your children, how much more will the Father in heaven give the holy Spirit* to those who ask him?"

Jesus and Beelzebul.ᵉ ¹⁴He was driving out a demon [that was] mute, and when the demon had gone out, the mute person spoke and the crowds were <u>amazed</u>. [15]Some of them said, "By the power of Beelzebul, the prince of demons, he drives out demons."[f] [16]Others, to test him, asked him for a sign from heaven.[g] [17]But he knew their thoughts and said to them, "Every kingdom divided against itself will be laid waste and house will fall against house. [18]And if Satan is divided against himself, how will his kingdom stand? For you say that it is by Beelzebul that I drive out demons. [19]If I, then, drive out demons by Beelzebul, by whom do your own people* drive them out? Therefore they will be your judges. [20]But if it is by the finger of God that [I] drive out demons, then the kingdom of God has come upon you.[h] [21]When a strong man fully armed guards his palace, his possessions are safe. [22]But when one stronger* than he attacks and overcomes him, he takes away the armor on which he relied and distributes the spoils. [23]Whoever is not with me is against me, and whoever does not gather with me scatters.[i]

The Return of the Unclean Spirit.[j] [24]"When an unclean spirit goes out of someone, it roams through arid regions searching for rest but, finding none, it says, 'I shall return to my home from which I came.' [25]But upon returning, it finds it swept clean and put in order. [26]Then it goes and brings back seven other spirits more wicked than itself who move in and dwell there, and the last condition of that person is worse than the first."[k]

True Blessedness.* [27]While he was speaking, a woman from the crowd called out and said to him, "Blessed is the womb that carried you and the breasts at which you nursed."[l] [28]He replied, "Rather, blessed are those who <u>hear</u> the word of God and <u>observe</u> it."

The Demand for a Sign.[*] ²⁹While still more people gathered in the crowd, he said to them,^m "This generation is an evil generation; it seeks a sign, but no sign will be given it, except the sign of Jonah.ⁿ ³⁰Just as Jonah became a sign to the Ninevites, so will the Son of Man be to this generation. ³¹At the judgment the queen of the south will rise with the men of this generation and she will condemn them, because she came from the ends of the earth to hear the wisdom of Solomon, and there is something greater than Solomon here.^o ³²At the judgment the men of Nineveh will arise with this generation and condemn it, because at the preaching of Jonah they repented, and there is something greater than Jonah here.^p

The Simile of Light. ³³"No one who lights a lamp hides it away or places it [under a bushel basket], but on a lampstand so that those who enter might see the light.^q ³⁴The lamp of the body is your eye.^r When your eye is sound, then your whole body is filled with light, but when it is bad, then your body is in darkness. ³⁵Take care, then, that the light in you not become darkness. ³⁶If your whole body is full of light, and no part of it is in darkness, then it will be as full of light as a lamp illuminating you with its brightness."

Denunciation of the Pharisees and Scholars of the Law.[*] ³⁷After he had spoken, a Pharisee invited him to dine at his home. He entered and reclined at table to eat.^t ³⁸The Pharisee was amazed to see that he did not observe the prescribed washing before the meal.^u ³⁹The Lord said to him, "Oh you Pharisees!^v Although you cleanse the outside of the cup and the dish, inside you are filled with plunder and evil. ⁴⁰You fools! Did not the maker of the outside also make the inside? ⁴¹But as to what is within, give alms, and behold, everything will be clean for you. ⁴²Woe to you Pharisees! You pay tithes of mint and of rue and of every garden herb, but you pay no attention to judgment and to love for God. These you should have done, without overlooking the others.ʷ ⁴³Woe to you Pharisees! You love the seat of honor in synagogues and greetings in marketplaces.ˣ ⁴⁴Woe to you! You are like unseen graves* over which people unknowingly walk."ʸ

⁴⁵Then one of the scholars of the law* said to him in reply, "Teacher, by saying this you are insulting us too."ᶻ ⁴⁶And he said, "Woe also to you scholars of the law! You impose on people burdens hard to carry, but you yourselves do not lift one finger to touch them. ⁴⁷ᵃWoe to you! You build the memorials of the prophets whom your ancestors killed. ⁴⁸Consequently, you bear witness and give consent to the deeds of your ancestors, for they killed them and you do the building. ⁴⁹ᵇTherefore, the wisdom of God said, 'I will send to them prophets and apostles;* some of them they will kill and persecute' ⁵⁰in order that this generation might be charged with the blood of all the prophets shed since the foundation of the world, ⁵¹from the blood of Abel to the blood of Zechariah* who died between the altar and the temple building. Yes, I tell you, this generation will be charged with their blood!ᶜ ⁵²Woe to you, scholars of the law! You have taken away the key of knowledge. You yourselves did not enter and you stopped those trying to enter."ᵈ ⁵³When he left, the scribes and Pharisees began to act with hostility toward him and to interrogate him about many things,ᵉ ⁵⁴for they

were plotting to catch him at something he might say.*f*

---

a. [11:1–4] Mt 6:9–15.
b. [11:5–8] 18:1–5.
c. [11:9–13] Mt 7:7–11.
d. [11:9] Mt 21:22; Mk 11:24; Jn 14:13; 15:7; 1 Jn 5:14–15.
e. [11:14–23] Mt 12:22–30; Mk 3:20–27.
f. [11:15] Mt 9:34.
g. [11:16] Mt 12:38; 16:1; Mk 8:11; 1 Cor 1:22.
h. [11:20] Ex 8:19.
i. [11:23] 9:50; Mk 9:40.
j. [11:24–26] Mt 12:43–45.
k. [11:26] Jn 5:14.
l. [11:27] 1:28, 42, 48.
m. [11:29–32] Mt 12:38–42; Mk 8:12.
n. [11:29] Mt 16:1, 4; Jn 6:30; 1 Cor 1:22.
o. [11:31] 1 Kgs 10:1–10; 2 Chr 9:1–12.
p. [11:32] Jon 3:8, 10.
q. [11:33] 8:16; Mt 5:15; Mk 4:21.
r. [11:34–36] Mt 6:22–23.
s. [11:37–54] 20:45–47; Mt 23:1–36; Mk 12:38–40.
t. [11:37] 7:36; 14:1.
u. [11:38] Mk 15:2; Mk 7:2–5.
v. [11:39–41] Mt 23:25–26.
w. [11:42] Lv 27:30; Mt 23:23.
x. [11:43] 20:46; Mt 23:6; Mk 12:38–39.
y. [11:44] Mt 23:27.
z. [11:45] Mt 23:4.
a. [11:47–48] Mt 23:29–32.
b. [11:49–51] Mt 23:34–36.
c. [11:51] Gn 4:8; 2 Chr 24:20–22.
d. [11:52] Mt 23:13.
e. [11:53] 6:11; Mt 22:15–22.
f. [11:54] 20:20.

CHAPTER 12

The Leaven of the Pharisees.* ¹Meanwhile, so many people were crowding together that they were trampling one another underfoot.*a* He began to speak, first to his disciples, "Beware of the leaven—that is, the hypocrisy—of the Pharisees.

Courage Under Persecution.* *2b*"There is nothing concealed that will not be revealed, nor secret that will not be known.*c* ³Therefore whatever you have said in the darkness will be heard in the light, and what you have whispered behind closed doors will be proclaimed on the housetops. ⁴I tell you, my friends, do not be afraid of those who kill the body but after that can do no more. ⁵I shall show you whom to fear. Be afraid of the one who after killing has the power to cast into Gehenna;* yes, I tell you, be afraid of that one. ⁶Are not five sparrows sold for two small coins?* Yet not one of them has escaped the notice of God. ⁷Even the hairs of your head have all been counted. Do not be afraid. You are worth more than many sparrows.*d* ⁸I tell you, everyone who acknowledges me before others the Son of Man will acknowledge before the angels of God. ⁹But whoever denies me before others will be denied before the angels of God.*

Sayings About the Holy Spirit.* ¹⁰"Everyone who speaks a word against the Son of Man will be forgiven, but the one who blasphemes against the holy Spirit will not be forgiven.*¹¹When they take you before synagogues and before rulers and authorities,* do not worry about how or what your defense will be or about what you are to say. ¹²For the holy Spirit will teach you at that moment what you should say."

Saying Against Greed. ¹³*Someone in the crowd said to him, "Teacher, tell my brother to share the inheritance with me." ¹⁴He replied to him, "Friend, who appointed me as your judge and arbitrator?"* ¹⁵Then he said to the crowd, "Take care to guard against all greed, for though one may be rich, one's life does not consist of possessions."*

Parable of the Rich Fool. ¹⁶Then he told them a parable. "There was a rich man whose land produced a bountiful harvest. ¹⁷He asked himself, 'What shall I do, for I do not have space to store my harvest?' ¹⁸And he said, 'This is what I shall do: I shall tear down my barns and build larger ones. There I shall store all my grain and other goods ¹⁹and I shall say to myself, "Now as for you, you have so many good things stored up for many years, rest, eat, drink, be merry!"'* ²⁰But God said to him, 'You fool, this night your life will be demanded of you; and the things you have prepared, to whom will they belong?' ²¹Thus will it be for the one who stores up treasure for himself but is not rich in what matters to God.'"

Dependence on God. ²²*He said to [his] disciples, "Therefore I tell you, do not worry about your life and what you will eat, or about your body and what you will wear. ²³For life is more than food and the body more than clothing. ²⁴Notice the ravens: they do not sow or reap; they have neither storehouse nor barn, yet God feeds them. How much more important are you than birds!^m ²⁵Can any of you by worrying add a moment to your life-span? ²⁶If even the smallest things are beyond your control, why are you anxious about the rest? ²⁷Notice how the flowers grow. They do not toil or spin. But I tell you, not even Solomon in all his splendor was dressed like one of them.^n ²⁸If God so clothes the grass in the field that grows today and is thrown into the oven tomorrow, will he not much more provide for you, O you of little faith? ²⁹As for you, do not seek what you are to eat and what you are to drink, and do not worry anymore. ³⁰All the nations of the world seek for these things,

and your Father knows that you need them. ³¹Instead, seek his kingdom, and these other things will be given you besides. ³²Do not be afraid any longer, little flock, for your Father is pleased to give you the kingdom.^o ³³Sell your belongings and give alms. Provide money bags for yourselves that do not wear out, an inexhaustible treasure in heaven that no thief can reach nor moth destroy.^p ³⁴For where your treasure is, there also will your heart be.

Vigilant and Faithful Servants.^* ³⁵q"Gird your loins and light your lamps ³⁶and be like servants who await their master's return from a wedding, ready to open immediately when he comes and knocks.^r ³⁷Blessed are those servants whom the master finds vigilant on his arrival. Amen, I say to you, he will gird himself, have them recline at table, and proceed to wait on them. ³⁸And should he come in the second or third watch and find them prepared in this way, blessed are those servants. [39s]Be sure of this: if the master of the house had known the hour when the thief was coming, he would not have let his house be broken into. [40]You also must be prepared, for at an hour you do not expect, the Son of Man will come."

[41]Then Peter said, "Lord, is this parable meant for us or for everyone?" [42]And the Lord replied, "Who, then, is the faithful and prudent steward whom the master will put in charge of his servants to distribute [the] food allowance at the proper time? [43]Blessed is that servant whom his master on arrival finds doing so. [44]Truly, I say to you, he will put him in charge of all his property. [45]But if that servant says to himself, 'My master is delayed in coming,' and begins to beat the menservants and the maidservants, to eat and drink and get drunk, [46]then that servant's master will come on an unexpected day and at an unknown hour and will punish him severely and assign him a place with the unfaithful. [47]That servant who knew his master's will but did not make preparations nor act in accord with his will shall be beaten severely;[t] [48]and the servant who was ignorant of his master's will but acted in a way deserving of a severe beating shall be beaten only lightly. Much will be required of the person entrusted with much, and still more will be demanded of the person entrusted with more.

Jesus: A Cause of Division.[*] [49]"I have come to set the earth on fire, and how I wish it were already blazing! [50*]There is a baptism with which I must be baptized, and how great is my anguish until it is accomplished![u] [51]Do you think that I have come to establish peace on the earth?[v] No, I tell you,

but rather division.[w] [52]From now on a household of five will be divided, three against two and two against three; [53]a father will be divided against his son and a son against his father, a mother against her daughter and a daughter against her mother, a mother-in-law against her daughter-in-law and a daughter-in-law against her mother-in-law."[x]

Signs of the Times.[y] [54]He also said to the crowds, "When you see [a] cloud rising in the west you say immediately that it is going to rain—and so it does; [55]and when you notice that the wind is blowing from the south you say that it is going to be hot—and so it is. [56]You hypocrites! You know how to interpret the appearance of the earth and the sky; why do you not know how to interpret the present time?

Settlement with an Opponent.[z] [57]"Why do you not judge for yourselves what is right? [58]If you are to go with your opponent before a magistrate, make an effort to settle the matter on the way; otherwise your opponent will turn you over to the judge, and the judge hand you over to the constable, and the constable throw you into prison. [59]I say to you, you will not be released until you have paid the last penny."*

a. [12:1] Mt 16:6; Mk 8:15.
b. [12:2–9] Mt 10:26–33.
c. [12:2] 8:17; Mk 4:22.
d. [12:7] 12:24; 21:18; Acts 27:34.
e. [12:9] 9:26; Mk 8:38; 2 Tm 2:12.
f. [12:10] Mt 12:31–32; Mk 3:28–29.
g. [12:11–12] 21:12–15; Mt 10:17–20; Mk 13:11.
h. [12:14] Ex 2:14; Acts 7:27.
i. [12:15] 1 Tm 6:9–10.
j. [12:19–21] Mt 6:19–21; 1 Tm 6:17.
k. [12:19–20] Sir 11:19.
l. [12:22–32] Mt 6:25–34.
m. [12:24] 12:7.
n. [12:27] 1 Kgs 10:4–7; 2 Chr 9:3–6.
o. [12:32] 22:29; Rev 1:6.
p. [12:33] 18:22; Mt 6:20–21; Mk 10:21.
q. [12:35–46] Mt 24:45–51.
r. [12:36] Mt 25:1–13; Mk 13:35–37.
s. [12:39–40] Mt 24:43–44; 1 Thes 5:2.
t. [12:47] Jas 4:17.
u. [12:50] Mk 10:38–39.
v. [12:51–53] Mt 10:34–35.
w. [12:51] 2:14.
x. [12:53] Mi 7:6.
y. [12:54–56] Mt 16:2–3.
z. [12:57–59] Mt 5:25–26.

CHAPTER 13

A Call to Repentance.* [1]At that time some people who

were present there told him about the Galileans whose blood Pilate* had mingled with the blood of their sacrifices. [2]He said to them in reply, "Do you think that because these Galileans suffered in this way they were greater sinners than all other Galileans?[a] [3]By no means! But I tell you, if you do not repent,[b] you will all perish as they did! [4]Or those eighteen people who were killed when the tower at Siloam fell on them*—do you think they were more guilty than everyone else who lived in Jerusalem? [5]By no means! But I tell you, if you do not repent, you will all perish as they did!"

The Parable of the Barren Fig Tree.* [6c]And he told them this parable: "There once was a person who had a fig tree planted in his orchard, and when he came in search of fruit on it but found none, [7]he said to the gardener, 'For three years now I have come in search of fruit on this fig tree but have found none. [So] cut it down. Why should it exhaust the soil?' [8]He said to him in reply, 'Sir, leave it for this year also, and I shall cultivate the ground around it and fertilize it; [9]it may bear fruit in the future. If not you can cut it down.'"

Cure of a Crippled Woman on the Sabbath.* [10]He was teaching in a synagogue on the sabbath. [11]And a woman was there who for eighteen years had been crippled by a spirit; she was bent over, completely incapable of standing erect. [12]When Jesus saw her, he called to her and said, "Woman, you are set free of your infirmity." [13]He laid his hands on her, and she at once stood up straight and glorified God. [14d]But the leader of the synagogue, indignant that Jesus had cured on the sabbath, said to the crowd in reply, "There are six days when work should be done. Come on those days to be cured, not on the sabbath day." [15*]The Lord said to him in reply, "Hypocrites! Does not each one of you on the sabbath untie his ox or his ass from the manger and lead it out for watering?[e] [16*]This daughter of Abraham, whom Satan has bound for eighteen years now, ought she not to have been set free on the sabbath day from this bondage?"[f] [17]When he said this, all his adversaries were humiliated; and the whole crowd rejoiced at all the splendid deeds done by him.

The Parable of the Mustard Seed.[g] [18*]Then he said, "What is the kingdom of God like? To what can I compare it? [19]It is like a mustard seed that a person took and planted in the garden. When it was fully grown, it became a large bush and 'the birds of the sky dwelt in its branches.'"[h]

The Parable of the Yeast.[i] [20]Again he said, "To what shall I compare the kingdom of God? [21]It is like yeast that a woman took and mixed [in] with three measures of wheat flour until the whole batch of dough was leavened."

The Narrow Door; Salvation and Rejection.[*] [22]He passed through towns and villages, teaching as he went and making his way to Jerusalem. [23]Someone asked him, "Lord, will only a few people be saved?" He answered them, [24j]"Strive to enter through the narrow door, for many, I tell you, will attempt to enter but will not be strong enough.[k] [25]After the master of the house has arisen and locked the door, then will you stand outside knocking and saying, 'Lord, open the door for us.' He will say to you in reply, 'I do not know where you are from.'[l] [26]And you will say, 'We ate and drank in your company and you taught in our streets.' [27m]Then he will say to you, 'I do not know where [you] are from. Depart from me, all you evildoers!' [28n]And there will be wailing and grinding of teeth when you see Abraham, Isaac, and Jacob and all the prophets in the kingdom of God and you yourselves cast out. [29]And people will come from the east and the west and from the north and the south and will recline at table in the kingdom of God.[o] [30]For behold, some are last who will be first, and some are first who will be last."[p]

Herod's Desire to Kill Jesus. [31]At that time some Pharisees came to him and said, "Go away, leave this area because Herod wants to kill you." [32]He replied, "Go and tell that fox, 'Behold, I cast out demons and I perform healings today and tomorrow, and on the third day I accomplish my purpose.' [33]Yet I must continue on my way today,[q] tomorrow, and the following

day, for it is impossible that a prophet should die outside of Jerusalem.'

The Lament over Jerusalem.[r] [34]"Jerusalem, Jerusalem, you who kill the prophets and stone those sent to you, how many times I yearned to gather your children together as a hen gathers her brood under her wings, but you were unwilling! [35]Behold, your house will be abandoned. [But] I tell you, you will not see me until [the time comes when] you say, 'Blessed is he who comes in the name of the Lord.'"[s]

a. [13:2] Jn 9:2.
b. [13:3–5] Jn 8:24.
c. [13:6–9] Jer 8:13; Heb 3:17; Mt 21:19; Mk 11:13.
d. [13:14] 6:7; 14:3; Ex 20:8–11; Dt 5:12–15; Mt 12:10; Mk 3:2–4; Jn 5:16; 7:23; 9:14, 16.
e. [13:15] 14:5; Dt 22:4; Mt 12:11.
f. [13:16] 19:9.
g. [13:18–19] Mt 13:31–32; Mk 4:30–32.
h. [13:19] Ez 17:23–24; 31:6.
i. [13:20–21] Mt 13:33.
j. [13:24–30] Mt 7:13–14, 21–23.
k. [13:24] Mk 10:25.
l. [13:25] Mt 25:10–12.
m. [13:27] Ps 6:9; Mt 7:23; 25:41.
n. [13:28–29] Mt 8:11–12.
o. [13:29] Ps 107:2–3.
p. [13:30] Mt 19:20; 20:16; Mk 10:31.
q. [13:33] 2:38; Jn 6:30; 8:20.
r. [13:34–35] 19:41–44; Mt 23:37–39.
s. [13:35] 19:38; 1 Kgs 9:7–8; Ps 118:26; Jer 7:4–7, 13–15; 12:7; 22:5.

CHAPTER 14

Healing of the Man with Dropsy on the Sabbath.[*] [1a]On a sabbath he went to dine at the home of one of the leading Pharisees, and the people there were observing him carefully.[b] [2]In front of him there was a man suffering from dropsy.[*] [3]Jesus spoke to the scholars of the law and Pharisees in reply, asking, ("Is it lawful to cure on the sabbath or not?")[c] [4]But they kept silent; so he took the man and, after he had healed him, dismissed him. [5]Then he said to them, "Who among you, if your son or ox[*] falls into a cistern, would not immediately pull him out on the sabbath day?"[d] [6]But they were unable to answer his question.[e]

Conduct of Invited Guests and Hosts.[*] [7]He told a parable to those who had been invited, noticing how they were choosing the places of honor at the table. [8]"When you are invited by someone to a wedding banquet, do not recline at table in the place of honor. A more distinguished guest than you may have been invited by him, [9]and the host who invited both of you may approach you and say, 'Give your place to this man,' and then you would proceed with embarrassment to take the lowest place. [10]Rather, when you are invited, go and take the lowest place so that when the host comes to you he may say, 'My friend, move up to a higher position.' Then you will enjoy the esteem of your companions at the table. [11]For everyone who exalts himself will be humbled, but the one who humbles himself will be exalted."[h] [12]Then he said to the host who invited him, "When you hold a lunch or a dinner, do not invite your friends or your brothers or your relatives or your wealthy neighbors, in case they may invite you back and you have repayment.[i]

¹³Rather, when you hold a banquet, invite the poor, the crippled, the lame, the blind; ¹⁴blessed indeed will you be because of their inability to repay you. For you will be repaid at the resurrection of the righteous."ʲ

The Parable of the Great Feast.* ¹⁵One of his fellow guests on hearing this said to him, "Blessed is the one who will dine in the kingdom of God." ¹⁶ᵏHe replied to him, "A man gave a great dinner to which he invited many. ¹⁷When the time for the dinner came, he dispatched his servant to say to those invited, 'Come, everything is now ready.' ¹⁸But one by one, they all began to excuse themselves. The first said to him, 'I have purchased a field and must go to examine it; I ask you, consider me excused.' ¹⁹And another said, 'I have purchased five yoke of oxen and am on my way to evaluate them; I ask you, consider

me excused.' ²⁰And another said, 'I have just married a woman, and therefore I cannot come.' ²¹The servant went and reported this to his master. Then the master of the house in a rage commanded his servant, 'Go out quickly into the streets and alleys of the town and bring in here the poor and the crippled, the blind and the lame.' ²²The servant reported, 'Sir, your orders have been carried out and still there is room.' ²³The master then ordered the servant, 'Go out to the highways and hedgerows and make people come in that my home may be filled. ²⁴For, I tell you, none of those men who were invited will taste my dinner.'"

Sayings on Discipleship.* ²⁵Great crowds were traveling with him, and he turned and addressed them, ²⁶ˡ"If any one comes to me without hating his father* and mother, wife and children, brothers and sisters, and even his own life, he cannot be my disciple.*m* *27*Whoever does not carry his own cross and come after me cannot be my disciple.*n* *28*Which of you wishing to construct a tower does not first sit down and calculate the cost to see if there is enough for its completion? *29*Otherwise, after laying the foundation and finding himself unable to finish the work the onlookers should laugh at him *30*and say, 'This one began to build but did not have the resources to finish.' *31*Or what king marching into battle would not first sit down and decide whether with ten thousand troops he can successfully oppose another king advancing upon him with twenty thousand troops? *32*But if not, while he is still far away, he will send a delegation to ask for peace terms. *33*In the same way, everyone of you who does not renounce all his possessions cannot be my disciple.*o*

EVERYONE!

The Simile of Salt. *34*"Salt is good, but if salt itself loses its taste, with what can its flavor be restored?*p* *35*It is fit neither for the soil nor for the manure pile; it is thrown out. Whoever has ears to hear ought to hear."*q*

---

a. [14:1–6] 6:6–11; 13:10–17.
b. [14:1] 11:37.
c. [14:3] 6:9; Mk 3:4.
d. [14:5] 13:15; Dt 22:4; Mt 12:11.
e. [14:6] Mt 22:46.
f. [14:7] 11:43; Mt 23:6; Mk 12:38–39.
g. [14:8–10] Prv 25:6–7.
h. [14:11] 18:14.
i. [14:12] 6:32–35.
j. [14:14] Jn 5:29.
k. [14:16–24] Mt 22:2–10.
l. [14:26–27] Mt 10:37–38.
m. [14:26] 9:57–62; 18:29; Jn 12:25.
n. [14:27] 9:23; Mt 16:24; Mk 8:34.
o. [14:33] 5:11.
p. [14:34] Mt 5:13; Mk 9:50.
q. [14:35] 8:8; Mt 11:15; 13:9; Mk 4:9, 23.

CHAPTER 15

The Parable of the Lost Sheep.*a* *1*The tax collectors and sinners were all drawing near to listen to him, *2*but the Pharisees and scribes began to complain, saying, "This man welcomes sinners and eats with them."*b* *3*So to them he addressed this parable. *4*"What man among you having a hundred sheep and losing one of them would not leave the ninety-nine in the desert and go after the lost one[d] until he finds it?[e] [5]And when he does find it, he sets it on his shoulders with great joy [6]and, upon his arrival home, he calls together his friends and neighbors and says to them, 'Rejoice with me because I have found my lost sheep.' [7]I tell you, in just the same way there will be more joy in heaven over one sinner who repents than over ninety-nine righteous people who have no need of repentance.[f]

The Parable of the Lost Coin. [8]"Or what woman having ten coins* and losing one would not light a lamp and sweep the house, searching carefully until she finds it? [9]And when she does find it, she calls together her friends and neighbors and says to them, 'Rejoice with me because I have found the coin that I lost.' [10]In just the same way, I tell you, there will be rejoicing among the angels of God over one sinner who repents."

The Parable of the Lost Son. [11]Then he said, "A man had two sons, [12]and the younger son said to his father, 'Father, give me the share of your estate that should come to me.' So the father divided the property between them. [13]After a few days, the younger son collected all his belongings and set off to a distant country where he squandered his inheritance on a life of dissipation.[g] [14]When he had freely spent everything, a severe famine struck that country, and he found himself in dire need. [15]So he hired himself out to one of the local citizens who sent him to his farm to tend the swine. [16]And he longed to eat his fill of the pods on which the swine fed, but nobody gave him any. [17]Coming to his senses he thought, 'How many of my father's hired workers have more than enough food to eat, but here am I, dying from hunger. [18]I shall get up and go to my father and I shall say to him, "Father, I have sinned against heaven and against you. [19]I no longer deserve to be called your son; treat me as you would treat one of your hired workers.'" [20]So he got up and went back to his father. While he was still a long way off, his father caught sight of him, and was filled with compassion. He ran to his son, embraced him and kissed him. [21]His son said to him, 'Father, I have sinned against heaven and against you; I no longer deserve to be called your son.'/[22]But his father ordered his servants, 'Quickly bring the finest robe and put it on him; put a ring on his finger and sandals on his feet. [23]Take the fattened calf and slaughter it. Then let us celebrate with a feast, [24]because this son of mine was dead, and has come to life again; he was lost, and has been found.' Then the celebration began. [25]Now the older son had been out in the field and, on his way back, as he neared the house, he heard the sound of music and dancing. [26]He called one of the servants and asked what this might mean. [27]The servant said to him, 'Your brother has returned and your father has slaughtered the fattened calf because he has him back safe and sound.' [28]He became angry, and when he refused to enter the house, his father came out and pleaded with him. [29]He said to his father in reply, 'Look, all these years I served you and not once did I disobey your orders; yet you never gave me even a young goat to feast on with my friends. [30]But when your son returns who swallowed up your property with prostitutes, for him you slaughter the fattened calf.' [31]He said to him, 'My son, you are here with me always; everything I have is yours. ³²But now we must celebrate and rejoice, because your brother was dead and has come to life again; he was lost and has been found.'"

a. [15:1–7] Mt 9:10–13.
b. [15:2] 5:30; 19:7.
c. [15:4–7] Mt 18:12–14.
d. [15:4–6] 19:10.
e. [15:4] Ez 34:11–12, 16.
f. [15:7] Ez 18:23.
g. [15:13] Prv 29:3.

CHAPTER 16

The Parable of the Dishonest Steward.[*] ¹Then he also said to his disciples, "A rich man had a steward who was reported to him for squandering his property. ²He summoned him and said, 'What is this I hear about you? Prepare a full account of your stewardship, because you can no longer be my steward.' ³The steward said to himself, 'What shall I do, now that my master is taking the position of steward away from me? I am not strong enough to dig and I am ashamed to beg. ⁴I know what I shall do so that, when I am removed from the stewardship, they may welcome me into their homes.' ⁵He called in his master's debtors one by one. To the first he said, 'How much do you owe my master?' ⁶He replied, 'One hundred measures of olive oil.' He said to him, 'Here is your promissory note. Sit down and quickly write one for fifty.' ⁷Then to another he said, 'And you, how much do you owe?' He replied, 'One hundred kors[*] of wheat.' He said to him, 'Here is your promissory note; write one for eighty.' ⁸And the master commended that dishonest steward for acting prudently.

Application of the Parable.[*] "For the children of this world are more prudent in dealing with their own generation than are the children of light."^a ⁹I tell you, make friends for yourselves with dishonest wealth,[*] so that when it fails, you will be welcomed into eternal dwellings.[b] [10]"The person who is trustworthy in very small matters is also trustworthy in great ones; and the person who is dishonest in very small matters is also dishonest in great ones.[c] [11]If, therefore, you are not trustworthy with dishonest wealth, who will trust you with true wealth? [12]If you are not trustworthy with what belongs to another, who will give you what is yours? [13]No servant can serve two masters.[*] He will either hate one and love the other, or be devoted to one and despise the other. (You cannot serve God and mammon."[d])

A Saying Against the Pharisees. [14*]The Pharisees, who loved money,[*] heard all these things and sneered at him. [15]And he said to them, "You justify yourselves in the sight of others, but God knows your hearts; for what is of human esteem is an abomination in the sight of God.[e]

Sayings About the Law. [16]"The law and the prophets lasted until John;[*] but from then on the kingdom of God is proclaimed, and everyone who enters does so with violence.[f] [17]It is easier for heaven and earth to pass away than for the smallest part of a letter of the law to become invalid.[g]

Sayings About Divorce. [18]"Everyone who divorces his wife and marries another commits adultery, and the one who marries a woman divorced from her husband commits adultery.[h]

The Parable of the Rich Man and Lazarus.[*] [19]"There was a rich man[*] who dressed in purple garments and fine linen and dined sumptuously each day. [20]And lying at his door was a poor man named Lazarus, covered with sores,[i] [21]who would gladly have eaten his fill of the scraps that fell from the rich man's table. Dogs even used to come and lick his sores. ²²When the poor man died, he was carried away by angels to the bosom of Abraham. The rich man also died and was buried, ²³and from the netherworld,* where he was in torment, he raised his eyes and saw Abraham far off and Lazarus at his side. ²⁴And he cried out, 'Father Abraham, have pity on me. Send Lazarus to dip the tip of his finger in water and cool my tongue, for I am suffering torment in these flames.' ²⁵Abraham replied, 'My child, remember that you received what was good during your lifetime while Lazarus likewise received what was bad; but now he is comforted here, whereas you are tormented.ʲ ²⁶Moreover, between us and you a great chasm is established to prevent anyone from crossing who might wish to go from our side to yours or from your side to ours.' ²⁷He said, 'Then I beg you, father, send

him to my father's house, ²⁸for I have five brothers, so that he may warn them, lest they too come to this place of torment.' ²⁹But Abraham replied, 'They have Moses and the prophets. Let them listen to them.' ³⁰He said, 'Oh no, father Abraham, but if someone from the dead goes to them, they will repent.' ³¹Then Abraham said, 'If they will not listen to Moses and the prophets, neither will they be persuaded if someone should rise from the dead.'"ᵏ

a. [16:8] Eph 5:8; 1 Thes 5:5.
b. [16:9] 12:33.
c. [16:10] 19:17; Mt 25:20–23.
d. [16:13] Mt 6:24.
e. [16:15] 18:9–14.
f. [16:16] Mt 11:12–13.
g. [16:17] Mt 5:18.
h. [16:18] Mt 5:32; 19:9; Mk 10:11–12; 1 Cor 7:10–11.
i. [16:20] Mt 15:27; Mk 7:28.
j. [16:25] 6:24–25.
k. [16:31] Jn 5:46–47; 11:44–48.

CHAPTER 17

Temptations to Sin. ¹ᵃHe said to his disciples, "Things that cause sin will inevitably occur, but woe to the person through whom they occur. ²It would be better for him if a millstone were put around his neck and he be thrown into the sea than for him to cause one of these little ones to sin. ³Be on your guard!' If your brother sins, rebuke him; and if he repents, forgive him.ᵇ ⁴And if he wrongs you seven times in one day and returns to you seven times saying, 'I am sorry,' you should forgive him."ᶜ

Saying of Faith. ⁵And the apostles said to the Lord, "Increase our faith." ⁶The Lord replied, "If you have faith the size of a mustard seed, you would say to [this] mulberry tree, 'Be uprooted and planted in the sea,' and it would obey you.ᵈ

Attitude of a Servant. * ⁷"Who among you would say to your servant who has just come in from plowing or tending sheep in the field, 'Come here immediately and take your place at table'? ⁸Would he not rather say to him, 'Prepare something for me to eat.

Put on your apron and wait on me while I eat and drink. You may eat and drink when I am finished'? ⁹Is he grateful to that servant because he did what was commanded? ¹⁰So should it be with you. When you have done all you have been commanded, say, 'We are unprofitable servants; we have done what we were obliged to do.'"

The Cleansing of Ten Lepers. * ¹¹As he continued his journey to Jerusalem,ᵉ he traveled through Samaria and Galilee. * ¹²As he was entering a village, ten lepers met [him]. They stood at a distance from him ¹³and raised their voice, saying, "Jesus, Master! Have pity on us!"ᶠ ¹⁴And when he saw them, he said, "Go show yourselves to the priests.'" As they were going they were cleansed.ᵍ ¹⁵And one of them, realizing he had been healed, returned, glorifying God in a loud voice; ¹⁶and he fell at the feet of Jesus and thanked him. He was a <u>Samaritan</u>. [17]Jesus said in reply, "Ten were cleansed, were they not? Where are the other nine? [18]Has none but this <u>foreigner</u> returned to give thanks to God?" [19]Then he said to him, "Stand up and go; your faith has saved you."[h]

The Coming of the Kingdom of God. [20]*Asked by the Pharisees when the kingdom of God would come, he said in reply, "The coming of the kingdom of God cannot be observed,[i] [21]*and no one will announce, 'Look, here it is,' or, 'There it is.'[j] For behold, the kingdom of God is among you."

The Day of the Son of Man. [22]Then he said to his disciples, "The days will come when you will long to see one of the days of the Son of Man, but you will not see it. [23]There will be those who will say to you, 'Look, there he is,' [or] 'Look, here he is.' Do not go off, do not run in pursuit.[k] [24]For just as lightning flashes and lights up the sky from one side to the other, so will the Son of Man be [in his day].[l] [25]But first he must suffer greatly and be rejected by this generation.[m] [26]As it was in the days of Noah,[n] so it will be in the days of the Son of Man; [27]they were eating and drinking, marrying and giving in marriage up to the day that Noah entered the ark, and the flood came and destroyed them all. [28]Similarly, as it was in the days of Lot: they were eating, drinking, buying, selling, planting, building; [29]on the day when Lot left Sodom, fire and brimstone rained from the sky to destroy them all. [30]So it will be on <u>the day the Son of Man is revealed.</u> [31][p]On that day, a person who is on the housetop and whose belongings are in the house must not go down to get them, and likewise a person in the field must not return to what was

[handwritten: moments of light]

left behind.*q* ³²Remember the wife of Lot. ³³Whoever seeks to preserve his life will lose it, but whoever loses it will save it.*r* ³⁴I tell you, on that night there will be two people in one bed; one will be taken, the other left. ³⁵*s*And there will be two women grinding meal together; one will be taken, the other left." [³⁶]* ³⁷They said to him in reply, "Where, Lord?" He said to them, "Where the body is, there also the vultures will gather."*t*

---

a. [17:1–2] Mt 18:6–7.
b. [17:3] Mt 18:15.
c. [17:4] Mt 6:14; 18:21–22, 35; Mk 11:25.
d. [17:6] Mt 17:20; 21:21; Mk 11:23.
e. [17:11] 9:51–53; 13:22, 33; 18:31; 19:28; Jn 4:4.
f. [17:13] 18:38; Mt 9:27; 15:22.
g. [17:14] 5:14; Lv 14:2–32; Mt 8:4; Mk 1:44.
h. [17:19] 7:50; 18:42.
i. [17:20] Jn 3:3.
j. [17:21] 17:23; Mt 24:23; Mk 13:21.
k. [17:23] 17:21; Mt 24:23, 26; Mk 13:21.
l. [17:24] Mt 24:27.
m. [17:25] 9:22; 18:32–33; Mt 16:21; 17:22–23; 20:18–19; Mk 8:31; 9:31; 10:33–34.
n. [17:26–27] Gn 6–8; Mt 24:37–39.
o. [17:28–29] Gn 18:20–21; 19:1–29.
p. [17:31–32] Gn 19:17, 26.
q. [17:31] Mt 24:17–18; Mk 13:15–16.
r. [17:33] 9:24; Mt 10:39; 16:25; Mk 8:35; Jn 12:25.
s. [17:35] Mt 24:40–41.
t. [17:37] Jb 39:30; Mt 24:28.

CHAPTER 18

The Parable of the Persistent Widow. ¹*Then he told them a parable about the necessity for them to pray always without becoming weary.*a* He said, ²"There was a judge in a certain town who neither feared God nor respected any human being. ³And a widow in that town used to come to him and say, 'Render a just decision for me against my adversary.' ⁴For a long time the judge was unwilling, but eventually he thought, 'While it is true that I neither fear God nor respect any human being, ⁵*b*because this widow keeps bothering me I shall deliver a just decision for her lest she finally come and strike me.'" ⁶The Lord said, "Pay attention to what the dishonest judge says. ⁷Will not God then secure the rights of his chosen ones who call out to him day and night? Will he be slow to answer them? ⁸I tell you, he will see to it that justice is done for them speedily. But when the Son of Man comes, will he find faith on earth?"

The Parable of the Pharisee and the Tax Collector. [9]He then addressed this parable to those who were convinced of their own righteousness and despised everyone else.[c] [10]"Two people went up to the temple area to pray; one was a Pharisee and the other was a tax collector. [11]The Pharisee took up his position and spoke this prayer to himself, 'O God, I thank you that I am not like the rest of humanity—greedy, dishonest, adulterous—or even like this tax collector. [12]I fast twice a week, and I pay tithes on my whole income.'[d] [13]But the tax collector stood off at a distance and would not even raise his eyes to heaven but beat his breast and prayed, 'O God, be merciful to me a sinner.'[e] [14]I tell you, the latter went home justified, not the former; for everyone who exalts himself will be humbled, and the one who humbles himself will be exalted."[f]

Saying on Children and the Kingdom. [15]People were bringing even infants to him that he might touch them, and when the disciples saw this, they rebuked them.[g] [16]Jesus, however, called the children to himself and said, "Let the children come to me and do not prevent them; for the kingdom of God belongs to such as these. [17]Amen, I say to you, whoever does not accept the kingdom of God like a child will not enter it."[h]

The Rich Official. [18i]An official asked him this question, "Good teacher, what must I do to inherit eternal life?"[j] [19]Jesus answered him, "Why do you call me good? No one is good but God alone. [20]You know the commandments, 'You shall not commit adultery; you shall not kill; you shall not steal; you shall not bear false witness; honor your father and your mother.'"[k] [21]And he replied, "All of these I have observed from my youth." [22*l]When Jesus heard this he said to him, "There is still one thing left for you: <u>sell all</u> that you have and <u>distribute</u> it to the <u>poor</u>, and you will have a treasure in heaven. Then come, <u>follow me</u>." [23]But when he heard this he became quite sad, for he was <u>very rich</u>.

On Riches and Renunciation. ([24]Jesus looked at him) [now sad] and said, "How hard it is for those who have <u>wealth</u> to enter the kingdom of God! [25]For it is easier for a camel to pass through the eye of a needle than for a <u>rich</u> person to enter the kingdom of God." [26]Those who heard this said, "Then who can be saved?" [27]And he said, ("What is impossible for human beings is possible for God."[m]) [28]Then Peter said, "We have given up our possessions and followed you." [29n]He said to them, "Amen, I say to you, there is no one who has given up house or wife or brothers or parents or children for the sake of the kingdom of God [30]who will not receive [back] an overabundant return in this present age and eternal life in the age to come."

The Third Prediction of the Passion.[o] [31*]Then he took the Twelve aside and said to them, "Behold, we are going up to Jerusalem and everything written by the prophets about the Son of Man will be fulfilled.[*] [32p]He will be handed over to the Gentiles and he will be mocked and insulted and spat upon; [33]and after they have scourged him they will kill him, but on the third day he will rise." [34]But they understood nothing of this; the word remained hidden from them and they failed to comprehend what he said.[q]

The Healing of the Blind Beggar.[r] [35]Now as he approached Jericho a blind man was sitting by the roadside begging, [36]and hearing a crowd going by, he inquired what was happening. [37]They told him, "Jesus of Nazareth is passing by." [38s]He shouted, "Jesus, Son of David,* have pity on me!" [39]The people walking in front rebuked him, telling him to be silent, but he kept calling out all the more, "Son of David, have pity on me!" [40]Then Jesus stopped and ordered that he be brought to him; and when he came near, Jesus asked him, [41]"What do you want me to do for you?" He replied, "Lord, please let me see."[t] [42]Jesus told him, "Have sight; your faith has saved you."[u] [43]He immediately received his sight and followed him, giving glory to God. When they saw this, all the people gave praise to God.

a. [18:1] Rom 12:12; Col 4:2; 1 Thes 5:17.
b. [18:5] 11:8.
c. [18:9] 16:5; Mt 23:25–28.
d. [18:12] Mt 23:23.
e. [18:13] Ps 51:3.
f. [18:14] 14:11; Mt 23:12.
g. [18:15–17] Mt 19:13–15; Mk 10:13–16.
h. [18:17] Mt 18:3.
i. [18:18–30] Mt 19:16–30; Mk 10:17–31.
j. [18:18] 10:25.
k. [18:20] Ex 20:12–16; Dt 5:16–20.
l. [18:22] 12:33; Sir 29:11; Mt 6:20.

m. [18:27] Mk 14:36.
n. [18:29–30] 14:26.
o. [18:31–34] 24:25–27, 44; Mt 20:17–19; Mk 10:32–34; Acts 3:18.
p. [18:32–33] 9:22, 44.
q. [18:34] Mk 9:32.
r. [18:35–43] Mt 20:29–34; Mk 10:46–52.
s. [18:38–39] 17:13; Mt 9:27; 15:22.
t. [18:41] Mk 10:36.
u. [18:42] 7:50; 17:19.

CHAPTER 19

Zacchaeus the Tax Collector. [1]He came to Jericho and ⟨intended⟩ to pass through the town. [2]Now a man there named Zacchaeus, who was a chief tax collector and also a wealthy man, [3]was seeking to see who Jesus was; but he could not see him because of the crowd, for he was short in stature. [4]So he ran ahead and climbed a sycamore tree in order to see Jesus, who was about to pass that way. [5]When he reached the place, Jesus looked up and said to him, "Zacchaeus, come down quickly, for ⟨today I must stay at your house."⟩ [6]And he came down quickly and received him with ⟨joy.⟩ [7]When they all saw this, they began to ⟨grumble,⟩ saying,

"He has gone to stay at the house of a sinner."*a* *8*But Zacchaeus stood there and said to the Lord, "Behold, half of my possessions, Lord, I shall give to the poor, and if I have extorted anything from anyone I shall repay it four times over."*b* *9**And Jesus said to him, "Today <u>salvation</u>*c* has come to this house because this man too is a descendant of Abraham. (*10*d*For the Son of Man has come to seek and to save what was lost.")

The Parable of the Ten Gold Coins.* *11e*While they were listening to him speak, he proceeded to tell a parable because he was near Jerusalem and they thought that the kingdom of God would appear there immediately. *12*So he said, "A nobleman went off to a distant country to obtain the kingship for himself and then to return.*f* *13*He called <u>ten</u> of his servants and gave them ten gold coins* and told them, 'Engage in trade with these

until I return.' *14*His fellow citizens, however, despised him and sent a delegation after him to announce, 'We do not want this man to be our king.' *15*But when he returned after obtaining the kingship, he had the servants called, to whom he had given the money, to learn what they had gained by trading. *16*The first came forward and said, 'Sir, your gold coin has earned ten additional ones.' *17*He replied, 'Well done, good servant! You have been faithful in this very small matter; take charge of ten cities.'*g* *18*Then the second came and reported, 'Your gold coin, sir, has earned five more.' *19*And to this servant too he said, 'You, take charge of five cities.' *20*Then the other servant came and said, 'Sir, here is your gold coin; I kept it stored away in a handkerchief, *21*for I was <u>afraid</u> of you, because you are a <u>demanding</u> person; you take up what you did not lay down and you harvest what you did not plant.'

[22]He said to him, 'With your own words I shall condemn you, you wicked servant. You knew I was a demanding person, taking up what I did not lay down and harvesting what I did not plant; [23]why did you not put my money in a bank? Then on my return I would have collected it with interest.' [24]And to those standing by he said, 'Take the gold coin from him and give it to the servant who has ten.' [25]But they said to him, 'Sir, he has ten gold coins.' [26]I tell you, to everyone who has, more will be given, but from the one who has not, even what he has will be taken away.[h] [27]Now as for those enemies of mine who did not want me as their king, bring them here and slay them before me.'"

VI. THE TEACHING MINISTRY IN JERUSALEM[*]

The Entry into Jerusalem.[i]

[28]After he had said this, he proceeded on his journey up to Jerusalem. [29]As he drew near to Bethphage and Bethany at the place called the Mount of Olives, he sent two of his disciples.[j] [30]He said, "Go into the village opposite you, and as you enter it you will find a colt tethered on which no one has ever sat. Untie it and bring it here.[k] [31]And if anyone should ask you, 'Why are you untying it?' you will answer, 'The Master has need of it.'" [32]So those who had been sent went off and found everything just as he had told them.[l] [33]And as they were untying the colt, its owners said to them, "Why are you untying this colt?" [34]They answered, "The Master has need of it." [35m]So they brought it to Jesus, threw their cloaks over the colt, and helped Jesus to mount. [36]As he rode along, the people were spreading their cloaks on the road; [37]and now as he was approaching the slope of the Mount of Olives, the

whole multitude of his disciples began to praise God aloud with joy for all the mighty deeds they had seen. [38]They proclaimed:

> "Blessed is the king who comes
>   in the name of the Lord.[*]
> Peace in heaven
>   and glory in the highest."[n]

[39]Some of the Pharisees in the crowd said to him, "Teacher, rebuke your disciples."[*] [40]He said in reply, "I tell you, if they keep silent, the stones will cry out!"

The Lament for Jerusalem.[*] [41o]As he drew near, he saw the city and wept over it,[p] [42]saying, "If this day you only knew what makes for peace— but now it is hidden from your eyes.[q] [43*]For the days are coming upon you when your enemies will raise a palisade against you; they will encircle you and hem you in on all sides.[r] [44]They will smash you to the ground and your children within you, and they will not leave one stone upon another within you because you did not recognize the time of your visitation."[s]

The Cleansing of the Temple. [45t]Then Jesus entered the temple area[*] and proceeded to drive out those who were selling things,[u] [46]saying to them, "It is written, 'My house shall be a house of prayer, but you have made it a den of thieves.'"[v] [47]And every day he was teaching in the temple area.[w] The chief priests, the scribes, and the leaders of the people, meanwhile, were seeking to put him to death,[x] [48]but they could find no way to accomplish their purpose because all the people were hanging on his words.

a. [19:7] 5:30; 15:2.
b. [19:8] Ex 21:37; Nm 5:6–7; 2 Sm 12:6.
c. [19:9] 13:16; Mt 21:31.
d. [19:10] 15:4–10; Ez 34:16.
e. [19:11–27] Mt 25:14–30.
f. [19:12] Mk 13:34.
g. [19:17] 16:10.
h. [19:26] 8:18; Mt 13:12; Mk 4:25.

i. [19:28–40] Mt 21:1–11; Mk 11:1–11; Jn 12:12–19.
j. [19:29] Zec 14:4.
k. [19:30] Nm 19:2; Dt 21:3; 1 Sm 6:7; Zec 9:9.
l. [19:32] 22:13.
m. [19:35–36] 2 Kgs 9:13.
n. [19:38] 2:14; Ps 118:26.
o. [19:41–44] 13:34–35.
p. [19:41] 2 Kgs 8:11–12; Jer 14:17; 15:5.
q. [19:42] 8:10; Is 6:9–10; Mt 13:14; Mk 4:12; Acts 28:26–27; Rom 11:8, 10:
r. [19:43] Is 29:3.
s. [19:44] 1:68; 21:6; Ps 137:9; Mt 24:2; Mk 13:2.
t. [19:45–46] Mt 21:12–13; Mk 11:15–17; Jn 2:13–17.
u. [19:45] 3:1 / Hos 9:15.
v. [19:46] Is 56:7; Jer 7:11.
w. [19:47–48] 20:19; 22:2; Mt 21:46; Mk 11:18; 12:12; 14:1–2; Jn 5:18; 7:30.
x. [19:47] 21:37; 22:53; Jn 18:20.

CHAPTER 20[*]

The Authority of Jesus Questioned.[a] [1]One day as he was teaching the people in the temple area and proclaiming the good news, the chief priests and scribes, together with the elders, approached him [2]and said to him, "Tell us, by what authority are you doing these things? Or who is the one who gave you this authority?"[b] [3]He said to them in reply, "I shall ask you a question. Tell me, [4]was John's baptism of heavenly or of human origin?"[c] [5]They discussed this among themselves, and said, "If we say, 'Of heavenly origin,' he will say, 'Why did you not believe him?'[d] [6]But if we say, 'Of human origin,' then all the people will stone us, for they are convinced that John was a prophet." [7]So they answered that they did not know from where it came. [8]Then Jesus said to them, "Neither shall I tell you by what authority I do these things."

The Parable of the Tenant Farmers.[*] [9e]Then he proceeded to tell the people this parable. "[A] man planted a vineyard, leased it to tenant farmers, and then went on a journey for a long time.[f] [10]At harvest time he sent a servant[g] to the tenant farmers to receive some of the produce of the vineyard. But they beat the servant and sent him away empty-handed. [11]So he proceeded to send another servant, but him also they beat and insulted and sent away empty-handed. [12]Then he proceeded to send a third, but this one too they wounded and threw out. [13]The owner of the vineyard said, 'What shall I do? I shall send my beloved son; maybe they will respect him.'[h] [14]But when the tenant farmers saw him they said to one another, 'This is the heir. Let us kill him that the inheritance may become ours.' [15]So they threw him out of the vineyard and killed him.[*] What will the owner of the vineyard do to them? [16]He will come and put those tenant farmers to death and turn over the vineyard to others." When the people heard this, they exclaimed, "Let it not be so!" [17]But he looked at them and asked, "What then does this scripture passage mean:

'The stone which the
     builders rejected
has become the
     cornerstone'?[i]

[18]Everyone who falls on that stone will be dashed to pieces; and it will crush anyone on whom it falls." [19]The scribes and chief priests sought to lay their hands on him at that very hour, but they feared the people, for they knew that he had addressed this parable to them.[j]

Paying Taxes to the Emperor.[k] [20]They watched him closely and sent agents pretending to be righteous who were to trap him in speech,[l] in order to hand him over to the authority and power of the governor. [21]They posed this question to him, "Teacher, we know that what you say and teach is correct, and you show no partiality, but teach the way of God in accordance with the truth.[m] [22]Is it lawful for us to pay tribute to Caesar or not?"[*] [23]Recognizing their craftiness he said to them, [24]"Show me a denarius;[*] whose image and name does it bear?" They replied, "Caesar's." [25]So he said to them, "Then repay to Caesar what belongs to Caesar and to God what belongs to God."[n] [26]They were unable to trap him by something he might say before the people, and so amazed were they at his reply that they fell silent.

The Question About the Resurrection.[o] [27]Some Sadducees,[*] those who deny that there is a resurrection, came forward and put this question to him,[p] [28*]saying, "Teacher, Moses wrote for us, 'If someone's brother dies leaving a wife but no child, his brother must take the wife and raise up descendants for his brother.'[q] [29]Now there were seven brothers; the first married a woman but died childless. [30]Then the second [31]and the third married her, and likewise all the seven died childless. [32]Finally the woman also died. [33]Now at the resurrection whose wife will that woman be? For all seven had been married to her." [34]Jesus said to them, "The children of this age marry and are given in marriage; [35]but those who are deemed worthy to attain to the coming age and to the resurrection of the dead neither marry nor are given in marriage. [36]They can no longer die, for they are like angels; and they are the children of God because they are the ones who will rise.[*] [37]That the dead will rise even Moses made known in the passage about the bush, when he called 'Lord' the God of Abraham, the God of Isaac, and the God of Jacob;[r] [38]and he is not God of the dead, but of the living, for to him all are alive."[s] [39]Some of the scribes said in reply, "Teacher, you have answered well." [40]And they no longer dared to ask him anything.[t]

The Question About David's Son.[*] [41u]Then he said to them, "How do they claim that the Messiah is the Son of David? [42]For David himself in the Book of Psalms says:[v]

'The Lord said to my lord,
  "Sit at my right hand
     [43]till I make your enemies your footstool."'

⁴⁴Now if David calls him 'lord,' how can he be his son?"

Denunciation of the Scribes.ʷ ⁴⁵Then, within the hearing of all the people, he said to [his] disciples, ⁴⁶"Be on guard against the scribes, who like to go around in long robes and love greetings in market-places, seats of honor in synagogues, and places of honor at banquets.ˣ ⁴⁷They devour the houses of widows and, as a pretext, recite lengthy prayers. They will receive a very severe condemnation."

a. [20:1–8] Mt 21:23–27; Mk 11:27–33.
b. [20:2] Acts 4:7.
c. [20:4] 3:3, 16.
d. [20:5] Mt 21:32.
e. [20:9–19] Mt 21:33–46; Mk 12:1–12.
f. [20:9] Is 5:1–7.
g. [20:10–12] 2 Chr 36:15–16.
h. [20:13] 3:22.
i. [20:17] Ps 118:22; Is 28:16.
j. [20:19] [9:47–48; 22:2; Mt 21:46; Mk 11:18; 12:12; 14:1–2; Jn 5:18; 7:30.
k. [20:20–26] Mt 22:15–22; Mk 12:13–17.
l. [20:20] 11:54.
m. [20:21] Jn 3:2.
n. [20:25] Rom 13:6–7.
o. [20:27–40] Mt 22:23–33; Mk 12:18–27.
p. [20:27] Acts 23:8.
q. [20:28] Gn 38:8; Dt 25:5.
r. [20:37] Ex 3:2, 6, 15–16.
s. [20:38] Rom 14:8–9.
t. [20:40] Mt 22:46; Mk 12:34.
u. [20:41–44] Mt 22:41–45; Mk 12:35–37.
v. [20:42–43] Ps 110:1.
w. [20:45–47] 11:37–54; Mt 23:1–36; Mk 12:38–40.
x. [20:46] 14:7–11.

CHAPTER 21

The Poor Widow's Contribution.* ¹ᵃWhen he looked up he saw some wealthy people putting their offerings into the treasury ²and he noticed a poor widow putting in two small coins. ³He said, "I tell you truly, this poor widow put in more than all the rest; ⁴for those others have all made offerings from their surplus wealth, but she, from her poverty, has offered her whole livelihood."

The Destruction of the Temple Foretold.ᵇ ⁵While some people were speaking about how the temple was adorned with costly stones and votive offerings, he said, ⁶"All that you see here—the days will come when there will not be left a stone upon another stone that will not be thrown down."ᶜ

The Signs of the End. ⁷ᵈThen they asked him, "Teacher, when will this happen? And what sign will there be when all these things are about to happen?" [8]He answered, "See that you not be deceived, for many will come in my name, saying, 'I am he,' and 'The time has come.'* Do not follow them![e] [9]When you hear of wars and insurrections, do not be terrified; for such things must happen first, but it will not immediately be the end." [10]Then he said to them, "Nation will rise against nation, and kingdom against kingdom.[f] [11]There will be powerful earthquakes, famines, and plagues from place to place; and awesome sights and mighty signs will come from the sky.

The Coming Persecution.
[12g]"Before all this happens,* however, they will seize and persecute you, they will hand you over to the synagogues and to prisons, and they will have you led before kings and governors because of my name.[h] [13]It will lead to your giving testimony. [14]Remember, you are not to prepare your defense beforehand, [15]for I myself shall give you a wisdom in speaking* that all your adversaries will be powerless to resist or refute. [16j]You will even be handed over by parents, brothers, relatives, and friends, and they will put some of you to death.[k] [17]You will be hated by all because of my name, [18]but not a hair on your head will be destroyed.[l] [19]By your perseverance you will secure your lives.[m]

The Great Tribulation. *
[20m]"When you see Jerusalem surrounded by armies, know that its desolation is at hand.[o] [21]Then those in Judea must flee to the mountains. Let those within the city escape from it, and let those in the countryside not enter the city,[p] [22]for these days are the time of punishment when all the scriptures are fulfilled. [23]Woe to pregnant women and nursing mothers in those days, for a terrible

calamity will come upon the earth and a wrathful judgment upon this people.*q* *24*They will fall by the edge of the sword and be taken as captives to all the Gentiles; and Jerusalem will be trampled underfoot by the Gentiles until the times of the Gentiles* are fulfilled.*r*

The Coming of the Son of Man.*s* *25*"There will be signs in the sun, the moon, and the stars, and on earth nations will be in dismay, perplexed by the roaring of the sea and the waves.*t* *26*People will die of fright in anticipation of what is coming upon the world, for the powers of the heavens* will be shaken.*u* *27*And then they will see the Son of Man coming in a cloud with power and great glory.*v* *28*But when these signs begin to happen, stand erect and raise your heads because your redemption is at hand."*w*

The Lesson of the Fig Tree.*x* *29*He taught them a lesson. "Consider the fig tree and all the other trees. *30*When their buds burst open, you see for yourselves and know that summer is now near; *31*in the same way, when you see these things happening, know that the kingdom of God is near. *32*Amen, I say to you, this generation will not pass away until all these things have taken place.*y* *33*Heaven and earth will pass away, but my words will not pass away.*z*

Exhortation to Be Vigilant. *34*"Beware that your hearts do not become drowsy from carousing and drunkenness and the anxieties of daily life, and that day catch you by surprise*a* *35*like a trap. For that day will assault everyone who lives on the face of the earth. *36*Be vigilant at all times and pray that you have the strength to escape the tribulations that are imminent and to stand before the Son of Man."*b*

Ministry in Jerusalem. *37*During the day, Jesus was teaching in the temple area, but at night he would leave and stay at the place called the Mount of Olives.[c] [38]And all the people would get up early each morning to listen to him in the temple area.

a. [21:1–4] Mk 12:41–44.
b. [21:5–6] Mt 24:1–2; Mk 13:1–2.
c. [21:6] 19:44.
d. [21:7–19] Mt 24:3–14; Mk 13:3–13.
e. [21:8] 17:23; Mk 13:5, 6, 21; 1 Jn 2:18.
f. [21:10] 2 Chr 15:6; Is 19:2.
g. [21:12–15] 12:11–12; Mt 10:17–20; Mk 13:9–11.
h. [21:12] Jn 16:2; Acts 25:24.
i. [21:15] Acts 6:10.
j. [21:16–18] Mt 10:21–22.
k. [21:16] 12:52–53.
l. [21:18] 12:7; 1 Sm 14:45; Mt 10:30; Acts 27:34.
m. [21:19] 8:15.
n. [21:20–24] Mt 24:15–21; Mk 13:14–19.
o. [21:20–22] 19:41–44.
p. [21:21] 17:31.
q. [21:23] 1 Cor 7:26.
r. [21:24] Tb 14:5; Ps 79:1; Is 63:18; Jer 21:7; Rom 11:25; Rev 11:2.
s. [21:25–28] Mt 24:29–31; Mk 13:24–27.
t. [21:25] Wis 5:22; Is 13:10; Ez 32:7; Jl 2:10; 3:3–4; 4:15; Rev 6:12–14.
u. [21:26] Hg 2:6, 21.
v. [21:27] Dn 7:13–14; Mt 26:64; Rev 1:7.
w. [21:28] 2:38.
x. [21:29–33] Mt 24:32–35; Mk 13:28–31.
y. [21:32] 9:27; Mt 16:28.
z. [21:33] 16:17.
a. [21:34] 12:45–46; Mt 24:48–50; 1 Thes 5:3, 6–7.
b. [21:36] Mk 13:33.
c. [21:37] 19:47; 22:39.

VII. THE PASSION NARRATIVE*

CHAPTER 22

The Conspiracy Against Jesus. [1a]Now the feast of Unleavened Bread, called the Passover,* was drawing near, [2b]and the chief priests and the scribes were seeking a way to put him to death, for they were afraid of the people. [3c]Then Satan entered into Judas,* the one surnamed Iscariot, who was counted among the Twelve,[d] [4]and he went to the chief priests and temple guards to discuss a plan for handing him over to them. [5]They were pleased and agreed to pay him money. [6]He accepted their offer and sought a favorable opportunity to hand him over to them in the absence of a crowd.

Preparations for the Passover.[e] [7]When the day of the feast of Unleavened Bread arrived, the day for sacrificing the Passover lamb,[f] [8]he sent out Peter and John, instructing them, "Go and make preparations for us to eat the Passover." [9]They asked him, "Where do you want us to make the preparations?"

[10]And he answered them, "When you go into the city, a man will meet you carrying a jar of water.* Follow him into the house that he enters [11]and say to the master of the house, 'The teacher says to you, "Where is the guest room where I may eat the Passover with my disciples?"' [12]He will show you a large upper room that is furnished. Make the preparations there." [13]Then they went off and found everything exactly as he had told them, and there they prepared the Passover.[g]

The Last Supper.[h] [14]When the hour came, he took his place at table with the apostles. [15]He said to them, "I have eagerly desired to eat this Passover* with you before I suffer, [16]for, I tell you, I shall not eat it [again] until there is fulfillment in the kingdom of God."[i] [17]Then he took a cup,* gave thanks, and said, "Take this and share it among yourselves; [18]for I tell you [that] from this time on I shall not drink of the fruit of the vine until the kingdom of God comes." [19]*[j]Then he took the bread, said the blessing, broke it, and gave it to them, saying, "This is my body, which will be given for you; do this in memory of me." [20]And likewise the cup after they had eaten, saying, "This cup is the new covenant in my blood, which will be shed for you.[k]

The Betrayal Foretold. [21]l"And yet behold, the hand of the one who is to betray me is with me on the table; [22]for the Son of Man indeed goes as it has been determined; but woe to that man by whom he is betrayed." [23]And they began to debate among themselves who among them would do such a deed.

The Role of the Disciples. [24]*Then an argument broke out among them[m] about which of them should be regarded as the greatest. [25]*[n]He said to them, "The kings of the Gentiles lord it over them and those in authority over them are addressed as 'Benefactors'; [26]but among you it shall not be so. Rather, let the greatest among you be as the youngest, and the leader as the servant.[o] [27]For who is greater: the one seated at table or the one who serves? Is it not the one seated at table? I am among you as the one who serves. [28]It is you who have stood by me in my trials; [29]and I confer a kingdom on you, just as my Father has conferred one on me,[p] [30]that you may eat and drink at my table in my kingdom; and you will sit on thrones judging the twelve tribes of Israel.[q]

Peter's Denial Foretold.[r] [31]"Simon, Simon, behold Satan has demanded to sift all of you[*] like wheat,[s] [32]but I have prayed that your own faith may not fail; and once you have turned back, you must strengthen your brothers." [33]He said to him, "Lord, I am prepared to go to prison and to die with you."[t] [34]But he replied, "I tell you, Peter, before the cock crows this day, you will deny three times that you know me."[u]

Instructions for the Time of Crisis. [35v]He said to them, "When I sent you forth without a money bag or a sack or sandals, were you in need of anything?" "No, nothing," they replied. [36w]He said to them,[*] "But now one who has a money bag should take it, and likewise a sack, and one who does not have a sword should sell his cloak and buy one. [37]For I tell you that this scripture must be fulfilled in me, namely, 'He was counted among the wicked'; and indeed what is written about me is coming to fulfillment."[x] [38]Then they said, "Lord, look, there are two swords here." But he replied, "It is enough!'"

The Agony in the Garden.[y] [39]Then going out he went, as was his custom, to the Mount of Olives, and the disciples followed him. [40]When he arrived at the place he said to them, "Pray that you may not undergo the test."[z] [41]After withdrawing about a stone's throw from them and kneeling, he prayed,[a] [42]saying, "Father, if you are willing, take this cup away from me; still, not my will but yours be done."[b] [[43]And to strengthen him an angel from heaven appeared to him. [44]He was in such agony and he prayed so fervently that his sweat became like drops of blood falling on the ground.] [45]When he rose from prayer and returned to his disciples, he found them sleeping from grief. [46]He said to them, "Why are you sleeping? Get up and pray that you may not undergo the test."[c]

The Betrayal and Arrest of Jesus.[d] [47]While he was still speaking, a crowd approached and in front was one of the Twelve, a man named Judas. He went up to Jesus to kiss him. [48]Jesus said to him, "Judas, are you betraying the Son of Man with a kiss?" [49]His disciples realized what was about to happen, and they asked, "Lord, shall we strike with a sword?"[e] [50]And one of them struck the high priest's servant and cut off his right ear.[f] [51]But Jesus said in reply, "Stop, no more of this!" Then he touched the servant's ear and healed him. [52]And Jesus said to the chief priests and temple guards and elders who had come for him, "Have you come out as against a robber, with swords and clubs?[g] [53]Day after day I was with you in the temple area, and you did not seize me; but this is your hour, the time for the power of darkness."[h]

Peter's Denial of Jesus. [54i]After arresting him they led him away and took him into the house of the high priest; Peter was following at a distance.[j] [55]They lit a fire in the middle of the courtyard and sat around it, and Peter sat down with them. [56]When a maid saw him seated in the light, she looked intently at him and said, "This man too was with him." [57]But he denied it saying, "Woman, I do not know him." [58]A short while later someone else saw him and said, "You too are one of them"; but Peter answered, "My friend, I am not." [59]About an hour later, still another insisted, "Assuredly, this man too was with him, for he also is a Galilean." [60]But Peter said, "My friend, I do not know what you are talking about." Just as he was saying this, the cock crowed, [61]and the Lord turned and looked at Peter; and Peter remembered the word of the Lord, how he had said to him, "Before the cock crows today, you will deny me three times."[k] [62]He went out and began to weep bitterly. [63][l]The men who held Jesus in custody were ridiculing and beating him. [64]They blindfolded him and questioned him, saying, "Prophesy! Who is it that struck you?" [65]And they reviled him in saying many other things against him.

Jesus Before the Sanhedrin.[*] [66][m]When day came the council of elders of the people met, both chief priests and scribes,[n] and they brought him before their Sanhedrin.[*] [67]They said, "If you are the Messiah, tell us," but he replied to them, "If I tell you, you will not believe,[o] [68]and if I question, you will not respond. [69]But from this time on the Son of Man will be seated at the right hand of the power of God."[p] [70]They all asked, "Are you then the Son of God?" He replied to them, "You say that I am." [71]Then they said, "What further need have we for testimony? We have heard it from his own mouth."

a. [22:1–2] Mt 26:1–5; Mk 14:1–2; Jn 11:47–53.
b. [22:2] 19:47–48; 20:19; Mt 21:46; Mk 12:12; Jn 5:18; 7:30.
c. [22:3–6] Mt 26:14–16; Mk 14:10–11; Jn 13:2, 27.
d. [22:3] Acts 1:17.
e. [22:7–13] Mt 26:17–19; Mk 14:12–16.
f. [22:7] Ex 12:6, 14–20.
g. [22:13] 19:32.
h. [22:14–20] Mt 26:20, 26–30; Mk 14:17, 22–26; 1 Cor 11:23–25.
i. [22:16] 13:29.
j. [22:19] 24:30; Acts 27:35.
k. [22:20] Ex 24:8; Jer 31:31; 32:40; Zec 9:11.
l. [22:21–23] Ps 41:10; Mt 26:21–25; Mk 14:18–21; Jn 13:21–30.
m. [22:24] 9:46; Mt 18:1; Mk 9:34.
n. [22:25–27] Mt 20:25–27; Mk 10:42–44; Jn 13:3–16.
o. [22:26] Mt 23:11; Mk 9:35.
p. [22:29] 12:32.
q. [22:30] Mt 19:28.
r. [22:31–34] Mt 26:33–35; Mk 14:29–31; Jn 13:37–38.
s. [22:31] Jb 1:6–12; Am 9:9.
t. [22:33] 22:54.
u. [22:34] 22:54–62.
v. [22:35] 9:3; 10:4; Mt 10:9–10; Mk 6:7–9.
w. [22:36] 22:49.
x. [22:37] Is 53:12.
y. [22:39–46] Mt 26:30, 36–46; Mk 14:26, 32–42; Jn 18:1–2.
z. [22:40] 22:46.
a. [22:41] Heb 5:7–8.
b. [22:42] Mt 6:10.
c. [22:46] 22:40.
d. [22:47–53] Mt 26:47–56; Mk 14:43–50; Jn 18:3–4.
e. [22:49] 22:36.
f. [22:50] Jn 18:26.
g. [22:52] 22:37.
h. [22:53] 19:47; 21:37; Jn 7:30; 8:20; Col 1:13.
i. [22:54–62] Mt 26:57–58, 69–75; Mk 14:53–54, 66–72; Jn 18:12–18, 25–27.
j. [22:54] 22:33.
k. [22:61] 22:34.
l. [22:63–65] Mt 26:67–68; Mk 14:65.
m. [22:66–71] Mt 26:59–66; Mk 14:55–64.
n. [22:66] Mt 27:1; Mk 15:1.
o. [22:67] Jn 3:12; 8:45; 10:24.
p. [22:69] Ps 110:1; Dn 7:13–14; Acts 7:56.

CHAPTER 23

Jesus Before Pilate.[a] [1]Then the whole assembly of them arose and brought him before Pilate. [2]They brought charges against him, saying, "We found this man misleading our people; he opposes the payment of taxes to Caesar and maintains that he is the Messiah, a king."[b] [3]Pilate asked him, "Are you the king of the Jews?" He said to him in reply, "You say so."[c] [4]Pilate then addressed the chief priests and the crowds, "I find this man not guilty." [5]But they were adamant and said, "He is inciting the people with his teaching throughout all Judea, from Galilee where he began even to here."[d]

Jesus Before Herod. [6]On hearing this Pilate asked if the man was a Galilean; [7]and upon learning that he was under Herod's jurisdiction, he sent him to Herod who was in Jerusalem at that time.[e] [8]Herod was very glad to see Jesus; he had been wanting to see him for a long time, for he had heard about him and had been hoping to see him perform some sign.*f* ⁹He questioned him at length, but he gave him no answer.*g* ¹⁰The chief priests and scribes, meanwhile, stood by accusing him harshly.*h* ¹¹[Even] Herod and his soldiers treated him contemptuously and mocked him, and after clothing him in resplendent garb, he sent him back to Pilate.*i* (¹²Herod and Pilate became friends that very day, even though they had been enemies formerly.) ¹³Pilate then summoned the chief priests, the rulers, and the people ¹⁴and said to them, "You brought this man to me and accused him of inciting the people to revolt. I have conducted my investigation in your presence and have not found this man guilty of the charges you have brought against him,*j* ¹⁵nor did Herod, for he sent him back to us. So no capital crime has been committed by him. ¹⁶*k*Therefore I shall have him flogged and then release him." [¹⁷]*

The Sentence of Death.·*l* ¹⁸But all together they shouted out, "Away with this man! Release Barabbas to us." ¹⁹(Now Barabbas had been imprisoned for a rebellion that had taken place in the city and for murder.) ²⁰Again Pilate addressed them, still wishing to release Jesus, ²¹but they continued their shouting, "Crucify him! Crucify him!" ²²Pilate addressed them a third time, "What evil has this man done? I found him guilty of no capital crime. Therefore I shall have him flogged and then release him." ²³With loud shouts, however, they persisted in calling for his crucifixion, and their voices prevailed. ²⁴The verdict of Pilate was that their demand should be granted. ²⁵So he released the man who had been imprisoned for rebellion and murder, for whom they asked, and he handed Jesus over to them to deal with as they wished.

The Way of the Cross.[*] [26][m]As they led him away they took hold of a certain Simon, a Cyrenian, who was coming in from the country; and after laying the cross on him, they made him carry it behind Jesus. [27]A large crowd of people followed Jesus, including many women who mourned and lamented him. [28][n]Jesus turned to them and said, "Daughters of Jerusalem, do not weep for me; weep instead for yourselves and for your children, [29]for indeed, the days are coming when people will say, 'Blessed are the barren, the wombs that never bore and the breasts that never nursed.' [30]At that time people will say to the mountains, 'Fall upon us!' and to the hills, 'Cover us!'[o] [31]for if these things are done when the wood is green what will happen when it is dry?" [32]Now two others, both criminals, were led away with him to be executed.

The Crucifixion.[p] [33]When they came to the place called the Skull, they crucified him and the criminals there, one on his right, the other on his left.[q] [34][Then Jesus said, "Father, forgive them, they know not what they do."][*] They divided his garments by casting lots.[r] [35]The people stood by and watched; the rulers, meanwhile, sneered at him and said,[s] "He saved others, let him save himself if he is the chosen one, the Messiah of God."[t] [36]Even the soldiers jeered at him. As they approached to offer him wine[u] [37]they called out, "If you are King of the Jews, save yourself." [38]Above him there was an inscription that read, "This is the King of the Jews."

[39][*]Now one of the criminals hanging there reviled Jesus, saying, "Are you not the Messiah? Save yourself and us." [40]The other, however, rebuking him, said in reply, "Have you no fear of God, for you are subject to the same

condemnation? [41]And indeed, we have been condemned justly, for the sentence we received corresponds to our crimes, but this man has done nothing criminal."[v] [42]Then he said, "Jesus, remember me when you come into your kingdom."[w] [43]He replied to him, "Amen, I say to you, today you will be with me in Paradise."[x]

The Death of Jesus.[y] [44]*It was now about noon[z] and darkness came over the whole land until three in the afternoon [45]because of an eclipse of the sun. Then the veil of the temple was torn down the middle.[a] [46]Jesus cried out in a loud voice, "Father, into your hands I commend my spirit"; and when he had said this he breathed his last.[b] [47]The centurion who witnessed what had happened glorified God and said, "This man was innocent* beyond doubt." [48]When all the people who had gathered for this spectacle saw what had happened, they returned home beating their breasts;[c] [49]but all his acquaintances stood at a distance, including the women who had followed him from Galilee and saw these events.[d]

The Burial of Jesus.[e] [50]Now there was a virtuous and righteous man named Joseph who, though he was a member of the council, [51]had not consented to their plan of action. He came from the Jewish town of Arimathea and was awaiting the kingdom of God. [52]He went to Pilate and asked for the body of Jesus. [53]After he had taken the body down, he wrapped it in a linen cloth and laid him in a rock-hewn tomb in which no one had yet been buried.[g] [54]It was the day of preparation, and the sabbath was about to begin. [55]The women who had come from Galilee with him followed behind, and when they had seen the tomb and the way in which his body was laid in it,*h* ⁵⁶they returned and prepared spices and perfumed oils. Then they rested on the sabbath according to the commandment.*i*

a. [23:1–5] Mt 27:1–2, 11–14; Mk 15:1–5; Jn 18:28–38.

b. [23:2] 20:22–25; Acts 17:7; 24:5.

c. [23:3] 22:70; 1 Tm 6:13.

d. [23:5] 23:14, 22, 41; Mt 27:24; Jn 19:4, 6; Acts 13:28.

e. [23:7] 3:1; 9:7.

f. [23:8] 9:9; Acts 4:27–28.

g. [23:9] Mk 15:5.

h. [23:10] Mt 27:12; Mk 15:3.

i. [23:11] Mt 27:28–30; Mk 15:17–19; Jn 19:2–3.

j. [23:14] 23:4, 22, 41.

k. [23:16] 23:22; Jn 19:12–14.

l. [23:18–25] Mt 27:20–26; Mk 15:6–7, 11–15; Jn 18:38b–40; 19:14–16; Acts 3:13–14.

m. [23:26–32] Mt 27:32, 38; Mk 15:21, 27; Jn 19:17.

n. [23:28–31] 19:41–44; 21:23–24.

o. [23:30] Hos 10:8; Rev 6:16.

p. [23:33–43] Mt 27:33–44; Mk 15:22–32; Jn 19:17–24.

q. [23:33] 22:37; Is 53:12.

r. [23:34] Nm 15:27–31; Ps 22:19; Mt 5:44; Acts 7:60.

s. [23:35–36] Ps 22:8–9.

t. [23:35] 4:23.

u. [23:36] Ps 69:22; Mt 27:48; Mk 15:36.

v. [23:41] 23:4, 14, 22.

w. [23:42] 9:27; 23:2, 3, 38.

x. [23:43] 2 Cor 12:3; Rev 2:7.

y. [23:44–49] Mt 27:45–56; Mk 15:33–41; Jn 19:25–30.

z. [23:44–45] Am 8:9.

a. [23:45] Ex 26:31–33; 36:35.

b. [23:46] Ps 31:6; Acts 7:59.

c. [23:48] 18:13; Zec 12:10.

d. [23:49] 8:1–3; 23:55–56; 24:10; Ps 38:12.

e. [23:51] 2:25, 38.

f. [23:51] 2:25, 38.

g. [23:53] 19:30; Acts 13:29.

h. [23:55] 8:2; 23:49; 24:10.

i. [23:56] Ex 12:16; 20:10; Dt 5:14.

VIII. THE RESURRECTION NARRATIVE*

CHAPTER 24

The Resurrection of Jesus. ¹*a*But at daybreak on the first day of the week they took the spices they had prepared and went to the tomb. ²They found the stone rolled away from the tomb; ³but when they entered, they did not find the body of the Lord Jesus. ⁴While they were puzzling over this, behold, two men in dazzling garments appeared to them.*b* ⁵They were terrified and bowed their faces to the ground. They said to them, "Why do you seek the living one among the dead?*c* ⁶He is not here, but he has been raised.* Remember what he said to you while he was still in Galilee, ⁷that the Son of Man must be handed over to sinners and be crucified, and rise on the third day."*d* ⁸And they remembered his words.*e*

⁹*ᶠThen they returned from the tomb and announced all these things to the eleven and to all the others. ¹⁰The women were (Mary Magdalene, Joanna, and Mary the mother of James;) the others who accompanied them also told this to the apostles,ᵍ ¹¹but their story seemed like nonsense and they did not believe them. ¹²*ʰBut Peter got up and ran to the tomb, bent down, and saw the burial cloths alone; then he went home amazed at what had happened.

The Appearance on the Road to Emmaus.˙ ¹³Now that very day two of them were going to a village seven miles˙ from Jerusalem called Emmaus,ⁱ ¹⁴and they were conversing about all the things that had occurred. ¹⁵And it happened that while they were conversing and debating, Jesus himself drew near and walked with them, ¹⁶*ʲbut their eyes were prevented from recognizing him. ¹⁷He asked them, "What are you discussing as you walk along?" They stopped, looking downcast. ¹⁸One of them, named Cleopas, said to him in reply, "Are you the only visitor to Jerusalem who does not know of the things that have taken place there in these days?" ¹⁹And he replied to them, "What sort of things?" They said to him, "The things that happened to Jesus the Nazarene, who was a prophet mighty in deed and word before God and all the people,ᵏ ²⁰how our chief priests and rulers both handed him over to a sentence of death and crucified him. ²¹ˡBut we were hoping that he would be the one to redeem Israel; and besides all this, it is now the third day since this took place. ²²ᵐSome women from our group, however, have astounded us: they were at the tomb early in the morning ²³and did not find his body; they came back and reported that they had indeed seen a vision of angels who announced that he was alive. [24n]Then some of those with us went to the tomb and found things just as the women had described, but him they did not see." [25o]And he said to them, ("Oh, how foolish you are! How slow of heart to believe all that the prophets spoke! [26]Was it not necessary that the Messiah should suffer* these things and enter into his glory?" [27]Then beginning with Moses and all the prophets, he interpreted to them what referred to him in all the scriptures.[p]) [28]As they approached the village to which they were going, he gave the impression that he was going on farther. [29]But they urged him, "Stay with us, for it is nearly evening and the day is almost over." So he went in to stay with them. [30]And it happened that, while he was with them at table, he took bread, said the blessing, broke it, and gave it to them.

[31]With that their eyes were opened and they recognized him, but he vanished from their sight. [32]Then they said to each other, "Were not our hearts burning [within us] while he spoke to us on the way and opened the scriptures to us?" [33]So they set out at once and returned to Jerusalem where they found gathered together the eleven and those with them [34]who were saying, "The Lord has truly been raised and has appeared to Simon!"[q] [35]Then the two recounted what had taken place on the way and how (he was made known to them in the breaking of the bread.)

The Appearance to the Disciples in Jerusalem. [36*]While they were still speaking about this,[r] he stood in their midst and said to them, "Peace be with you."[s] [37]But they were startled and terrified and thought that they were seeing a ghost.[t] [38]Then he said to them, "Why are you troubled? And why do questions arise in your hearts? ³⁹*Look at my hands and my feet, that it is I myself. Touch me and see, because a ghost does not have flesh and bones as you can see I have." ⁴⁰ᵘAnd as he said this, he showed them his hands and his feet. ⁴¹While they were still incredulous for joy and were amazed, he asked them, "Have you anything here to eat?" ⁴²They gave him a piece of baked fish;ᵛ ⁴³he took it and ate it in front of them.

⁴⁴He said to them, "These are my words that I spoke to you while I was still with you, that everything written about me in the law of Moses and in the prophets and psalms must be fulfilled."ʷ ⁴⁵Then he opened their minds to understand the scriptures.ˣ ⁴⁶*And he said to them,ʸ "Thus it is written that the Messiah would suffer and rise from the dead on the third day ⁴⁷and that repentance, for the forgiveness of sins, would be preached in his name to all the nations, beginning from Jerusalem.ᶻ ⁴⁸You are witnesses of these things.ᵃ ⁴⁹And [behold] I am sending the promise of my Father* upon you; but stay in the city until you are clothed with power from on high."ᵇ

The Ascension.* ⁵⁰ᶜThen he led them [out] as far as Bethany, raised his hands, and blessed them. ⁵¹As he blessed them he parted from them and was taken up to heaven. ⁵²They did him homage and then returned to Jerusalem with great joy,ᵈ ⁵³and they were continually in the temple praising God.*

---

a. [24:1–8] Mt 28:1–8; Mk 16:1–8; Jn 20:1–17.
b. [24:4] 2 Mc 3:26; Acts 1:10.
c. [24:5] Acts 2:9.
d. [24:7] 9:22, 44; 17:25; 18:32–33; Mt 16:21; 17:22–23; Mk 9:31; Acts 17:3.
e. [24:8] Jn 2:22.
f. [24:9–11] Mk 16:10–11; Jn 20:18.
g. [24:10] 8:2–3; Mk 16:9.
h. [24:12] Jn 20:3–7.
i. [24:13] Mk 16:12–13.
j. [24:16] Jn 20:14; 21:4.
k. [24:19] Mt 2:23; 21:11; Acts 2:22.
l. [24:21] 1:54, 68; 2:38.
m. [24:22–23] 24:1–11; Mt 28:1–8; Mk 16:1–8.
n. [24:24] Jn 20:3–10.
o. [24:25–26] 9:22; 18:31; 24:44; Acts 3:24; 17:3.

p. [24:27] 24:44; Dt 18:15; Ps 22:1–18; Is 53; 1 Pt 1:10–11.
q. [24:34] 1 Cor 15:4–5.
r. [24:36–53] Mk 16:14–19; Jn 20:19–20.
s. [24:36] 1 Cor 15:5.
t. [24:37] Mt 14:26.
u. [24:40–41] Jn 21:5, 9–10, 13.
v. [24:42] Acts 10:41.
w. [24:44] 18:31; 24:27; Mt 16:21; Jn 5:39, 46.
x. [24:45] Jn 20:9.
y. [24:46] 9:22; Is 53; Hos 6:2.
z. [24:47] Mt 3:2; 28:19–20; Mk 16:15–16; Acts 10:41.
a. [24:48] Acts 1:8.
b. [24:49] Jn 14:26; Acts 1:4; 2:3–4.
c. [24:50–51] Mk 16:19; Acts 1:9–11.
d. [24:52] Acts 1:12.

Notes

* [1:1–4] The Gospel according to Luke is the only one of the synoptic gospels to begin with a literary prologue. Making use of a formal, literary construction and vocabulary, the author writes the prologue in imitation of Hellenistic Greek writers and, in so doing, relates his story about Jesus to contemporaneous Greek and Roman literature. Luke is not only interested in the words and deeds of Jesus, but also in the larger context of the birth, ministry, death, and resurrection of Jesus as the fulfillment of the promises of God in the Old Testament. As a second- or third-generation Christian, Luke acknowledges his debt to earlier **eyewitnesses and ministers of the word**, but claims that his contribution to this developing tradition is a complete and accurate account, told in an orderly manner, and intended to provide **Theophilus** ("friend of God," literally) and other readers with certainty about earlier teachings they have received.

* [1:5–2:52] Like the Gospel according to Matthew, this gospel opens with an infancy narrative, a collection of stories about the birth and childhood of Jesus. The narrative uses early Christian traditions about the birth of Jesus, traditions about the birth and circumcision of John the Baptist, and canticles such as the Magnificat (Lk 1:46–55) and Benedictus (Lk 1:67–79), composed of phrases drawn from the Greek Old Testament. It is largely, however, the composition of Luke who writes in imitation of Old Testament birth stories, combining historical and legendary details, literary ornamentation and interpretation of scripture, to answer in advance the question, "Who is Jesus Christ?" The focus of the narrative, therefore, is primarily christological. In this section Luke announces many of the themes that will become prominent in the rest of the gospel: the centrality of Jerusalem and the temple, the journey motif, the universality of salvation, joy and peace, concern for the lowly, the importance of women, the presentation of Jesus as savior, Spirit-guided revelation and prophecy, and the fulfillment of Old Testament promises. The account presents parallel scenes (diptychs) of angelic announcements of the birth of John the Baptist and of Jesus, and of the birth, circumcision, and presentation of John and Jesus. In this parallelism, the ascendency of Jesus over John is stressed: John is prophet of the Most High (Lk 1:76); Jesus is Son of the Most High (Lk 1:32). John is great in the sight of the Lord (Lk 1:15); Jesus will be Great (a LXX attribute, used absolutely, of God) (Lk 1:32). John will go before the Lord (Lk 1:16–17); Jesus will be Lord (Lk 1:43; 2:11).

* [1:5] **In the days of Herod, King of Judea:** Luke relates the story of salvation history to events in contemporary world history. Here and in Lk 3:1–2 he connects his narrative with events in Palestinian history; in Lk 2:1–2 and Lk 3:1 he casts the Jesus story in the light of events of Roman history. Herod the Great, the son of the Idumean Antipater, was declared "King of Judea" by the Roman Senate in 40 B.C., but became the undisputed ruler of Palestine only in 37 B.C. He continued as king until his death in 4 B.C. **Priestly division of Abijah:** a reference to the eighth of the twenty-four divisions of priests who, for a week at a time, twice a year, served in the Jerusalem temple.

* [1:7] **They had no child:** though childlessness was looked upon in contemporaneous Judaism as a curse or punishment for sin, it is intended here to present Elizabeth in a situation similar to that of some of the great mothers of important Old Testament figures: Sarah (Gn 15:3; 16:1); Rebekah (Gn 25:21); Rachel (Gn 29:31; 30:1); the mother of Samson and wife of Manoah (Jgs 13:2–3); Hannah (1 Sm 1:2).

* [1:13] **Do not be afraid:** a stereotyped Old Testament phrase spoken to reassure the recipient of a heavenly vision (Gn 15:1; Jos 1:9; Dn 10:12, 19 and elsewhere in Lk 1:30; 2:10). **You shall name him John:** the name means "Yahweh has shown favor," an indication of John's role in salvation history.

* [1:15] **He will drink neither wine nor strong drink:** like Samson (Jgs 13:4–5) and Samuel (1 Sm 1:11 LXX and 4QSamª), John is to be consecrated by Nazirite vow and set apart for the Lord's service.

* [1:17] **He will go before him in the spirit and power of Elijah:** John is to be the messenger sent before Yahweh, as described in Mal 3:1–2. He is cast, moreover, in the role of the Old Testament fiery reformer, the prophet Elijah, who according to Mal 3:23 (Mal 4:5) is sent before "the great and terrible day of the Lord comes."

* [1:19] **I am Gabriel**: "the angel of the Lord" is identified as Gabriel, the angel who in Dn 9:20–25 announces the seventy weeks of years and the coming of an anointed one, a prince. By alluding to Old Testament themes in Lk 1:17, 19 such as the coming of the day of the Lord and the dawning of the messianic era, Luke is presenting his interpretation of the significance of the births of John and Jesus.

* [1:20] **You will be speechless and unable to talk**: Zechariah's becoming mute is the sign given in response to his question in v 18. When Mary asks a similar question in Lk 1:34, unlike Zechariah who was punished for his doubt, she, in spite of her doubt, is praised and reassured (Lk 1:35–37).

* [1:26–38] The announcement to Mary of the birth of Jesus is parallel to the announcement to Zechariah of the birth of John. In both the angel Gabriel appears to the parent who is troubled by the vision (Lk 1:11–12, 26–29) and then told by the angel not to fear (Lk 1:13, 30). After the announcement is made (Lk 1:14–17, 31–33) the parent objects (Lk 1:18, 34) and a sign is given to confirm the announcement (Lk 1:20, 36). The particular focus of the announcement of the birth of Jesus is on his identity as Son of David (Lk 1:32–33) and Son of God (Lk 1:32, 35).

* [1:32] **Son of the Most High**: cf. Lk 1:76 where John is described as "prophet of the Most High." "Most High" is a title for God commonly used by Luke (Lk 1:35, 76; 6:35; 8:28; Acts 7:48; 16:17).

* [1:34] Mary's questioning response is a denial of sexual relations and is used by Luke to lead to the angel's declaration about the Spirit's role in the conception of this child (Lk 1:35). According to Luke, the virginal conception of Jesus takes place through the holy Spirit, the power of God, and therefore Jesus has a unique relationship to Yahweh: he is Son of God.

* [1:36–37] The sign given to Mary in confirmation of the angel's announcement to her is the pregnancy of her aged relative Elizabeth. If a woman past the childbearing age could become pregnant, why, the angel implies, should there be doubt about Mary's pregnancy, for **nothing will be impossible for God**.

* [1:43] Even before his birth, Jesus is identified in Luke as the Lord.

* [1:45] **Blessed are you who believed**: Luke portrays Mary as a believer whose faith stands in contrast to the disbelief of Zechariah (Lk 1:20). Mary's role as believer in the infancy narrative should be seen in connection with the explicit mention of her presence among "those who believed" after the resurrection at the beginning of the Acts of the Apostles (Acts 1:14).

* [1:46–55] Although Mary is praised for being the mother of the Lord and because of her belief, she reacts as the servant in a psalm of praise, the Magnificat. Because there is no specific connection

of the canticle to the context of Mary's pregnancy and her visit to Elizabeth, the Magnificat (with the possible exception of v 48) may have been a Jewish Christian hymn that Luke found appropriate at this point in his story. Even if not composed by Luke, it fits in well with themes found elsewhere in Luke: joy and exultation in the Lord; the lowly being singled out for God's favor; the reversal of human fortunes; the fulfillment of Old Testament promises. The loose connection between the hymn and the context is further seen in the fact that a few Old Latin manuscripts identify the speaker of the hymn as Elizabeth, even though the overwhelming textual evidence makes Mary the speaker.

* [1:57–66] The birth and circumcision of John above all emphasize John's incorporation into the people of Israel by the sign of the covenant (Gn 17:1–12). The narrative of John's circumcision also prepares the way for the subsequent description of the circumcision of Jesus in Lk 2:21. At the beginning of his two-volume work Luke shows those who play crucial roles in the inauguration of Christianity to be wholly a part of the people of Israel. At the end of the Acts of the Apostles (Acts 21:20; 22:3; 23:6–9; 24:14–16; 26:2–8, 22–23) he will argue that Christianity is the direct descendant of Pharisaic Judaism.

* [1:59] The practice of Palestinian Judaism at this time was to name the child at birth; moreover, though naming a male child after the father is not completely unknown, the usual practice was to name the child after the grandfather (see Lk 1:61). The naming of the child John and Zechariah's recovery from his loss of speech should be understood as fulfilling the angel's announcement to Zechariah in Lk 1:13, 20.

* [1:68–79] Like the canticle of Mary (Lk 1:46–55) the canticle of Zechariah is only loosely connected with its context. Apart from Lk 1:76–77, the hymn in speaking of **a horn for our salvation** (Lk 1:69) and **the daybreak from on high** (Lk 1:78) applies more closely to Jesus and his work than to John. Again like Mary's canticle, it is largely composed of phrases taken from the Greek Old Testament and may have been a Jewish Christian hymn of praise that Luke adapted to fit the present context by inserting Lk 1:76–77 to give Zechariah's reply to the question asked in Lk 1:66.

* [1:69] **A horn for our salvation**: the horn is a common Old Testament figure for strength (Ps 18:3; 75:5–6; 89:18; 112:9; 148:14). This description is applied to God in Ps 18:2 and is here transferred to Jesus. The connection of the phrase with **the house of David** gives the title messianic overtones and may indicate an allusion to a phrase in Hannah's song of praise (1 Sm 2:10), "the horn of his anointed."

* [1:76] **You will go before the Lord**: here **the Lord** is most likely a reference to Jesus (contrast

Lk 1:15–17 where Yahweh is meant) and John is presented as the precursor of Jesus.

* [1:78] **The daybreak from on high**: three times in the LXX (Jer 23:5; Zec 3:8; 6:12), the Greek word used here for **daybreak** translates the Hebrew word for "scion, branch," an Old Testament messianic title.

* [2:1–2] Although universal registrations of Roman citizens are attested in 28 B.C., 8 B.C., and A.D. 14 and enrollments in individual provinces of those who are not Roman citizens are also attested, such a universal census of the Roman world under Caesar Augustus is unknown outside the New Testament. Moreover, there are notorious historical problems connected with Luke's dating the census **when Quirinius was governor of Syria**, and the various attempts to resolve the difficulties have proved unsuccessful. P. Sulpicius Quirinius became legate of the province of Syria in A.D. 6–7 when Judea was annexed to the province of Syria. At that time, a provincial census of Judea was taken up. If Quirinius had been legate of Syria previously, it would have to have been before 10 B.C. because the various legates of Syria from 10 B.C. to 4 B.C. (the death of Herod) are known, and such a dating for an earlier census under Quirinius would create additional problems for dating the beginning of Jesus' ministry (Lk 3:1, 23). A previous legateship after 4 B.C. (and before A.D. 6) would not fit with the dating of Jesus' birth in the days of Herod (Lk 1:5; Mt 2:1). Luke may simply be combining Jesus' birth in Bethlehem with his vague recollection of a census under Quirinius (see also Acts 5:37) to underline the significance of this birth for the whole Roman world: through this child born in Bethlehem peace and salvation come to the empire.

* [2:1] **Caesar Augustus**: the reign of the Roman emperor Caesar Augustus is usually dated from 27 B.C. to his death in A.D. 14. According to Greek inscriptions, Augustus was regarded in the Roman Empire as "savior" and "god," and he was credited with establishing a time of peace, the *pax Augusta*, throughout the Roman world during his long reign. It is not by chance that Luke relates the birth of Jesus to the time of Caesar Augustus: the real savior (Lk 2:11) and peacebearer (Lk 2:14; see also Lk 19:38) is the child born in Bethlehem. The great emperor is simply God's agent (like the Persian king Cyrus in Is 44:28–45:1) who provides the occasion for God's purposes to be accomplished. **The whole world**: that is, the whole Roman world: Rome, Italy, and the Roman provinces.

* [2:7] **Firstborn son**: the description of Jesus as **firstborn** son does not necessarily mean that Mary had other sons. It is a legal description indicating that Jesus possessed the rights and privileges of the firstborn son (Gn 27; Ex 13:2; Nm 3:12–13; 18:15–16; Dt 21:15–17). See notes

on Mt 1:25; Mk 6:3. **Wrapped him in swaddling clothes**: there may be an allusion here to the birth of another descendant of David, his son Solomon, who though a great king was wrapped in swaddling clothes like any other infant (Wis 7:4–6). **Laid him in a manger**: a feeding trough for animals. A possible allusion to Is 1:3 LXX.

* [2:8–20] The announcement of Jesus' birth to the shepherds is in keeping with Luke's theme that the lowly are singled out as the recipients of God's favors and blessings (see also Lk 1:48, 52).

* [2:11] The basic message of the infancy narrative is contained in the angel's announcement: this child is **savior**, **Messiah**, and **Lord**. Luke is the only synoptic gospel writer to use the title **savior** for Jesus (Lk 2:11; Acts 5:31; 13:23; see also Lk 1:69; 19:9; Acts 4:12). As savior, Jesus is looked upon by Luke as the one who rescues humanity from sin and delivers humanity from the condition of alienation from God. The title *christos*, "Christ," is the Greek equivalent of the Hebrew *māšiaḥ*, "Messiah," "anointed one." Among certain groups in first-century Palestinian Judaism, the title was applied to an expected royal leader from the line of David who would restore the kingdom to Israel (see Acts 1:6). The political overtones of the title are played down in Luke and instead the Messiah of the Lord (Lk 2:26) or the Lord's anointed is the one who now brings salvation to all humanity, Jew and Gentile (Lk 2:29–32). Lord is the most frequently used title for Jesus in Luke and Acts. In the New Testament it is also applied to Yahweh, as it is in the Old Testament. When used of Jesus it points to his transcendence and dominion over humanity.

* [2:14] **On earth peace to those on whom his favor rests**: the peace that results from the Christ event is for those whom God has favored with his grace. This reading is found in the oldest representatives of the Western and Alexandrian text traditions and is the preferred one; the Byzantine text tradition, on the other hand, reads: "on earth peace, good will toward men." The peace of which Luke's gospel speaks (Lk 2:14; 7:50; 8:48; 10:5–6; 19:38, 42; 24:36) is more than the absence of war of the *pax Augusta*; it also includes the security and well-being characteristic of peace in the Old Testament.

* [2:21] Just as John before him had been incorporated into the people of Israel through his circumcision, so too this child (see note on Lk 1:57–66).

* [2:22–40] The presentation of Jesus in the temple depicts the parents of Jesus as devout Jews, faithful observers of the law of the Lord (Lk 2:23–24, 39), i.e., the law of Moses. In this respect, they are described in a fashion similar to the parents of John (Lk 1:6) and Simeon (Lk 2:25) and Anna (Lk 2:36–37).

* [2:22] **Their purification**: syntactically, **their** must refer to Mary and Joseph, even though the

Mosaic law never mentions the purification of the husband. Recognizing the problem, some Western scribes have altered the text to read "his purification," understanding the presentation of Jesus in the temple as a form of purification; the Vulgate version has a Latin form that could be either "his" or "her." According to the Mosaic law (Lv 12:2–8), the woman who gives birth to a boy is unable for forty days to touch anything sacred or to enter the temple area by reason of her legal impurity. At the end of this period she is required to offer a year-old lamb as a burnt offering and a turtledove or young pigeon as an expiation of sin. The woman who could not afford a lamb offered instead two turtledoves or two young pigeons, as Mary does here. **They took him up to Jerusalem to present him to the Lord:** as the firstborn son (Lk 2:7) Jesus was consecrated to the Lord as the law required (Ex 13:2, 12), but there was no requirement that this be done at the temple. The concept of a presentation at the temple is probably derived from 1 Sm 1:24–28, where Hannah offers the child Samuel for sanctuary services. The law further stipulated (Nm 3:47–48) that the firstborn son should be redeemed by the parents through their payment of five shekels to a member of a priestly family. About this legal requirement Luke is silent.

* [2:25] **Awaiting the consolation of Israel:** Simeon here and later Anna who speak about the child to all who were awaiting the redemption of Jerusalem represent the hopes and expectations of faithful and devout Jews who at this time were looking forward to the restoration of God's rule in Israel. The birth of Jesus brings these hopes to fulfillment.

* [2:35] **(And you yourself a sword will pierce):** Mary herself will not be untouched by the various reactions to the role of Jesus (Lk 2:34). Her blessedness as mother of the Lord will be challenged by her son who describes true blessedness as "hearing the word of God and observing it" (Lk 11:27–28 and Lk 8:20–21).

* [2:41–52] This story's concern with an incident from Jesus' youth is unique in the canonical gospel tradition. It presents Jesus in the role of the faithful Jewish boy, raised in the traditions of Israel, and fulfilling all that the law requires. With this episode, the infancy narrative ends just as it began, in the setting of the Jerusalem temple.

* [2:49] **I must be in my Father's house:** this phrase can also be translated, "I must be about my Father's work." In either translation, Jesus refers to God as his Father. His divine sonship, and his obedience to his heavenly Father's will, take precedence over his ties to his family.

---

* [3:1–20] Although Luke is indebted in this section to his sources, the Gospel of Mark and a collection of sayings of John the Baptist, he has clearly

marked this introduction to the ministry of Jesus with his own individual style. Just as the gospel began with a long periodic sentence (Lk 1:1–4), so too this section (Lk 3:1–2). He casts the call of John the Baptist in the form of an Old Testament prophetic call (Lk 3:2) and extends the quotation from Isaiah found in Mk 1:3 (Is 40:3) by the addition of Is 40:4–5 in Lk 3:5–6. In doing so, he presents his theme of the universality of salvation, which he has announced earlier in the words of Simeon (Lk 2:30–32). Moreover, in describing the expectation of the people (Lk 3:15), Luke is characterizing the time of John's preaching in the same way as he had earlier described the situation of other devout Israelites in the infancy narrative (Lk 2:25–26, 37–38). In Lk 3:7–18 Luke presents the preaching of John the Baptist who urges the crowds to reform in view of **the coming wrath** (Lk 3:7, 9: eschatological preaching), and who offers the crowds certain standards for reforming social conduct (Lk 3:10–14: ethical preaching), and who announces to the crowds the coming of **one mightier than** he (Lk 3:15–18: messianic preaching).

* [3:1] **Tiberius Caesar:** Tiberius succeeded Augustus as emperor in A.D. 14 and reigned until A.D. 37. The fifteenth year of his reign, depending on the method of calculating his first regnal year, would have fallen between A.D. 27 and 29. **Pontius Pilate:** prefect of Judea from A.D. 26 to 36. The Jewish historian Josephus describes him as a greedy and ruthless prefect who had little regard for the local Jewish population and their religious practices (see Lk 13:1). **Herod:** i.e., Herod Antipas, the son of Herod the Great. He ruled over Galilee and Perea from 4 B.C. to A.D. 39. His official title **tetrarch** means literally, "ruler of a quarter," but came to designate any subordinate prince. **Philip:** also a son of Herod the Great, tetrarch of the territory to the north and east of the Sea of Galilee from 4 B.C. to A.D. 34. Only two small areas of this territory are mentioned by Luke. **Lysanias:** nothing is known about this Lysanias who is said here to have been tetrarch of Abilene, a territory northwest of Damascus.

* [3:2] **During the high priesthood of Annas and Caiaphas:** after situating the call of John the Baptist in terms of the civil rulers of the period, Luke now mentions the religious leadership of Palestine (see note on Lk 1:5). Annas had been high priest A.D. 6–15. After being deposed by the Romans in A.D. 15 he was succeeded by various members of his family and eventually by his son-in-law, Caiaphas, who was high priest A.D. 18–36. Luke refers to Annas as high priest at this time (but see Jn 18:13, 19), possibly because of the continuing influence of Annas or because the title continued to be used for the ex-high priest. **The word of God came to John:** Luke is alone among the New Testament writers in associating the preaching of John with a call from God. Luke is thereby identifying John with the prophets whose ministries began with similar calls. In Lk 7:26 John will be described as "more than a prophet"; he is also the precursor of Jesus (Lk 7:27), a transitional figure inaugurating the period of the fulfillment of prophecy and promise.

* [3:3] See note on Mt 3:2.

* [3:4] The Essenes from Qumran used the same passage to explain why their community was in the desert studying and observing the law and the prophets (1QS 8:12–15).

* [3:16] **He will baptize you with the holy Spirit and fire**: in contrast to John's baptism with water, Jesus is said to baptize with the holy Spirit and with fire. From the point of view of the early Christian community, the Spirit and fire must have been understood in the light of the fire symbolism of the pouring out of the Spirit at Pentecost (Acts 2:1–4); but as part of John's preaching, the Spirit and fire should be related to their purifying and refining characteristics (Ez 36:25–27; Mal 3:2–3). See note on Mt 3:11.

* [3:17] **Winnowing fan**: see note on Mt 3:12.

* [3:19–20] Luke separates the ministry of John the Baptist from that of Jesus by reporting the imprisonment of John before the baptism of Jesus (Lk 3:21–22). Luke uses this literary device to serve his understanding of the periods of salvation history. With John the Baptist, the time of promise, the period of Israel, comes to an end; with the baptism of Jesus and the descent of the Spirit upon him, the time of fulfillment, the period of Jesus, begins. In his second volume, the Acts of the Apostles, Luke will introduce the third epoch in salvation history, the period of the church.

* [3:21–22] This episode in Luke focuses on the heavenly message identifying Jesus as Son and, through the allusion to Is 42:1, as Servant of Yahweh. The relationship of Jesus to the Father has already been announced in the infancy narrative (Lk 1:32, 35; 2:49); it occurs here at the beginning of Jesus' Galilean ministry and will reappear in Lk 9:35 before another major section of Luke's gospel, the travel narrative (Lk 9:51–19:27). Elsewhere in Luke's writings (Lk 4:18; Acts 10:38), this incident will be interpreted as a type of anointing of Jesus.

* [3:21] **Was praying**: Luke regularly presents Jesus at prayer at important points in his ministry: here at his baptism; at the choice of the Twelve (Lk 6:12); before Peter's confession (Lk 9:18); at the transfiguration (Lk 9:28); when he teaches his disciples to pray (Lk 11:1); at the Last Supper (Lk 22:32); on the Mount of Olives (Lk 22:41); on the cross (Lk 23:46).

* [3:22] **You are my beloved Son; with you I am well pleased**: this is the best attested reading in the Greek manuscripts. The Western reading, "You are my Son, this day I have begotten you," is derived from Ps 2:7.

* [3:23–38] Whereas Mt 1:2 begins the genealogy of Jesus with Abraham to emphasize Jesus' bonds with the people of Israel, Luke's universalism leads him to trace the descent of Jesus beyond Israel to Adam and beyond that to God (Lk 3:38) to stress again Jesus' divine sonship.

* [3:31] **The son of Nathan, the son of David**: in keeping with Jesus' prophetic role in Luke and Acts (e.g., Lk 7:16, 39; 9:8; 13:33; 24:19; Acts 3:22–23; 7:37) Luke traces Jesus' Davidic ancestry through the prophet Nathan (see 2 Sm 7:2) rather than through King Solomon, as Mt 1:6–7.

---

* [4:1–13] See note on Mt 4:1–11.

* [4:1] **Filled with the holy Spirit**: as a result of the descent of the Spirit upon him at his baptism (Lk 3:21–22), Jesus is now equipped to overcome the devil. Just as the Spirit is prominent at this early stage of Jesus' ministry (Lk 4:1, 14, 18), so too it will be at the beginning of the period of the church in Acts (Acts 1:4; 2:4, 17).

* [4:2] **For forty days**: the mention of forty days recalls the forty years of the wilderness wanderings of the Israelites during the Exodus (Dt 8:2).

* [4:9] **To Jerusalem**: the Lucan order of the temptations concludes on the parapet of the temple in Jerusalem, the city of destiny in Luke-Acts. It is in Jerusalem that Jesus will ultimately face his destiny (Lk 9:51; 13:33).

* [4:13] **For a time**: the devil's opportune time will occur before the passion and death of Jesus (Lk 22:3, 31–32, 53).

* [4:14] **News of him spread**: a Lucan theme; see Lk 4:37; 5:15; 7:17.

* [4:16–30] Luke has transposed to the beginning of Jesus' ministry an incident from his Marcan source, which situated it near the end of the Galilean ministry (Mk 6:1–6a). In doing so, Luke turns the initial admiration (Lk 4:22) and subsequent rejection of Jesus (Lk 4:28–29) into a foreshadowing of the whole future ministry of Jesus. Moreover, the rejection of Jesus in his own hometown hints at the greater rejection of him by Israel (Acts 13:46).

* [4:16] **According to his custom**: Jesus' practice of regularly attending synagogue is carried on by the early Christians' practice of meeting in the temple (Acts 2:46; 3:1; 5:12).

* [4:18] **The Spirit of the Lord is upon me, because he has anointed me**: see note on Lk 3:21–22. As this incident develops, Jesus is portrayed as a prophet whose ministry is compared to that of the prophets Elijah and Elisha. Prophetic anointings are known in first-century Palestinian Judaism from the Qumran literature that speaks of prophets as God's anointed ones. **To bring glad tidings to the poor**: more than any other gospel writer Luke is concerned with Jesus' attitude toward the economically and socially poor (see Lk 6:20, 24; 12:16–21; 14:12–14; 16:19–26; 19:8).

At times, the poor in Luke's gospel are associated with the downtrodden, the oppressed and afflicted, the forgotten and the neglected (Lk 4:18; 6:20–22; 7:22; 14:12–14), and it is they who accept Jesus' message of salvation.

* [4:21] **Today this scripture passage is fulfilled in your hearing**: this sermon inaugurates the time of fulfillment of Old Testament prophecy. Luke presents the ministry of Jesus as fulfilling Old Testament hopes and expectations (Lk 7:22); for Luke, even Jesus' suffering, death, and resurrection are done in fulfillment of the scriptures (Lk 24:25–27, 44–46; Acts 3:18).

* [4:23] **The things that we heard were done in Capernaum**: Luke's source for this incident reveals an awareness of an earlier ministry of Jesus in Capernaum that Luke has not yet made use of because of his transposition of this Nazareth episode to the beginning of Jesus' Galilean ministry. It is possible that by use of the future tense **you will quote me…**, Jesus is being portrayed as a prophet.

* [4:25–26] The references to Elijah and Elisha serve several purposes in this episode: they emphasize Luke's portrait of Jesus as a prophet like Elijah and Elisha; they help to explain why the initial admiration of the people turns to rejection; and they provide the scriptural justification for the future Christian mission to the Gentiles.

* [4:26] **A widow in Zarephath in the land of Sidon**: like Naaman the Syrian in Lk 4:27, a non-Israelite becomes the object of the prophet's ministry.

* [4:31–44] The next several incidents in Jesus' ministry take place in Capernaum and are based on Luke's source, Mk 1:21–39. To the previous portrait of Jesus as prophet (Lk 4:16–30) they now add a presentation of him as teacher (Lk 4:31–32), exorcist (Lk 4:32–37, 41), healer (Lk 4:38–40), and proclaimer of God's kingdom (Lk 4:43).

* [4:34] **What have you to do with us?**: see note on Jn 2:4. **Have you come to destroy us?**: the question reflects the current belief that before the day of the Lord control over humanity would be wrested from the evil spirits, evil destroyed, and God's authority over humanity reestablished. The synoptic gospel tradition presents Jesus carrying out this task.

* [4:38] **The house of Simon**: because of Luke's arrangement of material, the reader has not yet been introduced to Simon (cf. Mk 1:16–18, 29–31). Situated as it is before the call of Simon (Lk 5:1–11), it helps the reader to understand Simon's eagerness to do what Jesus says (Lk 5:5) and to follow him (Lk 5:11).

* [4:41] **They knew that he was the Messiah**: that is, the Christ (see note on Lk 2:11).

* [4:42] **They tried to prevent him from leaving them**: the reaction of these strangers in Capernaum is presented in contrast to the reactions of those in his hometown who rejected him (Lk 4:28–30).

* [4:44] **In the synagogues of Judea**: instead of **Judea**, which is the best reading of the manuscript tradition, the Byzantine text tradition and other manuscripts read "Galilee," a reading that harmonizes Luke with Mt 4:23 and Mk 1:39. Up to this point Luke has spoken only of a ministry of Jesus in Galilee. Luke may be using **Judea** to refer to the land of Israel, the territory of the Jews, and not to a specific portion of it.

---

* [5:1–11] This incident has been transposed from his source, Mk 1:16–20, which places it immediately after Jesus makes his appearance in Galilee. By this transposition Luke uses this example of Simon's acceptance of Jesus to counter the earlier rejection of him by his hometown people, and since several incidents dealing with Jesus' power and authority have already been narrated, Luke creates a plausible context for the acceptance of Jesus by Simon and his partners. Many commentators have noted the similarity between the wondrous catch of fish reported here (Lk 4:4–9) and the post-resurrectional appearance of Jesus in Jn 21:1–11. There are traces in Luke's story that the post-resurrectional context is the original one: in Lk 4:8 Simon addresses Jesus as **Lord** (a post-resurrectional title for Jesus—see Lk 24:34; Acts 2:36—that has been read back into the historical ministry of Jesus) and recognizes himself as a sinner (an appropriate recognition for one who has denied knowing Jesus—Lk 22:54–62). As used by Luke, the incident looks forward to Peter's leadership in Luke-Acts (Lk 6:14; 9:20; 22:31–32; 24:34; Acts 1:15; 2:14–40; 10:11–18; 15:7–12) and symbolizes the future success of Peter as fisherman (Acts 2:41).

* [5:11] **They left everything**: in Mk 1:16–20 and Mt 4:18–22 the fishermen who follow Jesus leave their nets and their father; in Luke, they leave **everything** (see also Lk 5:28; 12:33; 14:33; 18:22), an indication of Luke's theme of complete detachment from material possessions.

* [5:12] **Full of leprosy**: see note on Mk 1:40.

* [5:14] **Show yourself to the priest…what Moses prescribed**: this is a reference to Lv 14:2–9 that gives detailed instructions for the purification of one who had been a victim of leprosy and thereby excluded from contact with others (see Lv 13:45–46, 49; Nm 5:2–3). **That will be proof for them**: see note on Mt 8:4.

* [5:17–6:11] From his Marcan source, Luke now introduces a series of controversies with Pharisees: controversy over Jesus' power to forgive sins (Lk 5:17–26); controversy over his eating and drinking with tax collectors and sinners (Lk 5:27–32); controversy over not fasting (Lk 5:33–36); and finally two episodes narrating controversies over observance of the sabbath (Lk 5:1–11).

* [5:17] **Pharisees**: see note on Mt 3:7.

* [5:19] **Through the tiles**: Luke has adapted the story found in Mark to his non-Palestinian audience by changing "opened up the roof" (Mk 2:4, a reference to Palestinian straw and clay roofs) to **through the tiles**, a detail that reflects the Hellenistic Greco-Roman house with tiled roof.

* [5:20] **As for you, your sins are forgiven**: literally, "O man, your sins are forgiven you." The connection between the forgiveness of sins and the cure of the paralytic reflects the belief of first-century Palestine (based on the Old Testament: Ex 20:5; Dt 5:9) that sickness and infirmity are the result of sin, one's own or that of one's ancestors (see also Lk 13:2; Jn 5:14; 9:2).

* [5:21] **The scribes**: see note on Mk 2:6.

* [5:24] See notes on Mt 9:6 and Mk 2:10.

* [5:28] **Leaving everything behind**: see note on Lk 5:11.

* [5:34–35] See notes on Mt 9:15 and Mk 2:19.

* [5:34] **Wedding guests**: literally, "sons of the bridal chamber."

* [5:36–39] See notes on Mt 9:16–17 and Mk 2:19.

* [5:39] **The old is good**: this saying is meant to be ironic and offers an explanation for the rejection by some of the new wine that Jesus offers: satisfaction with old forms will prevent one from sampling the new.

---

* [6:1–11] The two episodes recounted here deal with gathering grain and healing, both of which were forbidden on the sabbath. In his defense of his disciples' conduct and his own charitable deed, Jesus argues that satisfying human needs such as hunger and performing works of mercy take precedence even over the sacred sabbath rest. See also notes on Mt 12:1–14 and Mk 2:25–26.

* [6:4] **The bread of offering**: see note on Mt 12:5–6.

* [6:12–16] See notes on Mt 10:1–11:1 and Mk 3:14–15.

* [6:12] **Spent the night in prayer**: see note on Lk 3:21.

* [6:13] **He chose Twelve**: the identification of this group as the **Twelve** is a part of early Christian tradition (see 1 Cor 15:5), and in Matthew and Luke, the **Twelve** are associated with the twelve tribes of Israel (Lk 22:29–30; Mt 19:28). After the fall of Judas from his position among the Twelve, the need is felt on the part of the early community to reconstitute this group before the Christian mission begins at Pentecost (Acts 1:15–26). From Luke's perspective, they are an important group who because of their association with Jesus from the time of his baptism to his ascension (Acts 1:21–22) provide the continuity between the historical Jesus and the church of Luke's day and who as the original eyewitnesses guarantee the fidelity of the church's beliefs and practices to the teachings of Jesus (Lk 1:1–4).

Whom he also named apostles: only Luke among the gospel writers attributes to Jesus the bestowal of the name **apostles** upon the Twelve. See note on Mt 10:2–4. "Apostle" becomes a technical term in early Christianity for a missionary sent out to preach the word of God. Although Luke seems to want to restrict the title to the Twelve (only in Acts 4:4, 14 are Paul and Barnabas termed apostles), other places in the New Testament show an awareness that the term was more widely applied (1 Cor 15:5–7; Gal 1:19; 1 Cor 1:1; 9:1; Rom 16:7).

* [6:14] **Simon, whom he named Peter**: see note on Mk 3:16.

* [6:15] **Simon who was called a Zealot**: the Zealots were the instigators of the First Revolt of Palestinian Jews against Rome in A.D. 66–70. Because the existence of the Zealots as a distinct group during the lifetime of Jesus is the subject of debate, the meaning of the identification of Simon as a Zealot is unclear.

* [6:16] **Judas Iscariot**: the name **Iscariot** may mean "man from Kerioth."

* [6:17] **The coastal region of Tyre and Sidon**: not only Jews from Judea and Jerusalem, but even Gentiles from outside Palestine come to hear Jesus (see Lk 2:31–32; 3:6; 4:24–27).

* [6:20–49] Luke's "Sermon on the Plain" is the counterpart to Matthew's "Sermon on the Mount" (Mt 5:1–7:27). It is addressed to the disciples of Jesus, and, like the sermon in Matthew, it begins with beatitudes (Lk 6:20–22) and ends with the parable of the two houses (Lk 6:46–49). Almost all the words of Jesus reported by Luke are found in Matthew's version, but because Matthew includes sayings that were related to specifically Jewish Christian problems (e.g., Mt 5:17–20; 6:1–8, 16–18) that Luke did not find appropriate for his predominantly Gentile Christian audience, the "Sermon on the Mount" is considerably longer. Luke's sermon may be outlined as follows: an introduction consisting of blessings and woes (Lk 6:20–26); the love of one's enemies (Lk 6:27–36); the demands of loving one's neighbor (Lk 6:37–42); good deeds as proof of one's goodness (Lk 6:43–45); a parable illustrating the result of listening to and acting on the words of Jesus (Lk 6:46–49). At the core of the sermon is Jesus' teaching on the love of one's enemies (Lk 6:27–36) that has as its source of motivation God's graciousness and compassion for all humanity (Lk 6:35–36) and Jesus' teaching on the love of one's neighbor (Lk 6:37–42) that is characterized by forgiveness and generosity.

* [6:20–26] The introductory portion of the sermon consists of blessings and woes that address the real economic and social conditions of humanity (the poor—the rich; the hungry—the satisfied; those grieving—those laughing; the outcast—the socially acceptable). By contrast, Matthew emphasizes the religious and spiritual

values of disciples in the kingdom inaugurated by Jesus ("poor in spirit," Mt 5:3; "hunger and thirst for righteousness," Mt 5:6). In the sermon, **blessed** extols the fortunate condition of persons who are favored with the blessings of God; the woes, addressed as they are to the disciples of Jesus, threaten God's profound displeasure on those so blinded by their present fortunate situation that they do not recognize and appreciate the real values of God's kingdom. In all the blessings and woes, the present condition of the persons addressed will be reversed in the future.

* [6:27–36] See notes on Mt 5:43–48 and Mt 5:48.

* [6:37–42] See notes on Mt 7:1–12; 7:1; 7:5.

* [6:43–46] See notes on Mt 7:15–20 and 12:33.

* [6:47–49] See note on Mt 7:24–27.

---

* [7:1–8:3] The episodes in this section present a series of reactions to the Galilean ministry of Jesus and reflect some of Luke's particular interests: the faith of a Gentile (Lk 7:1–10); the prophet Jesus' concern for a widowed mother (Lk 7:11–17); the ministry of Jesus directed to the afflicted and unfortunate of Is 61:1 (Lk 7:18–23); the relation between John and Jesus and their role in God's plan for salvation (Lk 7:24–35); a forgiven sinner's manifestation of love (Lk 7:36–50); the association of women with the ministry of Jesus (Lk 8:1–3).

* [7:1–10] This story about the faith of the centurion, a Gentile who cherishes the Jewish nation (Lk 7:5), prepares for the story in Acts of the conversion by Peter of the Roman centurion Cornelius who is similarly described as one who is generous to the Jewish nation (Acts 10:2). See also Acts 10:34–35 in the speech of Peter: "God shows no partiality…whoever fears him and acts righteously is acceptable to him." See also notes on Mt 8:5–13 and Jn 4:43–54.

* [7:2] **A centurion**: see note on Mt 8:5.

* [7:6] **I am not worthy to have you come under my roof**: to enter the house of a Gentile was considered unclean for a Jew; cf. Acts 10:28.

* [7:11–17] In the previous incident Jesus' power was displayed for a Gentile whose servant was dying; in this episode it is displayed toward a widowed mother whose only son has already died. Jesus' power over death prepares for his reply to John's disciples in Lk 7:22: "the dead are raised." This resuscitation in alluding to the prophet Elijah's resurrection of the only son of a widow of Zarephath (1 Kgs 7:8–24) leads to the reaction of the crowd: "A great prophet has arisen in our midst" (Lk 7:16).

* [7:18–23] In answer to John's question, **Are you the one who is to come?**—a probable reference to the return of the fiery prophet of reform, Elijah, "before the day of the Lord comes, the great and terrible day" (Mal 3:23)—Jesus responds that his role is rather to bring the blessings spoken of in Is 61:1 to the oppressed and neglected of society (Lk 7:22; cf. Lk 4:18).

* [7:23] **Blessed is the one who takes no offense at me**: this beatitude is pronounced on the person who recognizes Jesus' true identity in spite of previous expectations of what "the one who is to come" would be like.

* [7:24–30] In his testimony to John, Jesus reveals his understanding of the relationship between them: John is the precursor of Jesus (Lk 7:27); John is the messenger spoken of in Mal 3:1 who in Mal 3:23 is identified as Elijah. Taken with the previous episode, it can be seen that Jesus identifies John as precisely the person John envisioned Jesus to be: the Elijah who prepares the way for the coming of the day of the Lord.

* [7:31–35] See note on Mt 11:16–19.

* [7:36–50] In this story of the pardoning of the sinful woman Luke presents two different reactions to the ministry of Jesus. A Pharisee, suspecting Jesus to be a prophet, invites Jesus to a festive banquet in his house, but the Pharisee's self-righteousness leads to little forgiveness by God and consequently little love shown toward Jesus. The sinful woman, on the other hand, manifests a faith in God (Lk 7:50) that has led her to seek forgiveness for her sins, and because so much was forgiven, she now overwhelms Jesus with her display of love; cf. the similar contrast in attitudes in Lk 18:9–14. The whole episode is a powerful lesson on the relation between forgiveness and love.

* [7:36] **Reclined at table**: the normal posture of guests at a banquet. Other oriental banquet customs alluded to in this story include the reception by the host with a kiss (Lk 7:45), washing the feet of the guests (Lk 7:44), and the anointing of the guests' heads (Lk 7:46).

* [7:41] **Days' wages**: one denarius is the normal daily wage of a laborer.

* [7:47] **Her many sins have been forgiven; hence, she has shown great love**: literally, "her many sins have been forgiven, seeing that she has loved much." That the woman's sins have been forgiven is attested by the great love she shows toward Jesus. Her love is the consequence of her forgiveness. This is also the meaning demanded by the parable in Lk 7:41–43.

---

* [8:1–3] Luke presents Jesus as an itinerant preacher traveling in the company of the Twelve and of the Galilean women who are sustaining them out of their means. These Galilean women will later accompany Jesus on his journey to Jerusalem and become witnesses to his death (Lk 23:49) and resurrection (Lk 24:9–11, where Mary Magdalene and Joanna are specifically mentioned; cf. also Acts 1:14). The association of women with the ministry of Jesus is most unusual in the light of the attitude of first-century Palestinian

Judaism toward women. The more common attitude is expressed in Jn 4:27, and early rabbinic documents caution against speaking with women in public.

* [8:4–21] The focus in this section is on how one should hear the word of God and act on it. It includes the parable of the sower and its explanation (Lk 8:4–15), a collection of sayings on how one should act on the word that is heard (Lk 8:16–18), and the identification of the mother and brothers of Jesus as the ones who hear the word and act on it (Lk 8:19–21). See also notes on Mt 13:1–53 and Mk 4:1–34.

* [8:4–8] See note on Mt 13:3–8.

* [8:11–15] On the interpretation of the parable of the sower, see note on Mt 13:18–23.

* [8:16–18] These sayings continue the theme of responding to the word of God. Those who hear the word must become a light to others (Lk 8:16); even the mysteries of the kingdom that have been made known to the disciples (Lk 8:9–10) must come to light (Lk 8:17); a generous and persevering response to the word of God leads to a still more perfect response to the word.

* [8:19] His brothers: see note on Mk 6:3.

* [8:21] The family of Jesus is not constituted by physical relationship with him but by obedience to the word of God. In this, Luke agrees with the Marcan parallel (Mk 3:31–35), although by omitting Mk 3:33 and especially Mk 3:20–21 Luke has softened the Marcan picture of Jesus' natural family. Probably he did this because Mary has already been presented in Lk 1:38 as the obedient handmaid of the Lord who fulfills the requirement for belonging to the eschatological family of Jesus; cf. also Lk 11:27–28.

* [8:22–56] This section records four miracles of Jesus that manifest his power and authority: (1) the calming of a storm on the lake (Lk 8:22–25); (2) the exorcism of a demoniac (Lk 8:26–39); (3) the cure of a hemorrhaging woman (Lk 8:40–48); (4) the raising of Jairus's daughter to life (Lk 8:49–56). They parallel the same sequence of stories at Mk 4:35–5:43.

* [8:26] Gerasenes: other manuscripts read Gadarenes or Gergesenes. See also note on Mt 8:28. Opposite Galilee: probably Gentile territory (note the presence in the area of pigs—unclean animals to Jews) and an indication that the person who receives salvation (Lk 8:36) is a Gentile.

* [8:30] What is your name?: the question reflects the popular belief that knowledge of the spirit's name brought control over the spirit. Legion: to Jesus' question the demon replies with a Latin word transliterated into Greek. The Roman legion at this period consisted of 5,000 to 6,000 foot soldiers; hence the name implies a very large number of demons.

* [8:31] Abyss: the place of the dead (Rom 10:7) or the prison of Satan (Rev 20:3) or the subterranean "watery deep" that symbolizes the chaos before the order imposed by creation (Gn 1:2).

* [8:35] Sitting at his feet: the former demoniac takes the position of a disciple before the master (Lk 10:39; Acts 22:3).

* [8:40–56] Two interwoven miracle stories, one a healing and the other a resuscitation, present Jesus as master over sickness and death. In the Lucan account, faith in Jesus is responsible for the cure (Lk 8:48) and for the raising to life (Lk 8:50).

* [8:42] An only daughter: cf. the son of the widow of Nain whom Luke describes as an "only" son (Lk 7:12; see also Lk 9:38).

* [8:43] Afflicted with hemorrhages for twelve years: according to the Mosaic law (Lv 15:25–30) this condition would render the woman unclean and unfit for contact with other people.

* [8:52] Sleeping: her death is a temporary condition; cf. Jn 11:11–14.

* [9:1–6] Armed with the power and authority that Jesus himself has been displaying in the previous episodes, the Twelve are now sent out to continue the work that Jesus has been performing throughout his Galilean ministry: (1) proclaiming the kingdom (Lk 4:43; 8:1); (2) exorcising demons (Lk 4:33–37, 41; 8:26–39) and (3) healing the sick (Lk 4:38–40; 5:12–16, 17–26; 6:6–10; 7:1–10, 17, 22; Lk 8:40–56).

* [9:3] Take nothing for the journey: the absolute detachment required of the disciple (Lk 14:33) leads to complete reliance on God (Lk 12:22–31).

* [9:5] Shake the dust from your feet: see note on Mt 10:14.

* [9:7–56] This section in which Luke gathers together incidents that focus on the identity of Jesus is introduced by a question that Herod is made to ask in this gospel: "Who then is this about whom I hear such things?"(Lk 9:9) In subsequent episodes, Luke reveals to the reader various answers to Herod's question: Jesus is one in whom God's power is present and who provides for the needs of God's people (Lk 9:10–17); Peter declares Jesus to be "the Messiah of God" (Lk 9:18–21); Jesus says he is the suffering Son of Man (Lk 9:22, 43–45); Jesus is the Master to be followed, even to death (Lk 9:23–27); Jesus is God's son, his Chosen One (Lk 9:28–36).

* [9:7] Herod the tetrarch: see note on Lk 3:1.

* [9:9] And he kept trying to see him: this indication of Herod's interest in Jesus prepares for Lk 13:31–33 and for Lk 23:8–12 where Herod's curiosity about Jesus' power to perform miracles remains unsatisfied.

* [9:16] Then taking . . . : the actions of Jesus recall the institution of the Eucharist in Lk 22:19; see also note on Mt 14:19.

* [9:18–22] This incident is based on Mk 8:27–33, but Luke has eliminated Peter's refusal to accept Jesus as suffering Son of Man (Mk 8:32) and the rebuke of Peter by Jesus (Mk 8:33). Elsewhere in the gospel, Luke softens the harsh portrait of Peter and the other apostles found in his Marcan source (cf. Lk 22:39–46, which similarly lacks a rebuke of Peter that occurs in the source, Mk 14:37–38).

* [9:18] **When Jesus was praying in solitude**: see note on Lk 3:21.

* [9:20] **The Messiah of God**: on the meaning of this title in first-century Palestinian Judaism, see notes on Lk 2:11 and on Mt 16:13–20 and Mk 8:27–30.

* [9:23] **Daily**: this is a Lucan addition to a saying of Jesus, removing the saying from a context that envisioned the imminent suffering and death of the disciple of Jesus (as does the saying in Mk 8:34–35) to one that focuses on the demands of daily Christian existence.

* [9:28–36] Situated shortly after the first announcement of the passion, death, and resurrection, this scene of Jesus' transfiguration provides the heavenly confirmation to Jesus' declaration that his suffering will end in glory (Lk 9:32); see also notes on Mt 17:1–8 and Mk 9:2–8.

* [9:28] **Up the mountain to pray**: the "mountain" is the regular place of prayer in Luke (see Lk 6:12; 22:39–41).

* [9:30] **Moses and Elijah**: the two figures represent the Old Testament law and the prophets. At the end of this episode, the heavenly voice will identify Jesus as the one to be listened to now (Lk 9:35). See also note on Mk 9:5.

* [9:31] **His exodus that he was going to accomplish in Jerusalem**: Luke identifies the subject of the conversation as the **exodus** of Jesus, a reference to the death, resurrection, and ascension of Jesus that will take place in Jerusalem, the city of destiny (see Lk 9:51). The mention of exodus, however, also calls to mind the Israelite Exodus from Egypt to the promised land.

* [9:32] **They saw his glory**: the **glory** that is proper to God is here attributed to Jesus (see Lk 24:26).

* [9:33] **Let us make three tents**: in a possible allusion to the feast of Tabernacles, Peter may be likening his joy on the occasion of the transfiguration to the joyful celebration of this harvest festival.

* [9:34] **Over them**: it is not clear whether **them** refers to Jesus, Moses, and Elijah, or to the disciples. For the cloud casting its shadow, see note on Mk 9:7.

* [9:35] Like the heavenly voice that identified Jesus at his baptism prior to his undertaking the Galilean ministry (Lk 3:22), so too here before the journey to the city of destiny is begun (Lk 9:51) the heavenly voice again identifies Jesus as Son.

Listen to him: the two representatives of Israel of old depart (Lk 9:33) and Jesus is left alone (Lk 9:36) as the teacher whose words must be heeded (see also Acts 3:22).

* [9:36] **At that time**: i.e., before the resurrection.

* [9:37–43a] See note on Mk 9:14–29.

* [9:46–50] These two incidents focus on attitudes that are opposed to Christian discipleship: rivalry and intolerance of outsiders.

* [9:51–18:14] The Galilean ministry of Jesus finishes with the previous episode and a new section of Luke's gospel begins, the journey to Jerusalem. This journey is based on Mk 10:1–52 but Luke uses his Marcan source only in Lk 18:15–19:27. Before that point he has inserted into his gospel a distinctive collection of sayings of Jesus and stories about him that he has drawn from Q, a collection of sayings of Jesus used also by Matthew, and from his own special traditions. All of the material collected in this section is loosely organized within the framework of a journey of Jesus to Jerusalem, the city of destiny, where his exodus (suffering, death, resurrection, ascension) is to take place (Lk 9:31), where salvation is accomplished, and from where the proclamation of God's saving word is to go forth (Lk 24:47; Acts 1:8). Much of the material in the Lucan travel narrative is teaching for the disciples. During the course of this journey Jesus is preparing his chosen Galilean witnesses for the role they will play after his exodus (Lk 9:31): they are to be his witnesses to the people (Acts 10:39; 13:31) and thereby provide certainty to the readers of Luke's gospel that the teachings they have received are rooted in the teachings of Jesus (Lk 1:1–4).

* [9:51–55] Just as the Galilean ministry began with a rejection of Jesus in his hometown, so too the travel narrative begins with the rejection of him by Samaritans. In this episode Jesus disassociates himself from the attitude expressed by his disciples that those who reject him are to be punished severely. The story alludes to 2 Kgs 1:10, 12 where the prophet Elijah takes the course of action Jesus rejects, and Jesus thereby rejects the identification of himself with Elijah.

* [9:51] **Days for his being taken up**: like the reference to his exodus in Lk 9:31 this is probably a reference to all the events (suffering, death, resurrection, ascension) of his last days in Jerusalem. **He resolutely determined**: literally, "he set his face."

* [9:52] **Samaritan**: Samaria was the territory between Judea and Galilee west of the Jordan river. For ethnic and religious reasons, the Samaritans and the Jews were bitterly opposed to one another (see Jn 4:9).

* [9:57–62] In these sayings Jesus speaks of the severity and the unconditional nature of Christian discipleship. Even family ties and filial obligations, such as burying one's parents, cannot distract one

no matter how briefly from proclaiming the kingdom of God. The first two sayings are paralleled in Mt 8:19–22; see also notes there.

* [9:60] **Let the dead bury their dead**: i.e., let the spiritually dead (those who do not follow) bury their physically dead. See also note on Mt 8:22.

---

* [10:1–12] Only the Gospel of Luke contains two episodes in which Jesus sends out his followers on a mission: the first (Lk 9:1–6) is based on the mission in Mk 6:6b–13 and recounts the sending out of the Twelve; here in Lk 10:1–12 a similar report based on Q becomes the sending out of seventy-two in this gospel. The episode continues the theme of Jesus preparing witnesses to himself and his ministry. These witnesses include not only the Twelve but also the seventy-two who may represent the Christian mission in Luke's own day. Note that the instructions given to the Twelve and to the seventy-two are similar and that what is said to the seventy-two in Lk 10:4 is directed to the Twelve in Lk 22:35.

* [10:1] **Seventy[-two]**: important representatives of the Alexandrian and Caesarean text types read "seventy," while other important Alexandrian texts and Western readings have "seventy-two."

* [10:4] **Carry no money bag…greet no one along the way**: because of the urgency of the mission and the singlemindedness required of missionaries, attachment to material possessions should be avoided and even customary greetings should not distract from the fulfillment of the task.

* [10:5] **First say, 'Peace to this household'**: see notes on Lk 2:14 and Mt 10:13.

* [10:6] **A peaceful person**: literally, "a son of peace."

* [10:13–16] The call to repentance that is a part of the proclamation of the kingdom brings with it a severe judgment for those who hear it and reject it.

* [10:15] **The netherworld**: the underworld, the place of the dead (Acts 2:27, 31) here contrasted with heaven; see also note on Mt 11:23.

* [10:18] **I have observed Satan fall like lightning**: the effect of the mission of the seventy-two is characterized by the Lucan Jesus as a symbolic fall of Satan. As the kingdom of God is gradually being established, evil in all its forms is being defeated; the dominion of Satan over humanity is at an end.

* [10:21] **Revealed them to the childlike**: a restatement of the theme announced in Lk 8:10: the mysteries of the kingdom are revealed to the disciples. See also note on Mt 11:25–27.

* [10:25–37] In response to a question from a Jewish legal expert about inheriting eternal life, Jesus illustrates the superiority of love over legalism through the story of the good Samaritan. The law of love proclaimed in the "Sermon on the Plain" (Lk 6:27–36) is exemplified by one whom

the legal expert would have considered ritually impure (see Jn 4:9). Moreover, the identity of the "neighbor" requested by the legal expert (Lk 10:29) turns out to be a Samaritan, the enemy of the Jew (see note on Lk 9:52).

* [10:25] **Scholar of the law**: an expert in the Mosaic law, and probably a member of the group elsewhere identified as the scribes (Lk 5:21).

* [10:31–32] **Priest…Levite**: those religious representatives of Judaism who would have been expected to be models of "neighbor" to the victim pass him by.

* [10:38–42] The story of Martha and Mary further illustrates the importance of hearing the words of the teacher and the concern with women in Luke.

* [10:39] **Sat beside the Lord at his feet**: it is remarkable that for first-century Palestinian Judaism that a woman would assume the posture of a disciple at the master's feet (see also Lk 8:35; Acts 22:3), and it reveals a characteristic attitude of Jesus toward women in this gospel (see Lk 8:2–3).

* [10:42] **There is need of only one thing**: some ancient versions read, "there is need of few things"; another important, although probably inferior, reading found in some manuscripts is, "there is need of few things, or of one."

---

* [11:1–13] Luke presents three episodes concerned with prayer. The first (Lk 11:1–4) recounts Jesus teaching his disciples the Christian communal prayer, the "Our Father"; the second (Lk 11:5–8), the importance of persistence in prayer; the third (Lk 11:9–13), the effectiveness of prayer.

* [11:1–4] The Matthean form of the "Our Father" occurs in the "Sermon on the Mount" (Mt 6:9–15); the shorter Lucan version is presented while Jesus is at prayer (see note on Lk 3:21) and his disciples ask him to teach them to pray just as John taught his disciples to pray. In answer to their question, Jesus presents them with an example of a Christian communal prayer that stresses the fatherhood of God and acknowledges him as the one to whom the Christian disciple owes daily sustenance (Lk 11:3), forgiveness (Lk 11:4), and deliverance from the final trial (Lk 11:4). See also notes on Mt 6:9–13.

* [11:2] **Your kingdom come**: in place of this petition, some early church Fathers record: "May your holy Spirit come upon us and cleanse us," a petition that may reflect the use of the "Our Father" in a baptismal liturgy.

* [11:3–4] **Daily bread**: see note on Mt 6:11. **The final test**: see note on Mt 6:13.

* [11:13] **The holy Spirit**: this is a Lucan editorial alteration of a traditional saying of Jesus (see Mt 7:11). Luke presents the gift of the holy Spirit as the response of the Father to the prayer of the Christian disciple.

* [11:19] **Your own people**: the Greek reads "your sons." Other Jewish exorcists (see Acts 19:13–20), who recognize that the power of God is active in the exorcism, would themselves convict the accusers of Jesus. See also note on Mt 12:27.

* [11:22] **One stronger**: i.e., Jesus. Cf. Lk 3:16 where John the Baptist identifies Jesus as "mightier than I."

* [11:27–28] The beatitude in Lk 11:28 should not be interpreted as a rebuke of the mother of Jesus; see note on Lk 8:21. Rather, it emphasizes (like Lk 2:35) that attentiveness to God's word is more important than biological relationship to Jesus.

* [11:29–32] The "sign of Jonah" in Luke is the preaching of the need for repentance by a prophet who comes from afar. Cf. Mt 12:38–42 (and see notes there) where the "sign of Jonah" is interpreted by Jesus as his death and resurrection.

* [11:37–54] This denunciation of the Pharisees (Lk 11:39–44) and the scholars of the law (Lk 11:45–52) is set by Luke in the context of Jesus' dining at the home of a Pharisee. Controversies with or reprimands of Pharisees are regularly set by Luke within the context of Jesus' eating with Pharisees (see Lk 5:29–39; 7:36–50; 14:1–24). A different compilation of similar sayings is found in Mt 23 (see also notes there).

* [11:44] **Unseen graves**: contact with the dead or with human bones or graves (see Nm 19:16) brought ritual impurity. Jesus presents the Pharisees as those who insidiously lead others astray through their seeming attention to the law.

* [11:45] **Scholars of the law**: see note on Lk 10:25.

* [11:49] **I will send to them prophets and apostles**: Jesus connects the mission of the church (apostles) with the mission of the Old Testament prophets who often suffered the rebuke of their contemporaries.

* [11:51] **From the blood of Abel to the blood of Zechariah**: the murder of Abel is the first murder recounted in the Old Testament (Gn 4:8). The Zechariah mentioned here may be the Zechariah whose murder is recounted in 2 Chr 24:20–22, the last murder presented in the Hebrew canon of the Old Testament.

* [12:1] See notes on Mk 8:15 and Mt 16:5–12.

* [12:2–9] Luke presents a collection of sayings of Jesus exhorting his followers to acknowledge him and his mission fearlessly and assuring them of God's protection even in times of persecution. They are paralleled in Mt 10:26–33.

* [12:5] **Gehenna**: see note on Mt 5:22.

* [12:6] **Two small coins**: the Roman copper coin, the assarion (Latin *as*), was worth about one-sixteenth of a denarius (see note on Lk 7:41).

* [12:10–12] The sayings about the holy Spirit are set in the context of fearlessness in the face of persecution (Lk 12:2–9; cf. Mt 12:31–32). The holy Spirit will be presented in Luke's second volume, the Acts of the Apostles, as the power responsible for the guidance of the Christian mission and the source of courage in the face of persecution.

* [12:13–34] Luke has joined together sayings contrasting those whose focus and trust in life is on material possessions, symbolized here by the rich fool of the parable (Lk 12:16–21), with those who recognize their complete dependence on God (Lk 12:21), those whose radical detachment from material possessions symbolizes their heavenly treasure (Lk 12:33–34).

* [12:21] **Rich in what matters to God**: literally, "rich for God."

* [12:35–48] This collection of sayings relates to Luke's understanding of the end time and the return of Jesus. Luke emphasizes for his readers the importance of being faithful to the instructions of Jesus in the period before the parousia.

* [12:45] **My master is delayed in coming**: this statement indicates that early Christian expectations for the imminent return of Jesus had undergone some modification. Luke cautions his readers against counting on such a delay and acting irresponsibly. Cf. the similar warning in Mt 24:48.

* [12:49–53] Jesus' proclamation of the kingdom is a refining and purifying fire. His message that meets with acceptance or rejection will be a source of conflict and dissension even within families.

* [12:50] **Baptism**: i.e., his death.

* [12:59] **The last penny**: Greek, **lepton**, a very small amount. Mt 5:26 has for "the last penny" the Greek word *kodrantēs* (Latin *quadrans*, "farthing").

---

* [13:1–5] The death of the Galileans at the hands of Pilate (Lk 13:1) and the accidental death of those on whom the tower fell (Lk 13:4) are presented by the Lucan Jesus as timely reminders of the need for all to repent, for the victims of these tragedies should not be considered outstanding sinners who were singled out for punishment.

* [13:1] The slaughter of the Galileans by Pilate is unknown outside Luke; but from what is known about Pilate from the Jewish historian Josephus, such a slaughter would be in keeping with the character of Pilate. Josephus reports that Pilate had disrupted a religious gathering of the Samaritans on Mount Gerizim with a slaughter of the participants (*Antiquities* 18:86–87), and that on another occasion Pilate had killed many Jews who had opposed him when he appropriated money from the temple treasury to build an aqueduct in Jerusalem (*Jewish War* 2:175–77; *Antiquities* 18:60–62).

* [13:4] Like the incident mentioned in Lk 13:1 nothing of this accident in Jerusalem is known outside Luke and the New Testament.

* [13:6–9] Following on the call to repentance in Lk 13:1–5, the parable of the barren fig tree presents a story about the continuing patience of

God with those who have not yet given evidence of their repentance (see Lk 3:8). The parable may also be alluding to the delay of the end time, when punishment will be meted out, and the importance of preparing for the end of the age because the delay will not be permanent (Lk 13:8–9).

* [13:10–17] The cure of the crippled woman on the sabbath and the controversy that results furnishes a parallel to an incident that will be reported by Luke in 14:1–6, the cure of the man with dropsy on the sabbath. A characteristic of Luke's style is the juxtaposition of an incident that reveals Jesus' concern for a man with an incident that reveals his concern for a woman; cf., e.g., Lk 7:11–17 and Lk 8:49–56.

* [13:15–16] If the law as interpreted by Jewish tradition allowed for the untying of bound animals on the sabbath, how much more should this woman who has been bound by Satan's power be freed on the sabbath from her affliction.

* [13:16] **Whom Satan has bound:** affliction and infirmity are taken as evidence of Satan's hold on humanity. The healing ministry of Jesus reveals the gradual wresting from Satan of control over humanity and the establishment of God's kingdom.

* [13:18–21] Two parables are used to illustrate the future proportions of the kingdom of God that will result from its deceptively small beginning in the preaching and healing ministry of Jesus. They are paralleled in Mt 13:31–33 and Mk 4:30–32.

* [13:22–30] These sayings of Jesus follow in Luke upon the parables of the kingdom (Lk 13:18–21) and stress that great effort is required for entrance into the kingdom (Lk 13:24) and that there is an urgency to accept the present opportunity to enter because the narrow door will not remain open indefinitely (Lk 13:25). Lying behind the sayings is the rejection of Jesus and his message by his Jewish contemporaries (Lk 13:26) whose places at table in the kingdom will be taken by Gentiles from the four corners of the world (Lk 13:29). Those called last (the Gentiles) will precede those to whom the invitation to enter was first extended (the Jews). See also Lk 14:15–24.

* [13:32] Nothing, not even Herod's desire to kill Jesus, stands in the way of Jesus' role in fulfilling God's will and in establishing the kingdom through his exorcisms and healings.

* [13:33] **It is impossible that a prophet should die outside of Jerusalem:** Jerusalem is the city of destiny and the goal of the journey of the prophet Jesus. Only when he reaches the holy city will his work be accomplished.

---

* [14:1–6] See note on Lk 13:10–17.

* [14:2] **Dropsy:** an abnormal swelling of the body because of the retention and accumulation of fluid.

* [14:5] **Your son or ox:** this is the reading of many of the oldest and most important New Testament manuscripts. Because of the strange collocation of **son** and **ox,** some copyists have altered it to "your ass or ox," on the model of the saying in Lk 13:15.

* [14:7–14] The banquet scene found only in Luke provides the opportunity for these teachings of Jesus on humility and presents a setting to display Luke's interest in Jesus' attitude toward the rich and the poor (see notes on Lk 4:18; 6:20–26; 12:13–34).

* [14:15–24] The parable of the great dinner is a further illustration of the rejection by Israel, God's chosen people, of Jesus' invitation to share in the banquet in the kingdom and the extension of the invitation to other Jews whose identification as the poor, crippled, blind, and lame (Lk 14:21) classifies them among those who recognize their need for salvation, and to Gentiles (Lk 14:23). A similar parable is found in Mt 22:1–10.

* [14:25–33] This collection of sayings, most of which are peculiar to Luke, focuses on the total dedication necessary for the disciple of Jesus. No attachment to family (Lk 14:26) or possessions (Lk 14:33) can stand in the way of the total commitment demanded of the disciple. Also, acceptance of the call to be a disciple demands readiness to accept persecution and suffering (Lk 14:27) and a realistic assessment of the hardships and costs (Lk 14:28–32).

* [14:26] **Hating his father . . . :** cf. the similar saying in Mt 10:37. The disciple's family must take second place to the absolute dedication involved in following Jesus (see also Lk 9:59–62).

* [14:34–35] The simile of salt follows the sayings of Jesus that demanded the disciple total dedication and detachment from family and possessions and illustrates the condition of one who does not display this total commitment. The halfhearted disciple is like salt that cannot serve its intended purpose. See the simile of salt in Mt 5:13 and the note there.

---

* [15:1–32] To the parable of the lost sheep (Lk 15:1–7) that Luke shares with Matthew (Mt 18:12–14), Luke adds two parables (the lost coin, Lk 15:8–10; the prodigal son, Lk 15:11–32) from his own special tradition to illustrate Jesus' particular concern for the lost and God's love for the repentant sinner.

* [15:8] **Ten coins:** literally, "ten drachmas." A drachma was a Greek silver coin.

---

* [16:1–8a] The parable of the dishonest steward has to be understood in the light of the Palestinian custom of agents acting on behalf of their masters and the usurious practices common to such agents. The dishonesty of the steward consisted in the squandering of his master's property (Lk 16:1) and not in any subsequent graft. The master

commends the dishonest steward who has forgone his own usurious commission on the business transaction by having the debtors write new notes that reflected only the real amount owed the master (i.e., minus the steward's profit). The dishonest steward acts in this way in order to ingratiate himself with the debtors because he knows he is being dismissed from his position (Lk 16:3). The parable, then, teaches the prudent use of one's material goods in light of an imminent crisis.

* [16:6] **One hundred measures**: literally, "one hundred baths." A bath is a Hebrew unit of liquid measurement equivalent to eight or nine gallons.

* [16:7] **One hundred kors**: a kor is a Hebrew unit of dry measure for grain or wheat equivalent to ten or twelve bushels.

* [16:8b–13] Several originally independent sayings of Jesus are gathered here by Luke to form the concluding application of the parable of the dishonest steward.

* [16:8b–9] The first conclusion recommends the prudent use of one's wealth (in the light of the coming of the end of the age) after the manner of the children of this world, represented in the parable by the dishonest steward.

* [16:9] **Dishonest wealth**: literally, "mammon of iniquity." Mammon is the Greek transliteration of a Hebrew or Aramaic word that is usually explained as meaning "that in which one trusts." The characterization of this wealth as **dishonest** expresses a tendency of wealth to lead one to dishonesty. **Eternal dwellings**: or, "eternal tents," i.e., heaven.

* [16:10–12] The second conclusion recommends constant fidelity to those in positions of responsibility.

* [16:13] The third conclusion is a general statement about the incompatibility of serving God and being a slave to riches. To be dependent upon wealth is opposed to the teachings of Jesus who counseled complete dependence on the Father as one of the characteristics of the Christian disciple (Lk 12:22–39). **God and mammon**: see note on Lk 16:9. Mammon is used here as if it were itself a god.

* [16:14–18] The two parables about the use of riches in chap. 16 are separated by several isolated sayings of Jesus on the hypocrisy of the Pharisees (Lk 16:14–15), on the law (Lk 16:16–17), and on divorce (Lk 16:18).

* [16:14–15] The Pharisees are here presented as examples of those who are slaves to wealth (see Lk 16:13) and, consequently, they are unable to serve God.

* [16:16] John the Baptist is presented in Luke's gospel as a transitional figure between the period of Israel, the time of promise, and the period of Jesus, the time of fulfillment. With John, the fulfillment of the Old Testament promises has begun.

* [16:19–31] The parable of the rich man and Lazarus again illustrates Luke's concern with

Jesus' attitude toward the rich and the poor. The reversal of the fates of the rich man and Lazarus (Lk 16:22–23) illustrates the teachings of Jesus in Luke's "Sermon on the Plain" (Lk 6:20–21, 24–25).

* [16:19] The oldest Greek manuscript of Luke dating from ca. A.D. 175–225 records the name of the rich man as an abbreviated form of "Nineveh," but there is very little textual support in other manuscripts for this reading. "Dives" of popular tradition is the Latin Vulgate's translation for "rich man" (Lk 16:19–31).

* [16:23] **The netherworld**: see note on Lk 10:15.

* [16:30–31] A foreshadowing in Luke's gospel of the rejection of the call to repentance even after Jesus' resurrection.

---

* [17:3] **Be on your guard**: the translation takes Lk 17:3a as the conclusion to the saying on scandal in Lk 17:1–2. It is not impossible that it should be taken as the beginning of the saying on forgiveness in Lk 17:3b–4.

* [17:7–10] These sayings of Jesus, peculiar to Luke, which continue his response to the apostles' request to increase their faith (Lk 17:5–6), remind them that Christian disciples can make no claim on God's graciousness; in fulfilling the exacting demands of discipleship, they are only doing their duty.

* [17:11–19] This incident recounting the thankfulness of the cleansed Samaritan leper is narrated only in Luke's gospel and provides an instance of Jesus holding up a non-Jew (Lk 17:18) as an example to his Jewish contemporaries (cf. Lk 10:33 where a similar purpose is achieved in the story of the good Samaritan). Moreover, it is the faith in Jesus manifested by the foreigner that has brought him salvation (Lk 17:19; cf. the similar relationship between faith and salvation in Lk 7:50; 8:48, 50).

* [17:11] **Through Samaria and Galilee**: or, "between Samaria and Galilee."

* [17:14] See note on Lk 5:14.

* [17:20–37] To the question of the Pharisees about the time of the coming of God's kingdom, Jesus replies that the kingdom is **among you** (Lk 17:20–21). The emphasis has thus been shifted from an imminent observable coming of the kingdom to something that is already present in Jesus' preaching and healing ministry. Luke has also appended further traditional sayings of Jesus about the unpredictable suddenness of the day of the Son of Man, and assures his readers that in spite of the delay of that day (Lk 12:45), it will bring judgment unexpectedly on those who do not continue to be vigilant.

* [17:21] **Among you**: the Greek preposition translated as **among** can also be translated as "within." In the light of other statements in Luke's gospel about the presence of the kingdom (see Lk 10:9, 11; 11:20) "among" is to be preferred.

* [17:36] The inclusion of Lk 17:36, "There will be two men in the field; one will be taken, the other left behind," in some Western manuscripts appears to be a scribal assimilation to Mt 24:40.

* [18:1–14] The particularly Lucan material in the travel narrative concludes with two parables on prayer. The first (Lk 18:1–8) teaches the disciples the need of persistent prayer so that they not fall victims to apostasy (Lk 18:8). The second (Lk 18:9–14) condemns the self-righteous, critical attitude of the Pharisee and teaches that the fundamental attitude of the Christian disciple must be the recognition of sinfulness and complete dependence on God's graciousness. The second parable recalls the story of the pardoning of the sinful woman (Lk 7:36–50) where a similar contrast is presented between the critical attitude of the Pharisee Simon and the love shown by the pardoned sinner.

* [18:5] **Strike me**: the Greek verb translated as strike means "to strike under the eye" and suggests the extreme situation to which the persistence of the widow might lead. It may, however, be used here in the much weaker sense of "to wear one out."

* [18:15–19:27] Luke here includes much of the material about the journey to Jerusalem found in his Marcan source (Lk 10:1–52) and adds to it the story of Zacchaeus (Lk 19:1–10) from his own particular tradition and the parable of the gold coins (minas) (Lk 19:11–27) from Q, the source common to Luke and Matthew.

* [18:15–17] The sayings on children furnish a contrast to the attitude of the Pharisee in the preceding episode (Lk 18:9–14) and that of the wealthy official in the following one (Lk 18:18–23) who think that they can lay claim to God's favor by their own merit. The attitude of the disciple should be marked by the receptivity and trustful dependence characteristic of the child.

* [18:22] Detachment from material possessions results in the total dependence on God demanded of one who would inherit eternal life. **Sell all that you have**: the original saying (cf. Mk 10:21) has characteristically been made more demanding by Luke's addition of "all."

* [18:31–33] The details included in this third announcement of Jesus' suffering and death suggest that the literary formulation of the announcement has been directed by the knowledge of the historical passion and death of Jesus.

* [18:31] **Everything written by the prophets… will be fulfilled**: this is a Lucan addition to the words of Jesus found in the Marcan source (Mk 10:32–34). Luke understands the events of Jesus' last days in Jerusalem to be the fulfillment of Old Testament prophecy, but, as is usually the case in Luke-Acts, the author does not specify which Old Testament prophets he has in mind; cf. Lk 24:25, 27, 44; Acts 3:8; 13:27; 26:22–23.

* [18:38] **Son of David**: the blind beggar identifies Jesus with a title that is related to Jesus' role as Messiah (see note on Lk 2:11). Through this Son of David, salvation comes to the blind man. Note the connection between salvation and house of David mentioned earlier in Zechariah's canticle (Lk 1:69). See also note on Mt 9:27.

* [19:1–10] The story of the tax collector Zacchaeus is unique to this gospel. While a rich man (Lk 19:2), Zacchaeus provides a contrast to the rich man of Lk 18:18–23 who cannot detach himself from his material possessions to become a follower of Jesus. Zacchaeus, according to Luke, exemplifies the proper attitude toward wealth: he promises to give half of his possessions to the poor (Lk 19:8) and consequently is the recipient of salvation (Lk 19:9–10).

* [19:9] **A descendant of Abraham**: literally, "a son of Abraham." The tax collector Zacchaeus, whose repentance is attested by his determination to amend his former ways, shows himself to be a true descendant of Abraham, the true heir to the promises of God in the Old Testament. Underlying Luke's depiction of Zacchaeus as a descendant of Abraham, the father of the Jews (Lk 1:73; 16:22–31), is his recognition of the central place occupied by Israel in the plan of salvation.

* [19:10] This verse sums up for Luke his depiction of the role of Jesus as savior in this gospel.

* [19:11–27] In this parable Luke has combined two originally distinct parables: (1) a parable about the conduct of faithful and productive servants (Lk 19:13, 15b–26) and (2) a parable about a rejected king (Lk 19:12, 14–15a, 27). The story about the conduct of servants occurs in another form in Mt 25:14–20. The story about the rejected king may have originated with a contemporary historical event. After the death of Herod the Great, his son Archelaus traveled to Rome to receive the title of king. A delegation of Jews appeared in Rome before Caesar Augustus to oppose the request of Archelaus. Although not given the title of king, Archelaus was made ruler over Judea and Samaria. As the story is used by Luke, however, it furnishes a correction to the expectation of the imminent end of the age and of the establishment of the kingdom in Jerusalem (Lk 19:11). Jesus is not on his way to Jerusalem to receive the kingly power; for that, he must go away and only after returning from the distant country (a reference to the parousia) will reward and judgment take place.

* [19:13] **Ten gold coins**: literally, "ten minas." A mina was a monetary unit that in ancient Greece was the equivalent of one hundred drachmas.

* [19:28–21:38] With the royal entry of Jesus into Jerusalem, a new section of Luke's gospel begins, the ministry of Jesus in Jerusalem before his death and resurrection. Luke suggests that this was a lengthy ministry in Jerusalem (Lk 19:47;

20:1; 21:37–38; 22:53) and it is characterized by Jesus' daily teaching in the temple (Lk 21:37–38). For the story of the entry of Jesus into Jerusalem, see also Mt 21:1–11; Mk 11:1–10; Jn 12:12–19 and the notes there.

* [19:38] **Blessed is the king who comes in the name of the Lord**: only in Luke is Jesus explicitly given the title **king** when he enters Jerusalem in triumph. Luke has inserted this title into the words of Ps 118:26 that heralded the arrival of the pilgrims coming to the holy city and to the temple. Jesus is thereby acclaimed as **king** (see Lk 1:32) and as the one **who comes** (see Mal 3:1; Lk 7:19). **Peace in heaven . . .** : the acclamation of the disciples of Jesus in Luke echoes the announcement of the angels at the birth of Jesus (Lk 2:14). The peace Jesus brings is associated with the salvation to be accomplished here in Jerusalem.

* [19:39] **Rebuke your disciples**: this command, found only in Luke, was given so that the Roman authorities would not interpret the acclamation of Jesus as king as an uprising against them; cf. Lk 23:2–3.

* [19:41–44] The lament for Jerusalem is found only in Luke. By not accepting Jesus (the one who mediates peace), Jerusalem will not find peace but will become the victim of devastation.

* [19:43–44] Luke may be describing the actual disaster that befell Jerusalem in A.D. 70 when it was destroyed by the Romans during the First Revolt.

* [19:45–46] Immediately upon entering the holy city, Jesus in a display of his authority enters the temple (see Mal 3:1–3) and lays claim to it after cleansing it that it might become a proper place for his teaching ministry in Jerusalem (Lk 19:47; 20:1; 21:37; 22:53). See Mt 21:12–17; Mk 11:15–19; Jn 2:13–17 and the notes there.

---

* [20:1–47] The Jerusalem religious leaders or their representatives, in an attempt to incriminate Jesus with the Romans and to discredit him with the people, pose a number of questions to him (about his authority, Lk 20:2; about payment of taxes, Lk 20:22; about the resurrection, Lk 20:28–33).

* [20:9–19] This parable about an absentee landlord and a tenant farmers' revolt reflects the social and economic conditions of rural Palestine in the first century. The synoptic gospel writers use the parable to describe how the rejection of the landlord's son becomes the occasion for the vineyard to be taken away from those to whom it was entrusted (the religious leadership of Judaism that rejects the teaching and preaching of Jesus; Lk 20:19).

* [20:15] **They threw him out of the vineyard and killed him**: cf. Mk 12:8. Luke has altered his Marcan source and reports that the murder of the son takes place outside the vineyard to reflect the tradition of Jesus' death outside the walls of the city of Jerusalem (see Heb 13:12).

* [20:20] **The governor**: i.e., Pontius Pilate, the Roman administrator responsible for the collection of taxes and maintenance of order in Palestine.

* [20:22] Through their question the agents of the Jerusalem religious leadership hope to force Jesus to take sides on one of the sensitive political issues of first-century Palestine. The issue of nonpayment of taxes to Rome becomes one of the focal points of the First Jewish Revolt (A.D. 66–70) that resulted in the Roman destruction of Jerusalem and the temple. See also note on Mt 22:15–22.

* [20:24] **Denarius**: a Roman silver coin (see note on Lk 7:41).

* [20:27] **Sadducees**: see note on Mt 3:7.

* [20:28–33] The Sadducees' question, based on the law of levirate marriage recorded in Dt 25:5–10, ridicules the idea of the resurrection. Jesus rejects their naive understanding of the resurrection (Lk 20:35–36) and then argues on behalf of the resurrection of the dead on the basis of the written law (Lk 20:37–38) that the Sadducees accept. See also notes on Mt 22:23–33.

* [20:36] **Because they are the ones who will rise**: literally, "being sons of the resurrection."

* [20:41–44] After successfully answering the three questions of his opponents, Jesus now asks them a question. Their inability to respond implies that they have forfeited their position and authority as the religious leaders of the people because they do not understand the scriptures. This series of controversies between the religious leadership of Jerusalem and Jesus reveals Jesus as the authoritative teacher whose words are to be listened to (see Lk 9:35). See also notes on Mt 22:41–46.

---

* [21:1–4] The widow is another example of the poor ones in this gospel whose detachment from material possessions and dependence on God leads to their blessedness (Lk 6:20). Her simple offering provides a striking contrast to the pride and pretentiousness of the scribes denounced in the preceding section (Lk 20:45–47). The story is taken from Mk 12:41–44.

* [21:5–36] Jesus' eschatological discourse in Luke is inspired by Mk 13 but Luke has made some significant alterations to the words of Jesus found there. Luke maintains, though in a modified form, the belief in the early expectation of the end of the age (see Lk 21:27, 28, 31, 32, 36), but, by focusing attention throughout the gospel on the importance of the day-to-day following of Jesus and by reinterpreting the meaning of some of the signs of the end from Mk 13 he has come to terms with what seemed to be an early Christian community to be a delay of the parousia. Mark, for example, described the desecration of the Jerusalem temple by the Romans (Mk 13:14) as the apocalyptic symbol (see Dn 9:27; 12:11) accompanying

the end of the age and the coming of the Son of Man. Luke (Lk 21:20–24), however, removes the apocalyptic setting and separates the historical destruction of Jerusalem from the signs of the coming of the Son of Man by a period that he refers to as "the times of the Gentiles" (Lk 21:24). See also notes on Mt 24:1–36 and Mk 13:1–37.

* [21:8] **The time has come:** in Luke, the proclamation of the imminent end of the age has itself become a false teaching.

* [21:12] **Before all this happens . . . :** to Luke and his community, some of the signs of the end just described (Lk 21:10–11) still lie in the future. Now in dealing with the persecution of the disciples (Lk 21:12–19) and the destruction of Jerusalem (Lk 21:20–24) Luke is pointing to eschatological signs that have already been fulfilled.

* [21:15] **A wisdom in speaking:** literally, "a mouth and wisdom."

* [21:20–24] The actual destruction of Jerusalem by Rome in A.D. 70 upon which Luke and his community look back provides the assurance that, just as Jesus' prediction of Jerusalem's destruction was fulfilled, so too will be his announcement of their final redemption (Lk 21:27–28).

* [21:24] **The times of the Gentiles:** a period of indeterminate length separating the destruction of Jerusalem from the cosmic signs accompanying the coming of the Son of Man.

* [21:26] **The powers of the heavens:** the heavenly bodies mentioned in Lk 21:25 and thought of as cosmic armies.

* [22:1–23:56a] The passion narrative. Luke is still dependent upon Mark for the composition of the passion narrative but has incorporated much of his own special tradition into the narrative. Among the distinctive sections in Luke are: (1) the tradition of the institution of the Eucharist (Lk 22:15–20); (2) Jesus' farewell discourse (Lk 22:21–38); (3) the mistreatment and interrogation of Jesus (Lk 22:63–71); (4) Jesus before Herod and his second appearance before Pilate (Lk 23:6–16); (5) words addressed to the women followers on the way to the crucifixion (Lk 23:27–32); (6) words to the penitent thief (Lk 23:39–41); (7) the death of Jesus (Lk 23:46, 47b–49). Luke stresses the innocence of Jesus (Lk 23:4, 14–15, 22) who is the victim of the powers of evil (Lk 22:3, 31, 53) and who goes to his death in fulfillment of his Father's will (Lk 22:42, 46). Throughout the narrative Luke emphasizes the mercy, compassion, and healing power of Jesus (Lk 22:51; 23:43) who does not go to death lonely and deserted, but is accompanied by others who follow him on the way of the cross (Lk 23:26–31, 49).

* [22:1] **Feast of Unleavened Bread, called the Passover:** see note on Mk 14:1.

* [22:3] **Satan entered into Judas:** see note on Lk 4:13.

* [22:10] **A man will meet you carrying a jar of water:** see note on Mk 14:13.

* [22:15] **This Passover:** Luke clearly identifies this last supper of Jesus with the apostles as a Passover meal that commemorated the deliverance of the Israelites from slavery in Egypt. Jesus reinterprets the significance of the Passover by setting it in the context of the kingdom of God (Lk 22:16). The "deliverance" associated with the Passover finds its new meaning in the blood that will be shed (Lk 22:20).

* [22:17] Because of a textual problem in Lk 22:19–20 some commentators interpret this cup as the eucharistic cup.

* [22:19c–20] **Which will be given…do this in memory of me:** these words are omitted in some important Western text manuscripts and a few Syriac manuscripts. Other ancient text types, including the oldest papyrus manuscript of Luke dating from the late second or early third century, contain the longer reading presented here. The Lucan account of the words of institution of the Eucharist bears a close resemblance to the words of institution in the Pauline tradition (see 1 Cor 11:23–26). See also notes on Mt 26:26–29; 26:27–28; and Mk 14:22–24.

* [22:24–38] The Gospel of Luke presents a brief farewell discourse of Jesus; compare the lengthy farewell discourses and prayer in Jn 13–17.

* [22:25] **'Benefactors':** this word occurs as a title of rulers in the Hellenistic world.

* [22:31–32] Jesus' prayer for Simon's faith and the commission to strengthen his brothers anticipates the post-resurrectional prominence of Peter in the first half of Acts, where he appears as the spokesman for the Christian community and the one who begins the mission to the Gentiles (Acts 10–11).

* [22:31] **All of you:** literally, "you." The translation reflects the meaning of the Greek text that uses a second person plural pronoun here.

* [22:36] In contrast to the ministry of the Twelve and of the seventy-two during the period of Jesus (Lk 9:3; 10:4), in the future period of the church the missionaries must be prepared for the opposition they will face in a world hostile to their preaching.

* [22:38] **It is enough!:** the farewell discourse ends abruptly with these words of Jesus spoken to the disciples when they take literally what was intended as figurative language about being prepared to face the world's hostility.

* [22:43–44] These verses, though very ancient, were probably not part of the original text of Luke. They are absent from the oldest papyrus manuscripts of Luke and from manuscripts of wide geographical distribution.

* [22:51] **And healed him:** only Luke recounts this healing of the injured servant.

* [22:61] Only Luke recounts that **the Lord turned and looked at Peter.** This look of Jesus leads to Peter's weeping bitterly over his denial (Lk 22:62).

* [22:66–71] Luke recounts one daytime trial of Jesus (Lk 22:66–71) and hints at some type of preliminary nighttime investigation (Lk 22:54–65). Mark (and Matthew who follows Mark) has transferred incidents of this day into the nighttime interrogation with the result that there appear to be two Sanhedrin trials of Jesus in Mark (and Matthew); see note on Mk 14:53.

* [22:66] **Sanhedrin:** the word is a Hebraized form of a Greek word meaning a "council," and refers to the elders, chief priests, and scribes who met under the high priest's leadership to decide religious and legal questions that did not pertain to Rome's interests. Jewish sources are not clear on the competence of the Sanhedrin to sentence and to execute during this period.

* [23:1–5, 13–25] Twice Jesus is brought before Pilate in Luke's account, and each time Pilate explicitly declares Jesus innocent of any wrongdoing (Lk 23:4, 14, 22). This stress on the innocence of Jesus before the Roman authorities is also characteristic of John's gospel (Jn 18:38; 19:4, 6). Luke presents the Jerusalem Jewish leaders as the ones who force the hand of the Roman authorities (Lk 23:1–2, 5, 10, 13, 18, 21, 23–25).

* [23:6–12] The appearance of Jesus before Herod is found only in this gospel. Herod has been an important figure in Luke (Lk 9:7–9; 13:31–33) and has been presented as someone who was curious about Jesus for a long time. His curiosity goes unrewarded. It is faith in Jesus, not curiosity, that is rewarded (Lk 7:50; 8:48, 50; 17:19).

* [23:17] This verse, "He was obliged to release one prisoner for them at the festival," is not part of the original text of Luke. It is an explanatory gloss from Mk 15:6 (also Mt 27:15) and is not found in many early and important Greek manuscripts. On its historical background, see notes on Mt 27:15–26.

* [23:26–32] An important Lucan theme throughout the gospel has been the need for the Christian disciple to follow in the footsteps of Jesus. Here this theme comes to the fore with the story of Simon of Cyrene who takes up the cross and follows Jesus (see Lk 9:23; 14:27) and with the large crowd who likewise follow Jesus on the way of the cross. See also note on Mk 15:21.

* [23:34] **[Then Jesus said, "Father, forgive them, they know not what they do."]:** this portion of Lk 23:34 does not occur in the oldest papyrus manuscript of Luke and in other early Greek manuscripts and ancient versions of wide geographical distribution.

* [23:39–43] This episode is recounted only in this gospel. The penitent sinner receives salvation through the crucified Jesus. Jesus' words to the penitent thief reveal Luke's understanding that the destiny of the Christian is "to be with Jesus."

* [23:44] **Noon...three in the afternoon:** literally, the sixth and ninth hours. See note on Mk 15:25.

* [23:47] **This man was innocent:** or, "This man was righteous."

* [24:1–53] The resurrection narrative in Luke consists of five sections: (1) the women at the empty tomb (Lk 23:56b–24:12); (2) the appearance to the two disciples on the way to Emmaus (Lk 24:13–35); (3) the appearance to the disciples in Jerusalem (Lk 24:36–43); (4) Jesus' final instructions (Lk 24:44–49); (5) the ascension (Lk 24:50–53). In Luke, all the resurrection appearances take place in and around Jerusalem; moreover, they are all recounted as having taken place on Easter Sunday. A consistent theme throughout the narrative is that the suffering, death, and resurrection of Jesus were accomplished in fulfillment of Old Testament promises and of Jewish hopes (Lk 24:19a, 21, 26–27, 44, 46). In his second volume, Acts, Luke will argue that Christianity is the fulfillment of the hopes of Pharisaic Judaism and its logical development (see Acts 24:10–21).

* [24:6] **He is not here, but he has been raised:** this part of the verse is omitted in important representatives of the Western text tradition, but its presence in other text types and the slight difference in wording from Mt 28:6 and Mk 16:6 argue for its retention.

* [24:9] The women in this gospel do not flee from the tomb and tell no one, as in Mk 16:8 but return and tell the disciples about their experience. The initial reaction to the testimony of the women is disbelief (Lk 24:11).

* [24:12] This verse is missing from the Western textual tradition but is found in the best and oldest manuscripts of other text types.

* [24:13–35] This episode focuses on the interpretation of scripture by the risen Jesus and the recognition of him in the breaking of the bread. The references to the quotations of scripture and explanation of it (Lk 24:25–27), the kerygmatic proclamation (Lk 24:34), and the liturgical gesture (Lk 24:30) suggest that the episode is primarily catechetical and liturgical rather than apologetic.

* [24:13] **Seven miles:** literally, "sixty stades." A stade was 607 feet. Some manuscripts read "160 stades" or more than eighteen miles. The exact location of Emmaus is disputed.

* [24:16] A consistent feature of the resurrection stories is that the risen Jesus was different and initially unrecognizable (Lk 24:37; Mk 16:12; Jn 20:14; 21:4).

* [24:26] **That the Messiah should suffer . . . :** Luke is the only New Testament writer to speak explicitly of a suffering Messiah (Lk 24:26, 46; Acts 3:18; 17:3; 26:23). The idea of a suffering Messiah is not found in the Old Testament or in other Jewish literature prior to the New Testament

period, although the idea is hinted at in Mk 8:31–33. See notes on Mt 26:63 and 26:67–68.

* [24:36–43, 44–49] The Gospel of Luke, like each of the other gospels (Mt 28:16–20; Mk 16:14–15; Jn 20:19–23), focuses on an important appearance of Jesus to the Twelve in which they are commissioned for their future ministry. As in Lk 24:6, 12, so in Lk 24:36, 40 there are omissions in the Western text.

* [24:39–42] The apologetic purpose of this story is evident in the concern with the physical details and the report that Jesus ate food.

* [24:46] See note on Lk 24:26.

* [24:49] **The promise of my Father**: i.e., the gift of the holy Spirit.

* [24:50–53] Luke brings his story about the time of Jesus to a close with the report of the ascension. He will also begin the story of the time of the church with a recounting of the ascension. In the gospel, Luke recounts the ascension of Jesus on Easter Sunday night, thereby closely associating it with the resurrection. In Acts 1:3, 9–11; 13:31 he historicizes the ascension by speaking of a forty-day period between the resurrection and the ascension. The Western text omits some phrases in Lk 24:51, 52 perhaps to avoid any chronological conflict with Acts 1 about the time of the ascension.

* [24:53] The Gospel of Luke ends as it began (Lk 1:9), in the Jerusalem temple.

THE GOSPEL ACCORDING TO JOHN

INTRODUCTION

The Gospel according to John is quite different in character from the three synoptic gospels. It is highly literary and symbolic. It does not follow the same order or reproduce the same stories as the synoptic gospels. To a much greater degree, it is the product of a developed theological reflection and grows out of a different circle and tradition. It was probably written in the 90s of the first century.

The Gospel of John begins with a magnificent prologue, which states many of the major themes and motifs of the gospel, much as an overture does for a musical work. The prologue proclaims Jesus as the preexistent and incarnate Word of God who has revealed the Father to us. The rest of the first chapter forms the introduction to the gospel proper and consists of the Baptist's testimony about Jesus (there is no baptism of Jesus in this gospel—John simply points him out as the Lamb of God), followed by stories of the call of the first disciples, in which various titles predicated of Jesus in the early church are presented.

The gospel narrative contains a series of "signs"—the gospel's word for the wondrous deeds of Jesus. The author is primarily interested in the significance of these deeds, and so interprets them for the reader by various reflections, narratives, and discourses. The first sign is the transformation of water into wine at Cana (Jn 2:1–11); this represents the replacement of the Jewish ceremonial washings and symbolizes the entire creative and transforming work of Jesus. The second sign, the cure of the royal official's son (Jn 4:46–54) simply by the word of Jesus at a distance, signifies the power of Jesus' life-giving word. The same theme is further developed by other signs, probably for a total of seven. The third sign, the cure of the paralytic at the pool with five porticoes in chap. 5, continues the theme of water offering newness of life. In the preceding chapter, to the woman at the well in Samaria Jesus had offered living water springing up to eternal life, a symbol of the revelation that Jesus brings; here Jesus' life-giving word replaces the water of the pool that failed to bring life. Jn 6 contains two signs, the multiplication of loaves and the walking on the waters of the Sea of Galilee. These signs are connected much as the manna and the crossing of the Red Sea are in the Passover narrative and symbolize a new exodus. The multiplication of the loaves is interpreted for the reader by the discourse that follows, where the bread of life is used first as a figure for the revelation of God in Jesus and then for the Eucharist. After a series of dialogues reflecting Jesus' debates with the Jewish authorities at the Feast of Tabernacles in Jn 7; 8, the sixth sign is presented in Jn 9, the sign of the young man born blind. This is a narrative illustration of the theme of conflict in the preceding two chapters; it proclaims the triumph of light over darkness, as Jesus is presented as the Light of the world. This is interpreted by a narrative of controversy between the Pharisees and the young man who had been given his sight by Jesus, ending with a discussion of spiritual blindness and spelling out the symbolic meaning of the cure. And finally, the seventh sign, the raising of Lazarus in chap. 11, is the climax of signs. Lazarus is presented as a token of the real life that Jesus, the Resurrection and the Life, who will now ironically be put to death because of his gift of life to Lazarus, will give to all who believe in him once he has been raised from the dead.

After the account of the seven signs, the "hour" of Jesus arrives, and the author passes from sign to reality, as he moves into the discourses in the upper room that interpret the meaning of the passion, death, and resurrection narratives that follow. The whole gospel of John is a progressive revelation of the glory of God's only Son, who comes to reveal the Father and then returns in glory to the Father. The author's purpose is clearly expressed in what must have been the original ending of the gospel at the end of Jn 20: "Now Jesus did many other signs in the presence of [his] disciples that are not written in this book. But these are written that you may [come to] believe that Jesus is the Messiah, the Son of God, and that through this belief you may have life in his name."

Critical analysis makes it difficult to accept the idea that the gospel as it now stands was written by one person. Jn 21 seems to have been added after the gospel was completed; it exhibits a Greek style somewhat different from that of the rest of the work. The prologue (Jn 1:1–18) apparently contains an independent hymn, subsequently adapted to serve as a preface to the gospel. Within the gospel itself there are also some inconsistencies, e.g., there are two endings of Jesus' discourse in the upper room (Jn 14:31; 18:1). To solve these problems, scholars have proposed various rearrangements that would produce a smoother order. However, most have come to the conclusion that the inconsistencies were probably produced by subsequent editing in which homogeneous materials were added to a shorter original.

Other difficulties for any theory of eyewitness authorship of the gospel in its present form are presented by its highly developed theology and by certain elements of its literary style. For instance, some of the wondrous deeds of Jesus have been worked into highly effective dramatic scenes (Jn 9); there has been a careful attempt to have these followed by discourses that explain them (Jn 5; 6); and the sayings of Jesus have been woven into long discourses of a quasi-poetic form resembling the speeches of personified Wisdom in the Old Testament.

The gospel contains many details about Jesus not found in the synoptic gospels, e.g., that Jesus engaged in a baptizing ministry (Jn 3:22) before he changed to one of preaching and signs; that Jesus' public ministry lasted for several years (see note on Jn 2:13); that he traveled to Jerusalem for various festivals and met serious opposition long before his death (Jn 2:14–25; 5; 7–8); and that he was put to death on the day before Passover (Jn 18:28). These events are not always in chronological order because of the development and editing that took place. However, the accuracy of much of the detail of the fourth gospel constitutes a strong argument that the Johannine tradition rests upon the testimony of an eyewitness. Although tradition identified this person as John, the son of Zebedee, most modern scholars find that the evidence does not support this.

The fourth gospel is not simply history; the narrative has been organized and adapted to serve the evangelist's theological purposes as well. Among them are the opposition to the synagogue of the day and to John the Baptist's followers, who tried to exalt their master at Jesus' expense, the desire to show that Jesus was the Messiah, and the desire to convince Christians that their religious belief and practice must be rooted in Jesus. Such theological purposes have impelled the evangelist to emphasize motifs that were not so clear in the synoptic account of Jesus' ministry, e.g., the explicit emphasis on his divinity.

The polemic between synagogue and church produced bitter and harsh invective, especially regarding the hostility toward Jesus of the authorities—Pharisees and Sadducees—who are combined and referred to frequently as "the Jews" (see note on Jn 1:19). These opponents are even described in Jn 8:44 as springing from their father the devil, whose conduct they imitate in opposing God by rejecting Jesus, whom God has sent. On the other hand, the author of this gospel seems to take pains to show that women are not inferior to men in the Christian community: the woman at the well in Samaria (Jn 4) is presented as a prototype of a missionary (Jn 4:4–42), and the first witness of the resurrection is a woman (Jn 20:11–18).

The final editing of the gospel and arrangement in its present form probably dates from between A.D. 90 and 100. Traditionally, Ephesus has been favored as the place of composition, though many support a location in Syria, perhaps the city of Antioch, while some have suggested other places, including Alexandria.

The principal divisions of the Gospel according to John are the following:

I.   Prologue (1:1–18)
II.   The Book of Signs (1:19–12:50)
III.   The Book of Glory (13:1–20:31)
IV.   Epilogue: The Resurrection Appearance in Galilee (21:1–25)

I. PROLOGUE[*]

CHAPTER 1

[1]In the beginning[*] was the
Word,
and the Word was with
God,
and the Word was God.[a]
[2]He was in the beginning
with God.
[3][*]All things came to be
through him,
and without him noth-
ing came to be.[b]
What came to be [4]through
him was life,
and this life was the
light of the human
race;[c]
[5][*]the light shines in the
darkness,[d]
and the darkness has
not overcome it.

[6][*]A man named John was
sent from God.[e] [7]He came for
testimony,[*] to testify to the
light, so that all might believe
through him.[f] [8]He was not
the light, but came to testify
to the light.[g] [9]The true light,
which enlightens everyone,
was coming into the world.[h]

[10]He was in the world,
and the world came to
be through him,
but the world did not
know him.
[11]He came to what was his
own,
but his own people[*] did
not accept him.

[12][i]But to those who did
accept him he gave power
to become children of God,
to those who believe in his
name, [13][*][j]who were born not
by natural generation nor by
human choice nor by a man's
decision but of God.

[14]And the Word became
flesh[*]
and made his dwelling
among us,
and we saw his glory,
the glory as of the
Father's only Son,
full of grace and truth.[k]

15*John testified to him and cried out, saying, "This was he of whom I said,[l] 'The one who is coming after me ranks ahead of me because he existed before me.'" 16From his fullness we have all received, grace in place of grace,* 17because while the law was given through Moses, grace and truth came through Jesus Christ.[m] 18No one has ever seen God. The only Son, God,* who is at the Father's side, has revealed him.[n]

II. THE BOOK OF SIGNS

John the Baptist's Testimony to Himself. 19*And this is the testimony of John. When the Jews* from Jerusalem sent priests and Levites [to him] to ask him, "Who are you?" 20*he admitted and did not deny it, but admitted,[o] "I am not the Messiah." 21So they asked him, "What are you then? Are you Elijah?"* And he said, "I am not." "Are you the Prophet?" He answered, "No."[p] 22So they said to him, "Who are you, so we can give an answer to those who sent us? What do you have to say for yourself?" 23He said:

> "I am 'the voice of one crying out in the desert,[q]
> "Make straight the way of the Lord,"'*

as Isaiah the prophet said." 24Some Pharisees* were also sent. 25They asked him, "Why then do you baptize if you are not the Messiah or Elijah or the Prophet?"[r] 26John answered them, "I baptize with water;* but there is one among you whom you do not recognize,[s] 27the one who is coming after me, whose sandal strap I am not worthy to untie." 28This happened in Bethany across the Jordan,* where John was baptizing.

John the Baptist's Testimony to Jesus. 29The next day he saw Jesus coming toward him and said, ("Behold, the Lamb of God,* who takes away the sin of the world.*) [30]"He is the one of whom I said,[u] 'A man is coming after me who ranks ahead of me because he existed before me.' [31]I did not know him,* but the reason why I came baptizing with water was that he might be made known to Israel." [32]John testified further, saying, "I saw the Spirit come down like a dove* from the sky and remain upon him. [33]I did not know him,[v] but the one who sent me to baptize with water told me, 'On whomever you see the Spirit come down and remain, he is the one who will baptize with the holy Spirit.'[w] [34]*Now I have seen and testified that he is the Son of God."

The First Disciples.[y] [35]The next day John was there again with two of his disciples, [36]and as he watched Jesus walk by, he said, ("Behold, the Lamb of God."* [37]The two disciples* heard what he said and followed Jesus. [38]Jesus turned and saw them following him and said to them, "What are you looking for?" They said to him, "Rabbi" (which translated means Teacher), "where are you staying?" [39]He said to them, "Come, and you will see." So they went and saw where he was staying, and they stayed with him that day. It was about four in the afternoon.* [40]Andrew, the brother of Simon Peter, was one of the two who heard John and followed Jesus. [41]He first found his own brother Simon and told him, "We have found the Messiah"* (which is translated Anointed).[z] [42]Then he brought him to Jesus. Jesus looked at him and said, "You are Simon the son of John;* you will be called Cephas" (which is translated Peter).[a]

[43]The next day he* decided to go to Galilee, and he found Philip. And Jesus said to him, "Follow me." [44]Now Philip

was from Bethsaida, the town of Andrew and Peter. ⁴⁵Philip found Nathanael and told him, "We have found the one about whom Moses wrote in the law, and also the prophets, Jesus son of Joseph, from Nazareth."ᵇ ⁴⁶But Nathanael said to him, "Can anything good come from Nazareth?" Philip said to him, "Come and see." ⁴⁷Jesus saw Nathanael coming toward him and said of him, "Here is a true Israelite.* There is no duplicity in him." ⁴⁸*ᶜNathanael said to him, "How do you know me?" Jesus answered and said to him, "Before Philip called you, I saw you under the fig tree." ⁴⁹Nathanael answered him, "Rabbi, you are the Son of God;* you are the King of Israel."ᵈ ⁵⁰Jesus answered and said to him, "Do you believe because I told you that I saw you under the fig tree?* You will see greater things than this." ⁵¹And he said to him, "Amen, amen,* I say to you, you will see the sky opened and the angels of God ascending and descending on the Son of Man."ᵉ

---

a. [1:1] 10:30; Gn 1:1–5; Jb 28:12–27; Prv 8:22–25; Wis 9:1–2; 1 Jn 1:1–2; Col 1:1, 15; Rev 3:14; 19:13.

b. [1:3] Ps 33:9; Wis 9:1; Sir 42:15; 1 Cor 8:6; Col 1:16; Heb 1:2; Rev 3:14.

c. [1:4] 5:26; 8:12; 1 Jn 1:2.

d. [1:5] 3:19; 8:12; 9:5; 12:35, 46; Wis 7:29–30; 1 Thes 5:4; 1 Jn 2:8.

e. [1:6] Mt 3:1; Mk 1:4; Lk 3:2–3.

f. [1:7] 1:19–34; 5:33.

g. [1:8] 5:35.

h. [1:9] 3:19; 8:12; 9:39; 12:46.

i. [1:12] 3:11–12; 5:43–44; 12:46–50; Gal 3:26; 4:6–7; Eph 1:5; 1 Jn 3:2.

j. [1:13] 3:5–6.

k. [1:14] 6:51; 14:10; 24:17; 25:8–9; 33:22; 34:6; Sir 24:4, 8; Is 60:1; Ez 43:7; Jl 4:17; Heb 2:14; 1 Jn 1:2; 4:2; 2 Jn 7.

l. [1:15] 1:30; 3:27–30.

m. [1:17] 7:19; Ex 31:18; 34:28.

n. [1:18] 5:37; 6:46; Ex 33:20; Jgs 13:21–22; 1 Tm 6:16; 1 Jn 4:12.

o. [1:20] 3:28; Lk 3:15; Acts 13:25.

p. [1:21] Dt 18:15, 18; 2 Kgs 2:11; Sir 48:10; Mal 3:1, 23; Mt 11:14; 17:11–13; Mk 9:13; Acts 3:22.

q. [1:23] Is 40:3; Mt 3:3; Mk 1:2; Lk 3:4.

r. [1:25] Ez 36:25; Zec 13:1; Mt 16:14.

s. [1:26] Mt 3:11; Mk 1:7–8; Lk 3:16; Acts 13:25.

t. [1:29] 1:36; Ex 12; Is 53:7; Rev 5–7; 17:14.

u. [1:30] 1:15; Mt 3:11; Mk 1:7; Lk 3:16.

v. [1:33] Sg 5:2; Is 11:2; Hos 11:11; Mt 3:16; Mk 1:10; Lk 3:21–22.

w. [1:33] Is 42:1; Mt 3:11; Mk 1:8; Lk 3:16.

x. [1:34] Is 42:1; Mt 3:17; Mk 1:11; Lk 9:35.

y. [1:35–51] Mt 4:18–22; Mk 1:16–20; Lk 5:1–11.

z. [1:41] 4:25.

a. [1:42] Mt 16:18; Mk 3:16.

b. [1:45] 21:2.

c. [1:48] Mi 4:4; Zec 3:10.

d. [1:49] 12:13; Ex 4:22; Dt 14:1; 2 Sm 7:14; Jb 1:6; 2:1; 38:7; Ps 2:7; 29:1; 89:27; Wis 2:18; Sir 4:10; Dn 3:92; Hos 11:1; Mt 14:33; 16:16; Mk 13:32.

e. [1:51] Gn 28:10–17; Dn 7:13.

CHAPTER 2

The Wedding at Cana. ¹On the third day there was a

wedding* in Cana* in Galilee, and the mother of Jesus was there.*[a] ²Jesus and his disciples were also invited to the wedding. ³When the wine ran short, the mother of Jesus said to him, "They have no wine." ⁴*[And] Jesus said to her, "Woman, how does your concern affect me? My hour has not yet come."*[b] ⁵His mother said to the servers, "Do whatever he tells you."*[c] ⁶*Now there were six stone water jars there for Jewish ceremonial washings,*[d] each holding twenty to thirty gallons. ⁷Jesus told them, "Fill the jars with water." So they filled them to the brim. ⁸Then he told them, "Draw some out now and take it to the headwaiter." So they took it. ⁹And when the headwaiter tasted the water that had become wine, without knowing where it came from (although the servers who had drawn the water knew), the headwaiter called the bridegroom ¹⁰and said to him,

"Everyone serves good wine first, and then when people have drunk freely, an inferior one; but you have kept the good wine until now." ¹¹Jesus did this as the beginning of his signs* in Cana in Galilee and so revealed his glory, and his disciples began to believe in him.*[e]

¹²*After this, he and his mother, [his] brothers, and his disciples went down to Capernaum and stayed there only a few days.*

Cleansing of the Temple.
¹³*Since the Passover* of the Jews was near,*[f] Jesus went up to Jerusalem. ¹⁴He found in the temple area those who sold oxen, sheep, and doves,* as well as the money-changers seated there.*[g] ¹⁵He made a whip out of cords and drove them all out of the temple area, with the sheep and oxen, and spilled the coins of the money-changers and overturned their tables, ¹⁶and to those who sold doves he

said, "Take these out of here, and stop making my Father's house a marketplace."[h] [17]His disciples recalled the words of scripture,[i] "Zeal for your house will consume me." [18]At this the Jews answered and said to him, "What sign can you show us for doing this?"[j] [19]Jesus answered and said to them,[*] [k]"Destroy this temple and in three days I will raise it up." [20]The Jews said, "This temple has been under construction for forty-six years,[*] and you will raise it up in three days?" [21]But he was speaking about the temple of his body. [22]Therefore, when he was raised from the dead, his disciples remembered that he had said this, and they came to believe the scripture and the word Jesus had spoken.[l]

[23]While he was in Jerusalem for the feast of Passover, many began to believe in his name when they saw the signs he was doing.[m] [24]But Jesus would not trust himself to them because he knew them all, [25]and did not need anyone to testify about human nature. He himself understood it well."[n]

a. [2:1] 4:46; Jgs 14:12; Tb 11:8.
b. [2:4] 7:30; 8:20; 12:23; 13:1; Jgs 11:12; 1 Kgs 17:18; 2 Kgs 3:13; 2 Chr 35:21; Hos 14:9; Mk 1:24; 5:7; 7:30; 8:20; 12:23; 13:1.
c. [2:5] Gn 41:55.
d. [2:6] 3:25; Lv 11:33; Am 9:13–14; Mt 15:2; 23:25–26; Mk 7:2–4; Lk 11:38.
e. [2:11] 4:54.
f. [2:13–22] Mt 21:12–13; Mk 11:15–17; Lk 19:45–46.
g. [2:14] Ex 30:11–16; Lv 5:7.
h. [2:16] Zec 14:21.
i. [2:17] Ps 69:9.
j. [2:18] 6:30.
k. [2:19] Mt 24:2; 26:61; 27:40; Mk 13:2; 14:58; 15:29; Lk 21:6; Acts 6:14.
l. [2:22] 5:39; 12:16; 14:26; 20:9; Mt 12:6; Lk 24:6–8; Rev 21:22.
m. [2:23] 4:45.
n. [2:25] 1 Kgs 8:39; Ps 33:15; 94:11; Sir 42:18; Jer 17:10; 20:12.

CHAPTER 3

Nicodemus.[*] [1a]Now there was a Pharisee named Nicodemus, a ruler of the Jews.[*] [2]He came to Jesus at night and said to him, "Rabbi, we know that you are a teacher who has come from God, for no one can do these signs that you are doing unless God is with him."[b] [3]Jesus answered and said to him, "Amen, amen, I say to you, no one can see the kingdom of God without being born[*] from above."[b] [4]Nicodemus said to him, "How can a person once grown old be born again? Surely he cannot reenter his mother's womb and be born again, can he?"[c] [5]Jesus answered, "Amen, amen, I say to you, no one can enter the kingdom of God without being born of water and Spirit.[d] [6]What is born of flesh is flesh and what is born of spirit is spirit.[e] [7]Do not be amazed that I told you, 'You must be born from above.' [8]The wind[*] blows where it wills, and you can hear the sound it makes, but you do not know where it comes from or where it goes; so it is with everyone who is born of the Spirit."[f] [9]Nicodemus answered and said to him, "How can this happen?" [10]Jesus answered and said to him, "You are the teacher of Israel and you do not understand this? [11]Amen, amen, I say to you, we speak of what we know and we testify to

what we have seen, but you people do not accept our testimony.[g] [12]If I tell you about earthly things and you do not believe, how will you believe if I tell you about heavenly things?[h] [13]No one has gone up to heaven except the one who has come down from heaven, the Son of Man.[i] [14]And just as Moses lifted up[*] the serpent in the desert, so must the Son of Man be lifted up,[j] [15]so that everyone who believes in him may have eternal life."

[16]For God so loved the world that he gave[*] his only Son, so that everyone who believes in him might not perish but might have eternal life.[k] [17]For God did not send his Son into the world to condemn[*] the world, but that the world might be saved through him.[l] [18]Whoever believes in him will not be condemned, but whoever does not believe has already been condemned, because he has not believed in the name of the only Son of God.[m]

[19*]And this is the verdict,[n]
that the light came into the
world, but people preferred
darkness to light, because
their works were evil. [20]For
everyone who does wicked
things hates the light and
does not come toward the
light, so that his works might
not be exposed.[o] [21]But whoever lives the truth comes to
the light, so that his works
may be clearly seen as done
in God.[p]

Final Witness of the Baptist.
[22*]After this, Jesus and his disciples went into the region of
Judea, where he spent some
time with them baptizing.[q]
[23]John was also baptizing in
Aenon near Salim,[*] because
there was an abundance of
water there, and people came
to be baptized, [24*r]for John
had not yet been impris-
oned. [25]Now a dispute arose
between the disciples of John
and a Jew[*] about ceremonial
washings. [26]So they came
to John and said to him,
"Rabbi, the one who was
with you across the Jordan,
to whom you testified, here
he is baptizing and everyone 4:2
is coming to him."[s] [27]John
answered and said, "No one
can receive anything except
what has been given him
from heaven.[t] [28]You yourselves can testify that I said
[that] I am not the Messiah,
but that I was sent before
him.[u] [29]The one who has the
bride is the bridegroom; the
best man,[*] who stands and
listens to him, rejoices greatly
at the bridegroom's voice. So
this joy of mine has been
made complete.[v] [30]He must
increase; I must decrease."[w]

The One from Heaven.[*]
[31]The one who comes from
above is above all. The one
who is of the earth is earthly
and speaks of earthly things.
But the one who comes from
heaven [is above all].[x] [32]He
testifies to what he has seen
and heard, but no one accepts
his testimony.[y] [33]Whoever

does accept his testimony certifies that God is trustworthy.[z] ³⁴For the one whom God sent speaks the words of God. He does not ration his gift* of the Spirit. ³⁵The Father loves the Son and has given everything over to him.[a] ³⁶Whoever believes in the Son has eternal life, but whoever disobeys the Son will not see life, but the wrath of God remains upon him.[b]

a. [3:1] 7:50–51; 19:39.
b. [3:2] 9:4, 16, 33; 10:21; 11:10; 13:30; Mt 22:16; Mk 12:14; Lk 20:21.
c. [3:4] 1:13.
d. [3:5] 1:32; 7:39; 19:30, 34–35; Is 32:15; 44:3; Ez 36:25–27; Jl 3:1–2.
e. [3:6] 6:63; 1 Cor 15:44–50.
f. [3:8] Eccl 11:4–5; Acts 2:2–4.
g. [3:11] 3:32, 34; 8:14; Mt 11:27.
h. [3:12] 6:62–65; Wis 9:16–17; 1 Cor 15:40; 2 Cor 5:1; Phil 2:10; 3:19–20.
i. [3:13] 1:18; 6:62; Dn 7:13; Rom 10:6; Eph 4:9.
j. [3:14] 8:28; 12:32, 34; Nm 21:4–9; Wis 16:5–7.
k. [3:16] 1 Jn 4:9.
l. [3:17] 5:22, 30; 8:15–18; 12:47.
m. [3:18] 5:24; Mk 16:16.
n. [3:19] 1:5, 9–11; 8:12; 9:5.
o. [3:20] Jb 24:13–17.
p. [3:21] Gn 47:29 LXX; Jos 2:14 LXX; 2 Sm 2:6 LXX; 15:20 LXX; Tb 4:6 LXX; 13:6; Is 26:10 LXX; Mt 5:14–16.
q. [3:22–23] 4:1–2.
r. [3:24] Mt 4:12; 14:3; Mk 1:14; 6:17; Lk 3:20.
s. [3:26] 1:26, 32–34, 36.
t. [3:27] 19:11; 1 Cor 4:7; 2 Cor 3:5; Heb 5:4.
u. [3:28] 1:20–23; Lk 3:15.
v. [3:29] 15:11; 17:13; Mt 9:15.
w. [3:30] 2 Sm 3:1.
x. [3:31] 8:23.
y. [3:32] 3:11.
z. [3:33–34] 8:26; 12:44–50; 1 Jn 5:10.
a. [3:35] 13:3; Mt 11:27; 28:18; Lk 10:22.
b. [3:36] 3:16; 1 Jn 5:13.

CHAPTER 4

¹Now when Jesus learned that the Pharisees had heard that Jesus was making and baptizing more disciples than John ²(although Jesus himself was not baptizing, just his disciples),* ³he left Judea and returned to Galilee.

The Samaritan Woman. ⁴He had to* pass through Samaria. ⁵So he came to a town of Samaria called Sychar,* near the plot of land that Jacob had given to his son Joseph.[a] ⁶Jacob's well was there. Jesus, tired from his journey, sat down there at the well. It was about noon.

⁷A woman of Samaria came to draw water. Jesus said to her, "Give me a drink." ⁸His disciples had gone into the town to buy food. ⁹The Samaritan woman said to him, "How can you, a Jew, ask me, a Samaritan woman, for a drink?"[b] (For Jews use nothing in common with Samaritans.) ¹⁰*Jesus answered and

said to her,[c] "If you knew the gift of God and who is saying to you, 'Give me a drink,' you would have asked him and he would have given you living water." [11][The woman] said to him, "Sir,[*] you do not even have a bucket and the well is deep; where then can you get this living water? [12]Are you greater than our father Jacob, who gave us this well and drank from it himself with his children and his flocks?"[d] [13]Jesus answered and said to her, "Everyone who drinks this water will be thirsty again; [14]but whoever drinks the water I shall give will never thirst; the water I shall give will become in him a spring of water welling up to eternal life."[e] [15]The woman said to him, "Sir, give me this water, so that I may not be thirsty or have to keep coming here to draw water."

[16]Jesus said to her, "Go call your husband and come back." [17]The woman answered and said to him, "I do not have a husband." Jesus answered her, "You are right in saying, 'I do not have a husband.' [18]For you have had five husbands, and the one you have now is not your husband. What you have said is true."[f] [19]The woman said to him, "Sir, I can see that you are a prophet.[g] [20]Our ancestors worshiped on this mountain;[*] but you people say that the place to worship is in Jerusalem."[h] [21]Jesus said to her, "Believe me, woman, the hour is coming when you will worship the Father neither on this mountain nor in Jerusalem. [22]You people worship what you do not understand; we worship what we understand, because salvation is from the Jews.[i] [23]But the hour is coming, and is now here, when true worshipers will worship the Father in Spirit and truth;[*] and indeed the Father seeks such people to worship him. [24]God is Spirit, and those who worship him must worship

in Spirit and truth."[j] [25]"The woman said to him, "I know that the Messiah is coming,[k] the one called the Anointed; when he comes, he will tell us everything." [26]Jesus said to her, "I am he,* the one who is speaking with you."[l]

[27]At that moment his disciples returned, and were amazed that he was talking with a woman,* but still no one said, "What are you looking for?" or "Why are you talking with her?" [28]The woman left her water jar and went into the town and said to the people, [29]"Come see a man who told me everything I have done. Could he possibly be the Messiah?" [30]They went out of the town and came to him. [31]Meanwhile, the disciples urged him, "Rabbi, eat." [32]But he said to them, "I have food to eat of which you do not know." [33]So the disciples said to one another, "Could someone have brought him something to eat?" [34]Jesus said to them,

"My food is to do the will of the one who sent me and to finish his work.[m] [35]Do you not say, 'In four months* the harvest will be here'? I tell you, look up and see the fields ripe for the harvest.[n] [36]The reaper is already* receiving his payment and gathering crops for eternal life, so that the sower and reaper can rejoice together.[o] [37]For here the saying is verified that 'One sows and another reaps.'[p] [38]I sent you to reap what you have not worked for; others have done the work, and you are sharing the fruits of their work."

[39]Many of the Samaritans of that town began to believe in him (because of the word of the woman*) who testified, "He told me everything I have done." ([40]When the Samaritans came to him, they invited him to stay with them; and he stayed there two days.) [41]Many more began to believe in him because of his word, [42]and they said to the woman, "We no longer

believe because of your word; for we have heard for ourselves, and we know that this is truly the savior of the world."[q]

Return to Galilee. [43*]After the two days, he left there for Galilee. [44*r]For Jesus himself testified that a prophet has no honor in his native place. [45]When he came into Galilee, the Galileans welcomed him, since they had seen all he had done in Jerusalem at the feast; for they themselves had gone to the feast.

Second Sign at Cana. [46s]Then he returned to Cana in Galilee, where he had made the water wine. Now there was a royal official whose son was ill in Capernaum. [47]When he heard that Jesus had arrived in Galilee from Judea, he went to him and asked him to come down and heal his son, who was near death. [48]Jesus said to him, "Unless you people see signs and wonders, you will not believe."[t] [49]The royal official said to him, "Sir, come down before my child dies." [50]Jesus said to him, "You may go; your son will live." The man believed what Jesus said to him and left. [u] [51]While he was on his way back, his slaves met him and told him that his boy would live. [52]He asked them when he began to recover. They told him, "The fever left him yesterday, about one in the afternoon." [53]The father realized that just at that time Jesus had said to him, "Your son will live," and he and his whole household came to believe. [54][Now] this was the second sign Jesus did when he came to Galilee from Judea.[v]

---

a. [4:5] Gn 33:18–19; 48:22; Jos 24:32.
b. [4:9] Sir 50:25–26; Mt 10:5.
c. [4:10] Sir 24:20–21; Is 55:1; Jer 2:13.
d. [4:12] 8:53; Mt 12:41.
e. [4:14] 6:35, 58; 7:37–39; Is 44:3; 49:10; Jl 4:18; Rev 7:16; 21:6.
f. [4:18] 2 Kgs 17:24–34.
g. [4:19] 9:17; Hos 1:3.
h. [4:20] Dt 11:29; 27:4; Jos 8:33; Ps 122:1–5.
i. [4:22] 2 Kgs 17:27; Ps 76:2–3.
j. [4:24] 2 Cor 3:17.
k. [4:25] 1:41.
l. [4:26] 9:37.
m. [4:34] 5:30, 36; 6:38; 9:4; 17:4.
n. [4:35] Mt 9:37–38; Lk 10:2; Rev 14:15.
o. [4:36] Ps 126:5–6; Am 9:13–14.

p. [4:37] Dt 20:6; 28:30; Jb 31:8; Mi 6:15.
q. [4:42] 1 Jn 4:14.
r. [4:44] Mt 13:57; Mk 6:4; Lk 4:24.
s. [4:46–54] 2:1–11; Mt 8:5–13; 15:21–28; Mk 7:24–30; Lk 7:1–10.
t. [4:48] 2:18, 23; Wis 8:8; Mt 12:38; 1 Cor 1:22.
u. [4:50] 1 Kgs 17:23.
v. [4:54] 2:11.

CHAPTER 5*

Cure on a Sabbath. ¹After this, there was a feast* of the Jews, and Jesus went up to Jerusalem.ᵃ ²Now there is in Jerusalem at the Sheep [Gate]* a pool called in Hebrew Bethesda, with five porticoes.ᵇ ³In these lay a large number of ill, blind, lame, and crippled.* [⁴]* ⁵One man was there who had been ill for thirty-eight years. ⁶When Jesus saw him lying there and knew that he had been ill for a long time, he said to him, "Do you want to be well?" ⁷The sick man answered him, "Sir, I have no one to put me into the pool when the water is stirred up; while I am on my way, someone else gets down there before me." ⁸Jesus said to him, "Rise, take up your mat,

and walk."ᶜ ⁹Immediately the man became well, took up his mat, and walked.ᵈ

Now that day was a sabbath. ¹⁰So the Jews said to the man who was cured, "It is the sabbath, and it is not lawful for you to carry your mat."ᵉ ¹¹He answered them, "The man who made me well told me, 'Take up your mat and walk.'" ¹²They asked him, "Who is the man who told you, 'Take it up and walk'?" ¹³The man who was healed did not know who it was, for Jesus had slipped away, since there was a crowd there.ᶠ ¹⁴After this Jesus found him in the temple area and said to him,ᵍ "Look, you are well; do not sin any more, so that nothing worse may happen to you." ¹⁵The man went and told the Jews that Jesus was the one who had made him well. ¹⁶Therefore, the Jews began to persecute Jesus because he did this on a sabbath.ʰ ¹⁷But Jesus answered them,ⁱ "My Father is at work until now, so I am at work." [18]For this reason the Jews tried all the more to kill him, because he not only broke the sabbath but he also called God his own father, making himself equal to God.[j]

The Work of the Son. [19*]Jesus answered and said to them, "Amen, amen, I say to you, a son cannot do anything on his own, but only what he sees his father doing;[k] for what he does, his son will do also. [20]For the Father loves his Son and shows him everything that he himself does, and he will show him greater works than these, so that you may be amazed.[l] [21]For just as the Father raises the dead and gives life,* so also does the Son give life to whomever he wishes.[m] [22]Nor does the Father judge anyone, but he has given all judgment* to his Son,[n] [23]so that all may honor the Son just as they honor the Father. Whoever does not honor the Son does not honor the Father who sent him. [24]Amen, amen, I say to you, whoever hears my word and believes in the one who sent me has eternal life and will not come to condemnation, but has passed from death to life.[o] [25]Amen, amen, I say to you, the hour is coming and is now here when the dead will hear the voice of the Son of God, and those who hear will live.[p] [26]For just as the Father has life in himself, so also he gave to his Son the possession of life in himself.[q] [27]And he gave him power to exercise judgment, because he is the Son of Man.[r] [28*]Do not be amazed at this, because the hour is coming in which all who are in the tombs will hear his voice[s] [29]and will come out, those who have done good deeds to the resurrection of life, but those who have done wicked deeds to the resurrection of condemnation.[t]

[30]"I cannot do anything on my own; I judge as I hear, and

my judgment is just, because I do not seek my own will but the will of the one who sent me.[u]

Witnesses to Jesus. [31v]"If I testify on my own behalf, my testimony cannot be verified. [32]But there is another[*] who testifies on my behalf, and I know that the testimony he gives on my behalf is true. [33]You sent emissaries to John, and he testified to the truth.[w] [34]I do not accept testimony from a human being, but I say this so that you may be saved.[x] [35]He was a burning and shining lamp,[*] and for a while you were content to rejoice in his light.[y] [36]But I have testimony greater than John's. The works that the Father gave me to accomplish, these works that I perform testify on my behalf that the Father has sent me.[z] [37]Moreover, the Father who sent me has testified on my behalf. But you have never heard his voice nor seen his form,[a] [38]and you do not have his word remaining in you, because you do not believe in the one whom he has sent.[b] ([39]You search[*] the scriptures, because you think you have eternal life through them; even they testify on my behalf.[c] [40]But you do not want to come to me to have life.)

Unbelief of Jesus' Hearers. [41]"I do not accept human praise;[*] [42]moreover, I know that you do not have the love of God in you.[d] [43]I came in the name of my Father, but you do not accept me; yet if another comes in his own name, you will accept him.[e] [44]How can you believe, when you accept praise from one another and do not seek the praise that comes from the only God?[f] [45]Do not think that I will accuse you before the Father: the one who will accuse you is Moses, in whom you have placed your hope.[g] [46]For if you had believed Moses, you would have believed me, because he wrote about me.[h] 47But if you do not believe his writings, how will you believe my words?"

---

a. [5:1] 6:4.
b. [5:2] Neh 3:1, 32; 12:39.
c. [5:8] Mt 9:6; Mk 2:11; Lk 5:24; Acts 3:6.
d. [5:9] Mk 2:12; Lk 5:25; 9:14.
e. [5:10] Ex 20:8; Jer 17:21–27; Mk 3:2; Lk 13:10; 14:1.
f. [5:13] Mt 8:18; 13:36; Mk 4:36; 7:17.
g. [5:14] 8:11; 9:2; Ez 18:20.
h. [5:17] 7:23; Mt 12:8.
i. [5:17] Ex 20:11.
j. [5:18] 7:1, 25; 8:37, 40; 10:33, 36; 14:28; Gn 3:5–6; Wis 2:16; Mt 26:4; 2 Thes 2:4.
k. [5:19] 3:34; 8:26; 12:49; 9:4; 10:30.
l. [5:20] 3:35.
m. [5:21] 11:25; Dt 32:39; 1 Sm 2:6; 2 Kgs 5:7; Tb 13:2; Wis 16:13; Is 26:19; Dn 7:10, 13; 12:2; Rom 4:17; 2 Cor 1:9.
n. [5:22] Acts 10:42; 17:31.
o. [5:24] 3:18; 8:51; 1 Jn 3:14.
p. [5:25] 5:28; 8:51; 11:25–26; Eph 2:1; 5:14; Rev 3:1.
q. [5:26] 1:4; 1 Jn 5:11.
r. [5:27] 5:22; Dn 7:13, 22; Mt 25:31; Lk 21:36.
s. [5:28] 11:43.
t. [5:29] Dn 12:2; Mt 16:27; 25:46; Acts 24:15; 2 Cor 5:10.
u. [5:30] 6:38.
v. [5:31–32] 8:13–14, 18.
w. [5:33] 1:19–27; Mt 11:10–11.
x. [5:34] 1 Jn 5:9.
y. [5:35] 1:8; Ps 132:17; Sir 48:1.
z. [5:36] 10:25.
a. [5:37] 8:18; Dt 4:12, 15; 1 Jn 5:9.
b. [5:38] 1 Jn 2:14.
c. [5:39] 12:16; 19:28; 20:9; Lk 24:27, 44; 1 Pt 1:10.
d. [5:42] 1 Jn 2:15.
e. [5:43] Mt 24:5, 24.
f. [5:44] 12:43.
g. [5:45] Dt 31:26.
h. [5:46] 5:39; Dt 18:15; Lk 16:31; 24:44.

CHAPTER 6

Multiplication of the Loaves.[*] 1aAfter this, Jesus went across the Sea of Galilee [of Tiberias].[*] 2A large crowd followed him, because they saw the signs he was performing on the sick. 3Jesus went up on the mountain, and there he sat down with his disciples. 4The Jewish feast of Passover was near.[b] 5*When Jesus raised his eyes and saw that a large crowd was coming to him, he said to Philip,[c] "Where can we buy enough food for them to eat?" 6*He said this to test him, because he himself knew what he was going to do. 7Philip answered him, "Two hundred days' wages* worth of food would not be enough for each of them to have a little [bit]."[d] 8One of his disciples, Andrew, the brother of Simon Peter, said to him, 9"There is a boy here who has five barley loaves* and two fish; but what good are these for so many?"[e] 10Jesus said, "Have the people recline." Now there was a great deal of grass* in that place. So the men reclined, about five thousand in number.*f* 11Then Jesus took the loaves, gave thanks, and distributed them to those who were reclining, and also as much of the fish as they wanted.*g* 12When they had had their fill, he said to his disciples, "Gather the fragments left over, so that nothing will be wasted." 13So they collected them, and filled twelve wicker baskets* with fragments from the five barley loaves that had been more than they could eat. 14When the people saw the sign he had done, they said, "This is truly the Prophet,* the one who is to come into the world."*h* 15Since Jesus knew that they were going to come and carry him off to make him king, he withdrew again to the mountain alone.*i*

Walking on the Water.*

16jWhen it was evening, his disciples went down to the sea, 17embarked in a boat, and went across the sea to Capernaum. It had already grown dark, and Jesus had not yet come to them. 18The sea was stirred up because a strong wind was blowing. 19When they had rowed about three or four miles, they saw Jesus walking on the sea* and coming near the boat, and they began to be afraid.*k* 20But he said to them, "It is I.* Do not be afraid." 21They wanted to take him into the boat, but the boat immediately arrived at the shore to which they were heading.

The Bread of Life Discourse.

22*The next day, the crowd that remained across the sea saw that there had been only one boat there, and that Jesus had not gone along with his disciples in the boat, but only his disciples had left. 23*Other boats came from Tiberias near the place where they had eaten the bread when the Lord gave thanks. 24When the crowd saw that neither Jesus nor his disciples were there, they themselves got into boats and came to Capernaum looking for Jesus. [25]And when they found him across the sea they said to him, "Rabbi, when did you get here?" [26]Jesus answered them and said, "Amen, amen, I say to you, you are looking for me not because you saw signs but because you ate the loaves and were filled. [27]Do not work for food that perishes but for the food that endures for eternal life,[*] which the Son of Man will give you. For on him the Father, God, has set his seal."[l] [28]So they said to him, "What can we do to accomplish the works of God?" [29]Jesus answered and said to them, "This is the work of God, that you believe in the one he sent." [30]So they said to him, "What sign can you do, that we may see and believe in you? What can you do?[m] [31*]Our ancestors ate manna in the desert, as it is written:[n]

'He gave them bread from
heaven to eat.'"

[32]So Jesus said to them, "Amen, amen, I say to you, it was not Moses who gave the bread from heaven; my Father gives you the true bread from heaven.[o] [33]For the bread of God is that which comes down from heaven and gives life to the world."

[34p]So they said to him, "Sir, give us this bread always." [35*]Jesus said to them, "I am the bread of life; whoever comes to me will never hunger, and whoever believes in me will never thirst.[q] [36]But I told you that although you have seen [me], you do not believe.[r] [37]Everything that the Father gives me will come to me, and I will not reject anyone who comes to me, [38]because I came down from heaven not to do my own will but the will of the one who sent me.[s] [39]And this is the will of the one who sent me, that I should not lose anything

of what he gave me, but that I should raise it [on] the last day.*[t] [40]For this is the will of my Father, that everyone who sees the Son and believes in him may have eternal life, and I shall raise him [on] the last day."[u]

[41]The Jews murmured about him because he said, "I am the bread that came down from heaven," [42]and they said, "Is this not Jesus, the son of Joseph? Do we not know his father and mother? Then how can he say, 'I have come down from heaven'?"[v] [43]Jesus answered and said to them, "Stop murmuring* among yourselves.[w] [44]No one can come to me unless the Father who sent me draw him, and I will raise him on the last day. [45]It is written in the prophets:

'They shall all be taught by God.'

Everyone who listens to my Father and learns from him comes to me.[x] [46]Not that anyone has seen the Father except the one who is from God; he has seen the Father.[y] [47]Amen, amen, I say to you, whoever believes has eternal life. [48]I am the bread of life. [49]Your ancestors ate the manna in the desert, but they died;[z] [50]this is the bread that comes down from heaven so that one may eat it and not die. [51]I am the living bread that came down from heaven; (whoever eats this bread will live forever; and the bread that I will give is my flesh for the life of the world."[a])

[52]The Jews quarreled among themselves, saying, "How can this man give us [his] flesh to eat?" [53]Jesus said to them, "Amen, amen, I say to you, unless you eat the flesh of the Son of Man and drink his blood, you do not have life within you. ([54]Whoever eats* my flesh and drinks my blood has eternal life, and I will raise him on the last day.) [55]For my flesh is true food, and my blood is true drink.

⁵⁶Whoever eats my flesh and drinks my blood remains in me and I in him. ⁵⁷Just as the living Father sent me and I have life because of the Father, so also the one who feeds on me will have life because of me.*ᵇ* ⁵⁸This is the bread that came down from heaven. Unlike your ancestors who ate and still died, whoever eats this bread will live forever." ⁵⁹These things he said while teaching in the synagogue in Capernaum.

The Words of Eternal Life.ˣ ⁶⁰Then many of his disciples who were listening said, "This saying is hard; who can accept it?" ⁶¹Since Jesus knew that his disciples were murmuring about this, he said to them, "Does this shock you? ⁶²What if you were to see the Son of Man ascending to where he was before?ˣ ⁶³It is the spirit that gives life, while the flesh* is of no avail. The words I have spoken to you are spirit and life. ⁶⁴But there are some of you who do not believe." Jesus knew from the beginning the ones who would not believe and the one who would betray him.*ᶜ* ⁶⁵And he said, "For this reason I have told you that no one can come to me unless it is granted him by my Father."

⁶⁶As a result of this, many [of] his disciples returned to their former way of life and no longer accompanied him. ⁶⁷Jesus then said to the Twelve, "Do you also want to leave?" ⁶⁸Simon Peter answered him, "Master, to whom shall we go? You have the words of eternal life. ⁶⁹We have come to believe and are convinced that you are the Holy One of God."*ᵈ* ⁷⁰Jesus answered them, "Did I not choose you twelve? Yet is not one of you a devil?" ⁷¹He was referring to Judas, son of Simon the Iscariot; it was he who would betray him, one of the Twelve.*ᵉ*

a. [6:1–13] Mt 14:13–21; Mk 6:32–44; Lk 9:10–17.
b. [6:4] 2:13; 11:55.

c. [6:5] Nm 11:13.
d. [6:7] Mt 20:2.
e. [6:9] 2 Kgs 4:42–44.
f. [6:10] Mt 14:21; Mk 6:44.
g. [6:11] 21:13.
h. [6:14] Dt 18:15, 18; Mal 3:1, 23; Acts 3:22.
i. [6:15] 18:36.
j. [6:16–21] Mt 14:22–27; Mk 6:45–52.
k. [6:19] Jb 9:8; Ps 29:3–4; 77:20; Is 43:16.
l. [6:27] 6:50, 51, 54, 58.
m. [6:30] Mt 16:1–4; Lk 11:29–30.
n. [6:31] Ex 16:4–5; Nm 11:7–9; Ps 78:24.
o. [6:32] Mt 6:11.
p. [6:34] 4:15.
q. [6:35] Is 55:1–3; Am 8:11–13.
r. [6:36] 20:29.
s. [6:38] 4:34; Mt 26:39; Heb 10:9.
t. [6:39] 10:28–29; 17:12; 18:9.
u. [6:40] 1 Jn 2:25.
v. [6:42] Mt 13:54–57; Mk 6:1–4; Lk 4:22.
w. [6:43] Ex 16:2, 7, 8; Lk 4:22.
x. [6:45] Is 54:13; Jer 31:33–34.
y. [6:46] 1:18; 7:29; Ex 33:20.
z. [6:49] 1 Cor 10:3, 5.
a. [6:51] Mt 26:26–27; Lk 22:19.
b. [6:57] 5:26.
c. [6:64] 13:11.
d. [6:69] 11:27; Mt 16:16; Mk 1:24; Lk 4:34.
e. [6:71] 12:4; 13:2, 27.

CHAPTER 7

The Feast of Tabernacles. ¹*After this, Jesus moved about within Galilee; but he did not wish to travel in Judea, because the Jews were trying to kill him.*ᵃ ²But the Jewish feast of Tabernacles was near.ᵇ ³So his brothers* said to him, "Leave here and go to Judea, so that your disciples also may see the works you are doing. ⁴No one works in secret if he wants to be known publicly. If you do these things, manifest yourself to the world."ᶜ ⁵For his brothers did not believe in him.) ⁶So Jesus said to them, "My time is not yet here, but the time is always right for you. ⁷The world cannot hate you, but it hates me, because I testify to it that its works are evil.ᵈ ⁸You go up to the feast. I am not going up* to this feast, because my time has not yet been fulfilled." ⁹After he had said this, he stayed on in Galilee.

¹⁰But when his brothers had gone up to the feast, he himself also went up, not openly but [as it were] in secret. ¹¹The Jews were looking for him at the feast and saying, "Where is he?" ¹²And there was considerable murmuring about him in the crowds. Some said, "He is a good man," [while] others said, "No; on the contrary, he misleads the crowd." ¹³Still, no one spoke openly about

him because they were afraid of the Jews.[e]

The First Dialogue.[*] [14]When the feast was already half over, Jesus went up into the temple area and began to teach. [15][*][f]The Jews were amazed and said, "How does he know scripture without having studied?" [16]Jesus answered them and said, "My teaching is not my own but is from the one who sent me. [17]Whoever chooses to do his will[*] shall know whether my teaching is from God or whether I speak on my own.[g] [18]Whoever speaks on his own seeks his own glory, but whoever seeks the glory of the one who sent him is truthful, and there is no wrong in him. [19]Did not Moses give you the law? Yet none of you keeps the law. Why are you trying to kill me?"[h] [20]The crowd answered, "You are possessed![*] Who is trying to kill you?"[i] [21]Jesus answered and said to them, "I performed one work[*] and all of you are amazed[j] [22]because of it. Moses gave you circumcision—not that it came from Moses but rather from the patriarchs—and you circumcise a man on the sabbath.[k] [23]If a man can receive circumcision on a sabbath so that the law of Moses may not be broken, are you angry with me because I made a whole person well on a sabbath?[l] [24]Stop judging by appearances, but judge justly."[m]

[25]So some of the inhabitants of Jerusalem said, "Is he not the one they are trying to kill? [26]And look, he is speaking openly and they say nothing to him. Could the authorities[*] have realized that he is the Messiah? [27]But we know where he is from. When the Messiah comes, no one will know where he is from."[n] [28]So Jesus cried out in the temple area as he was teaching and said, "You know me and also know where I am from. Yet I did not come on my own, but the one who

sent me, whom you do not know, is true.[o] [29]I know him, because I am from him, and he sent me."[p] [30]So they tried to arrest him, but no one laid a hand upon him, because his hour had not yet come.[q] [31]But many of the crowd began to believe in him, and said, "When the Messiah comes, will he perform more signs than this man has done?"[r]

Officers Sent to Arrest Jesus.[*] [32]The Pharisees heard the crowd murmuring about him to this effect, and the chief priests and the Pharisees sent guards to arrest him. [33]So Jesus said, "I will be with you only a little while longer, and then I will go to the one who sent me.[s] [34]You will look for me but not find [me], and where I am you cannot come."[t] [35]So the Jews said to one another, "Where is he going that we will not find him? Surely he is not going to the dispersion[*] among the Greeks to teach the Greeks, is he? [36]What is the meaning of his saying, 'You will look for me and not find [me], and where I am you cannot come'?"

Rivers of Living Water.[*] [37]On the last and greatest day of the feast, Jesus stood up and exclaimed, "Let anyone who thirsts come to me and drink.[u] [38]Whoever believes in me, as scripture says:

'Rivers of living water[*]
will flow from within
him.'"[v]

[39]He said this in reference to the Spirit that those who came to believe in him were to receive. There was, of course, no Spirit yet,[*] because Jesus had not yet been glorified.[w]

Discussion About the Origins of the Messiah.[*] [40]Some in the crowd who heard these words said, "This is truly the Prophet."[x] [41]Others said, "This is the Messiah." But others said, "The Messiah will not come from Galilee, will he? ⁴²Does not scripture say that the Messiah will be of David's family and come from Bethlehem, the village where David lived?"ʸ ⁴³So a division occurred in the crowd because of him. ⁴⁴Some of them even wanted to arrest him, but no one laid hands on him.

⁴⁵So the guards went to the chief priests and Pharisees, who asked them, "Why did you not bring him?" ⁴⁶The guards answered, "Never before has anyone spoken like this one." ⁴⁷So the Pharisees answered them, "Have you also been deceived? ⁴⁸Have any of the authorities or the Pharisees believed in him?ᶻ ⁴⁹But this crowd, which does not know the law, is accursed." ⁵⁰Nicodemus, one of their members who had come to him earlier, said to them,ᵃ ⁵¹"Does our law condemn a person before it first hears him and finds out what he is doing?"ᵇ

⁵²They answered and said to him, "You are not from Galilee also, are you? Look and see that no prophet arises from Galilee."

a. [7:1] 5:18; 8:37, 40.
b. [7:2] Ex 23:16; Lv 23:34; Nm 29:12; Dt 16:13–16; Zec 14:16–19.
c. [7:4] 14:22.
d. [7:7] 15:18.
e. [7:13] 9:22; 19:38; 20:19.
f. [7:15] Lk 2:47.
g. [7:17] 6:29.
h. [7:19] Acts 7:53.
i. [7:20] 8:48–49; 10:20.
j. [7:21] 5:1–9.
k. [7:22] Gn 17:10; Lv 12:3.
l. [7:23] 5:2–9, 16; Mt 12:11–12; Lk 14:5.
m. [7:24] 8:15; Lv 19:15; Is 11:3–4.
n. [7:27] Heb 7:3.
o. [7:28] 8:19.
p. [7:29] 6:46; 8:55.
q. [7:30] 7:44; 8:20; Lk 4:29–30.
r. [7:31] 2:11; 10:42; 11:45.
s. [7:33] 13:33; 16:16.
t. [7:34] 8:21; 12:36; 13:33, 36; 16:5; Dt 4:29; Prv 1:28; Is 55:6; Hos 5:6.
u. [7:37] Rev 21:6.
v. [7:38] 4:10, 14; 19:34; Is 12:3; Ez 47:1.
w. [7:39] 16:7.
x. [7:40] Dt 18:15, 18.
y. [7:42] 2 Sm 7:12–14; Ps 89:3–4; 132:11; Mi 5:1; Mt 2:5–6.
z. [7:48] 12:42.
a. [7:50] 3:1; 19:39.
b. [7:51] Dt 1:16–17.

CHAPTER 8

A Woman Caught in Adultery.* [⁷:⁵³Then each went to his own house, ¹while Jesus went to the Mount of Olives.*ᵃ ²But early in the morning he arrived again in the temple area, and all the people

started coming to him, and he sat down and taught them. [3]Then the scribes and the Pharisees brought a woman who had been caught in adultery and made her stand in the middle. [4]They said to him, "Teacher, this woman was caught in the very act of committing adultery. [5]Now in the law, Moses commanded us to stone such women.[*] So what do you say?"[b] [6]They said this to test him, so that they could have some charge to bring against him. Jesus bent down and began to write on the ground with his finger.[*] [7*]But when they continued asking him, he straightened up and said to them,[c] "Let the one among you who is without sin be the first to throw a stone at her." [8]Again he bent down and wrote on the ground. [9]And in response, they went away one by one, beginning with the elders. So he was left alone with the woman before him. [10]Then Jesus straightened up and

said to her, "Woman, where are they? Has no one condemned you?"[d] [11]She replied, "No one, sir." Then Jesus said, "Neither do I condemn you. Go, [and] from now on do not sin any more."]e

The Light of the World.[*] [12]Jesus spoke to them again, saying, "I am the light of the world. Whoever follows me will not walk in darkness, but will have the light of life."[f] [13]So the Pharisees said to him, "You testify on your own behalf, so your testimony cannot be verified." [14]Jesus answered and said to them, "Even if I do testify on my own behalf, my testimony can be verified,[*] because I know where I came from and where I am going. But you do not know where I come from or where I am going.[g] [15]You judge by appearances,[*] but I do not judge anyone.[h] [16]And even if I should judge, my judgment is valid, because I am not alone, but it is I and

the Father who sent me.[i]
[17]Even in your law* it is written that the testimony of two
men can be verified.[j] [18]I testify on my behalf and so does
the Father who sent me."[k] [19]So
they said to him, "Where is
your father?" Jesus answered,
"You know neither me nor
my Father. If you knew me,
you would know my Father
also."[l] [20]He spoke these words
while teaching in the treasury in the temple area. But
no one arrested him, because
his hour had not yet come.[m]

Jesus, the Father's Ambassador.* [21]He said to them
again, "I am going away and
you will look for me, but you
will die in your sin.* Where I
am going you cannot come."[n]
[22*]So the Jews said, "He is not
going to kill himself, is he,
because he said, 'Where I am
going you cannot come'?"
[23]He said to them, "You
belong to what is below, I
belong to what is above. You
belong to this world, but I
do not belong to this world.[o]
[24]That is why I told you that
you will die in your sins. For
if you do not believe that I
AM,* you will die in your
sins."[p] [25*]So they said to him,
"Who are you?"[q] Jesus said to
them, "What I told you from
the beginning. [26]I have much
to say about you in condemnation. But the one who sent
me is true, and what I heard
from him I tell the world."[r]
[27]They did not realize that
he was speaking to them of
the Father. [28]So Jesus said [to
them], "When you lift up the
Son of Man, then you will
realize that I AM, and that I
do nothing on my own, but
I say only what the Father
taught me.[s] [29]The one who
sent me is with me. He has
not left me alone, because I
always do what is pleasing to
him." [30]Because he spoke this
way, many came to believe
in him.

Jesus and Abraham.* [31]Jesus
then said to those Jews who

believed in him,[s] "If you remain in my word, you will truly be my disciples, [32]and you will know the truth, and the truth will set you free."[t] [33]They answered him, "We are descendants of Abraham and have never been enslaved to anyone.[*] How can you say, 'You will become free'?"[u] [34]Jesus answered them, "Amen, amen, I say to you, everyone who commits sin is a slave of sin.[v] [35]A slave does not remain in a household forever, but a son[*] always remains."[w] [36]So if a son frees you, then you will truly be free. [37]I know that you are descendants of Abraham. But you are trying to kill me, because my word has no room among you. [38]I tell you what I have seen in the Father's presence; then do what you have heard from the Father."

[39]They answered and said to him, "Our father is Abraham." Jesus said to them,[x] "If you were Abraham's children, you would be doing the works of Abraham. [40]But now you are trying to kill me, a man who has told you the truth that I heard from God; Abraham did not do this. [41]You are doing the works of your father!" [So] they said to him, "We are not illegitimate. We have one Father, God."[y] [42]Jesus said to them, "If God were your Father, you would love me, for I came from God and am here; I did not come on my own, but he sent me.[z] [43]Why do you not understand what I am saying? Because you cannot bear to hear my word. [44]You belong to your father the devil and you willingly carry out your father's desires. He was a murderer from the beginning and does not stand in truth, because there is no truth in him. When he tells a lie, he speaks in character, because he is a liar and the father of lies.[a] [45]But because I speak the truth, you do not believe me. [46]Can any of you charge me

with sin? If I am telling the truth, why do you not believe me?[b] [47]Whoever belongs to God hears the words of God; for this reason you do not listen, because you do not belong to God."[c]

[48]The Jews answered and said to him, "Are we not right in saying that you are a Samaritan* and are possessed?" [49]Jesus answered, "I am not possessed; I honor my Father, but you dishonor me. [50]I do not seek my own glory; there is one who seeks it and he is the one who judges.[d] [51]Amen, amen, I say to you, whoever keeps my word will never see death."[e] [52][So] the Jews said to him, "Now we are sure that you are possessed. Abraham died, as did the prophets, yet you say, 'Whoever keeps my word will never taste death.' [53]Are you greater than our father Abraham,* who died? Or the prophets, who died? Who do you make yourself out to be?"[f] [54]Jesus answered, "If I glorify myself, my glory is worth nothing; but it is my Father who glorifies me, of whom you say, 'He is our God.' [55]You do not know him, but I know him. And if I should say that I do not know him, I would be like you a liar. But I do know him and I keep his word.[g] [56]Abraham your father rejoiced to see my day; he saw it* and was glad.[h] [57]So the Jews said to him, "You are not yet fifty years old and you have seen Abraham?"* [58]*Jesus said to them,[i] "Amen, amen, I say to you, before Abraham came to be, I AM." [59]So they picked up stones to throw at him; but Jesus hid and went out of the temple area.[j]

---

a.   [8:1–2] Lk 21:37–38.
b.   [8:5] Lv 20:10; Dt 22:22–29.
c.   [8:7] Dt 17:7.
d.   [8:10] Ez 33:11.
e.   [8:11] 5:14.
f.   [8:12] 1:4–5, 9; 12:46; Ex 13:22; Is 42:6; Zec 14:8.
g.   [8:14] 5:31.
h.   [8:15] 12:47; 1 Sm 16:7.
i.   [8:16] 5:30.
j.   [8:17] Dt 17:6; 19:15; Nm 35:30.
k.   [8:18] 5:23, 37.
l.   [8:19] 7:28; 14:7; 15:21.
m.   [8:20] 7:30.
n.   [8:21] 7:34; 13:33.
o.   [8:23] 3:31; 17:14; 18:36.
p.   [8:24] Ex 3:14; Dt 32:39; Is 43:10.
q.   [8:25] 10:24.
r.   [8:26] 12:44–50.
s.   [8:28] 3:14; 12:32, 34.
t.   [8:32] Is 42:7; Gal 4:31.

u.   [8:33] Mt 3:9.
v.   [8:34] Rom 6:16–17.
w. [8:35] Gn 21:10; Gal 4:30; Heb 3:5–6.
x.   [8:39] Gn 26:5; Rom 4:11–17; Jas 2:21–23.
y.   [8:41] Mal 2:10.
z.   [8:42] 1 Jn 5:1.
a.   [8:44] Gn 3:4; Wis 1:13; 2:24; Acts 13:10; 1 Jn
     3:8–15.
b.   [8:46] Heb 4:15; 1 Pt 2:22; 1 Jn 3:5.
c.   [8:47] 10:26; 1 Jn 4:6.
d.   [8:50] 7:18.
e.   [8:51] 5:24–29; 6:40, 47; 11:25–26.
f.   [8:53] 4:12.
g.   [8:55] 7:28–29.
h.   [8:56] Gn 17:17; Mt 13:17; Lk 17:22.
i.   [8:58] 1:30; 17:5.
j.   [8:59] 10:31, 39; 11:8; Lk 4:29–30.

CHAPTER 9

The Man Born Blind. [1]*As he passed by he saw a man blind from birth.[a] [2]*His disciples asked him,[b] "Rabbi, who sinned, this man or his parents, that he was born blind?" [3]Jesus answered, "Neither he nor his parents sinned; it is so that the works of God might be made visible through him.[c] [4]We have to do the works of the one who sent me while it is day. Night is coming when no one can work.[d] [5]While I am in the world, I am the light of the world."[e] [6]When he had said this, he spat on the ground and made clay with the saliva, and smeared the clay on his eyes,[f] [7]and said to him, "Go wash* in the Pool of Siloam" (which means Sent). So he went and washed, and came back able to see.[g]

[8]His neighbors and those who had seen him earlier as a beggar said, "Isn't this the one who used to sit and beg?" [9]Some said, "It is," but others said, "No, he just looks like him." He said, "I am." [10]So they said to him, "[So] how were your eyes opened?" [11]He replied, "The man called Jesus made clay and anointed my eyes and told me, 'Go to Siloam and wash.' So I went there and washed and was able to see." [12]And they said to him, "Where is he?" He said, "I don't know."

[13]They brought the one who was once blind to the Pharisees. [14]Now Jesus had made clay* and opened his eyes on a sabbath.[h] [15]So then the Pharisees also asked him how he was able to see. He said to them, "He put clay on my eyes, and I washed, and

now I can see." ¹⁶So some of the Pharisees said, "This man is not from God, because he does not keep the sabbath." [But] others said, "How can a sinful man do such signs?" And there was a division among them.^{i} ¹⁷So they said to the blind man again, "What do you have to say about him, since he opened your eyes?" He said, "He is a prophet."^{j}

¹⁸Now the Jews did not believe that he had been blind and gained his sight until they summoned the parents of the one who had gained his sight. ¹⁹They asked them, "Is this your son, who you say was born blind? How does he now see?" ²⁰His parents answered and said, "We know that this is our son and that he was born blind. ²¹We do not know how he sees now, nor do we know who opened his eyes. Ask him, he is of age; he can speak for himself." ²²^{*k}His parents said this because they were afraid of the Jews, for the Jews had already agreed that if anyone acknowledged him as the Messiah, he would be expelled from the synagogue. ²³For this reason his parents said, "He is of age; question him."^{l}

²⁴So a second time they called the man who had been blind and said to him, "Give God the praise!* We know that this man is a sinner."^{m} ²⁵He replied, "If he is a sinner, I do not know. One thing I do know is that I was blind and now I see." ²⁶So they said to him, "What did he do to you? How did he open your eyes?" ²⁷He answered them, "I told you already and you did not listen. Why do you want to hear it again? Do you want to become his disciples, too?" ²⁸They ridiculed him and said, "You are that man's disciple; we are disciples of Moses! ²⁹We know that God spoke to Moses, but we do not know where this one is from."^{n} ³⁰The man

answered and said to them, "This is what is so amazing, that you do not know where he is from, yet he opened my eyes. [31]We know that God does not listen to sinners, but if one is devout and does his will, he listens to him.[o] [32*]It is unheard of that anyone ever opened the eyes of a person born blind. [33]If this man were not from God, he would not be able to do anything."[p] [34]They answered and said to him, "You were born totally in sin, and are you trying to teach us?" Then they threw him out.

[35]When Jesus heard that they had thrown him out, he found him and said, "Do you believe in the Son of Man?" [36]He answered and said, "Who is he, sir, that I may believe in him?" [37]Jesus said to him, "You have seen him and the one speaking with you is he."[q] [38]He said, "I do believe, Lord," and he worshiped him. [39*]Then Jesus said, "I came into this world for judgment, so that those who do not see might see, and those who do see might become blind."[r]

[40]Some of the Pharisees who were with him heard this and said to him, "Surely we are not also blind, are we?"[s] [41]Jesus said to them, "If you were blind, you would have no sin; but now you are saying, 'We see,' so your sin remains.[t]

---

a. [9:1–2] Is 42:7.
b. [9:2] Ex 20:5; Ez 18:20; Lk 13:2.
c. [9:3] 5:14; 11:4.
d. [9:4] 11:9–10; 12:35–36.
e. [9:5] 8:12.
f. [9:6] 5:11; Mk 7:33; 8:23.
g. [9:7] 2 Kgs 5:10–14.
h. [9:14] 5:9.
i. [9:16] 3:2; Mt 12:10–11; Lk 13:10–11; 14:1–4.
j. [9:17] 4:19.
k. [9:22] 7:13; 12:42; 16:2; 19:38.
l. [9:23] 12:42.
m. [9:24] Jos 7:19; 1 Sm 6:5 LXX.
n. [9:29] Ex 33:11.
o. [9:31] 10:21; Ps 34:16; 66:18; Prv 15:29; Is 1:15.
p. [9:33] 3:2.
q. [9:37] 4:26; Dn 7:13.
r. [9:39] Mt 13:33–35.
s. [9:40] Mt 15:14; 23:26; Rom 2:19.
t. [9:41] 15:22.

CHAPTER 10

The Good Shepherd.

[1*]"Amen, amen, I say to you,[a] whoever does not enter a sheepfold* through the gate

Jesus = gate (v. 7)

but climbs over elsewhere is a thief and a robber. ²But whoever enters (through the gate) is the shepherd of the sheep. ³The gatekeeper opens it for him, and the sheep hear his voice, as he calls his own sheep by name and leads them out. ⁴*When he has driven out all his own, he walks ahead of them, and the sheep follow him,*ᵇ* because they recognize his voice. ⁵But they will not follow a stranger; they will run away from him, because they do not recognize the voice of strangers." ⁶Although Jesus used this figure of speech,* they did not realize what he was trying to tell them.

⁷*So Jesus said again, "Amen, amen, I say to you, I am the gate for the sheep. ⁸*All who came [before me] are thieves and robbers, but the sheep did not listen to them. ⁹I am the gate. Whoever enters through me will be saved, and will come in and go out and find pasture. ¹⁰A thief comes only to steal and slaughter and destroy; (I came so that they might have life and have it more abundantly.)¹¹I am the good shepherd. A good shepherd lays down his life for the sheep.*ᶜ* ¹²A hired man, who is not a shepherd and whose sheep are not his own, sees a wolf coming and leaves the sheep and runs away, and the wolf catches and scatters them.*ᵈ* ¹³This is because he works for pay and has no concern for the sheep. ¹⁴I am the good shepherd, and I know mine and mine know me, ¹⁵just as the Father knows me and I know the Father; and I will lay down my life for the sheep.*ᵉ* ¹⁶I have other sheep* that do not belong to this fold. These also I must lead, and they will hear my voice, and there will be one flock, one shepherd.*ᶠ* ¹⁷This is why the Father loves me, because I lay down my life in order to take it up again.*ᵍ* ¹⁸No one takes it from me, but I lay it down on my own. I have power to lay it

down, and power to take it up again.* This command I have received from my Father."[h]

[19] Again there was a division among the Jews because of these words.[i] [20] Many of them said, "He is possessed and out of his mind; why listen to him?"[j] [21] Others said, "These are not the words of one possessed; surely a demon cannot open the eyes of the blind, can he?"[k]

Feast of the Dedication.
[22] The feast of the Dedication* was then taking place in Jerusalem. It was winter.[l] [23]* And Jesus walked about in the temple area on the Portico of Solomon. [24] So the Jews gathered around him and said to him, "How long are you going to keep us in suspense?* If you are the Messiah, tell us plainly."[m] [25] Jesus answered them, "I told you* and you do not believe. The works I do in my Father's name testify to me.[n] [26] But you do not believe, because you are not among

my sheep.[o] [27] My sheep hear my voice; I know them, and they follow me. [28] I give them eternal life, and they shall never perish. No one can take them out of my hand.[p] [29] My Father, who has given them to me, is greater than all,* and no one can take them out of the Father's hand.[q] [30]* The Father and I are one."[r]

[31] The Jews again picked up rocks to stone him.[s] [32] Jesus answered them, "I have shown you many good works from my Father. For which of these are you trying to stone me?" [33] The Jews answered him, "We are not stoning you for a good work but for blasphemy. You, a man, are making yourself God."[t] [34] Jesus answered them,[u] "Is it not written in your law, 'I said, "You are gods"'? [35] If it calls them gods to whom the word of God came, and scripture cannot be set aside, [36] can you say that the one whom the Father has consecrated* and sent into the

world blasphemes because I said, 'I am the Son of God'?*[v] ³⁷If I do not perform my Father's works, do not believe me; ³⁸but if I perform them, even if you do not believe me, believe the works, so that you may realize [and understand] that (the Father is in me and I am in the Father."*[w] ³⁹[Then] they tried again to arrest him; but he escaped from their power.

⁴⁰He went back across the Jordan to the place where John first baptized, and there he remained.*[x] ⁴¹Many came to him and said, "John performed no sign,* but everything John said about this man was true." ⁴²And many there began to believe in him.*[y]

a. [10:1–5] Gn 48:15; 49:24; Ps 23:1–4; 80:2; Jer 23:1–4; Ez 34:1–31; Mi 7:14.
b. [10:4] Mi 2:12–13.
c. [10:11] Ps 23:1–4; Is 40:11; 49:9–10; Heb 13:20; Rev 7:17.
d. [10:12] Zec 11:17.
e. [10:15] 15:13; 1 Jn 3:16.
f. [10:16] 11:52; Is 56:8; Jer 23:3; Ez 34:23; 37:24; Mi 2:12.
g. [10:17] Heb 10:10.
h. [10:18] 19:11.
i. [10:19] 7:43; 9:16.
j. [10:20] 7:20; 8:48.
k. [10:21] 3:2.
l. [10:22] 1 Mc 4:54, 59.
m. [10:24] Lk 22:67.

n. [10:25] 8:25 / 5:36; 10:38.
o. [10:26] 8:45, 47.
p. [10:28] Dt 32:39.
q. [10:29] Wis 3:1; Is 43:13.
r. [10:30] 1:1; 12:45; 14:9; 17:21.
s. [10:31] 8:59.
t. [10:33] 5:18; 19:7; Lv 24:16.
u. [10:34] Ps 82:6.
v. [10:36] 5:18.
w. [10:38] 14:10–11, 20.
x. [10:40] 1:28.
y. [10:42] 2:23; 7:31; 8:30.

CHAPTER 11

The Raising of Lazarus.[*] ¹Now a man was ill, Lazarus from Bethany,*[a] the village of Mary and her sister Martha. ²Mary was the one who had anointed the Lord with perfumed oil and dried his feet with her hair; it was her brother Lazarus who was ill. ³So the sisters sent word to him, saying, "Master, the one you love is ill." ⁴When Jesus heard this he said, "This illness is not to end in death,* but is for the glory of God, that the Son of God may be glorified through it."*[b] ⁵Now Jesus loved Martha and her sister and Lazarus. ⁶So when he heard that he was ill, he remained for two days in the place where he was. ⁷Then after this he said to his disciples, "Let us go back to Judea." [8]The disciples said to him, "Rabbi, the Jews were just trying to stone you, and you want to go back there?"[c] [9]Jesus answered, "Are there not twelve hours in a day? If one walks during the day,[d] he does not stumble, because he sees the light of this world.[e] [10]But if one walks at night, he stumbles, because the light is not in him."[*] [11]He said this, and then told them, "Our friend Lazarus is asleep, but I am going to awaken him." [12]So the disciples said to him, "Master, if he is asleep, he will be saved." [13]But Jesus was talking about his death, while they thought that he meant ordinary sleep.[f] [14]So then Jesus said to them clearly, "Lazarus has died. [15]And I am glad for you that I was not there, that you may believe. Let us go to him." [16]So Thomas, called Didymus,[*] said to his fellow disciples, "Let us also go to die with him."[g]

[17]When Jesus arrived, he found that Lazarus had already been in the tomb for four days. [18]Now Bethany was near Jerusalem, only about two miles[*] away. [19]And many of the Jews had come to Martha and Mary to comfort them about their brother.[h] [20]When Martha heard that Jesus was coming, she went to meet him; but Mary sat at home. [21]Martha said to Jesus, "Lord, if you had been here, my brother would not have died.[i] [22][But] even now I know that whatever you ask of God, God will give you." [23]Jesus said to her, "Your brother will rise." [24]Martha said to him, "I know he will rise, in the resurrection on the last day."[j] [25]Jesus told her, "I am the resurrection and the life; whoever believes in me, even if he dies, will live,[k] [26]and everyone who lives and believes in me will never die. Do you believe this?" [27][*]She

said to him, "Yes, Lord. I have come to believe that you are the Messiah, the Son of God, the one who is coming into the world."

²⁸When she had said this, she went and called her sister Mary secretly, saying, "The teacher is here and is asking for you." ²⁹As soon as she heard this, she rose quickly and went to him. ³⁰For Jesus had not yet come into the village, but was still where Martha had met him. ³¹So when the Jews who were with her in the house comforting her saw Mary get up quickly and go out, they followed her, presuming that she was going to the tomb to weep there. ³²When Mary came to where Jesus was and saw him, she fell at his feet and said to him, "Lord, if you had been here, my brother would not have died." ³³When Jesus saw her weeping and the Jews who had come with her weeping, he became perturbed* and deeply troubled, ³⁴and said,

"Where have you laid him?" They said to him, "Sir, come and see." ³⁵And Jesus wept.ᵐ ³⁶So the Jews said, "See how he loved him." ³⁷But some of them said, "Could not the one who opened the eyes of the blind man have done something so that this man would not have died?"

³⁸So Jesus, perturbed again, came to the tomb. It was a cave, and a stone lay across it. ³⁹Jesus said, "Take away the stone." Martha, the dead man's sister, said to him, "Lord, by now there will be a stench; he has been dead for four days." ⁴⁰Jesus said to her, "Did I not tell you that if you believe you will see the glory of God?" ⁴¹So they took away the stone. And Jesus raised his eyes and said, "Father,* I thank you for hearing me. ⁴²I know that you always hear me; but because of the crowd here I have said this, that they may believe that you sent me."ⁿ ⁴³And when he had said this, he cried out in

a loud voice,* "Lazarus, come out!" [44]The dead man came out, tied hand and foot with burial bands, and his face was wrapped in a cloth. So Jesus said to them, "Untie him and let him go."

Session of the Sanhedrin. [45]Now many of the Jews who had come to Mary and seen what he had done began to believe in him.*[o] [46]But some of them went to the Pharisees and told them what Jesus had done. [47]So the chief priests and the Pharisees convened the Sanhedrin and said, "What are we going to do? This man is performing many signs.*[p] [48]If we leave him alone, all will believe in him, and the Romans will come* and take away both our land and our nation." [49q]But one of them, Caiaphas, who was high priest that year,* said to them, "You know nothing, [50]nor do you consider that it is better for you that one man should die instead of the people, so that the whole nation may not perish." [51]He did not say this on his own, but since he was high priest for that year, he prophesied (that Jesus was going to die for the nation, [52]and not only for the nation, but also to gather into one the dispersed children of God.*)[53]So from that day on they planned to kill him.*[r]

[54]So Jesus no longer walked about in public among the Jews, but he left for the region near the desert, to a town called Ephraim,* and there he remained with his disciples.

The Last Passover. [55]Now the Passover of the Jews was near, and many went up from the country to Jerusalem before Passover to purify* themselves.*[s] [56]They looked for Jesus and said to one another as they were in the temple area, "What do you think? That he will not come to the feast?" [57]For the chief priests and the Pharisees had given orders that if any-one knew where he was, he should inform them, so that they might arrest him.

a. [11:1–2] 12:1–8; Lk 10:38–42; 16:19–31.
b. [11:4] 9:3, 24.
c. [11:8] 8:59; 10:31.
d. [11:9–10] 12:35; 1 Jn 2:10.
e. [11:9] 8:12; 9:4.
f. [11:13] Mt 9:24.
g. [11:16] 14:5, 22.
h. [11:19] 12:9, 17–18.
i. [11:21] 11:32.
j. [11:24] 5:29; 6:39–40, 44, 54; 12:48; Is 2:2; Mi 4:1; Acts 23:8; 24:15.
k. [11:25] 5:24; 8:51; 14:6; Dn 12:2.
l. [11:27] 1:9; 6:69.
m. [11:35] Lk 19:41.
n. [11:42] 12:30.
o. [11:45] Lk 16:31.
p. [11:47] 12:19; Mt 26:3–5; Lk 22:2; Acts 4:16.
q. [11:49–50] 18:13–14.
r. [11:53] 5:18; 7:1; Mt 12:14.
s. [11:55] 2:13; 5:1; 6:4; 18:28; Ex 19:10–11, 15; Nm 9:6–14; 19:12; Dt 16:6; 2 Chr 30:1–3, 15–18.

CHAPTER 12

The Anointing at Bethany.[a] ¹Six days before Passover Jesus came to Bethany, where Lazarus was, whom Jesus had raised from the dead.[b] ²They gave a dinner for him there, and Martha served, while Lazarus was one of those reclining at table with him.[c] ³Mary took a liter of costly perfumed oil made from genuine aromatic nard and anointed the feet of Jesus* and dried them with her hair; the house was filled with the fragrance of the oil.[d] ⁴Then Judas the Iscariot, one [of] his disciples, and the one who would betray him, said, ⁵"Why was this oil not sold for three hundred days' wages* and given to the poor?" ⁶He said this not because he cared about the poor but because he was a thief and held the money bag and used to steal the contributions.[e] ⁷So Jesus said, "Leave her alone. Let her keep this for the day of my burial.* ⁸You always have the poor with you, but you do not always have me."[f]

⁹[The] large crowd of the Jews found out that he was there and came, not only because of Jesus, but also to see Lazarus, whom he had raised from the dead.[g] ¹⁰And the chief priests plotted to kill Lazarus too, ¹¹because many of the Jews were turn-ing away and believing in Jesus because of him.[h]

The Entry into Jerusalem.[*]

[12i]On the next day, when the great crowd that had come to the feast heard that Jesus was coming to Jerusalem, [13]they took palm branches[*] and went out to meet him, and cried out:

"Hosanna!
Blessed is he who comes in
    the name of the Lord,
    [even] the king of
    Israel."[j]

[14]Jesus found an ass and sat upon it, as is written:

[15]"Fear no more, O daugh-
    ter Zion;[*]
see, your king comes,
    seated upon an ass's
    colt."[k]

[16]His disciples did not understand this at first, but when Jesus had been glorified they remembered that these things were written about him and that they had done this[*] for him.[l] [17*]So the crowd that was with him when he called Lazarus from the tomb and raised him from death continued to testify. [18]This was [also] why the crowd went to meet him, because they heard that he had done this sign. [19]So the Pharisees said to one another, "You see that you are gaining nothing. Look, the whole world[*] has gone after him."[m]

The Coming of Jesus' Hour.[*]

[20]Now there were some Greeks[*] among those who had come up to worship at the feast.[n] [21*]They came to Philip, who was from Bethsaida in Galilee, and asked him, "Sir, we would like to see Jesus."[o] [22]Philip went and told Andrew; then Andrew and Philip went and told Jesus.[p] [23*]Jesus answered them,[q] "The hour has come for the Son of Man to be glorified. [24*]Amen, amen, I say to you, unless a grain of wheat falls to the ground and dies, it remains just a grain of wheat;[r] but if it dies, it produces much fruit.

²⁵Whoever loves his life* loses it, and whoever hates his life in this world will preserve it for eternal life.ˢ ²⁶Whoever serves me must follow me, and where I am, there also will my servant be. The Father will honor whoever serves me.ᵗ

²⁷"I am troubled* now. Yet what should I say? 'Father, save me from this hour'? But it was for this purpose that I came to this hour.ᵘ ²⁸Father, glorify your name." Then a voice came from heaven, "I have glorified it and will glorify it again."ᵛ ²⁹The crowd there heard it and said it was thunder; but others said, "An angel has spoken to him."ʷ ³⁰Jesus answered and said, "This voice did not come for my sake but for yours.ˣ ³¹Now is the time of judgment on this world; now the ruler of this world* will be driven out.ʸ ³²And when I am lifted up from the earth, I will draw everyone to myself."ᶻ ³³He said this indicating the kind of death he would die. ³⁴So the crowd answered him, "We have heard from the law that the Messiah remains forever.* Then how can you say that the Son of Man must be lifted up? Who is this Son of Man?"ᵃ ³⁵Jesus said to them, "The light will be among you only a little while. Walk while you have the light, so that darkness may not overcome you. Whoever walks in the dark does not know where he is going.ᵇ ³⁶While you have the light, believe in the light, so that you may become children of the light."ᶜ

Unbelief and Belief Among the Jews. After he had said this, Jesus left and hid from them. ³⁷*ᵈAlthough he had performed so many signs in their presence they did not believe in him, ³⁸*in order that the word which Isaiah the prophet spoke might be fulfilled:

"Lord, who has believed
    our preaching,

to whom has the might of the Lord been revealed?"[e]

[39]For this reason they could not believe, because again Isaiah said:

[40]"He blinded their eyes
and hardened their heart,
so that they might not see
with their eyes
and understand with
their heart and be
converted,
and I would heal them."[f]

[41]Isaiah said this because he saw his glory* and spoke about him.[g] [42]Nevertheless, many, even among the authorities, believed in him, but because of the Pharisees they did not acknowledge it openly in order not to be expelled from the synagogue.[h] [43]For they preferred human praise to the glory of God.[i]

Recapitulation. [44]Jesus cried out and said, "Whoever believes in me believes not only in me but also in the one who sent me,[j] [45]and whoever sees me sees the one who sent me.[k] [46]I came into the world as light, so that everyone who believes in me might not remain in darkness.[l] [47]And if anyone hears my words and does not observe them, I do not condemn him, for I did not come to condemn the world but to save the world.[m] [48]Whoever rejects me and does not accept my words has something to judge him: the word that I spoke, it will condemn him on the last day,[n] [49]because I did not speak on my own, but the Father who sent me commanded me what to say and speak.[o] [50]And I know that his commandment is eternal life. So what I say, I say as the Father told me."

a. [12:1–11] Mt 26:6–13; Mk 14:3–9.
b. [12:1–2] 11:1.
c. [12:2] Lk 10:38–42.
d. [12:3] 11:2.

e.   [12:6] 13:29.
f.   [12:8] Dt 15:11.
g.   [12:9] 11:19.
h.   [12:11] 11:45.
i.   [12:12–19] Mt 21:1–16; Mk 11:1–10; Lk
     19:28–40.
j.   [12:13] 1:49; Lv 23:40; 1 Mc 13:51; 2 Mc 10:7;
     Rev 7:9.
k.   [12:15] Is 40:9; Zec 9:9.
l.   [12:16] 2:22.
m. [12:19] 11:47–48.
n.   [12:20] Acts 10:2.
o.   [12:21] 1:44.
p.   [12:22] 1:40.
q.   [12:23] 2:4.
r.   [12:24] Is 53:10–12; 1 Cor 15:36.
s.   [12:25] Mt 10:39; 16:25; Mk 9:24; 17:33.
t.   [12:26] 14:3; 17:24; Mt 16:24; Mk 8:34; Lk 9:23.
u.   [12:27] 6:38; 18:11; Mt 26:38–39; Mk 14:34–36;
     Lk 42:42; Heb 5:7–8.
v.   [12:28] 2:11; 17:5; Dn 4:31, 34.
w.   [12:29] Ex 9:28; 2 Sm 22:14; Jb 37:4; Ps 29:3; Lk
     22:43; Acts 23:9.
x.   [12:30] 11:42.
y.   [12:31] 16:11; Lk 10:18; Rev 12:9.
z.   [12:32] 3:14; 8:28; Is 52:13.
a.   [12:34] Ps 89:5; 110:4; Is 9:7; Dn 7:13–14; Rev
     20:1–6.
b.   [12:35] 9:4; 11:10; Jb 5:14.
c.   [12:36] Eph 5:8.
d.   [12:37–43] Dt 29:2–4; Mk 4:11–12; Rom 9–11.
e.   [12:38] Is 53:1; Rom 10:16.
f.   [12:40] Is 6:9–10; Mt 13:13–15; Mk 4:12.
g.   [12:41] 5:39; Is 6:1, 4.
h.   [12:42] 9:22.
i.   [12:43] 5:44.
j.   [12:44] 13:20; 14:1.
k.   [12:45] 14:7–9.
l.   [12:46] 1:9; 8:12.
m. [12:47] 3:17.
n.   [12:48] Lk 10:16; Heb 4:12.
o.   [12:49] 14:10, 31; Dt 18:18–19.

III. THE BOOK OF GLORY*

CHAPTER 13

The Washing of the Disciples' Feet. * ¹Before the feast of Passover,* Jesus knew that his hour had come to pass from this world to the Father. (He loved his own in the world and he loved them to the end.*) ²The devil had already induced* Judas, son of Simon the Iscariot, to hand him over. So, during supper,*ᵇ ³fully aware that the Father had put everything into his power and that he had come from God and was returning to God,*ᶜ ⁴he rose from supper and took off his outer garments. He took a towel and tied it around his waist. ⁵Then he poured water into a basin and began to wash the disciples' feetᵈ and dry them with the towel around his waist. ⁶He came to Simon Peter, who said to him, "Master, are you going to wash my feet?" ⁷Jesus answered and said to him, "What I am doing, you do not understand now, but you will understand later." ⁸Peter said to him, "You will never wash my feet." Jesus answered him, "Unless I wash you, you will have no inheritance with me."[e] [9]Simon Peter said to him, "Master, then not only my feet, but my hands and head as well." [10]Jesus said to him, "Whoever has bathed[*] has no need except to have his feet washed, for he is clean all over; so you are clean, but not all."[f] [11]For he knew who would betray him; for this reason, he said, "Not all of you are clean."[g]

[12]So when he had washed their feet [and] put his garments back on and reclined at table again, he said to them, "Do you realize what I have done for you? [13]You call me 'teacher' and 'master,' and rightly so, for indeed I am.[h] [14]If I, therefore, the master and teacher, have washed your feet, you ought to wash one another's feet. [15]I have given you a model to follow, so that as I have done for you, you should also do.[i] [16]Amen, amen, I say to you, no slave is greater than his master nor any messenger[*] greater than

the one who sent him.[j] [17]If you understand this, blessed are you if you do it. [18]I am not speaking of all of you. I know those whom I have chosen. But so that the scripture might be fulfilled, 'The one who ate my food has raised his heel against me.'[k] [19]From now on I am telling you before it happens, so that when it happens you may believe that I AM. [20]Amen, amen, I say to you, whoever receives the one I send receives me, and whoever receives me receives the one who sent me."[l]

Announcement of Judas's Betrayal.[m] [21]When he had said this, Jesus was deeply troubled and testified, "Amen, amen, I say to you, one of you will betray me." [22]The disciples looked at one another, at a loss as to whom he meant. [23]One of his disciples, the one whom Jesus loved,[*] was reclining at Jesus' side.[n] [24]So Simon Peter nodded to him to find out whom he meant. 25 He leaned back against Jesus' chest and said to him, "Master, who is it?"[o] 26 Jesus answered, "It is the one to whom I hand the morsel* after I have dipped it." So he dipped the morsel and [took it and] handed it to Judas, son of Simon the Iscariot. 27 After he took the morsel, Satan entered him. So Jesus said to him, "What you are going to do, do quickly."[p] 28 [Now] none of those reclining at table realized why he said this to him. 29 Some thought that since Judas kept the money bag, Jesus had told him, "Buy what we need for the feast," or to give something to the poor.[q] 30 So he took the morsel and left at once. And it was night.

The New Commandment. 31 *When he had left, Jesus said,* "Now is the Son of Man glorified, and God is glorified in him. 32 [If God is glorified in him,] God will also glorify him in himself, and he will glorify him at once.[r] 33 My children, I will be with you only a little while longer. You will look for me, and as I told the Jews, 'Where I go you cannot come,' so now I say it to you.[s] 34 I give you a new commandment:* love one another. As I have loved you, so you also should love one another.[t] 35 This is how all will know that you are my disciples, if you have love for one another."

Peter's Denial Predicted. 36 Simon Peter said to him, "Master, where are you going?" Jesus answered [him], "Where I am going, you cannot follow me now, though you will follow later."[u] 37 Peter said to him, "Master, why can't I follow you now? I will lay down my life for you." 38 Jesus answered, "Will you lay down your life for me? Amen, amen, I say to you, the cock will not crow before you deny me three times."[v]

a. [13:1] 2:4; 7:30; 8:20; Mt 26:17, 45; Mk 14:12, 41; Lk 22:7.
b. [13:2] 6:71; 17:12; Mt 26:20–21; Mk 14:17–18; Lk 22:3.
c. [13:3] 3:35.
d. [13:5] 1 Sm 25:41.
e. [13:8] 2 Sm 20:1.
f. [13:10] 15:3.
g. [13:11] 6:70.
h. [13:13] Mt 23:8, 10.
i. [13:15] Lk 22:27; 1 Pt 2:21.
j. [13:16] 15:20; Mt 10:24; Lk 6:40.
k. [13:18] Ps 41:10.
l. [13:20] Mt 10:40; Mk 9:37; Lk 9:48.
m. [13:21–30] Mt 26:21–25; Mk 14:18–21; Lk 22:21–23.
n. [13:23] 19:26; 20:2; 21:7, 20; Mt 10:37.
o. [13:25] 21:20.
p. [13:27] 13:2; Lk 22:3;
q. [13:29] 12:5–6.
r. [13:32] 17:1–5.
s. [13:33] 7:33; 8:21.
t. [13:34] 15:12–13, 17; Lv 19:18; 1 Thes 4:9; 1 Jn 2:7–10; 3:23; 2 Jn 5.
u. [13:36] Mk 14:27; Lk 22:23.
v. [13:38] 18:27; Mt 26:33–35; Mk 14:29–31; Lk 22:33–34.

CHAPTER 14

Last Supper Discourses. [1]"Do not let your hearts be troubled. You have faith* in God; have faith also in me. [2]In my Father's house there are many dwelling places. If there were not, would I have told you that I am going to prepare a place for you? [3]*And if I go and prepare a place for you, I will come back again and take you to myself, so that where I am you also may be.ᵃ [4]Where [I] am going you know the way."* [5]Thomas said to him, "Master, we do not know where you are going; how can we know the way?" [6]Jesus said to him, "I am the way and the truth* and the life. No one comes to the Father except through me.ᵇ [7]If you know me, then you will also know my Father.* From now on you do know him and have seen him."ᶜ [8]Philip said to him, "Master, show us the Father,* and that will be enough for us."ᵈ [9]Jesus said to him, "Have I been with you for so long a time and you still do not know me, Philip? Whoever has seen me has seen the Father. How can you say, 'Show us the Father'?ᵉ [10]Do you not believe that I am in the Father and the Father is in me? The words that I speak to you I do not speak on my own. The Father who dwells in me is doing his works.ᶠ [11]Believe me that I am in the Father and the Father is in me, or else, believe because

of the works themselves.*g*
12Amen, amen, I say to you,
whoever believes in me will
do the works that I do, and
will do greater ones than
these, because I am going to
the Father.*h* 13And whatever
you ask in my name, I will do,
so that the Father may be glorified in the Son.*i* 14If you ask
anything of me in my name, I
will do it.

The Advocate. 15"If you
love me, you will keep my
commandments.*j* 16And I will
ask the Father, and he will
give you another Advocate*
to be with you always,*k* 17the
Spirit of truth,* which the
world cannot accept, because
it neither sees nor knows it.
But you know it, because it
remains with you, and will
be in you.*l* 18I will not leave
you orphans; I will come to
you.* 19In a little while the
world will no longer see me,
but you will see me, because
I live and you will live.*m* 20On
that day you will realize that I
am in my Father and you are
in me and I in you."*n* 21Who-
ever has my commandments
and observes them is the one
who loves me. And whoever
loves me will be loved by my
Father, and I will love him
and reveal myself to him."*o*
22Judas, not the Iscariot,* said
to him, "Master, [then] what
happened that you will reveal
yourself to us and not to the
world?"*p* 23Jesus answered
and said to him, "Whoever
loves me will keep my word,
and my Father will love him,
and we will come to him and
make our dwelling with him.*q*
24Whoever does not love me
does not keep my words;
yet the word you hear is not
mine but that of the Father
who sent me.

25"I have told you this
while I am with you. 26The
Advocate, the holy Spirit
that the Father will send
in my name—he will teach
you everything and remind
you of all that [I] told you.*r*
27Peace* I leave with you; my

peace I give to you. Not as the world gives do I give it to you. Do not let your hearts be troubled or afraid.[s] [28]You heard me tell you, 'I am going away and I will come back to you.'[t] If you loved me, you would rejoice that I am going to the Father; for the Father is greater than I. [29]And now I have told you this before it happens, so that when it happens you may believe.[u] [30]I will no longer speak much with you, for the ruler of the world[*] is coming. He has no power over me, [31]but the world must know that I love the Father and that I do just as the Father has commanded me. Get up, let us go.[v]

a. [14:3] 12:26; 17:24; 1 Jn 2:28.
b. [14:6] 8:31–47.
c. [14:7] 8:19; 12:45.
d. [14:8] Ex 24:9–10; 33:18.
e. [14:9] 1:18; 10:30; 12:45; 2 Cor 4:4; Col 1:15; Heb 1:3.
f. [14:10] 1:1; 10:37–38; 12:49.
g. [14:11] 10:38.
h. [14:12] 1:50; 5:20.
i. [14:13] 15:7, 16; 16:23–24; Mt 7:7–11.
j. [14:15] 15:10; Dt 6:4–9; Ps 119; Wis 6:18; 1 Jn 5:3; 2 Jn 6.
k. [14:16] 15:26; Lk 24:49; 1 Jn 2:1.
l. [14:17] 16:13; Mt 28:20; 2 Jn 1–2.
m. [14:19] 16:16.
n. [14:20] 10:38; 17:21; Is 2:17; 4:2–3.
o. [14:21] 16:27; 1 Jn 2:5; 3:24.
p. [14:22] 7:4; Acts 10:40–41.
q. [14:23] Rev 3:20.
r. [14:26] 15:26; 16:7, 13–14; Ps 51:13; Is 63:10.
s. [14:27] 16:33; Eph 2:14–18.
t. [14:28] 8:40.
u. [14:29] 13:19; 16:4.
v. [14:31] 6:38.

CHAPTER 15

The Vine and the Branches.

[1]"I am the true vine,[*] and my Father is the vine grower.[a] [2]He takes away every branch in me that does not bear fruit, and every one that does he prunes[*] so that it bears more fruit. [3]You are already pruned because of the word that I spoke to you. [4]Remain in me, as I remain in you. Just as a branch cannot bear fruit on its own unless it remains on the vine, so neither can you unless you remain in me. [5]I am the vine, you are the branches. Whoever remains in me and I in him will bear much fruit, because without me you can do nothing. [6]Anyone who does not remain in me will be thrown out like a branch and wither; people will gather them and throw them into a fire and

remain – 10 x

they will be burned. ⁷If you remain in me and my words remain in you, ask for whatever you want and it will be done for you.*^d* ⁸By this is my Father glorified, that you bear much fruit and become my disciples.*^e* ⁹As the Father loves me, so I also love you. Remain in my love.*^f* ¹⁰If you keep my commandments, you will remain in my love, just as I have kept my Father's commandments and remain in his love.*^g*

¹¹"I have told you this so that <u>my joy may be in you</u> and <u>your joy may be complete</u>.*^h* ¹²This is my commandment: love one another as I love you.*ⁱ* ¹³No one has greater love than this,*^j* to lay down one's life for one's friends. ¹⁴You are my friends if you do what I command you. ¹⁵I no longer call you slaves, because a slave does not know what his master is doing. I have called you friends,* because I have told you everything I have heard from my Father.*^k* ¹⁶It was not you who chose me, but I who chose you and appointed you to go and <u>bear fruit</u> <u>that will remain</u>, so that whatever you ask the Father in my name he may give you.*^l* ¹⁷<u>This I command you: love one another</u>.*^m*

The World's Hatred.[*] ¹⁸"If the world hates you, realize that it hated me first."*ⁿ* ¹⁹If you belonged to the world, the world would love its own; but because you do not belong to the world, and I have chosen you out of the world, the world hates you.*^o* ²⁰Remember <u>the word</u> I spoke to you,* 'No slave is greater than his master.' If they persecuted me, they will also persecute you. If they kept my word, they will also keep yours.*^p* ²¹And they will do all these things to you on account of my name,* because they do not know the one who sent me.*^q* ²²If I had not come and spoken* to them, they would have no sin; but as it is they have no excuse for their sin.[r] [23]Whoever hates me also hates my Father.[s] [24]If I had not done works among them that no one else ever did, they would not have sin; but as it is, they have seen and hated both me and my Father.[t] [25]But in order that the word written in their law might be fulfilled, 'They hated me without cause.'[u]

[26]"When the Advocate comes whom I will send you from the Father, the Spirit of truth that proceeds from the Father, he will testify to me.[v] [27]And you also testify, because you have been with me from the beginning.[w]

a. [15:1] Ps 80:9–17; Is 5:1–7; Jer 2:21; Ez 15:2; 17:5–10; 19:10.
b. [15:3] 13:10.
c. [15:6] Ez 15:6–7; 19:10–14.
d. [15:7] 14:13; Mt 7:7; Mk 11:24; 1 Jn 5:14.
e. [15:8] Mt 5:16.
f. [15:9] 17:23.
g. [15:10] 8:29; 14:15.
h. [15:11] 16:22; 17:13.
i. [15:12] 13:34.
j. [15:13] Rom 5:6–8; 1 Jn 3:16.
k. [15:15] Dt 34:5; Jos 24:29; 2 Chr 20:7; Ps 89:21; Is 41:8; Rom 8:15; Gal 4:7; Jas 2:23.
l. [15:16] 14:13; Dt 7:6.
m. [15:17] 13:34; 1 Jn 3:23; 4:21.
n. [15:18] 7:7; 14:17; Mt 10:22; 24:9; Mk 13:13; Lk 6:22; 1 Jn 3:13.
o. [15:19] 17:14–16; 1 Jn 4:5.
p. [15:20] 13:16; Mt 10:24.
q. [15:21] 8:19; 16:3.
r. [15:22] 8:21, 24; 9:41.
s. [15:23] 5:23; Lk 10:16; 1 Jn 2:23.
t. [15:24] 3:2; 9:32; Dt 4:32–33.
u. [15:25] Ps 35:19; 69:4.
v. [15:26] 14:16, 26; Mt 10:19–20.
w. [15:27] Lk 1:2; Acts 1:8.

CHAPTER 16

[1]"I have told you this so that you may not fall away. [2]They will expel you from the synagogues; in fact, the hour is coming when everyone who kills you will think he is offering worship to God.[a] [3]They will do this because they have not known either the Father or me.[b] [4]I have told you this so that when their hour comes you may remember that I told you.[c]

Jesus' Departure; Coming of the Advocate. "I did not tell you this from the beginning, because I was with you. [5]But now I am going to the one who sent me, and not one of you asks me, 'Where are you going?'[d] [6]But because I told you this, grief has filled your hearts. [7]But I tell you the truth, it is better for you that I go. For if I do not go, the Advocate will not come to you.*e* But if I go, I will send him to you. ⁸*And when he comes he will convict the world in regard to sin and righteousness and condemnation: ⁹sin, because they do not believe in me;*f* ¹⁰righteousness, because I am going to the Father and you will no longer see me; ¹¹condemnation, because the ruler of this world has been condemned.*g*

¹²"I have much more to tell you, but you cannot bear it now. ¹³*But when he comes, the Spirit of truth, he will guide you to all truth.*h* He will not speak on his own, but he will speak what he hears, and will declare to you the things that are coming. ¹⁴He will glorify me, because he will take from what is mine and declare it to you. ¹⁵Everything that the Father has is mine; for this reason I told you that he will take from what is mine and declare it to you.

¹⁶"A little while and you will no longer see me, and again a little while later and you will see me."*i* ¹⁷So some of his disciples said to one another, "What does this mean that he is saying to us, 'A little while and you will not see me, and again a little while and you will see me,' and 'Because I am going to the Father'?" ¹⁸So they said, "What is this 'little while' [of which he speaks]? We do not know what he means." ¹⁹Jesus knew that they wanted to ask him, so he said to them, "Are you discussing with one another what I said, 'A little while and you will not see me, and again a little while and you will see me'? ²⁰Amen, amen, I say to you, you will weep and mourn, while the world rejoices; you will grieve, but your grief will become joy.*j* ²¹When a woman is in labor, she is in anguish because her hour has arrived; but when she has given birth to a child, she no longer remembers the

pain because of her joy that a child has been born into the world.[k] [22]So you also are now in anguish. But I will see you again, and your hearts will rejoice, and no one will take your joy away from you.[l] [23]On that day you will not question me about anything. Amen, amen, I say to you, whatever you ask the Father in my name he will give you.[m] [24]Until now you have not asked anything in my name; ask and you will receive, so that your joy may be complete.

[25][*][n]"I have told you this in figures of speech. The hour is coming when I will no longer speak to you in figures but I will tell you clearly about the Father. [26]On that day you will ask in my name, and I do not tell you that I will ask the Father for you.[o] [27]For the Father himself loves you, because you have loved me and have come to believe that I came from God. [28]I came from the Father and have come into the world. Now I am leaving the world and going back to the Father."[p] [29]His disciples said, "Now you are talking plainly, and not in any figure of speech. [30]Now we realize that you know everything and that you do not need to have anyone question you. Because of this we believe that you came from God." [31]Jesus answered them, "Do you believe now? [32]Behold, the hour is coming and has arrived when each of you will be scattered[*] to his own home and you will leave me alone. But I am not alone, because the Father is with me.[q] [33]I have told you this so that you might have peace in me. In the world you will have trouble, but take courage, I have conquered the world."[r]

a. [16:2] 9:22; 12:42; Mt 10:17; Lk 21:12; Acts 26:11.
b. [16:3] 15:21.
c. [16:4] 13:19; 14:29.
d. [16:5] 7:33; 13:36; 14:5.
e. [16:7] 7:39; 14:16–17, 26; 15:26.
f. [16:9] 8:21–24; 15:22.
g. [16:11] 12:31.
h. [16:13] 14:17, 26; 15:26; Ps 25:5; 143:10; 1 Jn 2:27; Rev 7:17.
i. [16:16] 7:33; 14:19.
j. [16:20] Ps 126:6.
k. [16:21] Is 26:17–18; Jer 31:13; Mi 4:9.

l.   [16:22] 14:19; 15:11; 20:20.
m.   [16:23] 14:13.
n.   [16:25] Mt 13:34–35.
o.   [16:26] 14:13.
p.   [16:28] 1:1.
q.   [16:32] 8:29; Zec 13:7; Mt 26:31; Mk 14:27.
r.   [16:33] 14:27.

CHAPTER 17

The Prayer of Jesus.* ¹When Jesus had said this, he raised his eyes to heaven* and said, "Father, the hour has come. Give glory to your son, so that your son may glorify you,*ᵃ* (²*just as you gave him authority over all people,*ᵇ* so that he may give eternal life to all you gave him.) ³*Now this is eternal life,*ᶜ* that they should know you, the only true God, and the one whom you sent, Jesus Christ. ⁴I glorified you on earth by accomplishing the work that you gave me to do. ⁵Now glorify me, Father, with you, with the glory that I had with you before the world began.*ᵈ*

⁶"I revealed your name* to those whom you gave me out of the world. They belonged to you, and you gave them to me, and they have kept your word. ⁷Now they know that everything you gave me is from you, ⁸because the words you gave to me I have given to them, and they accepted them and truly understood that I came from you, and they have believed that you sent me. ⁹I pray for them. I do not pray for the world but for the ones you have given me, because they are yours,*ᵉ* ¹⁰and everything of mine is yours and everything of yours is mine, and I have been glorified in them.*ᶠ* ¹¹And now I will no longer be in the world, but they are in the world, while I am coming to you. Holy Father, keep them in your name that you have given me, so that they may be one just as we are. ¹²When I was with them I protected them in your name that you gave me, and I guarded them, and none of them was lost except the son of destruction, in order that the scripture might be fulfilled.*ᵍ* ¹³But now

I am coming to you. I speak this in the world so that they may share my joy completely.[h] [14]I gave them your word, and the world hated them, because they do not belong to the world any more than I belong to the world.[i] [15]I do not ask that you take them out of the world[j] but (that you keep them from the evil one.) [16]They do not belong to the world any more than I belong to the world. [17]Consecrate them in the truth. Your word is truth.[k] [18]As you sent me into the world, so I sent them into the world.[l] [19]And I consecrate myself for them, so that they also may be consecrated in truth.

[20]"I pray not only for them, but also for those who will believe in me through their word, [21]so that they may all be one, as you, Father, are in me and I in you, that they also may be in us, that the world may believe that you sent me.[m] [22]And I have given them the glory you gave me, so that they may be one, as we are one, [23]I in them and you in me, that they may be brought to perfection as one, that the world may know that you sent me, and that you loved them even as you loved me. [24]Father, they are your gift to me. I wish that where I am* they also may be with me, that they may see my glory that you gave me, because you loved me before the foundation of the world.[n] [25]Righteous Father, the world also does not know you, but I know you, and they know that you sent me.[o] [26]I made known to them your name and I will make it known,* that the love with which you loved me may be in them and I in them."

a. [17:1] 13:31.
b. [17:2] 3:35; Mt 28:18.
c. [17:3] 1:17; Wis 14:7; 15:3; 1 Jn 5:20.
d. [17:5] 1:1, 2; 12:28; Phil 2:6, 9–11.
e. [17:9] 17:20.
f. [17:10] 16:15; 2 Thes 1:10, 12.
g. [17:12] 13:18; 18:9; Ps 41:10; Mt 26:24; Acts 1:16.
h. [17:13] 15:11.
i. [17:14] 15:19.
j. [17:15] Mt 6:13; 2 Thes 3:3; 1 Jn 5:18.
k. [17:17] 1 Pt 1:22.
l. [17:18] 20:21–22.
m. [17:21] 10:30; 14:10–11, 20.
n. [17:24] 14:3; 1 Thes 4:17.
o. [17:25] 1:10.

CHAPTER 18

Jesus Arrested.[*] ¹When he had said this, Jesus went out[*] with his disciples across the Kidron valley to where there was a garden, into which he and his disciples entered.[a] ²Judas his betrayer also knew the place, because Jesus had often met there with his disciples. ³So Judas got a band of soldiers[*] and guards from the chief priests and the Pharisees and went there with lanterns, torches, and weapons.[b] ⁴Jesus, knowing everything that was going to happen to him, went out and said to them, "Whom are you looking for?" ⁵They answered him, "Jesus the Nazorean."[*] He said to them, "I AM." Judas his betrayer was also with them. ⁶When he said to them, "I AM," they turned away and fell to the ground. ⁷So he again asked them, "Whom are you looking for?" They said, "Jesus the Nazorean." ⁸Jesus answered, "I told you that I AM. So if you are looking for me, let these men go." ⁹[*c]This was to fulfill what he had said, "I have not lost any of those you gave me." ¹⁰Then Simon Peter, who had a sword, drew it, struck the high priest's slave, and cut off his right ear. The slave's name was Malchus.[*] ¹¹Jesus said to Peter, "Put your sword into its scabbard. Shall I not drink the cup[*] that the Father gave me?"[d]

¹²[e]So the band of soldiers, the tribune, and the Jewish guards seized Jesus, bound him, ¹³and brought him to Annas[*] first. He was the father-in-law of Caiaphas, who was high priest that year.[f] ¹⁴It was Caiaphas who had counseled the Jews that it was better that one man should die rather than the people.[g]

Peter's First Denial.[h] ¹⁵Simon Peter and another disciple[*] followed Jesus. Now the other disciple was known to the high priest, and he entered the courtyard of the high priest with Jesus. [16]But Peter stood at the gate outside. So the other disciple, the acquaintance of the high priest, went out and spoke to the gatekeeper and brought Peter in. [17]Then the maid who was the gatekeeper said to Peter, "You are not one of this man's disciples, are you?" He said, "I am not." [18]Now the slaves and the guards were standing around a charcoal fire that they had made, because it was cold, and were warming themselves. Peter was also standing there keeping warm.

The Inquiry Before Annas.[i]
[19]The high priest questioned Jesus about his disciples and about his doctrine. [20]Jesus answered him, "I have spoken publicly to the world. I have always taught in a synagogue or in the temple area* where all the Jews gather, and in secret I have said nothing.[j] [21]Why ask me? Ask those who heard me what I said to them. They know what I said." [22]When he had said this, one of the temple guards standing there struck Jesus and said, "Is this the way you answer the high priest?"[k] [23]Jesus answered him, "If I have spoken wrongly, testify to the wrong; but if I have spoken rightly, why do you strike me?" [24]Then Annas sent him bound to Caiaphas* the high priest.[l]

Peter Denies Jesus Again.[m]
[25]Now Simon Peter was standing there keeping warm. And they said to him, "You are not one of his disciples, are you?" He denied it and said, "I am not." [26]One of the slaves of the high priest, a relative of the one whose ear Peter had cut off, said, "Didn't I see you in the garden with him?" [27]Again Peter denied it. And immediately the cock crowed.*

The Trial Before Pilate.
[28][n]Then they brought Jesus

from Caiaphas to the praetorium.* It was morning. And they themselves did not enter the praetorium, in order not to be defiled so that they could eat the Passover. 29So Pilate came out to them and said, "What charge do you bring [against] this man?" 30They answered and said to him, "If he were not a criminal, we would not have handed him over to you." 31At this, Pilate said to them, "Take him yourselves, and judge him according to your law." The Jews answered him, "We do not have the right to execute anyone,"* 32*in order that the word of Jesus might be fulfilled that he said indicating the kind of death[o] he would die. 33So Pilate went back into the praetorium and summoned Jesus and said to him, "Are you the King of the Jews?" 34Jesus answered, "Do you say this on your own or have others told you about me?" 35Pilate answered, "I am not a Jew, am I? Your own nation and the chief priests handed you over to me. What have you done?"[p] 36Jesus answered, "My kingdom does not belong to this world. If my kingdom did belong to this world, my attendants [would] be fighting to keep me from being handed over to the Jews. But as it is, my kingdom is not here."[q] 37So Pilate said to him, "Then you are a king?" Jesus answered, "You say I am a king.* For this I was born and for this I came into the world, to testify to the truth. Everyone who belongs to the truth listens to my voice."[r] 38Pilate said to him, "What is truth?"[s]

When he had said this, he again went out to the Jews and said to them, "I find no guilt in him. 39But you have a custom that I release one prisoner to you at Passover.* Do you want me to release to you the King of the Jews?" 40They cried out again, "Not this one but Barabbas!"* Now Barabbas was a revolutionary.

a. [18:1] 2 Sm 15:23; Mt 26:30, 36; Mk 14:26, 32; Lk 22:39.
b. [18:3] Mt 26:47–51; Mk 14:43–44; Lk 22:47.
c. [18:9] 6:39; 10:28; 17:12.
d. [18:11] Mt 20:22; 26:39; Mk 10:38; Lk 22:42.
e. [18:12–14] Mt 26:57–58; Mk 14:53–54; Lk 22:54–55.
f. [18:13] Lk 3:2.
g. [18:14] 11:49–50.
h. [18:15–18] Mt 26:58, 69–70; Mk 14:54, 66–68; Lk 22:54–57.
i. [18:19–24] Mt 26:59–66; Mk 14:55–64; Lk 22:66–71.
j. [18:20] 6:59; 7:14, 26; Is 48:16; Mt 26:55; Mk 4:23; Lk 19:47; 22:53.
k. [18:22] Acts 23:2.
l. [18:24] Mt 26:57.
m. [18:25–27] Mt 26:71–75; Mk 14:69–72; Lk 22:58–62.
n. [18:28–38a] Mt 27:1–2, 11–25; Mk 15:1–5; Lk 23:1–5.
o. [18:32] 3:14; 8:28; 12:32–33.
p. [18:35] 1:11.
q. [18:36] 1:10; 8:23.
r. [18:37] 8:47; 1 Tm 6:13.
s. [18:38b–40] Mt 27:15–26; Mk 15:6–15; Lk 23:18–25; Acts 3:14.

CHAPTER 19

1 [a]Then Pilate took Jesus and had him scourged. 2And the soldiers wove a crown out of thorns and placed it on his head, and clothed him in a purple cloak, 3and they came to him and said, "Hail, King of the Jews!" And they struck him repeatedly. 4Once more Pilate went out and said to them, "Look, I am bringing him out to you, so that you may know that I find no guilt in him." [b] 5So Jesus came out, wearing the crown of thorns and the purple cloak. And he said to them, "Behold, the man!" [c] 6When the chief priests and the guards saw him they cried out, "Crucify him, crucify him!" Pilate said to them, "Take him yourselves and crucify him. I find no guilt in him." [d] 7The Jews answered, [e] "We have a law, and according to that law he ought to die, because he made himself the Son of God." 8Now when Pilate heard this statement, he became even more afraid, 9and went back into the praetorium and said to Jesus, "Where are you from?" Jesus did not answer him. [f] 10So Pilate said to him, "Do you not speak to me? Do you not know that I have power to release you and I have power to crucify you?" 11Jesus answered [him], "You would have no power over me if it had not been given to you from above. For this reason the one who handed me over to you has the greater sin." [g]

[12]Consequently, Pilate tried to release him; but the Jews cried out, "If you release him, you are not a Friend of Caesar.* Everyone who makes himself a king opposes Caesar."[h]

[13]When Pilate heard these words he brought Jesus out and seated him* on the judge's bench in the place called Stone Pavement, in Hebrew, Gabbatha. [14]It was preparation day for Passover, and it was about noon.* And he said to the Jews, "Behold, your king!" [15]They cried out, "Take him away, take him away! Crucify him!" Pilate said to them, "Shall I crucify your king?" The chief priests answered, "We have no king but Caesar." [16]Then he handed him over to them to be crucified.*

The Crucifixion of Jesus. So they took Jesus, [17]*and carrying the cross himself* he went out to what is called the Place of the Skull, in Hebrew, Golgotha. [18]There they crucified him, and with him two others, one on either side, with Jesus in the middle. [19]*Pilate also had an inscription written and put on the cross. It read, "Jesus the Nazorean, the King of the Jews." [20]Now many of the Jews read this inscription, because the place where Jesus was crucified was near the city; and it was written in Hebrew, Latin, and Greek. [21]So the chief priests of the Jews said to Pilate, "Do not write 'The King of the Jews,' but that he said, 'I am the King of the Jews.'"[j] [22]Pilate answered, "What I have written, I have written."

[23]*When the soldiers had crucified Jesus,[k] they took his clothes and divided them into four shares, a share for each soldier.[l] They also took his tunic, but the tunic was seamless, woven in one piece from the top down. [24]So they said to one another, "Let's not tear it, but cast lots for it to see whose it will be," in order

that the passage of scripture might be fulfilled [that says]:

> "They divided my gar-
> ments among them,
> and for my vesture they
> cast lots."

This is what the soldiers did. [25]*[m]Standing by the cross of Jesus were his mother and his mother's sister, Mary the wife of Clopas, and Mary of Magdala. [26]When Jesus saw his mother* and the disciple there whom he loved, he said to his mother, "Woman, behold, your son."[n] [27]Then he said to the disciple, "Behold, your mother." And from that hour the disciple took her into his home.

[28o]After this, aware that everything was now finished, in order that the scripture might be fulfilled, Jesus said, "I thirst."[p] [29]There was a vessel filled with common wine. So they put a sponge soaked in wine on a sprig of hyssop and put it up to his mouth.

[30†]When Jesus had taken the wine, he said, "It is finished."[q] And bowing his head, he handed over the spirit.

The Blood and Water. [31]Now since it was preparation day, in order that the bodies might not remain on the cross on the sabbath, for the sabbath day of that week was a solemn one, the Jews asked Pilate that their legs be broken and they be taken down.[r] [32]So the soldiers came and broke the legs of the first and then of the other one who was crucified with Jesus. [33]But when they came to Jesus and saw that he was already dead, they did not break his legs, [34]*[s]but one soldier thrust his lance into his side, and immediately blood and water flowed out. [35]An eyewitness has testified, and his testimony is true; he knows* that he is speaking the truth, so that you also may [come to] believe.[t] [36]For this happened so that the scripture passage might be fulfilled:

"Not a bone of it will be broken."[u]

[37]And again another passage says:

"They will look upon
him whom they have
pierced."[v]

The Burial of Jesus.[*] [38w]After this, Joseph of Arimathea, secretly a disciple of Jesus for fear of the Jews, asked Pilate if he could remove the body of Jesus. And Pilate permitted it. So he came and took his body. [39]Nicodemus, the one who had first come to him at night, also came bringing a mixture of myrrh and aloes weighing about one hundred pounds.[x] [40]They took the body of Jesus and bound it with burial cloths along with the spices, according to the Jewish burial custom. [41]Now in the place where he had been crucified there was a garden, and in the garden a new tomb, in which no one had yet been buried. [42]So they laid Jesus there because of the Jewish preparation day; for the tomb was close by.

---

a. [19:1–16] Mt 27:27–31; Mk 15:16–20; Lk 23:13–25.
b. [19:4] 18:38.
c. [19:5] Is 52:14.
d. [19:6] 18:31; 19:15.
e. [19:7] 10:33–36; Lv 24:16.
f. [19:9] 7:28.
g. [19:11] 3:27; 10:18; Rom 13:1.
h. [19:12] Acts 17:7.
i. [19:17–28] Mt 27:32–37; Mk 15:21–26; Lk 23:26–35.
j. [19:21] 18:33; Lk 19:14.
k. [19:23–27] Mt 27:38–44; Mk 15:27–32; Lk 23:36–43.
l. [19:23–24] Ps 22:19; Mt 27:35; Mk 15:24; Lk 23:34.
m. [19:25] Mt 27:55; Mk 15:40–41; Lk 8:2; 23:49.
n. [19:26] 13:23.
o. [19:28–30] Mt 27:45–56; Mk 15:33–41; Lk 23:44–49.
p. [19:28] Ps 22:16; 69:22.
q. [19:30] 4:34; 10:18; 17:4; Lk 23:46.
r. [19:31] Ex 12:16; Dt 21:23.
s. [19:34] Nm 20:11; 1 Jn 5:6.
t. [19:35] 7:37–39; 21:24.
u. [19:36] Ex 12:46; Nm 9:12; Ps 34:21.
v. [19:37] Nm 21:9; Zec 12:10; Rev 1:7.
w. [19:38–42] Mt 27:57–60; Mk 15:42–46; Lk 23:46–49.
x. [19:39] 3:1–2; 7:50; Ps 45:9.

CHAPTER 20[*]

The Empty Tomb.[*] [1]On the first day of the week,[a] Mary of Magdala came to the tomb early in the morning, while it was still dark,[*] and saw the stone removed from the tomb.[b] [2]So she ran[*] and went to Simon Peter and to the other disciple whom Jesus loved, and told them, "They have taken the Lord from the tomb, and we don't know where they put him." ³*So Peter and the other disciple went out and came to the tomb. ⁴They both ran, but the other disciple ran faster than Peter and arrived at the tomb first; ⁵he bent down and saw the burial cloths there, but did not go in. ⁶*When Simon Peter arrived after him, he went into the tomb and saw the burial cloths* there, ⁷and the cloth that had covered his head, not with the burial cloths but rolled up in a separate place.ᵈ ⁸Then the other disciple also went in, the one who had arrived at the tomb first, and he saw and believed. ⁹*ᵉFor they did not yet understand the scripture that he had to rise from the dead. ¹⁰Then the disciples returned home.

The Appearance to Mary of Magdala.* ¹¹But Mary stayed outside the tomb weeping.ᶠ And as she wept, she bent over into the tomb ¹²and saw two angels in white sitting there, one at the head and one at the feet where the body of Jesus had been. ¹³And they said to her, "Woman, why are you weeping?" She said to them, "They have taken my Lord, and I don't know where they laid him." ¹⁴When she had said this, she turned around and saw Jesus there, but did not know it was Jesus.ᵍ ¹⁵Jesus said to her, "Woman, why are you weeping? Whom are you looking for?"ʰ She thought it was the gardener and said to him, "Sir, if you carried him away, tell me where you laid him, and I will take him." ¹⁶Jesus said to her, "Mary!" She turned and said to him in Hebrew, "Rabbouni,"* which means Teacher. ¹⁷Jesus said to her, "Stop holding on to me,* for I have not yet ascended to the Father. But go to my brothers and tell them, 'I am going to my Father and your Father, to my God and your God.'"ⁱ

[18]Mary of Magdala went and announced to the disciples, "I have seen the Lord," and what he told her.

Appearance to the Disciples.[*] [19]On the evening of that first day of the week,[j] when the doors were locked, where the disciples[*] were, for fear of the Jews, Jesus came and stood in their midst and said to them, "Peace be with you." [20]When he had said this, he showed them his hands and his side.[*] The disciples rejoiced when they saw the Lord.[k] [21][*][Jesus] said to them again,[l] "Peace be with you. As the Father has sent me, so I send you." [22][*]And when he had said this, he breathed on them and said to them,[m] "Receive the holy Spirit. [23][*][n]Whose sins you forgive are forgiven them, and whose sins you retain are retained."

Thomas. [24]Thomas, called Didymus, one of the Twelve, was not with them when Jesus came. [25]So the other disciples said to him, "We have seen the Lord." But he said to them, "Unless I see the mark of the nails in his hands and put my finger into the nailmarks and put my hand into his side, I will not believe."[o] [26]Now a week later his disciples were again inside and Thomas was with them. Jesus came, although the doors were locked, and stood in their midst and said, "Peace be with you."[p] [27]Then he said to Thomas, "Put your finger here and see my hands, and bring your hand and put it into my side, and do not be unbelieving, but <u>believe</u>." [28][*][q]Thomas answered and said to him, "My Lord and my God!" [29]Jesus said to him, "Have you come to believe because you have seen me?[r] Blessed are those who have not seen and have believed."

Conclusion.[*] [30]Now Jesus did many other signs in the presence of [his] disciples that are not written in this book.[s] [31]But these are written that you may [come to] believe that Jesus is the Messiah, the Son of God, and that through this belief you may have life in his name.[t]

a. [20:1–10] Mt 28:1–10; Mk 16:1–11; Lk 24:1–12.
b. [20:1] 19:25.
c. [20:6] Lk 24:12.
d. [20:7] 11:44; 19:40.
e. [20:9] Acts 2:26–27; 1 Cor 15:4.
f. [20:11–18] Mk 16:9–11.
g. [20:14] 21:4; Mk 16:12; Lk 24:16; 1 Cor 15:43–44.
h. [20:15–17] Mt 28:9–10.
i. [20:17] Acts 1:9.
j. [20:19–23] Mt 28:16–20; Mk 16:14–18; Lk 24:36–44.
k. [20:20] 14:27.
l. [20:21] 17:18; Mt 28:19; Mk 16:15; Lk 24:47–48.
m. [20:22] Gn 2:7; Ez 37:9; 1 Cor 15:45.
n. [20:23] Mt 16:19; 18:18.
o. [20:25] 1 Jn 1:1.
p. [20:26] 21:14.
q. [20:28] 1:1.
r. [20:29] 4:48; Lk 1:45; 1 Pt 1:8.
s. [20:30] 21:25.
t. [20:31] 3:14, 15; 1 Jn 5:13.

IV. EPILOGUE: THE RESURRECTION APPEARANCE IN GALILEE

CHAPTER 21

The Appearance to the Seven Disciples. [1]After this, Jesus revealed himself again to his disciples at the Sea of Tiberias. He revealed himself in this way.[a] [2]Together were Simon Peter, Thomas called Didymus, Nathanael from Cana in Galilee, Zebedee's sons,[b] and two others of his disciples. [3]Simon Peter said to them, "I am going fishing." They said to him, "We also will come with you." So they went out and got into the boat, but that night they caught nothing.[b] [4]When it was already dawn, Jesus was standing on the shore; but the disciples did not realize that it was Jesus.[c] [5]Jesus said to them, "Children, have you caught anything to eat?" They answered him, "No."[d] [6]So he said to them, "Cast the net over the right side of the boat and you will find something." So they cast it, and were not able to pull it in because of the number of fish. [7]So the disciple whom Jesus loved said to Peter, "It is the Lord." When Simon Peter heard that it was the Lord, he tucked in his garment, for he was lightly clad, and jumped into the sea.

[8]The other disciples came in the boat, for they were not far from shore, only about a hundred yards, dragging the net with the fish. [9]*e*When they climbed out on shore, they saw a charcoal fire with fish on it and bread. [10]Jesus said to them, "Bring some of the fish you just caught." [11]So Simon Peter went over and dragged the net ashore full of <u>one hundred fifty-three</u>* large fish. Even though there were so many, the net was not torn.*f* [12]Jesus said to them, "Come, have breakfast." And none of the disciples dared to ask him,* "Who are you?" because they realized it was the Lord. [13]Jesus came over and took the bread and gave it to them, and in like manner the fish.*g* [14]This was now the third time*h* Jesus was revealed to his disciples after being raised from the dead.

Jesus and Peter.** [15]When they had finished breakfast, Jesus said to Simon Peter,* "Simon, son of John, do you love me more than these?"** He said to him, "Yes, Lord, you know that I love you." He said to him, "Feed my lambs." [16]He then said to him a second time, "Simon, son of John, do you love me?" He said to him, "Yes, Lord, you know that I love you." He said to him, "Tend my sheep." [17]He said to him the third time, "Simon, son of John, do you love me?" Peter was distressed that he had said to him a third time, "Do you love me?" and he said to him, "Lord, you know everything; you know that I love you." [Jesus] said to him, "Feed my sheep.*i* [18]*Amen, amen, I say to you,*j* when you were younger, you used to dress yourself and go where you wanted; but when you grow old, you will stretch out your hands, and someone else will dress you and lead you where you do not want to go." [19]He said this signifying by what kind of death he would glorify God. And when he had said this, he said to him, "Follow me."[k]

The Beloved Disciple. [20]Peter turned and saw the disciple following whom Jesus loved, the one who had also reclined upon his chest during the supper and had said, "Master, who is the one who will betray you?"[l] [21]When Peter saw him, he said to Jesus, "Lord, what about him?" [22]Jesus said to him, "What if I want him to remain until I come?* What concern is it of yours? You follow me."[m] [23]So the word spread among the brothers that that disciple would not die. But Jesus had not told him that he would not die, just "What if I want him to remain until I come? [What concern is it of yours?]"

Conclusion. [24]It is this disciple who testifies to these things and has written them,* and we know that his testimony is true.[n] [25]There are also many other things that Jesus did, but if these were to be described individually, I do not think the whole world would contain the books that would be written.[o]

a. [21:1] Mt 26:32; 28:7.
b. [21:3] Mt 4:18; Lk 5:4–10.
c. [21:4] 20:14; Mt 28:17; Lk 24:16.
d. [21:5] Lk 24:41.
e. [21:9] Lk 24:41–43.
f. [21:11] 2 Chr 2:16.
g. [21:13] Lk 24:42.
h. [21:14] 20:19, 26.
i. [21:17] 13:37–38; 18:15–18, 25–27; Mt 26:69–75; Mk 14:66–72; Lk 22:55–62.
j. [21:18] Acts 21:11, 14; 2 Pt 1:14.
k. [21:19] 13:36.
l. [21:20] 13:25.
m. [21:22] Mt 16:28.
n. [21:24] 19:35.
o. [21:25] 20:30.

Notes

* [1:1–18] The prologue states the main themes of the gospel: life, light, truth, the world, testimony, and the preexistence of Jesus Christ, the incarnate *Logos*, who reveals God the Father. In origin, it was probably an early Christian hymn. Its closest parallel is in other christological hymns, Col 1:15–20 and Phil 2:6–11. Its core (Jn 1:1–5, 10–11, 14) is poetic in structure, with short phrases linked by "staircase parallelism," in which the last word of one phrase becomes the first word of the next. Prose inserts (at least Jn 1:6–8, 15) deal with John the Baptist.

* [1:1] **In the beginning**: also the first words of the Old Testament (Gn 1:1). **Was**: this verb is used three times with different meanings in this verse: existence, relationship, and predication. **The Word** (Greek *logos*): this term combines God's dynamic, creative word (Genesis), personified preexistent Wisdom as the instrument of God's creative activity (Proverbs), and the ultimate intelligibility of reality (Hellenistic philosophy). **With God**: the Greek preposition here connotes communication with another. **Was God**: lack of a definite article with "God" in Greek signifies predication rather than identification.

* [1:3] **What came to be**: while the oldest manuscripts have no punctuation here, the corrector of Bodmer Papyrus P^{75}, some manuscripts, and the Ante-Nicene Fathers take this phrase with what follows, as staircase parallelism. Connection with Jn 1:3 reflects fourth-century anti-Arianism.

* [1:5] The ethical dualism of light and darkness is paralleled in intertestamental literature and in the Dead Sea Scrolls. **Overcome**: "comprehend" is another possible translation, but cf. Jn 12:35; Wis 7:29–30.

* [1:6] John was **sent** just as Jesus was "sent" (Jn 4:34) in divine mission. Other references to John the Baptist in this gospel emphasize the differences between them and John's subordinate role.

* [1:7] **Testimony**: the testimony theme of John is introduced, which portrays Jesus as if on trial throughout his ministry. All testify to Jesus: John the Baptist, the Samaritan woman, scripture, his works, the crowds, the Spirit, and his disciples.

* [1:11] **What was his own . . . his own people**: first a neuter, literally, "his own property/possession" (probably = Israel), then a masculine, "his own people" (the Israelites).

* [1:13] Believers in Jesus become children of God not through any of the three natural causes mentioned but through God who is the immediate cause of the new spiritual life. **Were born**: the Greek verb can mean "begotten" (by a male) or "born" (from a female or of parents). The variant "he who was begotten," asserting Jesus' virginal conception, is weakly attested in Old Latin and Syriac versions.

* [1:14] **Flesh**: the whole person, used probably against docetic tendencies (cf. 1 Jn 4:2; 2 Jn 7). **Made his dwelling**: literally, "pitched his tent/tabernacle." Cf. the tabernacle or tent of meeting that was the place of God's presence among his people (Ex 25:8–9). The incarnate Word was the new mode of God's presence among his people. The Greek verb has the same consonants as the Aramaic word for God's presence (Shekinah). **Glory**: God's visible manifestation of majesty in power, which once filled the tabernacle (Ex 40:34) and the temple (1 Kgs 8:10–11, 27), is now centered in Jesus. **Only Son**: Greek, *monogenēs*, but see note on Jn 1:18. **Grace and truth**: these words may represent two Old Testament terms describing Yahweh in covenant relationship with Israel (cf. Ex 34:6), thus God's "love" and "fidelity." The Word shares Yahweh's covenant qualities.

* [1:15] This verse, interrupting Jn 1:14, 16 seems drawn from Jn 1:30.

* [1:16] **Grace in place of grace**: replacement of the Old Covenant with the New (cf. Jn 1:17). Other possible translations are "grace upon grace" (accumulation) and "grace for grace" (correspondence).

* [1:18] **The only Son, God**: while the vast majority of later textual witnesses have another reading, "the Son, the only one" or "the only Son,"

the translation above follows the best and earliest manuscripts, *monogenēs theos*, but takes the first term to mean not just "Only One" but to include a filial relationship with the Father, as at Lk 9:38 ("only child") or Heb 11:17 ("only son") and as translated at Jn 1:14. The Logos is thus "only Son" and God but not Father/God.

* [1:19–51] The testimony of John the Baptist about the Messiah and Jesus' self-revelation to the first disciples. This section constitutes the introduction to the gospel proper and is connected with the prose inserts in the prologue. It develops the major theme of testimony in four scenes: John's negative testimony about himself; his positive testimony about Jesus; the revelation of Jesus to Andrew and Peter; the revelation of Jesus to Philip and Nathanael.

* [1:19] **The Jews**: throughout most of the gospel, the "Jews" does not refer to the Jewish people as such but to the hostile authorities, both Pharisees and Sadducees, particularly in Jerusalem, who refuse to believe in Jesus. The usage reflects the atmosphere, at the end of the first century, of polemics between church and synagogue, or possibly it refers to Jews as representative of a hostile world (Jn 1:10–11).

* [1:20] **Messiah**: the anointed agent of Yahweh, usually considered to be of Davidic descent. See further the note on Jn 1:41.

* [1:21] **Elijah**: the Baptist did not claim to be Elijah returned to earth (cf. Mal 3:19; Mt 11:14). **The Prophet**: probably the prophet like Moses (Dt 18:15; cf. Acts 3:22).

* [1:23] This is a repunctuation and reinterpretation (as in the synoptic gospels and Septuagint) of the Hebrew text of Is 40:3 which reads, "A voice cries out: In the desert prepare the way of the LORD."

* [1:24] **Some Pharisees**: other translations, such as "Now they had been sent from the Pharisees," misunderstand the grammatical construction. This is a different group from that in Jn 1:19; the priests and Levites would have been Sadducees, not Pharisees.

* [1:26] **I baptize with water**: the synoptics add "but he will baptize you with the holy Spirit" (Mk 1:8) or ". . . holy Spirit and fire" (Mt 3:11; Lk 3:16). John's emphasis is on purification and preparation for a better baptism.

* [1:28] **Bethany across the Jordan**: site unknown. Another reading is "Bethabara."

* [1:29] **The Lamb of God**: the background for this title may be the victorious apocalyptic lamb who would destroy evil in the world (Rev 5–7; 17:14); the paschal lamb, whose blood saved Israel (Ex 12); and/or the suffering servant led like a lamb to the slaughter as a sin-offering (Is 53:7, 10).

* [1:30] **He existed before me**: possibly as Elijah (to come, Jn 1:27); for the evangelist and his

audience, Jesus' preexistence would be implied (see note on Jn 1:1).

* [1:31] **I did not know him**: this gospel shows no knowledge of the tradition (Lk 1) about the kinship of Jesus and John the Baptist. **The reason why I came baptizing with water**: in this gospel, John's baptism is not connected with forgiveness of sins; its purpose is revelatory, that Jesus may be made known to Israel.

* [1:32] **Like a dove**: a symbol of the new creation (Gn 8:8) or the community of Israel (Hos 11:11). **Remain**: the first use of a favorite verb in John, emphasizing the permanency of the relationship between Father and Son (as here) and between the Son and the Christian. Jesus is the permanent bearer of the Spirit.

* [1:34] **The Son of God**: this reading is supported by good Greek manuscripts, including the Chester Beatty and Bodmer Papyri and the Vatican Codex, but is suspect because it harmonizes this passage with the synoptic version: "This is my beloved Son" (Mt 3:17; Mk 1:11; Lk 3:22). The poorly attested alternate reading, "God's chosen One," is probably a reference to the Servant of Yahweh (Is 42:1).

* [1:36] John the Baptist's testimony makes his disciples' following of Jesus plausible.

* [1:37] **The two disciples**: Andrew (Jn 1:40) and, traditionally, John, son of Zebedee (see note on Jn 13:23).

* [1:39] **Four in the afternoon**: literally, the tenth hour, from sunrise, in the Roman calculation of time. Some suggest that the next day, beginning at sunset, was the sabbath; they would have stayed with Jesus to avoid travel on it.

* [1:41] **Messiah**: the Hebrew word *māšîaḥ*, "anointed one" (see note on Lk 2:11), appears in Greek as the transliterated *messias* only here and in Jn 4:25. Elsewhere the Greek translation *christos* is used.

* [1:42] **Simon, the son of John**: in Mt 16:17, Simon is called *Bariōna*, "son of Jonah," a different tradition for the name of Simon's father. **Cephas**: in Aramaic = the Rock; cf. Mt 16:18. Neither the Greek equivalent **Petros** nor, with one isolated exception, **Cephas** is attested as a personal name before Christian times.

* [1:43] **He**: grammatically, could be Peter, but logically is probably Jesus.

* [1:47] **A true Israelite. There is no duplicity in him**: Jacob was the first to bear the name "Israel" (Gn 32:29), but Jacob was a man of duplicity (Gn 27:35–36).

* [1:48] **Under the fig tree**: a symbol of messianic peace (cf. Mi 4:4; Zec 3:10).

* [1:49] **Son of God**: this title is used in the Old Testament, among other ways, as a title of adoption for the Davidic king (2 Sm 7:14; Ps 2:7; 89:27), and thus here, with **King of Israel**, in a messianic sense. For the evangelist, **Son of God** also points to Jesus' divinity (cf. Jn 20:28).

* [1:50] Possibly a statement: "You [singular] believe because I saw you under the fig tree."

* [1:51] The double "Amen" is characteristic of John. **You** is plural in Greek. The allusion is to Jacob's ladder (Gn 28:12).

---

* [2:1–6:71] Signs revealing Jesus as the Messiah to all Israel. "Sign" (*sēmeion*) is John's symbolic term for Jesus' wondrous deeds (see Introduction). The Old Testament background lies in the Exodus story (cf. Dt 11:3; 29:2). John is interested primarily in what the *sēmeia* signify: God's intervention in human history in a new way through Jesus.

* [2:1–11] The first sign. This story of replacement of Jewish ceremonial washings (Jn 2:6) presents the initial revelation about Jesus at the outset of his ministry. He manifests his glory; the disciples believe. There is no synoptic parallel.

* [2:1] **Cana**: unknown from the Old Testament. **The mother of Jesus**: she is never named in John.

* [2:4] This verse may seek to show that Jesus did not work miracles to help his family and friends, as in the apocryphal gospels. **Woman**: a normal, polite form of address, but unattested in reference to one's mother. Cf. also Jn 19:26. **How does your concern affect me?**: literally, "What is this to me and to you?"—a Hebrew expression of either hostility (Jgs 11:12; 2 Chr 35:21; 1 Kgs 17:18) or denial of common interest (Hos 14:9; 2 Kgs 3:13). Cf. Mk 1:24; 5:7 used by demons to Jesus. **My hour has not yet come**: the translation as a question ("Has not my hour now come?"), while preferable grammatically and supported by Greek Fathers, seems unlikely from a comparison with Jn 7:6, 30. The "hour" is that of Jesus' passion, death, resurrection, and ascension (Jn 13:1).

* [2:6] **Twenty to thirty gallons**: literally, "two or three measures"; the Attic liquid measure contained 39.39 liters. The vast quantity recalls prophecies of abundance in the last days; cf. Am 9:13–14; Hos 14:7; Jer 31:12.

* [2:8] **Headwaiter**: used of the official who managed a banquet, but there is no evidence of such a functionary in Palestine. Perhaps here a friend of the family acted as master of ceremonies; cf. Sir 32:1.

* [2:11] **The beginning of his signs**: the first of seven (see Introduction).

* [2:12–3:21] The next three episodes take place in Jerusalem. Only the first is paralleled in the synoptic gospels.

* [2:12] This transitional verse may be a harmonization with the synoptic tradition in Lk 4:31 and Mt 4:13. There are many textual variants. John depicts no extended ministry in Capernaum as do the synoptics.

* [2:13–22] This episode indicates the post-resurrectional replacement of the temple by the person of Jesus.

* [2:13] **Passover**: this is the first Passover mentioned in John; a second is mentioned in Jn 6:4; a third in Jn 13:1. Taken literally, they point to a ministry of at least two years.

* [2:14–22] The other gospels place the cleansing of the temple in the last days of Jesus' life (Matthew, on the day Jesus entered Jerusalem; Mark, on the next day). The order of events in the gospel narratives is often determined by theological motives rather than by chronological data.

* [2:14] **Oxen, sheep, and doves**: intended for sacrifice. The doves were the offerings of the poor (Lv 5:7). **Money-changers**: for a temple tax paid by every male Jew more than nineteen years of age, with a half-shekel coin (Ex 30:11–16), in Syrian currency. See note on Mt 17:24.

* [2:17] Ps 69:10, changed to future tense to apply to Jesus.

* [2:19] This saying about the destruction of the temple occurs in various forms (Mt 24:2; 27:40; Mk 13:2; 15:29; Lk 21:6; cf. Acts 6:14). Mt 26:61 has: "I *can* destroy the temple of God. . ."; see note there. In Mk 14:58, there is a metaphorical contrast with a new temple: "I will destroy this temple *made with hands* and within three days I will build another *not made with hands*." Here it is symbolic of Jesus' resurrection and the resulting community (see Jn 2:21 and Rev 21:2). **In three days**: an Old Testament expression for a short, indefinite period of time; cf. Hos 6:2.

* [2:20] **Forty-six years**: based on references in Josephus (*Jewish Wars* 1:401; *Antiquities* 15:380), possibly the spring of A.D. 28. Cf. note on Lk 3:1.

* [3:1–21] Jesus instructs Nicodemus on the necessity of a new birth from above. This scene in Jerusalem at Passover exemplifies the faith engendered by signs (Jn 2:23). It continues the self-manifestation of Jesus in Jerusalem begun in Jn 2. This is the first of the Johannine discourses, shifting from dialogue to monologue (Jn 3:11–15) to reflection of the evangelist (Jn 3:16–21). The shift from singular through Jn 3:10 to plural in Jn 3:11 may reflect the early church's controversy with the Jews.

* [3:1] **A ruler of the Jews**: most likely a member of the Jewish council, the Sanhedrin; see note on Mk 8:31.

* [3:3] **Born**: see note on Jn 1:13. **From above**: the Greek adverb *anōthen* means both "from above" and "again." Jesus means "from above" (see Jn 3:31) but Nicodemus misunderstands it as "again." This misunderstanding serves as a springboard for further instruction.

* [3:8] **Wind**: the Greek word *pneuma* (as well as the Hebrew *rûah*) means both "wind" and "spirit." In the play on the double meaning, "wind" is primary.

* [3:14] **Lifted up**: in Nm 21:9, Moses simply "mounted" a serpent upon a pole. John here substitutes a verb implying glorification. Jesus, exalted to glory at his cross and resurrection, represents healing for all.

* [3:15] **Eternal life**: used here for the first time in John, this term stresses quality of life rather than duration.

* [3:16] **Gave**: as a gift in the incarnation, and also "over to death" in the crucifixion; cf. Rom 8:32.

* [3:17–19] **Condemn**: the Greek root means both judgment and condemnation. Jesus' purpose is to save, but his coming provokes judgment; some condemn themselves by turning from the light.

* [3:19] Judgment is not only future but is partially realized here and now.

* [3:22–26] Jesus' ministry in Judea is only loosely connected with Jn 2:13–3:21; cf. Jn 1:19–36. Perhaps John the Baptist's further testimony was transposed here to give meaning to "water" in Jn 3:5. Jesus is depicted as baptizing (Jn 3:22); contrast Jn 4:2.

* [3:23] **Aenon near Salim**: site uncertain, either in the upper Jordan valley or in Samaria.

* [3:24] A remark probably intended to avoid objections based on a chronology like that of the synoptics (Mt 4:12; Mk 1:14).

* [3:25] **A Jew**: some think Jesus is meant. Many manuscripts read "Jews."

* [3:29] **The best man**: literally, "the friend of the groom," the *shoshben* of Jewish tradition, who arranged the wedding. Competition between him and the groom would be unthinkable.

* [3:31–36] It is uncertain whether these are words by the Baptist, Jesus, or the evangelist. They are reflections on the two preceding scenes.

* [3:34] **His gift**: of God or to Jesus, perhaps both. This verse echoes Jn 3:5, 8.

* [4:1–42] Jesus in Samaria. The self-revelation of Jesus continues with his second discourse, on his mission to "half-Jews." It continues the theme of replacement, here with regard to cult (Jn 4:21). Water (Jn 4:7–15) serves as a symbol (as at Cana and in the Nicodemus episode).

* [4:2] An editorial refinement of Jn 3:22, perhaps directed against followers of John the Baptist who claimed that Jesus imitated him.

* [4:4] **He had to**: a theological necessity; geographically, Jews often bypassed Samaria by taking a route across the Jordan.

* [4:5] **Sychar**: Jerome identifies this with Shechem, a reading found in Syriac manuscripts.

* [4:9] Samaritan women were regarded by Jews as ritually impure, and therefore Jews were forbidden to drink from any vessel they had handled.

* [4:10] **Living water**: the water of life, i.e., the revelation that Jesus brings; the woman thinks of "flowing water," so much more desirable than stagnant well water. On John's device of such misunderstanding, cf. note on Jn 3:3.

* [4:11] **Sir**: the Greek *kyrios* means "master" or "lord," as a respectful mode of address for a human being or a deity; cf. Jn 4:19. It is also the word used in the Septuagint for the Hebrew *'adōnai*, substituted for the tetragrammaton YHWH.

* [4:20] **This mountain**: Gerizim, on which a temple was erected in the fourth century B.C. by Samaritans to rival Mount Zion in Jerusalem; cf. Dt 27:4 (Mount Ebal = the Jews' term for Gerizim).

* [4:23] **In Spirit and truth**: not a reference to an interior worship within one's own spirit. The Spirit is the spirit given by God that reveals truth and enables one to worship God appropriately (Jn 14:16–17). Cf. "born of water and Spirit" (Jn 3:5).

* [4:25] The expectations of the Samaritans are expressed here in Jewish terminology. They did not expect a messianic king of the house of David but a prophet like Moses (Dt 18:15).

* [4:26] **I am he**: it could also be translated "I am," an Old Testament self-designation of Yahweh (Is 43:3, etc.); cf. Jn 6:20; 8:24, 28, 58; 13:19; 18:5–6, 8. See note on Mk 6:50.

* [4:27] **Talking with a woman**: a religious and social restriction that Jesus is pictured treating as unimportant.

* [4:35] '**In four months . . .** ': probably a proverb; cf. Mt 9:37–38.

* [4:36] **Already**: this word may go with the preceding verse rather than with Jn 4:36.

* [4:39] The woman is presented as a missionary, described in virtually the same words as the disciples are in Jesus' prayer (Jn 17:20).

* [4:43–54] Jesus' arrival in Cana in Galilee; the second sign. This section introduces another theme, that of the life-giving word of Jesus. It is explicitly linked to the first sign (Jn 2:11). The royal official believes (Jn 4:50): the natural life given his son is a sign of eternal life.

* [4:44] Probably a reminiscence of a tradition as in Mk 6:4. Cf. Gospel of Thomas 31: "No prophet is acceptable in his village, no physician heals those who know him."

* [4:46–54] The story of the cure of the royal official's son may be a third version of the cure of the centurion's son (Mt 8:5–13) or servant (Lk 7:1–10). Cf. also Mt 15:21–28; Mk 7:24–30.

---

* [5:1–47] The self-revelation of Jesus continues in Jerusalem at a feast. The third sign (cf. Jn 2:11; 4:54) is performed, the cure of a paralytic by Jesus' life-giving word. The water of the pool fails to bring life; Jesus' word does.

* [5:1] The reference in Jn 5:45–46 to Moses suggests that the feast was Pentecost. The connection

of that feast with the giving of the law to Moses on Sinai, attested in later Judaism, may already have been made in the first century. The feast could also be Passover (cf. Jn 6:4). John stresses that the day was a sabbath (Jn 5:9).

* [5:2] There is no noun with **Sheep**. "Gate" is supplied on the grounds that there must have been a gate in the NE wall of the temple area where animals for sacrifice were brought in; cf. Neh 3:1, 32; 12:39. **Hebrew**: more precisely, Aramaic. **Bethesda**: preferred to variants "Be(th)zatha" and "Bethsaida"; *bêt-'ešdatayîn* is given as the name of a double pool northeast of the temple area in the Qumran Copper Roll. **Five porticoes**: a pool excavated in Jerusalem actually has five porticoes.

* [5:3] The Caesarean and Western recensions, followed by the Vulgate, add "waiting for the movement of the water." Apparently an intermittent spring in the pool bubbled up occasionally (see Jn 5:7). This turbulence was believed to cure.

* [5:4] Toward the end of the second century in the West and among the fourth-century Greek Fathers, an additional verse was known: "For [from time to time] an angel of the Lord used to come down into the pool; and the water was stirred up, so the first one to get in [after the stirring of the water] was healed of whatever disease afflicted him." The angel was a popular explanation of the turbulence and the healing powers attributed to it. This verse is missing from all early Greek manuscripts and the earliest versions, including the original Vulgate. Its vocabulary is markedly non-Johannine.

* [5:14] While the cure of the paralytic in Mk 2:1–12 is associated with the forgiveness of sins, Jesus never drew a one-to-one connection between sin and suffering (cf. Jn 9:3; Lk 12:1–5), as did Ez 18:20.

* [5:17] Sabbath observance (Jn 5:10) was based on God's resting on the seventh day (cf. Gn 2:2–3; Ex 20:11). Philo and some rabbis insisted that God's providence remains active on the sabbath, keeping all things in existence, giving life in birth and taking it away in death. Other rabbis taught that God rested from creating, but not from judging (= ruling, governing). Jesus here claims the same authority to work as the Father, and, in the discourse that follows, the same divine prerogatives: power over life and death (Jn 5:21, 24–26) and judgment (Jn 5:22, 27).

* [5:19] This proverb or parable is taken from apprenticeship in a trade: the activity of a son is modeled on that of his father. Jesus' dependence on the Father is justification for doing what the Father does.

* [5:21] **Gives life**: in the Old Testament, a divine prerogative (Dt 32:39; 1 Sm 2:6; 2 Kgs 5:7; Tb 13:2; Is 26:19; Dn 12:2).

* [5:22] **Judgment**: another divine prerogative, often expressed as acquittal or condemnation (Dt 32:36; Ps 43:1).

* [5:28–29] While Jn 5:19–27 present realized eschatology, Jn 5:28–29 are future eschatology; cf. Dn 12:2.

* [5:32] **Another**: likely the Father, who in four different ways gives testimony to Jesus, as indicated in the verse groupings Jn 5:33–34, 36, 37–38, 39–40.

* [5:35] **Lamp**: cf. Ps 132:17—"I will place a lamp for my anointed (= David)," and possibly the description of Elijah in Sir 48:1. But only **for a while**, indicating the temporary and subordinate nature of John's mission.

* [5:39] **You search**: this may be an imperative: "Search the scriptures, because you think that you have eternal life through them."

* [5:41] **Praise**: the same Greek word means "praise" or "honor" (from others) and "glory" (from God). There is a play on this in Jn 5:44.

* [6:1–15] This story of the multiplication of the loaves is the fourth sign (cf. note on Jn 5:1–47). It is the only miracle story found in all four gospels (occurring twice in Mark and Matthew). See notes on Mt 14:13–21; 15:32–39. John differs on the roles of Philip and Andrew, the proximity of Passover (Jn 6:4), and the allusion to Elisha (see Jn 6:9). The story here symbolizes the food that is really available through Jesus. It connotes a new exodus and has eucharistic overtones.

* [6:1] [**Of Tiberias**]: the awkward apposition represents a later name of the Sea of Galilee. It was probably originally a marginal gloss.

* [6:5] Jesus takes the initiative (in the synoptics, the disciples do), possibly pictured as (cf. Jn 6:14) the new Moses (cf. Nm 11:13).

* [6:6] Probably the evangelist's comment; in this gospel Jesus is never portrayed as ignorant of anything.

* [6:7] **Days' wages**: literally, "denarii"; a Roman denarius is a day's wage in Mt 20:2.

* [6:9] **Barley loaves**: the food of the poor. There seems to be an allusion to the story of Elisha multiplying the barley bread in 2 Kgs 4:42–44.

* [6:10] **Grass**: implies springtime, and therefore **Passover**. **Five thousand**: so Mk 6:39, 44 and parallels.

* [6:13] **Baskets**: the word describes the typically Palestinian wicker basket, as in Mk 6:43 and parallels.

* [6:14] **The Prophet**: probably the prophet like Moses (see note on Jn 1:21). **The one who is to come into the world**: probably Elijah; cf. Mal 3:1, 23.

* [6:16–21] The fifth sign is a nature miracle, portraying Jesus sharing Yahweh's power. Cf. the parallel stories following the multiplication of the loaves in Mk 6:45–52 and Mt 14:22–33.

* [6:19] **Walking on the sea**: although the Greek (cf. Jn 6:16) could mean "on the seashore" or "by the sea" (cf. Jn 21:1), the parallels, especially Mt 14:25, make clear that Jesus walked upon the water. John may allude to Jb 9:8: God "treads upon the crests of the sea."

* [6:20] **It is I**: literally, "I am." See also notes on Jn 4:26 and Mk 6:50.

* [6:22–71] Discourse on the bread of life; replacement of the manna. Jn 6:22–34 serve as an introduction, Jn 6:35–59 constitute the discourse proper, Jn 6:60–71 portray the reaction of the disciples and Peter's confession.

* [6:23] Possibly a later interpolation, to explain how the crowd got to Capernaum.

* [6:27] **The food that endures for eternal life**: cf. Jn 4:14, on water "springing up to eternal life."

* [6:31] **Bread from heaven**: cf. Ex 16:4, 15, 32–34 and the notes there; Ps 78:24. The manna, thought to have been hidden by Jeremiah (2 Mc 2:5–8), was expected to reappear miraculously at Passover, in the last days.

* [6:35–59] Up to Jn 6:50 "bread of life" is a figure for God's revelation in Jesus; in Jn 6:51–58, the eucharistic theme comes to the fore. There may thus be a break between Jn 6:50–51.

* [6:43] **Murmuring**: the word may reflect the Greek of Ex 16:2, 7–8.

* [6:54–58] **Eats**: the verb used in these verses is not the classical Greek verb used of human eating, but that of animal eating: "munch," "gnaw." This may be part of John's emphasis on the reality of the flesh and blood of Jesus (cf. Jn 6:55), but the same verb eventually became the ordinary verb in Greek meaning "eat."

* [6:60–71] These verses refer more to themes of Jn 6:35–50 than to those of Jn 6:51–58 and seem to be addressed to members of the Johannine community who found it difficult to accept the high christology reflected in the bread of life discourse.

* [6:62] This unfinished conditional sentence is obscure. Probably there is a reference to Jn 6:49–51. Jesus claims to be **the bread that comes down from heaven** (Jn 6:50); this claim provokes incredulity (Jn 6:60); and so Jesus is pictured as asking what his disciples will say when he goes up to heaven.

* [6:63] **Spirit . . . flesh**: probably not a reference to the eucharistic body of Jesus but to the supernatural and the natural, as in Jn 3:6. **Spirit and life**: all Jesus said about the bread of life is the revelation of the Spirit.

* [7–8] These chapters contain events about the feast of Tabernacles (Sukkoth, Ingathering: Ex 23:16; Tents, Booths: Dt 16:13–16), with its symbols of booths (originally built to shelter harvesters), rain (water from Siloam poured on the temple altar), and lights (illumination of the four torches in the Court of the Women). They

continue the theme of the replacement of feasts (Passover, Jn 2:13; 6:4; Hanukkah, Jn 10:22; Pentecost, Jn 5:1), here accomplished by Jesus as the Living Water. These chapters comprise seven miscellaneous controversies and dialogues. There is a literary inclusion with Jesus in hiding in Jn 7:4, 10; 8:59. There are frequent references to attempts on his life: Jn 7:1, 13, 19, 25, 30, 32, 44; 8:37, 40, 59.

* [7:3] **Brothers**: these relatives (cf. Jn 2:12 and see note on Mk 6:3) are never portrayed as disciples until after the resurrection (Acts 1:14). Mt 13:55 and Mk 6:3 give the names of four of them. Jesus has already performed works/signs in Judea; cf. Jn 2:23; 3:2; 4:45; 5:8.

* [7:6] **Time**: the Greek word means "opportune time," here a synonym for Jesus' "hour" (see note on Jn 2:4), his death and resurrection. In the wordplay, any time is suitable for Jesus' brothers, because they are not dependent on God's will.

* [7:8] **I am not going up**: an early attested reading "not yet" seems a correction, since Jesus in the story does go up to the feast. "Go up," in a play on words, refers not only to going up to Jerusalem but also to exaltation at the cross, resurrection, and ascension; cf. Jn 3:14; 6:62; 20:17.

* [7:14–31] Jesus teaches in the temple; debate with the Jews.

* [7:15] **Without having studied**: literally, "How does he know letters without having learned?" Children were taught to read and write by means of the scriptures. But here more than Jesus' literacy is being discussed; the people are wondering how he can teach like a rabbi. Rabbis were trained by other rabbis and traditionally quoted their teachers.

* [7:17] **To do his will**: presumably a reference back to the "work" of Jn 6:29: belief in the one whom God has sent.

* [7:20] **You are possessed**: literally, "You have a demon." The insane were thought to be possessed by a demoniacal spirit.

* [7:21] **One work**: the cure of the paralytic (Jn 5:1–9) because of the reference to the sabbath (Jn 7:22; 5:9–10).

* [7:26] **The authorities**: the members of the Sanhedrin (same term as Jn 3:1).

* [7:32–36] Jesus announces his approaching departure (cf. also Jn 8:21; 12:36; 13:33) and complete control over his destiny.

* [7:35] **Dispersion**: or "diaspora": Jews living outside Palestine. **Greeks**: probably refers to the Gentiles in the Mediterranean area; cf. Jn 12:20.

* [7:37, 39] Promise of living water through the Spirit.

* [7:38] **Living water**: not an exact quotation from any Old Testament passage; in the gospel context the gift of the Spirit is meant; cf. Jn 3:5. **From within him**: either Jesus or the believer; if Jesus, it continues the Jesus-Moses motif (water from the rock, Ex 17:6; Nm 20:11) as well as Jesus

as the new temple (cf. Ez 47:1). Grammatically, it goes better with the believer.

* [7:39] **No Spirit yet**: Codex Vaticanus and early Latin, Syriac, and Coptic versions add "given." In this gospel, the sending of the Spirit cannot take place until Jesus' glorification through his death, resurrection, and ascension; cf. Jn 20:22.

* [7:40–53] Discussion of the Davidic lineage of the Messiah.

* [7:53–8:11] The story of the woman caught in adultery is a later insertion here, missing from all early Greek manuscripts. A Western text-type insertion, attested mainly in Old Latin translations, it is found in different places in different manuscripts: here, or after Jn 7:36 or at the end of this gospel, or after Jn 21:38, or at the end of that gospel. There are many non-Johannine features in the language, and there are also many doubtful readings within the passage. The style and motifs are similar to those of Luke, and it fits better with the general situation at the end of Lk 21, but it was probably inserted here because of the allusion to Jer 17:13 (cf. note on Jn 8:6) and the statement, "I do not judge anyone," in Jn 8:15. The Catholic Church accepts this passage as canonical scripture.

* [8:1] **Mount of Olives**: not mentioned elsewhere in the gospel tradition outside of passion week.

* [8:5] Lv 20:10 and Dt 22:22 mention only death, but Dt 22:23–24 prescribes stoning for a betrothed virgin.

* [8:6] Cf. Jer 17:13 (RSV): "Those who turn away from thee shall be written in the earth, for they have forsaken the LORD, the fountain of living water"; cf. Jn 7:38.

* [8:7] The first stones were to be thrown by the witnesses (Dt 17:7).

* [8:12–20] Jesus the light of the world. Jesus replaces the four torches of the illumination of the temple as the light of joy.

* [8:14] **My testimony can be verified**: this seems to contradict Jn 5:31, but the emphasis here is on Jesus' origin from the Father and his divine destiny. **Where I am going**: indicates Jesus' passion and glorification.

* [8:15] **By appearances**: literally, "according to the flesh." **I do not judge anyone**: superficial contradiction of Jn 5:22, 27, 30; here the emphasis is that the judgment is not by material standards.

* [8:17] **Your law**: a reflection of later controversy between church and synagogue.

* [8:21–30] He whose ambassador I am is with me. Jesus' origin is from God; he can reveal God.

* [8:21] **You will die in your sin**: i.e., of disbelief; cf. Jn 8:24. **Where I am going you cannot come**: except through faith in Jesus' passion-resurrection.

* [8:22] The Jews suspect that he is referring to his death. Johannine irony is apparent here; Jesus' death will not be self-inflicted but destined by God.

* [8:24, 28] **I AM**: an expression that late Jewish tradition understood as Yahweh's own self-designation (Is 43:10); see note on Jn 4:26. Jesus is here placed on a par with Yahweh.

* [8:25] **What I told you from the beginning**: this verse seems textually corrupt, with several other possible translations: "(I am) what I say to you"; "Why do I speak to you at all?" The earliest attested reading (Bodmer Papyrus P⁶⁶) has (in a second hand), "I told you at the beginning what I am also telling you (now)." The answer here (cf. Prv 8:22) seems to hinge on a misunderstanding of Jn 8:24 "*that* I AM" as "*what* I am."

* [8:31–59] Jesus' origin ("before Abraham") and destiny are developed; the truth will free them from sin (Jn 8:34) and death (Jn 8:51).

* [8:31] **Those Jews who believed in him**: a rough editorial suture, since in Jn 8:37 they are described as trying to kill Jesus.

* [8:33] **Have never been enslaved to anyone**: since, historically, the Jews were enslaved almost continuously, this verse is probably Johannine irony, about slavery to sin.

* [8:35] **A slave . . . a son**: an allusion to Ishmael and Isaac (Gn 16; 21), or to the release of a slave after six years (Ex 21:2; Dt 15:12).

* [8:38] **The Father**: i.e., God. It is also possible, however, to understand the second part of the verse as a sarcastic reference to descent of the Jews from the devil (Jn 8:44), "You do what you have heard from [your] father."

* [8:39] **The works of Abraham**: Abraham believed; cf. Rom 4:11–17; Jas 2:21–23.

* [8:48] **Samaritan**: therefore interested in magical powers; cf. Acts 7:14–24.

* [8:53] **Are you greater than our father Abraham?**: cf. Jn 4:12.

* [8:56] **He saw it**: this seems a reference to the birth of Isaac (Gn 17:7; 21:6), the beginning of the fulfillment of promises about Abraham's seed.

* [8:57] The evidence of the third-century Bodmer Papyrus P⁷⁵ and the first hand of Codex Sinaiticus indicates that the text originally read: "How can Abraham have seen you?"

* [8:58] **Came to be, I AM**: the Greek word used for "came to be" is the one used of all creation in the prologue, while the word used for "am" is the one reserved for the Logos.

* [9:1–10:21] Sabbath healing of the man born blind. This sixth sign is introduced to illustrate the saying, "I am the light of the world" (Jn 8:12; 9:5). The narrative of conflict about Jesus contrasts Jesus (light) with the Jews (blindness, Jn 9:39–41). The theme of water is reintroduced in the reference to the pool of Siloam. Ironically, Jesus is being judged by the Jews, yet the Jews are judged by the Light of the world; cf. Jn 3:19–21.

* [9:2] See note on Jn 5:14, and Ex 20:5, that parents' sins were visited upon their children. Jesus denies such a cause and emphasizes the purpose: the infirmity was providential.

* [9:7] **Go wash**: perhaps a test of faith; cf. 2 Kgs 5:10–14. The water tunnel Siloam (= Sent) is used as a symbol of Jesus, sent by his Father.

* [9:14] In using spittle, kneading clay, and healing, Jesus had broken the sabbath rules laid down by Jewish tradition.

* [9:22] This comment of the evangelist (in terms used again in Jn 12:42; 16:2) envisages a situation after Jesus' ministry. Rejection/excommunication from the synagogue of Jews who confessed Jesus as Messiah seems to have begun ca. A.D. 85, when the curse against the *minim* or heretics was introduced into the "Eighteen Benedictions."

* [9:24] **Give God the praise!**: an Old Testament formula of adjuration to tell the truth; cf. Jos 7:19; 1 Sm 6:5 LXX. Cf. Jn 5:41.

* [9:32] **A person born blind**: the only Old Testament cure from blindness is found in Tobit (cf. Tb 7:7; 11:7–13; 14:1–2), but Tobit was not born blind.

* [9:39–41] These verses spell out the symbolic meaning of the cure; the Pharisees are not the innocent blind, willing to accept the testimony of others.

* [10:1–21] The good shepherd discourse continues the theme of attack on the Pharisees that ends Jn 9. The figure is allegorical: the hired hands are the Pharisees who excommunicated the cured blind man. It serves as a commentary on Jn 9. For the shepherd motif, used of Yahweh in the Old Testament, cf. Ex 34; Gn 48:15; 49:24; Mi 7:14; Ps 23:1–4; 80:1.

* [10:1] **Sheepfold**: a low stone wall open to the sky.

* [10:4] **Recognize his voice**: the Pharisees do not recognize Jesus, but the people of God, symbolized by the blind man, do.

* [10:6] **Figure of speech**: John uses a different word for illustrative speech than the "parable" of the synoptics, but the idea is similar.

* [10:7–10] In Jn 10:7–8, the figure is of a gate for the shepherd to come to the sheep; in Jn 10:9–10, the figure is of a gate for the sheep to **come in and go out**.

* [10:8] [**Before me**]: these words are omitted in many good early manuscripts and versions.

* [10:16] **Other sheep**: the Gentiles, possibly a reference to "God's dispersed children" of Jn 11:52 destined to be gathered into one, or "apostolic Christians" at odds with the community of the beloved disciple.

* [10:18] **Power to take it up again**: contrast the role of the Father as the efficient cause of the

resurrection in Acts 2:24; 4:10; etc.; Rom 1:4; 4:24. Yet even here is added: **This command I have received from my Father**.

* [10:22] **Feast of the Dedication**: an eight-day festival of lights (Hebrew, Hanukkah) held in December, three months after the feast of Tabernacles (Jn 7:2), to celebrate the Maccabees' rededication of the altar and reconsecration of the temple in 164 B.C., after their desecration by Antiochus IV Epiphanes (Dn 8:13; 9:27; cf. 1 Mc 4:36–59; 2 Mc 1:18–2:19; 10:1–8).

* [10:23] **Portico of Solomon**: on the east side of the temple area, offering protection against the cold winds from the desert.

* [10:24] **Keep us in suspense**: literally, "How long will you take away our life?" Cf. Jn 11:48–50. **If you are the Messiah, tell us plainly**: cf. Lk 22:67. This is the climax of Jesus' encounters with the Jewish authorities. There has never yet been an open confession before them.

* [10:25] **I told you**: probably at Jn 8:25 which was an evasive answer.

* [10:29] The textual evidence for the first clause is very divided; it may also be translated: "As for the Father, what he has given me is greater than all," or "My Father is greater than all, in what he has given me."

* [10:30] This is justification for Jn 10:29; it asserts unity of power and reveals that the words and deeds of Jesus are the words and deeds of God.

* [10:34] This is a reference to the judges of Israel who, since they exercised the divine prerogative to judge (Dt 1:17), were called "gods"; cf. Ex 21:6, besides Ps 82:6, from which the quotation comes.

* [10:36] **Consecrated**: this may be a reference to the rededicated altar at the Hanukkah feast; see note on Jn 10:22.

* [10:41] **Performed no sign**: this is to stress the inferior role of John the Baptist. The Transjordan topography recalls the great witness of John the Baptist to Jesus, as opposed to the hostility of the authorities in Jerusalem.

* [11:1–44] The raising of Lazarus, the longest continuous narrative in John outside of the passion account, is the climax of the signs. It leads directly to the decision of the Sanhedrin to kill Jesus. The theme of life predominates. Lazarus is a token of the real life that Jesus dead and raised will give to all who believe in him. Johannine irony is found in the fact that Jesus' gift of life leads to his own death. The story is not found in the synoptics, but cf. Mk 5:21 and parallels; Lk 7:11–17. There are also parallels between this story and Luke's parable of the rich man and poor Lazarus (Lk 16:19–31). In both a man named Lazarus dies; in Luke, there is a request that he return to convince his contemporaries of the need for faith and repentance, while in John, Lazarus does return and some believe but others do not.

* [11:4] **Not to end in death**: this is misunderstood by the disciples as referring to physical death, but it is meant as spiritual death.

* [11:10] **The light is not in him**: the ancients apparently did not grasp clearly the entry of light *through* the eye; they seem to have thought of it as being *in* the eye; cf. Lk 11:34; Mt 6:23.

* [11:16] **Called Didymus**: **Didymus** is the Greek word for twin. **Thomas** is derived from the Aramaic word for twin; in an ancient Syriac version and in the Gospel of Thomas (80:11–12) his given name, Judas, is supplied.

* [11:18] **About two miles**: literally, "about fifteen stades"; a stade was 607 feet.

* [11:27] The titles here are a summary of titles given to Jesus earlier in the gospel.

* [11:33] **Became perturbed**: a startling phrase in Greek, literally, "He snorted in spirit," perhaps in anger at the presence of evil (death).

* [11:41] **Father**: in Aramaic, '*abbā*'. See note on Mk 14:36.

* [11:43] **Cried out in a loud voice**: a dramatization of Jn 5:28; "the hour is coming when all who are in the tombs will hear his voice."

* [11:48] **The Romans will come**: Johannine irony; this is precisely what happened after Jesus' death.

* [11:49] **That year**: emphasizes the conjunction of the office and the year. Actually, Caiaphas was high priest A.D. 18–36. The Jews attributed a gift of prophecy, sometimes unconscious, to the high priest.

* [11:52] **Dispersed children of God**: perhaps the "other sheep" of Jn 10:16.

* [11:54] **Ephraim** is usually located about twelve miles northeast of Jerusalem, where the mountains descend into the Jordan valley.

* [11:55] **Purify**: prescriptions for purity were based on Ex 19:10–11, 15; Nm 9:6–14; 2 Chr 30:1–3, 15–18.

* [12:1–8] This is probably the same scene of anointing found in Mk 14:3–9 (see note there) and Mt 26:6–13. The anointing by a penitent woman in Lk 7:36–38 is different. Details from these various episodes have become interchanged.

* [12:3] **The feet of Jesus**: so Mk 14:3; but in Mt 26:6, Mary anoints Jesus' head as a sign of regal, messianic anointing.

* [12:5] **Days' wages**: literally, "denarii." A denarius is a day's wage in Mt 20:2; see note on Jn 6:7.

* [12:7] Jesus' response reflects the rabbinical discussion of what was the greatest act of mercy, almsgiving or burying the dead. Those who favored proper burial of the dead thought it an essential condition for sharing in the resurrection.

* [12:12–19] In John, the entry into Jerusalem follows the anointing whereas in the synoptics it

precedes. In John, the crowd, not the disciples, are responsible for the triumphal procession.

* [12:13] **Palm branches**: used to welcome great conquerors; cf. 1 Mc 13:51; 2 Mc 10:7. They may be related to the *lûlāb*, the twig bundles used at the feast of Tabernacles. **Hosanna**: see Ps 118:25–26. The Hebrew word means: "(O Lord), grant salvation." **He who comes in the name of the Lord**: referred in Ps 118:26 to a pilgrim entering the temple gates, but here a title for Jesus (see notes on Mt 11:3 and Jn 6:14; 11:27). **The king of Israel**: perhaps from Zep 3:14–15, in connection with the next quotation from Zec 9:9.

* [12:15] **Daughter Zion**: Jerusalem. **Ass's colt**: symbol of peace, as opposed to the war horse.

* [12:16] **They had done this**: the antecedent of **they** is ambiguous.

* [12:17–18] There seem to be two different crowds in these verses. There are some good witnesses to the text that have another reading for Jn 12:17: "Then the crowd that was with him began to testify that he had called Lazarus out of the tomb and raised him from the dead."

* [12:19] **The whole world**: the sense is that everyone is following Jesus, but John has an ironic play on **world**; he alludes to the universality of salvation (Jn 3:17; 4:42).

* [12:20–36] This announcement of glorification by death is an illustration of "the whole world" (Jn 12:19) going after him.

* [12:20] **Greeks**: not used here in a nationalistic sense. These are probably Gentile proselytes to Judaism; cf. Jn 7:35.

* [12:21–22] **Philip . . . Andrew**: the approach is made through disciples who have distinctly Greek names, suggesting that access to Jesus was mediated to the Greek world through his disciples. Philip and Andrew were from Bethsaida (Jn 1:44); Galileans were mostly bilingual. **See**: here seems to mean "have an interview with."

* [12:23] Jesus' response suggests that only after the crucifixion could the gospel encompass both Jew and Gentile.

* [12:24] This verse implies that through his death Jesus will be accessible to all. **It remains just a grain of wheat**: this saying is found in the synoptic triple and double traditions (Mk 8:35; Mt 16:25; Lk 9:24; Mt 10:39; Lk 17:33). John adds the phrases (Jn 12:25) **in this world** and **for eternal life**.

* [12:25] **His life**: the Greek word *psychē* refers to a person's natural life. It does not mean "soul," for Hebrew anthropology did not postulate body/soul dualism in the way that is familiar to us.

* [12:27] **I am troubled**: perhaps an allusion to the Gethsemane agony scene of the synoptics.

* [12:31] **Ruler of this world**: Satan.

* [12:34] There is no passage in the Old Testament that states precisely what the **Messiah remains forever**. Perhaps the closest is Ps 89:37.

* [12:37–50] These verses, on unbelief of the Jews, provide an epilogue to the Book of Signs.

* [12:38–41] John gives a historical explanation of the disbelief of the Jewish people, not a psychological one. The Old Testament had to be fulfilled; the disbelief that met Isaiah's message was a foreshadowing of the disbelief that Jesus encountered. In Jn 12:42 and also in Jn 3:20 we see that there is no negation of freedom.

* [12:41] **His glory**: Isaiah saw the glory of Yahweh enthroned in the heavenly temple, but in John the antecedent of **his** is Jesus.

---

* [13:1–19:42] The Book of Glory. There is a major break here; the word "sign" is used again only in Jn 20:30. In this phase of Jesus' return to the Father, the discourses (Jn 13–17) precede the traditional narrative of the passion (Jn 18–20) to interpret them for the Christian reader. This is the only extended example of esoteric teaching of disciples in John.

* [13:1–20] Washing of the disciples' feet. This episode occurs in John at the place of the narration of the institution of the Eucharist in the synoptics. It may be a dramatization of Lk 22:27—"I am your servant." It is presented as a "model" ("pattern") of the crucifixion. It symbolizes cleansing from sin by sacrificial death.

* [13:1] **Before the feast of Passover**: this would be Thursday evening, before the day of preparation; in the synoptics, the Last Supper is a Passover meal taking place, in John's chronology, on Friday evening. **To the end**: or, "completely."

* [13:2] **Induced**: literally, "the devil put into the heart that Judas should hand him over."

* [13:5] The act of washing another's feet was one that could not be required of the lowliest Jewish slave. It is an allusion to the humiliating death of the crucifixion.

* [13:10] **Bathed**: many have suggested that this passage is a symbolic reference to baptism. The Greek root involved is used in baptismal contexts in 1 Cor 6:11; Eph 5:26; Ti 3:5; Heb 10:22.

* [13:16] **Messenger**: the Greek has *apostolos*, the only occurrence of the term in John. It is not used in the technical sense here.

* [13:23] **The one whom Jesus loved**: also mentioned in Jn 19:26; 20:2; 21:7. A disciple, called "another disciple" or "the other disciple," is mentioned in Jn 18:15 and Jn 20:2; in the latter reference he is identified with the disciple whom Jesus loved. There is also an unnamed disciple in Jn 1:35–40; see note on Jn 1:37.

* [13:26] **Morsel**: probably the bitter herb dipped in salt water.

* [13:31–17:26] Two farewell discourses and a prayer. These seem to be Johannine compositions, including sayings of Jesus at the Last Supper and on other occasions, modeled on similar farewell discourses in Greek literature and the Old Testament (of Moses, Joshua, David).

* [13:31–38] **Introduction: departure and return.** Terms of coming and going predominate. These verses form an introduction to the last discourse of Jesus, which extends through Jn 14–17. In it John has collected Jesus's words to his own (Jn 13:1). There are indications that several speeches have been fused together, e.g., in Jn 14:31 and Jn 17:1.

* [13:34] **I give you a new commandment:** this puts Jesus on a par with Yahweh. The commandment itself is not new; cf. Lv 19:18 and the note there.

* [14:1–31] Jesus' departure and return. This section is a dialogue marked off by a literary inclusion in Jn 14:1, 27: "Do not let your hearts be troubled."

* [14:1] **You have faith:** could also be imperative: "Have faith."

* [14:3] **Come back again:** a rare Johannine reference to the parousia; cf. 1 Jn 2:28.

* [14:4] **The way:** here, of Jesus himself; also a designation of Christianity in Acts 9:2; 19:9, 23; 22:4; 24:14, 22.

* [14:6] **The truth:** in John, the divinely revealed reality of the Father manifested in the person and works of Jesus. The possession of truth confers knowledge and liberation from sin (Jn 8:32).

* [14:7] An alternative reading, "If you know me, then you would have known my Father also," would be a rebuke, as in Jn 8:19.

* [14:8] **Show us the Father:** Philip is pictured asking for a theophany like Ex 24:9–10; 33:18.

* [14:16] **Another Advocate:** Jesus is the first advocate (*paraclete*); see 1 Jn 2:1, where Jesus is an advocate in the sense of intercessor in heaven. The Greek term derives from legal terminology for an advocate or defense attorney, and can mean spokesman, mediator, intercessor, comforter, consoler, although none of these terms encompasses the meaning in John. The Paraclete in John is a teacher, a witness to Jesus, and a prosecutor of the world, who represents the continued presence on earth of the Jesus who has returned to the Father.

* [14:17] **The Spirit of truth:** this term is also used at Qumran, where it is a moral force put into a person by God, as opposed to the spirit of perversity. It is more personal in John; it will teach the realities of the new order (Jn 14:26), and testify to the truth (Jn 14:6). While it has been customary to use masculine personal pronouns in English for the Advocate, the Greek word for "spirit" is neuter, and the Greek text and manuscript variants fluctuate between masculine and neuter pronouns.

* [14:18] **I will come to you:** indwelling, not parousia.

* [14:22] **Judas, not the Iscariot:** probably not the brother of Jesus in Mk 6:3 // Mt 13:55 or the apostle named Jude in Lk 6:16, but Thomas (see note on Jn 11:16), although other readings have "Judas the Cananean."

* [14:27] **Peace:** the traditional Hebrew salutation *šālôm;* but Jesus' "Shalom" is a gift of salvation, connoting the bounty of messianic blessing.

* [14:28] **The Father is greater than I:** because he **sent, gave,** etc., and Jesus is "a man who has told you the truth that I heard from God" (Jn 8:40).

* [14:30] **The ruler of the world:** Satan; cf. Jn 12:31; 16:11.

* [15:1–16:4] Discourse on the union of Jesus with his disciples. His words become a monologue and go beyond the immediate crisis of the departure of Jesus.

* [15:1–17] Like Jn 10:1–5, this passage resembles a parable. Israel is spoken of as a vineyard at Is 5:1–7; Mt 21:33–46 and as a vine at Ps 80:9–17; Jer 2:21; Ez 15:2; 17:5–10; 19:10; Hos 10:1. The identification of the vine as the Son of Man in Ps 80:15 and Wisdom's description of herself as a vine in Sir 24:17 are further background for portrayal of Jesus by this figure. There may be secondary eucharistic symbolism here; cf. Mk 14:25, "the fruit of the vine."

* [15:2] **Takes away . . . prunes:** in Greek there is a play on two related verbs.

* [15:6] Branches were cut off and dried on the wall of the vineyard for later use as fuel.

* [15:13] **For one's friends:** or: "those whom one loves." In Jn 15:9–13a, the words for love are related to the Greek *agapaō.* In Jn 15:13b–15, the words for love are related to the Greek *phileō.* For John, the two roots seem synonymous and mean "to love"; cf. also Jn 21:15–17. The word *philos* is used here.

* [15:15] **Slaves . . . friends:** in the Old Testament, Moses (Dt 34:5), Joshua (Jos 24:29), and David (Ps 89:21) were called "servants" or "slaves of Yahweh"; only Abraham (Is 41:8; 2 Chr 20:7; cf. Jas 2:23) was called a "friend of God."

* [15:18–16:4] The hostile reaction of the world. There are synoptic parallels, predicting persecution, especially at Mt 10:17–25; 24:9–10.

* [15:20] **The word I spoke to you:** a reference to Jn 13:16.

* [15:21] **On account of my name:** the idea of persecution for Jesus' name is frequent in the New Testament (Mt 10:22; 24:9; Acts 9:14). For John, association with Jesus' name implies union with Jesus.

* [15:22, 24] Jesus' words (**spoken**) and deeds (**works**) are the great motives of credibility. **They have seen and hated:** probably means that they have seen his works and still have hated; but the Greek can be read: "have seen both me and my Father and still have hated both me and my

Father." **Works . . . that no one else ever did**: so Yahweh in Dt 4:32–33.

* [15:25] **In their law**: law is here used as a larger concept than the Pentateuch, for the reference is to Ps 35:19 or Ps 69:5. See notes on Jn 10:34; 12:34. Their law reflects the argument of the church with the synagogue.

* [15:26] **Whom I will send**: in Jn 14:16, 26, the Paraclete is to be sent by the Father, at the request of Jesus. Here the Spirit comes from both Jesus and the Father in mission; there is no reference here to the eternal procession of the Spirit.

* [16:2] **Hour**: of persecution, not Jesus' "hour" (see note on Jn 2:4).

* [16:4b–33] A duplicate of Jn 14:1–31 on departure and return.

* [16:5] **Not one of you asks me**: the difficulty of reconciling this with Simon Peter's question in Jn 13:36 and Thomas' words in Jn 14:5 strengthens the supposition that the last discourse has been made up of several collections of Johannine material.

* [16:8–11] These verses illustrate the forensic character of the Paraclete's role: in the forum of the disciples' conscience he prosecutes the world. He leads believers to see (a) that the basic sin was and is refusal to believe in Jesus; (b) that, although Jesus was found guilty and apparently died in disgrace, in reality righteousness has triumphed, for Jesus has returned to his Father; (c) finally, that it is the ruler of this world, Satan, who has been condemned through Jesus' death (Jn 12:32).

* [16:13] **Declare to you the things that are coming**: not a reference to new predictions about the future, but interpretation of what has already occurred or been said.

* [16:25] See note on Jn 10:6. Here, possibly a reference to Jn 15:1–16 or Jn 16:21.

* [16:30] The reference is seemingly to the fact that Jesus could anticipate their question in Jn 16:19. The disciples naively think they have the full understanding that is the climax of "the hour" of Jesus' death, resurrection, and ascension (Jn 16:25), but the only part of the hour that is at hand for them is their share in the passion (Jn 16:32).

* [16:32] **You will be scattered**: cf. Mk 14:27 and Mt 26:31, where both cite Zec 13:7 about the sheep being dispersed.

* [17:1–26] Climax of the last discourse(s). Since the sixteenth century, this chapter has been called the "high priestly prayer" of Jesus. He speaks as intercessor, with words addressed directly to the Father and not to the disciples, who supposedly only overhear. Yet the prayer is one of petition, for immediate (Jn 17:6–19) and future (Jn 17:20–21) disciples. Many phrases reminiscent of the Lord's Prayer occur. Although still in the world (Jn

17:13), Jesus looks on his earthly ministry as a thing of the past (Jn 17:4, 12). Whereas Jesus has up to this time stated that the disciples could follow him (Jn 13:33, 36), now he wishes them to be with him in union with the Father (Jn 17:12–14).

* [17:1] The action of looking up to heaven and the address Father are typical of Jesus at prayer; cf. Jn 11:41 and Lk 11:2.

* [17:2] Another possible interpretation is to treat the first line of the verse as parenthetical and the second as an appositive to the clause that ends v 1: **so that your son may glorify you (just as . . . all people), so that he may give eternal life. . . .**

* [17:3] This verse was clearly added in the editing of the gospel as a reflection on the preceding verse; Jesus nowhere else refers to himself as Jesus Christ.

* [17:6] **I revealed your name**: perhaps the name **I AM**; cf. Jn 8:24, 28, 58; 13:19.

* [17:15] Note the resemblance to the petition of the Lord's Prayer, "deliver us from the evil one." Both probably refer to the devil rather than to abstract evil.

* [17:24] **Where I am**: Jesus prays for the believers ultimately to join him in heaven. Then they will not see his glory as in a mirror but clearly (2 Cor 3:18; 1 Jn 3:2).

* [17:26] **I will make it known**: through the Advocate.

* [18:1–14] John does not mention the agony in the garden and the kiss of Judas, nor does he identify the place as Gethsemane or the Mount of Olives.

* [18:1] **Jesus went out**: see Jn 14:31, where it seems he is leaving the supper room. **Kidron valley**: literally, "the winter-flowing Kidron"; this wadi has water only during the winter rains.

* [18:3] **Band of soldiers**: seems to refer to Roman troops, either the full cohort of 600 men (1/10 of a legion), or more likely the maniple of 200 under their tribune (Jn 18:12). In this case, John is hinting at Roman collusion in the action against Jesus before he was brought to Pilate. The lanterns and torches may be symbolic of the hour of darkness.

* [18:5] **Nazorean**: the form found in Mt 26:71 (see note on Mt 2:23) is here used, not **Nazarene** of Mark. **I AM**: or "I am he," but probably intended by the evangelist as an expression of divinity (cf. their appropriate response in Jn 18:6); see note on Jn 8:24. John sets the confusion of the arresting party against the background of Jesus' divine majesty.

* [18:9] The citation may refer to Jn 6:39; 10:28; or 17:12.

* [18:10] Only John gives the names of the two antagonists; both John and Luke mention the right ear.

* [18:11] The theme of the cup is found in the synoptic account of the agony (Mk 14:36 and parallels).

* [18:13] **Annas**: only John mentions an inquiry before Annas; cf. Jn 18:16, 19–24; see note on Lk 3:2. It is unlikely that this nighttime interrogation before Annas is the same as the trial before Caiaphas placed by Matthew and Mark at night and by Luke in the morning.

* [18:15–16] **Another disciple . . . the other disciple**: see note on Jn 13:23.

* [18:20] **I have always taught . . . in the temple area**: cf. Mk 14:49 for a similar statement.

* [18:24] **Caiaphas**: see Mt 26:3, 57; Lk 3:2; and the notes there. John may leave room here for the trial before Caiaphas described in the synoptic gospels.

* [18:27] Cockcrow was the third Roman division of the night, lasting from midnight to 3 a.m.

* [18:28] **Praetorium**: see note on Mt 27:27. **Morning**: literally, "the early hour," or fourth Roman division of the night, 3 to 6 a.m. **The Passover**: the synoptic gospels give the impression that the Thursday night supper was the Passover meal (Mk 14:12); for John that meal is still to be eaten Friday night.

* [18:31] **We do not have the right to execute anyone**: only John gives this reason for their bringing Jesus to Pilate. Jewish sources are not clear on the competence of the Sanhedrin at this period to sentence and to execute for political crimes.

* [18:32] The Jewish punishment for blasphemy was stoning (Lv 24:16). In coming to the Romans to ensure that Jesus would be crucified, the Jewish authorities fulfilled his prophecy that he would be exalted (Jn 3:14; 12:32–33). There is some historical evidence, however, for Jews crucifying Jews.

* [18:37] **You say I am a king**: see Mt 26:64 for a similar response to the high priest. It is at best a reluctant affirmative.

* [18:39] See note on Mt 27:15.

* [18:40] **Barabbas**: see note on Mt 27:16–17. **Revolutionary**: a guerrilla warrior fighting for nationalistic aims, though the term can also denote a robber. See note on Mt 27:38.

* [19:1] Luke places the mockery of Jesus at the midpoint in the trial when Jesus was sent to Herod. Mark and Matthew place the scourging and mockery at the end of the trial after the sentence of death. Scourging was an integral part of the crucifixion penalty.

* [19:7] **Made himself the Son of God**: this question was not raised in John's account of the Jewish interrogations of Jesus as it was in the synoptic account. Nevertheless, see Jn 5:18; 8:53; 10:36.

* [19:12] **Friend of Caesar**: a Roman honorific title bestowed upon high-ranking officials for merit.

* [19:13] **Seated him**: others translate "(Pilate) sat down." In John's thought, Jesus is the real judge of the world, and John may here be portraying him seated on the judgment bench. **Stone Pavement**: in Greek *lithostrotos*; under the fortress Antonia, one of the conjectured locations of the praetorium, a massive stone pavement has been excavated. **Gabbatha** (Aramaic rather than Hebrew) probably means "ridge, elevation."

* [19:14] **Noon**: Mk 15:25 has Jesus crucified "at the third hour," which means either 9 a.m. or the period from 9 to 12 noon, the time when, according to John, Jesus was sentenced to death, the hour at which the priests began to slaughter Passover lambs in the temple; see Jn 1:29.

* [19:16] **He handed him over to them to be crucified**: in context this would seem to mean "handed him over to the chief priests." Lk 23:25 has a similar ambiguity. There is a polemic tendency in the gospels to place the guilt of the crucifixion on the Jewish authorities and to exonerate the Romans from blame. But John later mentions the Roman soldiers (Jn 19:23), and it was to these soldiers that Pilate handed Jesus over.

* [19:17] **Carrying the cross himself**: a different picture from that of the synoptics, especially Lk 23:26, where Simon of Cyrene is made to carry the cross, walking behind Jesus. In John's theology, Jesus remained in complete control and master of his destiny (cf. Jn 10:18). **Place of the Skull**: the Latin word for skull is *Calvaria*; hence "Calvary." **Golgotha** is actually an Aramaic rather than a Hebrew word.

* [19:19] The inscription differs with slightly different words in each of the four gospels. John's form is fullest and gives the equivalent of the Latin *INRI = Iesus Nazarenus Rex Iudaeorum*. Only John mentions its polyglot character (Jn 19:20) and Pilate's role in keeping the title unchanged (Jn 19:21–22).

* [19:23–25a] While all four gospels describe the soldiers casting lots to divide Jesus' garments (see note on Mt 27:35), only John quotes the underlying passage in Ps 22:19, and only John sees each line of the poetic parallelism literally carried out in two separate actions (Jn 19:23–24).

* [19:25] It is not clear whether four women are meant, or three (i.e., **Mary the wife of Cl[e]opas** [cf. Lk 24:18] is in apposition with **his mother's sister**) or two (his mother and his mother's sister, i.e., Mary of Cl[e]opas and Mary of Magdala). Only John mentions the mother of Jesus here. The synoptics have a group of women looking on from a distance at the cross (Mk 15:40).

* [19:26–27] This scene has been interpreted literally, of Jesus' concern for his mother; and symbolically, e.g., in the light of the Cana story in Jn 2

(the presence of the mother of Jesus, the address **woman**, and the mention of the **hour**) and of the upper room in Jn 13 (the presence of the beloved disciple; the **hour**). Now that the hour has come (Jn 19:28), Mary (a symbol of the church?) is given a role as the mother of Christians (personified by the beloved disciple); or, as a representative of those seeking salvation, she is supported by the disciple who interprets Jesus' revelation; or Jewish and Gentile Christianity (or Israel and the Christian community) are reconciled.

* [19:28] **The scripture . . . fulfilled**: either in the scene of Jn 19:25–27, or in the **I thirst** of Jn 19:28. If the latter, Ps 22:16; 69:22 deserve consideration.

* [19:29] **Wine**: John does not mention the drugged wine, a narcotic that Jesus refused as the crucifixion began (Mk 15:23), but only this final gesture of kindness at the end (Mk 15:36). **Hyssop**, a small plant, is scarcely suitable for carrying a sponge (Mark mentions a reed) and may be a symbolic reference to the hyssop used to daub the blood of the paschal lamb on the doorpost of the Hebrews (Ex 12:22).

* [19:30] **Handed over the spirit**: there is a double nuance of dying (giving up the last breath or spirit) and that of passing on the holy Spirit; see Jn 7:39, which connects the giving of the Spirit with Jesus' glorious return to the Father, and Jn 20:22, where the author portrays the conferral of the Spirit.

* [19:34–35] John probably emphasizes these verses to show the reality of Jesus' death, against the docetic heretics. In the blood and water there may also be a symbolic reference to the Eucharist and baptism.

* [19:35] **He knows**: it is not certain from the Greek that this **he** is the **eyewitness** of the first part of the sentence. **May [come to] believe**: see note on Jn 20:31.

* [19:38–42] In the first three gospels there is no anointing on Friday. In Matthew and Luke the women come to the tomb on Sunday morning precisely to anoint Jesus.

* [20:1–31] The risen Jesus reveals his glory and confers the Spirit. This story fulfills the basic need for testimony to the resurrection. What we have here is not a record but a series of single stories.

* [20:1–10] The story of the empty tomb is found in both the Matthean and the Lucan traditions; John's version seems to be a fusion of the two.

* [20:1] **Still dark**: according to Mark the sun had risen, Matthew describes it as "dawning," and Luke refers to early dawn. Mary sees the stone removed, not the empty tomb.

* [20:2] Mary runs away, not directed by an angel/young man as in the synoptic accounts. The plural "we" in the second part of her statement might reflect a tradition of more women going to the tomb.

* [20:3–10] The basic narrative is told of Peter alone in Lk 24:12, a verse missing in important manuscripts and which may be borrowed from tradition similar to John. Cf. also Lk 24:24.

* [20:6–8] Some special feature about the state of the burial cloths caused the beloved disciple to believe. Perhaps the details emphasized that the grave had not been robbed.

* [20:9] Probably a general reference to the scriptures is intended, as in Lk 24:26 and 1 Cor 15:4. Some individual Old Testament passages suggested are Ps 16:10; Hos 6:2; Jon 2:1, 2, 10.

* [20:11–18] This appearance to Mary is found only in John, but cf. Mt 28:8–10 and Mk 16:9–11.

* [20:16] **Rabbouni**: Hebrew or Aramaic for "my master."

* [20:17] **Stop holding on to me**: see Mt 28:9, where the women take hold of his feet. **I have not yet ascended**: for John and many of the New Testament writers, the ascension in the theological sense of going to the Father to be glorified took place with the resurrection as one action. This scene in John dramatizes such an understanding, for by Easter night Jesus is glorified and can give the Spirit. Therefore his ascension takes place immediately after he has talked to Mary. In such a view, the ascension after forty days described in Acts 1:1–11 would be simply a termination of earthly appearances or, perhaps better, an introduction to the conferral of the Spirit upon the early church, modeled on Elisha's being able to have a (double) share in the spirit of Elijah if he saw him being taken up (same verb as ascending) into heaven (2 Kgs 2:9–12). **To my Father and your Father, to my God and your God**: this echoes Ru 1:16: "Your people shall be my people, and your God my God." The Father of Jesus will now become the Father of the disciples because, once ascended, Jesus can give them the Spirit that comes from the Father and they can be reborn as God's children (Jn 3:5). That is why he calls them **my brothers**.

* [20:19–29] The appearances to the disciples, without or with Thomas (cf. Jn 11:16; 14:5), have rough parallels in the other gospels only for Jn 20:19–23; cf. Lk 24:36–39; Mk 16:14–18.

* [20:19] **The disciples**: by implication from Jn 20:24 this means ten of the Twelve, presumably in Jerusalem. **Peace be with you**: although this could be an ordinary greeting, John intends here to echo Jn 14:27. The theme of rejoicing in Jn 20:20 echoes Jn 16:22.

* [20:20] **Hands and . . . side**: Lk 24:39–40 mentions "hands and feet," based on Ps 22:17.

* [20:21] By means of this sending, the Eleven were made apostles, that is, "those sent" (cf. Jn 17:18), though John does not use the noun in reference to them (see note on Jn 13:16). A solemn mission or "sending" is also the subject of the

* [20:22] This action recalls Gn 2:7, where God breathed on the first man and gave him life; just as Adam's life came from God, so now the disciples' new spiritual life comes from Jesus. Cf. also the revivification of the dry bones in Ez 37. This is the author's version of Pentecost. Cf. also the note on Jn 19:30.

* [20:23] The Council of Trent defined that this power to forgive sins is exercised in the sacrament of penance: See Mt 16:19; 18:18.

* [20:28] **My Lord and my God**: this forms a literary inclusion with the first verse of the gospel: "and the Word was God."

* [20:29] This verse is a beatitude on future generations; faith, not sight, matters.

* [20:30–31] These verses are clearly a conclusion to the gospel and express its purpose. While many manuscripts read **come to believe**, possibly implying a missionary purpose for John's gospel, a small number of quite early ones read "continue to believe," suggesting that the audience consists of Christians whose faith is to be deepened by the book; cf. Jn 19:35.

---

* [21:1–23] There are many non-Johannine peculiarities in this chapter, some suggesting Lucan Greek style; yet this language is closer to John than Jn 7:53–8:11. There are many Johannine features as well. Its closest parallels in the synoptic gospels are found in Lk 5:1–11 and Mt 14:28–31. Perhaps the tradition was ultimately derived from John but preserved by some disciple other than the writer of the rest of the gospel. The appearances narrated seem to be independent of those in Jn 20. Even if a later addition, the chapter was added before publication of the gospel, for it appears in all manuscripts.

* [21:2] **Zebedee's sons**: the only reference to James and John in this gospel (but see note on Jn 1:37). Perhaps the phrase was originally a gloss to identify, among the five, the **two others of his disciples**. The anonymity of the latter phrase is more Johannine (Jn 1:35). The total of seven may suggest the community of the disciples in its fullness.

* [21:3–6] This may be a variant of Luke's account of the catch of fish; see note on Lk 5:1–11.

* [21:9, 12–13] It is strange that Jesus already has fish since none have yet been brought ashore. This meal may have had eucharistic significance for early Christians since Jn 21:13 recalls Jn 6:11 which uses the vocabulary of Jesus' action at the Last Supper; but see also note on Mt 14:19.

* [21:11] The exact number 153 is probably meant to have a symbolic meaning in relation to the apostles' universal mission; Jerome claims that Greek zoologists catalogued 153 species of fish. Or 153 is the sum of the numbers from 1 to 17. Others invoke Ez 47:10.

* [21:12] **None . . . dared to ask him**: is Jesus' appearance strange to them? Cf. Lk 24:16; Mk 16:12; Jn 20:14. The disciples do, however, recognize Jesus **before** the breaking of the bread (opposed to Lk 24:35).

* [21:14] This verse connects Jn 20 and 21; cf. Jn 20:19, 26.

* [21:15–23] This section constitutes Peter's rehabilitation and emphasizes his role in the church.

* [21:15–17] In these three verses there is a remarkable variety of synonyms: two different Greek verbs for **love** (see note on Jn 15:13); two verbs for **feed/tend**; two nouns for **sheep**; two verbs for **know**. But apparently there is no difference of meaning. The threefold confession of Peter is meant to counteract his earlier threefold denial (Jn 18:17, 25, 27). The First Vatican Council cited these verses in defining that Jesus after his resurrection gave Peter the jurisdiction of supreme shepherd and ruler over the whole flock.

* [21:15] **More than these**: probably "more than these disciples do" rather than "more than you love them" or "more than you love these things [fishing, etc.]."

* [21:18] Originally probably a proverb about old age, now used as a figurative reference to the crucifixion of Peter.

* [21:22] **Until I come**: a reference to the parousia.

* [21:23] This whole scene takes on more significance if the disciple is already dead. The death of the apostolic generation caused problems in the church because of a belief that Jesus was to have returned first. Loss of faith sometimes resulted; cf. 2 Pt 3:4.

* [21:24] **Who . . . has written them**: this does not necessarily mean he wrote them with his own hand. The same expression is used in Jn 19:22 of Pilate, who certainly would not have written the inscription himself. **We know**: i.e., the Christian community; cf. Jn 1:14, 16.

THE ACTS OF
THE APOSTLES

INTRODUCTION

The Acts of the Apostles, the second volume of Luke's two-volume work, continues Luke's presentation of biblical history, describing how the salvation promised to Israel in the Old Testament and accomplished by Jesus has now under the guidance of the holy Spirit been extended to the Gentiles. This was accomplished through the divinely chosen representatives (Acts 10:41) whom Jesus prepared during his historical ministry (Acts 1:21–22) and commissioned after his resurrection as witnesses to all that he taught (Acts 1:8; 10:37–43; Lk 24:48). Luke's preoccupation with the Christian community as the Spirit-guided bearer of the word of salvation rules out of his book detailed histories of the activity of most of the preachers. Only the main lines of the roles of Peter and Paul serve Luke's interest.

Peter was the leading member of the Twelve (Acts 1:13, 15), a miracle worker like Jesus in the gospel (Acts 3:1–10; 5:1–11, 15; 9:32–35, 36–42), the object of divine care (Acts 5:17–21; 12:6–11), and the spokesman for the Christian community (Acts 2:14–36; 3:12–26; 4:8–12; 5:29–32; 10:34–43; 15:7–11), who, according to Luke, was largely responsible for the growth of the community in the early days (Acts 2:4; 4:4). Paul eventually joined the community at Antioch (Acts 11:25–26), which subsequently commissioned him and Barnabas to undertake the spread of the gospel to Asia Minor. This missionary venture generally failed to win the Jews of the diaspora to the gospel but enjoyed success among the Gentiles (Acts 13:14–14:27).

Paul's refusal to impose the Mosaic law upon his Gentile converts provoked very strong objection among the Jewish Christians of Jerusalem (Acts 15:1), but both Peter and James supported his position (Acts 15:6–21). Paul's second and third missionary journeys (Acts 16:36–21:16) resulted in the same pattern of failure among the Jews generally but of some success among the Gentiles. Paul, like Peter, is presented as a miracle worker (Acts 14:8–18; 19:12; 20:7–12; 28:7–10) and the object of divine care (Acts 16:25–31).

In Acts, Luke has provided a broad survey of the church's development from the resurrection of Jesus to Paul's first Roman imprisonment, the point at which the book ends. In telling this story, Luke describes the emergence of Christianity from its origins in Judaism to its position as a religion of worldwide status and appeal. Originally a Jewish Christian community in Jerusalem, the church was placed in circumstances impelling it to include within its membership people of other cultures: the Samaritans (Acts 8:4–25), at first an occasional Gentile (Acts 8:26–30; 10:1–48), and finally the Gentiles on principle (Acts 11:20–21). Fear on the part of the Jewish people that Christianity, particularly as preached to the Gentiles, threatened their own cultural heritage caused them to be suspicious of Paul's gospel (Acts 13:42–45; 15:1–5; 28:17–24). The inability of Christian missionaries to allay this apprehension inevitably created a situation in which the gospel was preached more and more to the Gentiles. Toward the end of Paul's career, the Christian communities, with the exception of those in Palestine itself (Acts 9:31), were mainly of Gentile membership. In tracing the emergence of Christianity from Judaism, Luke is insistent upon the prominence of Israel in the divine plan of salvation (see note on Acts 1:26; see also Acts 2:5–6; 3:13–15; 10:36; 13:16–41; 24:14–15) and that the extension of salvation to the Gentiles has been a part of the divine plan from the beginning (see Acts 15:13–18; 26:22–23).

In the development of the church from a Jewish Christian origin in Jerusalem, with its roots in Jewish religious tradition, to a series of Christian communities among the Gentiles of the Roman empire, Luke perceives the action of God in history laying open the heart of all humanity to the divine message of salvation. His approach to the history of the church is motivated by his theological interests. His history of the apostolic church is the story of a Spirit-guided community and a Spirit-guided spread of the Word of God (Acts 1:8). The travels of Peter and Paul are in reality the travels of the Word of God as it spreads from Jerusalem, the city of destiny for Jesus, to Rome, the capital of the civilized world of Luke's day. Nonetheless, the historical data he utilizes are of value for the understanding of the church's early life and development and as general background to the Pauline epistles. In the interpretation of Acts, care must be exercised to determine Luke's theological aims and interests and to evaluate his historical data without either exaggerating their literal accuracy or underestimating their factual worth.

Finally, an apologetic concern is evident throughout Acts. By stressing the continuity between Judaism and Christianity (Acts 13:16–41; 23:6–9; 24:10–21; 26:2–23), Luke argues that Christianity is deserving of the same toleration accorded Judaism by Rome. Part of Paul's defense before Roman authorities is to show that Christianity is not a disturber of the peace of the Roman Empire (Acts 24:5, 12–13; 25:7–8). Moreover, when he stands before Roman authorities, he is declared innocent of any crime against the empire (Acts 18:13–15; 23:29; 25:25–27; 26:31–32). Luke tells his story with the hope that Christianity will be treated as fairly.

Concerning the date of Acts, see the Introduction to the Gospel according to Luke.

The principal divisions of the Acts of the Apostles are the following:

I.   The Preparation for the Christian Mission (1:1–2:13)
II.   The Mission in Jerusalem (2:14–8:3)
III. The Mission in Judea and Samaria (8:4–9:43)
IV.   The Inauguration of the Gentile Mission (10:1–15:35)
V.   The Mission of Paul to the Ends of the Earth
      (15:36–28:31)

I. THE PREPARATION FOR THE CHRISTIAN MISSION

CHAPTER 1*

The Promise of the Spirit. [1]In the first book,[a] Theophilus, I dealt with all that Jesus did and taught [2]until the day he was taken up, after giving instructions through the holy Spirit to the apostles whom he had chosen.[b] [3]He presented himself alive to them by many proofs after he had suffered, appearing to them during forty days* and speaking about the kingdom of God.[c] [4]While meeting with them, he enjoined them not to depart from Jerusalem, but to wait for "the promise of the Father* about which you have heard me speak;[d] [5]for John baptized with water, but in a few days you will be baptized with the holy Spirit."[e]

The Ascension of Jesus. [6]When they had gathered together they asked him, "Lord, are you at this time going* to restore the kingdom to Israel?" [7]He answered them,[f] "It is not for you to know the times or seasons that the Father has established by his own authority. [8]But you will receive power when the holy Spirit comes upon you,[g] and you will be my witnesses in Jerusalem, throughout Judea and Samaria, and to the ends of the earth." [9]When he had said this, as they were looking on, he was lifted up, and a cloud took him from their sight.[h] [10]While they were looking intently at the sky as he was going, suddenly two men dressed in white garments stood beside them.[i] [11]They said, "Men of Galilee, why are you standing there looking at the sky? This Jesus who has been taken up from you into heaven will return in the same way as you have seen him going into heaven."[j] [12k]Then they returned to Jerusalem from the mount called Olivet, which is near Jerusalem, a sabbath day's journey away.

The First Community in Jerusalem. [13]When they entered the city they went to the upper room where they were staying, Peter and John and James and Andrew, Philip and Thomas, Bartholomew and Matthew, James son of Alphaeus, Simon the Zealot, and Judas son of James. [14]All these devoted themselves with one accord to prayer, together with some women, and Mary the mother of Jesus, and his brothers.[l]

The Choice of Judas's Successor. [15]During those days Peter stood up in the midst of the brothers (there was a group of about one hundred and twenty persons in the one place). He said, [16]"My brothers, the scripture had to be fulfilled which the holy Spirit spoke beforehand through the mouth of David, concerning Judas, who was the guide for those who arrested Jesus.[m] [17]He was numbered among us and was allotted a share in this ministry. [18n]He bought a parcel of land with the wages of his iniquity, and falling headlong, he burst open in the middle, and all his insides spilled out.[.] [19]This became known to everyone who lived in Jerusalem, so that the parcel of land was called in their language 'Akeldama,' that is, Field of Blood. [20]For it is written in the Book of Psalms:

'Let his encampment
　　become desolate,
　and may no one dwell
　　in it.'

And:

'May another take his
　　office.'[o]

[21]Therefore, it is necessary that one of the men who

accompanied us the whole time the Lord Jesus came and went among us, ²²beginning from the baptism of John until the day on which he was taken up from us, become with us a witness to his resurrection."^p ²³So they proposed two, Joseph called Barsabbas, who was also known as Justus, and Matthias. ²⁴Then they prayed, "You, Lord, who know the hearts of all, show which one of these two you have chosen ²⁵to take the place in this apostolic ministry from which Judas turned away to go to his own place." ²⁶*^qThen they gave lots to them, and the lot fell upon Matthias, and he was counted with the eleven apostles.

a. [1:1] Lk 1:1–4.
b. [1:2] Mt 28:19–20; Lk 24:44–49; Jn 20:22; 1 Tm 3:16.
c. [1:3] 10:41; 13:31.
d. [1:4] Jn 14:16, 17, 26.
e. [1:5] 11:16; Mt 3:11; Mk 1:8; Lk 3:16; Jn 1:26; Eph 1:13.
f. [1:7] Mt 24:36; 1 Thes 5:1–2.
g. [1:8] 2:1–13; 10:39; Is 43:10; Mt 28:19; Lk 24:47–48.
h. [1:9] 2 Kgs 2:11; Mk 16:19; Lk 24:51.
i. [1:10] Jn 20:17.
j. [1:11] Lk 24:51; Eph 4:8–10; 1 Pt 3:22; Rev 1:7.
k. [1:12–14] Lk 6:14–16.
l. [1:14] Lk 23:49.
m. [1:16] Ps 41:10; Lk 22:47.
n. [1:18] Mt 27:3–10.
o. [1:20] Ps 69:26; 109:8; Jn 17:12.
p. [1:22] 1:8–9; 10:39.
q. [1:26] Prv 16:33.

CHAPTER 2

The Coming of the Spirit.

¹*When the time for Pentecost was fulfilled, they were all in one place together.^a ²And suddenly there came from the sky a noise like a strong driving wind,* and it filled the entire house in which they were.^b ³Then there appeared to them tongues as of fire,* which parted and came to rest on each one of them.^c ⁴And they were all filled with the holy Spirit and began to speak in different tongues,* as the Spirit enabled them to proclaim.^d

⁵Now there were devout Jews from every nation under heaven staying in Jerusalem. ⁶At this sound, they gathered in a large crowd, but they were confused because each one heard them speaking in his own language. ⁷They were astounded, and in amazement

they asked, "Are not all these people who are speaking Galileans?*[e] [8]Then how does each of us hear them in his own native language? [9]We are Parthians, Medes, and Elamites, inhabitants of Mesopotamia, Judea and Cappadocia, Pontus and Asia, [10]Phrygia and Pamphylia, Egypt and the districts of Libya near Cyrene, as well as travelers from Rome, [11]both Jews and converts to Judaism, Cretans and Arabs, yet we hear them speaking in our own tongues of the mighty acts of God."[f] [12]They were all astounded and bewildered, and said to one another, "What does this mean?" [13]But others said, scoffing, "They have had too much new wine."[g]

II. THE MISSION IN JERUSALEM

Peter's Speech at Pentecost. [14]Then Peter stood up with the Eleven, raised his voice, and proclaimed to them, "You who are Jews, indeed all of you staying in Jerusalem. Let this be known to you, and listen to my words. [15]These people are not drunk, as you suppose, for it is only nine o'clock in the morning. [16]No, this is what was spoken through the prophet Joel:

[17]'It will come to pass in
        the last days,' God
        says,
   'that I will pour out a
        portion of my spirit
        upon all flesh.
Your sons and your
        daughters shall
        prophesy,
   your young men shall
        see visions,
   your old men shall
        dream dreams.[h]
[18]Indeed, upon my
        servants and my
        handmaids
   I will pour out a portion
        of my spirit in those
        days,
        and they shall
        prophesy.

¹⁹And I will work wonders
in the heavens above
and signs on the earth
below:
blood, fire, and a
cloud of smoke.
²⁰The sun shall be turned
to darkness,
and the moon to blood,
before the coming
of the great and
splendid day of the
Lord,
²¹and it shall be that every-
one shall be saved
who calls on the name
of the Lord.'ⁱ

²²You who are Israelites,
hear these words. Jesus the
Nazorean was a man com-
mended to you by God with
mighty deeds, wonders, and
signs, which God worked
through him in your midst, as
you yourselves know.^j ²³This
man, delivered up by the set
plan and foreknowledge of
God, you killed, using lawless
men to crucify him.^k ²⁴But
God raised him up, releasing

him from the throes of death,
because it was impossible for
him to be held by it.^l ²⁵For
David says of him:

'I saw the Lord ever before
me,^m
with him at my right
hand I shall not be
disturbed.
²⁶Therefore my heart has
been glad and my
tongue has exulted;
my flesh, too, will dwell
in hope,
²⁷because you will not
abandon my soul to
the netherworld,
nor will you suffer
your holy one to see
corruption.ⁿ
²⁸You have made known to
me the paths of life;
you will fill me with joy
in your presence.'

²⁹My brothers, one can con-
fidently say to you about the
patriarch David that he died
and was buried, and his tomb
is in our midst to this day.

30 But since he was a prophet and knew that God had sworn an oath to him that he would set one of his descendants upon his throne,[o] 31 he foresaw and spoke of the resurrection of the Messiah, that neither was he abandoned to the netherworld nor did his flesh see corruption.[p] 32 God raised this Jesus; of this we are all witnesses. 33 Exalted at the right hand of God,* he received the promise of the holy Spirit from the Father and poured it forth, as you [both] see and hear.[q] 34 For David did not go up into heaven, but he himself said:

'The Lord said to my Lord,
"Sit at my right hand[r]
35 until I make your enemies your footstool."'

36 Therefore let the whole house of Israel know for certain that God has made him both Lord and Messiah, this Jesus whom you crucified."[s]

37 Now when they heard this, they were cut to the heart, and they asked Peter and the other apostles, "What are we to do, my brothers?"[t] 38 Peter [said] to them, "Repent and be baptized,* every one of you, in the name of Jesus Christ for the forgiveness of your sins; and you will receive the gift of the holy Spirit.[u] 39 For the promise is made to you and to your children and to all those far off, whomever the Lord our God will call."[v] 40 He testified with many other arguments, and was exhorting them, "Save yourselves from this corrupt generation."[w] 41 Those who accepted his message were baptized, and about three thousand persons were added that day.[x]

Communal Life.* 42[y] They devoted themselves to the teaching of the apostles and to the communal life, to the breaking of the bread and to the prayers.[z] 43 Awe came upon everyone, and many wonders and signs were done through the apostles.[a] [44]All who believed were together and had all things in common;[b] [45]they would sell their property and possessions and divide them among all according to each one's need. [46]Every day they devoted themselves to meeting together in the temple area and to breaking bread in their homes. They ate their meals with exultation and sincerity of heart, [47]praising God and enjoying favor with all the people. And every day the Lord added to their number those who were being saved.

a.   [2:1] Lv 23:15–21; Dt 16:9–11.
b.   [2:2–3] Jn 3:8.
c.   [2:3] Lk 3:16.
d.   [2:4] 1:5; 4:31; 8:15, 17; 10:44; 11:15–16; 15:8; 19:6; Ps 104:30; Jn 20:33.
e.   [2:7] 1:11.
f.   [2:11] 10:46.
g.   [2:13] 1 Cor 14:23.
h.   [2:17] Is 2:2; 44:3; Jl 3:1–5.
i.   [2:21] Rom 10:13.
j.   [2:22] 10:38; Lk 24:19.
k.   [2:23] 1 Thes 2:15.
l.   [2:24] 13:34.
m. [2:25–28] Ps 16:8–11.
n.   [2:27] 13:35.
o.   [2:30] 2 Sm 7:12; Ps 132:11.
p.   [2:31] 13:35; Ps 16:10.
q.   [2:33] 1:4–5.
r.   [2:34–35] Ps 110:1.
s.   [2:36] 9:22; Rom 10:9; Phil 2:11.
t.   [2:37] Lk 3:10.
u.   [2:38] 3:19; 16:31; Lk 3:3.
v.   [2:39] Is 57:19; Jl 3:5; Eph 2:17.
w.   [2:40] Dt 32:5; Ps 78:8; Lk 9:41; Phil 2:15.
x.   [2:41] 2:47; 4:4; 5:14; 6:7; 11:21, 24; 21:20.
y.   [2:42–47] 4:32–35.
z.   [2:42] 1:14; 6:4.
a.   [2:43] 5:12–16.
b.   [2:44] 4:32, 34–35.

CHAPTER 3

Cure of a Crippled Beggar.

[1]*Now Peter and John were going up to the temple area for the three o'clock hour of prayer.* [2a]And a man crippled from birth was carried and placed at the gate of the temple called "the Beautiful Gate" every day to beg for alms from the people who entered the temple. [3]When he saw Peter and John about to go into the temple, he asked for alms. [4]But Peter looked intently at him, as did John, and said, "Look at us." [5]He paid attention to them, expecting to receive something from them. [6]*Peter said, "I have neither silver nor gold, but what I do have I give you: in the name of Jesus

Christ the Nazorean, [rise and] walk."[b] [7]Then Peter took him by the right hand and raised him up, and immediately his feet and ankles grew strong. [8]He leaped up, stood, and walked around, and went into the temple with them, walking and jumping and praising God.[c] [9]When all the people saw him walking and praising God, [10]they recognized him as the one who used to sit begging at the Beautiful Gate of the temple, and they were filled with amazement and astonishment at what had happened to him.

Peter's Speech. [11]As he clung to Peter and John, all the people hurried in amazement toward them in the portico called "Solomon's Portico."[d] [12]When Peter saw this, he addressed the people, "You Israelites, why are you amazed at this, and why do you look so intently at us as if we had made him walk by our own power or piety?[e] [13]The God of Abraham, [the God] of Isaac, and [the God] of Jacob, the God of our ancestors, has glorified* his servant Jesus whom you handed over and denied in Pilate's presence, when he had decided to release him.[f] [14]You denied the Holy and Righteous One* and asked that a murderer be released to you.[g] [15]The author of life you put to death, but God raised him from the dead; of this we are witnesses.[h] [16]And by faith in his name, this man, whom you see and know, his name has made strong, and the faith that comes through it has given him this perfect health, in the presence of all of you. [17]Now I know, brothers, that you acted out of ignorance,* just as your leaders did;[i] [18]but God has thus brought to fulfillment what he had announced beforehand through the mouth of all the prophets,* that his Messiah would suffer.[j] [19]Repent, therefore, and be converted, that your sins may be wiped away,[k] [20]and that the Lord may grant you times of refreshment and send you the Messiah already appointed for you, Jesus,* [21]whom heaven must receive until the times of universal restoration* of which God spoke through the mouth of his holy prophets from of old. [22]For Moses said:*

'A prophet like me will the
     Lord, your God, raise
     up for you
   from among your own
     kinsmen;
to him you shall listen in
     all that he may say to
     you.[l]
[23]Everyone who does not
     listen to that prophet
   will be cut off from the
     people.'[m]

[24]Moreover, all the prophets who spoke, from Samuel and those afterwards, also announced these days. [25]You are the children of the prophets and of the covenant that God made with your ancestors when he said to Abraham, 'In your offspring all the families of the earth shall be blessed.'[n] [26]For you first, God raised up his servant and sent him to bless you by turning each of you from your evil ways."[o]

a. [3:2–8] 14:8–10.
b. [3:6] 4:10.
c. [3:8] Is 35:6; Lk 7:22.
d. [3:11] 5:12; Jn 10:23.
e. [3:12] 14:15.
f. [3:13] Ex 3:6, 15; Is 52:13; Lk 23:14–25.
g. [3:14] Mt 27:20–21; Mk 15:11; Lk 23:18; Jn 18:40.
h. [3:15] 4:10; 5:31 / 1:8; 2:32.
i. [3:17] 13:27; Lk 23:34; 1 Cor 2:8; 1 Tm 1:13.
j. [3:18] Lk 18:31.
k. [3:19] 2:38.
l. [3:22] 7:37; Dt 18:15, 18.
m. [3:23] Lv 23:29; Dt 18:19.
n. [3:25] Gn 12:3; 18:18; 22:18; Sir 44:19–21; Gal 3:8–9.
o. [3:26] 13:46; Rom 1:16.

CHAPTER 4

[1]While they were still speaking to the people, the priests, the captain of the temple guard, and the Sadducees* confronted them, [2]disturbed that they were teaching the people and proclaiming in Jesus the resurrection of the dead.[a] [3]They laid hands on them and put them in custody until the next day, since

it was already evening. [4]But many of those who heard the word came to believe and [the] number of men grew to [about] five thousand.

Before the Sanhedrin. [5]On the next day, their leaders, elders, and scribes were assembled in Jerusalem, [6]with Annas the high priest, Caiaphas, John, Alexander, and all who were of the high-priestly class. [7]They brought them into their presence and questioned them, "By what power or by what name have you done this?" [8]Then Peter, filled with the holy Spirit, answered them, "Leaders of the people and elders:[b] [9]If we are being examined today about a good deed done to a cripple, namely, by what means he was saved, [10]then all of you and all the people of Israel should know that it was in the name of Jesus Christ the Nazorean whom you crucified, whom God raised from the dead; in his

name this man stands before you healed. [11c]He is 'the stone rejected by you,' the builders, which has become the cornerstone.' [12*d]There is no salvation through anyone else, nor is there any other name under heaven given to the human race by which we are to be saved."

[13]Observing the boldness of Peter and John and perceiving them to be uneducated, ordinary men, they were amazed, and they recognized them as the companions of Jesus. [14]Then when they saw the man who had been cured standing there with them, they could say nothing in reply. [15]So they ordered them to leave the Sanhedrin, and conferred with one another, saying, [16]"What are we to do with these men? Everyone living in Jerusalem knows that a remarkable sign was done through them, and we cannot deny it. [17]But so that it may not be spread any further among the people, let us

give them a stern warning never again to speak to anyone in this name."[e]

[18]So they called them back and ordered them not to speak or teach at all in the name of Jesus. [19]Peter and John, however, said to them in reply, "Whether it is right in the sight of God for us to obey you rather than God, you be the judges.[f] [20]It is impossible for us not to speak about what we have seen and heard." [21]After threatening them further, they released them, finding no way to punish them, on account of the people who were all praising God for what had happened. [22]For the man on whom this sign of healing had been done was over forty years old.

Prayer of the Community. [23]After their release they went back to their own people and reported what the chief priests and elders had told them. [24]And when they heard it, they raised their voices to God with one accord and said, "Sovereign Lord, maker of heaven and earth and the sea and all that is in them, [25]you said by the holy Spirit through the mouth of our father David, your servant:

'Why did the Gentiles rage[g]
     and the peoples entertain folly?
[26]The kings of the earth took their stand
     and the princes gathered together
          against the Lord
          and against his anointed.'

[27]Indeed they gathered in this city against your holy servant Jesus whom you anointed, Herod* and Pontius Pilate, together with the Gentiles and the peoples of Israel,[h] [28]to do what your hand and [your] will had long ago planned to take place. [29]And now, Lord, take note of their threats, and enable your

servants to speak your word with all boldness, [30]as you stretch forth [your] hand to heal, and signs and wonders are done through the name of your holy servant Jesus." [31]*As they prayed, the place where they were gathered shook, and they were all filled with the holy Spirit and continued to speak the word of God with boldness.[i]

Life in the Christian Community.* [32]The community of believers was of one heart and mind, and no one claimed that any of his possessions was his own, but they had everything in common. [33]With great power the apostles bore witness to the resurrection of the Lord Jesus, and great favor was accorded them all. [34]*There was no needy person among them, for those who owned property or houses would sell them, bring the proceeds of the sale, [35]and put them at the feet of the apostles, and they were distributed to each according to need.

[36]*[k]Thus Joseph, also named by the apostles Barnabas (which is translated "son of encouragement"), a Levite, a Cypriot by birth, [37]sold a piece of property that he owned, then brought the money and put it at the feet of the apostles.

---

a. [4:2] 23:6–8; 24:21.
b. [4:8] Mt 10:20.
c. [4:11] Ps 118:22; Is 28:16; Mt 21:42; Mk 12:10; Lk 20:17; Rom 9:33; 1 Pt 2:7.
d. [4:12] Mt 1:21; 1 Cor 3:11.
e. [4:17] 5:28.
f. [4:19] 5:29–32.
g. [4:25–26] Ps 2:1–2.
h. [4:27] Lk 23:12–13.
i. [4:31] 2:4.
j. [4:34–35] 2:44–45.
k. [4:36–37] 9:27; 11:22, 30; 12:25; 13:15; 1 Cor 9:6; Gal 2:1, 9, 13; Col 4:10.

CHAPTER 5

Ananias and Sapphira.* [1]A man named Ananias, however, with his wife Sapphira, sold a piece of property. [2]He retained for himself, with his wife's knowledge, some of the purchase price, took the remainder, and put it at the feet of the apostles. [3]But Peter said, "Ananias, why has Satan filled your heart so that you lied to the holy Spirit and retained part of the price of the land?[a] [4]While it remained unsold, did it not remain yours? And when it was sold, was it not still under your control? Why did you contrive this deed? You have lied not to human beings, but to God." [5]When Ananias heard these words, he fell down and breathed his last, and great fear came upon all who heard of it. [6]The young men came and wrapped him up, then carried him out and buried him.

[7]After an interval of about three hours, his wife came in, unaware of what had happened. [8]Peter said to her, "Tell me, did you sell the land for this amount?" She answered, "Yes, for that amount." [9]Then Peter said to her, "Why did you agree to test the Spirit of the Lord? Listen, the footsteps of those who have buried your husband are at the door, and they will carry you out." [10]At once, she fell down at his feet and breathed her last. When the young men entered they found her dead, so they carried her out and buried her beside her husband. [11]And great fear came upon the whole church and upon all who heard of these things.[b]

Signs and Wonders of the Apostles. [12]Many signs and wonders were done among the people at the hands of the apostles. They were all together in Solomon's portico.[c] [13]None of the others dared to join them, but the people esteemed them. [14]Yet more than ever, believers in the Lord, great numbers of men and women, were added to them. [15]Thus they even carried the sick out into the streets and laid them on cots and mats so that when Peter came by, at least his shadow might fall on one or another of them.[d] [16]A large number of people from the towns in the vicinity of Jerusalem also gathered, bringing the sick and those disturbed by unclean spirits, and they were all cured.

Trial Before the Sanhedrin.[*] [17]Then the high priest rose up and all his companions, that is, the party of the Sadducees, and, filled with jealousy,[e] [18]laid hands upon the apostles and put them in the public jail. [19]But during the night, the angel of the Lord opened the doors of the prison, led them out, and said,[f] [20]"Go and take your place in the temple area, and tell the people everything about this life." [21]When they heard this, they went to the temple early in the morning and taught. When the high priest and his companions arrived, they convened the Sanhedrin, the full senate of the Israelites, and sent to the jail to have them brought in. [22]But the court officers who went did not find them in the prison, so they came back and reported, [23]"We found the jail securely locked and the guards stationed outside the doors, but when we opened them, we found no one inside." [24]When they heard this report, the captain of the temple guard and the chief priests were at a loss about them, as to what this would come to. [25]Then someone came in and reported to them, "The men whom you put in prison are in the temple area and are teaching the people." [26]Then the captain and the court officers went and brought them in, but without force, because they were afraid of being stoned by the people.[g]

[27]When they had brought them in and made them stand before the Sanhedrin, the high priest questioned them, [28]"We gave you strict orders [did we not?] to stop teaching in that name. Yet you have filled Jerusalem with your teaching and want to bring this man's blood upon us."[h] [29]But Peter and the apostles said

in reply, "We must obey God rather than men.[i] [30*]The God of our ancestors raised Jesus,[j] though you had him killed by hanging him on a tree. [31]God exalted him at his right hand[*] as leader and savior to grant Israel repentance and forgiveness of sins.[k] [32]We are witnesses of these things, as is the holy Spirit that God has given to those who obey him."[l]

[33]When they heard this, they became infuriated and wanted to put them to death. [34*]But a Pharisee in the Sanhedrin named Gamaliel, a teacher of the law, respected by all the people, stood up, ordered the men to be put outside for a short time,[m] [35]and said to them, "Fellow Israelites, be careful what you are about to do to these men. [36*]Some time ago, Theudas appeared, claiming to be someone important, and about four hundred men joined him, but he was killed, and all those who were loyal to him were disbanded and came to nothing. [37]After him came Judas the Galilean at the time of the census. He also drew people after him, but he too perished and all who were loyal to him were scattered. [38]So now I tell you, have nothing to do with these men, and let them go. For if this endeavor or this activity is of human origin, it will destroy itself. [39]But if it comes from God, you will not be able to destroy them; you may even find yourselves fighting against God." They were persuaded by him. [40]After recalling the apostles, they had them flogged, ordered them to stop speaking in the name of Jesus, and dismissed them.[n] [41]So they left the presence of the Sanhedrin, rejoicing that they had been found worthy to suffer dishonor for the sake of the name.[o] [42]And all day long, both at the temple and in their homes, they did not stop teaching and proclaiming the Messiah, Jesus.[p]

a. [5:3] Lk 22:3; Jn 13:2.
b. [5:11] 2:43; 5:5; 19:17.

c. [5:12] 2:43; 6:8; 14:3; 15:12.
d. [5:15] 19:11–12; Mk 6:56.
e. [5:17] 4:1–3, 6.
f. [5:19] 12:7–10; 16:25–26.
g. [5:26] Lk 20:19.
h. [5:28] Mt 27:25.
i. [5:29] 4:19.
j. [5:30] 2:23–24.
k. [5:31] 2:38.
l. [5:32] Lk 24:48; Jn 15:26.
m. [5:34] 22:3.
n. [5:40] Mt 10:17; Acts 4:17–18.
o. [5:41] Mt 5:10–11; 1 Pt 4:13.
p. [5:42] 2:46; 5:20–21, 25; 8:35; 17:3; 18:5, 28; 19:4–5.

CHAPTER 6

The Need for Assistants. [1]*At that time, as the number of disciples continued to grow, the Hellenists complained against the Hebrews because their widows were being neglected in the daily distribution.[a] [2]*So the Twelve called together the community of the disciples and said, "It is not right for us to neglect the word of God to serve at table.* [3]Brothers, select from among you seven reputable men, filled with the Spirit and wisdom, whom we shall appoint to this task, [4]whereas we shall devote ourselves to prayer and to the ministry of the word." [5]The proposal was acceptable to the whole community, so they chose Stephen, a man filled with faith and the holy Spirit, also Philip, Prochorus, Nicanor, Timon, Parmenas, and Nicholas of Antioch, a convert to Judaism. [6b]They presented these men to the apostles who prayed and laid hands on them.* [7]The word of God continued to spread, and the number of the disciples in Jerusalem increased greatly; even a large group of priests were becoming obedient to the faith.[c]

Accusation Against Stephen. [8]*Now Stephen, filled with grace and power, was working great wonders and signs among the people. [9]Certain members of the so-called Synagogue of Freedmen, Cyrenians, and Alexandrians, and people from Cilicia and Asia, came forward and debated with Stephen, [10]but they could not withstand the wisdom and the spirit with which he spoke.[d] [11]Then they instigated some men to say, "We have heard him speaking blasphemous words against Moses and God."[e] [12]They stirred up the people, the elders, and the scribes, accosted him, seized him, and brought him before the Sanhedrin. [13]They presented false witnesses* who testified, "This man never stops saying things against [this] holy place and the law. [14]For we have heard him claim that this Jesus the Nazorean will destroy this place and change the customs that Moses handed down to us."[f] [15]All those who sat in the Sanhedrin looked intently at him and saw that his face was like the face of an angel.

---

a. [6:1] 2:45; 4:34–35.
b. [6:6] 1:24; 13:3; 14:23.
c. [6:7] 9:31; 12:24; 16:5; 19:20; 28:30–31.
d. [6:10] Lk 21:15.
e. [6:11] Mt 26:59–61; Mk 14:55–58; Acts 21:21.
f. [6:14] Mt 26:59–61; 27:40; Jn 2:19.

CHAPTER 7

Stephen's Discourses. [1]Then the high priest asked, "Is this

so?" [2a]And he replied,* "My brothers and fathers, listen. The God of glory appeared to our father Abraham while he was in Mesopotamia,* before he had settled in Haran, [3]and said to him, 'Go forth from your land and [from] your kinsfolk to the land that I will show you.'[b] [4]So he went forth from the land of the Chaldeans and settled in Haran. And from there, after his father died, he made him migrate to this land where you now dwell.[c] [5]Yet he gave him no inheritance in it, not even a foot's length, but he did promise to give it to him and his descendants as a possession, even though he was childless.[d] [6]And God spoke thus;[e] 'His descendants shall be aliens in a land not their own, where they shall be enslaved and oppressed for four hundred years; [7]but I will bring judgment on the nation they serve,' God said, 'and after that they will come out and worship me in this place.*f* [8]Then he gave him the covenant of circumcision, and so he became the father of Isaac, and circumcised him on the eighth day, as Isaac did Jacob, and Jacob the twelve patriarchs.*g*

[9]"And the patriarchs, jealous of Joseph, sold him into slavery in Egypt; but God was with him*h* [10]and rescued him from all his afflictions. He granted him favor and wisdom before Pharaoh, the king of Egypt, who put him in charge of Egypt and [of] his entire household.*i* [11]Then a famine and great affliction struck all Egypt and Canaan, and our ancestors could find no food;*j* [12]but when Jacob heard that there was grain in Egypt, he sent our ancestors there a first time.*k* [13]The second time, Joseph made himself known to his brothers, and Joseph's family became known to Pharaoh.*l* [14]Then Joseph sent for his father Jacob, inviting him and his whole clan, seventy-five persons;*m* [15]and Jacob went down to Egypt. And he and our ancestors died*n* [16]and were brought back to Shechem and placed in the tomb that Abraham had purchased for a sum of money from the sons of Hamor at Shechem.*o*

[17]"When the time drew near for the fulfillment of the promise that God pledged to Abraham, the people had increased and become very numerous in Egypt,*p* [18]until another king who knew nothing of Joseph came to power [in Egypt].*q* [19]He dealt shrewdly with our people and oppressed [our] ancestors by forcing them to expose their infants, that they might not survive. [20]At this time Moses was born, and he was extremely beautiful. For three months he was nursed in his father's house;*r* [21]but when he was exposed, Pharaoh's daughter adopted him and brought him up as her own son.*s* [22]Moses was educated [in] all the wisdom of

the Egyptians and was powerful in his words and deeds.

²³ᵗ"When he was forty years old, he decided to visit his kinsfolk, the Israelites. ²⁴When he saw one of them treated unjustly, he defended and avenged the oppressed man by striking down the Egyptian. ²⁵He assumed [his] kinsfolk would understand that God was offering them deliverance through him, but they did not understand. ²⁶ᵘThe next day he appeared to them as they were fighting and tried to reconcile them peacefully, saying, 'Men, you are brothers. Why are you harming one another?' ²⁷Then the one who was harming his neighbor pushed him aside, saying, 'Who appointed you ruler and judge over us? ²⁸Are you thinking of killing me as you killed the Egyptian yesterday?' ²⁹Moses fled when he heard this and settled as an alien in the land of Midian, where he became the father of two sons.ᵛ

³⁰ʷ"Forty years later, an angel appeared to him in the desert near Mount Sinai in the flame of a burning bush. ³¹When Moses saw it, he was amazed at the sight, and as he drew near to look at it, the voice of the Lord came, ³²'I am the God of your fathers, the God of Abraham, of Isaac, and of Jacob.' Then Moses, trembling, did not dare to look at it. ³³But the Lord said to him, 'Remove the sandals from your feet, for the place where you stand is holy ground. ³⁴I have witnessed the affliction of my people in Egypt and have heard their groaning, and I have come down to rescue them. Come now, I will send you to Egypt.' ³⁵This Moses, whom they had rejected with the words, 'Who appointed you ruler and judge?' God sent as [both] ruler and deliverer, through the angel who appeared to him in the bush.ˣ ³⁶This man led them out, performing wonders and

signs in the land of Egypt, at the Red Sea, and in the desert for forty years.[y] [37]It was this Moses who said to the Israelites, 'God will raise up for you, from among your own kinsfolk, a prophet like me.'[z] [38]It was he who, in the assembly in the desert, was with the angel who spoke to him on Mount Sinai and with our ancestors, and he received living utterances to hand on to us.[a]

[39]"Our ancestors were unwilling to obey him; instead, they pushed him aside and in their hearts turned back to Egypt,[b] [40]saying to Aaron, 'Make us gods who will be our leaders. As for that Moses who led us out of the land of Egypt, we do not know what has happened to him.'[c] [41d]So they made a calf in those days, offered sacrifice to the idol, and reveled in the works of their hands. [42]Then God turned and handed them over to worship the host of heaven, as it is written in the book of the prophets:[e]

'Did you bring me sacrifices and offerings
   for forty years in the
   desert, O house of
   Israel?[f]
[43]No, you took up the tent
   of Moloch
   and the star of [your]
   god Rephan,
   the images that you
   made to worship.
So I shall take you into
   exile beyond Babylon.'

[44]Our ancestors had the tent of testimony in the desert just as the One who spoke to Moses directed him to make it according to the pattern he had seen.[g] [45]Our ancestors who inherited it brought it with Joshua when they dispossessed the nations that God drove out from before our ancestors, up to the time of David,[h] [46]who found favor in the sight of God and asked that he might find a dwelling

place for the house of Jacob.^{i} ^{47}But Solomon built a house for him.^{j} ^{48}Yet the Most High does not dwell in houses made by human hands. As the prophet says:^{k}

^{49}'The heavens are my throne,
the earth is my footstool.
What kind of house can you build for me?
says the Lord,
or what is to be my resting place?^{l}
^{50}Did not my hand make all these things?'

Conclusion. ^{51}"You stiff-necked people, uncircumcised in heart and ears, you always oppose the holy Spirit; you are just like your ancestors. ^{52}Which of the prophets did your ancestors not persecute? They put to death those who foretold the coming of the righteous one, whose betrayers and murderers you have now become.^{m} ^{53}You received the law as transmitted by angels, but you did not observe it."^{n}

Stephen's Martyrdom. ^{54}When they heard this, they were infuriated, and they ground their teeth at him. ^{55}But he, filled with the holy Spirit, looked up intently to heaven and saw the glory of God and Jesus standing at the right hand of God,* ^{56}and he said, "Behold, I see the heavens opened and the Son of Man standing at the right hand of God." ^{57}But they cried out in a loud voice, covered their ears,* and rushed upon him together. ^{58}They threw him out of the city, and began to stone him. The witnesses laid down their cloaks at the feet of a young man named Saul.^{p} ^{59}As they were stoning Stephen,^{q} he called out, "Lord Jesus, receive my spirit."* ^{60}Then he fell to his knees and cried out in a loud voice, "Lord, do not hold this sin against them"; and when he said this, he fell asleep.^{r}

a. [7:2] Gn 11:31; 12:1; Ps 29:3.
b. [7:3] Gn 12:1.
c. [7:4] Gn 12:5; 15:7.
d. [7:5] Gn 12:7; 13:15; 15:2; 16:1; Dt 2:5.
e. [7:6–7] Gn 15:13–14.
f. [7:7] Ex 3:12.
g. [7:8] Gn 17:10–14; 21:2–4.
h. [7:9] Gn 37:11, 28; 39:2, 3, 21, 23.
i. [7:10] Gn 41:37–43; Ps 105:21; Wis 10:13–14.
j. [7:11] Gn 41:54–57; 42:5.
k. [7:12] Gn 42:1–2.
l. [7:13] Gn 45:3–4, 16.
m. [7:14] Gn 45:9–11, 18–19; 46:27; Ex 1:5 LXX; Dt 10:22.
n. [7:15] Gn 46:5–6; 49:33.
o. [7:16] Gn 23:3–20; 33:19; 49:29–30; 50:13; Jos 24:32.
p. [7:17] Ex 1:7.
q. [7:18] Ex 1:8.
r. [7:20] Ex 2:2; Heb 11:23.
s. [7:21] Ex 2:3–10.
t. [7:23–24] Ex 2:11–12.
u. [7:26–28] Ex 2:13–14.
v. [7:29] Ex 2:15, 21–22; 18:3–4.
w. [7:30–34] Ex 3:2–3.
x. [7:35] Ex 2:14.
y. [7:36] Ex 7:3, 10; 14:21; Nm 14:33.
z. [7:37] Dt 18:15; Acts 3:22.
a. [7:38] Ex 19:3; 20:1–17; Dt 5:4–22; 6:4–25.
b. [7:39] Nm 14:3.
c. [7:40] Ex 32:1, 23.
d. [7:41] Ex 32:4–6.
e. [7:42–43] Am 5:25–27.
f. [7:42] Jer 7:18; 8:2; 19:13.
g. [7:44] Ex 25:9, 40.
h. [7:45] Jos 3:14–17; 18:1; 2 Sm 7:5–7.
i. [7:46] 2 Sm 7:1–2; 1 Kgs 8:17; Ps 132:1–5.
j. [7:47] 1 Kgs 6:1; 1 Chr 17:12.
k. [7:48] 17:24.
l. [7:49] Is 66:1–2.
m. [7:52] 2 Chr 36:16; Mt 23:31, 34.
n. [7:53] Gal 3:19; Heb 2:2.
o. [7:55–56] Mt 26:64; Mk 14:62; Lk 22:69; Acts 2:34.
p. [7:58] 22:20.
q. [7:59] Ps 31:6; Lk 23:46.
r. [7:60] Mt 27:46, 50; Mk 15:34; Lk 23:46.

CHAPTER 8

¹Now Saul was consenting to his execution.[a]

Persecution of the Church. On that day, there broke out a severe persecution* of the church in Jerusalem, and all were scattered throughout the countryside of Judea and Samaria, except the apostles.* ²Devout men buried Stephen and made a loud lament over him. ³Saul, meanwhile, was trying to destroy the church;* entering house after house and dragging out men and women, he handed them over for imprisonment.[b]

III. THE MISSION IN JUDEA AND SAMARIA

Philip in Samaria. ⁴Now those who had been scattered went about preaching the word.[c] ⁵Thus Philip went down to [the] city of Samaria and proclaimed the Messiah to them.[d] ⁶With one accord, the crowds paid attention to what was said by Philip when they heard it and saw the signs he was doing. ⁷For unclean spirits, crying out in a loud voice, came out of many possessed people, and many paralyzed and crippled people were cured.*e* *8*There was great joy in that city.

Simon the Magician. *9*A man named Simon used to practice magic* in the city and astounded the people of Samaria, claiming to be someone great. *10*All of them, from the least to the greatest, paid attention to him, saying, "This man is the 'Power of God' that is called 'Great.'" *11*They paid attention to him because he had astounded them by his magic for a long time, *12*but once they began to believe Philip as he preached the good news about the kingdom of God and the name of Jesus Christ, men and women alike were baptized.*f* *13*Even Simon himself believed and, after being baptized, became devoted to Philip; and when he saw the signs and mighty deeds that were occurring, he was astounded.

*14*Now when the apostles in Jerusalem heard that Samaria had accepted the word of God, they sent them Peter and John, *15*who went down and prayed for them, that they might receive the holy Spirit, *16*for it had not yet fallen upon any of them; they had only been baptized in the name of the Lord Jesus.* *17*Then they laid hands on them and they received the holy Spirit.*g*

*18*When Simon saw that the Spirit was conferred by the laying on of the apostles' hands, he offered them money *19*and said, "Give me this power too, so that anyone upon whom I lay my hands may receive the holy Spirit." *20*But Peter said to him, "May your money perish with you, because you thought that you could buy the gift of God with money. *21*You have no share or lot in this matter, for your heart is not upright before God. *22*Repent of this wickedness of yours and pray to the Lord that, if possible, your intention may be forgiven. ²³For I see that you are filled with bitter gall and are in the bonds of iniquity." ²⁴Simon said in reply, "Pray for me to the Lord, that nothing of what you have said may come upon me." ²⁵So when they had testified and proclaimed the word of the Lord, they returned to Jerusalem and preached the good news to many Samaritan villages.

Philip and the Ethiopian.[*] ²⁶Then the angel of the Lord spoke to Philip, "Get up and head south on the road that goes down from Jerusalem to Gaza, the desert route." ²⁷So he got up and set out. Now there was an Ethiopian eunuch, a court official of the Candace,[*] that is, the queen of the Ethiopians, in charge of her entire treasury, who had come to Jerusalem to worship,[h] ²⁸and was returning home. Seated in his chariot, he was reading the prophet Isaiah. ²⁹The Spirit said to

Philip, "Go and join up with that chariot." ³⁰Philip ran up and heard him reading Isaiah the prophet and said, "Do you understand what you are reading?" ³¹He replied, "How can I, unless someone instructs me?" So he invited Philip to get in and sit with him.[i] ³²This was the scripture passage he was reading:[j]

"Like a sheep he was led to
the slaughter,
and as a lamb before its
shearer is silent,
so he opened not his
mouth.
³³In [his] humiliation jus-
tice was denied him.
Who will tell of his
posterity?
For his life is taken
from the earth."

³⁴Then the eunuch said to Philip in reply, "I beg you, about whom is the prophet saying this? About himself, or about someone else?" ³⁵Then Philip opened his mouth and,

beginning with this scripture passage, he proclaimed Jesus to him. ³⁶ᵏAs they traveled along the road they came to some water, and the eunuch said, "Look, there is water. What is to prevent my being baptized?" [³⁷]* ³⁸Then he ordered the chariot to stop, and Philip and the eunuch both went down into the water, and he baptized him. ³⁹When they came out of the water, the Spirit of the Lord snatched Philip away, and the eunuch saw him no more, but continued on his way rejoicing.ˡ ⁴⁰Philip came to Azotus, and went about proclaiming the good news to all the towns until he reached Caesarea.ᵐ

CHAPTER 9

Saul's Conversion. ¹Now Saul, still breathing murderous threats against the disciples of the Lord,ᵃ went to the high priestᵇ ²and asked him for letters to the synagogues in Damascus, that, if he should find any men or women who belonged to the Way,* he might bring them back to Jerusalem in chains. ³On his journey, as he was nearing Damascus, a light from the sky suddenly flashed around him.ᶜ ⁴He fell to the ground and heard a voice saying to him, "Saul, Saul, why are you persecuting me?"ᵈ ⁵He said, "Who are you, sir?" The reply came, "I am Jesus, whom you are persecuting.ᵉ ⁶Now get up and go into the city and you will be told what you must do."ᶠ ⁷The men who were traveling with him stood speechless, for they heard the voice but could see no one.ᵍ ⁸Saul got up from the ground, but when he opened his eyes he

a. [8:1] 22:20.
b. [8:3] 9:1, 13; 22:4; 26:9–11; 1 Cor 5:9; Gal 1:13.
c. [8:4] 11:19.
d. [8:5] 6:5; 21:8–9.
e. [8:7] Mk 16:17.
f. [8:12] 1:3; 19:8; 28:23, 31.
g. [8:17] 2:4; 4:31; 10:44–47; 15:8–9; 19:2, 6.
h. [8:27] Is 56:3–5.
i. [8:31] Jn 16:13.
j. [8:32–33] Is 53:7–8 LXX.
k. [8:36] 10:47.
l. [8:39] 1 Kgs 18:12.
m. [8:40] 21:8.

could see nothing;* so they led him by the hand and brought him to Damascus.[h] [9]For three days he was unable to see, and he neither ate nor drank.

Saul's Baptism. [10i]There was a disciple in Damascus named Ananias, and the Lord said to him in a vision, "Ananias." He answered, "Here I am, Lord." [11]The Lord said to him, "Get up and go to the street called Straight and ask at the house of Judas for a man from Tarsus named Saul. He is there praying,[j] [12]and [in a vision] he has seen a man named Ananias come in and lay [his] hands on him, that he may regain his sight." [13]But Ananias replied, "Lord, I have heard from many sources about this man, what evil things he has done to your holy ones* in Jerusalem.[k] [14]And here he has authority from the chief priests to imprison all who call upon your name."[l] [15]But the Lord said to him, "Go, for this man

is a chosen instrument of mine to carry my name before Gentiles, kings, and Israelites,[m] [16]and I will show him what he will have to suffer for my name." [17]So Ananias went and entered the house; laying his hands on him, he said, "Saul, my brother, the Lord has sent me, Jesus who appeared to you on the way by which you came, that you may regain your sight and be filled with the holy Spirit." [18]Immediately things like scales fell from his eyes and he regained his sight. He got up and was baptized, [19]and when he had eaten, he recovered his strength.*

Saul Preaches in Damascus. He stayed some days with the disciples in Damascus, [20]and he began at once to proclaim Jesus in the synagogues, that he is the Son of God.* [21]All who heard him were astounded and said, "Is not this the man who in Jerusalem ravaged those who call upon this name, and came here expressly to take them back in chains to the chief priests?" [22]But Saul grew all the stronger and confounded [the] Jews who lived in Damascus, proving that this is the Messiah.

Saul Visits Jerusalem. [23]After a long time had passed, the Jews conspired to kill him, [24n]but their plot became known to Saul. Now they were keeping watch on the gates day and night so as to kill him, [25]but his disciples took him one night and let him down through an opening in the wall, lowering him in a basket. [26o]When he arrived in Jerusalem[*] he tried to join the disciples, but they were all afraid of him, not believing that he was a disciple. [27]Then Barnabas took charge of him and brought him to the apostles, and he reported to them how on the way he had seen the Lord and that he had spoken to him, and how in Damascus he had spoken out boldly in the name of Jesus.

[28]He moved about freely with them in Jerusalem, and spoke out boldly in the name of the Lord. [29]He also spoke and debated with the Hellenists,[*] but they tried to kill him. [30]And when the brothers learned of this, they took him down to Caesarea and sent him on his way to Tarsus.[p]

The Church at Peace. [31]"The church throughout all Judea, Galilee, and Samaria was at peace. It was being built up and walked in the fear of the Lord, and with the consolation of the holy Spirit it grew in numbers.

Peter Heals Aeneas at Lydda. [32]As Peter was passing through every region, he went down to the holy ones living in Lydda. [33]There he found a man named Aeneas, who had been confined to bed for eight years, for he was paralyzed. [34]Peter said to him, "Aeneas, Jesus Christ heals you. Get up and make your bed." He got up at once.

³⁵And all the inhabitants of Lydda and Sharon saw him, and they turned to the Lord.

Peter Restores Tabitha to Life. ³⁶Now in Joppa there was a disciple named Tabitha (which translated means Dorcas).[*] She was completely occupied with good deeds and almsgiving. ³⁷Now during those days she fell sick and died, so after washing her, they laid [her] out in a room upstairs. ³⁸Since Lydda was near Joppa, the disciples, hearing that Peter was there, sent two men to him with the request, "Please come to us without delay." ³⁹So Peter got up and went with them. When he arrived, they took him to the room upstairs where all the widows came to him weeping and showing him the tunics and cloaks that Dorcas had made while she was with them. ⁴⁰Peter sent them all out and knelt down and prayed. Then he turned to her body and said, "Tabitha,

rise up." She opened her eyes, saw Peter, and sat up.^q ⁴¹He gave her his hand and raised her up, and when he had called the holy ones and the widows, he presented her alive. ⁴²This became known all over Joppa, and many came to believe in the Lord. ^{43*r}And he stayed a long time in Joppa with Simon, a tanner.

---

a. [9:1] 8:3; 9:13; 22:4; 1 Cor 15:9; Gal 1:13–14.
b. [9:1–2] 9:14; 26:10.
c. [9:3] 1 Cor 9:1; 15:8; Gal 1:16.
d. [9:4] 22:6; 26:14.
e. [9:5] 22:8; 26:15; Mt 25:40.
f. [9:6] 22:10; 26:16.
g. [9:7] 22:9; 26:13–14.
h. [9:8] 22:11.
i. [9:10–19] 22:12–16.
j. [9:11] 21:39.
k. [9:13] 8:3; 9:1.
l. [9:14] 9:1–2; 26:10; 1 Cor 1:2; 2 Tm 2:22.
m. [9:15] 22:15; 26:1; 27:24.
n. [9:24–25] 2 Cor 11:32–33.
o. [9:26–27] Gal 1:18.
p. [9:30] 11:25.
q. [9:40] Mk 5:40–41.
r. [9:43] 10:6.

IV. THE INAUGURATION OF THE GENTILE MISSION

CHAPTER 10

The Vision of Cornelius.^a ^{1*}Now in Caesarea there was a man named Cornelius, a centurion of the Cohort called the Italica,* [2]devout and God-fearing along with his whole household, who used to give alms generously* to the Jewish people and pray to God constantly. [3]One afternoon about three o'clock,* he saw plainly in a vision an angel of God come in to him and say to him, "Cornelius." [4]He looked intently at him and, seized with fear, said, "What is it, sir?" He said to him, "Your prayers and almsgiving have ascended as a memorial offering before God. [5]Now send some men to Joppa and summon one Simon who is called Peter. [6]He is staying with another Simon, a tanner, who has a house by the sea."[b] [7]When the angel who spoke to him had left, he called two of his servants and a devout soldier* from his staff, [8]explained everything to them, and sent them to Joppa.

The Vision of Peter. [9]*The next day, while they were on their way and nearing the city, Peter went up to the roof terrace to pray at about noontime.* [10]He was hungry and wished to eat, and while they were making preparations he fell into a trance. [11]He saw heaven opened and something resembling a large sheet coming down, lowered to the ground by its four corners. [12]In it were all the earth's four-legged animals and reptiles and the birds of the sky. [13]A voice said to him, "Get up, Peter. Slaughter and eat." [14]But Peter said, "Certainly not, sir. For never have I eaten anything profane and unclean."[d] [15]The voice spoke to him again, a second time, "What God has made clean, you are not to call profane."[e] [16]This happened three times, and then the object was taken up into the sky.

[17]*While Peter was in doubt about the meaning of the vision he had seen, the men

sent by Cornelius asked for Simon's house and arrived at the entrance. ¹⁸They called out inquiring whether Simon, who is called Peter, was staying there. ¹⁹As Peter was pondering the vision, the Spirit said [to him], "There are three men here looking for you.*f* ²⁰So get up, go downstairs, and accompany them without hesitation, because I have sent them." ²¹Then Peter went down to the men and said, "I am the one you are looking for. What is the reason for your being here?" ²²They answered, "Cornelius, a centurion, an upright and God-fearing man, respected by the whole Jewish nation, was directed by a holy angel to summon you to his house and to hear what you have to say."*g* ²³So he invited them in and showed them hospitality.

The next day he got up and went with them, and some of the brothers from Joppa went with him. ²⁴*On the following day he entered Caesarea.

Cornelius was expecting them and had called together his relatives and close friends. ²⁵*h*When Peter entered, Cornelius met him and, falling at his feet, paid him homage. ²⁶Peter, however, raised him up, saying, "Get up. I myself am also a human being." ²⁷While he conversed with him, he went in and found many people gathered together ²⁸*i*and said to them, "You know that it is unlawful for a Jewish man to associate with, or visit, a Gentile, but God has shown me that I should not call any person profane or unclean.* ²⁹And that is why I came without objection when sent for. May I ask, then, why you summoned me?"

³⁰Cornelius replied, "Four days ago* at this hour, three o'clock in the afternoon, I was at prayer in my house when suddenly a man in dazzling robes stood before me and said, ³¹'Cornelius, your prayer has been heard and your almsgiving remembered

before God. [32]Send therefore to Joppa and summon Simon, who is called Peter. He is a guest in the house of Simon, a tanner, by the sea.' [33]So I sent for you immediately, and you were kind enough to come. Now therefore we are all here in the presence of God to listen to all that you have been commanded by the Lord."

Peter's Speech.[*] [34]Then Peter proceeded to speak and said,[*] "In truth, I see that God shows no partiality.[j] [35]Rather, in every nation whoever fears him and acts uprightly is acceptable to him. [36*]You know the word [that] he sent to the Israelites[*] as he proclaimed peace through Jesus Christ, who is Lord of all,[k] [37]what has happened all over Judea, beginning in Galilee after the baptism that John preached,[l] [38]how God anointed Jesus of Nazareth[*] with the holy Spirit and power. He went about doing good and healing all those oppressed by the devil, for God was with him.[m] [39]We are witnesses[*] of all that he did both in the country of the Jews and [in] Jerusalem. They put him to death by hanging him on a tree. [40]This man God raised [on] the third day and granted that he be visible, [41]not to all the people, but to us, the witnesses chosen by God in advance, who ate and drank with him after he rose from the dead.[n] [42]He commissioned us[o] to preach to the people and testify that he is the one appointed by God as judge of the living and the dead.[*] [43]To him all the prophets bear witness, that everyone who believes in him will receive forgiveness of sins through his name."

The Baptism of Cornelius. [44p]While Peter was still speaking these things, the holy Spirit fell upon all who were listening to the word.[*] [45]The circumcised believers who had accompanied Peter were astounded that the gift of the holy Spirit should have been poured out on the Gentiles also, ⁴⁶for they could hear them speaking in tongues and glorifying God. Then Peter responded, ⁴⁷"Can anyone withhold the water for baptizing these people, who have received the holy Spirit even as we have?"^q ⁴⁸He ordered them to be baptized in the name of Jesus Christ. ⁴⁹Then they invited him to stay for a few days.

a. [10:1–8] 10:30–33.
b. [10:6] 9:43.
c. [10:11–20] 11:5–12.
d. [10:14] Lv 11:1–47; Ez 4:14.
e. [10:15] Mk 7:15–19; Gal 2:12.
f. [10:19] 13:2.
g. [10:22] Lk 7:4–5.
h. [10:25–26] 14:13–15; Rev 19:10.
i. [10:28] Gal 2:11–16.
j. [10:34] Dt 10:17; 2 Chr 19:7; Jb 34:19; Wis 6:7; Rom 2:11; Gal 2:6; Eph 6:9; 1 Pt 1:17.
k. [10:36] Is 52:7; Na 2:1.
l. [10:37] Mt 4:12; Mk 1:14; Lk 4:14.
m. [10:38] Is 61:1; Lk 4:18.
n. [10:41] Lk 24:41–43.
o. [10:42] 1:8; 3:15; 17:31; Lk 24:48; Rom 14:9; 2 Tm 4:1.
p. [10:44] 11:15; 15:8.
q. [10:47] 8:36.

CHAPTER 11

The Baptism of the Gentiles Explained.[*] ¹Now the apostles and the brothers who were in Judea heard that the Gentiles too had accepted the word of God. ²So when Peter went up to Jerusalem the circumcised believers confronted him, ³saying, "You entered[*] the house of uncircumcised people and ate with them." ⁴Peter began and explained it to them step by step, saying, ^{5a}"I was at prayer in the city of Joppa when in a trance I had a vision, something resembling a large sheet coming down, lowered from the sky by its four corners, and it came to me. ⁶Looking intently into it, I observed and saw the four-legged animals of the earth, the wild beasts, the reptiles, and the birds of the sky. ⁷I also heard a voice say to me, 'Get up, Peter. Slaughter and eat.' ⁸But I said, 'Certainly not, sir, because nothing profane or unclean has ever entered my mouth.' ⁹But a second time a voice from heaven answered, 'What God has made clean, you are not to call profane.' ¹⁰This happened three times, and then everything was drawn up again into the sky. ¹¹Just then three men appeared at the house where we were, who had been sent to me from Caesarea. ¹²The Spirit told me to accompany them without discriminating. These six brothers* also went with me, and we entered the man's house. ¹³He related to us how he had seen [the] angel standing in his house, saying, 'Send someone to Joppa and summon Simon, who is called Peter,ᵇ ¹⁴who will speak words to you by which you and all your household will be saved.' ¹⁵As I began to speak, the holy Spirit fell upon them as it had upon us at the beginning.ᶜ ¹⁶and I remembered the word of the Lord, how he had said, 'John baptized with water but you will be baptized with the holy Spirit.'ᵈ ¹⁷If then God gave them the same gift he gave to us when we came to believe in the Lord Jesus Christ, who was I to be able to hinder God?"ᵉ ¹⁸When they heard this, they stopped objecting and glorified God, saying, "God has then granted life-giving repentance to the Gentiles too."

The Church at Antioch. ¹⁹Now those who had been scattered by the persecution that arose because of Stephen went as far as Phoenicia, Cyprus, and Antioch, preaching the word to no one but Jews.ᶠ ²⁰There were some Cypriots and Cyrenians among them, however, who came to Antioch and began to speak to the Greeks as well, proclaiming the Lord Jesus. ²¹The hand of the Lord was with them and a great number who believed turned to the Lord. ²²The news about them reached the ears of the church in Jerusalem, and they sent Barnabas [to go] to Antioch. ²³When he arrived and saw the grace of God, he rejoiced and encouraged them all to remain faithful to the Lord in firmness of heart, [24]for he was a good man, filled with the holy Spirit and faith. And a large number of people was added to the Lord. [25]Then he went to Tarsus to look for Saul, [26]and when he had found him he brought him to Antioch. For a whole year they met with the church and taught a large number of people, and it was in Antioch that the disciples were first called Christians.[*]

The Prediction of Agabus.[*] [27]At that time some prophets came down from Jerusalem to Antioch, [28]and one of them named Agabus stood up and predicted by the Spirit that there would be a severe famine all over the world, and it happened under Claudius.[g] [29]So the disciples determined that, according to ability,[h] each should send relief to the brothers who lived in Judea.

[30]This they did, sending it to the presbyters in care of Barnabas and Saul.

---

a. [11:5–12] 10:11–20.
b. [11:13] 10:3–5, 22, 30–32.
c. [11:15] 10:44.
d. [11:16] 1:5; 19:4; Lk 3:16.
e. [11:17] 15:8–9.
f. [11:19] 8:1–4.
g. [11:28] 21:10.
h. [11:29–30] 12:25.

CHAPTER 12

Herod's Persecution of the Christians.[*] [1]About that time King Herod laid hands upon some members of the church to harm them. [2]He had James, the brother of John,[*] killed by the sword, [3][*]and when he saw that this was pleasing to the Jews he proceeded to arrest Peter also. (It was [the] feast of Unleavened Bread.) [4]He had him taken into custody and put in prison under the guard of four squads of four soldiers each. He intended to bring him before the people after Passover. [5]Peter thus was being kept in prison, but prayer by the church was fervently being made to God on his behalf.[a]

6On the very night before Herod was to bring him to trial, Peter, secured by double chains, was sleeping between two soldiers, while outside the door guards kept watch on the prison. 7Suddenly the angel of the Lord stood by him and a light shone in the cell. He tapped Peter on the side and awakened him, saying, "Get up quickly." The chains fell from his wrists. 8The angel said to him, "Put on your belt and your sandals." He did so. Then he said to him, "Put on your cloak and follow me." 9So he followed him out, not realizing that what was happening through the angel was real; he thought he was seeing a vision. 10They passed the first guard, then the second, and came to the iron gate leading out to the city, which opened for them by itself. They emerged and made their way down an alley, and suddenly the angel left him. 11Then Peter recovered his senses and said, "Now I know for certain that [the] Lord sent his angel and rescued me from the hand of Herod and from all that the Jewish people had been expecting." 12When he realized this, he went to the house of Mary, the mother of John who is called Mark, where there were many people gathered in prayer.[b] 13When he knocked on the gateway door, a maid named Rhoda came to answer it. 14She was so overjoyed when she recognized Peter's voice that, instead of opening the gate, she ran in and announced that Peter was standing at the gate. 15They told her, "You are out of your mind," but she insisted that it was so. But they kept saying, "It is his angel." 16But Peter continued to knock, and when they opened it, they saw him and were astounded. 17He motioned to them with his hand to be quiet and explained [to them] how the Lord had led him out of the prison, and said, "Report this to James* and the brothers." Then he left and went to another place. ¹⁸At daybreak there was no small commotion among the soldiers over what had become of Peter.ᶜ ¹⁹Herod, after instituting a search but not finding him, ordered the guards tried and executed. Then he left Judea to spend some time in Caesarea.

Herod's Death. ²⁰*He had long been very angry with the people of Tyre and Sidon, who now came to him in a body. After winning over Blastus, the king's chamberlain, they sued for peace because their country was supplied with food from the king's territory. ²¹On an appointed day, Herod, attired in royal robes, [and] seated on the rostrum, addressed them publicly. ²²The assembled crowd cried out, "This is the voice of a god, not of a man." ²³At once the angel of the Lord struck him down because he did not ascribe the honor to God, and he was eaten by worms and breathed his last. ²⁴But the word of God continued to spread and grow.ᵈ

Mission of Barnabas and Saul. ²⁵After Barnabas and Saul completed their relief mission, they returned to Jerusalem,* taking with them John, who is called Mark.ᵉ

a. [12:5] Jas 5:16.
b. [12:12] 12:25; 15:37.
c. [12:18] 5:22–24.
d. [12:24] 6:7.
e. [12:25] 11:29–30.

CHAPTER 13

¹*Now there were in the church at Antioch prophets and teachers: Barnabas, Symeon who was called Niger, Lucius of Cyrene, Manaen who was a close friend of Herod the tetrarch, and Saul. ²While they were worshiping the Lord and fasting, the

holy Spirit said, "Set apart for me Barnabas and Saul for the work to which I have called them." ³Then, completing their fasting and prayer, they laid hands on them and sent them off.

First Mission Begins in Cyprus. ⁴*So they, sent forth by the holy Spirit, went down to Seleucia and from there sailed to Cyprus. ⁵When they arrived in Salamis, they proclaimed the word of God in the Jewish synagogues. They had John* also as their assistant. ⁶When they had traveled through the whole island as far as Paphos, they met a magician named Bar-Jesus who was a Jewish false prophet.* ⁷He was with the proconsul Sergius Paulus, a man of intelligence, who had summoned Barnabas and Saul and wanted to hear the word of God. ⁸But Elymas the magician (for that is what his name means) opposed them in an attempt to turn the proconsul away from the faith. ⁹But Saul, also known as Paul,* filled with the holy Spirit, looked intently at him ¹⁰and said, "You son of the devil, you enemy of all that is right, full of every sort of deceit and fraud. Will you not stop twisting the straight paths of [the] Lord? ¹¹Even now the hand of the Lord is upon you. You will be blind, and unable to see the sun for a time." Immediately a dark mist fell upon him, and he went about seeking people to lead him by the hand. ¹²When the proconsul saw what had happened, he came to believe, for he was astonished by the teaching about the Lord.

Paul's Arrival at Antioch in Pisidia. ¹³From Paphos, Paul and his companions set sail and arrived at Perga in Pamphylia. But John left them and returned to Jerusalem.ᵃ ¹⁴They continued on from Perga and reached Antioch in

Pisidia. On the sabbath they entered [into] the synagogue and took their seats. ¹⁵After the reading of the law and the prophets, the synagogue officials sent word to them, "My brothers, if one of you has a word of exhortation for the people, please speak."

Paul's Address in the Synagogue. ¹⁶So Paul got up, motioned with his hand, and said, "Fellow Israelites and you others who are God-fearing,* listen. ¹⁷The God of this people Israel chose our ancestors and exalted the people during their sojourn in the land of Egypt.ᵇ With uplifted arm he led them out of it ¹⁸and for about forty years he put up with* them in the desert.ᶜ ¹⁹When he had destroyed seven nations in the land of Canaan, he gave them their land as an inheritanceᵈ ²⁰at the end of about four hundred and fifty years.* After these things he provided judges up to Samuel [the] prophet.ᵉ ²¹Then they asked for a king. God gave them Saul, son of Kish, a man from the tribe of Benjamin, for forty years.ᶠ ²²Then he removed him and raised up David as their king; of him he testified, 'I have found David, son of Jesse, a man after my own heart; he will carry out my every wish.'ᵍ ²³From this man's descendants God, according to his promise, has brought to Israel a savior, Jesus.ʰ ²⁴John heralded his coming by proclaiming a baptism of repentance to all the people of Israel;ⁱ ²⁵and as John was completing his course, he would say, 'What do you suppose that I am? I am not he. Behold, one is coming after me; I am not worthy to unfasten the sandals of his feet.'ʲ

²⁶"My brothers, children of the family of Abraham, and those others among you who are God-fearing, to us this word of salvation has been sent. ²⁷The inhabitants

of Jerusalem and their leaders failed to recognize him, and by condemning him they fulfilled the oracles of the prophets that are read sabbath after sabbath. ²⁸For even though they found no grounds for a death sentence, they asked Pilate to have him put to death,^{k 29}and when they had accomplished all that was written about him, they took him down from the tree and placed him in a tomb.^l ³⁰But God raised him from the dead,^m ³¹and for many days he appeared to those who had come up with him from Galilee to Jerusalem.ⁿ These are [now] his witnesses before the people.[•] ³²We ourselves are proclaiming this good news to you that what God promised our ancestors ³³he has brought to fulfillment for us, [their] children, by raising up Jesus, as it is written in the second psalm, 'You are my son; this day I have begotten you.'^o ³⁴And that he raised him from the

dead never to return to corruption he declared in this way, 'I shall give you the benefits assured to David.'^p ³⁵That is why he also says in another psalm, 'You will not suffer your holy one to see corruption.'^q ³⁶Now David, after he had served the will of God in his lifetime, fell asleep, was gathered to his ancestors, and did see corruption.^r ³⁷But the one whom God raised up did not see corruption. ³⁸You must know, my brothers, that through him forgiveness of sins is being proclaimed to you, [and] in regard to everything from which you could not be justified[•] under the law of Moses, ³⁹in him every believer is justified.^s ⁴⁰Be careful, then, that what was said in the prophets not come about:

⁴¹'Look on, you scoffers,
   be amazed and
   disappear.
For I am doing a work in
   your days,

a work that you will never believe even if someone tells you.'"[t]

[42]As they were leaving, they invited them to speak on these subjects the following sabbath. [43]After the congregation had dispersed, many Jews and worshipers who were converts to Judaism followed Paul and Barnabas, who spoke to them and urged them to remain faithful to the grace of God.

Address to the Gentiles. [44]On the following sabbath almost the whole city gathered to hear the word of the Lord. [45]When the Jews saw the crowds, they were filled with jealousy and with violent abuse contradicted what Paul said. [46]Both Paul and Barnabas spoke out boldly and said, "It was necessary that the word of God be spoken to you first, but since you reject it and condemn yourselves as unworthy of eternal life, we now turn to the Gentiles.[*] [47]For so the Lord has commanded us, 'I have made you a light to the Gentiles, that you may be an instrument of salvation to the ends of the earth.'"[v]

[48]The Gentiles were delighted when they heard this and glorified the word of the Lord. All who were destined for eternal life came to believe, [49]and the word of the Lord continued to spread through the whole region. [50]The Jews, however, incited the women of prominence who were worshipers and the leading men of the city, stirred up a persecution against Paul and Barnabas, and expelled them from their territory. [51w]So they shook the dust from their feet in protest against them and went to Iconium.[*] [52]The disciples were filled with joy and the holy Spirit.

---

a.   [13:13] 15:38.
b.   [13:17] Ex 6:1, 6; 12:51.
c.   [13:18] Ex 16:1, 35; Nm 14:34.
d.   [13:19] Dt 7:1; Jos 14:1–2.
e.   [13:20] Jgs 2:16; 1 Sm 3:20.
f.   [13:21] 1 Sm 8:5, 19; 9:16; 10:1, 20–21, 24; 11:15.

g. [13:22] 1 Sm 13:14; 16:12–13; Ps 89:20–21.
h. [13:23] Is 11:1.
i. [13:24] Mt 3:1–2; Mk 1:4–5; Lk 3:2–3.
j. [13:25] Mt 3:11; Mk 1:7; Lk 3:16; Jn 1:20, 27.
k. [13:28] Mt 27:20, 22–23; Mk 15:13–14; Lk 23:4, 14–15, 21–23; Jn 19:4–6, 15.
l. [13:29] Mt 27:59–60; Mk 15:46; Lk 23:53; Jn 19:38, 41–42.
m. [13:30] 2:24, 32; 3:15; 4:10; 17:31.
n. [13:31] 1:3, 8; 10:39, 41; Mt 28:8–10, 16–20; Mk 16:9, 12–20; Lk 24:13–53; Jn 20:11–29; 21:1–23.
o. [13:33] Ps 2:7.
p. [13:34] Is 55:3.
q. [13:35] Ps 16:10.
r. [13:36] 2:29; 1 Kgs 2:10.
s. [13:39] Rom 3:20.
t. [13:41] Heb 1:5.
u. [13:46] 3:26; Rom 1:16.
v. [13:47] Is 49:6.
w. [13:51] Mt 10:14; Mk 6:11; Lk 9:5; 10:11.

CHAPTER 14

Paul and Barnabas at Iconium. [1]In Iconium they entered the Jewish synagogue together and spoke in such a way that a great number of both Jews and Greeks came to believe, [2]although the disbelieving Jews stirred up and poisoned the minds of the Gentiles against the brothers. [3]So they stayed for a considerable period, speaking out boldly for the Lord, who confirmed the word about his grace by granting signs and wonders to occur through their hands.[a] [4]The people of the city were divided: some were with the Jews; others, with the apostles. [5]When there was an attempt by both the Gentiles and the Jews, together with their leaders, to attack and stone them,[b] [6]they realized it and fled to the Lycaonian cities of Lystra and Derbe and to the surrounding countryside, [7]where they continued to proclaim the good news.

Paul and Barnabas at Lystra. [8]At Lystra there was a crippled man, lame from birth, who had never walked. [9]He listened to Paul speaking, who looked intently at him, saw that he had the faith to be healed, [10]and called out in a loud voice, "Stand up straight on your feet." He jumped up and began to walk about. [11]When the crowds saw what Paul had done, they cried out in Lycaonian, "The gods have come down to us in human form."[c] [12]They called Barnabas "Zeus" and Paul "Hermes," because he was the chief speaker. [13]And the priest of Zeus, whose temple was at the entrance to the city, brought oxen and garlands to the gates, for he together with the people intended to offer sacrifice.

[14]The apostles Barnabas and Paul tore their garments* when they heard this and rushed out into the crowd, shouting, [15]*"Men, why are you doing this? We are of the same nature as you, human beings. We proclaim to you good news that you should turn from these idols to the living God, 'who made heaven and earth and sea and all that is in them.'[d] [16]In past generations he allowed all Gentiles to go their own ways;[e] [17]yet, in bestowing his goodness, he did not leave himself without witness, for he gave you rains from heaven and fruitful seasons, and filled you with nourishment and gladness for your hearts."[f] [18]Even with these words, they scarcely restrained the crowds from offering sacrifice to them.

[19]*However, some Jews from Antioch and Iconium arrived and won over the crowds. They stoned Paul and dragged him out of the city, supposing that he was dead. [20]But when the disciples gathered around him, he got up and entered the city. On the following day he left with Barnabas for Derbe.

End of the First Mission. [21]After they had proclaimed the good news to that city and made a considerable number of disciples, they returned to Lystra and to Iconium and to Antioch. [22]They strengthened the spirits of the disciples and exhorted them to persevere in the faith, saying, "It is necessary for us to undergo many hardships to enter the kingdom of God."[h] [23]They appointed presbyters* for them in each church and, with prayer and fasting, commended them to the Lord in whom they had put their faith. ²⁴Then they traveled through Pisidia and reached Pamphylia. ²⁵After proclaiming the word at Perga they went down to Attalia. ²⁶From there they sailed to Antioch, where they had been commended to the grace of God for the work they had now accomplished.ⁱ ²⁷And when they arrived, they called the church together and reported what God had done with them and how he had opened the door of faith to the Gentiles. ²⁸Then they spent no little time with the disciples.

a. [14:3] Mk 16:17–20.
b. [14:5] 2 Tm 3:11.
c. [14:11] 28:6.
d. [14:15] 3:12; 10:26; Ex 20:11; Ps 146:6.
e. [14:16] 17:30.
f. [14:17] Wis 13:1.
g. [14:19–20] 2 Cor 11:25; 2 Tm 3:11.
h. [14:22] 1 Thes 3:3.
i. [14:26] 13:1–3.

CHAPTER 15

Council of Jerusalem. ¹*Some who had come down from Judea were instructing the brothers,ᵃ "Unless you are circumcised according to the Mosaic practice,ᵇ you cannot be saved."* ²Because there arose no little dissension and debate by Paul and Barnabas with them, it was decided that Paul, Barnabas, and some of the others should go up to Jerusalem to the apostles and presbyters about this question. ³They were sent on their journey by the church, and passed through Phoenicia and Samaria telling of the conversion of the Gentiles, and brought great joy to all the brothers. ⁴When they arrived in Jerusalem, they were welcomed by the church, as well as by the apostles and the presbyters, and they reported what God had done with them. ⁵But some from the party of the Pharisees who had become believers stood up and said, "It is necessary to circumcise them and direct them to observe the Mosaic law."

⁶*The apostles and the presbyters met together to see about this matter. ⁷*After

much debate had taken place, Peter got up and said to them, "My brothers, you are well aware that from early days God made his choice among you that through my mouth the Gentiles would hear the word of the gospel and believe.*c* 8And God, who knows the heart, bore witness by granting them the holy Spirit just as he did us.*d* 9He made no distinction between us and them, for by faith he purified their hearts.*e* 10Why, then, are you now putting God to the test by placing on the shoulders of the disciples a yoke that neither our ancestors nor we have been able to bear?*f* 11On the contrary, we believe that we are saved through the grace of the Lord Jesus,*g* in the same way as they."* 12The whole assembly fell silent, and they listened while Paul and Barnabas described the signs and wonders God had worked among the Gentiles through them.

James on Dietary Law. 13*After they had fallen silent, James responded, "My brothers, listen to me. 14Symeon* has described how God first concerned himself with acquiring from among the Gentiles a people for his name. 15The words of the prophets agree with this, as is written:

16'After this I shall return*h*
    and rebuild the fallen
        hut of David;
from its ruins I shall
        rebuild it
    and raise it up again,
17so that the rest of
        humanity may seek
        out the Lord,
    even all the Gentiles on
        whom my name is
        invoked.
Thus says the Lord who
        accomplishes these
        things,
18known from of old.'

19iIt is my judgment, therefore, that we ought to stop troubling the Gentiles who turn to God, [20]but tell them by letter to avoid pollution from idols, unlawful marriage, the meat of strangled animals, and blood.[j] [21]For Moses, for generations now, has had those who proclaim him in every town, as he has been read in the synagogues every sabbath."

Letter of the Apostles. [22]Then the apostles and presbyters, in agreement with the whole church, decided to choose representatives and to send them to Antioch with Paul and Barnabas. The ones chosen were Judas, who was called Barsabbas, and Silas, leaders among the brothers. [23]This is the letter delivered by them: "The apostles and the presbyters, your brothers, to the brothers in Antioch, Syria, and Cilicia of Gentile origin: greetings. [24]Since we have heard that some of our number [who went out] without any mandate from us have upset you with their teachings and disturbed your peace of mind, [25]we have with one accord decided to choose representatives and to send them to you along with our beloved Barnabas and Paul, [26]who have dedicated their lives to the name of our Lord Jesus Christ. [27]So we are sending Judas and Silas who will also convey this same message by word of mouth: [28][k]It is the decision of the holy Spirit and of us not to place on you any burden beyond these necessities, [29]namely, to abstain from meat sacrificed to idols, from blood, from meats of strangled animals, and from unlawful marriage. If you keep free of these, you will be doing what is right. Farewell.'"[l]

Delegates at Antioch. [30]And so they were sent on their journey. Upon their arrival in Antioch they called the assembly together and delivered the letter. [31]When the people read it, they were delighted with the exhortation. [32]Judas and Silas, who were themselves prophets, exhorted and strengthened the brothers with many words. [33]After they had spent some time there, they were sent off with greetings of peace from the brothers to those who had commissioned them. [[34]]* [35]But Paul and Barnabas remained in Antioch, teaching and proclaiming with many others the word of the Lord.

V. THE MISSION OF PAUL TO THE ENDS OF THE EARTH

Paul and Barnabas Separate. [36]*After some time, Paul said to Barnabas, "Come, let us make a return visit to see how the brothers are getting on in all the cities where we proclaimed the word of the Lord." [37]Barnabas wanted to take with them also John, who was called Mark, [38]but Paul insisted that they should not take with them someone who had deserted them at Pamphylia and who had not continued with them in their work.[m] [39]So sharp was their disagreement that they separated. Barnabas took Mark and sailed to Cyprus. [40]But Paul chose Silas and departed after being commended by the brothers to the grace of the Lord. [41]He traveled through Syria and Cilicia bringing strength to the churches.

a. [15:1–4] Gal 2:1–9.
b. [15:1] Lv 12:3; Gal 5:2.
c. [15:7] 10:27–43.
d. [15:8] 10:44–48.
e. [15:9] 10:34–35.
f. [15:10] Mt 23:4; Gal 5:1.
g. [15:11] Gal 2:16; 3:11; Eph 2:5–8.
h. [15:16–17] Am 9:11–12.
i. [15:19–20] 15:28–29; 21:25.
j. [15:20] Gn 9:4; Lv 3:17; 17:10–14.
k. [15:28–29] 15:19–20.
l. [15:29] Gn 9:4; Lv 3:17; 17:10–14.
m. [15:38] 13:13.

CHAPTER 16

Paul in Lycaonia: Timothy. [1]He reached [also] Derbe and Lystra where there was a disciple named Timothy, the son of a Jewish woman who was a believer, but his father was a Greek.[a] [2]The brothers in Lystra and Iconium spoke highly of him,[b] [3]and Paul wanted him to come along with him. On account of the Jews of that region, Paul had him circumcised,[*] for they all knew that his father was a Greek. [4]As they traveled from city to city, they handed on to the people for observance the decisions reached by the apostles and presbyters in Jerusalem. [5]Day after day the churches grew stronger in faith and increased in number.

Through Asia Minor. [6]They traveled through the Phrygian and Galatian territory because they had been prevented by the holy Spirit from preaching the message in the province of Asia. [7]When they came to Mysia, they tried to go on into Bithynia, but the Spirit of Jesus[*] did not allow them, [8]so they crossed through Mysia and came down to Troas. [9]During [the] night Paul had a vision. A Macedonian stood before him and implored him with these words, "Come over to Macedonia and help us." [10]When he had seen the vision, we[*] sought passage to Macedonia at once, concluding that God had called us to proclaim the good news to them.

Into Europe. [11*]We set sail from Troas, making a straight run for Samothrace, and on the next day to Neapolis, [12]and from there to Philippi, a leading city in that district of Macedonia and a Roman colony. We spent some time in that city. [13]On the sabbath we went outside the city gate along the river where we thought there would be a place of prayer. We sat and spoke with the women who had gathered there. [14]One of them, a woman named Lydia, a dealer in purple cloth, from the city of Thyatira, a worshiper of God,[*] listened, and the Lord opened her heart to pay attention to what Paul was saying. [15]After she and her household had been baptized, she offered us an invitation, "If you consider me a believer in the Lord, come and stay at my home," and she prevailed on us.

Imprisonment at Philippi. [16]As we were going to the place of prayer, we met a slave girl with an oracular spirit,* who used to bring a large profit to her owners through her fortune-telling. [17]She began to follow Paul and us, shouting, "These people are slaves of the Most High God, who proclaim to you a way of salvation." [18]She did this for many days. Paul became annoyed, turned, and said to the spirit, "I command you in the name of Jesus Christ to come out of her." Then it came out at that moment.

[19]When her owners saw that their hope of profit was gone, they seized Paul and Silas and dragged them to the public square before the local authorities. [20]They brought them before the magistrates* and said, "These people are Jews and are disturbing our city [21]and are advocating customs that are not lawful for us Romans to adopt or practice." [22c]The crowd joined in the attack on them, and the magistrates had them stripped and ordered them to be beaten with rods. [23]After inflicting many blows on them, they threw them into prison and instructed the jailer to guard them securely. [24]When he received these instructions, he put them in the innermost cell and secured their feet to a stake.

Deliverance from Prison. [25]About midnight, while Paul and Silas were praying and singing hymns to God as the prisoners listened, [26]there was suddenly such a severe earthquake that the foundations of the jail shook; all the doors flew open, and the chains of all were pulled loose. [27]When the jailer woke up and saw the prison doors wide open, he drew [his] sword and was about to kill himself, thinking that the prisoners had escaped. [28]But Paul shouted out in a loud voice, "Do no harm to yourself; we are all here." [29]He asked for a light and rushed in and, trembling with fear, he fell down before Paul and Silas. [30]Then he brought them out and said, "Sirs, what must I do to be saved?" [31]And they said, "Believe in the Lord Jesus and you and your household will be saved." [32]So they spoke the word of the Lord to him and to everyone in his house. [33]He took them in at that hour of the night and bathed their wounds; then he and all his family were baptized at once. [34]He brought them up into his house and provided a meal and with his household rejoiced at having come to faith in God.

[35]But when it was day, the magistrates sent the lictors[*] with the order, "Release those men." [36]The jailer reported the[se] words to Paul, "The magistrates have sent orders that you be released. Now, then, come out and go in peace." [37]But Paul said to them, "They have beaten us publicly, even though we are Roman citizens and have not been tried, and have thrown us into prison.[d] And now, are they going to release us secretly? By no means. Let them come themselves and lead us out." [38]The lictors reported these words to the magistrates, and they became alarmed when they heard that they were Roman citizens.[e] [39]So they came and placated them, and led them out and asked that they leave the city. [40]When they had come out of the prison, they went to Lydia's house where they saw and encouraged the brothers, and then they left.

a.　[16:1] 1 Tm 1:2; 2 Tm 1:5.
b.　[16:2] Phil 2:20.
c.　[16:22–23] 2 Cor 11:25; Phil 1:30; 1 Thes 2:2.
d.　[16:37] 22:25.
e.　[16:38] 22:29.

CHAPTER 17

Paul in Thessalonica. ¹When they took the road through Amphipolis and Apollonia, they reached Thessalonica, where there was a synagogue of the Jews.ª ²Following his usual custom, Paul joined them, and for three sabbaths he entered into discussions with them from the scriptures, ³expounding and demonstrating that the Messiah had to suffer and rise from the dead, and that "This is the Messiah, Jesus, whom I proclaim to you."ᵇ ⁴Some of them were convinced and joined Paul and Silas; so, too, a great number of Greeks who were worshipers, and not a few of the prominent women. ⁵But the Jews became jealous and recruited some worthless men loitering in the public square, formed a mob, and set the city in turmoil. They marched on the house of Jason,ᶜ intending to bring them before the people's assembly. ⁶When they could not find them, they dragged Jason and some of the brothers before the city magistrates, shouting, "These people who have been creating a disturbance all over the world have now come here, ⁷and Jason has welcomed them.ᵈ They all act in opposition to the decrees of Caesar and claim instead that there is another king, Jesus."* ⁸They stirred up the crowd and the city magistrates who, upon hearing these charges, ⁹took a surety payment from Jason and the others before releasing them.

Paul in Beroea. ¹⁰The brothers immediately sent Paul and Silas to Beroea during the night. Upon arrival they went to the synagogue of the Jews. ¹¹These Jews were more fair-minded than those in Thessalonica, for they received the word with all willingness and examined the scriptures daily to determine whether these things were so.[e] [12]Many of them became believers, as did not a few of the influential Greek women and men. [13]But when the Jews of Thessalonica learned that the word of God had now been proclaimed by Paul in Beroea also, they came there too to cause a commotion and stir up the crowds. [14]So the brothers at once sent Paul on his way to the seacoast, while Silas and Timothy remained behind.[f] [15]After Paul's escorts had taken him to Athens, they came away with instructions for Silas and Timothy to join him as soon as possible.

Paul in Athens.[*] [16]While Paul was waiting for them in Athens, he grew exasperated at the sight of the city full of idols. [17]So he debated in the synagogue with the Jews and with the worshipers, and daily in the public square with whoever happened to be there. [18]Even some of the Epicurean and Stoic philosophers[*] engaged him in discussion. Some asked, "What is this scavenger trying to say?" Others said, "He sounds like a promoter of foreign deities," because he was preaching about 'Jesus' and 'Resurrection.' [19]They took him and led him to the Areopagus[*] and said, "May we learn what this new teaching is that you speak of?[g] [20]For you bring some strange notions to our ears; we should like to know what these things mean." [21]Now all the Athenians as well as the foreigners residing there used their time for nothing else but telling or hearing something new.

Paul's Speech at the Areopagus. [22]Then Paul stood up at the Areopagus and said:[*]

"You Athenians, I see that in every respect you are very

religious. ²³For as I walked around looking carefully at your shrines, I even discovered an altar inscribed, 'To an Unknown God.'" What therefore you unknowingly worship, I proclaim to you. ²⁴The God who made the world and all that is in it, the Lord of heaven and earth, does not dwell in sanctuaries made by human hands,ʰ ²⁵nor is he served by human hands because he needs anything. Rather it is he who gives to everyone life and breath and everything. ²⁶He made from one⁎ the whole human race to dwell on the entire surface of the earth, and he fixed the ordered seasons and the boundaries of their regions, ²⁷so that people might seek God, even perhaps grope for him and find him, though indeed he is not far from any one of us.ⁱ ²⁸For 'In him we live and move and have our being,'⁎ as even some of your poets have said, 'For we too are his offspring.' ²⁹Since

therefore we are the offspring of God, we ought not to think that the divinity is like an image fashioned from gold, silver, or stone by human art and imagination.ʲ ³⁰God has overlooked the times of ignorance, but now he demands that all people everywhere repent ³¹because he has established a day on which he will 'judge the world with justice' through a man he has appointed, and he has provided confirmation for all by raising him from the dead."ᵏ

³²When they heard about resurrection of the dead, some began to scoff, but others said, "We should like to hear you on this some other time." ³³And so Paul left them. ³⁴But some did join him, and became believers. Among them were Dionysius, a member of the Court of the Areopagus, a woman named Damaris, and others with them.

---

a. [17:1] 1 Thes 2:1–2.
b. [17:3] 3:18; Lk 24:25–26, 46.
c. [17:5] Rom 16:21.
d. [17:7] Lk 23:2; Jn 19:12–15.

e. [17:11] Jn 5:39.
f. [17:14] 1 Thes 3:1–2.
g. [17:19] 1 Cor 1:22.
h. [17:24] 7:48–50; Gn 1:1; 1 Kgs 8:27; Is 42:5.
i. [17:27] Jer 23:23; Wis 13:6; Rom 1:19.
j. [17:29] 19:26; Is 40:18–20; 44:10–17; Rom 1:22–23.
k. [17:31] 10:42.

CHAPTER 18

Paul in Corinth. [1]After this he left Athens and went to Corinth. [2]There he met a Jew named Aquila,[a] a native of Pontus, who had recently come from Italy with his wife Priscilla* because Claudius had ordered all the Jews to leave Rome. He went to visit them [3]and, because he practiced the same trade, stayed with them and worked, for they were tentmakers by trade. [4]Every sabbath, he entered into discussions in the synagogue, attempting to convince both Jews and Greeks.

[5]When Silas and Timothy came down from Macedonia, Paul began to occupy himself totally with preaching the word, testifying to the Jews that the Messiah was Jesus. [6]When they opposed him and reviled him, he shook out his garments* and said to them, "Your blood be on your heads! I am clear of responsibility. From now on I will go to the Gentiles."[b] [7]So he left there and went to a house belonging to a man named Titus Justus, a worshiper of God;* his house was next to a synagogue.[c] [8]Crispus,* the synagogue official,[d] came to believe in the Lord along with his entire household, and many of the Corinthians who heard believed and were baptized. [9e]One night in a vision the Lord said to Paul, "Do not be afraid. Go on speaking, and do not be silent, [10]for I am with you. No one will attack and harm you, for I have many people in this city." [11]He settled there for a year and a half and taught the word of God among them.

Accusations Before Gallio. [12]But when Gallio was proconsul of Achaia,* the Jews rose up together against Paul and brought him to the tribunal, [13]saying, "This man is inducing people to worship God contrary to the law.'" [14]When Paul was about to reply, Gallio spoke to the Jews, "If it were a matter of some crime or malicious fraud, I should with reason hear the complaint of you Jews; [15]but since it is a question of arguments over doctrine and titles and your own law, see to it yourselves. I do not wish to be a judge of such matters." [16]And he drove them away from the tribunal. [17]They all seized Sosthenes, the synagogue official, and beat him in full view of the tribunal. But none of this was of concern to Gallio.

Return to Syrian Antioch. [18]Paul remained for quite some time, and after saying farewell to the brothers he sailed for Syria, together with Priscilla and Aquila. At Cenchreae he had his hair cut[f] because he had taken a vow.[*]

[19]When they reached Ephesus, he left them there, while he entered the synagogue and held discussions with the Jews. [20]Although they asked him to stay for a longer time, he did not consent, [21]but as he said farewell he promised, "I shall come back to you again, God willing." Then he set sail from Ephesus. [22]Upon landing at Caesarea, he went up and greeted the church[*] and then went down to Antioch. [23*]After staying there some time, he left and traveled in orderly sequence through the Galatian country and Phrygia, bringing strength to all the disciples.

Apollos. [24]A Jew named Apollos,[g] a native of Alexandria, an eloquent speaker, arrived in Ephesus. He was an authority on the scriptures.[*] [25]He had been instructed in the Way of the Lord and, with ardent spirit, spoke and taught accurately about Jesus, although he knew only the baptism of John. ²⁶He began to speak boldly in the synagogue; but when Priscilla and Aquila heard him, they took him aside and explained to him the Way [of God]^e more accurately. ²⁷And when he wanted to cross to Achaia, the brothers encouraged him and wrote to the disciples there to welcome him. After his arrival he gave great assistance to those who had come to believe through grace. ²⁸He vigorously refuted the Jews in public, establishing from the scriptures that the Messiah is Jesus.

a. [18:2] Rom 16:3.
b. [18:6] 13:51; Mt 10:14; 27:24–25; Mk 6:11; Lk 9:5; 10:10–11.
c. [18:7] 13:46–47; 28:28.
d. [18:8] 1 Cor 1:14.
e. [18:9–10] Jer 1:8.
f. [18:18] 21:24; Nm 6:18.
g. [18:24] 1 Cor 1:12.

CHAPTER 19

Paul in Ephesus. ¹*While Apollos was in Corinth, Paul traveled through the interior of the country and came [down] to Ephesus where he found some disciples. ²He said to them, "Did you receive the holy Spirit when you became believers?" They answered him, "We have never even heard that there is a holy Spirit." ³He said, "How were you baptized?" They replied, "With the baptism of John." ⁴Paul then said, "John baptized with a baptism of repentance, telling the people to believe in the one who was to come after him, that is, in Jesus."^a ⁵When they heard this, they were baptized in the name of the Lord Jesus. ⁶And when Paul laid [his] hands on them, the holy Spirit came upon them, and they spoke in tongues and prophesied.^b ⁷Altogether there were about twelve men.

⁸He entered the synagogue, and for three months debated boldly with persuasive arguments about the kingdom of God. ⁹But when some in their obstinacy and disbelief disparaged the Way before the assembly, he withdrew and

took his disciples with him and began to hold daily discussions in the lecture hall of Tyrannus. ¹⁰This continued for two years with the result that all the inhabitants of the province of Asia heard the word of the Lord, Jews and Greeks alike. ¹¹So extraordinary were the mighty deeds God accomplished at the hands of Paul ¹²that when face cloths or aprons that touched his skin were applied to the sick, their diseases left them and the evil spirits came out of them.*

The Jewish Exorcists. ¹³Then some itinerant Jewish exorcists tried to invoke the name of the Lord Jesus over those with evil spirits, saying, "I adjure you by the Jesus whom Paul preaches." ¹⁴When the seven sons of Sceva, a Jewish high priest, tried to do this, ¹⁵the evil spirit said to them in reply, "Jesus I recognize, Paul I know, but who are you?" ¹⁶The person with

the evil spirit then sprang at them and subdued them all. He so overpowered them that they fled naked and wounded from that house. ¹⁷When this became known to all the Jews and Greeks who lived in Ephesus, fear fell upon them all, and the name of the Lord Jesus was held in great esteem. ¹⁸Many of those who had become believers came forward and openly acknowledged their former practices. ¹⁹Moreover, a large number of those who had practiced magic collected their books and burned them in public. They calculated their value and found it to be fifty thousand silver pieces. ²⁰Thus did the word of the Lord continue to spread with influence and power.

Paul's Plans. ²¹When this was concluded, Paul made up his mind to travel through Macedonia and Achaia, and then to go on to Jerusalem, saying, "After I have been there,

I must visit Rome also."[d] [22]Then he sent to Macedonia two of his assistants, Timothy and Erastus, while he himself stayed for a while in the province of Asia.

The Riot of the Silversmiths. [23]About that time a serious disturbance broke out concerning the Way. [24]There was a silversmith named Demetrius who made miniature silver shrines of Artemis* and provided no little work for the craftsmen. [25]He called a meeting of these and other workers in related crafts and said, "Men, you know well that our prosperity derives from this work. [26]As you can now see and hear, not only in Ephesus but throughout most of the province of Asia this Paul has persuaded and misled a great number of people by saying that gods made by hands are not gods at all.[e] [27]The danger grows, not only that our business will be discredited, but also that the temple of the great goddess Artemis will be of no account, and that she whom the whole province of Asia and all the world worship will be stripped of her magnificence."

[28]When they heard this, they were filled with fury and began to shout, "Great is Artemis of the Ephesians!" [29]The city was filled with confusion, and the people rushed with one accord into the theater, seizing Gaius and Aristarchus, the Macedonians, Paul's traveling companions.[f] [30]Paul wanted to go before the crowd, but the disciples would not let him, [31]and even some of the Asiarchs* who were friends of his sent word to him advising him not to venture into the theater. [32]Meanwhile, some were shouting one thing, others something else; the assembly was in chaos, and most of the people had no idea why they had come together. [33]Some of the crowd prompted Alexander, as the Jews pushed

him forward, and Alexander signaled with his hand that he wished to explain something to the gathering. ³⁴But when they recognized that he was a Jew, they all shouted in unison, for about two hours, "Great is Artemis of the Ephesians!" ³⁵Finally the town clerk restrained the crowd and said, "You Ephesians, what person is there who does not know that the city of the Ephesians is the guardian of the temple* of the great Artemis and of her image that fell from the sky? ³⁶Since these things are undeniable, you must calm yourselves and not do anything rash. ³⁷The men you brought here are not temple robbers, nor have they insulted our goddess. ³⁸If Demetrius and his fellow craftsmen have a complaint against anyone, courts are in session, and there are proconsuls. Let them bring charges against one another. ³⁹If you have anything further to investigate, let the matter be settled in the lawful assembly, ⁴⁰for, as it is, we are in danger of being charged with rioting because of today's conduct. There is no cause for it. We shall [not]* be able to give a reason for this demonstration." With these words he dismissed the assembly.

a. [19:4] 1:5; 11:16; 13:24–25; Mt 3:11; Mk 1:8; Lk 3:16.
b. [19:6] 8:15–17; 10:44, 46.
c. [19:12] 5:15–16; Lk 8:44–47.
d. [19:21] 23:11; Rom 1:13; 15:22–32.
e. [19:26] 17:29.
f. [19:29] Col 4:10.

CHAPTER 20

Journey to Macedonia and Greece. ¹When the disturbance was over, Paul had the disciples summoned and, after encouraging them, he bade them farewell and set out on his journey to Macedonia.ᵃ ²As he traveled throughout those regions, he provided many words of encouragement for them. Then he arrived in Greece, ³where he stayed for three months. But when a plot was made against him by the Jews as he was about to set sail for Syria, he decided to return by way of Macedonia.

Return to Troas. [4b]Sopater, the son of Pyrrhus, from Beroea, accompanied him, as did Aristarchus and Secundus from Thessalonica, Gaius from Derbe, Timothy, and Tychicus and Trophimus from Asia [5]who went on ahead and waited for us* at Troas.* [6]We sailed from Philippi after the feast of Unleavened Bread,* and rejoined them five days later in Troas, where we spent a week.

Eutychus Restored to Life. [7]On the first day of the week* when we gathered to break bread, Paul spoke to them because he was going to leave on the next day, and he kept on speaking until midnight. [8]There were many lamps in the upstairs room where we were gathered, [9]and a young man named Eutychus who was sitting on the window sill was sinking into a deep sleep as Paul talked on and on. Once overcome by sleep, he fell down from the third story and when he was picked up, he was dead. [10d]Paul went down,* threw himself upon him, and said as he embraced him, "Don't be alarmed; there is life in him." [11]Then he returned upstairs, broke the bread, and ate; after a long conversation that lasted until daybreak, he departed. [12]And they took the boy away alive and were immeasurably comforted.

Journey to Miletus. [13]We went ahead to the ship and set sail for Assos where we were to take Paul on board, as he had arranged, since he was going overland. [14]When he met us in Assos, we took him aboard and went on to Mitylene. [15]We sailed away from there on the next day and reached a point off Chios, and a day later we reached Samos, and on the following day we arrived at Miletus.

¹⁶ᵉPaul had decided to sail past Ephesus in order not to lose time in the province of Asia, for he was hurrying to be in Jerusalem, if at all possible, for the day of Pentecost.

Paul's Farewell Speech at Miletus. ¹⁷From Miletus he had the presbyters of the church at Ephesus summoned. ¹⁸When they came to him, he addressed them, "You know how I lived among you the whole time from the day I first came to the province of Asia. ¹⁹I served the Lord with all humility and with the tears and trials that came to me because of the plots of the Jews, ²⁰and I did not at all shrink from telling you what was for your benefit, or from teaching you in public or in your homes. ²¹I earnestly bore witness for both Jews and Greeks to repentance before God and to faith in our Lord Jesus. ²²But now, compelled by the Spirit, I am going to Jerusalem. What will happen to me there I do not know, ²³except that in one city after another the holy Spirit has been warning me that imprisonment and hardships await me.ᵉ ²⁴Yet I consider life of no importance to me, if only I may finish my course and the ministry that I received from the Lord Jesus, to bear witness to the gospel of God's grace.ᶠ

²⁵"But now I know that none of you to whom I preached the kingdom during my travels will ever see my face again. ²⁶And so I solemnly declare to you this day that I am not responsible for the blood of any of you, ²⁷for I did not shrink from proclaiming to you the entire plan of God. ²⁸ᵍKeep watch over yourselves and over the whole flock of which the holy Spirit has appointed you overseers,* in which you tend the church of God that he acquired with his own blood. ²⁹I know that after my departure savage wolves

will come among you, and they will not spare the flock.[h] [30]And from your own group, men will come forward perverting the truth to draw the disciples away after them.[i] [31]So be vigilant and remember that for three years, night and day, I unceasingly admonished each of you with tears.[j] [32]And now I commend you to God and to that gracious word of his that can build you up and give you the inheritance among all who are consecrated. [33]I have never wanted anyone's silver or gold or clothing. [34]You know well that these very hands have served my needs and my companions.[k] [35]In every way I have shown you that by hard work of that sort we must help the weak, and keep in mind the words of the Lord Jesus who himself said, 'It is more blessed to give than to receive.'"[l]

[36]When he had finished speaking he knelt down and prayed with them all. [37]They were all weeping loudly as they threw their arms around Paul and kissed him, [38]for they were deeply distressed that he had said that they would never see his face again. Then they escorted him to the ship.

a. [20:1] 1 Cor 16:1.
b. [20:4] Rom 16:21.
c. [20:5] 21:29; 2 Tm 4:20.
d. [20:10] 1 Kgs 17:17–24; 2 Kgs 4:30–37; Mt 9:24; Mk 5:39; Lk 8:52.
e. [20:23] 9:16.
f. [20:24] 2 Tm 4:7.
g. [20:28] Jn 21:15–17; 1 Pt 5:2.
h. [20:29] Jn 10:12.
i. [20:30] Mt 7:15; 2 Pt 2:1–3; 1 Jn 2:18–19.
j. [20:31] 1 Thes 2:11.
k. [20:34] 1 Cor 4:12; 1 Thes 2:9; 2 Thes 3:8.
l. [20:35] Sir 4:31.

CHAPTER 21

Arrival at Tyre. [1*]When we had taken leave of them we set sail, made a straight run for Cos, and on the next day for Rhodes, and from there to Patara. [2]Finding a ship crossing to Phoenicia, we went on board and put out to sea. [3]We caught sight of Cyprus but passed by it on our left and sailed on toward Syria and put in at Tyre where the ship was to unload cargo. [4]There we sought out the disciples and stayed for a week. They kept telling Paul through the Spirit not to embark for Jerusalem. [5]At the end of our stay we left and resumed our journey. All of them, women and children included, escorted us out of the city, and after kneeling on the beach to pray, [6]we bade farewell to one another. Then we boarded the ship, and they returned home.

Arrival at Ptolemais and Caesarea. [7]We continued the voyage and came from Tyre to Ptolemais, where we greeted the brothers and stayed a day with them. [8]On the next day we resumed the trip and came to Caesarea, where we went to the house of Philip the evangelist, who was one of the Seven,* and stayed with him.[a] [9]He had four virgin daughters gifted with prophecy. [10]We had been there several days when a prophet named Agabus* came down from Judea. [11b]He came up to us, took Paul's belt, bound

his own feet and hands with it, and said, "Thus says the holy Spirit: This is the way the Jews will bind the owner of this belt in Jerusalem, and they will hand him over to the Gentiles."* [12]When we heard this, we and the local residents begged him not to go up to Jerusalem. [13]Then Paul replied, "What are you doing, weeping and breaking my heart? I am prepared not only to be bound but even to die in Jerusalem for the name of the Lord Jesus." [14c]Since he would not be dissuaded we let the matter rest, saying,[d] "The Lord's will be done."*

Paul and James in Jerusalem. [15]After these days we made preparations for our journey, then went up to Jerusalem. [16]Some of the disciples from Caesarea came along to lead us to the house of Mnason, a Cypriot, a disciple of long standing, with whom we were to stay. [17*]When we reached Jerusalem the brothers welcomed us warmly. [18]The next day, Paul accompanied us on a visit to James, and all the presbyters were present. [19]He greeted them, then proceeded to tell them in detail what God had accomplished among the Gentiles through his ministry. [20]They praised God when they heard it but said to him, "Brother, you see how many thousands of believers there are from among the Jews, and they are all zealous observers of the law. [21]They have been informed that you are teaching all the Jews who live among the Gentiles to abandon Moses and that you are telling them not to circumcise their children or to observe their customary practices. [22]What is to be done? They will surely hear that you have arrived. [23]*So do what we tell you. We have four men who have taken a vow.[e] [24]Take these men and purify yourself with them, and pay their expenses* that

they may have their heads shaved. In this way everyone will know that there is nothing to the reports they have been given about you but that you yourself live in observance of the law. [25]*As for the Gentiles who have come to believe, we sent them our decision that they abstain from meat sacrificed to idols, from blood, from the meat of strangled animals, and from unlawful marriage."* [26]So Paul took the men, and on the next day after purifying himself together with them entered the temple to give notice of the day when the purification would be completed and the offering made for each of them.[g]

Paul's Arrest. [27]When the seven days were nearly completed, the Jews from the province of Asia noticed him in the temple, stirred up the whole crowd, and laid hands on him, [28h]shouting, "Fellow Israelites, help us. This is the man who is teaching everyone everywhere against the people and the law and this place, and what is more, he has even brought Greeks into the temple and defiled this sacred place." [29]For they had previously seen Trophimus the Ephesian in the city with him and supposed that Paul had brought him into the temple. [30]The whole city was in turmoil with people rushing together. They seized Paul and dragged him out of the temple, and immediately the gates were closed. [31]While they were trying to kill him, a report reached the cohort commander* that all Jerusalem was rioting. [32]He immediately took soldiers and centurions and charged down on them. When they saw the commander and the soldiers they stopped beating Paul. [33]The cohort commander came forward, arrested him, and ordered him to be secured with two chains; he tried to find out who he might be and what he had done. [34]Some in the mob shouted one thing, others something else; so, since he was unable to ascertain the truth because of the uproar, he ordered Paul to be brought into the compound. [35]When he reached the steps, he was carried by the soldiers because of the violence of the mob, [36]*ifor a crowd of people followed and shouted, "Away with him!"

[37]Just as Paul was about to be taken into the compound, he said to the cohort commander, "May I say something to you?" He replied, "Do you speak Greek? [38]So then you are not the Egyptian* who started a revolt some time ago and led the four thousand assassins into the desert?"j [39]Paul answered, "I am a Jew, of Tarsus in Cilicia, a citizen of no mean city; I request you to permit me to speak to the people." [40]When he had given his permission, Paul stood on the steps

and motioned with his hand to the people; and when all was quiet he addressed them in Hebrew.[*]

a. [21:8] 6:5; 8:5–6.
b. [21:11] 11:28; 20:23.
c. [21:14] 19:15–16.
d. [21:14] Mt 6:10; 26:39; Mk 14:36; Lk 22:42.
e. [21:23–27] 18:18; Nm 6:1–21.
f. [21:25] 15:19–20, 28–29.
g. [21:26] 1 Cor 9:20.
h. [21:28] Rom 15:31.
i. [21:36] 22:22; Lk 23:18; Jn 19:15.
j. [21:38] 5:36–37.

CHAPTER 22

Paul's Defense Before the Jerusalem Jews.[*] [1]"My brothers and fathers, listen to what I am about to say to you in my defense."[*] [2]When they heard him addressing them in Hebrew they became all the more quiet. And he continued, [3]"I am a Jew, born in Tarsus in Cilicia, but brought up in this city. At the feet of Gamaliel I was educated strictly in our ancestral law and was zealous for God, just as all of you are today.[a] [4]I persecuted this Way to death, binding both men and women and delivering them to prison.[b] [5]Even the high priest and the whole council of elders can testify on my behalf. For from them I even received letters to the brothers and set out for Damascus to bring back to Jerusalem in chains for punishment those there as well.

[6]"On that journey as I drew near to Damascus, about noon a great light from the sky suddenly shone around me.[c] [7]I fell to the ground and heard a voice saying to me, 'Saul, Saul, why are you persecuting me?'[d] [8]I replied, 'Who are you, sir?' And he said to me, 'I am Jesus the Nazorean whom you are persecuting.'[e] [9]My companions saw the light but did not hear the voice of the one who spoke to me.[f] [10]I asked, 'What shall I do, sir?' The Lord answered me, 'Get up and go into Damascus, and there you will be told about everything appointed for you to do.'[g] [11]Since I could see nothing because of the brightness

of that light, I was led by hand by my companions and entered Damascus.[h]

[12i]"A certain Ananias, a devout observer of the law, and highly spoken of by all the Jews who lived there, [13]came to me and stood there and said, 'Saul, my brother, regain your sight.' And at that very moment I regained my sight and saw him. [14]Then he said, 'The God of our ancestors designated you to know his will, to see the Righteous One, and to hear the sound of his voice; [15]for you will be his witness[*] before all to what you have seen and heard. [16]Now, why delay? Get up and have yourself baptized and your sins washed away, calling upon his name.'

[17]"After I had returned to Jerusalem and while I was praying in the temple, I fell into a trance [18]and saw the Lord saying to me, 'Hurry, leave Jerusalem at once, because they will not accept your testimony about me.'

[19]But I replied, 'Lord, they themselves know that from synagogue to synagogue I used to imprison and beat those who believed in you.[j] [20]And when the blood of your witness Stephen was being shed, I myself stood by giving my approval and keeping guard over the cloaks of his murderers.'[k] [21]Then he said to me,[l] 'Go, I shall send you far away to the Gentiles.'"[*]

Paul Imprisoned. [22m]They listened to him until he said this, but then they raised their voices and shouted, "Take such a one as this away from the earth. It is not right that he should live."[*] [23]And as they were yelling and throwing off their cloaks and flinging dust into the air, [24]the cohort commander ordered him to be brought into the compound and gave instruction that he be interrogated under the lash to determine the reason why they were making such an outcry against him. [25n]But when they had stretched him out for the whips, Paul said to the centurion on duty, "Is it lawful for you to scourge a man who is a Roman citizen and has not been tried?" [26]When the centurion heard this, he went to the cohort commander and reported it, saying, "What are you going to do? This man is a Roman citizen." [27]Then the commander came and said to him, "Tell me, are you a Roman citizen?" "Yes," he answered. [28]The commander replied, "I acquired this citizenship for a large sum of money." Paul said, "But I was born one." [29]At once those who were going to interrogate him backed away from him, and the commander became alarmed when he realized that he was a Roman citizen and that he had had him bound.

Paul Before the Sanhedrin.
[30]The next day, wishing to determine the truth about

why he was being accused by the Jews, he freed him and ordered the chief priests and the whole Sanhedrin to convene. Then he brought Paul down and made him stand before them.

a. [22:3] 5:34; 26:4–5; 2 Cor 11:22; Gal 1:13–14; Phil 3:5–6.
b. [22:4] 8:3; 9:1–2; 22:19; 26:9–11; Phil 3:6.
c. [22:6] 9:3; 26:13; 1 Cor 15:8.
d. [22:7] 9:4; 26:14.
e. [22:8] 9:5; 26:15; Mt 25:40.
f. [22:9] 9:7; 26:13–14.
g. [22:10] 9:6; 26:16.
h. [22:11] 9:8.
i. [22:12–16] 9:10–19.
j. [22:19] 8:3; 9:1–2; 22:4–5; 26:9–11.
k. [22:20] 7:58; 8:1.
l. [22:21] 9:15; Gal 2:7–9.
m. [22:22] 21:36; Lk 23:18; Jn 19:15.
n. [22:25] 16:37.

CHAPTER 23

[1]Paul looked intently at the Sanhedrin and said, "My brothers, I have conducted myself with a perfectly clear conscience before God to this day."[a] [2]The high priest Ananias* ordered his attendants to strike his mouth. [3]Then Paul said to him, "God will strike you,* you whitewashed wall. Do you indeed sit in judgment upon me according to the law and

yet in violation of the law order me to be struck?"[b] [4]The attendants said, "Would you revile God's high priest?" [5]Paul answered, "Brothers, I did not realize he was the high priest. For it is written,[c] 'You shall not curse a ruler of your people.'"*

[6]Paul was aware that some were Sadducees and some Pharisees, so he called out before the Sanhedrin, "My brothers, I am a Pharisee, the son of Pharisees; [I] am on trial for hope in the resurrection of the dead."[d] [7]When he said this, a dispute broke out between the Pharisees and Sadducees, and the group became divided. [8]For the Sadducees say that there is no resurrection or angels or spirits, while the Pharisees acknowledge all three.[e] [9]A great uproar occurred, and some scribes belonging to the Pharisee party stood up and sharply argued, "We find nothing wrong with this man. Suppose a spirit or an angel has spoken to him?" [10]The dispute was so serious that the commander, afraid that Paul would be torn to pieces by them, ordered his troops to go down and rescue him from their midst and take him into the compound. [11][f]The following night the Lord stood by him and said, "Take courage. For just as you have borne witness to my cause in Jerusalem, so you must also bear witness in Rome."

Transfer to Caesarea. [12]When day came, the Jews made a plot and bound themselves by oath not to eat or drink until they had killed Paul. [13]There were more than forty who formed this conspiracy. [14]They went to the chief priests and elders and said, "We have bound ourselves by a solemn oath to taste nothing until we have killed Paul. [15]You, together with the Sanhedrin, must now make an official request to the commander to have him bring him down to you, as though you meant to investigate his case more thoroughly. We on our part are prepared to kill him before he arrives." ¹⁶The son of Paul's sister, however, heard about the ambush; so he went and entered the compound and reported it to Paul. ¹⁷Paul then called one of the centurions* and requested, "Take this young man to the commander; he has something to report to him." ¹⁸So he took him and brought him to the commander and explained, "The prisoner Paul called me and asked that I bring this young man to you; he has something to say to you." ¹⁹The commander took him by the hand, drew him aside, and asked him privately, "What is it you have to report to me?" ²⁰He replied, "The Jews have conspired to ask you to bring Paul down to the Sanhedrin tomorrow, as though they meant to inquire

about him more thoroughly, ²¹but do not believe them. More than forty of them are lying in wait for him; they have bound themselves by oath not to eat or drink until they have killed him. They are now ready and only wait for your consent." ²²As the commander dismissed the young man he directed him, "Tell no one that you gave me this information."

²³Then he summoned two of the centurions and said, "Get two hundred soldiers ready to go to Caesarea by nine o'clock tonight,* along with seventy horsemen and two hundred auxiliaries. ²⁴Provide mounts for Paul to ride and give him safe conduct to Felix the governor." ²⁵Then he wrote a letter with this content: ²⁶*"Claudius Lysias to his excellency the governor Felix, greetings.* ²⁷This man, seized by the Jews and about to be murdered by them, I rescued after intervening with my

troops when I learned that he was a Roman citizen.[g] [28]I wanted to learn the reason for their accusations against him so I brought him down to their Sanhedrin. [29]I discovered that he was accused in matters of controversial questions of their law and not of any charge deserving death or imprisonment.[h] [30]Since it was brought to my attention that there will be a plot against the man, I am sending him to you at once, and have also notified his accusers to state [their case] against him before you."

[31]So the soldiers, according to their orders, took Paul and escorted him by night to Antipatris. [32]The next day they re turned to the compound, leaving the horsemen to complete the journey with him. [33]When they arrived in Caesarea they delivered the letter to the governor and presented Paul to him. [34]When he had read it and asked to what province he belonged,

and learned that he was from Cilicia, [35]he said, "I shall hear your case when your accusers arrive." Then he ordered that he be held in custody in Herod's praetorium.

---

a. [23:1] 24:16.
b. [23:3] Ez 13:10–15; Mt 23:27.
c. [23:5] Ex 22:27.
d. [23:6] 24:15, 21; 26:5; Phil 3:5.
e. [23:8] Mt 22:23; Lk 20:27.
f. [23:11] 19:21.
g. [23:27] 21:30–34; 22:27.
h. [23:29] 18:14–15; 25:18–19.

CHAPTER 24

Trial Before Felix. [1]Five days later the high priest Ananias came down with some elders and an advocate, a certain Tertullus, and they presented formal charges against Paul to the governor. [2]When he was called, Tertullus began to accuse him, saying, "Since we have attained much peace through you, and reforms have been accomplished in this nation through your provident care, [3]we acknowledge this in every way and everywhere, most excellent Felix, with all gratitude. [4]But in order not to detain you further, I ask you to give us a brief hearing with your customary graciousness. ⁵ᵃWe found this man to be a pest; he creates dissension among Jews all over the world and is a ringleader of the sect of the Nazoreans.* ⁶He even tried to desecrate our temple, but we arrested him.*ᵇ [⁷]* ⁸If you examine him you will be able to learn from him for yourself about everything of which we are accusing him." ⁹The Jews also joined in the attack and asserted that these things were so.

¹⁰*Then the governor motioned to him to speak and Paul replied, "I know that you have been a judge over this nation for many years and so I am pleased to make my defense before you. ¹¹As you can verify, not more than twelve days have passed since I went up to Jerusalem to worship. ¹²Neither in the temple, nor in the synagogues, nor anywhere in the city did they find me arguing with anyone or instigating a riot among the people. ¹³Nor can they prove to you the accusations they are now making against me. ¹⁴But this I do admit to you, that according to the Way, which they call a sect, I worship the God of our ancestors and I believe everything that is in accordance with the law and written in the prophets.*ᶜ ¹⁵I have the same hope in God as they themselves have that there will be a resurrection of the righteous and the unrighteous.*ᵈ ¹⁶Because of this, I always strive to keep my conscience clear before God and man.*ᵉ ¹⁷After many years, I came to bring alms for my nation and offerings.*ᶠ ¹⁸While I was so engaged, they found me, after my purification, in the temple without a crowd or disturbance.*ᵍ ¹⁹But some Jews from the province of Asia, who should be here before you to make whatever accusation they might have against me— ²⁰or let these

men themselves state what crime they discovered when I stood before the Sanhedrin, [21]unless it was my one outcry as I stood among them, that 'I am on trial before you today for the resurrection of the dead.'"[h]

[22]Then Felix, who was accurately informed about the Way, postponed the trial, saying, "When Lysias the commander comes down, I shall decide your case." [23]He gave orders to the centurion that he should be kept in custody but have some liberty, and that he should not prevent any of his friends from caring for his needs.

Captivity in Caesarea. [24]Several days later Felix came with his wife Drusilla, who was Jewish. He had Paul summoned and listened to him speak about faith in Christ Jesus. [25]But as he spoke about righteousness and self-restraint and the coming judgment, Felix

became frightened and said, "You may go for now; when I find an opportunity I shall summon you again." [26]At the same time he hoped that a bribe would be offered him by Paul, and so he sent for him very often and conversed with him.

[27]Two years passed and Felix was succeeded by Porcius Festus. Wishing to ingratiate himself with the Jews, Felix left Paul in prison.

---

a. [24:5] 24:14; Lk 23:2.
b. [24:6] 21:28.
c. [24:14] 24:5.
d. [24:15] Dn 12:2; Jn 5:28–29.
e. [24:16] 23:1.
f. [24:17] Rom 15:25–26; Gal 2:10.
g. [24:18–19] 21:26–30.
h. [24:21] 23:6; 24:15.

CHAPTER 25

Appeal to Caesar. [1]Three days after his arrival in the province, Festus went up from Caesarea to Jerusalem [2]where the chief priests and Jewish leaders presented him their formal charges against Paul. They asked him [3]as a favor to have him sent to

Jerusalem, for they were plotting to kill him along the way. [4]Festus replied that Paul was being held in custody in Caesarea and that he himself would be returning there shortly. [5]He said, "Let your authorities come down with me, and if this man has done something improper, let them accuse him."

[6]After spending no more than eight or ten days with them, he went down to Caesarea, and on the following day took his seat on the tribunal and ordered that Paul be brought in. [7]When he appeared, the Jews who had come down from Jerusalem surrounded him and brought many serious charges against him, which they were unable to prove. [8]In defending himself Paul said, "I have committed no crime either against the Jewish law or against the temple or against Caesar." [9]Then Festus, wishing to ingratiate himself with the Jews, said to Paul in reply,

"Are you willing to go up to Jerusalem and there stand trial before me on these charges?" [10]Paul answered, "I am standing before the tribunal of Caesar; this is where I should be tried. I have committed no crime against the Jews, as you very well know. [11]If I have committed a crime or done anything deserving death, I do not seek to escape the death penalty; but if there is no substance to the charges they are bringing against me, then no one has the right to hand me over to them. I appeal to Caesar." [12]Then Festus, after conferring with his council, replied, "You have appealed to Caesar. To Caesar you will go."

Paul Before King Agrippa. [13]When a few days had passed, King Agrippa and Bernice* arrived in Caesarea on a visit to Festus. [14]Since they spent several days there, Festus referred Paul's case to the king, saying, "There is a man here left in custody by Felix.ᵃ ¹⁵When I was in Jerusalem the chief priests and the elders of the Jews brought charges against him and demanded his condemnation. ¹⁶I answered them that it was not Roman practice to hand over an accused person before he has faced his accusers and had the opportunity to defend himself against their charge. ¹⁷So when [they] came together here, I made no delay; the next day I took my seat on the tribunal and ordered the man to be brought in. ¹⁸ᵇHis accusers stood around him, but did not charge him with any of the crimes I suspected. ¹⁹Instead they had some issues with him about their own religion and about a certain Jesus who had died but who Paul claimed was alive. ²⁰Since I was at a loss how to investigate this controversy, I asked if he were willing to go to Jerusalem and there stand trial on these charges. ²¹And

when Paul appealed that he be held in custody for the Emperor's decision, I ordered him held until I could send him to Caesar." ²²Agrippa said to Festus, "I too should like to hear this man." He replied, "Tomorrow you will hear him."

²³The next day Agrippa and Bernice came with great ceremony and entered the audience hall in the company of cohort commanders and the prominent men of the city and, by command of Festus, Paul was brought in. ²⁴And Festus said, "King Agrippa and all you here present with us, look at this man about whom the whole Jewish populace petitioned me here and in Jerusalem, clamoring that he should live no longer. ²⁵I found, however, that he had done nothing deserving death, and so when he appealed to the Emperor, I decided to send him. ²⁶But I have nothing definite to write about him to our sovereign;

therefore I have brought him before all of you, and particularly before you, King Agrippa, so that I may have something to write as a result of this investigation. ²⁷For it seems senseless to me to send up a prisoner without indicating the charges against him."

---

a. [25:14] 24:27.
b. [25:18–19] 18:14–15; 23:29.

CHAPTER 26

King Agrippa Hears Paul. ¹Then Agrippa said to Paul, "You may now speak on your own behalf." So Paul stretched out his hand and began his defense. ²"I count myself fortunate, King Agrippa, that I am to defend myself before you today against all the charges made against me by the Jews, ³especially since you are an expert in all the Jewish customs and controversies. And therefore I beg you to listen patiently. ⁴My manner of living from my youth, a life spent from the beginning among my people[*] and in Jerusalem, all [the] Jews know. ^{5a}They have known about me from the start, if they are willing to testify, that I have lived my life as a Pharisee, the strictest party of our religion. ^{6b}But now I am standing trial because of my hope in the promise made by God to our ancestors. ⁷Our twelve tribes hope to attain to that promise as they fervently worship God day and night; and on account of this hope I am accused by Jews, O king. ⁸Why is it thought unbelievable among you that God raises the dead? ⁹I myself once thought that I had to do many things against the name of Jesus the Nazorean, ¹⁰and I did so in Jerusalem. I imprisoned many of the holy ones with the authorization I received from the chief priests, and when they were to be put to death I cast my vote against them.^d ¹¹Many times, in synagogue after synagogue, I punished them in an attempt to force them to blaspheme; I was so enraged against them that I pursued them even to foreign cities.

¹²"On one such occasion I was traveling to Damascus with the authorization and commission of the chief priests. ¹³ᵉAt midday, along the way, O king, I saw a light from the sky, brighter than the sun, shining around me and my traveling companions.ᶠ ¹⁴We all fell to the ground and I heard a voice saying to me in Hebrew, 'Saul, Saul, why are you persecuting me?ᵍ It is hard for you to kick against the goad.' ¹⁵And I said, 'Who are you, sir?' And the Lord replied, 'I am Jesus whom you are persecuting.ʰ ¹⁶Get up now, and stand on your feet.ⁱ I have appeared to you for this purpose, to appoint you as a servant and witness of what you have seen [of me] and what you will be shown.' ¹⁷I shall deliver you from this people and from the Gentiles to whom I send you,ʲ ¹⁸to open their eyes* that they may turn from darkness to light and from the power of Satan to God, so that they may obtain forgiveness of sins and an inheritance among those who have been consecrated by faith in me.'ᵏ

¹⁹"And so, King Agrippa, I was not disobedient to the heavenly vision. ²⁰On the contrary, first to those in Damascus and in Jerusalem and throughout the whole country of Judea, and then to the Gentiles, I preached the need to repent and turn to God, and to do works giving evidence of repentance. ²¹ˡThat is why the Jews seized me [when I was] in the temple and tried to kill me. ²²ᵐBut I have enjoyed God's help to this very day, and so I stand here testifying to small and great alike, saying nothing different from what the prophets and Moses foretold,* ²³that the Messiah must suffer* and that, as the first to rise

from the dead, he would proclaim light both to our people and to the Gentiles."[n]

Reactions to Paul's Speech. [24]While Paul was so speaking in his defense, Festus said in a loud voice, "You are mad, Paul; much learning is driving you mad." [25]But Paul replied, "I am not mad, most excellent Festus; I am speaking words of truth and reason. [26]The king knows about these matters and to him I speak boldly, for I cannot believe that [any] of this has escaped his notice; this was not done in a corner.[*] [27]King Agrippa, do you believe the prophets?[*] I know you believe." [28]Then Agrippa said to Paul, "You will soon persuade me to play the Christian." [29]Paul replied, "I would pray to God that sooner or later not only you but all who listen to me today might become as I am except for these chains."

[30]Then the king rose, and with him the governor and Bernice and the others who sat with them. [31*]And after they had withdrawn they said to one another, "This man is doing nothing [at all] that deserves death or imprisonment." [32]And Agrippa said to Festus, "This man could have been set free if he had not appealed to Caesar."[o]

---

a. [26:5] Phil 3:5–6; Gal 1:13–14; 2 Cor 11:22.
b. [26:6–8] 23:6; 24:15, 21; 28:20.
c. [26:9–11] 8:3; 9:1–2; 22:19; Phil 3:6.
d. [26:10] 9:14.
e. [26:13–14] 9:7.
f. [26:13] 9:3; 22:6.
g. [26:14] 9:4; 22:7.
h. [26:15] 9:5; 22:8; Mt 25:40.
i. [26:16] 9:6; 22:10; Ez 2:1.
j. [26:17] Jer 1:7.
k. [26:18] Is 42:7, 16; 61:1 LXX; Col 1:13.
l. [26:21] 21:31.
m. [26:22–23] 3:18; Lk 24:26–27, 44–47.
n. [26:23] Is 42:6; 49:6; Lk 2:32; 1 Cor 15:20–23.
o. [26:32] 25:11–12.

CHAPTER 27

Departure for Rome. [1*]When it was decided that we should sail to Italy, they handed Paul and some other prisoners over to a centurion named Julius of the Cohort Augusta.[*] [2]We went on board a ship from Adramyttium bound for ports in the province of Asia and set sail. Aristarchus, a Macedonian from Thessalonica, was with us.*a* ³On the following day we put in at Sidon where Julius was kind enough to allow Paul to visit his friends who took care of him. ⁴From there we put out to sea and sailed around the sheltered side of Cyprus because of the headwinds, ⁵and crossing the open sea off the coast of Cilicia and Pamphylia we came to Myra in Lycia.

Storm and Shipwreck. ⁶There the centurion found an Alexandrian ship that was sailing to Italy and put us on board. ⁷For many days we made little headway, arriving at Cnidus only with difficulty, and because the wind would not permit us to continue our course we sailed for the sheltered side of Crete off Salmone. ⁸We sailed past it with difficulty and reached a place called Fair Havens, near which was the city of Lasea.

⁹Much time had now passed and sailing had become hazardous because the time of the fast* had already gone by, so Paul warned them,*b* ¹⁰"Men, I can see that this voyage will result in severe damage and heavy loss not only to the cargo and the ship, but also to our lives." ¹¹The centurion, however, paid more attention to the pilot and to the owner of the ship than to what Paul said. ¹²Since the harbor was unfavorably situated for spending the winter, the majority planned to put out to sea from there in the hope of reaching Phoenix, a port in Crete facing west-northwest, there to spend the winter.

¹³A south wind blew gently, and thinking they had attained their objective, they weighed anchor and sailed along close to the coast of Crete. ¹⁴Before long an offshore wind of hurricane force called a "Northeaster" struck. ¹⁵Since the ship was caught up in it and could

not head into the wind we gave way and let ourselves be driven. [16]We passed along the sheltered side of an island named Cauda and managed only with difficulty to get the dinghy under control. [17]They hoisted it aboard, then used cables to undergird the ship. Because of their fear that they would run aground on the shoal of Syrtis, they lowered the drift anchor and were carried along in this way. [18]We were being pounded by the storm so violently that the next day they jettisoned some cargo, [19]and on the third day with their own hands they threw even the ship's tackle overboard. [20]Neither the sun nor the stars were visible for many days, and no small storm raged. Finally, all hope of our surviving was taken away.

[21]When many would no longer eat, Paul stood among them and said, "Men, you should have taken my advice and not have set sail from Crete and you would have avoided this disastrous loss. [22]I urge you now to keep up your courage; not one of you will be lost, only the ship. [23]For last night an angel of the God to whom [I] belong and whom I serve stood by me [24]and said, 'Do not be afraid, Paul. You are destined to stand before Caesar; and behold, for your sake, God has granted safety to all who are sailing with you.'[c] [25]Therefore, keep up your courage, men; I trust in God that it will turn out as I have been told. [26]We are destined to run aground on some island."

[27]On the fourteenth night, as we were still being driven about on the Adriatic Sea, toward midnight the sailors began to suspect that they were nearing land. [28]They took soundings and found twenty fathoms; a little farther on, they again took soundings and found fifteen fathoms. [29]Fearing that we would run aground on

a rocky coast, they dropped four anchors from the stern and prayed for day to come. ³⁰The sailors then tried to abandon ship; they lowered the dinghy to the sea on the pretext of going to lay out anchors from the bow. ³¹But Paul said to the centurion and the soldiers, "Unless these men stay with the ship, you cannot be saved." ³²So the soldiers cut the ropes of the dinghy and set it adrift.

³³Until the day began to dawn, Paul kept urging all to take some food. He said, "Today is the fourteenth day that you have been waiting, going hungry and eating nothing. ³⁴I urge you, therefore, to take some food; it will help you survive. Not a hair of the head of anyone of you will be lost." ³⁵When he said this, he took bread,* gave thanks to God in front of them all, broke it, and began to eat.^d ³⁶They were all encouraged, and took some food themselves. ³⁷In all, there were two hundred seventy-six of us on the ship. ³⁸After they had eaten enough, they lightened the ship by throwing the wheat into the sea.

³⁹When day came they did not recognize the land, but made out a bay with a beach. They planned to run the ship ashore on it, if they could. ⁴⁰So they cast off the anchors and abandoned them to the sea, and at the same time they unfastened the lines of the rudders, and hoisting the foresail into the wind, they made for the beach. ⁴¹But they struck a sandbar and ran the ship aground. The bow was wedged in and could not be moved, but the stern began to break up under the pounding [of the waves]. ⁴²The soldiers planned to kill the prisoners so that none might swim away and escape, ⁴³but the centurion wanted to save Paul and so kept them from carrying out their plan. He ordered those who could

swim to jump overboard first and get to the shore, [44]and then the rest, some on planks, others on debris from the ship. In this way, all reached shore safely.

a. [27:2] 19:29; 20:4.
b. [27:9] Lv 16:29–31.
c. [27:24] 23:11.
d. [27:35] Mt 15:36; Mk 6:41; 8:6; Lk 22:19; 1 Cor 11:23–24.

CHAPTER 28

Winter in Malta. [1]Once we had reached safety we learned that the island was called Malta. [2]The natives showed us extraordinary hospitality; they lit a fire and welcomed all of us because it had begun to rain and was cold. [3]Paul had gathered a bundle of brushwood and was putting it on the fire when a viper, escaping from the heat, fastened on his hand. [4]When the natives saw the snake hanging from his hand, they said to one another, "This man must certainly be a murderer; though he escaped the sea, Justice* has not let him remain alive." [5]But he shook the snake off into the fire and suffered no harm. [6]They were expecting him to swell up or suddenly to fall down dead but, after waiting a long time and seeing nothing unusual happen to him, they changed their minds and began to say that he was a god.[a] [7]In the vicinity of that place were lands belonging to a man named Publius, the chief of the island. He welcomed us and received us cordially as his guests for three days. [8]It so happened that the father of Publius was sick with a fever and dysentery. Paul visited him and, after praying, laid his hands on him and healed him. [9]After this had taken place, the rest of the sick on the island came to Paul and were cured. [10]They paid us great honor and when we eventually set sail they brought us the provisions we needed.

Arrival in Rome. [11]Three months later we set sail on

a ship that had wintered at the island. It was an Alexandrian ship with the Dioscuri[*] as its figurehead. ¹²We put in at Syracuse and stayed there three days, ¹³and from there we sailed round the coast and arrived at Rhegium. After a day, a south wind came up and in two days we reached Puteoli. ¹⁴There we found some brothers and were urged to stay with them for seven days. And thus we came to Rome. ¹⁵The brothers from there heard about us and came as far as the Forum of Appius and Three Taverns to meet us. On seeing them, Paul gave thanks to God and took courage. ¹⁶When he entered Rome,[*] Paul was allowed to live by himself, with the soldier who was guarding him.

Testimony to Jews in Rome. ¹⁷Three days later he called together the leaders of the Jews. When they had gathered he said to them, "My brothers, although I had done nothing against our people or our ancestral customs, I was handed over to the Romans as a prisoner from Jerusalem.[b] ¹⁸After trying my case the Romans wanted to release me, because they found nothing against me deserving the death penalty.[c] ¹⁹But when the Jews objected, I was obliged to appeal to Caesar, even though I had no accusation to make against my own nation.[d] ²⁰This is the reason, then, I have requested to see you and to speak with you, for it is on account of the hope of Israel[*] that I wear these chains."[e] ²¹They answered him, "We have received no letters from Judea about you, nor has any of the brothers arrived with a damaging report or rumor about you. ²²But we should like to hear you present your views, for we know that this sect is denounced everywhere."[f]

²³So they arranged a day with him and came to his

lodgings in great numbers. From early morning until evening, he expounded his position to them, bearing witness to the kingdom of God and trying to convince them about Jesus from the law of Moses and the prophets. ²⁴Some were convinced by what he had said, while others did not believe. ²⁵*Without reaching any agreement among themselves they began to leave; then Paul made one final statement. "Well did the holy Spirit speak to your ancestors through the prophet Isaiah, saying:

²⁶'Go to this people and say:ᵍ
You shall indeed hear but
    not understand.
  You shall indeed look
    but never see.
²⁷Gross is the heart of this
    people;
  they will not hear with
    their ears;
  they have closed
    their eyes,

so they may not see with
    their eyes
  and hear with their ears
and understand with
    their heart and be
    converted,
  and I heal them.'

²⁸ʰLet it be known to you that this salvation of God has been sent to the Gentiles; they will listen." [²⁹]*

³⁰*He remained for two full years in his lodgings. He received all who came to him, ³¹and with complete assurance and without hindrance he proclaimed the kingdom of God and taught about the Lord Jesus Christ.

a. [28:6] 14:11.
b. [28:17] 24:12–13; 25:8.
c. [28:18] 23:29; 25:25; 26:31–32.
d. [28:19] 25:11.
e. [28:20] 23:6; 24:15, 21; 26:6–8.
f. [28:22] 24:5, 14.
g. [28:26] Is 6:9–10; Mt 13:14–15; Mk 4:12; Lk 8:10; Jn 12:40; Rom 11:8.
h. [28:28] 13:46; 18:6; Ps 67:2; Is 40:5 LXX; Lk 3:6.

Notes

* [1:1–26] This introductory material (Acts 1:1–2) connects Acts with the Gospel of Luke, shows that the apostles were instructed by the risen Jesus (Acts 1:3–5), points out that the parousia or second coming in glory of Jesus will occur as

certainly as his ascension occurred (Acts 1:6–11), and lists the members of the Twelve, stressing their role as a body of divinely mandated witnesses to his life, teaching, and resurrection (Acts 1:12–26).

* [1:3] **Appearing to them during forty days**: Luke considered especially sacred the interval in which the appearances and instructions of the risen Jesus occurred and expressed it therefore in terms of the sacred number forty (cf. Dt 8:2). In his gospel, however, Luke connects the ascension of Jesus with the resurrection by describing the ascension on Easter Sunday evening (Lk 24:50–53). What should probably be understood as one event (resurrection, glorification, ascension, sending of the Spirit—the paschal mystery) has been historicized by Luke when he writes of a visible ascension of Jesus after forty days and the descent of the Spirit at Pentecost. For Luke, the ascension marks the end of the appearances of Jesus except for the extraordinary appearance to Paul. With regard to Luke's understanding of salvation history, the ascension also marks the end of the time of Jesus (Lk 24:50–53) and signals the beginning of the time of the church.

* [1:4] **The promise of the Father**: the holy Spirit, as is clear from the next verse. This gift of the Spirit was first promised in Jesus' final instructions to his chosen witnesses in Luke's gospel (Lk 24:49) and formed part of the continuing instructions of the risen Jesus on the kingdom of God, of which Luke speaks in Acts 1:3.

* [1:6] The question of the disciples implies that in believing Jesus to be the Christ (see note on Lk 2:11) they had expected him to be a political leader who would restore self-rule to Israel during his historical ministry. When this had not taken place, they ask if it is to take place at this time, the period of the church.

* [1:7] This verse echoes the tradition that the precise time of the parousia is not revealed to human beings; cf. Mk 13:32; 1 Thes 5:1–3.

* [1:8] Just as Jerusalem was the city of destiny in the Gospel of Luke (the place where salvation was accomplished), so here at the beginning of Acts, Jerusalem occupies a central position. It is the starting point for the mission of the Christian disciples to "the ends of the earth," the place where the apostles were situated and the doctrinal focal point in the early days of the community (Acts 15:2, 6). **The ends of the earth**: for Luke, this means Rome.

* [1:18] Luke records a popular tradition about the death of Judas that differs from the one in Mt 27:5, according to which Judas hanged himself. Here, although the text is not certain, Judas is depicted as purchasing a piece of property with the betrayal money and being killed on it in a fall.

* [1:26] The need to replace Judas was probably dictated by the symbolism of the number twelve,

recalling the twelve tribes of Israel. This symbolism also indicates that for Luke (see Lk 22:30) the Christian church is a reconstituted Israel.

* [2:1–41] Luke's pentecostal narrative consists of an introduction (Acts 2:1–13), a speech ascribed to Peter declaring the resurrection of Jesus and its messianic significance (Acts 2:14–36), and a favorable response from the audience (Acts 2:37–41). It is likely that the narrative telescopes events that took place over a period of time and on a less dramatic scale. The Twelve were not originally in a position to proclaim publicly the messianic office of Jesus without incurring immediate reprisal from those religious authorities in Jerusalem who had brought about Jesus' death precisely to stem the rising tide in his favor.

* [2:2] **There came from the sky a noise like a strong driving wind**: wind and spirit are associated in Jn 3:8. The sound of a great rush of wind would herald a new action of God in the history of salvation.

* [2:3] **Tongues as of fire**: see Ex 19:18 where fire symbolizes the presence of God to initiate the covenant on Sinai. Here the holy Spirit acts upon the apostles, preparing them to proclaim the new covenant with its unique gift of the Spirit (Acts 2:38).

* [2:4] **To speak in different tongues**: ecstatic prayer in praise of God, interpreted in Acts 2:6, 11 as speaking in foreign languages, symbolizing the worldwide mission of the church.

* [2:14–36] The first of six discourses in Acts (along with Acts 3:12–26; 4:8–12; 5:29–32; 10:34–43; 13:16–41) dealing with the resurrection of Jesus and its messianic import. Five of these are attributed to Peter, the final one to Paul. Modern scholars term these discourses in Acts the "kerygma," the Greek word for proclamation (cf. 1 Cor 15:11).

* [2:33] **At the right hand of God**: or "by the right hand of God."

* [2:38] **Repent and be baptized**: repentance is a positive concept, a change of mind and heart toward God reflected in the actual goodness of one's life. It is in accord with the apostolic teaching derived from Jesus (Acts 2:42) and ultimately recorded in the four gospels. Luke presents baptism in Acts as the expected response to the apostolic preaching about Jesus and associates it with the conferring of the Spirit (Acts 1:5; 10:44–48; 11:16).

* [2:42–47] The first of three summary passages (along with Acts 4:32–37; 5:12–16) that outline, somewhat idyllically, the chief characteristics of the Jerusalem community: adherence to the teachings of the Twelve and the centering of its religious life in the eucharistic liturgy (Acts 2:42); a system of distribution of goods that led wealthier Christians to sell their possessions when the

needs of the community's poor required it (Acts 2:44 and the note on Acts 4:32–37); and continued attendance at the temple, since in this initial stage there was little or no thought of any dividing line between Christianity and Judaism (Acts 2:46).

* [3:1–4:31] This section presents a series of related events: the dramatic cure of a lame beggar (Acts 3:1–10) produces a large audience for the kerygmatic discourse of Peter (Acts 3:11–26). The Sadducees, taking exception to the doctrine of resurrection, have Peter, John, and apparently the beggar as well, arrested (Acts 4:1–4) and brought to trial before the Sanhedrin. The issue concerns the authority by which Peter and John publicly teach religious doctrine in the temple (Acts 4:5–7). Peter replies with a brief summary of the kerygma, implying that his authority is prophetic (Acts 4:8–12). The court warns the apostles to abandon their practice of invoking prophetic authority in the name of Jesus (Acts 4:13–18). When Peter and John reply that the prophetic role cannot be abandoned to satisfy human objections, the court nevertheless releases them, afraid to do otherwise since the beggar, lame from birth and over forty years old, is a well-known figure in Jerusalem and the facts of his cure are common property (Acts 4:19–22). The narrative concludes with a prayer of the Christian community imploring divine aid against threats of persecution (Acts 4:23–31).

* [3:1] For the three o'clock hour of prayer: literally, "at the ninth hour of prayer." With the day beginning at 6 A.M., the ninth hour would be 3 P.M.

* [3:6–10] The miracle has a dramatic cast; it symbolizes the saving power of Christ and leads the beggar to enter the temple, where he hears Peter's proclamation of salvation through Jesus.

* [3:13] Has glorified: through the resurrection and ascension of Jesus, God reversed the judgment against him on the occasion of his trial. Servant: the Greek word can also be rendered as "son" or even "child" here and also in Acts 3:26; 4:25 (applied to David); Acts 4:27; and Acts 4:30. Scholars are of the opinion, however, that the original concept reflected in the words identified Jesus with the suffering Servant of the Lord of Is 52:13–53:12.

* [3:14] The Holy and Righteous One: so designating Jesus emphasizes his special relationship to the Father (see Lk 1:35; 4:34) and emphasizes his sinlessness and religious dignity that are placed in sharp contrast with the guilt of those who rejected him in favor of Barabbas.

* [3:15] The author of life: other possible translations of the Greek title are "leader of life" or "pioneer of life." The title clearly points to Jesus as the source and originator of salvation.

* [3:17] Ignorance: a Lucan motif, explaining away the actions not only of the people but also of their leaders in crucifying Jesus. On this basis the presbyters in Acts could continue to appeal to the Jews in Jerusalem to believe in Jesus, even while affirming their involvement in his death because they were unaware of his messianic dignity. See also Acts 13:27 and Lk 23:34.

* [3:18] Through the mouth of all the prophets: Christian prophetic insight into the Old Testament saw the crucifixion and death of Jesus as the main import of messianic prophecy. The Jews themselves did not anticipate a suffering Messiah; they usually understood the Servant Song in Is 52:13–53:12 to signify their own suffering as a people. In his typical fashion (cf. Lk 18:31; 24:25, 27, 44), Luke does not specify the particular Old Testament prophecies that were fulfilled by Jesus. See also note on Lk 24:26.

* [3:20] The Lord . . . and send you the Messiah already appointed for you, Jesus: an allusion to the parousia or second coming of Christ, judged to be imminent in the apostolic age. This reference to its nearness is the only explicit one in Acts. Some scholars believe that this verse preserves a very early christology, in which the title "Messiah" (Greek "Christ") is applied to him as of his parousia, his second coming (contrast Acts 2:36). This view of a future messiahship of Jesus is not found elsewhere in the New Testament.

* [3:21] The times of universal restoration: like "the times of refreshment" (Acts 3:20), an apocalyptic designation of the messianic age, fitting in with the christology of Acts 3:20 that associates the messiahship of Jesus with his future coming.

* [3:22] A loose citation of Dt 18:15, which teaches that the Israelites are to learn the will of Yahweh from no one but their prophets. At the time of Jesus, some Jews expected a unique prophet to come in fulfillment of this text. Early Christianity applied this tradition and text to Jesus and used them especially in defense of the divergence of Christian teaching from traditional Judaism.

* [4:1] The priests, the captain of the temple guard, and the Sadducees: the priests performed the temple liturgy; the temple guard was composed of Levites, whose captain ranked next after the high priest. The Sadducees, a party within Judaism at this time, rejected those doctrines, including bodily resurrection, which they believed alien to the ancient Mosaic religion. The Sadducees were drawn from priestly families and from the lay aristocracy.

* [4:11] Early Christianity applied this citation from Ps 118:22 to Jesus; cf. Mk 12:10; 1 Pt 2:7.

* [4:12] In the Roman world of Luke's day, salvation was often attributed to the emperor who was hailed as "savior" and "god." Luke, in the words of Peter, denies that deliverance comes through anyone other than Jesus.

* [4:27] **Herod**: Herod Antipas, ruler of Galilee and Perea from 4 B.C. to A.D. 39, who executed John the Baptist and before whom Jesus was arraigned; cf. Lk 23:6–12.

* [4:31] **The place . . . shook**: the earthquake is used as a sign of the divine presence in Ex 19:18; Is 6:4. Here the shaking of the building symbolizes God's favorable response to the prayer. Luke may have had as an additional reason for using the symbol in this sense the fact that it was familiar in the Hellenistic world. Ovid and Virgil also employ it.

* [4:32–37] This is the second summary characterizing the Jerusalem community (see note on Acts 2:42–47). It emphasizes the system of the distribution of goods and introduces Barnabas, who appears later in Acts as the friend and companion of Paul, and who, as noted here (Acts 4:37), endeared himself to the community by a donation of money through the sale of property. This sharing of material possessions continues a practice that Luke describes during the historical ministry of Jesus (Lk 8:3) and is in accord with the sayings of Jesus in Luke's gospel (Lk 12:33; 16:9, 11, 13).

* [5:1–11] The sin of Ananias and Sapphira did not consist in the withholding of part of the money but in their deception of the community. Their deaths are ascribed to a lie to the holy Spirit (Acts 5:3, 9), i.e., they accepted the honor accorded them by the community for their generosity, but in reality they were not deserving of it.

* [5:12–16] This, the third summary portraying the Jerusalem community, underscores the Twelve as its bulwark, especially because of their charismatic power to heal the sick; cf. Acts 2:42–47; 4:32–37.

* [5:17–42] A second action against the community is taken by the Sanhedrin in the arrest and trial of the Twelve; cf. Acts 4:1–3. The motive is the jealousy of the religious authorities over the popularity of the apostles (Acts 5:17) who are now charged with the defiance of the Sanhedrin's previous order to them to abandon their prophetic role (Acts 5:28; cf. Acts 4:18). In this crisis the apostles are favored by a miraculous release from prison (Acts 5:18–24). (For similar incidents involving Peter and Paul, see Acts 12:6–11; 16:25–29.) The real significance of such an event, however, would be manifest only to people of faith, not to unbelievers; since the Sanhedrin already judged the Twelve to be inauthentic prophets, it could disregard reports of their miracles. When the Twelve immediately resumed public teaching, the Sanhedrin determined to invoke upon them the penalty of death (Acts 5:33) prescribed in Dt 13:6–10. Gamaliel's advice against this course finally prevailed, but it did not save the Twelve from the punishment of scourging (Acts 5:40) in

a last endeavor to shake their conviction of their prophetic mission.

* [5:30] **Hanging him on a tree**: that is, crucifying him (cf. also Gal 3:13).

* [5:31] **At his right hand**: see note on Acts 2:33.

* [5:34] **Gamaliel**: in Acts 22:3, Paul identifies himself as a disciple of this Rabbi Gamaliel I who flourished in Jerusalem between A.D. 25 and 50.

* [5:36–37] Gamaliel offers examples of unsuccessful contemporary movements to argue that if God is not the origin of this movement preached by the apostles it will perish by itself. The movement initiated by Theudas actually occurred when C. Cuspius Fadus was governor, A.D. 44–46. Luke's placing of Judas the Galilean after Theudas and at the time of the census (see note on Lk 2:1–2) is an indication of the vagueness of his knowledge of these events.

* [6:1–7] **The Hellenists . . . the Hebrews**: the Hellenists were not necessarily Jews from the diaspora, but were more probably Palestinian Jews who spoke only Greek. The Hebrews were Palestinian Jews who spoke Hebrew or Aramaic and who may also have spoken Greek. Both groups belong to the Jerusalem Jewish Christian community. The conflict between them leads to a restructuring of the community that will better serve the community's needs. The real purpose of the whole episode, however, is to introduce Stephen as a prominent figure in the community whose long speech and martyrdom will be recounted in Acts 7.

* [6:2–4] The essential function of the Twelve is the "service of the word," including development of the kerygma by formulation of the teachings of Jesus.

* [6:2] **To serve at table**: some commentators think that it is not the serving of food that is described here but rather the keeping of the accounts that recorded the distribution of food to the needy members of the community. In any case, after Stephen and the others are chosen, they are never presented carrying out the task for which they are appointed (Acts 6:2–3). Rather, two of their number, Stephen and Philip, are presented as preachers of the Christian message. They, the Hellenist counterpart of the Twelve, are active in the ministry of the word.

* [6:6] **They . . . laid hands on them**: the customary Jewish way of designating persons for a task and invoking upon them the divine blessing and power to perform it.

* [6:8–8:1] The summary (Acts 6:7) on the progress of the Jerusalem community, illustrated by the conversion of the priests, is followed by a lengthy narrative regarding Stephen. Stephen's defense is not a response to the charges made against him but takes the form of a discourse that reviews the fortunes of God's word to Israel and

leads to a prophetic declaration: a plea for the hearing of that word as announced by Christ and now possessed by the Christian community.

The charges that Stephen depreciated the importance of the temple and the Mosaic law and elevated Jesus to a stature above Moses (Acts 6:13–14) were in fact true. Before the Sanhedrin, no defense against them was possible. With Stephen, who thus perceived the fuller implications of the teachings of Jesus, the differences between Judaism and Christianity began to appear. Luke's account of Stephen's martyrdom and its aftermath shows how the major impetus behind the Christian movement passed from Jerusalem, where the temple and law prevailed, to Antioch in Syria, where these influences were less pressing.

* [6:13] **False witnesses**: here, and in his account of Stephen's execution (Acts 7:54–60), Luke parallels the martyrdom of Stephen with the death of Jesus.

* [7:2–53] Stephen's speech represents Luke's description of Christianity's break from its Jewish matrix. Two motifs become prominent in the speech: (1) Israel's reaction to God's chosen leaders in the past reveals that the people have consistently rejected them; and (2) Israel has misunderstood God's choice of the Jerusalem temple as the place where he is to be worshiped.

* [7:2] **God . . . appeared to our father Abraham . . . in Mesopotamia**: the first of a number of minor discrepancies between the data of the Old Testament and the data of Stephen's discourse. According to Gn 12:1, God first spoke to Abraham in Haran. The main discrepancies are these: in Acts 7:16 it is said that Jacob was buried in Shechem, whereas Gn 50:13 says he was buried at Hebron; in the same verse it is said that the tomb was purchased by Abraham, but in Gn 33:19 and Jos 24:32 the purchase is attributed to Jacob himself.

* [7:55] **He . . . saw . . . Jesus standing at the right hand of God**: Stephen affirms to the Sanhedrin that the prophecy Jesus made before them has been fulfilled (Mk 14:62).

* [7:57] **Covered their ears**: Stephen's declaration, like that of Jesus, is a scandal to the court, which regards it as blasphemy.

* [7:59] Compare Lk 23:34, 46.

* [8:1–40] Some idea of the severity of the persecution that now breaks out against the Jerusalem community can be gathered from Acts 22:4 and Acts 26:9–11. Luke, however, concentrates on the fortunes of the word of God among people, indicating how the dispersal of the Jewish community resulted in the conversion of the Samaritans (Acts 8:4–17, 25). His narrative is further expanded to include the account of Philip's acceptance of an Ethiopian (Acts 8:26–39).

* [8:1] **All were scattered . . . except the apostles**: this observation leads some modern scholars to conclude that the persecution was limited to the Hellenist Christians and that the Hebrew Christians were not molested, perhaps because their attitude toward the law and temple was still more in line with that of their fellow Jews (see the charge leveled against the Hellenist Stephen in Acts 6:13–14). Whatever the facts, it appears that the Twelve took no public stand regarding Stephen's position, choosing, instead, to await the development of events.

* [8:3] **Saul . . . was trying to destroy the church**: like Stephen, Saul was able to perceive that the Christian movement contained the seeds of doctrinal divergence from Judaism. A pupil of Gamaliel, according to Acts 22:3, and totally dedicated to the law as the way of salvation (Gal 1:13–14), Saul accepted the task of crushing the Christian movement, at least insofar as it detracted from the importance of the temple and the law. His vehement opposition to Christianity reveals how difficult it was for a Jew of his time to accept a messianism that differed so greatly from the general expectation.

* [8:9–13, 18–24] Sorcerers were well known in the ancient world. Probably the incident involving Simon and his altercation with Peter is introduced to show that the miraculous charisms possessed by members of the Christian community (Acts 8:6–7) were not to be confused with the magic of sorcerers.

* [8:16] Here and in Acts 10:44–48 and Acts 19:1–6, Luke distinguishes between baptism in the name of the Lord Jesus and the reception of the Spirit. In each case, the Spirit is conferred through members of the Twelve (Peter and John) or their representative (Paul). This may be Luke's way of describing the role of the church in the bestowal of the Spirit. Elsewhere in Acts, baptism and the Spirit are more closely related (Acts 1:5; 11:16).

* [8:18–20] Simon attempts to buy the gift of God (Acts 8:20) with money. Peter's cursing of Simon's attempt so to use his money expresses a typically Lucan attitude toward material wealth (cf. Lk 6:24; 12:16–21; 16:13).

* [8:26–40] In the account of the conversion of the Ethiopian eunuch, Luke adduces additional evidence to show that the spread of Christianity outside the confines of Judaism itself was in accord with the plan of God. He does not make clear whether the Ethiopian was originally a convert to Judaism or, as is more probable, a "God-fearer" (Acts 10:1), i.e., one who accepted Jewish monotheism and ethic and attended the synagogue but did not consider himself bound by other regulations such as circumcision and

observance of the dietary laws. The story of his conversion to Christianity is given a strong supernatural cast by the introduction of an angel (Acts 8:26), instruction from the holy Spirit (Acts 8:29), and the strange removal of Philip from the scene (8:39).

* [8:27] **The Candace**: Candace is not a proper name here but the title of a Nubian queen.

* [8:30–34] Philip is brought alongside the carriage at the very moment when the Ethiopian is pondering the meaning of Is 53:7–8, a passage that Christianity, from its earliest origins, has applied to Jesus; cf. note on Acts 3:13.

* [8:37] The oldest and best manuscripts of Acts omit this verse, which is a Western text reading: "And Philip said, 'If you believe with all your heart, you may.' And he said in reply, 'I believe that Jesus Christ is the Son of God.'"

* [9:1–19] This is the first of three accounts of Paul's conversion (with Acts 22:3–16 and Acts 26:2–18) with some differences of detail owing to Luke's use of different sources. Paul's experience was not visionary but was precipitated by the appearance of Jesus, as he insists in 1 Cor 15:8. The words of Jesus, "Saul, Saul, why are you persecuting me?" related by Luke with no variation in all three accounts, exerted a profound and lasting influence on the thought of Paul. Under the influence of this experience he gradually developed his understanding of justification by faith (see the letters to the Galatians and Romans) and of the identification of the Christian community with Jesus Christ (see 1 Cor 12:27). That Luke would narrate this conversion three times is testimony to the importance he attaches to it. This first account occurs when the word is first spread to the Gentiles. At this point, the conversion of the hero of the Gentile mission is recounted. The emphasis in the account is on Paul as a divinely chosen instrument (Acts 9:15).

* [9:2] **The Way**: a name used by the early Christian community for itself (Acts 18:26; 19:9, 23; 22:4; 24:14, 22). The Essene community at Qumran used the same designation to describe its mode of life.

* [9:8] **He could see nothing**: a temporary blindness (Acts 9:18) symbolizing the religious blindness of Saul as persecutor (cf. Acts 26:18).

* [9:13] **Your holy ones**: literally, "your saints."

* [9:19–30] This is a brief resume of Paul's initial experience as an apostolic preacher. At first he found himself in the position of being regarded as an apostate by the Jews and suspect by the Christian community of Jerusalem. His acceptance by the latter was finally brought about through his friendship with Barnabas (Acts 9:27).

* [9:20] **Son of God**: the title "Son of God" occurs in Acts only here, but cf. the citation

of Ps 2:7 in Paul's speech at Antioch in Pisidia (Acts 13:33).

* [9:26] This visit of Paul to Jerusalem is mentioned by Paul in Gal 1:18.

* [9:29] **Hellenists**: see note on Acts 6:1–7.

* [9:31–43] In the context of the period of peace enjoyed by the community through the cessation of Paul's activities against it, Luke introduces two traditions concerning the miraculous power exercised by Peter as he was making a tour of places where the Christian message had already been preached. The towns of Lydda, Sharon, and Joppa were populated by both Jews and Gentiles and their Christian communities may well have been mixed.

* [9:36] **Tabitha** (**Dorcas**), respectively the Aramaic and Greek words for "gazelle," exemplifies the right attitude toward material possessions expressed by Jesus in the Lucan Gospel (Lk 6:30; 11:41; 12:33; 18:22; 19:8).

* [9:43] The fact that Peter lodged with a tanner would have been significant to both the Gentile and Jewish Christians, for Judaism considered the tanning occupation unclean.

* [10:1–48] The narrative centers on the conversion of Cornelius, a Gentile and a "God-fearer" (see note on Acts 8:26–40). Luke considers the event of great importance, as is evident from his long treatment of it. The incident is again related in Acts 11:1–18 where Peter is forced to justify his actions before the Jerusalem community and alluded to in Acts 15:7–11 where at the Jerusalem "Council" Peter supports Paul's missionary activity among the Gentiles. The narrative divides itself into a series of distinct episodes, concluding with Peter's presentation of the Christian kerygma (Acts 10:34–43) and a pentecostal experience undergone by Cornelius' household preceding their reception of baptism (Acts 10:44–48).

* [10:1] **The Cohort called the Italica**: this battalion was an auxiliary unit of archers formed originally in Italy but transferred to Syria shortly before A.D. 69.

* [10:2] **Used to give alms generously**: like Tabitha (Acts 9:36), Cornelius exemplifies the proper attitude toward wealth (see note on Acts 9:36).

* [10:3] **About three o'clock**: literally, "about the ninth hour." See note on Acts 3:1.

* [10:7] **A devout soldier**: by using this adjective, Luke probably intends to classify him as a "God-fearer" (see note on Acts 8:26–40).

* [10:9–16] The vision is intended to prepare Peter to share the food of Cornelius' household without qualms of conscience (Acts 10:48). The necessity of such instructions to Peter reveals that at first not even the apostles fully grasped the implications of Jesus' teaching on the law. In Acts, the initial insight belongs to Stephen.

* [10:9] **At about noontime**: literally, "about the sixth hour."

* [10:17–23] The arrival of the Gentile emissaries with their account of the angelic apparition illuminates Peter's vision: he is to be prepared to admit Gentiles, who were considered unclean like the animals of his vision, into the Christian community.

* [10:24–27] So impressed is Cornelius with the apparition that he invites close personal friends to join him in his meeting with Peter. But his understanding of the person he is about to meet is not devoid of superstition, suggested by his falling down before him. For a similar experience of Paul and Barnabas, see Acts 14:11–18.

* [10:28] Peter now fully understands the meaning of his vision; see note on Acts 10:17–23.

* [10:30] **Four days ago**: literally, "from the fourth day up to this hour."

* [10:34–43] Peter's speech to the household of Cornelius typifies early Christian preaching to Gentiles.

* [10:34–35] The revelation of God's choice of Israel to be the people of God did not mean he withheld the divine favor from other people.

* [10:36–43] These words are more directed to Luke's Christian readers than to the household of Cornelius, as indicated by the opening words, "You know." They trace the continuity between the preaching and teaching of Jesus of Nazareth and the proclamation of Jesus by the early community. The emphasis on this divinely ordained continuity (Acts 10:41) is meant to assure Luke's readers of the fidelity of Christian tradition to the words and deeds of Jesus.

* [10:36] **To the Israelites**: Luke, in the words of Peter, speaks of the prominent position occupied by Israel in the history of salvation.

* [10:38] **Jesus of Nazareth**: God's revelation of his plan for the destiny of humanity through Israel culminated in Jesus of Nazareth. Consequently, the ministry of Jesus is an integral part of God's revelation. This viewpoint explains why the early Christian communities were interested in conserving the historical substance of the ministry of Jesus, a tradition leading to the production of the four gospels.

* [10:39] **We are witnesses**: the apostolic testimony was not restricted to the resurrection of Jesus but also included his historical ministry. This witness, however, was theological in character; the Twelve, divinely mandated as prophets, were empowered to interpret his sayings and deeds in the light of his redemptive death and resurrection. The meaning of these words and deeds was to be made clear to the developing Christian community as the bearer of the word of salvation (cf. Acts 1:21–26). **Hanging him on a tree**: see note on 5:30.

* [10:42] **As judge of the living and the dead**: the apostolic preaching to the Jews appealed to their messianic hope, while the preaching to Gentiles stressed the coming divine judgment; cf. 1 Thes 1:10.

* [10:44] Just as the Jewish Christians received the gift of the Spirit, so too do the Gentiles.

* [11:1–18] The Jewish Christians of Jerusalem were scandalized to learn of Peter's sojourn in the house of the Gentile Cornelius. Nonetheless, they had to accept the divine directions given to both Peter and Cornelius. They concluded that the setting aside of the legal barriers between Jew and Gentile was an exceptional ordinance of God to indicate that the apostolic kerygma was also to be directed to the Gentiles. Only in Acts 15 at the "Council" in Jerusalem does the evangelization of the Gentiles become the official position of the church leadership in Jerusalem.

* [11:3] **You entered . . .**: alternatively, this could be punctuated as a question.

* [11:12] **These six brothers**: companions from the Christian community of Joppa (see Acts 10:23).

* [11:19–26] The Jewish Christian antipathy to the mixed community was reflected by the early missionaries generally. The few among them who entertained a different view succeeded in introducing Gentiles into the community at Antioch (in Syria). When the disconcerted Jerusalem community sent Barnabas to investigate, he was so favorably impressed by what he observed that he persuaded his friend Saul to participate in the Antioch mission.

* [11:26] **Christians**: "Christians" is first applied to the members of the community at Antioch because the Gentile members of the community enable it to stand out clearly from Judaism.

* [11:27–30] It is not clear whether the prophets from Jerusalem came to Antioch to request help in view of the coming famine or whether they received this insight during their visit there. The former supposition seems more likely. Suetonius and Tacitus speak of famines during the reign of Claudius (A.D. 41–54), while the Jewish historian Josephus mentions a famine in Judea in A.D. 46–48. Luke is interested, rather, in showing the charity of the Antiochene community toward the Jewish Christians of Jerusalem despite their differences on mixed communities.

* [11:30] **Presbyters**: this is the same Greek word that elsewhere is translated "elders," primarily in reference to the Jewish community.

* [12:1–19] Herod Agrippa ruled Judea A.D. 41–44. While Luke does not assign a motive for his execution of James and his intended execution of Peter, the broad background lies in Herod's

support of Pharisaic Judaism. The Jewish Christians had lost the popularity they had had in Jerusalem (Acts 2:47), perhaps because of suspicions against them traceable to the teaching of Stephen.

* [12:2] **James, the brother of John**: this James, the son of Zebedee, was beheaded by Herod Agrippa ca. A.D. 44.

* [12:3, 4] **Feast of Unleavened Bread . . . Passover**: see note on Lk 22:1.

* [12:17] **To James**: this James is not the son of Zebedee mentioned in Acts 12:2, but is James, the "brother of the Lord" (Gal 1:19), who in Acts 15; 21 is presented as leader of the Jerusalem Christian community. **He left and went to another place**: the conjecture that Peter left for Rome at this time has nothing to recommend it. His chief responsibility was still the leadership of the Jewish Christian community in Palestine (see Gal 2:7). The concept of the great missionary effort of the church was yet to come (see Acts 13:1–3).

* [12:20–23] Josephus gives a similar account of Herod's death that occurred in A.D. 44. Early Christian tradition considered the manner of it to be a divine punishment upon his evil life. See 2 Kgs 19:35 for the figure of the angel of the Lord in such a context.

* [12:25] **They returned to Jerusalem**: many manuscripts read "from Jerusalem," since Acts 11:30 implies that Paul and Barnabas are already in Jerusalem. This present verse could refer to a return visit or subsequent relief mission.

* [13:1–3] The impulse for the first missionary effort in Asia Minor is ascribed to the prophets of the Antiochene community, under the inspiration of the holy Spirit. Just as the Jerusalem community had earlier been the center of missionary activity, so too Antioch becomes the center from which the missionaries Barnabas and Saul are sent out.

* [13:4–14:27] The key event in Luke's account of the first missionary journey is the experience of Paul and Barnabas at Pisidian Antioch (Acts 13:14–52). The Christian kerygma proclaimed by Paul in the synagogue was favorably received. Some Jews and "God-fearers" (see note on Acts 8:26–40) became interested and invited the missionaries to speak again on the following sabbath (Acts 13:42). By that time, however, the appearance of a large number of Gentiles from the city had so disconcerted the Jews that they became hostile toward the apostles (Acts 13:44–50). This hostility of theirs appears in all three accounts of Paul's missionary journeys in Acts, the Jews of Iconium (Acts 14:1–2) and Beroea (Acts 17:11) being notable exceptions.

* [13:5] **John**: that is, John Mark (see Acts 12:12, 25).

* [13:6] **A magician named Bar-Jesus who was a Jewish false prophet**: that is, he posed as a prophet. Again Luke takes the opportunity to dissociate Christianity from the magical acts of the time (Acts 13:7–11); see also Acts 8:18–24.

* [13:9] **Saul, also known as Paul**: there is no reason to believe that his name was changed from Saul to Paul upon his conversion. The use of a double name, one Semitic (Saul), the other Greco-Roman (Paul), is well attested (cf. Acts 1:23, Joseph Justus; Acts 12:12, 25, John Mark).

* [13:16–41] This is the first of several speeches of Paul proclaiming that the Christian church is the logical development of Pharisaic Judaism (see also Acts 24:10–21; 26:2–23).

* [13:16] **Who are God-fearing**: see note on Acts 8:26–40.

* [13:18] **Put up with**: some manuscripts read "sustained."

* [13:20] **At the end of about four hundred and fifty years**: the manuscript tradition makes it uncertain whether the mention of four hundred and fifty years refers to the sojourn in Egypt before the Exodus, the wilderness period and the time of the conquest (see Ex 12:40–41), as the translation here suggests, or to the time between the conquest and the time of Samuel, the period of the judges, if the text is read, "After these things, for about four hundred and fifty years, he provided judges."

* [13:31] The theme of the Galilean witnesses is a major one in the Gospel of Luke and in Acts and is used to signify the continuity between the teachings of Jesus and the teachings of the church and to guarantee the fidelity of the church's teachings to the words of Jesus.

* [13:38–39] **Justified**: the verb is the same as that used in Paul's letters to speak of the experience of justification and, as in Paul, is here connected with the term "to have faith" ("every believer"). But this seems the only passage about Paul in Acts where justification is mentioned. In Lucan fashion it is paralleled with "forgiveness of sins" (a theme at Acts 2:38; 3:19; 5:31; 10:43) based on Jesus' resurrection (Acts 13:37) rather than his cross, and is put negatively (Acts 13:38). Therefore, some would translate, "in regard to everything from which you could not be acquitted . . . every believer is acquitted."

* [13:46] The refusal to believe frustrates God's plan for his chosen people; however, no adverse judgment is made here concerning their ultimate destiny. Again, Luke, in the words of Paul, speaks of the priority of Israel in the plan for salvation (see Acts 10:36).

* [13:51] See note on Lk 9:5.

* [14:8–18] In an effort to convince his hearers that the divine power works through his word, Paul cures the cripple. However, the pagan tradition of the occasional appearance of gods among human beings leads the people astray in interpreting the miracle. The incident reveals the cultural

difficulties with which the church had to cope. Note the similarity of the miracle worked here by Paul to the one performed by Peter in Acts 3:2–10.

* [14:12] **Zeus . . . Hermes**: in Greek religion, Zeus was the chief of the Olympian gods, the "father of gods and men"; Hermes was a son of Zeus and was usually identified as the herald and messenger of the gods.

* [14:14] **Tore their garments**: a gesture of protest.

* [14:15–17] This is the first speech of Paul to Gentiles recorded by Luke in Acts (cf. Acts 17:22–31). Rather than showing how Christianity is the logical outgrowth of Judaism, as he does in speeches before Jews, Luke says that God excuses past Gentile ignorance and then presents a natural theology arguing for the recognition of God's existence and presence through his activity in natural phenomena.

* [14:23] **They appointed presbyters**: the communities are given their own religious leaders by the traveling missionaries. The structure in these churches is patterned on the model of the Jerusalem community (Acts 11:30; 15:2, 5, 22; 21:18).

---

* [15:1–35] The Jerusalem "Council" marks the official rejection of the rigid view that Gentile converts were obliged to observe the Mosaic law completely. From here to the end of Acts, Paul and the Gentile mission become the focus of Luke's writing.

* [15:1–5] When some of the converted Pharisees of Jerusalem discover the results of the first missionary journey of Paul, they urge that the Gentiles be taught to follow the Mosaic law. Recognizing the authority of the Jerusalem church, Paul and Barnabas go there to settle the question of whether Gentiles can embrace a form of Christianity that does not include this obligation.

* [15:6–12] The gathering is possibly the same as that recalled by Paul in Gal 2:1–10. Note that in Acts 15:2 it is only the apostles and presbyters, a small group, with whom Paul and Barnabas are to meet. Here Luke gives the meeting a public character because he wishes to emphasize its doctrinal significance (see Acts 15:22).

* [15:7–11] Paul's refusal to impose the Mosaic law on the Gentile Christians is supported by Peter on the ground that within his own experience God bestowed the holy Spirit upon Cornelius and his household without preconditions concerning the adoption of the Mosaic law (see Acts 10:44–47).

* [15:11] In support of Paul, Peter formulates the fundamental meaning of the gospel: that all are invited to be saved through faith in the power of Christ.

* [15:13–35] Some scholars think that this apostolic decree suggested by James, the immediate leader of the Jerusalem community, derives from another historical occasion than the meeting in question. This seems to be the case if the meeting is the same as the one related in Gal 2:1–10. According to that account, nothing was imposed upon Gentile Christians in respect to Mosaic law; whereas the decree instructs Gentile Christians of mixed communities to abstain from meats sacrificed to idols and from blood-meats, and to avoid marriage within forbidden degrees of consanguinity and affinity (Lv 18), all of which practices were especially abhorrent to Jews. Luke seems to have telescoped two originally independent incidents here: the first a Jerusalem "Council" that dealt with the question of circumcision, and the second a Jerusalem decree dealing mainly with Gentile observance of dietary laws (see Acts 21:25 where Paul seems to be learning of the decree for the first time).

* [15:14] **Symeon**: elsewhere in Acts he is called either Peter or Simon. The presence of the name Symeon here suggests that, in the source Luke is using for this part of the Jerusalem "Council" incident, the name may have originally referred to someone other than Peter (see Acts 13:1 where the Antiochene Symeon Niger is mentioned). As the text now stands, however, it is undoubtedly a reference to Simon Peter (Acts 15:7).

* [15:34] Some manuscripts add, in various wordings, "But Silas decided to remain there."

* [15:36–18:22] This continuous narrative recounts Paul's second missionary journey. On the internal evidence of the Lucan account, it lasted about three years. Paul first visited the communities he had established on his first journey (Acts 16:1–5), then pushed on into Macedonia, where he established communities at Philippi, Thessalonica, and Beroea (Acts 16:7–17:5). To escape the hostility of the Jews of Thessalonica, he left for Greece and while resident in Athens attempted, without success, to establish an effective Christian community there. From Athens he proceeded to Corinth and, after a stay of a year and a half, returned to Antioch by way of Ephesus and Jerusalem (Acts 17:16–18:22). Luke does not concern himself with the structure or statistics of the communities but aims to show the general progress of the gospel in the Gentile world as well as its continued failure to take root in the Jewish community.

* [16:3] **Paul had him circumcised**: he did this in order that Timothy might be able to associate with the Jews and so perform a ministry among them. Paul did not object to the Jewish Christians' adherence to the law. But he insisted that the law could not be imposed on the Gentiles. Paul himself lived in accordance with the law, or as exempt from the law, according to particular circumstances (see 1 Cor 9:19–23).

* [16:7] **The Spirit of Jesus**: this is an unusual formulation in Luke's writings. The parallelism with Acts 16:6 indicates its meaning, the holy Spirit.

* [16:10–17] This is the first of the so-called "we-sections" in Acts, where Luke writes as one of Paul's companions. The other passages are Acts 20:5–15; 21:1–18; 27:1–28:16. Scholars debate whether Luke may not have used the first person plural simply as a literary device to lend color to the narrative. The realism of the narrative, however, lends weight to the argument that the "we" includes Luke or another companion of Paul whose data Luke used as a source.

* [16:11–40] The church at Philippi became a flourishing community to which Paul addressed one of his letters (see Introduction to the Letter to the Philippians).

* [16:14] **A worshiper of God**: a "God-fearer." See note on Acts 8:26–40.

* [16:16] **With an oracular spirit**: literally, "with a Python spirit." The Python was the serpent or dragon that guarded the Delphic oracle. It later came to designate a "spirit that pronounced oracles" and also a ventriloquist who, it was thought, had such a spirit in the belly.

* [16:20] **Magistrates**: in Greek, *stratēgoi*, the popular designation of the *duoviri*, the highest officials of the Roman colony of Philippi.

* [16:35] **The lictors**: the equivalent of police officers, among whose duties were the apprehension and punishment of criminals.

* [16:37] Paul's Roman citizenship granted him special privileges in regard to criminal process. Roman law forbade under severe penalty the beating of Roman citizens (see also Acts 22:25).

---

* [17:6–7] The accusations against Paul and his companions echo the charges brought against Jesus in Lk 23:2.

* [17:7] **There is another king, Jesus**: a distortion into a political sense of the apostolic proclamation of Jesus and the kingdom of God (see Acts 8:12).

* [17:16–21] Paul's presence in Athens sets the stage for the great discourse before a Gentile audience in Acts 17:22–31. Although Athens was a politically insignificant city at this period, it still lived on the glories of its past and represented the center of Greek culture. The setting describes the conflict between Christian preaching and Hellenistic philosophy.

* [17:18] **Epicurean and Stoic philosophers**: for the followers of Epicurus (342–271 B.C.), the goal of life was happiness attained through sober reasoning and the searching out of motives for all choice and avoidance. The Stoics were followers of Zeno, a younger contemporary of Alexander the Great. Zeno and his followers believed in a type of pantheism that held that the spark of divinity

was present in all reality and that, in order to be free, each person must live "according to nature." **This scavenger**: literally, "seed-picker," as of a bird that picks up grain. The word is later used of scrap collectors and of people who take other people's ideas and propagate them as if they were their own. **Promoter of foreign deities**: according to Xenophon, Socrates was accused of promoting new deities. The accusation against Paul echoes the charge against Socrates. **'Jesus' and 'Resurrection'**: the Athenians are presented as misunderstanding Paul from the outset; they think he is preaching about Jesus and a goddess named **Anastasis**, i.e., Resurrection.

* [17:19] **To the Areopagus**: the "Areopagus" refers either to the Hill of Ares west of the Acropolis or to the Council of Athens, which at one time met on the hill but which at this time assembled in the Royal Colonnade (**Stoa Basileios**).

* [17:22–31] In Paul's appearance at the Areopagus he preaches his climactic speech to Gentiles in the cultural center of the ancient world. The speech is more theological than christological. Paul's discourse appeals to the Greek world's belief in divinity as responsible for the origin and existence of the universe. It contests the common belief in a multiplicity of gods supposedly exerting their powers through their images. It acknowledges that the attempt to find God is a constant human endeavor. It declares, further, that God is the judge of the human race, that the time of the judgment has been determined, and that it will be executed through a man whom God raised from the dead. The speech reflects sympathy with pagan religiosity, handles the subject of idol worship gently, and appeals for a new examination of divinity, not from the standpoint of creation but from the standpoint of judgment.

* [17:23] **'To an Unknown God'**: ancient authors such as Pausanias, Philostratus, and Tertullian speak of Athenian altars with no specific dedication as altars of "unknown gods" or "nameless altars."

* [17:26] **From one**: many manuscripts read "from one blood." **Fixed . . . seasons**: or "fixed limits to the epochs."

* [17:28] **'In him we live and move and have our being'**: some scholars understand this saying to be based on an earlier saying of Epimenides of Knossos (6th century B.C.). **'For we too are his offspring'**: here Paul is quoting Aratus of Soli, a third-century B.C. poet from Cilicia.

---

* [18:2] **Aquila . . . Priscilla**: both may already have been Christians at the time of their arrival in Corinth (see Acts 18:26). According to 1 Cor 16:19, their home became a meeting place for Christians. **Claudius**: the Emperor Claudius expelled the Jews from Rome ca. A.D. 49. The Roman historian Suetonius gives as reason for

the expulsion disturbances among the Jews "at the instigation of Chrestos," probably meaning disputes about the messiahship of Jesus.

* [18:6] **Shook out his garments**: a gesture indicating Paul's repudiation of his mission to the Jews there; cf. Acts 28:17–31.

* [18:7] **A worshiper of God**: see note on Acts 8:26–40.

* [18:8] **Crispus**: in 1 Cor 1:14 Paul mentions that Crispus was one of the few he himself baptized at Corinth.

* [18:12] **When Gallio was proconsul of Achaia**: Gallio's proconsulship in Achaia is dated to A.D. 51–52 from an inscription discovered at Delphi. This has become an important date in establishing a chronology of the life and missionary work of Paul.

* [18:13] **Contrary to the law**: Gallio (Acts 18:15) understands this to be a problem of Jewish, not Roman, law.

* [18:18] **He had his hair cut because he had taken a vow**: a reference to a Nazirite vow (see Nm 6:1–21, especially Nm 6:18) taken by Paul (see also Acts 21:23–27).

* [18:22] **He went up and greeted the church**: "going up" suggests a visit to the church in Jerusalem.

* [18:23–21:16] Luke's account of Paul's third missionary journey devotes itself mainly to his work at Ephesus (Acts 19:1–20:1). There is a certain restiveness on Paul's part and a growing conviction that the Spirit bids him return to Jerusalem and prepare to come to Rome (Acts 19:21).

* [18:24–25] Apollos appears as a preacher who knows the teaching of Jesus in the context of John's baptism of repentance. Aquila and Priscilla instruct him more fully. He is referred to in 1 Cor 1:12; 3:5–6, 22.

* [18:26] **The Way [of God]**: for the Way, see note on Acts 9:2. Other manuscripts here read "the Way of the Lord," "the word of the Lord," or simply "the Way."

---

* [19:1–6] Upon his arrival in Ephesus, Paul discovers other people at the same religious stage as Apollos, though they seem to have considered themselves followers of Christ, not of the Baptist. On the relation between baptism and the reception of the Spirit, see note on Acts 8:16.

* [19:24] **Miniature silver shrines of Artemis**: the temple of Artemis at Ephesus was one of the seven wonders of the ancient world. Artemis, originally the Olympian virgin hunter, moon goddess, and goddess of wild nature, was worshiped at Ephesus as an Asian mother goddess and goddess of fertility. She was one of the most widely worshiped female deities in the Hellenistic world (see Acts 18:27).

* [19:31] **Asiarchs**: the precise status and role of the Asiarchs is disputed. They appear to have been

people of wealth and influence who promoted the Roman imperial cult and who may also have been political representatives in a league of cities in the Roman province of Asia.

* [19:35] **Guardian of the temple**: this title was accorded by Rome to cities that provided a temple for the imperial cult. Inscriptional evidence indicates that Ephesus was acknowledged as the temple keeper of Artemis and of the imperial cult. **That fell from the sky**: many scholars think that this refers to a meteorite that was worshiped as an image of the goddess.

* [19:40] Some manuscripts omit the negative in [not] be able, making the meaning, "There is no cause for which we shall be able to give a reason for this demonstration."

---

* [20:5] The second "we-section" of Acts begins here. See note on Acts 16:10–17.

* [20:6] **Feast of Unleavened Bread**: see note on Lk 22:1.

* [20:7] **The first day of the week**: the day after the sabbath and the first day of the Jewish week, apparently chosen originally by the Jerusalem community for the celebration of the liturgy of the Eucharist in order to relate it to the resurrection of Christ.

* [20:10] The action of Paul in throwing himself upon the dead boy recalls that of Elijah in 1 Kgs 17:21 where the son of the widow of Zarephath is revived and that of Elisha in 2 Kgs 4:34 where the Shunammite woman's son is restored to life.

* [20:16–35] Apparently aware of difficulties at Ephesus and neighboring areas, Paul calls the presbyters together at Miletus, about thirty miles from Ephesus. He reminds them of his dedication to the gospel (Acts 20:18–21), speaks of what he is about to suffer for the gospel (Acts 20:22–27), and admonishes them to guard the community against false prophets, sure to arise upon his departure (Acts 20:28–31). He concludes by citing a saying of Jesus (Acts 20:35) not recorded in the gospel tradition. Luke presents this farewell to the Ephesian presbyters as Paul's last will and testament.

* [20:28] **Overseers**: see note on Phil 1:1. **The church of God**: because the clause "that he acquired with his own blood" suggests "the church of God" suggests that "his own blood" refers to God's blood, some early copyists changed "the church of God" to "the church of the Lord." Some prefer the translation "acquired with the blood of his own," i.e., Christ.

---

* [21:1–18] The third "we-section" of Acts (see note on Acts 16:10–17).

* [21:8] **One of the Seven**: see note on Acts 6:2–4.

* [21:10] **Agabus**: mentioned in Acts 11:28 as the prophet who predicted the famine that occurred when Claudius was emperor.

* [21:11] The symbolic act of Agabus recalls those of Old Testament prophets. Compare Is 20:2; Ez 4:1; Jer 13:1.

* [21:14] The Christian disciples' attitude reflects that of Jesus (see Lk 22:42).

* [21:17–26] The leaders of the Jewish Christians of Jerusalem inform Paul that the Jews there believe he has encouraged the Jews of the diaspora to abandon the Mosaic law. According to Acts, Paul had no objection to the retention of the law by the Jewish Christians of Jerusalem and left the Jews of the diaspora who accepted Christianity free to follow the same practice.

* [21:23–26] The leaders of the community suggest that Paul, on behalf of four members of the Jerusalem community, make the customary payment for the sacrifices offered at the termination of the Nazirite vow (see Nm 6:1–24) in order to impress favorably the Jewish Christians in Jerusalem with his high regard for the Mosaic law. Since Paul himself had once made this vow (Acts 18:18), his respect for the law would be on public record.

* [21:24] **Pay their expenses**: according to Nm 6:14–15 the Nazirite had to present a yearling lamb for a holocaust, a yearling ewe lamb for a sin offering, and a ram for a peace offering, along with food and drink offerings, upon completion of the period of the vow.

* [21:25] Paul is informed about the apostolic decree, seemingly for the first time (see note on Acts 15:13–35). The allusion to the decree was probably introduced here by Luke to remind his readers that the Gentile Christians themselves were asked to respect certain Jewish practices deriving from the law.

* [21:28] The charges against Paul by the diaspora Jews are identical to the charges brought against Stephen by diaspora Jews in Acts 6:13. **Brought Greeks into the temple**: non-Jews were forbidden, under penalty of death, to go beyond the Court of the Gentiles. Inscriptions in Greek and Latin on a stone balustrade marked off the prohibited area.

* [21:31] **Cohort commander**: literally, "the leader of a thousand in a cohort." At this period the Roman cohort commander usually led six hundred soldiers, a tenth of a legion; but the number in a cohort varied.

* [21:36] **"Away with him!"**: at the trial of Jesus before Pilate in Lk 23:18, the people similarly shout, "Away with this man."

* [21:38] **The Egyptian**: according to the Jewish historian Josephus, an Egyptian gathered a large crowd on the Mount of Olives to witness the destruction of the walls of Jerusalem that would fall at the Egyptian "prophet's" word. The commotion was put down by the Roman authorities

and the Egyptian escaped, but only after thousands had been killed. **Four thousand assassins**: literally, *sicarii*. According to Josephus, these were political nationalists who removed their opponents by assassination with a short dagger, called in Latin a *sica*.

* [21:40] **In Hebrew**: meaning, perhaps, in Aramaic, which at this time was the Semitic tongue in common use.

---

* [22:1–21] Paul's first defense speech is presented to the Jerusalem crowds. Luke here presents Paul as a devout Jew (Acts 22:3) and zealous persecutor of the Christian community (Acts 22:4–5), and then recounts the conversion of Paul for the second time in Acts (see note on Acts 9:1–19).

* [22:15] **His witness**: like the Galilean followers during the historical ministry of Jesus, Paul too, through his experience of the risen Christ, is to be a witness to the resurrection (compare Acts 1:8; 10:39–41; Lk 24:48).

* [22:21] Paul endeavors to explain that his position on the law has not been identical with that of his audience because it has been his prophetic mission to preach to the Gentiles to whom the law was not addressed and who had no faith in it as a way of salvation.

* [22:22] Paul's suggestion that his prophetic mission to the Gentiles did not involve his imposing the law on them provokes the same opposition as occurred in Pisidian Antioch (Acts 13:45).

* [22:25] **Is it lawful for you to scourge a man who is a Roman citizen and has not been tried?**: see note on Acts 16:37.

---

* [23:2] **The high priest Ananias**: Ananias, son of Nedebaeus, was high priest from A.D. 47 to 59.

* [23:3] **God will strike you**: Josephus reports that Ananias was later assassinated in A.D. 66 at the beginning of the First Revolt.

* [23:5] Luke portrays Paul as a model of one who is obedient to the Mosaic law. Paul, because of his reverence for the law (Ex 22:27), withdraws his accusation of hypocrisy, "whitewashed wall" (cf. Mt 23:27), when he is told Ananias is the high priest.

* [23:11] The occurrence of the vision of Christ consoling Paul and assuring him that he will be his witness in Rome prepares the reader for the final section of Acts: the journey of Paul and the word he preaches to Rome under the protection of the Romans.

* [23:17] **Centurions**: a centurion was a military officer in charge of one hundred soldiers.

* [23:23] **By nine o'clock tonight**: literally, "by the third hour of the night." The night hours began at 6 p.m. **Two hundred auxiliaries**: the meaning of the Greek is not certain. It seems to

THE ACTS OF THE APOSTLES

refer to spearmen from the local police force and not from the cohort of soldiers, which would have numbered only 500–1000 men.

* [23:26–30] The letter emphasizes the fact that Paul is a Roman citizen and asserts the lack of evidence that he is guilty of a crime against the empire. The tone of the letter implies that the commander became initially involved in Paul's case because of his Roman citizenship, but this is not an exact description of what really happened (see Acts 21:31–33; 22:25–29).

* [23:26] M. Antonius Felix was procurator of Judea from A.D. 52 to 60. His procuratorship was marked by cruelty toward and oppression of his Jewish subjects.

* [24:5] **Nazoreans**: that is, followers of Jesus of Nazareth.

* [24:7] The Western text has added here a verse (really Acts 24:6b–8a) that is not found in the best Greek manuscripts. It reads, "and would have judged him according to our own law, but the cohort commander Lysias came and violently took him out of our hands and ordered his accusers to come before you."

* [24:10–21] Whereas the advocate Tertullus referred to Paul's activities on his missionary journeys, the apostle narrowed the charges down to the riot connected with the incident in the temple (see Acts 21:27–30; 24:17–20). In his defense, Paul stresses the continuity between Christianity and Judaism.

* [24:24, 25] The way of Christian discipleship greatly disquiets Felix, who has entered into an adulterous marriage with Drusilla, daughter of Herod Agrippa I. This marriage provides the background for the topics Paul speaks about and about which Felix does not want to hear.

* [24:27] Very little is known of Porcius Festus who was a procurator of Judea from A.D. 60 to 62.

* [25:2] Even after two years the animosity toward Paul in Jerusalem had not subsided (see Acts 24:27).

* [25:9–12] Paul refuses to acknowledge that the Sanhedrin in Jerusalem has any jurisdiction over him now (Acts 25:11). Paul uses his right as a Roman citizen to appeal his case to the jurisdiction of the Emperor (Nero, ca. A.D. 60) (Acts 25:12). This move broke the deadlock between Roman protective custody of Paul and the plan of his enemies to kill him (25:3).

* [25:13] **King Agrippa and Bernice**: brother and sister, children of Herod Agrippa I whose activities against the Jerusalem community are mentioned in Acts 12:1–19. Agrippa II was a petty ruler over small areas in northern Palestine and some villages in Perea. His influence on the Jewish population of Palestine was insignificant.

* [26:2–23] Paul's final defense speech in Acts is now made before a king (see Acts 9:15). In the speech Paul presents himself as a zealous Pharisee and Christianity as the logical development of Pharisaic Judaism. The story of his conversion is recounted for the third time in Acts in this speech (see note on Acts 9:1–19).

* [26:4] **Among my people**: that is, among the Jews.

* [26:14] **In Hebrew**: see note on Acts 21:40. **It is hard for you to kick against the goad**: this proverb is commonly found in Greek literature and in this context signifies the senselessness and ineffectiveness of any opposition to the divine influence in his life.

* [26:16] The words of Jesus directed to Paul here reflect the dialogues between Christ and Ananias (Acts 9:15) and between Ananias and Paul (Acts 22:14–15) in the two previous accounts of Paul's conversion.

* [26:18] **To open their eyes**: though no mention is made of Paul's blindness in this account (cf. Acts 9:8–9, 12, 18; 22:11–13), the task he is commissioned to perform is the removal of other people's spiritual blindness.

* [26:22] **Saying nothing different from what the prophets and Moses foretold**: see note on Lk 18:31.

* [26:23] **That the Messiah must suffer**: see note on Lk 24:26.

* [26:26] **Not done in a corner**: for Luke, this Greek proverb expresses his belief that he is presenting a story about Jesus and the church that is already well known. As such, the entire history of Christianity is public knowledge and incontestable. Luke presents his story in this way to provide "certainty" to his readers about the instructions they have received (Lk 1:4).

* [26:27–28] If the Christian missionaries proclaim nothing different from what the Old Testament prophets had proclaimed (Acts 26:22–23), then the logical outcome for the believing Jew, according to Luke, is to become a Christian.

* [26:31–32] In recording the episode of Paul's appearance before Agrippa, Luke wishes to show that, when Paul's case was judged impartially, no grounds for legal action against him were found (see Acts 23:29; 25:25).

* [27:1–28:16] Here Luke has written a stirring account of adventure on the high seas, incidental to his main purpose of showing how well Paul got along with his captors and how his prophetic influence saved the lives of all on board. The recital also establishes the existence of Christian communities in Puteoli and Rome. This account of the voyage and shipwreck also constitutes the final "we-section" in Acts (see note on Acts 16:10–17).

* [27:1] **Cohort Augusta**: the presence of a Cohort Augusta in Syria during the first century

A.D. is attested in inscriptions. Whatever the historical background to this information given by Luke may be, the name Augusta serves to increase the prominence and prestige of the prisoner Paul whose custodians bear so important a Roman name.

* [27:9] **The time of the fast**: the fast kept on the occasion of the Day of Atonement (Lv 16:29–31), which occurred in late September or early October.

* [27:35] **He took bread . . .**: the words recall the traditional language of the celebration of the Eucharist (see Lk 22:19).

---

* [28:4] **Justice**: in Greek mythology, the pursuing goddess of vengeance and justice.

* [28:11] **Dioscuri**: that is, the Twin Brothers, Castor and Pollux, the sons of Zeus and the patrons of the sailors.

* [28:16] With Paul's arrival in Rome, the programmatic spread of the word of the Lord to "the ends of the earth" (Acts 1:8) is accomplished. In Rome, Paul is placed under house arrest, and under this mild form of custody he is allowed to proclaim the word in the capital of the civilized world of his day.

* [28:17–22] Paul's first act in Rome is to learn from the leaders of the Jewish community whether the Jews of Jerusalem plan to pursue their case against him before the Roman jurisdiction. He is informed that no such plan is afoot, but that the Jews of Rome have heard the Christian teaching denounced. Paul's offer to explain it to them is readily accepted.

* [28:20] **The hope of Israel**: in the words of Paul (Acts 23:6), Luke has identified this hope as hope in the resurrection of the dead.

* [28:25–28] Paul's final words in Acts reflect a major concern of Luke's writings: how the salvation promised in the Old Testament, accomplished by Jesus, and offered first to Israel (Acts 13:26), has now been offered to and accepted by the Gentiles. Quoting Is 6:9–10, Paul presents the scriptural support for his indictment of his fellow Jews who refuse to accept the message he proclaims. Their rejection leads to its proclamation among the Gentiles.

* [28:29] The Western text has added here a verse that is not found in the best Greek manuscripts: "And when he had said this, the Jews left, seriously arguing among themselves."

* [28:30–31] Although the ending of Acts may seem to be abrupt, Luke has now completed his story with the establishment of Paul and the proclamation of Christianity in Rome. Paul's confident and unhindered proclamation of the gospel in Rome forms the climax to the story whose outline was provided in Acts 1:8—"You will be my witnesses in Jerusalem . . . and to the ends of the earth."

ONE CHURCH.
ONE MISSION.

The National Collections of the Church in the United States
www.usccb.org/nationalcollections

CATHOLIC RELIEF SERVICES eases suffering and provides assistance in 93 countries, touching the lives of 100 million people without regard to their race, religion, or nationality.

Go to *www.crs.org* to find out how you can help.

CRS serves Catholics in the United States by inviting them to live out their faith as part of one human family. As the official international humanitarian agency of the Catholic community in the United States, CRS has a special role to play in helping those in need overseas.

Photo by Jim Stipe, CRS

Immerse yourself
in Scripture with the

DAILY
MASS
READINGS
in text and audio.

www.usccb.org/bible

Get inspired each day!
With the USCCB

DAILY VIDEO
REFLECTIONS

www.usccb.org/bible/reflections

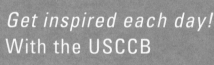

Made possible with parishioners' donations to the
USCCB's Catholic Communication Campaign